Pro NetBeans™ IDE 6 Rich Client Platform Edition

Adam Myatt

with Brian Leonard and Geertjan Wielenga

Apress®

Pro NetBeans™ IDE 6 Rich Client Platform Edition

ISBN-13 (pbk): 978-1-59059-895-5

ISBN-10 (pbk): 1-59059-895-4

ISBN-13 (electronic): 978-1-4302-0439-8

ISBN-10 (electronic): 1-4302-0439-7

Printed and bound in the United States of America 9 8 7 6 5 4 3 2 1

Lead Editor: Steve Anglin
Technical Reviewer: Sumit Pal
Editorial Board: Clay Andres, Steve Anglin, Ewan Buckingham, Tony Campbell, Gary Cornell, Jonathan Gennick, Kevin Goff, Matthew Moodie, Joseph Ottinger, Jeffrey Pepper, Frank Pohlmann, Ben Renow-Clarke, Dominic Shakeshaft, Matt Wade, Tom Welsh
Project Manager: Richard Dal Porto
Copy Editor: Elliot Simon
Associate Production Director: Kari Brooks-Copony
Production Editor: Jill Ellis
Compositor: Lynn L'Heureux
Proofreader: April Eddy
Indexer: Carol Burbo
Artist: April Milne
Cover Designer: Kurt Krames
Manufacturing Director: Tom Debolski

Distributed to the book trade worldwide by Springer-Verlag New York, Inc., 233 Spring Street, 6th Floor, New York, NY 10013. Phone 1-800-SPRINGER, fax 201-348-4505, e-mail orders-ny@springer-sbm.com, or visit http://www.springeronline.com.

For information on translations, please contact Apress directly at 2855 Telegraph Avenue, Suite 600, Berkeley, CA 94705. Phone 510-549-5930, fax 510-549-5939, e-mail info@apress.com, or visit http://www.apress.com.

Apress and friends of ED books may be purchased in bulk for academic, corporate, or promotional use. eBook versions and licenses are also available for most titles. For more information, reference our Special Bulk Sales–eBook Licensing web page at http://www.apress.com/info/bulksales.

The source code for this book is available to readers at http://www.apress.com.

To my wonderful wife, Morgan, for her love and support

Contents at a Glance

Contents

About the Author

ADAM MYATT currently works as the Principal Technologist of Software Development for GE Global Research, the worldwide R&D headquarters of General Electric, located in Niskayuna, New York. Adam is an experienced Java developer and a Sun Microsystems Certified Java Programmer. His work entails leading globally developed Java software and web applications through a rigorous software development life-cycle process, researching new technologies, and setting long-term strategies.

He is an active participant in a local Java users' group and is an avid enthusiast of open source software. Adam has previously published the book *Pro NetBeans IDE 5.5 Enterprise Edition* (Apress, 2007), which focuses on Java EE 5 technology and its use in NetBeans. He recently served on the Tools & Languages Track Committee for selecting presenters for JavaOne 2008.

Adam has also worked for several area software firms prior to joining General Electric. He is a graduate of the Computer Science Department at the State University of New York College at Potsdam.

In what little free time he has, Adam enjoys traveling to new and interesting places, fishing, and playing poker. Recently, Adam and his wife drove back and forth across the United States, covering 6,500 miles and 20 states, all with zero speeding tickets and zero traffic accidents.

About the Technical Reviewer

SUMIT PAL has about 14 years of experience with software architecture, design, and development on a variety of platforms, including Java, J2EE. Sumit has worked in the SQLServer Replication group while with Microsoft for two years and with Oracle's OLAP Server group while with Oracle for seven years.

Apart from certifications such as IEEE-CSDP and J2EE Architect, Sumit also has an MS in computer science.

Sumit has a keen interest in database internals, algorithms, and search engine technology.

He currently works as an OLAP Architect for LeapFrogRX.

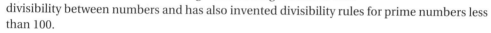

Sumit has invented some basic generalized algorithms to find divisibility between numbers and has also invented divisibility rules for prime numbers less than 100.

Sumit has a fierce desire to work for Google some day.

Acknowledgments

I would like to thank the many people without whom this book would not have been possible.

First, thanks to my editor, Steve Anglin, for his advice and guidance on this project. I also want to thank my project manager, Richard Dal Porto, for working hard to try to keep me on schedule and accountable. Thanks to my technical reviewer, Sumit Pal, who helped make this a stronger, more accurate book. You have my continued appreciation for your insightful suggestions and comments. A big thanks to my editors Elliot Simon and Jill Ellis for the fantastic job they did on making what I wrote actually read well and look good. I greatly appreciate the entire Apress team and all their efforts.

Many thanks to my contributing authors, Brian Leonard and Geertjan Wielenga, for providing Chapters 12 and 16, respectively. It's thrilling to work with well-known members of the NetBeans team and to be able to include their excellent contributions in this book.

I would also like to express my thanks to the entire GEGR ITMS organization for their support at work. Balancing work and personal projects can be difficult at times, but having a great team to work with certainly made it easier. This was especially true on the days when I would walk around like a zombie from having stayed up late writing on the previous night. Having patient co-workers, visiting the cafeteria to get Rich's pancakes, and guzzling gallons of Dr Pepper™ were often the only things that kept me going some days.

Finally I would like to express my heartfelt thanks to my wife, Morgan, who put up with my working on this new book nights and weekends, yet again, for far too long. Her love and support during this project made it all possible.

Preface

In the beginning, code was written using simple text-based tools like Notepad. For the purposes of this discussion, I'll define "beginning" as the early to mid-1990s, when Java first started to become popular. Using the combination of a text editor and command prompt, users could write and compile code.

It was quickly determined that this approach did not provide the most efficient development environment. For example, if you made a code syntax mistake in the text editor, there was no way to identify the problem until you saved and compiled the file. You would then review the compilation error, locate the offending line in the code, and attempt to determine the cause. Compilation errors are not always entirely helpful in diagnosing a problem with your code.

Many novice programmers start out using the Notepad and command-prompt environment. There is nothing inherently wrong with this approach, since some professionals still do the same thing. For an absolute beginner learning Java, using a plaintext editor can sometimes be the easiest and fastest approach. However, text editors do not provide assistance with language syntax, compiler integration, intelligent refactoring support, or other code-writing capabilities.

One of the useful features most text editors possess is called Find and Replace. With this simple capability, programmers could replace occurrences of a word or phrase with another. This worked for certain situations, but could cause problems. Suppose you created the following class:

```
public class SomeCode {

    public void myMethod1(String var) {

        String FirstName = var.toUpperCase();

        // do something with FirstName
    }

    public void myMethod2(String var) {

        String FirstName = var.toLowerCase();

        // do something else with FirstName
    }

}
```

The `SomeCode` class includes two methods: `myMethod1` and `myMethod2`. If you later needed to rename the `FirstName` variable in `myMethod1`, you could manually edit each line of code to alter the name. Obviously, this is a simple example, but if `myMethod1` happened to be a hundred lines long and FirstName appeared in many places, then manual editing of the code could take quite a long time. You could also use the text editor's Find and Replace functionality to quickly replace all occurrences of FirstName with the new variable name. However, the original change request specified only the FirstName variable in the myMethod1 method and *not* in the myMethod2 method. Using Find and Replace could incorrectly replace the wrong occurrences of FirstName in myMethod1 and myMethod2. Of course, it's possible to replace occurrences one by one, but that can take time and be prone to human error.

Some text editors provide more advanced support for programming languages. The popular Unix-based tool Emacs offers many interesting features, including advanced text matching and replacement capabilities. Through plugins, it can also provide Java syntax highlighting, code indentation, basic debugging, and compilation support. These are great pieces of functionality, but they still do not offer the most flexible and productive environment.

The first question anyone who uses Emacs or text editors might ask is, "Why use an IDE?" Some programmers tend to grow attached to a specific tool set or programming language and are resistant to change. An important quality in today's ever-changing world is the ability to adapt to new technology.

New tool sets can help professional programmers in many ways. As a programmer, your time should be spent writing code, rewriting code, and testing code. You shouldn't need to waste time trying to figure out how to rename methods across your code, generate project documentation, or correctly compile all the classes in a package. Once you have identified the action you need to perform, your tool should do it for you easily.

Integrated development environments (IDEs) literally provide an entire environment for your work. They bring together many different tools in a coherent way so that the services and actions you need are seamlessly integrated together.

Some technical benefits of IDEs include the following:

- Graphical user interface (GUI) for performing actions
- Grouping of source code and configuration files into the concept of a *project*
- Tight integration with the compiler
- Coupling with a source code repository
- Ability to performance tune, analyze, and load test code
- Integration with reusable test frameworks
- Capability to utilize third-party plugins and tools
- Ability to debug code by executing one line at a time
- Quick access to and ease of generating project documentation

Some of the more tangible business benefits of using an IDE include the following:

- Reduces the cycle time of development
- Increases the quality and reliability of your code
- Standardizes your software development processes
- Provides a common platform for programming staff to reduce training time

Some of these benefits are definitely arguable and can sometimes be realized only after careful analysis, implementation, and execution. Many other factors come into play, but a really good Java IDE tool can be the foundation for accomplishing important milestones such as the examples I provided.

NetBeans is my Java IDE of choice. This might be obvious, since I wrote this book, but I have many valid reasons for loving and using NetBeans. My experience with development tools covers a wide range of products, such as Notepad, TextPad, Emacs, vi, Macromedia UltraDeveloper, Macromedia Dreamweaver, Oracle JDeveloper, IntelliJ IDEA, Borland JBuilder, Microsoft Visual Studio, and Eclipse.

Each of these tools has its pros and cons. They all have devoted users and entire communities centered around them. After a while, distinguishing between the tools can be difficult, since they offer many similar features. I was on the fence deciding between IntelliJ IDEA and Eclipse. After only a few hours of working with NetBeans and viewing various tutorials, I was convinced. I downloaded, installed, and started working with it. I quickly discovered that the features were located in places I expected them to be, they functioned as I thought they would, and there were few or no configuration issues. In my opinion, that is how a tool should function out of the box.

In no particular order, the top ten reasons I think programmers should use NetBeans over another Java IDE are summarized as follows:

Intuitive and easy-to-use Matisse GUI designer for Swing development: With little or no Swing knowledge, users can be up and running, dragging-and-dropping elements into a WYSIWYG design window. The Matisse GUI designer actually generates real Swing code and not the usual boilerplate fluff code many tools tend to create. At the last JavaOne conference I attended, I sat next to a gentleman who used the GUI design capabilities of JBuilder. After only two minutes of watching me use Matisse, he was completely blown away and ran off to download it for himself.

Strong refactoring support: This is particularly true for the Jackpot engine, allowing for Java type-aware refactoring using a regular expression-like query language. Designed by James Gosling, the query language is quite simple to use and allows for pattern matching and replacement. The interesting aspect to the queries is that they can be tested to match specific Java types or instances of objects.

One of the best code profilers: Given that I haven't used every code profiler out there, but with an amazing array of options, I consider the NetBeans Profiler to be among the best. Users can profile for memory, CPU, and performance problems as well as monitor threads. The NetBeans 6 Profiler introduces the concept of profiling points. The Profiler can also be attached and detached from a currently running process or application. It provides 32-bit and 64-bit support as well as allows you to profile Enterprise JavaBeans (EJB) modules and enterprise applications. For those Mac fans in the crowd, it also supports profiling on Mac OS X Intel systems.

UML project support: Programmers can create a Unified Modeling Language (UML) project for modeling code, process steps, or design patterns. UML projects can be linked directly to Java projects. As a user creates and modifies the UML objects and diagrams, the corresponding Java code is generated automatically. If the source code in the linked Java project is changed, the diagram is also updated automatically. With the ability to export diagrams, generate code, and create web-based project reports, the UML project feature is one of the coolest additions to NetBeans that I have enjoyed using.

Ant integration: Java projects in NetBeans are structured using Ant build files. When a project is first created, the IDE generates the build script and associated targets. Users can then trigger specific targets or completely customize the structure of their build file to suit the needs of their project. For users unfamiliar with Ant, there is almost no impact, since execution of Ant targets is linked directly to the menus and buttons in NetBeans. Many users will also find it easy to import existing build files from external projects and quickly get up to speed. For beginners, it is ridiculously easy to use. For experts, it is ridiculously easy to customize.

J2ME mobile application support: Even if you don't do much mobile application development, after viewing the samples and reading an introductory tutorial, you should quickly see the power of NetBeans mobile tools. The sample applications provided are impressive enough as it is. With support for Java 2 Micro Edition (J2ME) Mobile Information Device Profile (MIDP) 2.0, a visual mobile designer, a wireless connection wizard, and over-the-air download testing, mobile application developers have some impressive and powerful tools.

Developer collaboration tools: Developers can log in to a public or private environment and share code. You can join public conversations or start your own restricted private ones. One of the greatest features I've seen in a while is the ability to drag-and-drop code or entire projects in the chat window and share code with one or more programmers. NetBeans supports multiuser team coding. As one user starts to change a block of code, it is highlighted and locked for the other users sharing it. In the current global economy, where development teams are spread across numerous locations, this tool can prove very beneficial.

Easy-to-use Update Center: The NetBeans Update Center allows you to quickly select which update distribution sites you wish to check for changes, updates, and new modules. You can also choose to install modules that you previously downloaded but chose not to install. The Update Center is more intuitive than many other Java IDE update tools and makes updating NetBeans a snap.

Out-of-the-box JSP and Tomcat support: NetBeans comes bundled with Apache Tomcat. Once you have used the New Project wizard to create a web application project, you can create your JavaServer Pages (JSP) files. Then you can right-click any JSP file and select Run File. The bundled Tomcat server starts immediately, your default Internet browser opens, and the JSP file executing in Tomcat is displayed. NetBeans is even smart enough to activate the HTTP Monitor.

NetBeans HTTP Monitor: I do a lot of web-related Java development. To me, this is one of the coolest and most unique features of any Java IDE on the market. The HTTP Monitor can be activated during the debugging or execution of a web application. It allows you to monitor the request, HTTP headers, cookies, session, servlet context, and client/server parameters. You no longer need to write server-side code to read these variables, output them to a log, and view the log file. Inside NetBeans, you can debug your code, step line by line through it, and watch the attributes you need.

These features are only a sampling of what NetBeans has to offer. Other Java IDEs may provide some of the capabilities described here, but none can match the NetBeans IDE's intuitive interface and integrated tool set. To learn about everything NetBeans has to offer, I invite you to continue reading the rest of the chapters in this book.

This book focuses on many new features of the NetBeans IDE 6. One can focus on many types of technologies and areas when learning NetBeans. With this latest release, developers have access to an impressive array of new and updated features, including, but not limited to,

- A new and improved Source Editor
- Improved refactoring capabilities
- Improved code completion
- Greatly improved Profiler with profiling points and HeapWalker
- Maven support
- JUnit 4 support
- Ruby and JRuby support

I wanted to write a book that really showcased the fantastic tools for working with these technologies.

Pro NetBeans IDE 6 Rich Client Platform Edition is meant for all levels of developers. Whether you are new to NetBeans, a student programmer, or an experienced professional, you will find this book provides direct explanations of features and straightforward examples. It also focuses on many of the core features of NetBeans that assist professional software developers, such as Ant, JUnit, CVS, Subversion, and static analysis tools, among others.

My personal web site, `www.ProNetBeans.com`, contains a variety of content, such as Java and NetBeans news, articles, and tutorials, among others. It will also contain updates, corrections, and errata to the book. If you have any questions or would like to provide feedback, please feel free to contact me at `adam@pronetbeans.com`.

CHAPTER 1

Downloading, Installing, and Customizing NetBeans

Since the NetBeans 5.5 release, many changes have been made in the core of the tool. One of these is the installation process. The NetBeans team has experimented with many different kinds of installation options over the years, such as bundled downloads, separate add-on packs, and individual downloadable modules.

To start using NetBeans, you merely need to download and install it. This chapter describes how to do that as well as how to check for updates and customize some NetBeans settings to suit your own preferences. Finally, we take a quick look at the NetBeans windows you'll use most often.

Downloading Files

Starting with the NetBeans 6 release, you have several types of bundled downloads you can use to install the IDE: basic, standard, and full.

Basic: The basic bundle comprises the stripped-down IDE and basic Java Standard Edition functionality, including the Profiler tool and GUI building capabilities.

Standard: The standard bundle expands on the basic by adding mobility, web, and Java EE features. It also includes several Java application servers, such as Apache Tomcat 6 and the latest build of GlassFish.

Full: The full bundle includes all the preceding features as well as the UML, SOA, and Ruby modules. This is the largest download. But unless you really want a stripped-down version of the IDE, I suggest downloading this bundle. During the installation process, you can pick and choose which features you actually want. If you download a smaller bundle, you have no such choice.

To download the NetBeans bundles, go to netbeans.org. This web site provides several different links for downloading the NetBeans software and related tools. The main download is typically linked off the homepage.

Depending on which path you follow to get to the download section, you may be presented with several choices. The specific operating system version you need will most likely be preselected for you. But if it is not, you can choose from Windows, Linux, Solaris, and MacOS X. At the time of this writing there are 64-bit options for Linux and Solaris, but this is subject to change. You should select the bundle you need and click the Download button. You will then be immediately prompted to download the file.

Installing the NetBeans IDE

Since NetBeans can be installed across numerous platforms, I will mention only the important installation concepts. NetBeans 6 can be installed on almost any operating system for which there is a Java Virtual Machine (JVM) that runs a minimum of Java 1.5.0.11 or later. I am running NetBeans using Java 6, unless otherwise specified.

On the download page at netbeans.org, a list of release documents is provided. In this list is a link to the installation instructions as recommended by NetBeans. These instructions cover the basic installation process for Windows, Solaris, Linux, and Macintosh OS X.

As of version 6.0 of the Profiler, it is recommended that you run it with JDK 1.5.11 or later as previously mentioned with NetBeans 6. However, for optimal performance I suggest using the most recent Java 6 release. In NetBeans 5.5 and 5.5.1 it is possible to profile against JDK 1.4, but an experimental add-on is needed to allow this functionality. Sun does not support the add-on, so you would be using it at your own risk. If your application is written for Java 1.4 and you want to use NetBeans 6 and its profiler, I recommend that you install the latest release of Java 6.0 and set the source compatibility in NetBeans to 1.4. This should resolve any issues with running the Profiler as well as maintain your Java 1.4–based code.

To set the source compatibility for a project, right-click the project name and select Properties from the context menu. With the Sources category selected, you should see a field called "Source Level." Using the drop-down list, you can set the version of Java with which your source code should be compatible.

The first time I downloaded and installed NetBeans, I used Sun's Java 5 on Windows XP, but I have since upgraded to Java 6. After executing the Windows installer, I clicked the Next button, accepted the license agreement, and selected a directory in which to install NetBeans. Personally, I like to group all my Java-related products in one location. I typically start with a `c:\java` directory. Within that directory, I install several JDKs, Java tools such as NetBeans, as well as a directory for all my Java-related projects and applications. I usually end up with the following:

- `c:\java\1.6.0.02`
- `c:\java\1.5.0.12`
- `c:\java\netbeans\6.0`
- `c:\java\projects`

When you execute the installation you will see the NetBeans 6 welcome page. Click the Customize button to select which features you want to install. The list may vary depending on the bundle you downloaded from netbeans.org. You can select or unselect the check box next to each item. By default, the Tomcat application is not checked, so to install the feature you must select it, as shown in Figure 1-1.

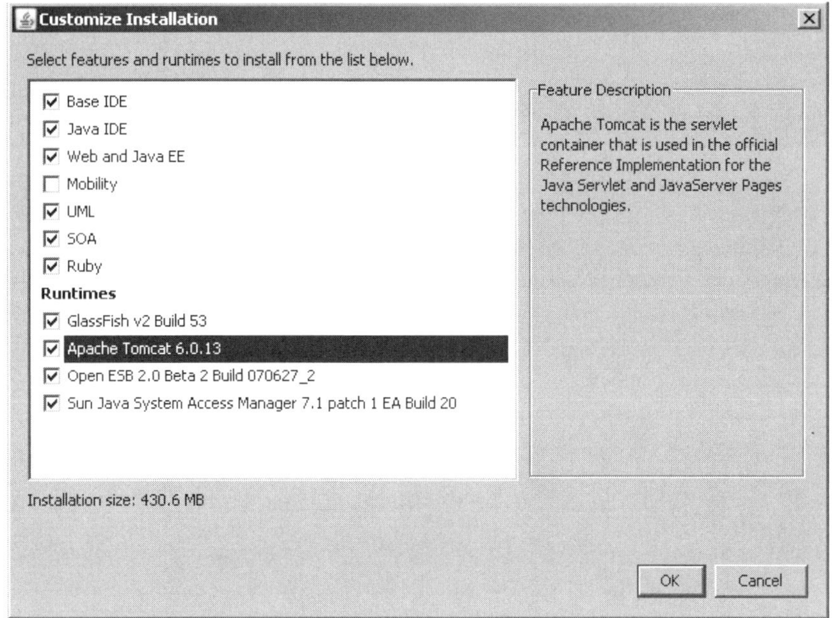

Figure 1-1. *List of features to include in the installation*

Once you have finished customizing the installation items, click the OK button to continue. The list of items you selected will be displayed. If any of the items under the Runtimes section were previously installed, then the text "Already Installed" will appear next to each name. If you click the OK button, the installation will initialize and display the license page and acknowledge.

Select the check box next to the text "I Accept the terms in the license agreement" and click the Next button. The installation wizard will search your local machine for JDKs and prompt you for several pieces of information. For the "Install NetBeans 6 IDE to" field, click the Browse button and select a directory. As mentioned earlier, I recommend a common directory structure such as `c:\java\netbeans\6.0`. For the "JDK for running NetBeans IDE" field, a JDK is already selected. You can click the Browse button to select a directory for the JDK as well. Click the Next button to proceed to the server runtimes installation configuration.

If you selected to have GlassFish installed, the installation wizard displays a configuration form with suggested values already filled out. The "Install GlassFish to" field specifies the directory where the application server will be installed. The form also allows you to specify which JDK you wish to use when running GlassFish in case it differs from the JDK you are using to run NetBeans. This is a convenient setting to have because you may very well be running GlassFish without having NetBeans open. The configuration form also allows you to set the admin username, password, and ports, as shown in Figure 1-2.

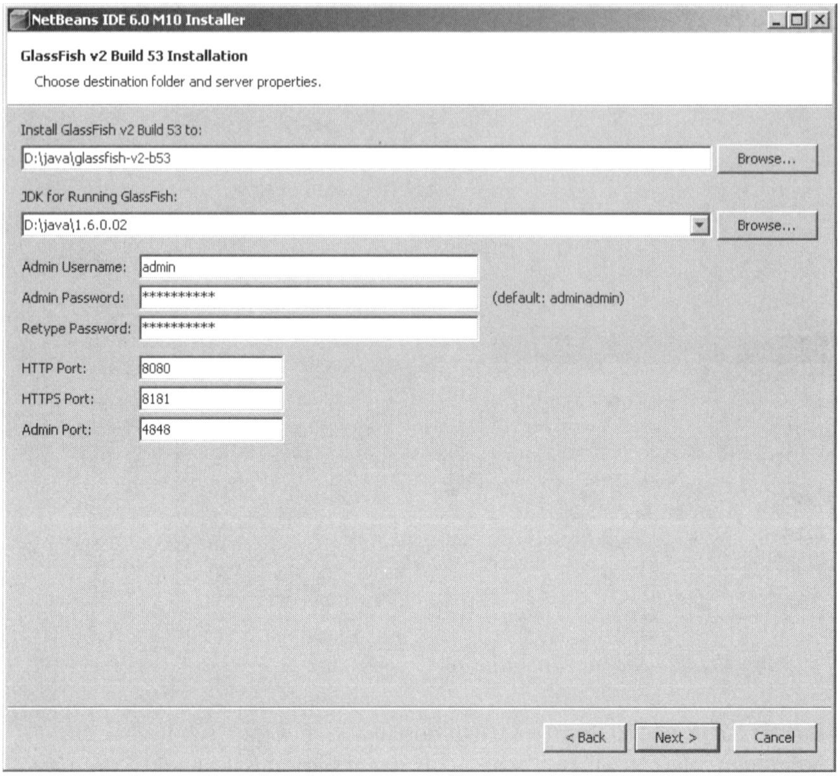

Figure 1-2. *The GlassFish application server installation configuration form*

When you have finished setting the GlassFish server fields, click the Next button to continue. Read the section on Java Application Servers in Chapter 13 if you want to know how to change these configuration settings. If you selected Tomcat to be installed, the installation wizard will display a Tomcat application server configuration form. The screen allows you to specify where to install Tomcat 6 by clicking the Browse button next to the "Installation Location" field. After you have set the location, click the Next button to proceed to the summary screen. The summary screen lists the various installation directories, the features you selected to install, and the estimated installation size of the entire package.

Click the Install button to execute the full installation. The installation process runs and installs the features. When installation is complete, click the Finish button to close the installation wizard.

When you load NetBeans for the first time, it creates a new `.netbeans` directory in the user directory. On Windows this is typically `c:\documents and settings\<username>\.netbeans`, and on Unix it's `/home/<username>/.netbeans`. You can safely remove this directory without hurting the core NetBeans installation. However, removing it will essentially undo all the configurations you have set in the IDE and uninstall all the modules you may have downloaded.

Starting with NetBeans 6, you no longer need to download and install the NetBeans Profiler separately. It is included in the core IDE. For usage instructions and best practices, see Chapter 5.

Customizing the NetBeans JVM Startup Options

One thing most people will probably never think to use is the ability to customize the NetBeans JVM startup options. By including several arguments in a NetBeans configuration file, you can tweak the memory usage settings for the JVM in which NetBeans starts up. You can also change the type of garbage-collection algorithm that is used.

If you are working on a semistandard computer (32-bit single processor), you probably won't benefit from changing the garbage-collection routine the JVM uses. However, if you use a JVM other than the Sun JVM or have a machine that is either multiprocessor, multicore, or 64-bit, you might want to consider these options. Your JVM vendor should provide some sort of documentation regarding the garbage-collection routines that run and how to configure them via command-line arguments. These can be passed along to NetBeans during startup.

In NetBeans, you can configure JVM startup arguments by editing the file `/etc/netbeans.conf` in your NetBeans home directory. In this file, you should see a property named `netbeans_default_options`. This property allows you to pass JVM customization arguments to NetBeans.

- The `-J-Xms32m` argument specifies that the initial heap size allocated to the JVM should be 32MB.
- The `-J-XX:+UseConcMarkSweepGC` argument specifies that the JVM should use a more efficient garbage-collection algorithm. It can be especially useful on multiprocessor and multicore machines.
- The `-J-XX:+CMSClassUnloadingEnabled` argument is used to enable class unloading.
- The `-J-XX:+CMSPermGenSweepingEnabled` argument must be used in conjunction with the `CMSClassUnloadingEnabled` argument.
- The `-J-Xmx256m` argument may not be present, by default; but if it is added, it specifies that the maximum heap size that can be allocated to the JVM should be 256MB.

Increasing the value of the `Xms` argument can improve performance in some applications, since the JVM would not have to keep reallocating heap space each time it needed to increase the available space. There is a lot of discussion in the Java industry about the correct way to set these parameters. The safest bet is to set the `Xms` argument to 64MB or 128MB and to set the `Xmx` argument to about 50 to 60 percent of the total memory on your system. This value may need to increase if you work with massive code bases.

You should also note that the `Xms` and `Xmx` arguments specify only the heap size of the JVM and not the total amount of memory the JVM will use, since there are items in the JVM that do not live inside the heap.

Managing Plugins and Updates

One of the most important aspects of a Java IDE tool is the ability to receive updates and fixes. Anyone who has ever written code knows that no program is ever perfect. Mistakes and bugs happen; when they do, the most important thing that can occur (other than fixing the bug) is to deliver the updated code to the users.

NetBeans allows you to check for, download, and install updates to the tools and plugins that are installed within your distribution through the Update Center. It is an integrated tool that checks one or more remote sites for any software updates that may be available. You can also check a remote site for new plugins as well as manually install an update module that was previously downloaded.

Using the Plugin Manager

In NetBeans 6 the Update Center and Module Manager are merged into one new tool named the Plugin Manager. This new tool enables you to

- Download NetBeans plugins to install into the IDE
- Manually install previously downloaded NetBeans modules
- Check for updates to existing NetBeans plugins
- Manage already installed plugins (and be able to deactivate them)
- Configure Update Centers to check for plugins

To access the Plugin Manager, select Tools ➤ Plugins. In the window that opens, you should see five tabs along the top: Updates, New Plugins, Downloaded, Installed, and Settings. I next cover them individually, although slightly out of the order in which they appear in the Plugin Manager.

Settings Tab

If you click the Settings tab you will see the list of Update Centers currently configured in NetBeans, as shown in Figure 1-3. As you download and install new plugins, various Update Centers are automatically added to the list.

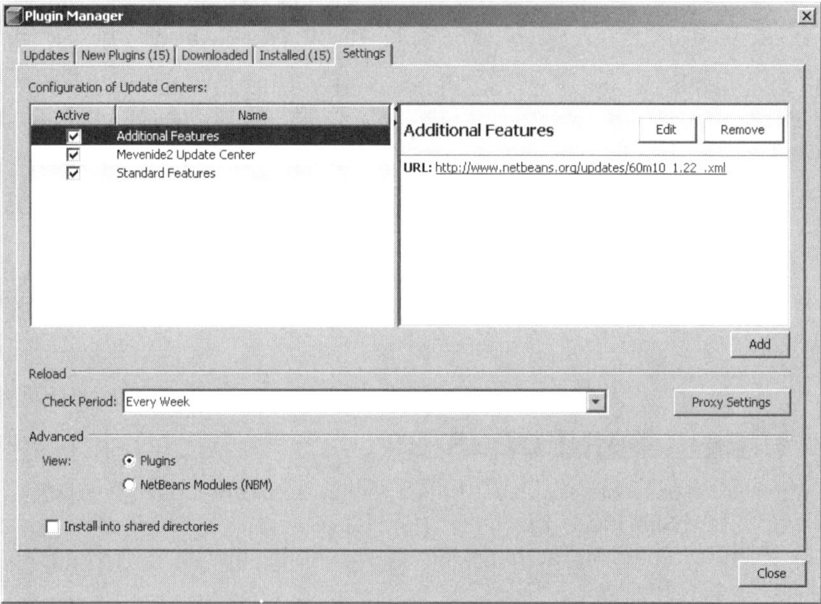

Figure 1-3. *The list of default Update Centers in the Plugin Manager*

The left pane of the Settings tab displays the list of Update Centers. If you unselect the check box next to an Update Center, it will not be searched for updates or new plugins. If you select an Update Center in the list, its information is displayed in the right pane. You can view the Update Center URL, and choose to edit or remove it from the list using the buttons displayed in the right pane, as shown in Figure 1-3.

If you wish to add a new Update Center manually, you can easily do so using the Add button at the center right of the Settings tab pane. If you click the Add button, the Update Center Customizer window is displayed, as shown in Figure 1-4. The window allows you to type in an arbitrary name to identify the Update Center as well as enter the Update Center's URL. If the check box next to the "Check for update automatically" field is selected, then the Update Center is automatically polled during the time frequency specified in the Check Period drop-down on the Settings tab. Once you have configured the desired settings for the Update Center, click the OK button and it will be added to the list.

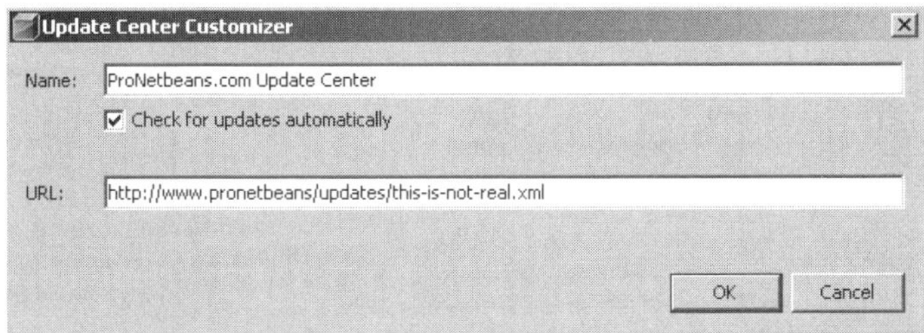

Figure 1-4. *The Update Center Customizer window*

Under the Advanced section at the bottom of the Settings tab are the View options. You can set this field to "Plugin" or "NetBeans Modules." If it is set to "NetBeans Modules," you will be able to view individual features and libraries. This setting can be useful if you are trying to understand a plugin's dependencies. If the View field is set to "Plugin," then you will not see the underlying libraries. Only the top-level plugins will be listed. This setting can make it much easier to see what is installed in your IDE without having to scroll through long lists of plugins.

The "Install into shared directories" field appears at the bottom of the Settings tab. If selected, this will install plugins into a shared folder so that they are available to all users and not to just the one who installed the plugin.

The last item to note on the Settings tab is the Proxy Settings button. If you click it, the Basic Options window will appear and display the General section. This is covered later in this chapter in the section "Setting a Proxy."

Updates Tab

The Updates tab displays any updated plugins or libraries that may have been posted to the Update Centers. You can check for updates by clicking the Reload Plugins button near the top of the pane. This will search the Update Centers and display any updated plugins by name and release date.

To install any updates that appear, simply click the check box next to each item and click the Updates button at the bottom of the pane. The features will be downloaded and installed. Depending on the module, you may be prompted to restart the IDE.

New Plugins Tab

The New Plugins tab will display a list of new plugins and libraries that have been released on the Update Centers. If you add new Update Centers, you can refresh the list of new plugins by clicking the Reload Plugins button.

You can click each plugin name and view the release date, source, and description in the right pane, as shown in Figure 1-5.

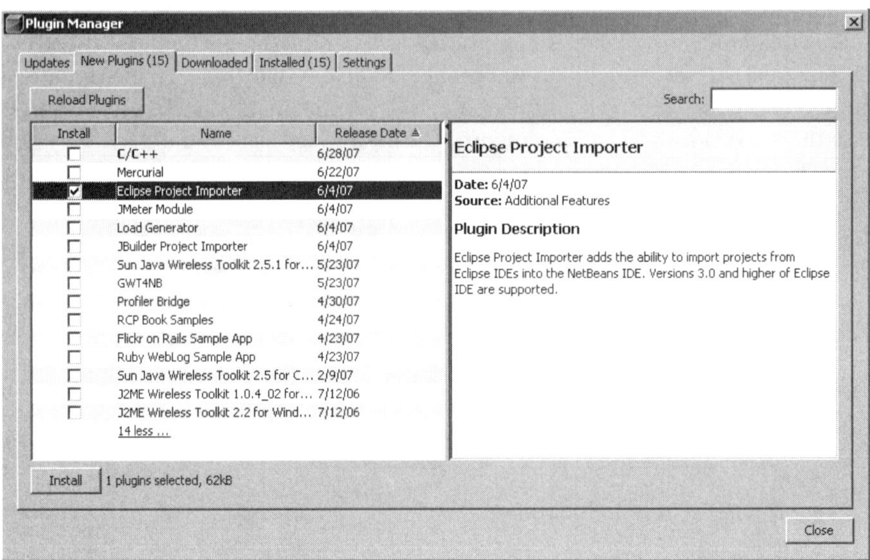

Figure 1-5. *The New Plugins tab displaying a list of plugins and libraries*

You can install each plugin by selecting the check box next to the name in the Install column. As you select each check box, a summary appears along the bottom of the window, displaying the number of plugins to be installed and the total installation size.

If the list of plugins is quite long (which it can be if you are viewing the list as NetBeans Modules versus Plugins), you can search the description text. A text box labeled Search appears in the upper right of the window. If you enter text into the Search field and press the Enter key, the list will be filtered to include only plugins that match the search criteria. This is especially useful if you are searching for plugin dependencies or libraries.

Once you have finished determining which plugins you want to install, click the Install button. A summary screen will pop open and display the plugins you selected. Review the items for correctness and click the Next button. The plugin installer will display a screen of license agreements.

In older versions of NetBeans you had to view and approve multiple licenses. In NetBeans 6 you can toggle back and forth between different license agreements and approve them all at once. You can view the different licenses by selecting them from the “Display license for” drop-down. You can then approve them all by clicking the radio button next to “I accept the terms in all license agreements” and clicking the Install button.

Each of the plugins will then download and be verified. When they are done downloading, click the Finish button. Depending on which plugins you chose to install, you may be prompted to restart the IDE. If the IDE does not need to be restarted, then you will see the list of plugins on the New Plugins tab refresh.

Installed Tab

The Installed tab lists the plugins and modules that you have previously installed. This section of the Plugin Manager allows you to uninstall and deactivate plugins and modules.

If you select a plugin from the list, you can view the date, source, description, and required modules in the right pane. You will also see a Deactivate button in the upper right. If you click the Deactivate button, it will disable the plugin without having to restart NetBeans.

■ **Tip** Disabling modules or features that you rarely use can improve the startup time and memory usage of NetBeans. When NetBeans opens, its splash screen displays several status messages, such as "Reading module storage," "Turning on modules," "Loading modules," and "Starting modules." Much of the processing and work that goes on behind the scenes during startup involves activating modules. The fewer modules NetBeans must activate, the better.

If a plugin is deactivated, it will appear in the plugin list with a red X icon in the Active column. If you select a deactivated plugin from the list, the right-hand information pane will display an Activate button. If you click the Activate button, the plugin will be enabled again.

You can also uninstall plugins by clicking the check box next to each plugin in the Uninstall column, as shown in Figure 1-6. After you have selected one or more plugins, click the Uninstall button. A popup window will appear listing each plugin you selected to uninstall. To finalize the process, click the Uninstall button, and the plugins will be uninstalled.

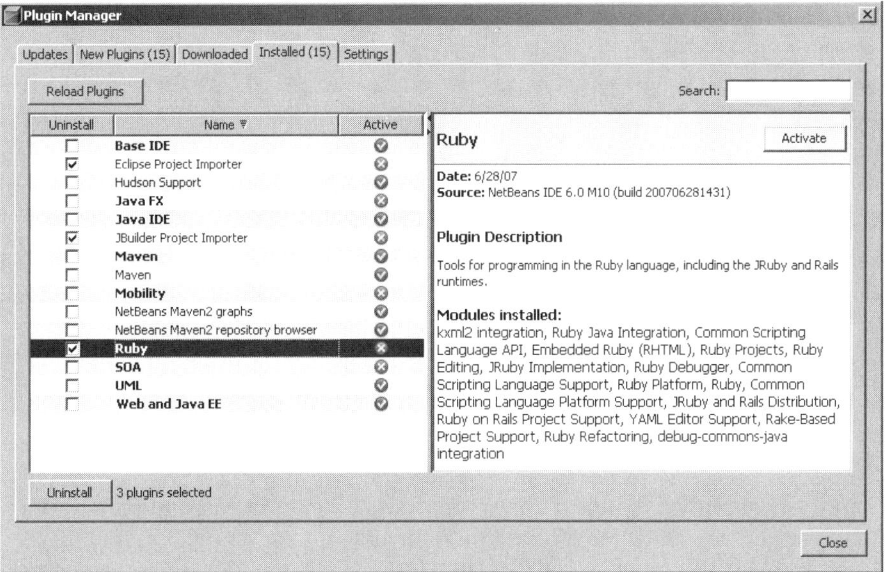

Figure 1-6. *Selecting plugins to uninstall in the Plugin Manager*

Downloaded Tab

The Downloaded tab allows you to install plugins you previously downloaded but never installed. It also allows you to install plugins you manually downloaded as .nbm files from a web site.

On the Downloaded tab, click the Add Plugins button to get a file dialog to appear. Navigate your file system, select one or more .nbm files, and click the Open button. The list of plugins to install will appear in a list. Once you have added the correct plugins to the list, click the Install button. A summary screen will pop up and allow you to review the plugins prior to installation. Click the Next button to finish installing the plugins.

Setting a Proxy

Many programmers, whether in corporations or on college campuses, need to work behind a proxy. The NetBeans IDE uses an Internet connection for numerous operations, such as downloading updates, linking to certain types of help documentation, and connecting to external database and web servers.

To configure the proxy settings for NetBeans, select Tools ➤ Options. The Basic Options window is displayed by default, and it contains a Proxy section. If it is not visible, click the General tab to see the proxy settings.

You can choose to select No Proxy, Use System Proxy Settings, or Manual Proxy Settings. If you select the radio button next to the Manual Proxy Settings label, then several fields will be enabled, allowing you to specify additional settings. The HTTP Proxy and Port text box allows you to enter specific proxy information. If you click the More button, you can view the Advanced Proxy Options window, as shown in Figure 1-7.

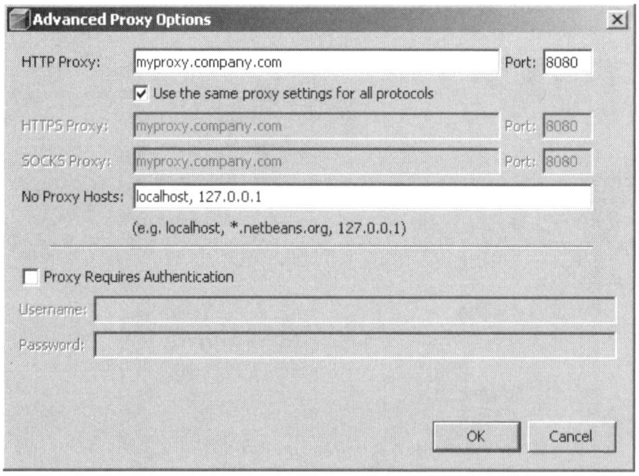

Figure 1-7. *The Advanced Proxy Options window*

The Advanced Proxy Options window allows you to enter the proxy host and port. You can also choose to select the "Use the same proxy settings for all protocols" check box. If this is selected, then the proxy you entered is used for HTTP, HTTPS, and SOCKS. If not selected, you can enter different proxies for each protocol.

An additional field, named No Proxy Hosts, will also appear in the Advanced Proxy Options window. This field allows you to specify a list of hosts to ignore that can be accessed by NetBeans without going through the proxy. If selected, the "Proxy Requires Authentication" check box allows you to specify a username and password that is used to authenticate to your proxy server. By default this field is not selected. Once you have configured the proxy settings to your needs, click the OK button to return to the Basic Options window. Click the OK button again to save the changes and exit the Basic Options window.

Customizing the IDE

Many Java IDE tools allow a wide array of customizations. NetBeans is no exception. Users can customize a variety of settings, such as fonts, colors, text messages, coding preferences, menus, toolbars, shortcuts, and much more. You could spend an exhaustive amount of time examining each and every possible customization, so I have highlighted several key items that I believe are the most relevant and useful.

Setting the Internal Web Browser

I personally do a lot of development with web-based content, so I need to be able to view that content in a convenient manner in the web browser of my choice. Sometimes I need to test web content in different browsers, especially if I am writing cross-browser JavaScript code. One of the nice features of NetBeans is the ability to set which Internet browser is used to view web content.

If you have a JSP file named `index.jsp` open and want to run it, select Run ➤ Run File ➤ Run and choose `index.jsp`. In the Output window, you will first see the application compiled, packaged, and deployed. Then the bundled Java application server will start, and finally a web browser will open.

NetBeans is initially configured to use the default browser for your system. You can change this by selecting Tools ➤ Options and selecting General in the top pane of the Options window. The Web Browser drop-down list offers Default System Browser and any browsers you have installed on your system. If you always prefer to test your web applications with Firefox, you could select it from the list.

Setting Code Editor Indentation

NetBeans allows some flexibility when configuring code indentation and formatting. When NetBeans formats source code (select Source ➤ Reformat Code) or autogenerates code, it applies several code styles. You can modify these by choosing Tools ➤ Options ➤ Editor and clicking the Indentation tab. As shown in Figure 1-8, this tab contains the code formatting options and a preview that displays how your code would be formatted if you toggled each of the available options. The following sections cover some of the more important settings.

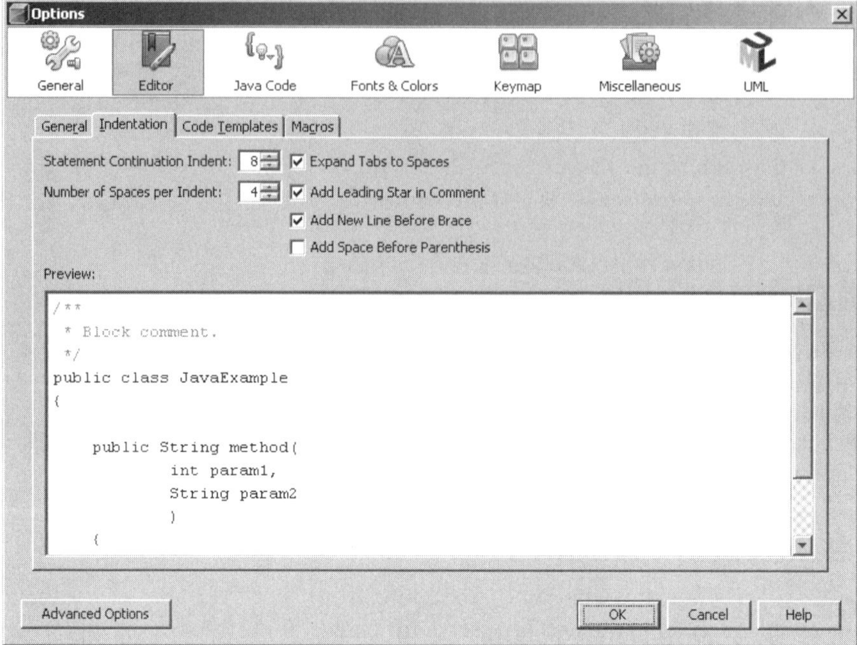

Figure 1-8. *Code indentation features*

Statement Continuation Indent

When writing code such as a method declaration with parameters, the line of characters can become quite long, as in this example:

```
public void setEmployeeData(String FirstName, String LastName)
```

Some coders believe it a best practice to leave the entire method declaration and defined parameters on one line. Popular practice is to separate long lines:

```
public void setEmployeeData(String FirstName,
                            String LastName)
```

or:

```
public void setEmployeeData(
        String FirstName,
        String LastName
        )
```

This type of syntax formatting is especially useful if you are defining a method with many parameters. It is far easier to read the parameter name and data type on a separate line than to have to scroll far to the right in a very long line.

In NetBeans, you can control the amount of space by which the continued code is indented. The Statement Continuation Indent option on the Indentation tab allows you to set the number of spaces the continued line is indented. The minimum indent is 1 space, and the maximum is 50 spaces. Try changing the number of spaces and watching the preview at the bottom of the tab.

Number of Spaces per Indent

Part of writing easy-to-maintain and legible code is indenting a statement such as `if-else`, `switch-case`, or any nested statement. Most modern IDE tools have some level of default indentation. When you finish typing a statement and press the Enter key, the cursor is positioned on the next line and indented one or more spaces.

In NetBeans, you can customize this formatting. The default number of spaces for indentation is four. The Number of Spaces per Indent option on the Indentation tab allows you to adjust this setting from 1 to 50. To see this in action, type a line of code like `if(myBooleanValue)` and the opening curly brace, and press Enter. You should see the following:

```
if(myBooleanValue) {
    //start here
}
```

The beginning of the comment marks where the cursor should be positioned. It should be indented four spaces from the position of the enclosing parent element. If you continued to press the Enter key and enter comments, you would see code like this:

```
if(myBooleanValue) {
    //start here
    //comment2
    //comment3
    //comment4
    //comment5
}
```

Notice that the line spacing for each of the lines inside the `if` block is the same. The IDE monitors the fact that all the statements you are typing have the same scope (I use this term loosely) and attempts to maintain similar spacing. After the fifth comment line, add another `if` block and see how the spacing is maintained. After typing `if(myNextBooleanValue)` and an opening curly brace, and pressing Enter, add several lines of comments. The following code should appear:

```
if(myBooleanValue) {
    //start here
    //comment2
    //comment3
    //comment4
    //comment5
    if(myNextBooleanValue) {
        // comment 6
        // comment 7
    }
}
```

If you want to see a better example of this, try setting the Number of Spaces per Indent option to 20 and typing several nested `if-else` blocks of code.

Expand Tabs to Spaces

When indenting code, some developers like to add tabs and some like spaces. For many people this is not a huge issue; but if you open code in different tools, it can cause formatting problems. If your development team works on a variety of operating systems or uses a variety of tools such as Emacs, vi, NetBeans, and Notepad, you may have run into this issue.

The Expand Tabs to Spaces option in NetBeans automatically converts any tab characters into an equivalent number of spaces. One tab character is the number of spaces set for the Number of Spaces per Indent option. This can help reduce formatting issues and spacing problems.

Add New Line Before Brace

A lot of development shops enforce a set of standard coding practices. One element of good coding is to use a consistent method of placing curly braces after method declarations, `if` blocks, `else` blocks, `switch` statements, `for` loops, and so on.

If you've ever worked on code that another developer created, you've probably seen bad coding styles. A typical piece of code for a method might look like this:

```
public int calculate(int x, int y, int z)
{
    int total = 0;
    if(x<y) {
        total = x + y;
    }
    else if(x > y)
    {
        total = x + z;
    }
    else {
        total = x+ y + z;
    }
    return total;
}
```

Notice that the opening curly brace for each block is either on the same line immediately following the statement or on the following line. Depending on how intricate your code is, this can lead to hard-to-read files, especially if numerous code blocks are embedded within code blocks embedded within code blocks.

I remember a project where I inherited code from another developer. I needed to trace what happened throughout a very long method. In the method were numerous loops and `if-else` blocks. Lining up curly braces to see where one block ended and another started soon grew frustrating. Using the NetBeans Add New Line Before Brace option and applying the formatting to the source code would have saved me a lot of headaches.

Choosing Fonts and Colors

NetBeans provides the ability to customize the overall appearance of fonts and colors. With the variety of development tools on the market, many developers are familiar with a different look and feel. For example, if you've been coding in Emacs and now are making the move to NetBeans, perhaps you want the code syntax to reflect the color scheme you used in Emacs. NetBeans provides several levels of customization.

Fonts and Color Profiles

The font and color customizations are grouped into a color profile. The profile contains the settings for customizing colors for language-specific syntax, highlighting, and annotations. Color profiles allow you to change numerous settings and toggle back and forth between them.

To customize color profiles, select Tools ➤ Options ➤ Fonts & Colors and select the Syntax tab. This tab displays the relevant settings, as shown in Figure 1-9.

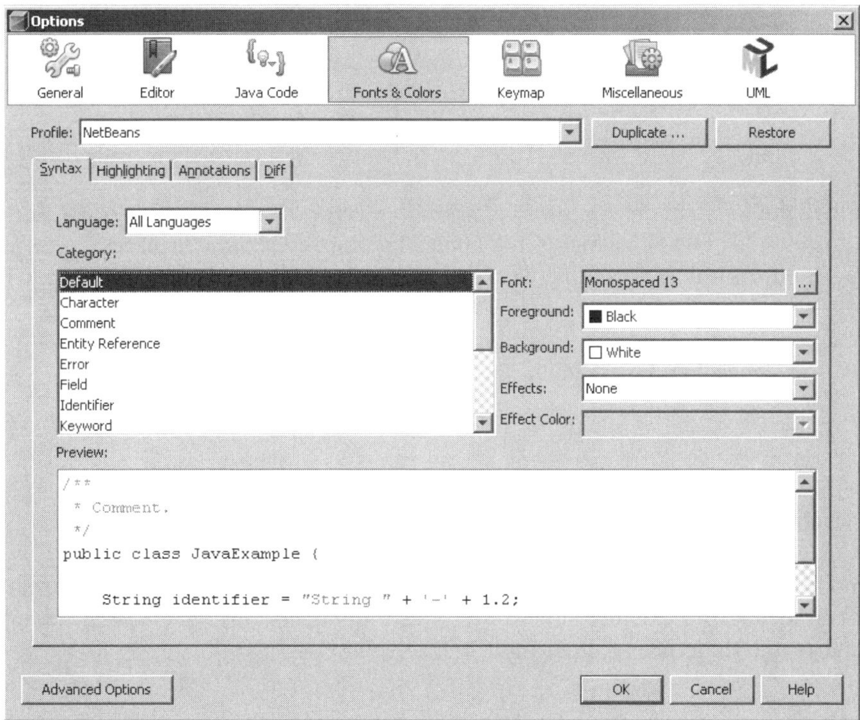

Figure 1-9. *Fonts & Colors settings in the Basic Options window*

NetBeans provides several color profiles: NetBeans, Earth, NetBeans 5.5, Norway Today, and City Lights. These can be modified as frequently as you wish and later restored to their initial settings by clicking the Restore button next to the Profile drop-down list. I recommend creating a copy of each of the NetBeans color profiles and modifying them as you see fit. You can do so by selecting the profile and clicking the Duplicate button to the right of the Profile drop-down list. This is useful because a profile that is a copy of another profile cannot be restored; it can only be deleted. The Duplicate button is also the mechanism for creating new color profiles. After clicking the Duplicate button, you are prompted for a new color profile name.

I use color profiles most often when giving presentations. For writing code, I typically use a color profile similar to the system default profile. When giving presentations, where I need to project my screen, I switch to an alternate profile that uses a larger font size and darker font color scheme.

The standard code syntax highlighting and coloring changed in NetBeans 6. Many developers used to the older NetBeans syntax coloring can switch to the NetBeans 5.5 profile by selecting it from the Profile drop-down.

Language-Specific Color Settings

For each color profile in the Fonts & Colors section, a list of language-specific settings is available. The list includes settings such as Java, JSP, HTML, SQL, XML, and more. By selecting one item from the list, you can customize the language-specific syntax elements. For example, if you select JSP, you will see a category list of items such as EL, HTML, JSP, and XML elements. Once you have selected an item from the category list, you can change the font size and color and other attributes using the options on the right (see Figure 1-9).

Highlighting

Through the Highlighting tab of the Fonts & Colors window, you can customize the foreground and background colors for elements that appear highlighted in various places in NetBean's Source Editor window. One possible use of this includes changing the color of the line numbers in the line number bar so that they are easier to see at a glance. I like to set the Code Folding Bar foreground to red so that the lines that appear next to each method stand out and are easier to trace when I am scrolling quickly through a class.

Diff Coloring

The Diff tab of the Fonts & Colors section allows you to specify the coloring for the new NetBeans 6 Diff tool. The Diff tool is used by the various version control modules and local history in NetBeans (see Chapter 6).

You can modify the color scheme for the Added, Changed, and Removed Text. If you select each field, you can specify the color using the Background drop-down at the right of the window. Then when you use the Diff tool, the color changes will display.

Annotation Coloring

The Annotations tab of the Fonts & Colors window allows you to customize several items related to glyphs that appear in the glyph margin. The glyph margin is the gray vertical strip that appears in the Source Editor to the immediate left of any source code. If you select View ➤ Show Line Numbers, the line numbers are also displayed in the glyph margin. You can change the foreground color and the background color of annotations as well as set the color of the Wave Underlined property for the Parser Annotation (Error) category. The Wave Underlined property pertains to the wavy line that appears under parser errors in your code, such as statements that will not compile.

Tip If you really want a parser error to stand out, you can set the background color to black, the foreground color to green, and the Wave Underlined property to red. Once you have done this, it should not be too difficult to spot compilation errors.

Configuring Keymaps

Every good software tool should provide shortcut keys (also known as hotkeys). NetBeans is no exception. Since the majority of the work carried out in NetBeans involves typing code, it is obviously convenient not to have to take your hands off the keyboard very often. Many menu commands, actions, and tools can be activated via keyboard shortcuts. NetBeans categorizes a group of shortcuts as a *keymap*.

Keymaps can be configured in the Basic Options window. Select Tools ➤ Options and choose Keymap from the top pane in the Options window. The default set of keyboard shortcuts (the keymap) is named NetBeans. You can copy any of the existing keymaps by selecting one from the Profile drop-down list and clicking the Duplicate button. The new keymap profile can then be customized any way you wish.

Tip The Profile drop-down contains an entry named Eclipse. If you select this option, then the NetBeans keymap will attempt to use the standard keyboard shortcuts prevalent in the Eclipse IDE. This is useful for developers who switch between the two IDEs.

To modify a specific keyboard shortcut, select the profile and locate which action you want to change. For example, you may want to change the shortcut used to compile a single file. To modify the shortcut, do the following:

1. Select the profile in the Keymap section of the Options window.
2. Click the plus sign next to the Build node.
3. Select the Compile File node under the Build node.
4. In the Shortcuts section at the bottom of the window, click the Remove button.
5. Click the Add button.
6. In the window that opens, press the key or keys that you want as the shortcut. The text representing those keys should be added to the Shortcut field.
7. Click the OK button.

NetBeans will prevent you from adding a duplicate keyboard shortcut. If the key or keys you pressed in the Shortcut pop-up window match another shortcut, then after clicking the OK button you will receive an error message. If the shortcut was successfully assigned to the action, it will be displayed in the Shortcuts list, as shown in Figure 1-10.

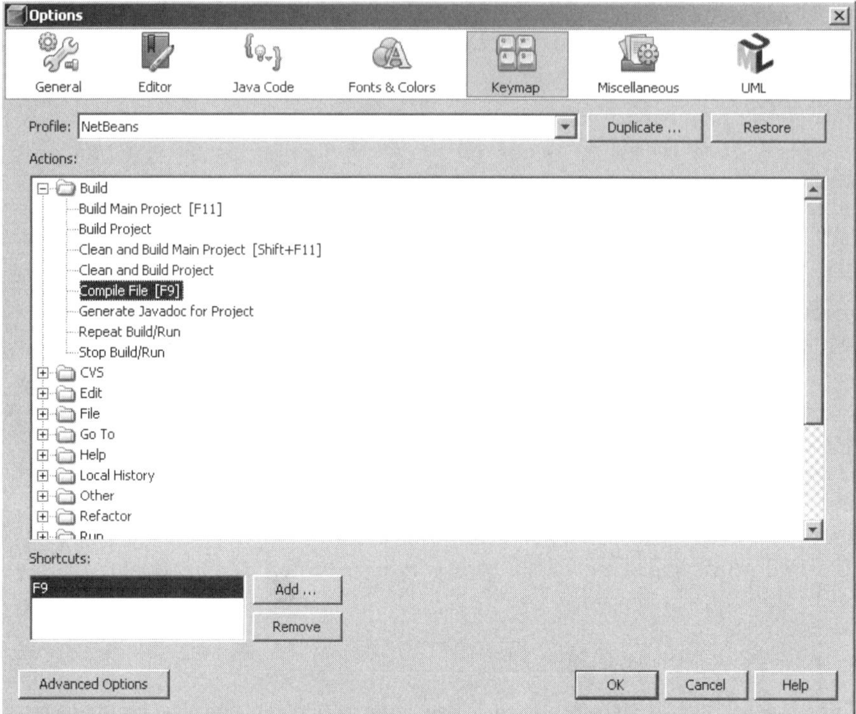

Figure 1-10. *Customizing keymaps in the Basic Options window*

Setting Advanced Options

In the Basic Options window (select Tools ➤ Options), you'll find a button to access the Advanced Options window. From the Advanced Options section, you can customize a wider variety of features than is possible through the Basic Options section. The settings for toolbars and menu bars are covered here. Other Advanced Options settings, such as those for system and external tools, are covered in later chapters.

Menu Bars

NetBeans allows you to customize the system menu bars. In the Advanced Options section, select IDE Configuration ➤ Look and Feel ➤ Menu Bar. Here, you can rename the menu options such as File, Edit, View, and so on. If you really wanted to, you could rename the View menu to Look At Stuff.

By right-clicking menu names, you can delete menus, change menu-item ordering, and add menu separators. By right-clicking menu items, you can cut or copy a menu item and paste it into another menu.

A useful application of this feature is to reorder menu items to be grouped in a manner that makes more sense to you. For example, on the Refactoring menu, I have rearranged the items I use most often to appear on the top, followed by a separator and the rest of the items. I have also found this functionality useful on the Run and Window menus.

Toolbars

NetBeans also allows you to customize toolbars in much the same way you customize menu bars. You can create new toolbars, reorder the elements of a toolbar, and copy and paste elements from one toolbar to another.

Being able to create custom toolbars is an important feature if you have installed a lot of plugins that are similar and want to group quick-access icons in one toolbar location.

Server and External Tool Settings

As previously mentioned, you can set a default web browser in the NetBeans Basic Options section. However, you were not previously able to determine where the browsers were located on your system or to add new ones. The Advanced Options window allows you to do so.

Navigate to IDE Configuration ➤ Server and External Tool Settings ➤ Web Browsers. Expand the Web Browsers node to view the list of Web Browsers that have automatically been configured. On a Windows machine you would typically only see a listing for Internet Explorer. If you installed Firefox, it would also be listed.

If the browser you want to use is not in the list but is installed on your machine, you can easily add it. Right-click the Web Browsers node and select New ➤ External Browser. In the New External Browser window that appears, type in the name of the browser and click the Finish button.

The new browser will appear under the Web Browsers node, allowing you to select it. Once you have selected it, the right pane of the Advanced Options window will display the Browser Executable property. This field specifies where on your machine NetBeans must look to find the browser. You can change this location anytime by clicking inside the field and typing or by clicking the ellipsis button next to it. If you click the ellipsis button, the Browser Executable Properties window will appear, as shown in Figure 1-11.

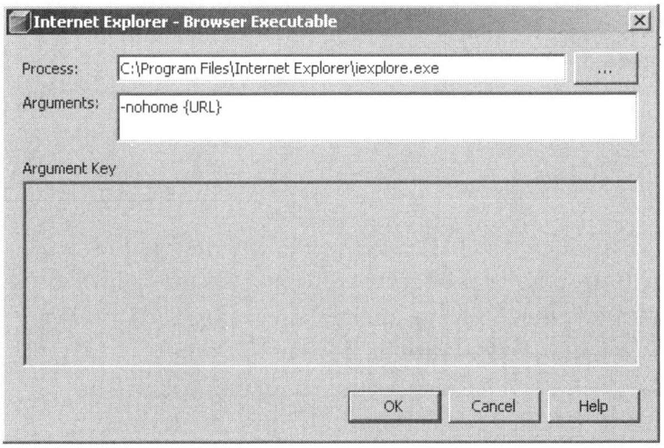

Figure 1-11. *The Browser Executable Properties window*

This window allows you to specify the path to the browser executable. You can also click the ellipsis button next to the field to display a File Open dialog to search for the executable. You can also specify command-line arguments using the Arguments text box. NetBeans passes the `-nohome` argument to Internet Explorer so that your default browser homepage will not load, saving time. The {URL} argument specifies a placeholder that NetBeans will replace with the actual URL you choose to load when you run a web application, single JSP or HTML file, etc.

There are a number of web browser–specific command-line arguments you can specify to assist you in web application development; see Tables 1-1 and 1-2. Once you have entered any command-line argument, click the OK button to close the window.

Table 1-1. *Firefox Command-Line Arguments*

Argument	Description
ProfileManager	Starts Firefox with a Profile Manager dialog. Allows you to specify which profile you wish to use to load Firefox.
Jsconsole	Loads a JavaScript console. This can be a big time saver when doing web development.
height	Specifies the height the browser window will be when it opens. Example: height 500.
width	Specifies the width the browser window will be when it opens. Example: width 500.
inspector	Displays the DOM inspector. Loads the DOM inspector into the top half of Firefox and the web page to be displayed in the bottom half.
{URL}	Loads the specified URL in Firefox when it opens.

Table 1-2. *Internet Explorer Command-Line Arguments*

Argument	Description
nohome	Specifies that the default browser homepage will not load
k	Specifies that the browser will open in full-screen mode
new	Specifies that the browser window will open a new browser, and thus a new process, instead of reloading in the same window

System

There are also several system settings you can customize in the Advanced Options window. Select IDE Configuration ➤ System ➤ System Settings. Several properties will appear in the right-hand pane, as shown in Figure 1-12. If you select the "Show Tool Tips in IDE" check box, then tool tips will be displayed throughout NetBeans as you mouse over various icons and features.

The "Confirm Delete" check box is a nice safety feature. If this is selected, you will be prompted to confirm a deletion before a file, folder, or other item can be deleted. I recommend leaving this checked, which it is by default, since even the most experienced users can mistakenly delete something.

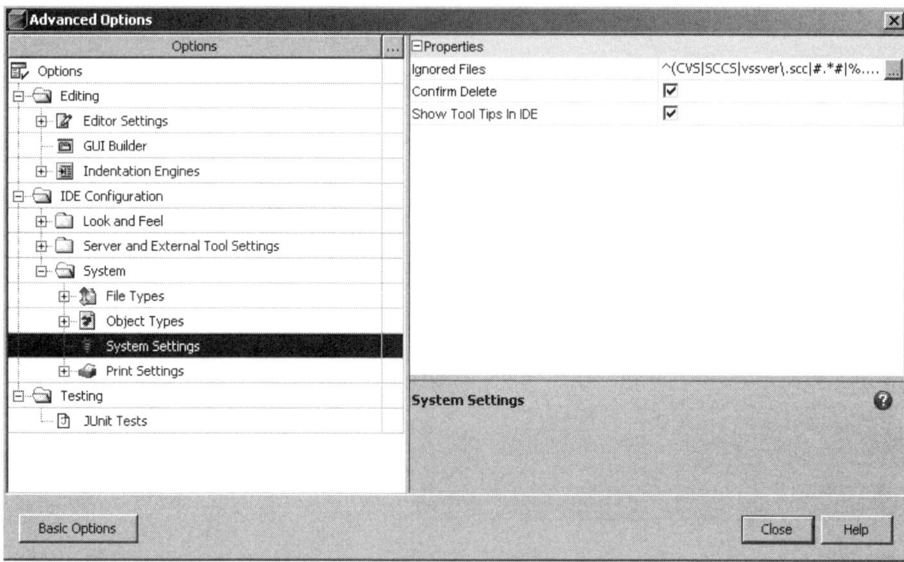

Figure 1-12. *The Confirm Delete setting in the Advanced Options window*

Navigating and Understanding the IDE Layout

Once you have installed NetBeans and customized it to your liking, it is time to start working on projects. But first you need to become familiar with the general layout of the NetBeans IDE. It provides numerous windows that enable you to view specific items or pieces of data.

Initial Layout

When the IDE first opens, the Projects, Files, and Services window is displayed on the left. The primary menu and toolbar are displayed along the top, allowing quick access to commonly used features. Other than those features, it is up to you to decide what to display and which windows you will use. See the following section ("Windows") for an explanation of some of the different windows.

The primary toolbar displayed along the top contains only a bare minimum of icons that allow you to perform frequently used operations, icons such as Open Project, New Project, New File, Cut, Copy, Paste, Build Main Project, and Run Main Project. You can customize the toolbars that are displayed and items that appear in them by right-clicking on an empty spot of the toolbar.

The context menu that appears allows you to select or unselect different toolbars from being displayed, such as Build, Debug, Edit, File, and Memory. You can also completely customize the toolbars by selecting Customize on the context menu. This will open the Customize Toolbars window, as shown in Figure 1-13. This window offers the same functionality as the toolbar configuration section in the Advanced Options window, but it has one additional benefit: you can click and drag icons from the Customize Toolbars window directly onto the primary toolbar in the IDE.

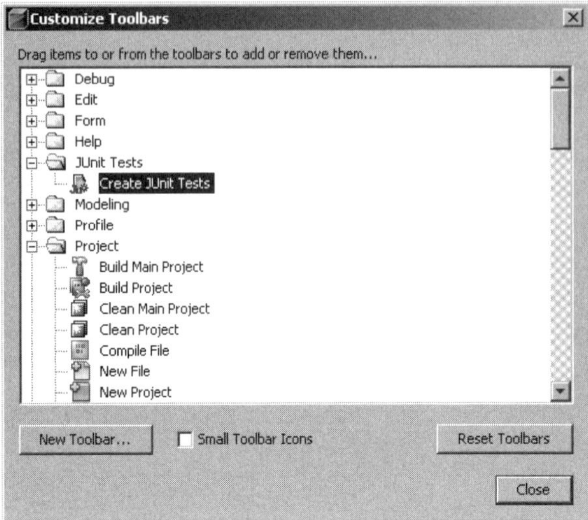

Figure 1-13. *The Customize Toolbars window*

One of the nice features on the toolbar context menu I like to use is the Small Toolbar Icons option. If this option is selected, then the primary toolbar in the IDE will shrink the icons to a smaller size. This saves space on the screen. (I like to have as much visual space as possible when working with code in the Source Editor.)

If you're programming an application and you have concerns about memory, I highly recommend selecting to display the Memory toolbar from the context menu that is displayed by right-clicking the primary toolbar. You can also activate it by going to View ➤ Toolbars ➤ Memory. This will display a JVM memory meter in the toolbar that lists the amount of memory currently used versus allocated. The memory toolbar can be useful when you launch web applications, since you can watch the memory allocated as a web application server starts up. This can be a quick and dirty way of monitoring memory usage without having to profile an application or use a tool such as JConsole.

■ **Tip** If you haven't already figured it out, you can click the Memory toolbar to force garbage collection. If you have a long-running process or a running application server started from inside NetBeans that is hogging resources, you can try to reclaim it.

Windows

There are multiple windows you can open and use throughout the IDE windowing system. Each window has a specific purpose and can be opened, minimized, or closed. Each window can also be dragged around and docked in virtually any place in NetBeans. I cover some of the more commonly used windows next.

Projects Window

The Projects window displays all the currently opened projects. It is the main entry point for NetBeans to categorize and group files for use in an application. A project can be a Java Application, an EJB Module, a Web Application, a Mobile Class Library, a NetBeans Module Project, or another type. If you need to jump quickly to the Projects window, you can toggle to it by pressing Ctrl+1.

The layout and usage of elements in the Projects window when working with files, folders, and projects is covered in more detail in various chapters throughout this book.

Files Window

The Files window provides a more normal file-based view of open projects. It contains the same information that is displayed in the Projects window but is organized in a manner that may be more familiar to you. The files in a project are organized in a folder-and-file structure that represents how your project would look if you used a file explorer outside NetBeans to view it. If the Files window is not active, you can toggle to it by pressing Ctrl+2.

Services Window

The Runtime window is where you can find important resources such as HTTP servers, database servers, web services, DTD and XML schema catalogs, and processes. You can access the Services window by selecting Window ➤ Runtime or pressing Ctrl+5.

Navigator Window

The Navigator window provides a quick-and-easy view of a node that has been selected in the Projects window or Source Editor. It can display the methods, constructors, and fields in a class in a traditional list view or as an inheritance tree. For classes with numerous methods, this can be a convenient way to jump back and forth between methods or fields. You can display the Navigator window by selecting Navigator from the Window menu or by pressing Ctrl+7.

Source Editor

The Source Editor window is where you edit code and other files. This is where the "magic" happens. When you open files, they appear in the Source Editor window as a tabbed view. The files displayed in this window can be arranged in several different ways (more on this in the next chapter, where you'll create your first Java application). If you have a file already open in the Source Editor, you can quickly toggle to it by pressing Ctrl+0.

Tip Pressing and holding Ctrl+Tab allows you to select and switch back and forth between open tabs in the Source Editor window, similar to how you can toggle between open applications in Windows using Alt+Tab.

Output Window

The Output window can display a variety of information. If you choose to build your project, compile a single file, or run a file that outputs text to the standard output or standard error stream, the information and results are displayed in the Output window. If the Output window is not displayed, you can select Window ➤ Output ➤ Output or press Ctrl+4 to open it.

Properties Window

The Properties window displays the attributes and properties of either the element currently selected in the Projects window or the item that is highlighted in the Source Editor. To see this in action, open the Properties window by selecting Window ➤ Properties or pressing Ctrl+Shift+7.

Once the Properties window opens, navigate through the Projects window and select a Java source file in an open project. The Properties window will display several attributes for the Java file, such as the filename, file size, last modified date, and classpath.

Double-click the source file. Once it opens in the Source Editor, select any method by clicking the method name. Notice that the Properties window changes to display the attributes of the method, such as the method name, access modifier, parameters, return type, any exceptions, and Javadoc comments.

The Properties window can be very convenient when used in conjunction with the Projects window for quickly navigating file structures and viewing attributes.

Palette Window

The Palette window displays a context-sensitive list of elements that are useful for the current file you are editing in the Source Editor. You can open the Palette window by selecting Window ➤ Palette or pressing Ctrl+Shift+8. If you selected a JSP file, the Palette window would display HTML, JSP, JSTL, and database elements. If you open a Java Swing source file in the Source Editor, the Palette window is filled with visual elements to be used in Swing projects.

Summary

In this chapter we discussed installing NetBeans, updating features, and customizing internal properties.

We covered installing NetBeans into standard directory structures and associating the correct JDK. We also covered how to customize the application server properties during the installation procedure. Performance considerations for the tool's startup time were also discussed. We reviewed several suggested settings that you may want to tweak to obtain optimal performance, such as altering the garbage collector that is used and specifying heap and memory arguments.

You can configure a variety of NetBeans settings based on your preferences. In this chapter we also discussed how to configure the Basic and Advanced Options (accessible from the Tools main menu) to set these properties. You can configure everything from code formatting to fonts and colors and menus and toolbars.

Lastly, we reviewed some of the windows that programmers will see and use most often. These windows provide various pieces of information and quick access to certain features. Understanding where and how to use them is critical to becoming an expert user of NetBeans.

CHAPTER 2

The Source Editor

The Source Editor is arguably one of the most important focal areas of NetBeans. It is where developers write new code, rework existing code, refine their documentation, and perform many important tasks.

The NetBeans Source Editor is not only a mechanism for writing text, but also a full-featured environment designed to assist you. Whether it's providing abbreviations for faster coding, automatic code completion, or navigation and documentation aids, the Source Editor aims to provide every possible convenience.

In this chapter I attempt to introduce the core features provided in the Source Editor. The NetBeans 6 Source Editor has a similar look and feel to that of previous versions of NetBeans, but it has an entirely new underlying architecture that affects syntax coloring, refactoring, code formatting, and more. Some of the Source Editor features are explained in more detail in other chapters, such as code completion (Chapter 3), debugging (Chapter 4), and Javadoc (Chapter 7). This chapter is intended to serve as a quick introduction and overview.

Working in the Projects Window

Before you can open and work with files in the Source Editor, you have to be able to navigate the Projects and Files windows. The Projects and Files windows are the places to go to open Java files in the Source Editor.

The Projects window is the primary location where you can view the files associated with your application. It is structured as a parent-child tree, where the parent node is the project and the child nodes are the categories into which NetBeans organizes the files.

For most Java project types, the files are sorted into four groups:

- Source Packages
- Libraries
- Test Packages
- Test Libraries

Source Packages

The Source Packages location is where you define the Java source code to be used in your application. Here, you can add and maintain the package statements you would normally use, such as `com.mycompany.projectname`. Adding packages is extremely easy. Right-click Source Packages and select New ➤ Java Package. In the New Java Package window, you can specify the name of the new package, such as `com.yourcompany.product`. Once you have decided on the name for your package, click the Finish button, and the new package name is added under Source Packages in the Projects window.

■ **Tip** Notice the icon next to the package name. If the icon is gray (which it is after you add a new package), then it is empty of classes. Once you have added at least one class into a package, the icon becomes orange. This small feature is useful once you have multiple hierarchies of package names.

You can right-click almost any node that appears in the Projects window, such as project names, packages, and Java source files. Each type of element displays different menu items on the context menu that appears.

Test Packages

The Test Packages node in the Projects window is nearly identical to the Source Packages node. However, the Test Packages node specifies the package structure for your application's test classes and JUnit tests. If you were to execute the project tests by going to the Run menu and selecting Test *MyProjectName*, the classes in the Test Packages node would be executed.

The source code for Test Packages is separate from the regular source code for Source Packages. You can see the difference by right-clicking the project name and selecting Properties. Make sure the Sources option is selected. In the Sources section in the Project Properties window, you will see a section for defining Source Package Folders and a different section for defining Test Package Folders, as shown in Figure 2-1. This allows you to reference one or more locations for Source Packages and Text Packages.

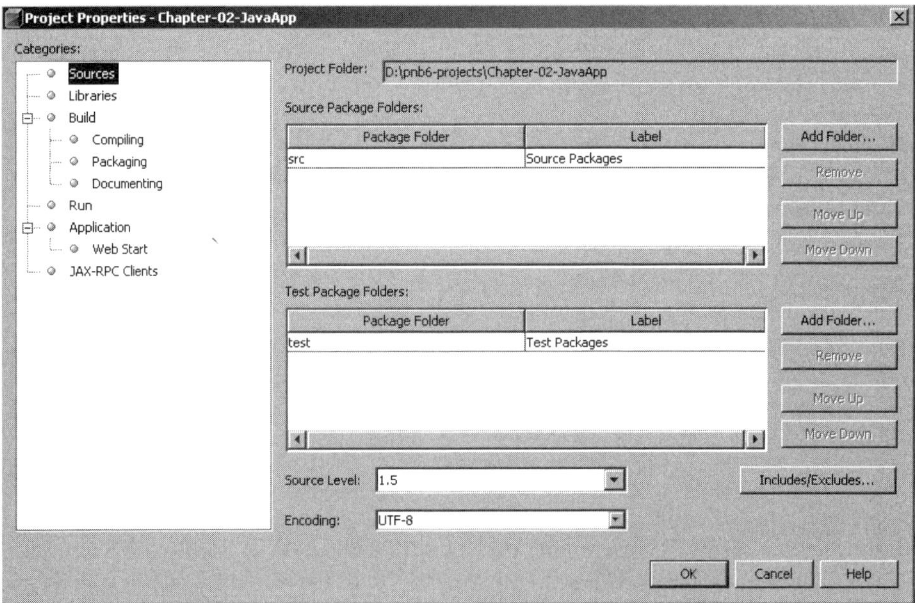

Figure 2-1. *Project Properties window specifying Source Package Folders and Test Package Folders*

Libraries

The Libraries node in the Projects window is for defining class libraries that your application will use. If you need to use nonstandard libraries or classes from an external project, you can define them under the Libraries node. To add a JAR file to the libraries for your project, right-click the Libraries node and select Add JAR/Folder.

Test Libraries

Similar to the Libraries node, the Test Libraries node contains class files or JAR files that your project test classes need to reference. You can add files to your test libraries by right-clicking the Test Libraries node and selecting Add JAR/Folder. The JAR file for JUnit exists by default in the Test Libraries section.

Working in the Files Window

As briefly introduced in Chapter 1, the Files window displays the same data as the Projects window, but in a more traditional file-and-folder view. In Figure 2-2, you can see a set of project files displayed in the Files window. The Files window shows an src folder for the Source Packages, a test folder for the Test Packages, and an nbproject folder, which contains the internal project-related settings NetBeans uses.

If you build the project, then a `build` directory will appear in the folder listing. If you have set the project to generate a JAR or WAR file, then a `dist` directory will also appear.

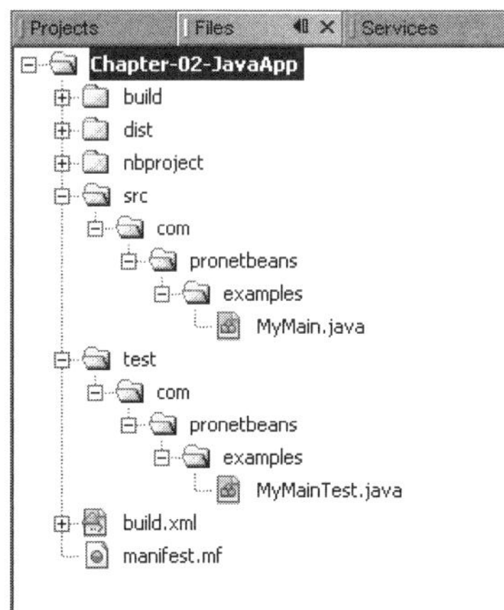

Figure 2-2. *Files window layout*

Arranging and Navigating

Now that you have learned where to go to find project files, you can open them in the Source Editor and begin working. One of the easiest concepts that is frequently overlooked when working in the Source Editor is the ability to arrange files.

Arranging Files in the Source Editor

The Source Editor allows you to arrange files in many different ways, giving you the maximum flexibility in working with files. The default viewing option for files is a tabbed approach, where all the files open in the same window with the names of each file appearing in a tab.

A different option is dual-file editing, where one file is displayed in the left portion of the Source Editor and another file is displayed in the right portion, as shown in Figure 2-3. Having two different files displayed at the same time can be convenient if you are writing code in one file that is based off another or uses a similar algorithm.

I use this occasionally when I am writing code that is subclassing another class. I display the superclass on the right and the subclass on the left. That way, I can line up method implementations and compare code without having to toggle repeatedly between two tabs.

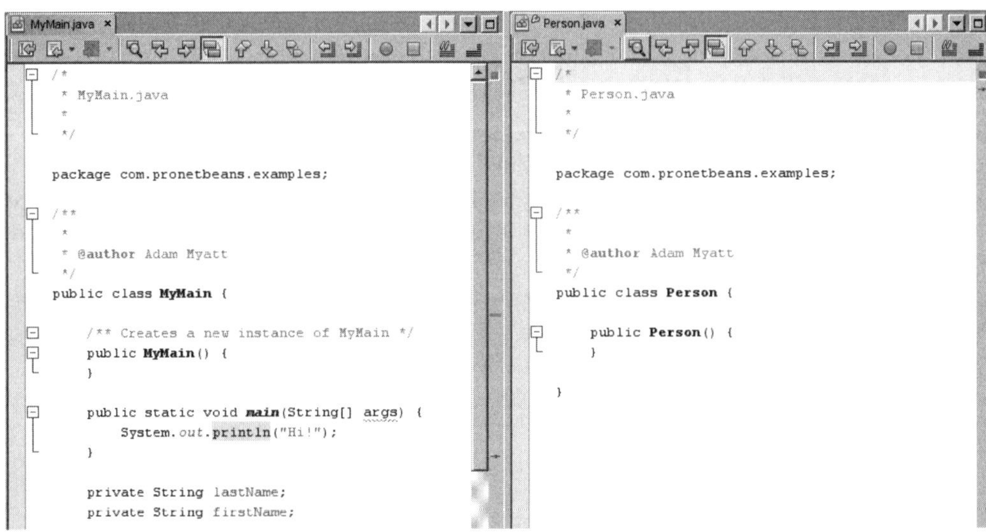

Figure 2-3. *Dual-window file display using left and right panels*

An additional method for displaying files in the Source Editor is top–bottom. Sometimes I need to edit one file and find myself constantly scrolling back and forth between two methods. Code folding comes in handy here, but it may not be convenient enough. If I could only view the same file in two places at once, my life would be much easier.

You can do this in the NetBeans Source Editor by right-clicking the Filename tab and selecting Clone Document. A second instance of the file will open in the Source Editor. Click and hold the Filename tab for the second file, and move your mouse to the lower half of the Source Editor. A highlighted outline of the file should be visible. Once you have it positioned correctly, release the mouse button. The result will be a split screen, as shown in Figure 2-4.

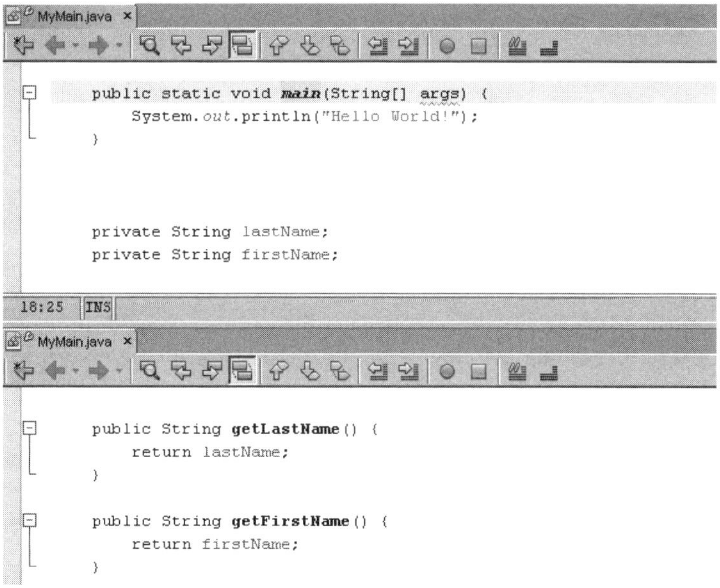

```
MyMain.java

    public static void main(String[] args) {
        System.out.println("Hello World!");
    }



    private String lastName;
    private String firstName;

18:25 INS
MyMain.java

    public String getLastName() {
        return lastName;
    }

    public String getFirstName() {
        return firstName;
    }
```

Figure 2-4. *Dual window top–bottom*

There are additional ways you can arrange files open in the Source Editor. To arrange the files click and drag the tab of one file around the inside of the Source Editor window. As you move the mouse around the edges of the window, you will notice an orange outline. If you release the mouse, the window you are moving will embed itself in that area of the Source Editor window that was defined by the outline. This sounds more difficult than it really is. Open several files in NetBeans and start experimenting with file layouts. You can even arrange a single source file to be displayed in four quadrants at the same time. Exactly why you would do so is beyond me, but it is in fact possible.

Navigating Files in the Source Editor

If multiple source files are open in the Source Editor, you can easily navigate between them. Depending on your screen width and the amount of visible space available to the Source Editor, the file tabs will not all display along the top of the Source Editor.

You can move back and forth between the open files in several ways. First you can do so without using a mouse. To switch between the tabs, press and hold the Ctrl key. Then press the Tab key. You will see a small pop-up window displaying the list of currently opened files. Each time you press Tab, you can toggle between the files. Once you have selected the file you wish to view, release the Ctrl key. The selected file should be displayed in the Source Editor.

You can also use the left, right, and down arrows that appear in the upper right of the Source Editor. If you click the down arrow a small pop-up window displaying the list of currently opened files will appear. It allows you to select a file and have it displayed in the Source Editor. If you use the left and right arrows, you can move through the list of open files one at a time in either direction (backward or forward).

Working in the Source Editor

The Source Editor window is where programmers will spend most of their time. This is where file contents are displayed when opened through the other windows or locations in NetBeans. The Source Editor displays all files, such as Java source files, XML files, and text files. The Source Editor provides a different set of tools and functionality based on the file type that is currently displayed or active.

Opening Files

As discussed in earlier sections of this chapter, you can display a file in the Source Editor by double-clicking the file in the Projects or Files window. It should open in the Source Editor portion of the IDE.

A toolbar at the top of the window allows for some convenient links to IDE functionality. It contains icons for searching for words, indenting code, and commenting lines of text. The icons displayed in this toolbar vary, depending on the type of file that is displayed. The same features can also be activated by viewing the corresponding menu items on the Edit, Navigate, and Source menus. Most of the features have keyboard shortcuts, which are noted on those main menus.

Line Numbers

In the Source Editor, line numbers are displayed along the left column. The line numbers provide a great way to track where certain pieces of code are as well as provide a quick way to trace the location of exceptions that are thrown. If the line numbers are not displayed, you can enable them by selecting View ➤ Show Line Numbers.

Code Folding

The next feature to notice in the Source Editor is code folding. For each section of Javadoc comments and each method name, notice the minus icon and the line extending below it. This denotes a piece of text that can be folded, or hidden. The obvious question from any user new to a modern Java IDE is "Why do I need this?"

If you have ever worked with a very long Java source file, you can start to see where I'm going with this. All too often, to edit code, I have needed to scroll up and down through a file between two methods. Every time you edit source code, you don't want to be rearranging where methods are in a file just to make it easier to work with them. With code folding, you can hide large blocks of code that you do not need to see.

Code folding can be enabled or disabled, depending on your personal preference. To disable code folding in NetBeans, select Tools ➤ Options ➤ Editor. On the top of the General tab is a check box labeled Use Code Folding. Uncheck this box and click OK. The code-folding lines and minus icons will disappear from the Source Editor.

In the same section in the Basic Options, you can also configure the default folding properties of Java source files. Below the Use Code Folding check box is a section called "Collapse by Default." Here you can enable folding for methods, inner classes, imports, Javadoc comments, and initial class comments. I typically enable code folding by default for methods and Javadoc comments but leave the rest of the options disabled. This is useful when you open a lot of Java source files and know exactly which method you need to find and edit.

If you have enabled code folding, several menu items in the IDE can be useful. Once you have opened a Java source file with all the methods and Javadoc folded, select View ➤ Code Folds. In this submenu are options for expanding all sections that are folded (Expand All), collapsing all sections that can be folded (Collapse All), expanding or collapsing just Javadoc comments, and expanding or collapsing all Java code blocks. This allows a great deal of flexibility when working with code folding in a file and saves you from manually scrolling through the file and collapsing each method.

Depending on the file type, code folding may or may not be supported when the file is displayed in the Source Editor. For example, if you open a web application's `web.xml` file in the Source Editor, then code folding is enabled. You can expand or collapse different tags in the XML file. Other file types may have code-folding support.

Tip The best shortcuts to remember when working with code folding are Ctrl+Shift+– (minus) to collapse all folds and Ctrl+Shift++ (plus) to expand all folds. If the cursor is inside a method, section of Javadoc, or other element where cold folding applies, you can also press the Ctrl+key combination to collapse or expand just that code block.

Current-Line Highlighting

A trivial but useful feature of the NetBeans Source Editor is current-line highlighting. The line that contains the cursor is lightly highlighted, so you always know exactly which line is being edited. You can see this by clicking anywhere in a Java source file and then using the up and down arrow keys to navigate through the file.

Syntax and Error Highlighting

In my humble opinion, code syntax-error highlighting might just be the greatest feature of modern Java IDE tools. I can still remember my early days of Java programming where I would type a lot of code and finally get around to compiling. There would always be several dozen errors that were mostly syntax related since I never remembered the exact case syntax of certain methods or forgot the semicolon at the end of each line.

When many programmers get inspired and literally fly through code, they don't want to stop and compile every few lines. This leads to long error lists when they finally do compile. Having a visual means of identifying errors immediately can be quite an asset.

NetBeans provides a great feature set for identifying errors in code. The first is the highlighting feature. If a programmer types a line of code and progresses line by line, the IDE scans the text of your source code in the background to determine if it will compile and, if not, shows the possible errors and warnings.

For example, if you were to open a Java source file, type `System.out.printlnnn("Hi");`, and press the Enter key, you would see a red wavy line appear under that piece of code. If you position the mouse over the error glyph in the left margin, a window will pop up with the message "cannot find symbol, symbol : method printlnnn(java.lang.String)."

Why is this one of the greatest features? Because it allows you to spot code syntax errors immediately, see exactly where in the code they occur, and get a helpful message telling you why the error exists. You do not have to wait until you compile the file and read the compiler output to discover that there is a problem.

In older versions of NetBeans, the entire line would be highlighted. In NetBeans 6, only the specific portion of the line causing the error is highlighted. Notice that the `System.out` portion of the line is displayed without problems, because it is syntactically correct, but only the `printlnnn` method is underlined as an error, as shown in Figure 2-5.

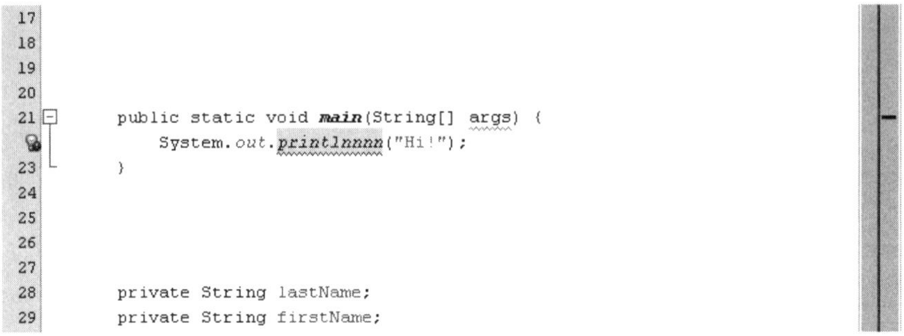

```
17
18
19
20
21      public static void main(String[] args) {
            System.out.printlnnnn("Hi!");
23      }
24
25
26
27
28      private String lastName;
29      private String firstName;
```

Figure 2-5. *The code highlighting for a syntax error in the Source Editor*

Annotation Glyphs and the Error Stripe

The annotation glyph margin (also called the *glyph gutter*) and the error stripe are two incredible features in NetBeans that allow a developer to perform fast error identification and resolution.

On the left side of the Source Editor, small icons, or glyphs, can appear in a vertical gray bar (or in place of line numbers if the line number feature is enabled). For example, in Figure 2-5, a glyph is displayed instead of the line numbers for line 22. The annotation glyph margin typically displays icons denoting the following:

- Errors
- Breakpoints for debugging
- Bookmarks
- Compiler warnings
- Suggestions
- Tasks
- Other code syntax notifications

The icons that appear in the glyph margin allow you to mouse over and read a brief description of the identified issue.

On the far-right side of the Source Editor window is a slim, vertical gray bar, which is the error stripe. The error stripe goes hand in hand with the glyph margin and code-syntax highlighting. The error stripe displays small, color-coded rectangles for specific issues that correspond to the glyphs in the glyph margin. The main difference is that as you scroll through a long file, the glyph margin and line numbers on the left scroll with you, while the error stripe bar on the right stays fixed. The error stripe represents the entire file, regardless of length. As the file grows longer, the error stripe stays the same length. Displayed on the error stripe are all syntax errors and warnings, highlighted items, breakpoints, and bookmarks.

As errors appear in the code and the glyph margin, they also appear in the error stripe bar. If you mouse over the small, red rectangle that appears in the error stripe signifying an error, it will display the exact error message, just like mousing over the error glyph icon in the left margin. If you click the red rectangle in the error stripe, it will take you directly to the line of code that is causing the problem. This is an important feature, since many times you have hundreds of lines of code but don't want to have to scroll through all of them just to find the one error that is being highlighted.

If you made an error that NetBeans thinks it can help you fix, then a Suggestion glyph icon will appear in the glyph margin. The following sample code demonstrates this.

```
package com.pronetbeans.examples;

/**
 * @author Adam Myatt
 */
public class Main {

    public static void main(String[] args)
    {
        Main MyObj = new Main();

        MyObj.doSomething();
    }
}
```

In the instance pictured in Figure 2-6, a method of an object was called that does not exist. The Suggestion glyph that appears suggests creating the method `Main.doSomething()` in the class to make the code valid (or at least compile).

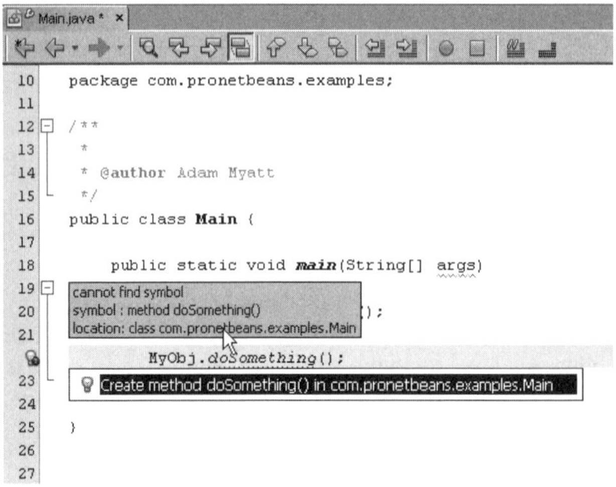

Figure 2-6. *Suggestion glyph icon in the glyph margin*

If you click on the Suggestion glyph icon, the blue highlighted text "Create method doSomething in com.pronetbeans.examples.Main" appears. You can also force it to appear by pressing the shortcut keys Alt+Enter. If you click the highlighted text or press the Enter key, NetBeans will implement the suggestion and the Suggestion glyph icon will disappear. The following code will have been added to the class:

```
private void doSomething() {
    throw new UnsupportedOperationException("Not yet implemented");
}
```

As you can see, it added a `private` method `doSomething` that throws an `UnsupportedOperationException` if executed. This allows your code to compile but throws the `Exception` if you execute the method without fully implementing it. The access modifier of `private` is the NetBeans way of making sure additional classes don't call the method until you explicitly make the decision to change it to `public`, `protected`, or `default`.

Some additional situations in which you might see Suggestion glyph icons are

When you need to surround a block with `try` and `catch` statements

When you use a class without first importing it or its package

When you type a local variable in a method's `return` statement without first having created the variable

When you define and reference a variable without first initializing it with a value

For the complete list of situations where NetBeans displays the Suggestion glyph icon, see the NetBeans help by navigating to Help ➤ Help Contents and searching the index for the word suggestions.

The last error-related feature I want to focus on here is the Output window. When code is built or executed, the output from the standard out and error streams is displayed in the Output window. If there is a compilation error, the standard error stream that is displayed in the Output window will be linked directly to the source code. For the following example, note that the semicolon is missing from the end of one of the lines.

```
public class Main {

    public static void main(String[] args) {

        Main MyObj = new Main()
        MyObj.doSomething();
    }
}
```

When the code is compiled, the Output window will display that a semicolon is expected and at which line the issue occurred. The line is also linked to the matching line in the source. As shown in Figure 2-7, the error line in the Output window is hyperlinked.

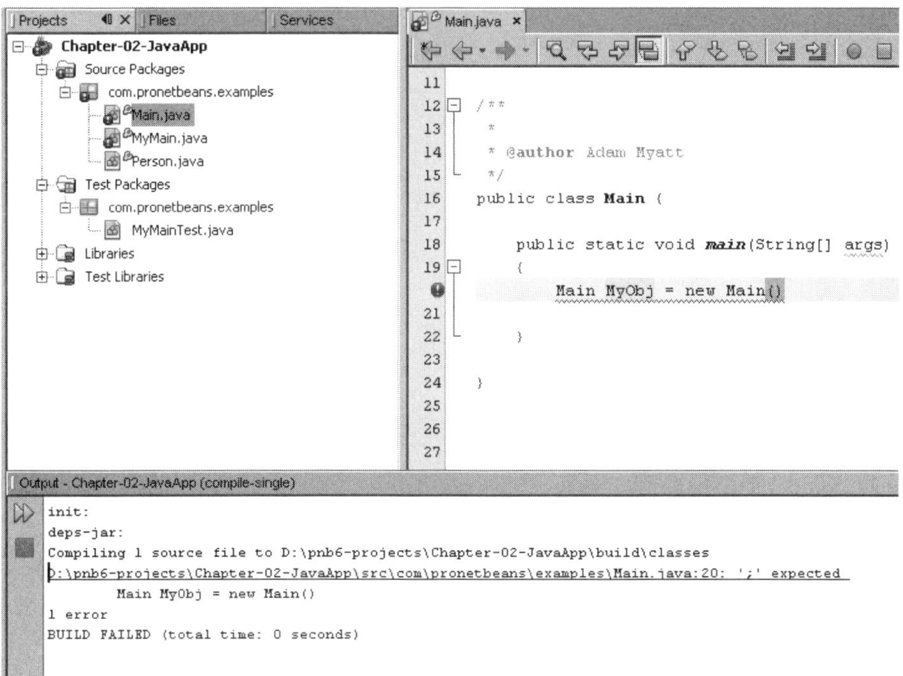

Figure 2-7. *The standard error output hyperlinked to the source code*

If you click the hyperlinked error message, then the matching code opens in the Source Editor and is scrolled to the line where the error occurred. This can be a very useful feature if you are compiling an entire package or project and numerous errors occur in the Output window. Not only do you see the errors, but NetBeans also intelligently links them directly to the source code, to save you time.

Code Indentation

Few programmers would argue that indenting code doesn't matter. Formatting your code and indenting each line properly makes the code more readable and easier to maintain. When code contains numerous nested blocks, it can sometimes be difficult to know where one `if` or `else` statement begins and another ends. Many programmers have played the "count the curly brackets" game to understand how some legacy code works. Look at the following code:

```
public class BadClass {

public BadClass() {

int x = 0;
int y = 1;
int z = 2;
int outputNum = 0;

if(x < y) {
System.out.println("X is less than Y");
if(x==0) {
outputNum = 9;
}
else if(x==1) {
x+=463;
}
else if(x==2) {
x+=x;
}
}
else if(x<z) {
z+=y;
}
}
}
```

At first glance (and maybe even second glance) it is not easily discernable which `else-if` blocks are nested inside which `if` blocks. It is the habit of a good programmer to indent the code using spaces and tabs so that it is easier to read and thus to maintain. Following some sort of standard indentation scheme is also important so that indentation is consistent across multiple files. NetBeans helps enforce this best practice.

NetBeans uses a standard indentation scheme. Combined with the Reformat Code option on the Sources main menu, you can create code and have NetBeans enforce good indentation. If you are dealing with a file created outside NetBeans, you can reformat it to use the correct indentation following the NetBeans standard.

To apply the formatting, go to the Source main menu and select Reformat Code. You can also press the shortcut Ctrl+Shift+F. After reformatting with indentation, our `BadClass` example should look like Figure 2-8.

```
public class BadClass {

    public BadClass() {

        int x = 0;
        int y = 1;
        int z = 2;
        int outputNum = 0;

        if (x < y) {
            System.out.println("X is less than Y");
            if (x == 0) {
                outputNum = 9;
            } else if (x == 1) {
                x += 463;
            } else if (x == 2) {
                x += x;
            }
        } else if (x < z) {
            z += y;
        }
    }
}
```

Figure 2-8. *The reformatted BadClass example with indentation applied*

In the reformatted code in Figure 2-8, notice that each nested block is properly indented. Each `if`, `else-if`, and `else` is easier to read, so you can quickly identify the start and end of the blocks. The important thing to note is that each block is indented a set number of spaces. This is a property that can be configured.

To set this and other indentation properties, go the Tools main menu and click Options. In the Basic Options window that appears, select Editor from the top pane and click the Indentation tab. The Indentation properties should be displayed as seen in Figure 2-9. You can set the Number of Spaces per Indent, which affects how far each line or block is indented. By default it is set to four. You can set this to whatever you want, but it should generally follow the default, especially if multiple developers work on the same code.

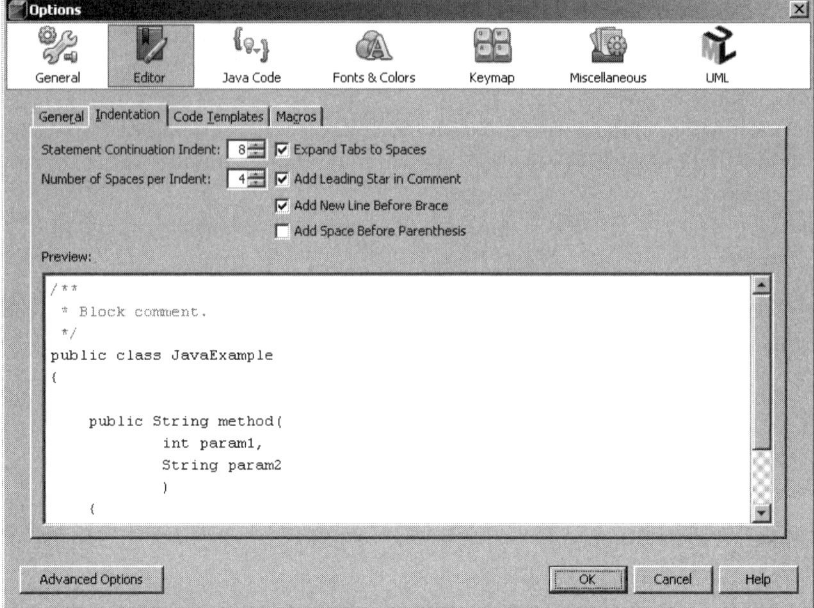

Figure 2-9. *Setting indentation properties*

Identifying Starting and Ending Braces

One of the improved features in NetBeans 6 is the ability to identify quickly and easily how curly braces line up. In the previous section I mentioned the importance of code indentation to make files easier to read and understand. Even then, it is sometimes still difficult to trace quickly where an `if` or `else-if` block ends.

Look back at the `BadClass` file in Figure 2-8. If you open the file in the Source Editor and click next to the curly brace at the end of line 21 that reads `if (x < y) {`, then that curly brace should be highlighted green, by default, and the matching curly brace that ends the `if` statement should be highlighted as well. The closing brace starts line 30 and reads `} else if (x < z) {`. The color may not show up, but review Figure 2-10 to see the curly brace highlighting.

```
20
21          if (x < y) {
22              System.out.println("X is less than Y");
23              if (x == 0) {
24                  outputNum = 9;
25              } else if (x == 1) {
26                  x += 463;
27              } else if (x == 2) {
28                  x += x;
29              }
30          } else if (x < z) {
31              z += y;
32          }
```

Figure 2-10. *The curly braces highlighted in the BadClass file*

This same type of highlighting can also be used with parentheses for method declarations, method calls, `if` statements, and more. Simply click next to any parenthesis or curly brace to see the matching element. This feature existed in previous versions of NetBeans, but it wasn't great. You always had to click inside and to the right of the brace or parenthesis, and it wasn't always perfect. In NetBeans 6 the feature works flawlessly.

Identifying Unused Imports

Another nice new feature of NetBeans 6 is the ability to see all unused imports highlighted as warnings. Using the `BadClass` file from the previous section, I have added several useful imports to various classes in the `java.util` package. In prior versions of NetBeans, you could use a keyboard shortcut or context menu selection to tell the IDE to remove unused imports. The same still applies, but now the unused imports are neatly highlighted in the source code, as shown in Figure 2-11.

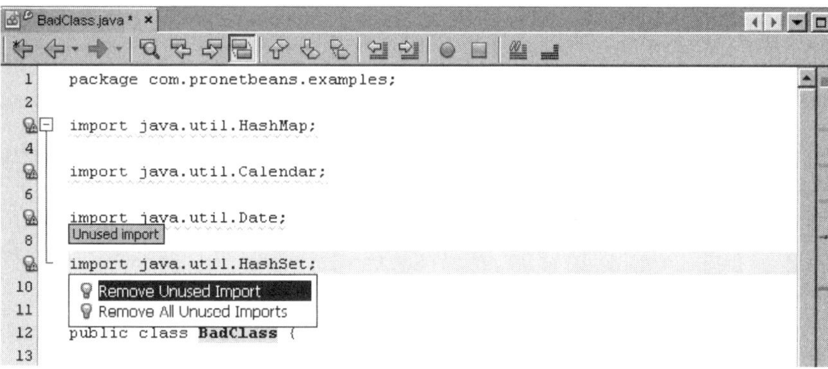

Figure 2-11. *Unused imports highlighted in source code*

Figure 2-11 shows four unused imports. The glyph margin displays a warning icon that you can click on to display several options. The first, Removed Unused Import, simply strips out the single line for the import you selected using the glyph in the margin. The second option, Remove All Unused Imports, will strip out all the invalid imports from the `BadClass` class.

Source Editor Menus

Several menus are specifically related to the Source Editor. These provide links to the most commonly used pieces of functionality that you will need as you are coding.

Context Menus

To activate the context menu in the Source Editor, simply right-click anywhere in the window. In the menu that appears are numerous options. Many of them are also available in the main menu structure in NetBeans, but if invoked here can be context sensitive to the file, section, line, or even word highlighted.

The first item to cover on the Source Editor context menu is the Go To option. This option has its own submenu and lists item selections such as Source, Declaration, Super Implementation, Test, Line, and Type. Depending on which option you select, you will get a slightly different result based on what is selected and/or highlighted. Each of the submenu options described next is also available from the main menu titled Navigate that is available in NetBeans.

Go To Source

The Go To Source menu option allows you to open the source code for an element. You can do this by either highlighting the name or placing the cursor inside the name of the element for which you wish to view the source code.

Assume you were not familiar with the `java.lang.System` class and wanted to discover how the internal code worked. For the code

```
System.out.println("How does this thing work?");
```

you can right-click anywhere inside the `System` class name and select Go To ➤ Source. You can also use the keyboard shortcut of Ctrl+Shift+B. The source file for the `System` class will open as a separate tab in the Source Editor.

■ **Tip** If the status bar along the bottom of the NetBeans IDE states that the source for the class cannot be found, then you need to locate the source for the platform or library you are using. Many open source projects, such as projects from the Sourceforge.net or the Apache Software Foundation, provide downloadable bundles of source code. Use the Library Manager or Java Platform Manager to link the source code bundle to the appropriate set of APIs. The manager features are located in the Tools main menu.

If the right-click occurred on the name of a method, then the source file will open and scroll to the specified method. This is extremely useful because you don't have to spend time scrolling through the file.

Overall I like to think of the Go To Source option as a convenience for a programmer who is curious about how code works. Using this submenu option you can quickly drill down through classes and methods, continuously opening the source code for each element you want to investigate. This functionality can allow you to learn quickly how a third-party API works.

Go To Declaration

The Go To Declaration submenu option allows you to jump directly to where a method or field is defined in the code. By right-clicking the element and selecting Go To ➤ Declaration or pressing Ctrl+B you can jump to the line where the element is defined. This can be a convenient feature if you need to jump to an element and see the details about the data type, access modifier, etc.

The `EmailClient` class defined as follows has a class member variable named `smtp`:

```
public class EmailClient {
    public static String smtp = "mail.mydomain.com";

    public static void main(String[] args) {
        System.out.println("Hello World!");
        System.out.println("SMTP = " + smtp);
    }
}
```

This variable is then logged to the standard output stream inside the `main` method. If the `EmailClient` class was hundreds of lines of code long, you would not want to have to scroll through the entire class to find the definition of the `smtp` member. By right-clicking on the `smtp` variable in the `System.out.println("SMTP = " + smtp);` line and activating the Go To Declaration feature, you cause the Source Editor window to jump immediately to the second line, where the `smtp` variable is declared.

Go To Super Implementation

The Go To Super Implementation submenu option allows you to jump directly to the declaration of the super interface for a class. By right-clicking the class, method, or field, selecting Go To ➤ Super Implementation, or pressing Ctrl+Shift+P, you can jump to the line where the element is defined in the super interface.

What exactly does this mean? In the following example we define a class interface named `MyInterface` and a class that implements the interface named `MyImpl`:

```
public interface MyInterface {

    public void doSomething();
}


public class MyImpl implements MyInterface {

    public void doSomething() {
        System.out.println("MyImpl.doSomething");
    }
}
```

The `MyImpl` class implements the `MyInterface` interface and provides a simple implementation of the `doSomething` method. If you were to activate the Go To Super Implementation feature after selecting the `MyImpl.doSomething` method, then the Source Editor would open the `MyInterface` file. The cursor in the file would start at the `MyInterface.doSomething` definition since `MyInterface` is the super implementation in this case.

Next examine the following, similar code:

```
public interface MySuperInterface {
    public void doSomething();
}
```

```
public interface MyInterface extends MySuperInterface {

    public void doSomething();
}


public class MyImpl implements MyInterface{

    public void doSomething() {
        System.out.println("MyImpl.doSomething");
    }
}
```

In this code, `MyImpl` implements `MyInterface`, which in turn extends `MySuperInterface`. `MySuperInterface.doSomething` thus becomes the super implementation for `MyImpl.doSomething`.

Go To Test

The Go To Test submenu option allows you to jump directly to the corresponding JUnit test for a class. By right-clicking inside the Source Editor window for a class and selecting Go To ➤ Test, as shown in Figure 2-12, you cause the corresponding test class to open. You can also use the shortcut keys of Ctrl+Shift+T to open the test class.

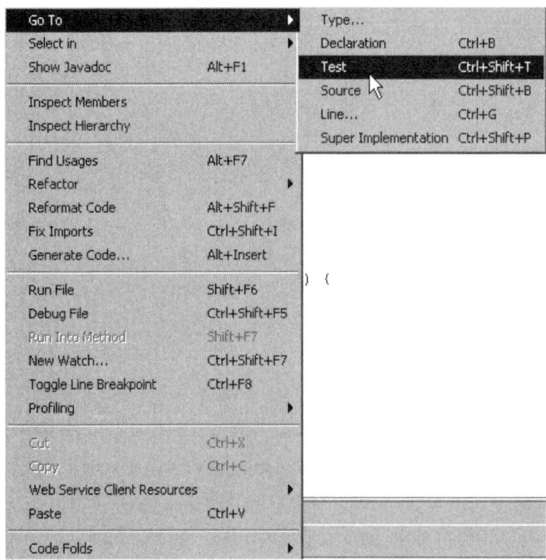

Figure 2-12. *The Go To Test context menu*

One thing to note is the context in which you activate the Go To Test feature. If you have the cursor anywhere inside a method for which a corresponding test method exists, then the test method is selected when the test class opens. Otherwise the test class opens without a particular area initially selected.

Go To Line

The Go To Line feature is a great navigation tool. As the name suggests it allows you to jump quickly and directly to a specific line in the code. You can use this feature by right-clicking in an open file in the Source Editor and selecting Go To ➤ Line from the context menu. The Go To Line window that appears is shown in Figure 2-13. You can also activate the feature for a file in the Source Editor by using the shortcut keys Ctrl+G.

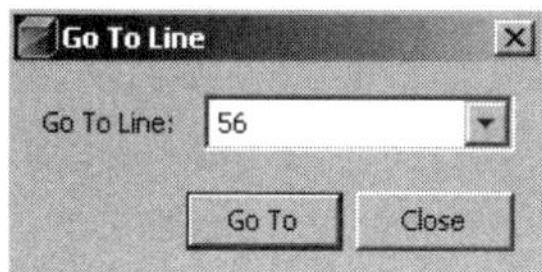

Figure 2-13. *The Go To Line dialog window*

This feature may seem unnecessary if you are dealing with small classes. However, when working with large classes it can save you a lot of scrolling in case you often need to jump back and forth between several sections. If you need to debug a class after reviewing an error stack trace, then you already know the line number and the Go To Line feature will help you jump directly to it.

Go to File

The Go to File tool allows you to search for and jump to any file in an open project or library. It does not appear on the context menu as did the others just described, but it is worth mentioning nonetheless. You can access the Go to File feature on the main menu item Navigate.

When the Go to File window opens, you will be prompted to enter a filename or search criterion. As you type, any files that match the text will appear in the list, as shown in Figure 2-14. You can modify this file matching by using the options in the window, such as Case Sensitive, Show Hidden Files, and Prefer Current Project.

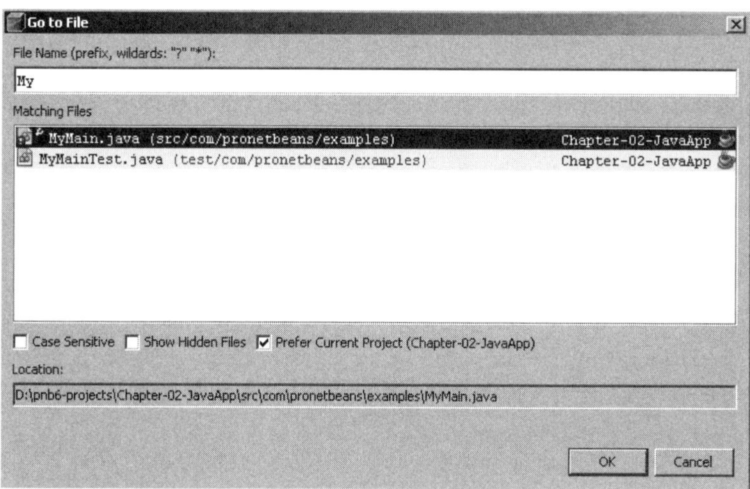

Figure 2-14. *The Go to File search fields and results*

Other Items

Additional menu items will appear on the context menu when you right-click inside a file in the Source Editor. These features are covered in later chapters on Javadoc (Chapter 7), refactoring (Chapter 10), and debugging (Chapter 4).

The only other feature I want to highlight on the context menu is the Select In option. This feature will trigger the file to be displayed and highlighted in the Projects, Files, or Favorites windows, depending on your selections. This can be useful if you have multiple projects and/or source files open and have lost track of where you opened the file. It can also be a convenient way to access other classes in the same package structure without having to click the nodes and drill down through the files.

Editor Menu (Toolbar)

The Editor menu is a toolbar with several links to useful tools. The functionality represented there is spread across several of the main menus, but the code editing and navigating features that benefit a developer are available via the icons. The Editor menu bar is displayed in Figure 2-15. Be aware that the exact arrangement of the icons on the menu bar is subject to change, based on ongoing development work and improvements in each edition of NetBeans. However, the core features should stay the same across versions.

Figure 2-15. *Icon menu in Source Editor*

Jump List

The first three icons represent the ability to navigate the jump list. The jump list is sort of like an Internet browser's history. You can click the second and third arrows to navigate back and forward between pages. The first arrow takes you back to the last code edit that was made, even if it wasn't in the currently opened file.

In NetBeans you can click Back and Forward to navigate between locations in code where you have opened source or made changes. If you are in a page of source and use the Go To Source feature to open the code of another class, the Back icon should become active. You can then click it and be returned to where you originated.

■ **Tip** Combined with the Go To Line feature, this is a very convenient tool if you are trying to debug code after reading an error stack trace. You can locate the line in the first class, drill down to the offending line in the next class using Go To Source, and be able to navigate your way back to where you started.

Find Text Selection

The next section of icons in Figure 2-15 deal with finding text. The sections on the toolbar should be easily distinguishable because of the vertical gray separator. From left to right in the section the icons are Find Selection, Find Previous Occurrence, Find Next Occurrence, and Toggle Highlight Search.

The text selection icons allow you to highlight one or more characters and locate all occurrences in the open file where that text appears. You can also place the cursor anywhere in or next to a class name, method, or variable and use the Find Selection icon to highlight the occurrences. The Previous Occurrence and Next Occurrence icons allow you to navigate back and forth between the different occurrences. The fourth and final icon, Toggle Highlight Search, allows you to turn off the highlighted search term so that each occurrence is not marked in the source code.

Bookmarks

The third section in Figure 2-15 contains three icons: Previous Bookmark, Next Bookmark, and Toggle Bookmark. By now you should be able to take an educated guess as to what these icons allow you to do. By using the Toggle Bookmark icon you can enable or disable bookmarks in your code.

Bookmarks are useful if you want to flag a line of code and come back to it later. Using the Next Bookmark and Previous Bookmark icons you can scroll through all the bookmarks you have set to navigate quickly and view what you wanted to remember.

Shifting Lines

The fifth section on the Editor menu deals with shifting lines. These two icons allow you to shift one or more lines of code to indent or unindent them. The number of spaces the lines are shifted can be set in the Options ➤ Editor section on the Indentation tab.

This feature comes in handy when you copy and paste in blocks of code and want to adjust the indentation. You can make the indentation line up with the rest of the file without necessarily having to format the entire source file. To shift lines left, you can use the shortcut of Alt+Shift+Left. To shift lines right, you can use the shortcut of Alt+Shift+Right.

Macros

The sixth section on the Editor menu is for working with macros. These two icons enable you to start and stop recording macros. This subject is covered in greater detail in this chapter's later section "Macros." Once you are comfortable working with macros, these icons can provide convenient access to starting and stopping the recording of them.

Commenting Code

The seventh and final section of the Editor menu deals with commenting code. No Java IDE can be called a Java IDE unless it provides this basic functionality. NetBeans holds true in this case, as do many other IDE tools. As a developer you will often write code where you want to comment out a line or block of code without having to add the comment characters manually.

The Comment icon allows you automatically to comment out the line that is currently active in the Source Editor window. If multiple lines are highlighted, then they are all commented out. You can also access the feature directly on the keyboard via the shortcut Ctrl+Slash.

Obviously the Uncomment icon performs the opposite action. Lines that were commented out can be quickly and easily uncommented using the Uncomment icon or by pressing Ctrl+Shift+Slash.

■ **Tip** If the different keyboard shortcuts for NetBeans 6 are starting to frazzle your nerves after having spent time learning them in NetBeans 5.5, you can easily switch them back. See the Chapter 1 section "Configuring Keymaps."

Source Editor Shortcuts

Table 2-1 presents a brief list of some of the most commonly used shortcut sets you might need while working with source code or in the Source Editor.

Table 2-1. *Partial List of Shortcuts Specific to the Source Editor*

Shortcut	Description
Ctrl+Minus	Collapse Fold
Ctrl+Plus	Expand Fold
Ctrl+Shift+Minus	Collapse All Folds
Ctrl+Shift+Plus	Expand All Folds
Alt+O	Go To Source
Alt+G	Go To Declaration
Ctrl+B	Go To Super Implementation
Alt+Shift+E	Go To Test
Ctrl+G	Go To Line
Alt+Shift+O	Go To Class
Ctrl+Shift+F	Reformat Code
F9	Compile File
F11	Build Main Project
Shift+F6	Run File
F6	Run Main Project
Ctrl+D	Shift Left
Ctrl+T	Shift Right
Ctrl+Shift+T	Comment Code
Ctrl+Shift+D	Uncomment Code

Supporting Features and Tools

Several features in NetBeans augment the Source Editor. They make working with files in the Source Editor significantly easier, so you should familiarize yourself with them in case they are useful in your daily work.

Macros

A macro is a set of automated keystrokes or repetitive behavior that can be reenacted over and over as needed. If you find yourself performing similar and repetitive actions, you might want to consider macros.

Macros differ from code templates in that templates are just template code with special markers that need to be inserted; they are not sets of steps. Macros provide the ability to automate numerous steps that can be triggered with a simple keyboard shortcut. You can record them or create them manually.

When you record a macro, you tell NetBeans to "watch" the set of steps you are about to perform. Once started, you perform the steps and NetBeans writes downs, or records, the names of the actions you take. When finished, you tell NetBeans to stop. You can then name the macro you just recorded and assign a keyboard shortcut to it. That set of steps, the macro, can then be replayed via your assigned shortcut.

You can use the Macro Editor to see a list of macros created in NetBeans. On the Tools main menu, select Options. Then select the Editor icon from the left pane and pick the Macros tab. The Macros Editor can be seen in Figure 2-16. There should be a list of macros displayed (name and shortcut); as you click each macro name, the corresponding macro code is displayed in the window at the bottom of the tab.

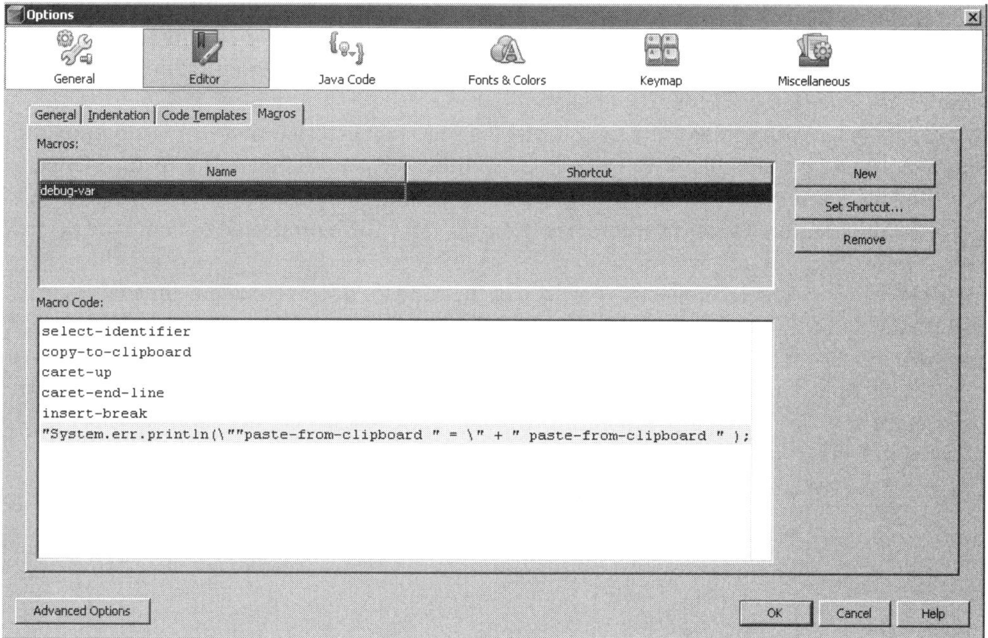

Figure 2-16. *The list of macros in NetBeans*

NetBeans is initially packaged with only one macro, named debug-var. This macro can be used to add an output statement for an identifier quickly. Here is the full code for the macro debug-var:

```
select-identifier
copy-to-clipboard
caret-end-line
insert-break
"System.err.println(\""paste-from-clipboard " = \" + " paste-from-clipboard " );
```

The names that appear in the code are individual macro actions that are performed during execution of the macro. In my humble opinion it is ridiculously easy to understand most of the action names. Only a few need explanation (see Table 2-2 for a list of some of the more common actions and a brief description of what they do).

In our example, the macro will select the current identifier, copy it, move the caret (a.k.a. the cursor) to the end of the line, add a line break, type the characters `System.err.print("`, paste the text from the clipboard, type the characters `= " +`, paste the text from the clipboard, and type the characters `);`.

Suppose you had the code `String FirstName = "Adam";`. If you placed the cursor inside the `FirstName` variable and activated the debug-var macro using its shortcut Ctrl+J, D, the code that would be created would look as follows:

```
String FirstName = "Adam";
System.err.println("FirstName = " + FirstName);
```

This is obviously a simple example, but with a wide variety of macro actions available there are many possibilities.

You can create your own macros manually by clicking the New button in the Macros Editor shown in Figure 2-16. This prompts you to name the macro. Using the editor you can then set the keyboard shortcut and type in the macro code. If this manual process does not appeal to you, you can also record your own macros.

The Source Editor toolbar shown in Figure 2-15 has two macro buttons. You can press the Start Recording button to begin. By default, no shortcut key is assigned to this feature. Once recording has started, simply perform the actions you want to automate. To finish, click the End Recording button. Once recording has stopped, you will be prompted to name the macro and set its keyboard shortcut.

Once you have created a macro, you can edit the code for the macro at any time by going back to the Macro Editor shown in Figure 2-16. This is a great feature when working with macros since you can record a long series of steps and manually edit and tweak them if necessary.

Table 2-2 presents a list of several different kinds of macro actions you might use. You can experiment and discover which actions are available by recording a macro and clicking every button and menu item possible to see what the macro records.

Table 2-2. *Partial List of Macro Actions in NetBeans*

Macro Action	Description
select-identifier	Select the identifier the cursor is currently on.
select-word	Select the word the cursor is currently on.
caret-forward	Move the caret (cursor) forward one space.
caret-backward	Move the caret (cursor) backward one space.
caret-end-line	Move the caret (cursor) to the end of the current line.
insert-break	Insert a line break after the current line.
bookmark-toggle	Toggle a bookmark on or off for the current line.
bookmark-next	Jump to the next bookmark.
bookmark-previous	Jump to the previous bookmark.
comment	Comment the current line or selection of code.
uncomment	Uncomment the current line or selection of code.
format	Cause the current source code file to be reformatted.
shift-line-right	Shift the current line or selection right by the default number of spaces.
shift-line-left	Shift the current line or selection left by the default number of spaces.
word-match-prev	Insert the previous matching word.
word-match-next	Insert the next matching word.
paste-from-clipboard	Paste the text from the clipboard.
copy-to-clipboard	Copy the currently selected text into the clipboard.
cut-to-clipboard	Cut and copy the currently selected text into the clipboard.
fix-imports	Run the Fix Imports refactoring.
try-catch	Surround the current selection or line with a `try-catch` statement.
collapse-fold	Collapse the code fold for the current block.
expand-fold	Expand the code fold for the current block.
collapse-all-folds	Collapse all the code folds in the file.
expand-all-folds	Expand all the code folds in the file.

Component Palette

The component Palette, or Palette window, is essentially a fancy toolbar that allows you quick access to language elements. To force the Palette window to open, go to Window ➤ Palette or press Ctrl+Shift+8. Based on the type of file you have open in the Source Editor, the palette will display custom elements and tags.

If you opened a JSP or an HTML file in the Source Editor, the Palette would display elements related to that content. See Figure 2-17. The HTML and JSP elements on the Palette can be dragged from the Palette into the currently open file. NetBeans does not have a WYSIWYG HTML/JSP editor like Dreamweaver or Frontpage. However, it still provides some nice features that help you save time when writing HTML code.

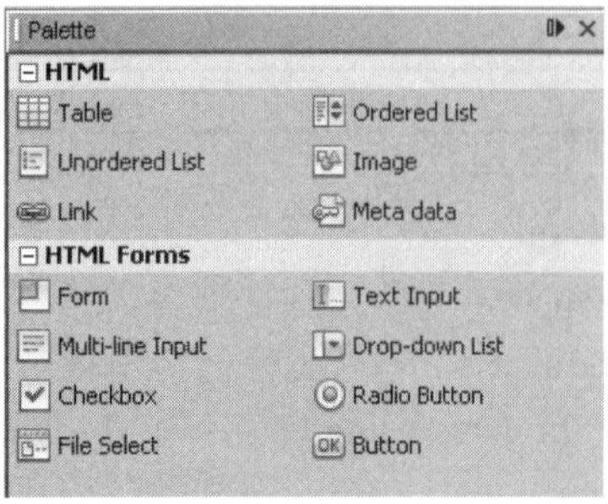

Figure 2-17. *The component Palette for HTML files*

Let's review the components available on the Palette. Say you needed to add an HTML table element. Click and drag the table element from the Palette into the open source file. As you move the mouse, the cursor follows inside the file. When the cursor is in the correct line and column where you want the `<table>` tag to appear, release the mouse button. The Insert Table wizard that appears is shown in Figure 2-18. 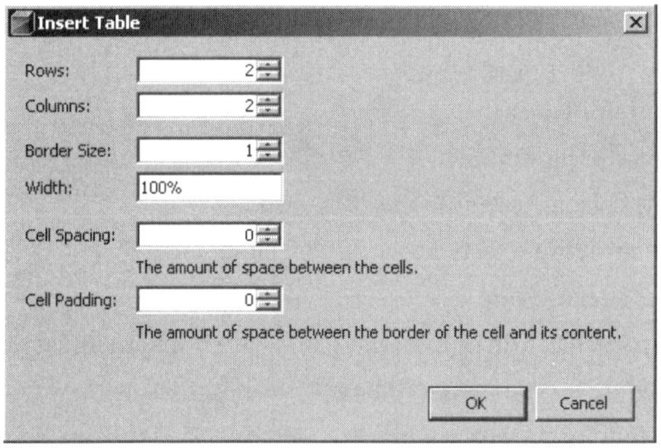

Figure 2-18. *The HTML Insert Table wizard*

Using this short wizard screen you can set several parameters about the table without having to write the code for them. The most convenient is the ability to set the numbers of rows and columns, as seen in Figure 2-18. If you are creating a large table with numerous columns, this can save you a lot of time from having to copy and paste repeatedly. If you try to add several additional elements from the Palette, you will see that NetBeans prompts you with an element-specific wizard in an attempt to save you coding and configuration. These prompts are nice, in that they simplify having to remember the exact syntax of each tag's attributes.

Another area where the Palette window comes in extremely handy is when working with Java Swing. If you are designing a Swing class that will contain Swing elements, it is almost mandatory for any tool to provide a palette or toolbar with the available elements. If you added a new class of type JFrame Form, then the Palette would contain the Swing elements seen in Figure 2-19.

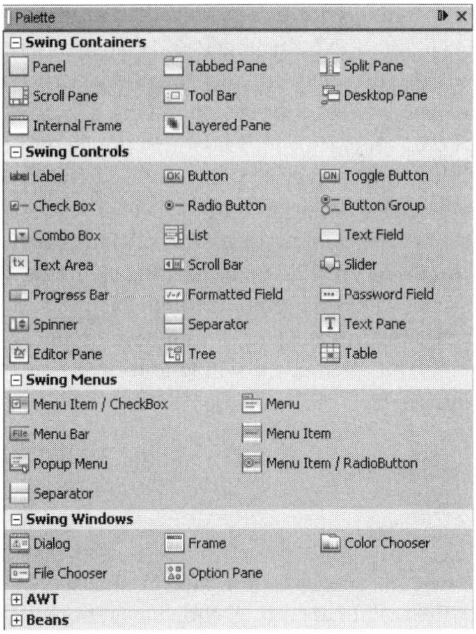

Figure 2-19. *The component Palette window for Swing*

You can perform some basic configuration tasks in the Palette window using the Palette Manager. From the main menu, go to Tools ➤ Palette and select the type of palette you want to configure. Let's assume you chose the HTML/JSP palette. The corresponding Palette Manager that is displayed will be as shown in Figure 2-20.

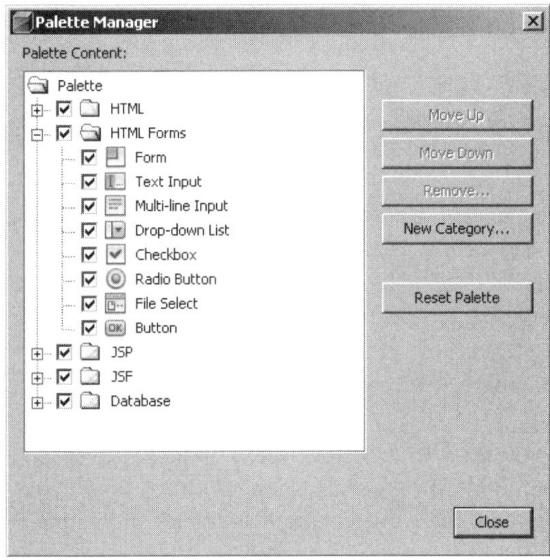

Figure 2-20. *The Palette Manager window*

With the Palette Manager, you can show and hide the different sections and elements that appear on the Palette. You can also sort and order the elements to be arranged and displayed as you see fit. To hide an element from displaying on the Palette, simply uncheck the check box next to the name of the element. To show the element again, check the check box. Only a limited set of features is available in the Palette Manager. The only other features that might not be obvious are the features available if you right-click on a palette category or element name. On the context menu that appears, you can sort the element in each category or sort the categories.

The last feature worthy of mention is the ability to create a new category by clicking the New Category button. You can name the category and then copy and paste existing elements from the Palette into that category. You cannot manually add new elements to the Palette.

Once you use the Palette window regularly it becomes an integral part of your development process. It offers quick access to commonly used pieces of functionality in a drag-and-drop manner. As NetBeans evolves, expect more and more features to be available in the Palette window for each file type.

Summary

This chapter presented a lot about working in the NetBeans Source Editor. Many topics were covered, but with a strong focus on how specific features relate to coding, code navigation, and automating development.

You saw that

Source file windows can be arranged in a variety of ways allowing for several viewing options (left-and-right, top-and-bottom, etc.).

Several context menu options are available for navigating through source code.

Many features and tools are available via a keyboard shortcut or a right-click menu.

The Editor menu bar along the top of the Source Editor provides quick access to code-related features.

This chapter also covered syntax and error highlighting. NetBeans provides several methods for identifying problems in code, navigating around files to locate errors, and providing suggestions for fixing the errors.

Developers should use the code indentation tools in NetBeans to format code in a readable manner so that the code is easy to maintain and understand. NetBeans attempts to enforce this best practice by automatically attempting to indent various blocks as you type lines of code. You also saw that you can reformat code at any time to conform to the indentation standards.

Macros are a feature that can be used in conjunction with code completion and code templates to save you time and keystrokes. You can record sequences of actions and have them played back using keyboard shortcuts.

Finally, the Palette window was briefly discussed. This feature lets you drag and drop context-specific elements into your source code. It also provides various wizards to assist you in adding the code without having to remember all the attribute names or syntax. In the end this translates to time saved.

Many of the features in this chapter, and in NetBeans as a whole, relate to saving you time as a developer. Learning all the ins and outs of these features can take time, but in the end the effort pays off dramatically in making you more productive.

CHAPTER 3

Code Completion and Templates

This chapter covers several important time-saving features NetBeans provides programmers: code completion, code templates, and file templates. Code completion allows you to enter the name of a class, interface, package, field, or method without having to type the entire name. A code template is a block of text or code that can be automatically inserted into your file by typing only a few characters. A file template is a placeholder for an entire file of content that can facilitate reuse and standardization.

All these features are related, in that they involve increasing your productivity and saving you time. The more you use features like code completion and templates, the more you will appreciate the benefits of using NetBeans. In the following sections we review each feature and how best to use them.

Code Completion

As you type in the NetBeans Source Editor, a pop-up window—also known as the code completion box—appears, showing a context-sensitive list of possibilities. As you type additional characters, the list is filtered further to display only those items that match what you have typed. This saves time and makes coding easier, since you don't have to remember the exact case-sensitive name of every construct in Java.

Configuring Code Completion

In NetBeans the code completion window can be enabled and disabled. You can also configure several additional parameters related to code completion for the IDE.

Basic Options

To see the code completion configuration options, select Tools ➤ Options ➤ Editor. The Code Completion section is in the lower half of the General tab, as shown in Figure 3-1.

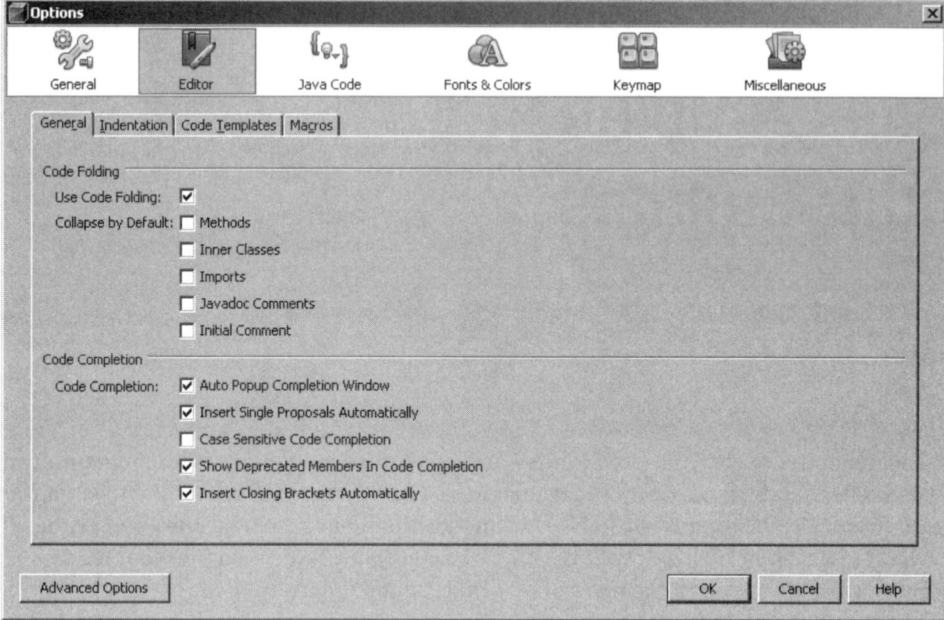

Figure 3-1. *Configuring code completion settings in the Basic Options window*

The Code Completion section has five check boxes:

Auto Popup Completion Window: If you turn off this option, the code completion window will not pop up while you are typing. You can still open it by pressing Ctrl+Spacebar.

Insert Single Proposals Automatically: With this option selected, the code completion box will not appear when there is only one possible completion for the current expression. Instead, the completion will be inserted automatically. One example of this option would be typing the text `System.current` and pressing the Enter key (you need to pause for half a second or so after typing the period). The text `System.currentTimeMillis();` will appear in the Source Editor window.

Case Sensitive Code Completion: As the name suggests, this option filters items from the code completion box based on the case of the character typed. Thus, typing `String.C` results in the suggestion of `String.CASE_INSENSITIVE_ORDER`. Items such as `String.copyValueOf` are filtered out of the list. This feature is most useful when working with custom-created classes. If your custom class has similarly named members and methods, you will find the case-sensitive filter helpful.

Show Deprecated Members In Code Completion: If you turn off this option, deprecated class elements are filtered out of the items displayed in the code completion box. If it's checked, deprecated items are displayed, but they have a line drawn through the name. In Figure 3-2, the code completion options for the `java.lang.System` class are displayed. Notice that the `runFinalizersOnExit(boolean b)` method has a line drawn through it. This method is deprecated in the version of the JDK I use with NetBeans. But if you have an older version, it may not be deprecated.

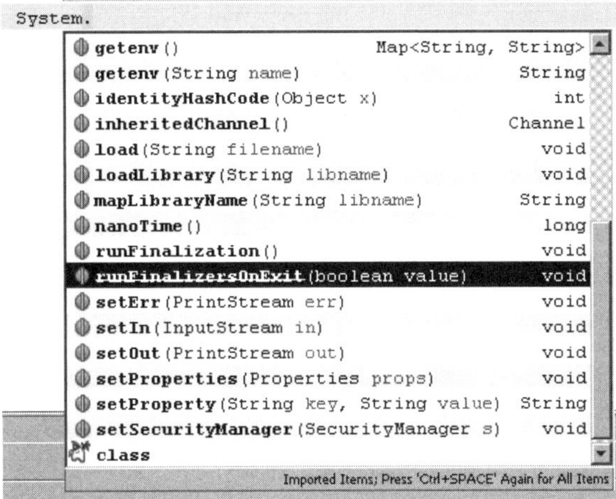

Figure 3-2. *Code completion window for the java.lang.System class showing a deprecated element*

Insert Closing Brackets Automatically: With this feature enabled, the Source Editor generates the closing parenthesis, bracket, brace, or quotation mark after you type the first one. Many Java IDE tools have similar functionality, but too often the autocompletion feature gets in the way. However, NetBeans handles the generating of closing elements very nicely, allowing you to type right over them and not inserting duplicate closing characters.

Advanced Options

To change additional code completion properties, click the Advanced Options button in the Options window. This changes the display and lists a variety of options in the left pane. Navigate the tree structure by drilling down to Editing ➤ Editor Settings ➤ Java Editor. In the right pane, a list of properties and expert options are displayed, as shown in Figure 3-3. The Auto Popup Completion Window check box allows you to disable/enable the code completion window. This has the same effect as the Auto Popup Completion Window check box in the Basic Options window.

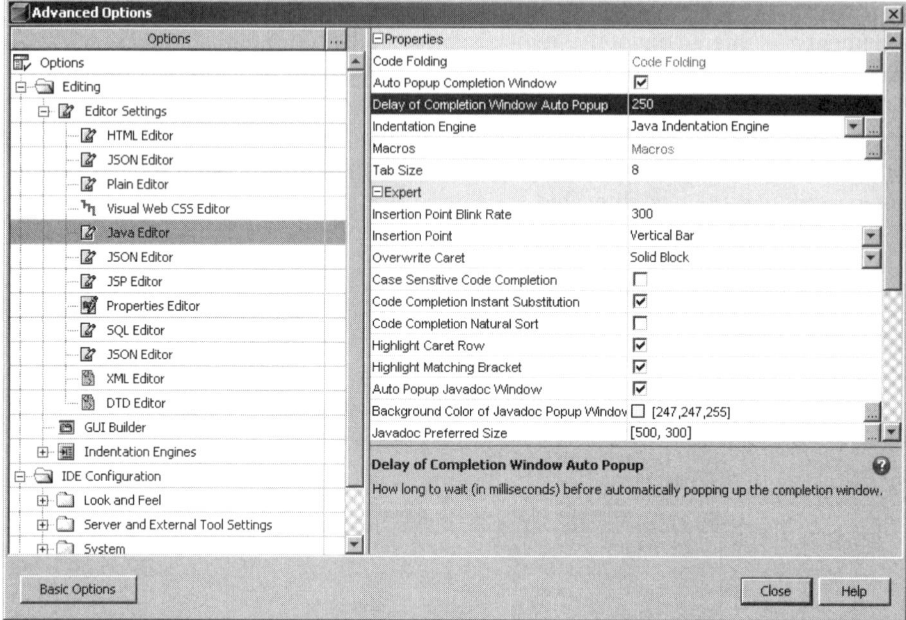

Figure 3-3. *The Java Editor properties in the Advanced Options window*

The Delay of Completion Window Auto Popup property is set to 250 by default. This value represents the time in milliseconds it takes for the code completion window to appear. A lot of developers change this value to 1000 (for 1 second).

The Code Completion Natural Sort check box, if enabled, sorts the results in the code completion box in natural order. If it's unchecked, the uppercase items are listed before the lowercase ones.

Code Completion Keystrokes

You can use various keyboard shortcuts to work with the code completion box, as listed in Table 3-1.

Table 3-1. *Keystrokes Affecting Code Completion*

Keystroke	Action
Ctrl+Space	Force the code completion pop-up to appear.
Enter	Insert the selected item into your code.
Escape	Close the code completion box and cancel any text insertions.
Up arrow	Scroll through list of items.
Down arrow	Scroll through list of items.
Page-Up	Scroll to top of visible list of items.
Page-Down	Scroll to bottom of visible list of items.
Home	Scroll to absolute top of the entire list of items.
End	Scroll to absolute bottom of the entire list of items.

Using Code Completion

Code completion is useful in many scenarios in Java coding. I've been coding Java for more than a few years, and I still cannot remember the name of every class, method, member, and exception that exists in the language. If you can, then congratulations! Code completion saves you the time of having to look up the Java API Javadocs every time you need a reminder of the methods of a class or the package structure of a set of APIs.

In the following sections, we look at several specific areas where you can use code completion.

Packages (Imports)

When working with packages, you sometimes have long combinations of text that define your class hierarchy. Many companies use package statements such as these:

```
com.mycompany.mydivision.myorganization.thisproduct.database;
com.mycompany.mydivision.myorganization.thisproduct.model;
com.mycompany.mydivision.myorganization.thisproduct.view;
```

or:

```
com.mycompany.product.client;
com.mycompany.product.server;
com.mycompany.product.server.threads;
com.mycompany.product.server.db;
```

Package names are not difficult to paste into your source code editor, but they can be annoying to try to remember. That's where code completion becomes useful.

Open any Java source file in the NetBeans Source Editor and try typing an `import` statement. After the first package element, press the Period key. The code completion box should appear, listing the next available package names. Depending on the package, the code completion box may contain classes and package names. Figure 3-4 shows an example of importing the `java.util` package.

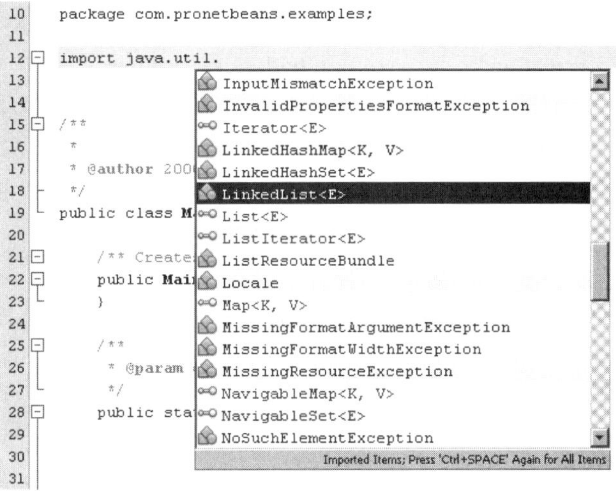

Figure 3-4. *The code completion listing for the java.util package*

Methods

The most frequent use of code completion is with methods. Whether you are trying to reference static or non-static methods, the code completion box will try to assist you. One intelligent feature NetBeans provides is static method code completion.

In the Source Editor, type `String` and press the Period key. The code completion box will appear with a list of suggestions. An interesting thing to note is that since you typed the name of a class, the items in the code completion box are only the static members and methods of the `String` class. See Figure 3-5.

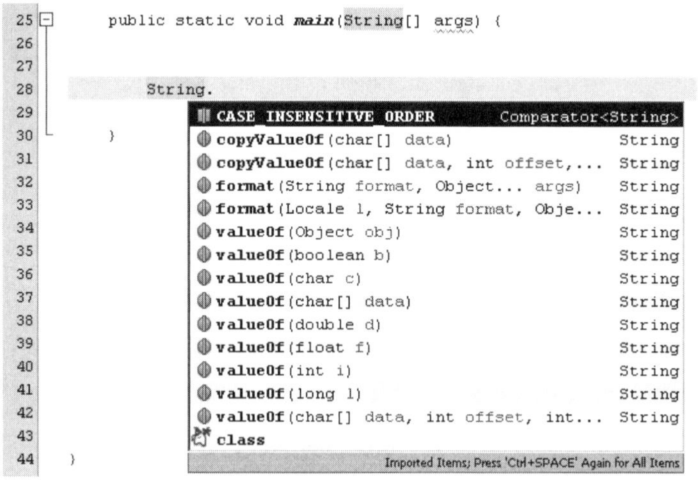

```
    public static void main(String[] args) {


        String.
    }
}
```

```
CASE_INSENSITIVE_ORDER                      Comparator<String>
copyValueOf(char[] data)                    String
copyValueOf(char[] data, int offset,...     String
format(String format, Object... args)       String
format(Locale l, String format, Obje...     String
valueOf(Object obj)                         String
valueOf(boolean b)                          String
valueOf(char c)                             String
valueOf(char[] data)                        String
valueOf(double d)                           String
valueOf(float f)                            String
valueOf(int i)                              String
valueOf(long l)                             String
valueOf(char[] data, int offset, int...     String
class
Imported Items; Press 'Ctrl+SPACE' Again for All Items
```

Figure 3-5. *Static elements from the String class displayed in the code completion box*

Let's look at an example of including both static and non-static items. Enter the following code in the Source Editor.

```
String MyString = "some string";
```

Then on the second line of your code, type the `MyString` variable name and press the Period key. The list that appears in the code completion box will contain *both* static and non-static items.

Class Members

The code completion box can also display class members. If you take a look at the `java.sql.ResultSet` interface, you will see that it contains a number of static integers, such as `TYPE_SCROLL_SENSITIVE`, `CONCUR_READ_ONLY`, and `FETCH_FORWARD`. These fields are mostly used when creating a `java.sql.Statement` object and specifying various parameters for the database operation you are about to perform.

For example, suppose you type this code:

```
Statement stmt = con.createStatement(
                 ResultSet.TYPE_SCROLL_SENSITIVE,
                 ResultSet.CONCUR_UPDATABLE);
```

Once you type the `ResultSet` class name and press the Period key, you should see the static members of the class. See Figure 3-6.

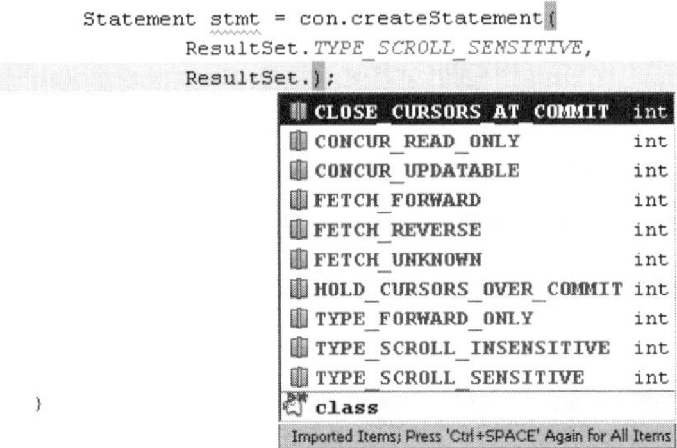

Figure 3-6. *Static elements of the java.sql.ResultSet class in the code completion box*

Constructors

Code completion can also be used when creating an instance of an object and selecting which constructor you need to use. For example, Figure 3-7 shows the code completion box for `java.lang.String`, which has numerous constructors.

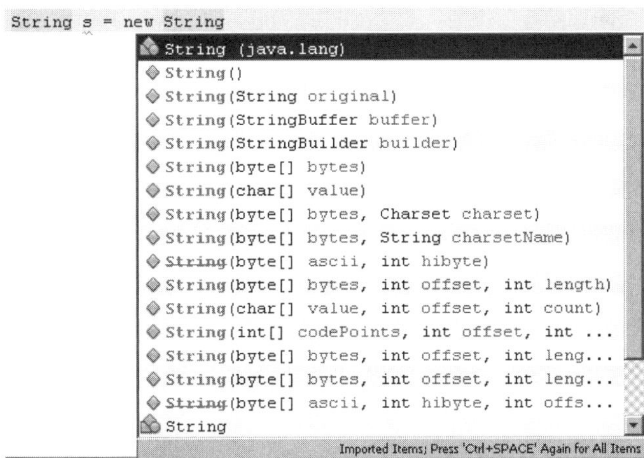

Figure 3-7. *Constructors for java.lang.String displayed on the code completion box*

The code completion box will not automatically appear for constructors. In the example, after typing the opening parenthesis for the `String` constructor, you need to press Ctrl+Spacebar to force the code completion box to appear.

super and this

You can use code completion immediately after `super` and `this`. Code completion referencing the `this` object is most useful if you are creating getter and setter methods and need to have quick access to class member variables. This is especially true if you have dozens of class member variables and you have scrolled down through the file.

For example, consider the following code:

```
public class MyMain {

    private String firstName;

    public void setFirstName(String firstName) {

    }
}
```

Inside the `setFirstName` method, if you were to type `this` and press the Period key, the code completion box would appear, as shown in Figure 3-8. From this list, you could quickly select the `firstName` member variable without having to remember the exact syntax or retype the entire name.

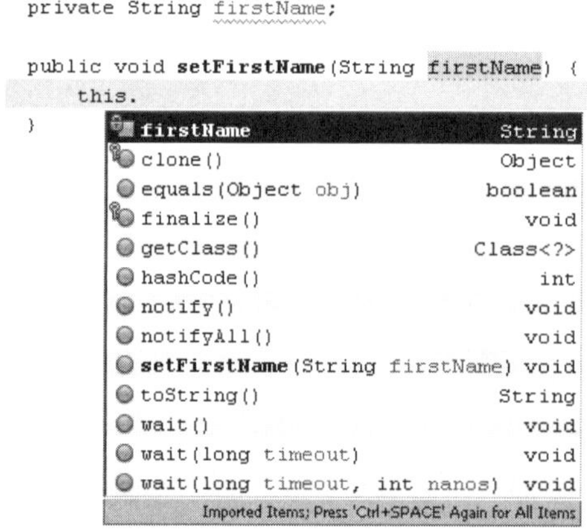

Figure 3-8. *Locating the class member variable firstName in the code completion box*

The new Operator

You can also use code completion when constructing a new instance of an object in conjunction with the `new` operator. Type the code `Map myMap = new`, and then press Ctrl+Spacebar to open the code completion box. You can start to type the name of the class for which you would like to create a new instance, and the list will filter accordingly, as shown in Figure 3-9.

```
public static void main(String[] args)
{

    Map myMap = new Hash
                         HashAttributeSet (javax.print.attribute)
}                        HashDocAttributeSet (javax.print.attribute)
                         HashMap<K, V> (java.util)
                         HashPrintJobAttributeSet (javax.print.attri...
                         HashPrintRequestAttributeSet (javax.print.a...
                         HashPrintServiceAttributeSet (javax.print.a...
                         HashSet<E> (java.util)
                         Hashtable<K, V> (java.util)
                         Hashtable (com.sun.org.apache.xalan.interna...
                         Hashtree2Node (com.sun.org.apache.xml.inter...
```

Figure 3-9. *Filtered list of classes in the code completion box*

In NetBeans 6, code completion has gotten a little smarter. When working with the `new` operator, NetBeans code completion can also factor in use of Java generics.

For example, consider the following code:

```
public class MyDataObject {

    Map<String, Object> MyMap = new
}
```

After typing the `new` operator, activate the code completion box by pressing Ctrl+Spacebar. The code completion box will display an intelligent list of matches (those classes in the classpath that implement the `Map` interface) as well as the correct object types originally stated by your use of generics, as shown in Figure 3-10.

Figure 3-10. *Filtered list of classes that implement the Map interface*

Code Templates

Code templates are interesting features of several Java IDE tools. They allow you to insert a block of code or text automatically by typing a few characters. This is similar to code completion, but the inserted code can be multiple lines of code or multiple method calls instead of a single class, package, or method name.

At first, it can be annoying to attempt to remember the correct abbreviation for the code template you want. Over time, as you develop code in NetBeans, you will learn the abbreviations (at least the important ones). Locating and customizing the list of available abbreviations is discussed later in this chapter ("Code Templates" section).

In addition to using the predefined code templates that come with NetBeans, you can create your own custom code templates.

Using Code Templates

Consider the following block of code in a Java source file:

```
System.out.println("print something to command line");
```

I can't even begin to count the number of times I have typed that statement or copied and pasted it repeatedly. Using the NetBeans code template and abbreviation functionality, you can simply type `sout` and press the Spacebar. The `sout` text is expanded into this:

```
System.out.println("");
```

Notice that the cursor rests inside the quotation marks. Once the `sout` statement has been expanded, you can begin typing the text you want to appear on the standard output stream.

A similar abbreviation is available for the standard error stream. Typing `serr` and pressing the Spacebar produces the following code:

```
System.err.println("");
```

The code template feature is nice to have for commonly used code phrases such as these. However, less useful abbreviations are available, such as `pu`, which expands into `public`, and `re`, which expands into `return`. Personally, if I need to type `public` in a block of code, it is usually faster for me to type the entire word than to try to remember the exact abbreviation. Some people would argue that since the abbreviation is only the first two characters of the word, it should be easy to remember. I prefer to save space in my brain for abbreviations that represent longer blocks of code. The following are some examples of truly useful code abbreviations that are predefined in NetBeans.

trycatch

Typing the abbreviation `trycatch` expands the text into the following:

```
try {

} catch (Exception exception) {

}
```

The object type, Exception, is highlighted, so as soon as you start typing, you overwrite the text with the name of the intended exception (NumberFormatException, NullPointerException, and so on). Once you are finished typing the name of the desired exception, press the Enter key. The cursor will jump to the first line of the try block. This allows you to start typing the expression that should be protected in a try-catch block.

ifelse

Typing the abbreviation ifelse expands the text into the following:

```
if (Boolean.TRUE)
{

}
else
{

}
```

The condition text that appears inside the if block is highlighted and overwritten as soon as you start typing. You can add any Boolean expression into this area and press the Enter key. The cursor should immediately jump to the first line of the if block.

fori

Typing the abbreviation fori expands the text into the following:

```
for (int i = 0; i < arr.length; i++)
{
    String string = args[i];
}
```

The integer variable name is highlighted by default once this piece of code is expanded from its abbreviation. You can type any variable name you like, and it will be changed in all three places in the code where it appears. Before pressing the Enter key to jump to the first line of the for block, you can press the Tab key to jump to and highlight the arr variable so that you can change the name if desired.

Customizing Templates

The code template abbreviations described in the previous sections represent only a small portion of what is available in NetBeans. The system provides a language-specific listing of code templates that can be completely customized. Additionally, you can add your own code templates.

Modifying Code Templates

To view the list of language-specific templates, select Tools ➤ Options ➤ Editor and click the Code Templates tab. From the Language drop-down list, select the programming or scripting language for the templates you wish to view. The Java language is selected by default. Scroll through the long list of templates, and you can see the abbreviations I mentioned in the previous sections, as shown in Figure 3-11. Click any of the Java code template abbreviations in the list to see the expanded text in the text box at the bottom of the tab. The expanded text is what the abbreviation itself is actually expanded into once you press the Spacebar after typing the abbreviation.

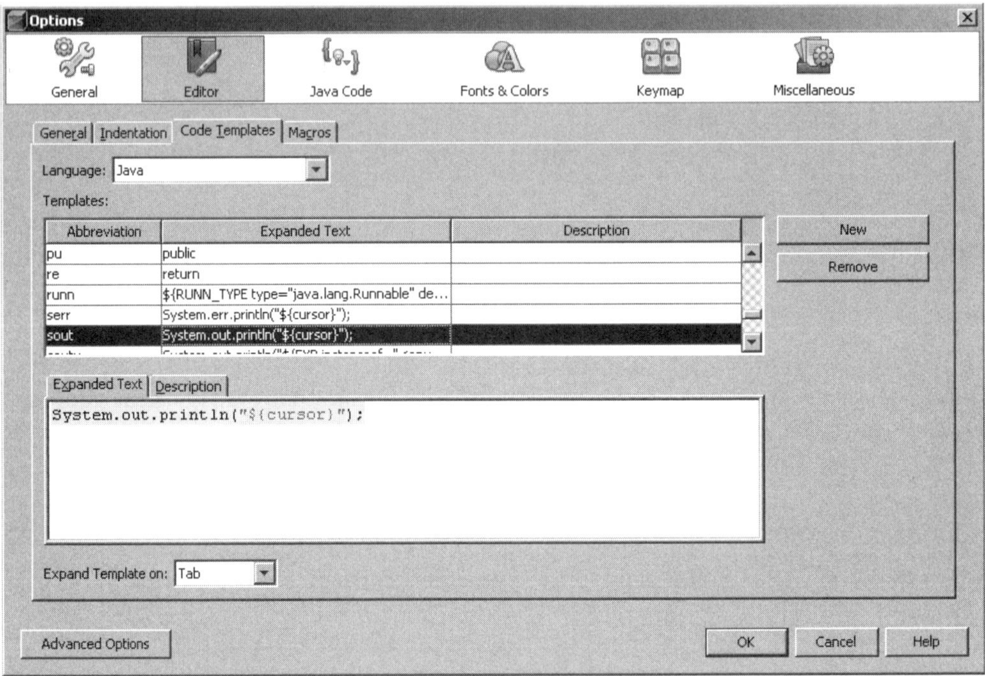

Figure 3-11. *List of code templates for Java*

For example, the following is the expanded text for the `trycatch` abbreviation:

```
try {
   ${selection line}${cursor}
} catch (${EX_TYPE uncaughtExceptionType default="Exception"} ➥
${EX newVarName default="e"}) {
}
```

Notice the text dollar sign–delimited markers that appear in the expanded text. These markers specify different bits of functionality for the template. The `${cursor}` text serves as a marker for where the actual cursor will jump to once you press the Enter key, thereby "exiting" the abbreviation sequence. When you use the code template abbreviation in the Source Editor, you will not actually see the text `${cursor}` in the code once the abbreviation has been expanded. It is only a behind-the-scenes marker.

The `trycatch` abbreviation is often used when coding, but a lot of Java error handling also uses the `try-catch-finally` form:

```
try {

}
catch(Exception e) {

} finally {

}
```

You can create an alternate template for this quite easily. Copy the expanded text for the trycatch abbreviation into the clipboard. In the Code Templates tab, click the New button. NetBeans displays a pop-up window that allows you to enter the new template's abbreviation. Type trycatchfinally and press the Enter key. The new abbreviation is added to the list. Paste the expanded text from the clipboard into the field at the bottom of the tab. Then modify it as follows:

```
try {
    ${cursor}
} catch (${Exception} e) {

} finally {

}
```

Creating a Code Template

The common code templates can prove to be very useful. However, I use many of my own custom code templates, which save me a lot of time. Much of the code I find myself rewriting is database related. Frequently, I write a method in a class that connects to a database, performs an SQL query, and iterates through the result to do something.

As an example, suppose you need to write a method that takes a java.sql.Connection object and an int as input variables, queries the database to retrieve some values, and returns some formatted text. You might code the following:

```
public String dbLookup(Connection conn, int Pkey) {

}
```

If we were coding this by hand, you would need to define other java.sql class objects, define the SQL statement, write the java.sql.ResultSet iteration code, and add the error handling. In NetBeans, I solve this problem by defining a code template with the abbreviation dblookupret. Notice the prefix of db, to signify a database operation. I use a naming convention for my code templates. I add the prefix db to all my code templates that perform database operations, such as select, insert, update, delete, stored procedure execution, and so on.

The expanded text for dblookupret is shown in Listing 3-1. This code is obviously not perfect, but you can tailor it to your needs. For brevity, I have left out issues like proper error handling and resource cleanup.

Listing 3-1. *Expanded Code for the dblookupret Code Abbreviation*

```
PreparedStatement pstmt = null;
ResultSet rs = null;
StringBuffer sb = new StringBuffer();

try {
          pstmt = conn.prepareStatement("SELECT COL1, COL2, COL3 FROM"
                       + " SOMETABLE WHERE INDEXCOL=?");

          pstmt.setInt(1, iPkey);
          rs = pstmt.executeQuery();
          sb = new StringBuffer();

          while(rs.hasNext()) {

                String sCol1 = rs.getString("COL1");
                String sCol2 = rs.getString("COL2");
                String sCol3 = rs.getString("COL3");

                sb.append(sCol1).append(",");
                sb.append(sCol2).append(",");
                sb.append(sCol3).append(",");
          }
} catch(Exception e) {
          // Good error handling goes here
          e.printStackTrace();
} finally {
          try {
                      if(rs!=null) {
                            rs.close();
                      }
                      if(pstmt!=null) {
                            pstmt.close();
                      }
          } catch(Exception e) { }
}

return sb.toString();
```

Setting up commonly used functions as code templates can save you a lot of time as well as help to enforce consistent coding methodologies. They should never be used in place of a good library or set of reusable classes, but they can provide a convenient place to store your commonly used code or expressions.

Code templates can be used for more than Java. They can also be defined for JSP, CSS, DTD, XML, SQL, HTML, plain text, and properties. For example, it is sometimes useful to group together commonly used pieces of SQL, such as date formatting or certain kinds of string parsing and formatting functions.

In one of my recent projects, I needed to make frequent use of the Oracle date functions. Rather than always having to look up the functions and their specific usage scenarios, I defined one slightly long SQL `SELECT` statement as a code template and assigned it the abbreviation `sqldates`. The SQL statement used most of the Oracle date functions in different ways. This way, the majority of the functions I might need would be readily available as an abbreviation. This trick can obviously be applied to HTML, XML, and CSS as well.

File Templates

A file template is similar to a code template in that it represents a block of precreated code. Whereas a code template is used to represent one or more lines of code, a file template represents an entire file of code. The file template contains elements that are populated with various pieces of metadata when you request that a file of that type be created.

These types of templates are useful, for many reasons. The first and most obvious reason is that they save you from having to type the same text over and over every time you create a file. Saving time often translates into increased productivity (or at least freeing up some time to make another run to the soda machine). The second and most valuable reason is standardization.

Using File Templates

NetBeans comes with file templates for the standard file types. For example, suppose you want to add an HTML file to your project. Right-click the project name and select New ➤ Other. In the New File window, choose the Web category and select the file type HTML. Click the Next button, name the file, and click Finish. The created file should look like the following:

```
<!DOCTYPE HTML PUBLIC "-//W3C//DTD HTML 4.01 Transitional//EN">
<html>
  <head>
    <title></title>
  </head>
  <body>

  </body>
</html>
```

This is a generic interpretation of the basic elements in an HTML file that you would need. However, there is nothing custom or specific in the file template based on the filename, the project, the current date and time, and so on.

Next, use the New File wizard to create a Java Class file type. Name the file `MyClassFromTemplate` and place it in the `com.pronetbeans.examples` package, as shown in Figure 3-12. After you click the Finish button, the class is created and added to your project.

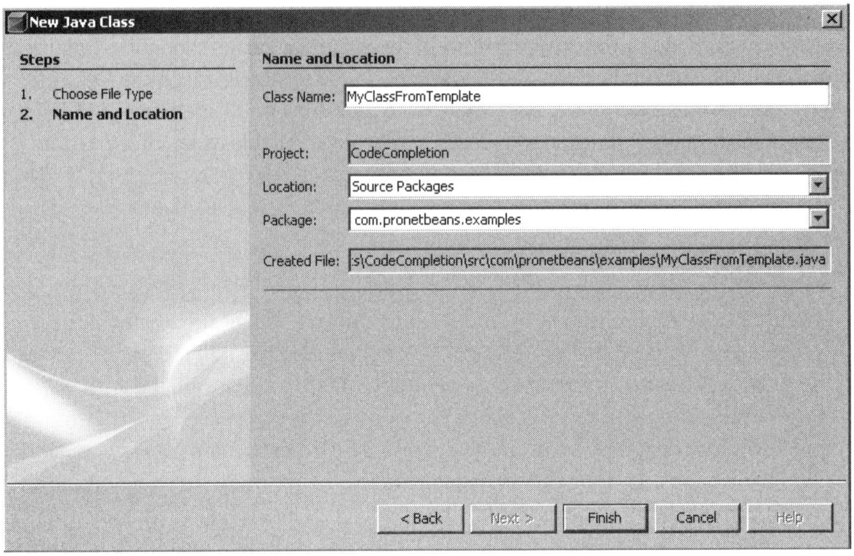

Figure 3-12. *The New File wizard for a creating a Java class*

When I open the class, I see the following code:

```
package com.pronetbeans.examples;

/**
 *
 * @author Adam Myatt
 */
public class MyClassFromTemplate {

    /** Creates a new instance of MyClassFromTemplate */
    public MyClassFromTemplate() {
    }

}
```

The NetBeans Java Class template has special markers for the name of the author, the name of the class, and the name of the constructor, to be inserted when the new file is generated.

NetBeans templates can be opened, manipulated directly in NetBeans, and customized to suit your needs.

Working with File Templates

To work with file templates, select Tools ➤ Templates. Using the Template Manager, you can add, view, and delete file templates. As shown in Figure 3-13, templates are arranged in folders, which represent the categories that appear in the New File wizard.

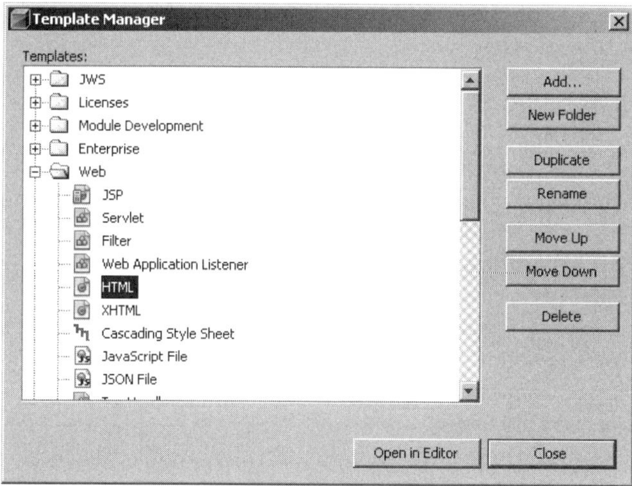

Figure 3-13. *The Template Manager*

To view a template, select an item and click the Open In Editor button. For example, select HTML under the Web folder. The template that opens should look exactly like the empty HTML file you created previously. There's little or no magic here.

Next, in the Java folder select the Java Class template and click the Open In Editor button. Notice that the template file that opens does *not* look exactly like the `MyClassFromTemplate` class you previously created. The template looks like the following:

```
<#assign licenseFirst = "/*">
<#assign licensePrefix = " * ">
<#assign licenseLast = " */">
<#include "../Licenses/license-${project.license}.txt">

<#if package?? && package != "">
package ${package};

</#if>
/**
 *
 * @author ${user}
 */
public class ${name} {

    public ${name}() {
    }
}
```

Notice the special `${user}` and `${name}` tags. These are replaced by the New File wizard when the actual file is created, based on the system values in the IDE and the values entered into the wizard. The `package ${package};` text is replaced with the package name of the class you create, and the name `${name}` is replaced with the actual name you specified.

If you make any changes to a template file and then save the file, they will be present in the generated file of that type the next time one is created.

Adding and Creating Templates

Many web developers maintain a large web site where pages have different content but follow a standard layout. Why create a file and copy and paste the different elements you need into it? Why save a copy of an existing file and try to remove all the information you don't need from it? Create a custom template that is specific to your needs, and avoid such hassles.

To add a new file template into NetBeans, click the Add button in the Template Manager. In the file system browser that opens, navigate to the template you previously created. If you had a category selected when you chose to add the template, it will be created inside that category. Otherwise, it will be added to the bottom of the list of category folders. You can then drag-and-drop it into the appropriate category folder.

If you want to create a file template inside NetBeans, you need to start with a file. The file can be of any type, such as HTML, Java, XML, and so on. In the Projects or Files window, you can right-click the file and select Save As Template from the context menu. The Save As Template dialog box will appear, as shown in Figure 3-14. Select the appropriate template category folder, and then click the OK button. The new template will then be available in the New File wizard.

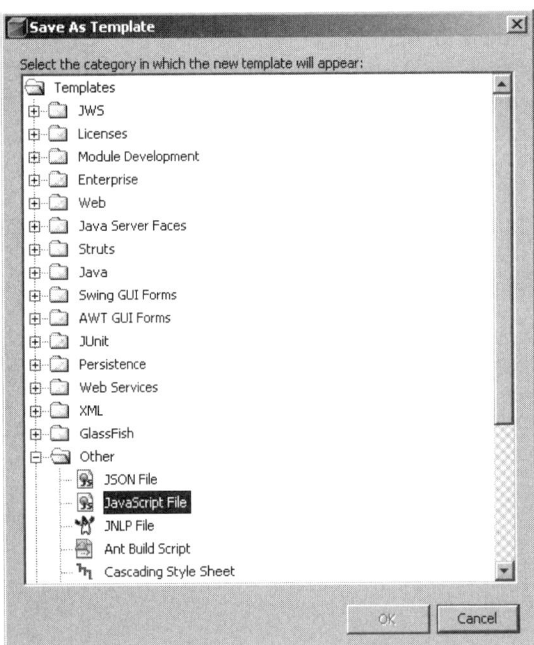

Figure 3-14. *The Save As Template window*

Tip When you make changes to the default templates or create your own, they are stored on the file system at `<user-directory> .netbeans\###\config\Templates`, where *###* is the version number of your installation. If you have created a large number of templates, I recommend periodically backing up this templates folder, in case your user directory is ever corrupted (which happens occasionally in Windows).

Summary

In this chapter we reviewed code completion, code templates, and file templates. NetBeans provides a rather intuitive method for discovering class, method, and field names or syntax. It also attempts to give hints as to the access level of the items referenced in the code completion box.

As a NetBeans user, you can customize and create code templates for several languages. This saves you time because you don't need to retype frequently used code snippets. It can also save you the hassle of repeatedly having to look up the Javadoc or the exact code syntax of a method or function. On the other hand, file templates allow you to reuse an entire file. You can create standard Java classes, HTML structures, and so on. These templates can be used when creating new files in the New File wizard, making code reuse quick and easy.

I never used to use templates, but after a while I got tired of telling myself it really didn't take *that* long to look up the exact syntax of some SQL function or to retype some piece of Java code.

CHAPTER 4

Debugging

Debugging code is one of the most frequently performed activities developers do while writing code. Developers use a variety of debugging methods, ranging from writing out program execution logic on paper to working it out step by step in their heads to littering their code with logging statements.

At one time or another virtually every Java programmer has written code such as the following:

```
public class BadDebugExample {

    public static void main(String[] args)
    {
        System.out.println("1");
        Calculator calc = new Calculator();

        System.out.println("2");
        String results = calc.doCalculation(4);

        System.out.println("3");
        String results2 = calc.doCalculation(5);

        System.out.println("4");
        String results3 = calc.doCalculation(6);
    }
}
```

This sample code was littered with `System.out.println` statements in an attempt to add visual markers to the standard output stream. Sometimes when programs fail, you don't always get a meaningful stack trace or line number where the error occurred. Adding `System.out.println` statements, as in the foregoing code, is an effective yet clumsy way of tracing program execution.

After writing debugging code like the preceding `BadDebugExample` class, you may start to get the feeling that you're doing something wrong or that there should be an easier way. Java IDEs like NetBeans offer that easier way by means of debugging tools.

What Is IDE Debugging?

Debugging Java code in an IDE involves stepping line by line through application code. You can pause program execution on specific lines (breakpoints) and even monitor the values of variables and objects.

Some common actions in IDE debugging include

- Pausing program execution on a specific line
- Executing code one line at a time
- Skipping over a line of code you don't want to execute
- Executing the application code until it reaches the current location of the cursor
- Viewing the call stack up to a specific line of code
- Monitoring the value of a local variable
- Monitoring the value of a class member variable
- Evaluating the return value of a method without stepping inside it
- Tracing program execution across multiple threads
- Conditionally halting program execution on specific lines
- Changing the runtime value of variables to see how it affects program behavior
- Changing code on the fly and proceeding with debugging without having to start over

The debugging tools in NetBeans add a lot of power and many capabilities to a developer's tool chest. Knowing how to use the debugging tools properly can save you a lot of time and many headaches.

Project-Level Debugging Settings

The only real debugging-related setting you can turn on and off is in the Project Properties. It can be enabled or disabled for each individual project and affects the Java source code in that project only.

To view the settings, right-click on any project name currently open in the Projects or Files window and select Properties. In the Project Properties window, click the Compiling node under the Build node, and you will see several properties in the right pane of the window, as shown in Figure 4-1.

The "Generate Debugging Info" property relates to debugging. If selected, it will instruct the compiler to add the necessary bytecode to all compiled Java classes for this project to allow the debugger to be used.

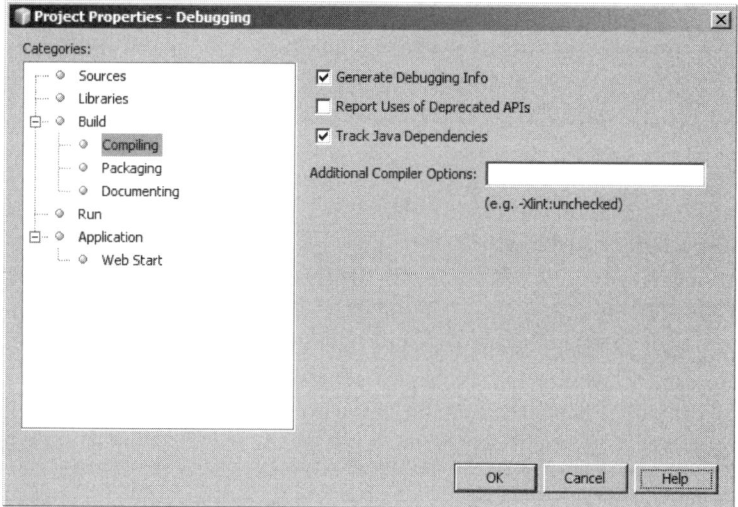

Figure 4-1. *Compilation properties in the Project Properties window*

Tip Leaving the "Generate Debugging Info" property selected results in slightly larger class files. If you intend on deploying your generated class files directly to a server, you may want to consider unchecking this option and recompiling them. While the number of bytes isn't significant, many people believe every little bit is important.

To see the effect of trying to debug your code without the property enabled, uncheck the check box next to the "Generate Debugging Info" field. Then click the OK button and open a Java class in the Source Editor, as shown in Listing 4-1.

Listing 4-1. *Sample Class for Testing Disabled Breakpoint*

```
public class DebugNotEnabled {

    public static void main(String[] args) {

        int x = 0;

        for (int i = 0; i < args.length; i++) {
            if (i > 0) {
                System.out.println("TEST");
            }
        }
    }
}
```

Add a breakpoint to the Java source file at the line `if (i > 0) {` and try activating the debugger. You will see the following error message in the Debugger Console tab that appears in the Output window:

```
User program running
Not able to submit breakpoint LineBreakpoint DebugNotEnabled.java : 23, reason: ➥
Line number information is missing in the class file.
Invalid LineBreakpoint DebugNotEnabled.java : 23
User program finished
```

Since the debugging info was not generated in the class file, the NetBeans Debugger had nothing to work. When working with code in the IDE it is highly recommended that you leave the "Generate Debugging Info" property enabled so that the NetBeans debugger *does* have something with which to work.

Breakpoints

Breakpoints are one of the most important concepts in debugging. They represent markers in the code where you want program execution to stop. Breakpoints can be set in several ways, including while a debugging session is active. This section reviews how to create, view, and work with breakpoints in application source code.

Adding a Breakpoint

There are several ways to add a breakpoint. The first is by clicking in the glyph margin on the left side of the Source Editor. This automatically creates a breakpoint for the line of code next to where you clicked, as shown in Figure 4-2.

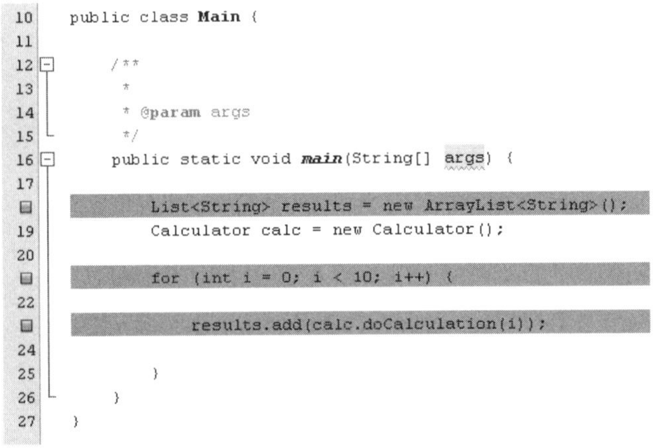

```
public class Main {

    /**
     *
     * @param args
     */
    public static void main(String[] args) {

        List<String> results = new ArrayList<String>();
        Calculator calc = new Calculator();

        for (int i = 0; i < 10; i++) {

            results.add(calc.doCalculation(i));

        }
    }
}
```

Figure 4-2. *Breakpoints added to several lines of code*

Each pink square that appears in the gutter denotes a breakpoint. When the program is debugged, program execution will halt on each of the lines where a breakpoint appears.

There are additional ways to add a breakpoint. Click in the line of code where you want the breakpoint, and select Run ➤ Toggle Line Breakpoint from the main menu. This will activate a breakpoint for that line of code. Other ways of adding different types of breakpoints are covered in the following sections.

Adding a Class Breakpoint

One type of breakpoint you can add is a *class breakpoint*. This allows you to halt program execution when a class is loaded or unloaded from the Java Virtual Machine. When you add a class breakpoint, it applies to any running code during the debug session.

In the Source Editor, open the class for which you need the breakpoint. Then select Run ➤ New Breakpoint from the main menu. This will open the New Breakpoint window. From the "Breakpoint Type" drop-down field, select Class. This will change the fields displayed in the New Breakpoint window, as shown in Figure 4-3.

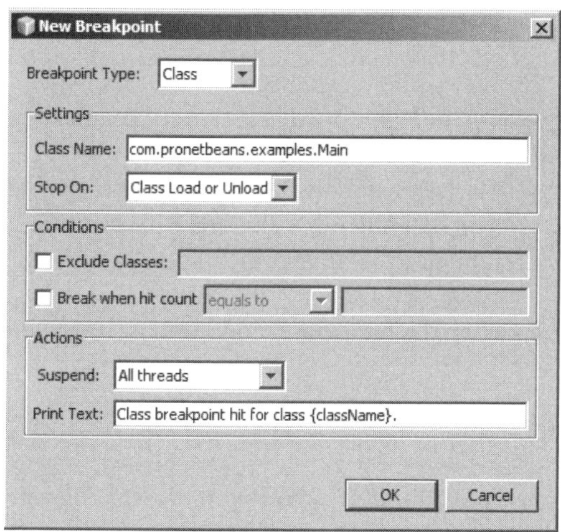

Figure 4-3. *Adding a class breakpoint using the New Breakpoint window*

Once the "Breakpoint Type" field is set to Class, you will see the Class Breakpoint–specific fields. In the Settings section, the "Class Name" field lists the fully qualified class name for which the breakpoint will be created. The "Stop On" drop-down contains several important values:

Class Load: The breakpoint will halt program execution when the specified class is loaded into the JVM.

Class Unload: The breakpoint will halt program execution when the specified class is unloaded from the JVM.

Class Load or Unload: The breakpoint will halt program execution when the specified class is loaded into or unloaded from the JVM.

The Conditions section allows you to specify an exclusion filter and a break hit count. This adds specified conditions to the breakpoint and is useful if you want the breakpoint to trigger if and only if a certain condition is true.

The "Exclude Classes" field lets you specify one or more classes to exclude from the class breakpoint. This can be used if you specified a package name in the "Class Name" field, such as `com.pronetbeans.example.*`.

The "Break when hit count" field allows you to specify a numerical condition such as equals to, greater than, or a multiple of a specified number. For example, if you specify equals to and a value of 5, then the breakpoint will halt program execution when the class is loaded or unloaded five times.

The Actions section is the area where you can specify what should happen when any of the breakpoint conditions is triggered. The "Suspend" drop-down field contains the following values:

No thread (continue)

Breakpoint thread

All threads

When the condition triggers, the text in the "Print Text" field will display in the Debugger tab of the Output window. If you specify the Suspend value "No thread (continue)," then program execution will not halt, but the Print text value will still print to the console.

If the "Suspend" field is set to "Breakpoint thread," then when the breakpoint condition is triggered, the thread where the breakpoint occurred will halt and other threads will continue. This can be useful in debugging multithread server applications where only a specific thread that meets the breakpoint condition will halt.

If the "Suspend" field is set to "All threads," then when the breakpoint condition is triggered, all threads executing in the JVM will be halted.

Adding an Exception Breakpoint

One type of breakpoint you can add is an *exception breakpoint*. This allows you to halt program execution when an exception is caught, uncaught, or merely encountered in the running code in the Java Virtual Machine.

Select Run ➤ New Breakpoint from the main menu. This will open the New Breakpoint window. From the "Breakpoint Type" drop-down field, select Exception. This will change the fields displayed in the New Breakpoint window, as shown in Figure 4-4.

In the Settings section, the "Exception Class Name" field is where you can specify the fully qualified class name for the exception you want to check for. The "Stop On" field allows you to specify Caught, Uncaught, or Caught or Uncaught. This lets you halt program execution if an exception is handled in the code, is not handled, or is thrown anywhere in the code regardless of whether it is caught or not.

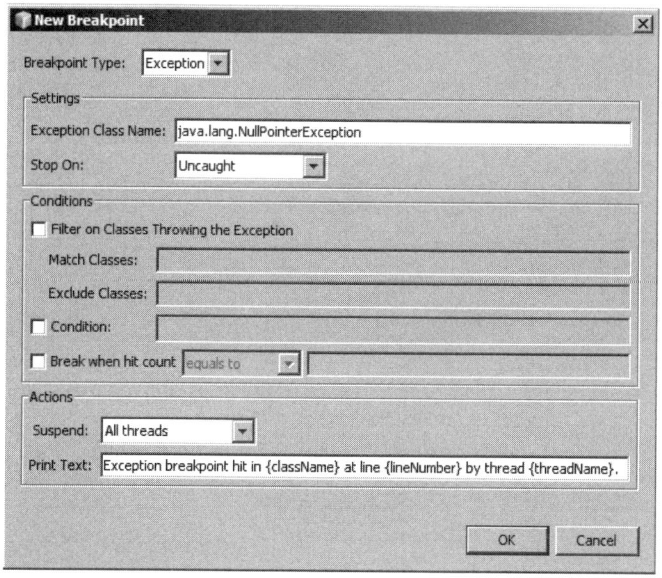

Figure 4-4. *Adding a breakpoint using the New Breakpoint window*

The Conditions section allows you to specify the specific conditions and filters to use to match the breakpoint type. If the "Filter on Classes Throwing the Exception" check box is selected, then you can enter values for the "Match Classes" and "Exclude Classes" fields. The "Match Classes" field lets you specify specific class names. If the class names specified throw the exception, then the breakpoint will be triggered. If a class not specified in the "Match Classes" field ends up throwing the exception, then the breakpoint will not be triggered.

The remaining fields in the New Breakpoint window function are as described in the previous section.

Adding a Method Breakpoint

Another type of breakpoint you can add is a *method breakpoint*. This type of breakpoint allows you to halt program execution when program execution enters or exits one or more methods of a specific class.

Open a Java source file in the Source Editor and place the cursor inside a method. Select Run ➤ New Breakpoint from the main menu. This will open the New Breakpoint window. The "Breakpoint Type" drop-down field should be preselected to the value Method. This will display the fields in the New Breakpoint window, as shown in Figure 4-5.

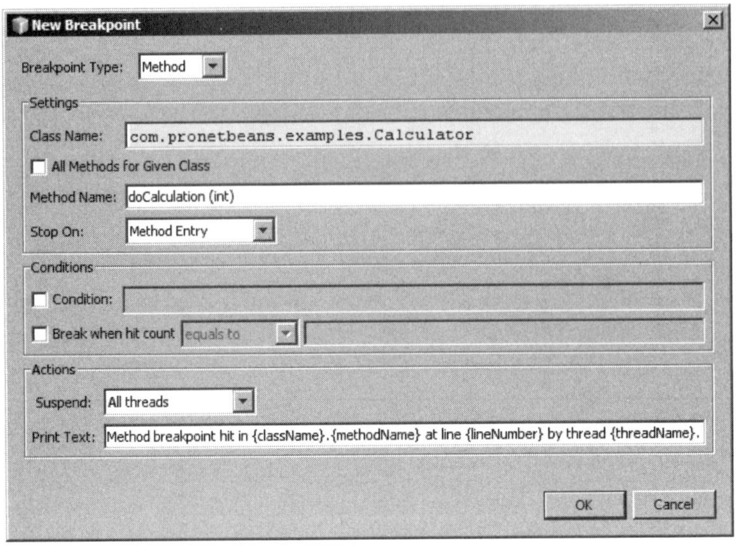

Figure 4-5. *Adding a method breakpoint using the New Breakpoint window*

The four important fields to mention here are the "Class Name," "All Methods for Given Class," "Method Name," and "Stop On" fields. The remaining fields function as described in the previous sections on adding breakpoints.

The "Class Name" field allows you to specify the fully qualified class name for the class to which the breakpoint is being added. It should initially be set to the name of the class that you opened in the Source Editor prior to activating the New Breakpoint window.

The "All Methods for Given Class" field lets you specify that the breakpoint condition should apply to every method in the class specified in the "Class Name" field. If selected, the "Method Name" will become grayed out and disabled.

The "Method Name" field allows you to specify the method name for which you want to add the breakpoint. If you had placed the cursor inside a method prior to activating the New Breakpoint window, the "Method Name" field should already be set. In Figure 4-5, the field is set to `doCalculation (int)`. You can manually change this field to point to any method in the class you want.

The "Stop On" drop-down field contains the following values:

Method Entry: The breakpoint condition is triggered if any thread enters the method.

Method Exit: The breakpoint condition is triggered when program execution exits the specified method or methods.

Method Entry or Exit: The breakpoint condition is triggered when program execution enters or exits the method or methods.

You can then set the remaining fields in the Conditions and Actions sections to finish adding the breakpoint.

Adding a Thread Breakpoint

A *thread breakpoint* is another type of breakpoint you can add via the New Breakpoint window. This type of breakpoint can be configured to halt program execution if a thread starts or finishes. This can be extremely useful in programming client-server applications or multithread server code.

To add a thread breakpoint, select Run ➤ New Breakpoint from the main menu. This will open the New Breakpoint window, as shown in Figure 4-6.

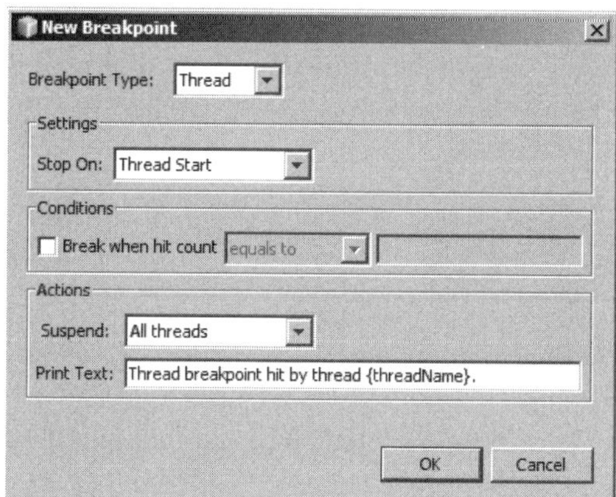

Figure 4-6. *Adding a thread breakpoint using the New Breakpoint window*

In the Settings section, the "Stop On" field allows you to specify the values Thread Start, Thread Death, and Thread Start or Death. These settings let you specify when the thread breakpoint is triggered.

The Conditions section lets you specify a condition to apply to the breakpoint such as having it trigger when the second thread starts or when all threads after the first thread start.

The Actions section performs identically as for the other breakpoint types. It lets you specify what should actually happen if the breakpoint condition and settings are triggered.

Adding a Field Breakpoint

The final type of breakpoint you can add is a *field breakpoint*. You can configure this type of breakpoint to halt program execution when a field is accessed, modified, or both.

To add a field breakpoint, you can click and highlight a class field in the Source Editor. Then select Run ➤ New Breakpoint from the main menu. The New Breakpoint window will open with the "Breakpoint Type" drop-down field set to Field, as shown in Figure 4-7. The "Class Name" field lets you specify a fully qualified class name. This should be the class that contains the field for the breakpoint.

The "Field Name" field lets you enter the name of the class variable used in the breakpoint.

The "Stop On" drop-down field allows you to specify Field Access, Field Modification, and Field Access or Modification. This lets you trigger the breakpoint when a class field is accessed or modified. This can be useful when trying to track down an elusive problem such as a hard-to-find field modification that is causing unexpected results.

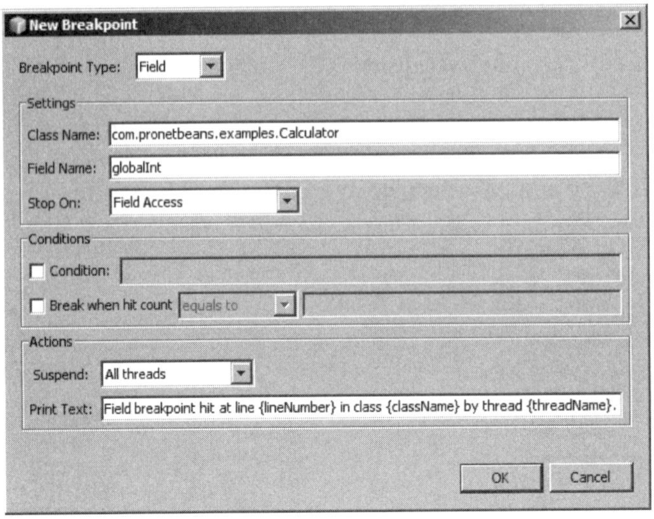

Figure 4-7. *Adding a field breakpoint using the New Breakpoint window*

The following class in Listing 4-2 contains a member field named `globalInt`. It is modified in the `doCalculation` method.

Listing 4-2. *Calculator Class*

```
public class Calculator {

    private int globalInt;

    public static void main(String[] args) {

        List<String> results = new ArrayList<String>();
        Calculator calc = new Calculator();

        for (int i = 0; i < 10; i++) {
            results.add(calc.doCalculation(i));
        }
        // do something with ArrayList
    }

    public String doCalculation(int x) {
        globalInt = 99;
        // do calculation with x
        return x+"";
    }
}
```

Add a field breakpoint, as described earlier, and set the "Stop On" drop-down to Field Modification. Make sure the "Field Name" field is set to `globalInt`.

When the class is debugged, program execution should halt on the line `globalInt = 99;` before the field is modified. This allows you to check the value before it is modified to ensure your code is working properly.

Disabling Breakpoints

You can also disable a breakpoint. This can be a nice option when you have added numerous breakpoints and want to disable them temporarily without deleting them. To disable a breakpoint, you can right-click the breakpoint glyph in the margin of the Source Editor and select Breakpoint ➤ Enabled, as shown in Figure 4-8.

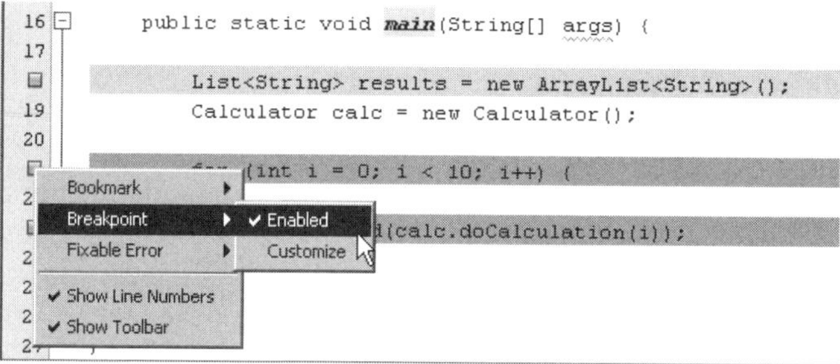

Figure 4-8. *The enable/disable breakpoint menu*

When a breakpoint is disabled, the breakpoint glyph and the corresponding line of code turn gray. The breakpoint has been disabled, but it has not been removed.

Deleting Breakpoints

Instead of disabling a breakpoint, you may want to delete it completely. To delete a breakpoint, click the breakpoint glyph in the Source Editor margin. Deleting a breakpoint removes the breakpoint glyph from the margin and any other trace of it from the Source Editor.

After debugging a section of code, you should delete all the breakpoints you used. Leaving breakpoints littered throughout your code isn't the end of the world, but it is generally considered bad practice. It can also cause problems when you later come back to debug code and it stops in places where you don't expect it to.

Customizing Breakpoints

Once you have added a breakpoint, you can customize or edit it at any time. To customize a breakpoint, locate one in the Source Editor and right-click it. On the context menu that appears, select Breakpoint ➤ Customize. The Customize Breakpoint window will open, as shown in Figure 4-9.

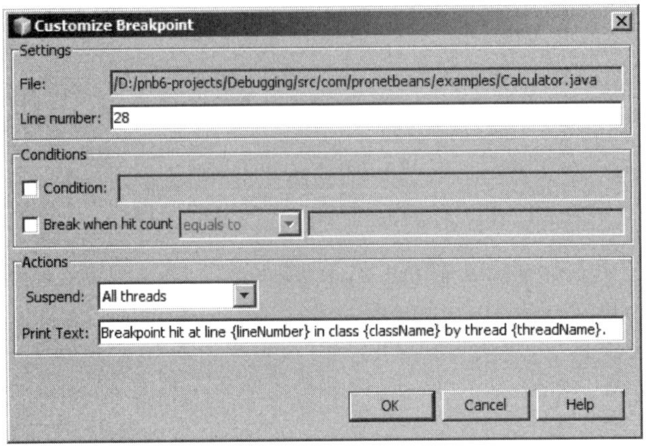

Figure 4-9. *The Customize Breakpoint window*

The Customize Breakpoint window contains many of the same fields as described in the sections on adding breakpoints. It also contains a "Line Number" field that lists the number of the precise line on which the breakpoint appears. You can alter any of the Conditions or Actions fields that you originally configured for the breakpoint. This is typically better than having to delete the breakpoint and add it over again simply to change one of the fields or the values.

Breakpoints Window

The Breakpoints window lists the currently set breakpoints in all open projects. It will list all disabled breakpoints in your code as well. The Breakpoints window can be accessed by going to the main menu and selecting Window ➤ Debugging ➤ Breakpoints. When the Breakpoints window opens, you should see two columns: Name and Enabled, as shown in Figure 4-10. The Name column contains a block of text that describes the breakpoint, its type, and its basic location. The Enabled column displays a check box for each breakpoint. If it is selected, then the breakpoint is enabled; otherwise it is disabled.

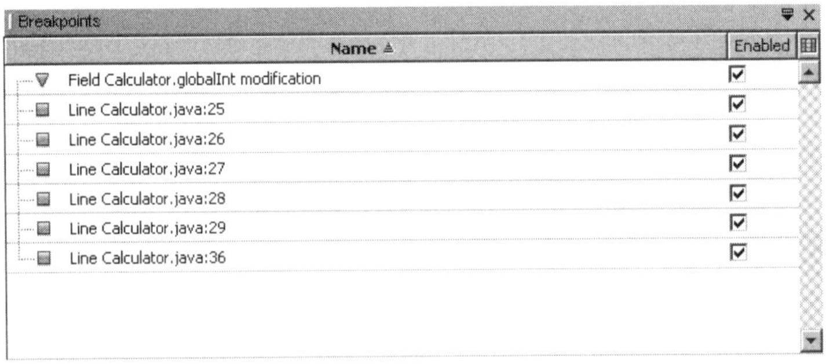

Figure 4-10. *The Breakpoints window*

The Breakpoints window serves as a single location where you can locate your breakpoints throughout your code. It also allows you to perform many of the common actions on breakpoints you would expect, such as disable, delete, and customize. Right-click a breakpoint and review the items that appear in the context menu, as listed in Table 4-1.

Table 4-1. *Context Menu Actions in the Breakpoints Window*

Action	Description
Go To Source	Jump directly to the class, method, or line in the Source Editor where the breakpoint is set. This same action is also triggered if you double-click the breakpoint name in the Breakpoints window.
Disable	Disable the specific breakpoint that you right-clicked in the Breakpoints window.
Delete	Delete the specific breakpoint that you right-clicked in the Breakpoints window.
Set Group Name	Assign a name to one or more breakpoints so that they can be handled collectively as a group. Discussed in the next section.
Enable All	Enable all the disabled breakpoints listed in the Breakpoints window.
Disable All	Disable all the enabled breakpoints listed in the Breakpoints window.
Delete All	Delete all the breakpoints listed in the Breakpoints window.
Customize	Customize the specific breakpoint you right-clicked in the Breakpoints window. This opens the Customize Breakpoint window.
List Options	Change the column ordering and display status of the fields displayed in the Breakpoints window.

Grouping Breakpoints

The idea of grouping breakpoints is quite simple and can often be amazingly effective. Review the list of breakpoints displayed in the Breakpoints window in Figure 4-10. If you wanted to disable or enable a set you could do so for each one. The list displayed in Figure 4-10 is not very long, but imagine it contained a hundred breakpoints. Disabling a specific set of 30-40 of them would probably take a few minutes.

The Breakpoints window allows you to select one or more breakpoints and assign a top-level group name to them. You can do so by holding your operating system's multiple-file-select key (the Ctrl key in Windows) and clicking each breakpoint listed in the Breakpoints window. Once you have selected your group of breakpoints, right-click any of them and select Set Group Name from the context menu.

A small pop-up window will appear and prompt you to specify a value in the "Name of Group" field. Enter a meaningful name or description, such as "Production Bug 56799" or "hanging DB connection issue" and click the OK button.

The breakpoints that you selected in the Breakpoints window will still appear, but they will be listed under a parent node, with the group name you specified, as shown in Figure 4-11. You can then hide or show the entire group of breakpoints by expanding or collapsing the group name's node. You can also disable all the breakpoints in the group by unselecting the check box in the Enabled column on the line for the group name. This will unselect all the check boxes for each breakpoint in that group. You can also delete the group by right-clicking it and selecting Delete All from the context menu. This will delete only the breakpoints in the selected group.

Breakpoints

Name	Enabled
Line Calculator.java:36	☑
Field Calculator.globalInt modification	☑
Breakpoints for main method	☑
Line Calculator.java:29	☑
Line Calculator.java:28	☑
Line Calculator.java:27	☑
Line Calculator.java:26	☑
Line Calculator.java:25	☑

Figure 4-11. *A set of grouped breakpoints*

Debugging Java Code

To begin debugging Java code, you need a good understanding and working knowledge of breakpoints and how to add, customize, disable, and delete them. I highly suggest reviewing the previous sections in this chapter that cover breakpoints until you have a firm grasp on working with them. Once you do, you can initiate your first debugging session and begin to learn the remaining debugging tools available in the NetBeans IDE.

Starting a Project Debug Session

There are multiple ways to initiate a debugging session in NetBeans. The primary method is to go to the main menu and select Run ➤ Debug Main Project. You can also use the keyboard shortcut Ctrl+F5. If the Main Project is not set, NetBeans will prompt you to select one from a provided list of open projects.

The IDE will then typically compile the code you are about to debug and open some of the debugging windows used (each is discussed in the following sections). If you open the Output window by selecting Window ➤ Output ➤ Output from the main menu (or pressing Ctrl+4), you will see two tabs: Debugging and Debugging Console, as shown in Figure 4-12. The Debugging tab provides basic control of the debugging session while it is running. You will see basic output that indicates the file or files that were compiled. You will also see two icons on the left side of the window that control the debugging session.

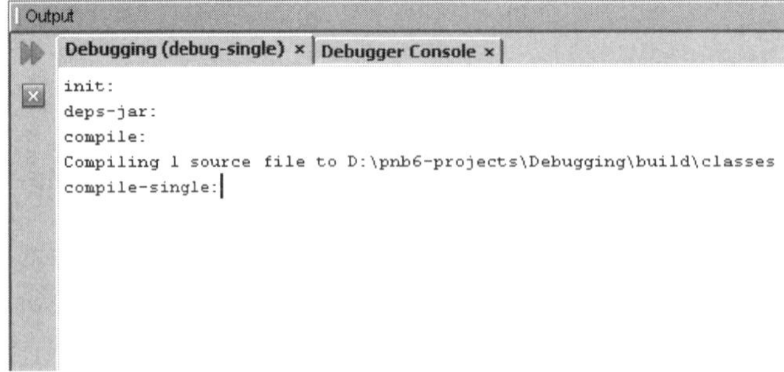

Figure 4-12. *The Debugging tab in the Output window during a debug session*

After a debugging session has completed, the right-pointing double arrow turns green and is able to be clicked. This icon allows you to rerun the previous debugging session. This is convenient because you don't have to remember the class with which you wanted to start debugging.

The red square with the X in the middle is the Stop icon. Clicking it will halt the debugging session and kill any debugging processes. If you click this icon accidentally, you can immediately rerun the debugging session using the rerun icon above it. This will start the session over and not from where you left off.

The Debugging Console tab in the Output window contains the standard output of the debug session. In Listing 4-2, I added a breakpoint on the following line of Java code:

```
results.add(calc.doCalculation(i));
```

When I started a debugging session, program execution paused, as expected, at the line. The NetBeans debugger output the following text to the Debugging Console tab:

```
User program running
LineBreakpoint Calculator.java : 29 successfully submitted.
Breakpoint hit at line 29 in class com.pronetbeans.examples.Calculator ➥
by thread main.
Thread main stopped at Calculator.java : 29.
```

This console text indicates that the debugging session started, that the breakpoint was valid, and that it triggered the breakpoint at the correct line and then halted program execution.

You can also start a debugging session for a project by right-clicking the project name in the Projects window and selecting Debug from the context menu. This is how you can quickly debug an open project if it is not set to be the main project.

Starting a File Debug Session

In addition to projects, you can debug individual files in NetBeans. This comes in handy since you will frequently want to debug a specific Java source file without having to step through dozens of classes to get to the one you want to test.

To debug a file, you can right-click it in the Projects or Files windows and select Debug File from the context menu. You can also use the keyboard shortcut Ctrl+Shift+F5, but the file must be selected.

You can also open a file in the Source Editor and use the main menu to start debugging. Select Run ➤ Run File ➤ Debug "Calculator.java," where "Calculator" is the name of the specific class or file you have selected in the Source Editor.

Stopping a Debug Session

Stopping a debugging session is quite simple and can be done from several places. You can locate a red square icon on the debug toolbar that is labeled "Finish Debugger Session" when you mouse over it. You can also use the keyboard shortcut Shift+F5 or navigate to the main menu and select Run ➤ Finish Debugger Session.

Finally, you can use the Sessions window to view and stop any active debugging sessions. You can access this window by navigating the main menu and selecting Window ➤ Debugging ➤ Sessions. You can also use the keyboard shortcut Alt+Shift+6. The Sessions window will open and display a list of current debugging sessions, as shown in Figure 4-13.

Figure 4-13. *The Sessions window during debugging*

The Sessions window displays the name of each session, the current state it is in, and the coding language. If you right-click a session name in the list, there are several options you can select from the context menu that appears, as detailed in Table 4-2.

Table 4-2. *Context Menu Actions in the Sessions Window*

Action	Description
Scope	Specifies the thread scope of execution for the current debugging sessions. You can set this field to Debug Current Thread or Debug All Threads, depending on your debug session needs.
Language	Specifies the programming language to which the current session applies.
Make Current	Sets a session as the current session. You can have multiple sessions active at once but only one can be set as the current session.
Finish	Finishes the selected debugging session.
Finish All	Finishes all active debugging sessions.
List Options	Allows you to change the sort order and column display status of the fields displayed in the Sessions window.

Stepping Through Code

Once you have learned how to set breakpoints and how to start and stop sessions, you are ready to do some serious debugging. One of the most powerful features of the NetBeans debugger is the ability to execute one line of code at a time.

While breakpoints will allow you to halt program execution at specific lines, you do not want to have to set a breakpoint at every single line. This is where the concept of "stepping" through code comes into play.

Step Into

Suppose you have a Java class in a Java Application project, such as the DebugStepping class displayed in Listing 4-3:

Listing 4-3. *The DebugStepping Class*

```
package com.pronetbeans.examples;

/**
 * Sample class to demonstrate debug stepping
 * @author Adam Myatt
 */
public class DebugStepping {

    public static void main(String[] args) {
        System.out.println("Step A");
        DebugStepping stepping = new DebugStepping();
    }

    public DebugStepping() {
        System.out.println("Step B");
    }
}
```

The class's main method is where the NetBeans debugger will first enter the class. You can easily debug and step through each line of the class without setting a breakpoint. Open the class in the Source Editor and go to the main menu. Select Run ➤ Step Into. A debugging session will start, and odds are that the Output tab will print the following text and then end:

```
Step A
Step B
```

This reflects the run configuration of the project. When I first created the Java Application project, I specified some other class as the Main class. When I activate the Step Into feature, I assume it will step into the main method of the class selected in the Source Editor. Unfortunately this is not so. The project has been configured to execute a main class by default. I can easily switch this to make the DebugStepping class the project's Main class.

You might be asking, "Why go through this hassle when you could just add a breakpoint to the first line of the DebugStepping.main method and then simply debug the file?" It makes no difference and is essentially the same action. On occasion I have found it useful to ensure that a debugging session starts precisely with the first line every time (without having to set a breakpoint).

You can also use the Step Into feature in other, more important ways. It allows you to execute each line of code and proceed to the next. The matching keyboard shortcut you can use is F7. This lets you quickly step through lines using F7 to get to the precise line you want to review.

For example, set a breakpoint at the line

```
System.out.println("Step A");
```

Then start a debug session and wait for program execution to halt at the breakpoint. Use the Step Into feature by pressing F7. The program execution proceeds to the line but does not execute it:

```
DebugStepping stepping = new DebugStepping();
```

Next, press F7 again, and you will see that program execution moves to the first line of the `DebugStepping` constructor:

```
public DebugStepping() {
```

Pressing F7 again will place program execution at the next line:

```
System.out.println("Step B");
```

Finally, press F7 two more times to return to the `main` method. Program execution will halt at the following line:

```
DebugStepping stepping = new DebugStepping();
```

The reason that program execution is back at this line for the second time is that the class constructor has executed, but the new instance of the class has not been assigned to the variable `stepping`. If you place the mouse over the `stepping` variable, you should see a pop-up tooltip that says

```
"stepping" is not a known variable in current context.
```

If you activate the Step Into feature again by pressing F7, the class instance will be assigned to the `stepping` variable. Program execution will proceed to the next line. If you mouse over the `stepping` variable again, the tooltip will read as follows:

```
stepping = (com.pronetbeans.examples.DebugStepping) ➥
 com.pronetbeans.examples.DebugStepping.
```

Step Out

The Step Out debugging feature will execute the code in the current method or constructor and move program execution back to the calling code of the method or constructor. This can best be illustrated with an example (see Listing 4-4).

Listing 4-4. *The DebugSteppingOut Class*

```
public class DebugSteppingOut {

    public static void main(String[] args) {
        System.out.println("Step A");
        DebugSteppingOut stepping = new DebugSteppingOut();
```

```
        stepping.doSomething();

        System.out.println("Step B");
    }

    public DebugSteppingOut() {
        System.out.println("Constructor Running");
    }

    public void doSomething() {
        int x = 0;
        int y = 0;
        int z = 0;
        int total = 0;

        total = x + y + z;

        System.out.println("Total = " + total);
    }
}
```

The DebugSteppingOut class shown in Listing 4-4 contains a doSomething method that simulates a calculation. It defines three ints, adds them together, and prints the total to the standard output stream. Realistically this method could be complex, time intensive, or 50 lines long.

Set a breakpoint at the following line of the main method:

```
System.out.println("Step A");
```

Start a debugging session. When program execution halts at the breakpoint, use the Step Into feature (F7) to step line by line until you are at the following line:

```
stepping.doSomething();
```

Press F7, and program execution will proceed into the doSomething.

If this method is exceptionally long and you do not want to step through every line, you can step out of the method. On the main menu select Run ➤ Step Out, or press Ctrl+F7. The doSomething method will execute and program execution will halt on the line after the call to the doSomething method:

```
System.out.println("Step B");
```

The Step Out feature can be very useful as you step through code. You might easily step into methods you want to skip. The Step Out feature allows you to skip a method. But it is not the only way to skip method and constructor calls. The Step Over feature, covered in the next section, provides a similar ability.

Step Over

The Step Over debugging feature will execute the current line of code and halt program execution on the next line of code. This may sound similar to the Step Into feature, but it has one important difference. If the line of code you executed contained a call to a method or constructor, the method or constructor is entered and executed.

This feature lets you execute methods or constructors without having to step through them. For an example of this review, see the code in Listing 4-4. Set a breakpoint at the following line in the `main` method:

```
System.out.println("Step A");
```

Activate a debugging session, and, when program execution halts at the breakpoint, step through each line by pressing F7 until program execution reaches the following line:

```
stepping.doSomething();
```

Now activate the Step Over debug feature. Go to the main menu and select Run ➤ Step Over, or use the keyboard shortcut F8. Program execution will proceed to the following line in the `main` method:

```
System.out.println("Step B");
```

It may look like the `doSomething` method was not executed. But if you review the Output window, you should see the `Total = X` expression in the standard output stream. This should indicate that the `doSomething` method did indeed execute.

The Step Over feature is very useful in that it allows you to execute methods and constructors without having to step through every line of code inside them. This can be a time-saving feature for developers.

Step Over Expression

The Step Over debugging feature has one flaw: multiple Java statements can be combined into one line. It's not unusual to see Java statements such as this:

```
someObject.setCustomerId( customer.getId() );
```

or

```
myArrayList.ensureCapacity(myHashMap.keySet().size());
```

In either of these scenarios, performing a Step Over of either line would execute the entire line. You would not be able to identify the values for `customer.getId()` and `myHashMap.keySet().size()` without actually stepping into each method call. The Step Over Expression debug feature lets you solve this problem by allowing you to see method return values without stepping into it.

Let's walk through an example so that you can understand how this important feature works. Review the code for the `DebugSteppingOverExp` class in Listing 4-5.

Listing 4-5. *The DebugSteppingOverExp Class*

```
public class DebugSteppingOutExp {

    public static void main(String[] args) {

        DebugSteppingOutExp stepping = new DebugSteppingOutExp();
```

```
        File myFile = new File("d:\\java\\test.txt");

        stepping.checkSize(myFile.length());

        System.out.println("Step Over Expression");
    }

    public void checkSize(long length) {

        if (length > 0) {
            System.out.println("length = " + length);
        } else {
            System.err.println("uh oh");
        }
    }
}
```

First, set a breakpoint at the following line:

```
stepping.checkSize(myFile.length());
```

Next, start a debugging session for the file and wait for program execution to halt at the breakpoint. Try mousing over the `myFile` variable. It should correctly list the reference to the file specified in the previous line (`d:\java\test.txt`). If you mouse over the `length()` method, the pop-up tooltip will state only that it is not recognized in the current context.

Go to the main menu and select Run ➤ Step Over Expression. Program execution will still be paused at the same line, but the `length()` method will be highlighted. This indicates that program execution will execute the method next. Activate the Step Over Expression feature one more time. Now the `length()` method will appear faintly underlined. If you mouse over it, you should see a pop-up tooltip that reads `MyFile.length(): (long) 10348920`.

The value `10348920` happens to be the number of bytes in the file on my machine. If you create your own test file, it should list the number of bytes in your file. This is the correct return value that the `length()` method should return. Program execution is still paused on the line `stepping.checkSize(myFile.length());` since the `checkSize(long length)` method has not yet been entered.

I have found the Step Over Expression feature very useful when debugging. It's not terribly time consuming to perform a Step Into operation to enter the method and then step out, but it changes what is visually displayed in the Source Editor. It interrupts your chain of thought much less when using the Step Over Expression feature.

Run to Cursor

The Run to Cursor debugging feature is simple and powerful. It is one of those things whose value you don't realize until you start using it. Activating the Run to Cursor feature while debugging will run all the lines of code in the source file between the current line (where program execution is currently halted) and the line where the cursor has been placed. It's a great way to jump quickly through long sections of code to specific locations without having to set breakpoints.

Run Into Method

The Run Into Method debug feature will run program execution from the current line of code to the first line of the method or constructor where the cursor was placed. This is a combination of the Run to Cursor and Step Into debug features. It allows you to execute the program quickly and to jump immediately into a method.

Review the `DebugRunIntoMethod` class displayed in Listing 4-6. It contains two methods of interest: `printStatement` and `getLogMessage`. The call to the `getLogMessage` method is embedded inside the call to the `printStatement` method. The Run Into Method debug feature will let you jump directly into the `getLogMessage` method.

Listing 4-6. *The DebugRunIntoMethod Class*

```
public class DebugRunIntoMethod {

    public static void main(String[] args) {

        DebugRunIntoMethod stepping = new DebugRunIntoMethod();

        stepping.printStatement(stepping.getLogMessage());

        System.out.println("Run Into Method finishing.");
    }

    public void printStatement(String logMessage) {
        // save logMessage to database

        // print to standard output for brevity
        System.out.println("logMessage = " + logMessage);
    }

    public String getLogMessage() {
        return "Adam Myatt was here";
    }
}
```

Set a breakpoint at the following line:

```
DebugRunIntoMethod stepping = new DebugRunIntoMethod();
```

Then activate a debugging session for the file. After program execution stops at the breakpoint, click and place the cursor inside the call to the `getLogMessage` method. Go to the main menu and select Run ➤ Run Into Method. The debugger will execute each line of the `main` method and pause at the first line inside the `getLogMessage` method.

If you activate the Run Into Method debug feature and there is no method selected by the cursor, you will see an error message pop up that reads "Put cursor on method call."

Evaluate Expression

One of the most interesting new features of the NetBeans debugger is the Evaluate Expression window. It allows you to enter Java expressions or methods calls and view the results. You can do so during a debugging session for any variable or object currently in scope of the program execution.

In Listing 4-7, the `DebugEvaluateExpression` class contains a `main` method that instantiates an instance of itself, declares two `int` variables, and adds them together. This code will demonstrate a very simple usage of the Evaluate Expression window during a debugging session.

Listing 4-7. *The DebugEvaluateExpression Class*

```
public class DebugEvaluateExpression {

    public static void main(String[] args) {

        int x = 0;
        int y = 0;

        int total = x + y;

    }

}
```

First set a breakpoint inside the first line of the `main` method at the line `int x = 0;`. Then start a debugging session for the class by selecting Run ➤ Run File ➤ Run DebugEvaluateExpression.java from the main menu. A debugging session will start, and program execution should pause at the breakpoint.

Open the Evaluate Expression window by going to the main menu and selecting Run ➤ Evaluate Expression. The window will open with no values displayed. You can now write a valid Java expression in the Expression field at the top of the window, such as the following:

```
((x + y) + 2) * 56 == 112
```

After you have entered the expression, click the Evaluate button along the bottom of the window. The expression will evaluate and display in the result table grid in the center of the window, as shown in Figure 4-14.

The first column in the data grid lists the name of the expression, the second column lists the data type of the result, and the third column lists the value of the result of the expression. The sample expression in Figure 4-14 is a `Boolean` result with a value of `true`, since 2 times 56 is equivalent to 112. This type of functionality can prove useful if you are trying to evaluate long or complex formulas, nested `Boolean` conditionals, or the like.

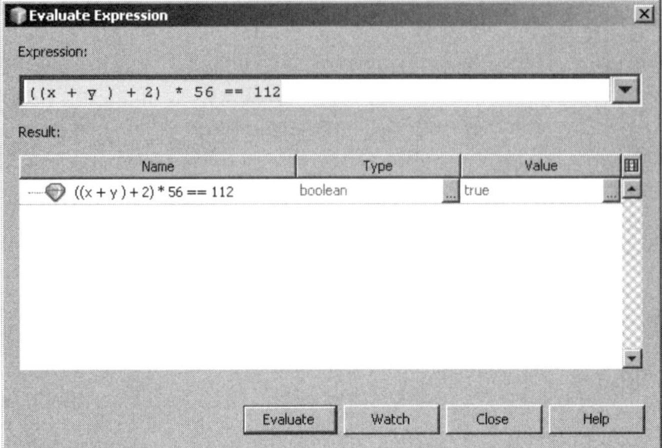

Figure 4-14. *The Evaluate Expression window with results*

You can also use the Evaluate Expression window for determining return values from method calls. Review the Java code in Listing 4-8.

Listing 4-8. *The DebugEvaluateExpression2 Class*

```
public class DebugEvaluateExpression2 {

    public static void main(String[] args) {

        DebugEvaluateExpression2 stepping = new DebugEvaluateExpression2();

        int id = 9;

        String personName = stepping.getNameById(id);
    }

    public String getNameById(int i) {

        String results = "";

        if(i > 5) {
            results = "Jones";
        } else {
            results = "Smith";
        }

        return results;
    }

}
```

The DebugEvaluateExpression2 class contains a main method that instantiates an instance of itself, defines an int with a value of 9, passes the int to the getNameById method, and retrieves the String result. The getNameById method simply takes in an int, performs some bogus logic on it, and returns one of two possible String values representing a name.

Set a breakpoint on any line in the main method and activate a debugging session. When program execution pauses, open the Evaluate Expression window by selecting Run ➤ Evaluate Expression from the main menu.

The Evaluate Expression window will open. Enter a value for the "Expression" field, such as stepping.getNameById(8);, and click the Evaluate button. This will actually execute the getNameById method, pass in the value 8, and return the result, as shown in Figure 4-15. All this occurs without advancing the actual program execution or the debugger. It stays paused at the breakpoint you set. This allows you to experiment with different input values for methods and see possible results without having to waste time running numerous debugging sessions.

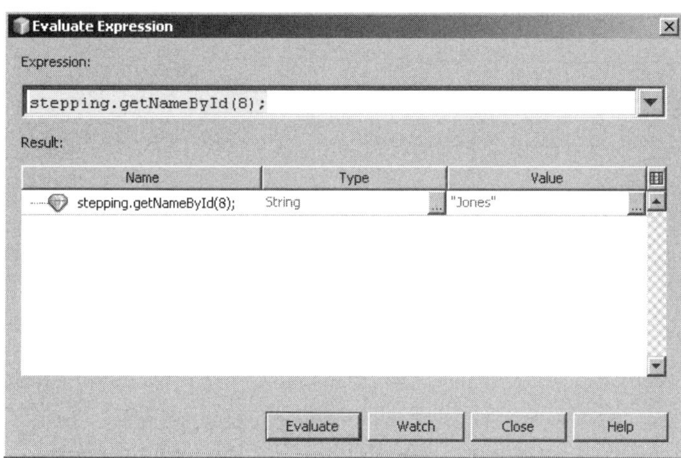

Figure 4-15. *The Evaluate Expression window with results*

One of the last things I want to mention about the Evaluate Expression window is the Watch button that appears next to the Evaluate button. Once you have evaluated an expression, you can easily create a new watch using that expression. To create the watch, simply click the Watch button. The expression will be added to the list of watches and be viewable in the Watches window, as discussed in the following section.

Debugging with Watches

A *watch* is a debugging feature that allows you to specify a Java statement and track its value during a debugging session. You can track fields, objects, or expressions in a window called the Watches window. The watches persist across debugging sessions, so you do not have to reset them each time you need them. This can help in debugging persistent problems in your code by enabling you to track and monitor the same fields and expressions.

You can open the Watches windows by navigating the main menu and selecting Window ➤ Debugging ➤ Watches. The Watches window will open with any existing watches listed, as shown in Figure 4-16.

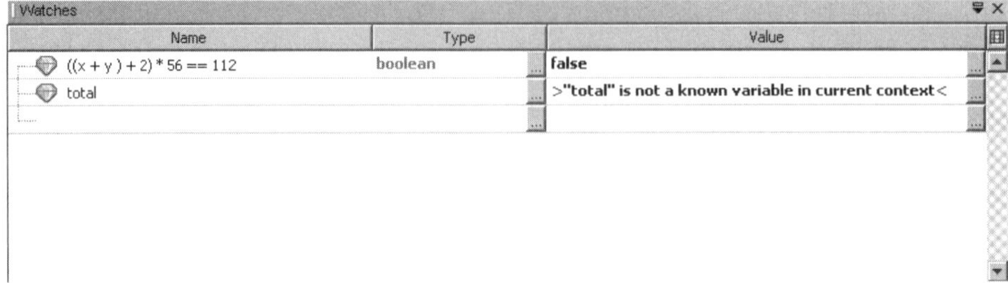

Figure 4-16. *The Watches window*

The Watches window contains three columns: Name, Type, and Value. The Name column displays the actual variable or expression that makes up the watch. The Type column displays the data type of the result, and the Value column displays the current value of the expression as it exists *in the current scope*.

This last point about scope is important to make clear. The first watch in Figure 4-16 is for the `total` variable. Let's assume the code for the current scope was for the following class:

```
public class DebugWatch {

    public static void main(String[] args) {
        int x = 1;
        int y = 2;
        int total = x + y;
    }
}
```

If program execution was paused at the line `int total = x + y;` but the line had not yet been executed, the Watches window would read as shown in Figure 4-16. The watch for the `total` variable will indicate that `total` is not a known variable in the current context. That is because it has not been defined and processed by the debugger. The other watch should evaluate to false:

```
((x + y ) + 2) * 56 == 112
```

Since x is 1 and y is 2, then adding 2 and multiplying by 56 should be equivalent to 280. If the watch was entered incorrectly, you can customize it by double-clicking the watch name. You can also right-click and select Customize from the context menu. This will open the Customize window that contains a "Watch Expression" field allowing you to edit the expression. You can change the watch expression to ensure it evaluates to `true`, as shown in Figure 4-17. Once you set the watch expression correctly, click the OK button to save the change.

Figure 4-17. *The Customize window for watch expressions*

The updated watch expression will be appear in the Watches window and should also display a value of `true`. You can now step through your code at any time and, by watching the expression in the Watches window, know if it ever evaluates to `true`.

There are several ways to add watch expressions in the NetBeans debugger. As discussed in the previous section, you can add a watch from the Evaluate Expression window. You can also highlight a variable or Java expression in code in the Source Editor and select Run ➤ New Watch.

The New Watch window will appear. The "Watch Expression" text field will be prepopulated with the text you selected in the Source Editor prior to invoking the New Watch command. You can leave the text as is or customize the expression. Click the OK button and the watch will be added to the list in the Watches window. You can also right-click any variable or expression in the Source Editor and select New Watch from the context menu. The matching keyboard shortcut is Ctrl+Shift+F7.

The Watches window contains several additional capabilities. You can right-click each watch in the list and select from the context menu that is displayed. Table 4-3 describes the actions available.

Table 4-3. *Context Menu Actions in the Watches Window*

Action	Description
Create Fixed Watch	Converts an existing watch to a fixed watch (explained further shortly).
New Watch	Displays the New Watch window, allowing you to enter a new watch.
Customize	Allows you to edit the watch expression using the Customize window.
Delete	Deletes the selected watch.
Delete All	Deletes all watches.
List Options	Allows you to change the sort order and column display status of the fields displayed in the Watches window.

One thing to note regards the concept of *fixed watches*. You can convert a watch to a fixed watch by selecting Create Fixed Watch from the right-click context menu in the Watches window. A fixed watch monitors the object reference assigned to a variable, as opposed to the value of the variable.

Local Variables Window

The Local Variables window is another important tool in the NetBeans debugging arsenal. It allows you to track the value of all variables and objects in the known scope of program execution during a debugging session. You are able to track primitive values, instances of objects, and even drill down to see the values of a `HashMap` stored inside an `ArrayList` that is stored inside a `Vector`.

Being able to track the value of all variables and objects can prove invaluable during debugging. Watches are useful, but only if you know the expression you want to monitor. The Local Variables window lets you monitor the values as they are created and modified throughout all classes and methods.

To open the Local Variables window, go to the main menu and select Run ➤ Window ➤ Debugging ➤ Local Variables. The Local Variables window will open and display no values.

Open the following class in the Source Editor as shown in Listing 4-9.

Listing 4-9. *The DebugLocalVariables Class*

```
public class DebugLocalVariables {

    private String country;

    public static void main(String[] args) {

       String s = "Adam was here!";
       int x = 123456789;

       DebugLocalVariables dlv = new DebugLocalVariables();
       dlv.country = "Brazil";

       System.out.println("Ending method");
    }
}
```

Set a breakpoint at the line `dlv.country = "Brazil";`. If you initiate a debugging session, program execution will pause at the breakpoint, and any of the classes' member variables as well as any locally scoped variables and objects should appear in the Local Variables window, as shown in Figure 4-18.

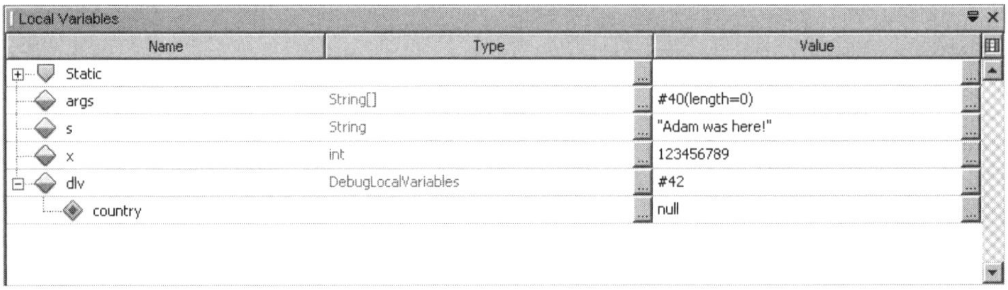

Local Variables

Name	Type	Value
Static		
args	String[]	#40(length=0)
s	String	"Adam was here!"
x	int	123456789
dlv	DebugLocalVariables	#42
country		null

Figure 4-18. *The Local Variables window*

The Local Variables window will display the list of variables recognized by the debugger in the current scope of program execution. Based on where the breakpoint is paused, the variables `args`, `s`, `x`, and `dlv` should be listed in the Local Variables window. The variable `dlv` has an instance of the `DebugLocalVariables` class instantiated and assigned to it, but the class member inside it, `country`, will not be initialized until the line `dlv.country = "Brazil";` runs.

As you step through the code, the data in the Value column changes as each variable or class changes. This can be a useful method for tracking data values through an application.

Another useful and powerful feature is the ability to edit the values of variables that appear in the Local Variables window. For most variables, you can click inside the text that appears in the Value column for a variable and type over it with a value of the same data type.

After typing the new value, press the Enter key. That variable has now been reassigned that value in the current scoped context.

If you click back inside the code in the Source Editor and mouse over the variable, the pop-up tooltip should display the new value. Going forward in the debugging session, your program now thinks the variable has the new value. This can be a great way to patch mistakes that crop up during long debugging sessions.

Summary

This chapter reviewed the concept of debugging code in NetBeans and why it can help save you time and trouble. Debugging tools can help you quickly identify errors, bugs, and mistaken assumptions in your code by allowing you to track specific variables and instances of classes and by monitoring Java expressions.

It reviewed the different types of breakpoints, including how to add, disable, delete, and customize them using the tools available in the Source Editor and the Breakpoints window. It discussed several scenarios in an attempt to clarify the impact that proper use of breakpoints can have on debugging errors.

The chapter went on to discuss the basics of how to start and stop different types of debugging sessions in NetBeans. You learned how to activate debugging for an entire project and a specific file. You also learned how to run multiple debugging sessions and how to switch between them.

The chapter reviewed in depth the concept of stepping through code. Stepping allows you to proceed through classes and methods line by line. This gives you fine-grained control over how to navigate your code during debugging.

The chapter went on to discuss watches and local variables. These are similar features and should be used together. Watches allow you to monitor simple variables or complex Java expressions during your debugging sessions. The Local Variables window allows you to track all variables, classes, and fields that exist in the JVM for your code that are in scope.

All these tools have been combined into a suite of debugging features available in NetBeans. When you use them correctly, they can assist you in identifying both simple and complex errors in your code.

CHAPTER 5

Profiling

One of the biggest problems with software applications is designing them efficiently so that they run under an optimal load. All too often applications work fine under an average number of users. When a higher-than-expected load of users accesses the application, problems typically occur, usually because of poorly designed algorithms or code that assumed only a specific load.

Performance problems can typically be fixed, but you just need to know where and why they are occurring. Enter the NetBeans Profiler. It allows a developer to examine the CPU performance and monitor the memory usage of a Java application. With the Profiler you can record and save performance data, examine results in detail, and get a true understanding of the bottlenecks in an application.

Prior to NetBeans 6, the Profiler was a separate add-on pack that had to be downloaded and installed. It therefore was an optional feature that some users never benefited from. Starting with NetBeans 6, the Profiler comes installed and is active by default. I think this was an excellent move. It raises the visibility of the tool and stresses the importance of profiling your code regularly.

Configuring Profiler Properties

The NetBeans Profiler has a number of configuration settings you can change to customize its behavior. To see the properties, open the Basic Options window by going to the main menu and selecting Tools ➤ Options. When the Basic Options window opens, click the Miscellaneous icon in the Windows toolbar and select the Profiler tab. The Profiler options will now be displayed, as shown in Figure 5-1.

There are three main sections on the Profiler tab on the Basic Options window: General, When Profiling Session Starts, and Miscellaneous. I next describe the fields available for each section.

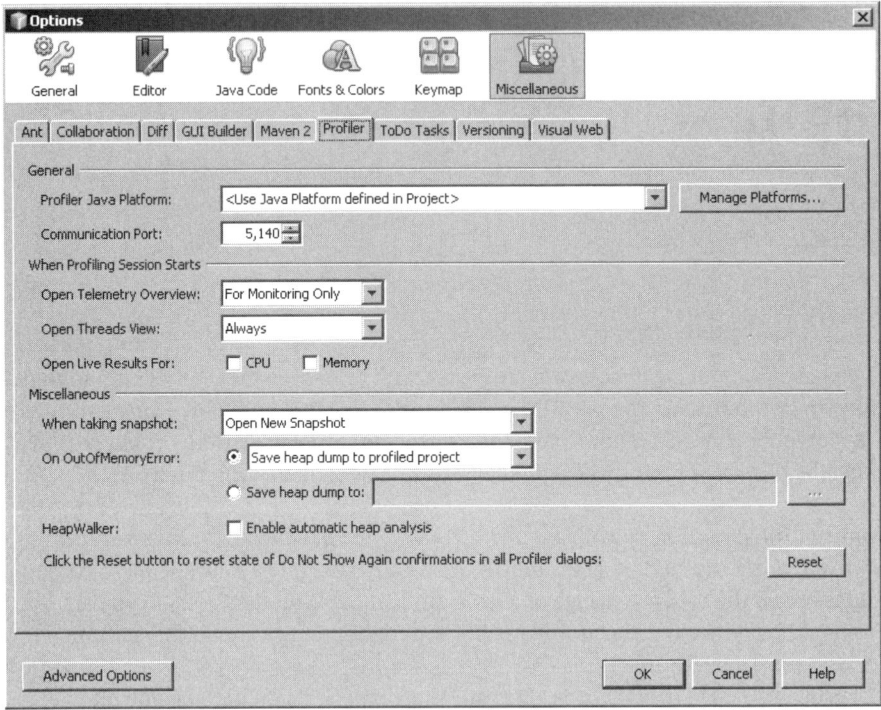

Figure 5-1. *Configuring Profiler properties in the Basic Options window*

The fields in the General section of the Profiler tab include:

Profiler Java Platform: The target JVM in which the Profiler runs. You can select any JDK that has been configured in the Java Platform Manager or set the field to "Use Java Platform defined in Project."

Communication Port: The TCP/IP port on which the Profiler listens. It is initially set to 5140.

The fields in the When Profiling Session Starts section of the Profiler tab include:

Open Telemetry Overview: Specifies when the Telemetry window will appear during a profiling session. If the field is set to "For Monitoring Only," it will appear automatically when you select to monitor an application during a profiling session. If the field is set to "Never," the Telemetry window will not appear automatically for any profiling session. You will have to open it manually. If the field is set to "Always," then the Telemetry window will appear for each profiling session. I typically set this to "Always."

Open Threads View: Specifies when the Threads View window will appear during a profiling session. If the field is set to "For Monitoring Only," it will appear automatically when you select to monitor an application during a profiling session. If the field is set to "Never," the Threads View window will not appear automatically for any profiling session. You will have to open it manually. If the field is set to "Always," then the Threads View window will appear for each profiling session. I typically change the default value and set this field to "For Monitoring Only."

Open Live Results For: Lets you select which type of profiling session should cause the Live Results window to open automatically. The two check boxes allow you to set this for both CPU and Memory profiling.

The fields in the Miscellaneous section of the Profiler tab include:

When taking snapshot: Specifies what action to take when you prompt the Profiler to take a snapshot of results. The field is set to "Open New Snapshot" by default. If this is set, then a snapshot will open in NetBeans when it is created. If the field is set to "Save New Snapshot," then the snapshot is in the list of snapshots but is not opened. If the field is set to "Open and Save New Snapshot," then the snapshot is saved in the list of snapshots and is opened in NetBeans for viewing. I typically set this field to "Save New Snapshot." When I'm viewing Live Results I may want to save multiple snapshots at different points and not have to deal with multiple snapshots that are open in the IDE.

On OutOfMemoryError: Specifies what action to take on an OutOfMemoryError. By default this field is set to "Save heap dump to profiled project." If an OutOfMemoryError occurs, then a special heap dump snapshot is saved into the list of snapshots for the project. The field can also be set to "Save heap dump to temporary directory" or to "Do nothing." There is also an additional radio button next to the "On OutOfMemoryError" field named "Save heap dump to." If this is selected, a text field next to it is enabled that allows you to specify a directory to which to save the heap dump.

HeapWalker: Provides a check box to enable automatic analysis of heap data.

Once you have configured the Profiler settings, click the OK button to save any changes and close the Basic Options window.

Profiler Calibration

The NetBeans Profiler needs to be calibrated before it can be used for the first time. Calibrating the Profiler allows it to provide realistic and accurate results based on different computers, operating systems, and hardware.

To activate Profiler calibration, go to the main menu and select Profile ➤ Advanced Commands ➤ Run Profiler Calibration. The Select Java Platform to Calibrate window will open, prompting you to select a JDK to calibrate. Select the target JDK and click the OK button. A pop-up window appears stating "Performing Calibration, please wait." When it finishes, an Information window will be displayed. Click the Show Details button and the window will display the calibration statistics, as shown in Figure 5-2.

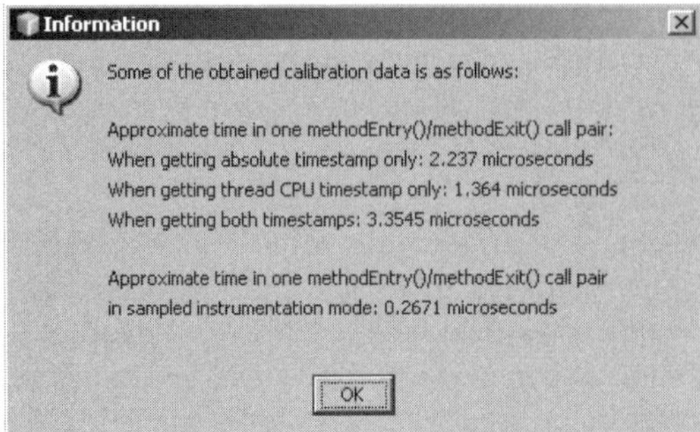

Figure 5-2. *Detailed statistics after running the Profiler calibration*

You don't have to trigger the calibration manually. If you attempt to profile a project and the target JDK has not yet been calibrated, you will be prompted to do so. You only have to do so once for each target JDK.

Profiling Java Applications

The NetBeans Profiler lets you profile almost every type of Java-related project. Once the Profiler has been configured and calibrated, you can begin using it in your projects.

Attaching the Profiler to a Project

When you profile a Java project in NetBeans for the first time, the Profiler modifies the project structure. You will see an information message pop up, as shown in Figure 5-3. It asks if it is OK to modify your project's build scripts. It also warns that any custom edits you may have made will be undone if you continue. Click the OK button in the pop-up window to continue profiling the project.

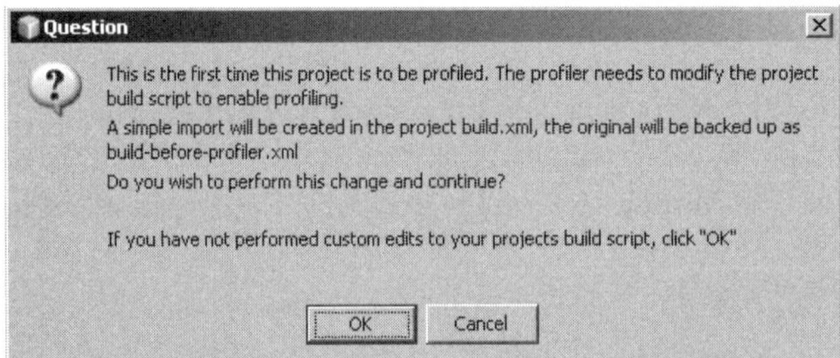

Figure 5-3. *Warning message when profiling a project for the first time*

When you OK the Profiler to modify your build scripts, the following events occur. First a backup of your project's `build.xml` file is copied and renamed to `build-before-profiler.xml`. Then an import statement is added to the `build.xml` as follows:

```
<import file="nbproject/profiler-build-impl.xml"/>
```

The import statement includes the contents of a new file, `profiler-build-impl.xml`, in the project build script. It adds Ant targets for profiling a single file, an entire project, an applet, or a test. The Ant targets are invoked directly by the NetBeans Profiler for the project when menu items and actions are selected.

Understanding the Profiler Control Panel Window

Before you can start profiling code, you need to understand the Profiler Control Panel window. The Profiler Control Panel window lets you access the various graphing and results monitoring tools you need in order to understand the results of the profiling session. You can open it by going to the main menu and selecting Window ➤ Profiling ➤ Profiler Control Panel.

The Profiler Control Panel window also lets you take snapshots of results, view basic telemetry, and control the profiling session. The window has multiple sections and is quite long, so I review it here in two pieces. The first half of the window contains the following sections, as shown in Figure 5-4:

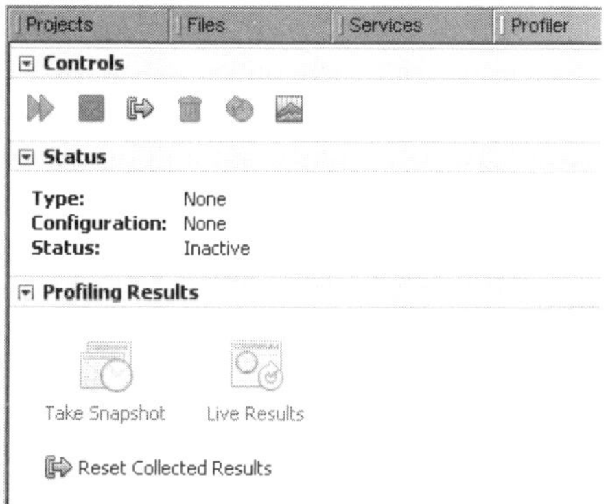

Figure 5-4. *The top half of the Profiler Control Panel window*

Controls: The Controls section lists the icons you can use to restart the profiling session, stop the profiling session, reset the collected results buffer, run garbage collection, modify the profiling session, and view the telemetry overview.

Status: The Status section lists the type of performance analysis, the configuration (Analyze Performance or Custom), and the status of the profiling session (stopped, starting, running, inactive, etc.).

Profiling Results: The Profiling Results section lets you perform several results-related actions. The first icon, labeled Take Snapshot, lets you take a snapshot of the current data that has been collected and display it in a results window. The second icon, labeled Live Results, lets you open the Live Results window to watch data accumulate as the code is profiled. The bottom of the Profiling Results section also contains a link to Reset Collected Results. Clicking it blanks the Live Results window, since the buffer of accumulated data is reset. Snapshots and live results are explained in more detail in the following sections of this chapter.

The second half of the Profiler Control Panel window contains the following sections, as shown in Figure 5-5:

Figure 5-5. *The bottom half of the Profiler Control Panel window*

Saved Snapshots: The list of result snapshots available for all open projects. You can click any snapshot that appears in the list and use the buttons to the right to open, delete, save as, or load a snapshot from disk. The saved snapshots in the list can present moments in time that occurred during a profiling session or the entire results from a profiling session.

View: The View section contains two icons: VM Telemetry and Threads. Clicking the VM Telemetry icon will open the VM Telemetry window. Clicking the Threads icon will open the Threads profiling window.

Basic Telemetry: The Basic Telemetry section contains information such as the number of instrumented methods, any filters applied to the session, the number of running threads, the total memory, the used memory, and the time spent in garbage collection.

The Profiler Control Panel window typically opens automatically when you start a profiling session. It is an integral part of profiling your code, so you should become familiar with the capabilities it provides and the icons located in it.

CPU Profiling

The first type of profiling I want to cover is CPU profiling. It involves measuring the runtime of each class, method, and constructor for the purpose of identifying performance bottlenecks.

For example, suppose you have a class that calls three methods and runs for 6 seconds. If you were able to identify that the total runtime for the first two methods was only 1 second, then you could examine the third method further to see why it is taking the majority of the runtime (5 seconds). The NetBeans Profiler lets you do just that.

Initializing CPU Profiling

In this section we discuss several ways to profile code. First, initialize a profiling session by selecting Profile ➤ Profile Main Project on the main menu. The Profile Project window will appear, as shown in Figure 5-6. When this window opens you can select from the three sections on the left: Monitor, CPU, and Memory. If CPU is not already selected, then click the CPU section to display the necessary options, as shown in Figure 5-6.

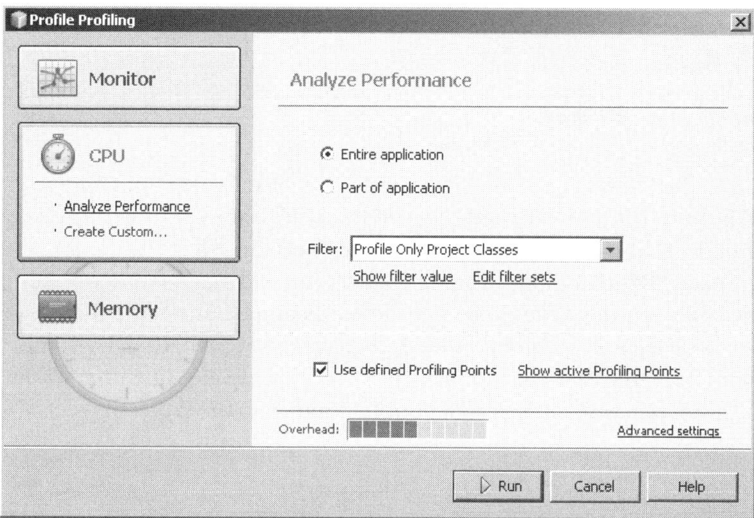

Figure 5-6. *The Profile Project window*

You will then be presented with the choice to profile the entire application or only part of the application. If you select "Entire application," then the project will be profiled starting at the main class's main method (assuming a Java application–type project with a main class set). If you select "Part of application," then you will be prompted to specify further which code will be profiled. A field will appear immediately to the right labeled "No root methods, define." Click the hyperlinked Define text to open the Specify Root Methods window.

This window requires you to pick, from one of several sources, which code the Profiler should use to begin profiling the project. It should be blank by default. If you click the Add From Project button, then the Select Root Methods window will open. This window displays all the projects open in NetBeans and lets you drill down through the source packages to select a method in a class, as shown in Figure 5-7.

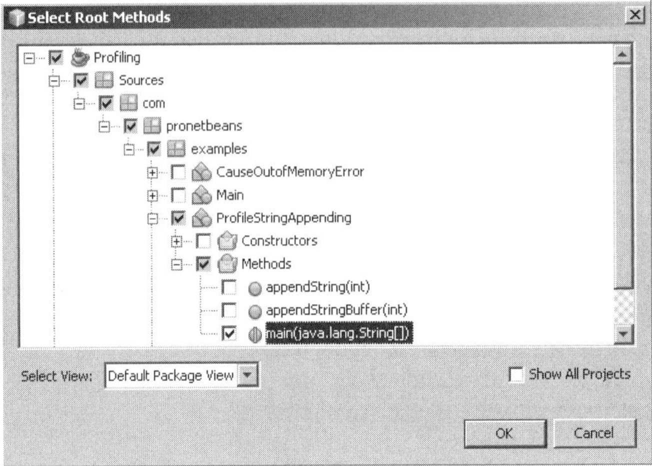

Figure 5-7. *The Select Root Methods window*

Once you have selected the method or methods that will serve as the root method for the profiler, click the OK button. The selected method(s) will then appear in the Specify Root Methods window. If one of the root methods was added in error, you can select it and click the Remove button. The Specify Root Methods window also lets you add a root method manually using the Add Manual button. When you click the Add Manual button, the Define New Root Method window opens. In this window you simply have to specify the package, the class name, the constructor or method name, and the constructor or method signature. When you are finished selecting root methods, click the OK button to return to the Profile Project window.

■ **Tip** Even if a class does not have a constructor specified (such as the default constructor), you can manually specify it in the "Method Name" field of the Define New Root Method window. For the `ProfileStringAppending` class, you could specify the constructor using the VM Signature of `()LprofileStringAppending()`.

The Profile Project window also contains a powerful filtering capability. With the filter fields that are available you can instruct the Profiler to profile only the project classes or all the classes, to exclude the Java core classes, or to include a custom quick filter.

By default the "Filter" field is set to Profile Only Project Classes. This instructs the Profiler to profile only the classes that appear in the Source Packages section of your project. You can see exactly what the Profiler will profile by clicking the Show Filter Value link that appears below the "Filter" drop-down field. A small pop-up window should appear that states precisely which packages and classes will be profiled for this profiling session.

The “Filter” drop-down also contains an item called Quick Filter. If you select it from the list, the Set Quick Filter window will appear, as shown in Figure 5-8. This window contains two fields: “Filter Type” and “Filter Value.” The “Filter Type” field can be set to Exclusive or Inclusive. If set to Exclusive, then the filter uses the class or classes specified in the “Filter Value” field and excludes them from the profiling session. If “Field Type” is set to Inclusive, then the filter uses the class or classes specified in the “Filter Value” field as the only classes to include in the profiling session.

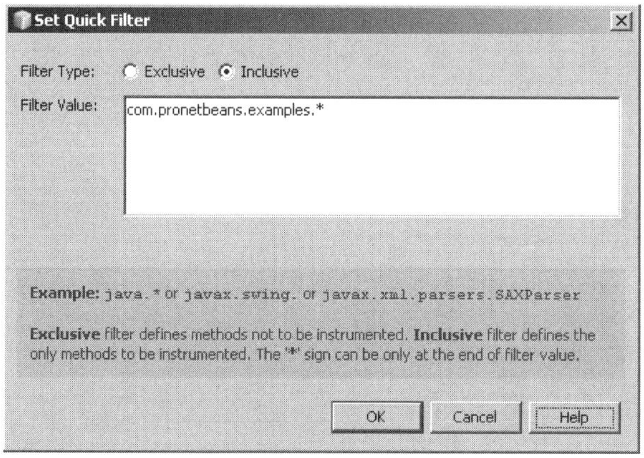

Figure 5-8. *The Set Quick Filter window*

Another filter option in the Profile Project window is the ability to manage *filter sets*. A filter set is what appears in the “Filter” drop-down list, such as Exclude Java Core Classes. Filter sets typically appear in the drop-down *below* the Quick Filter item and can be edited using the Edit Filter Sets link. Note that the filter sets *above* the Quick Filter item cannot be edited.

If you click the Edit Filter Sets link, the Customize Filter Sets window will open, as shown in Figure 5-9. The top portion of the window displays the list of defined filter sets. It also contains buttons that allow you to add and remove filter sets as well as manipulate the order in which they appear in the “Filter” drop-down field of the Profile Project window.

The middle of the window contains the basic filter properties, such as the name of the filter set and the filter set type: Exclusive or Inclusive.

The bottom of the window lists the global filters to apply to the filter set. Global filters are patterns of classes typically related to a special tool, framework, or application. For example, the global filter “Sun Java System Application Server (GlassFish) Classes” is made up of the pattern `com.iplanet., com.sun.appserv., com.sun.enterprise.`. These groups of patterns can be used to include or exclude lots of classes quickly from your profiling session.

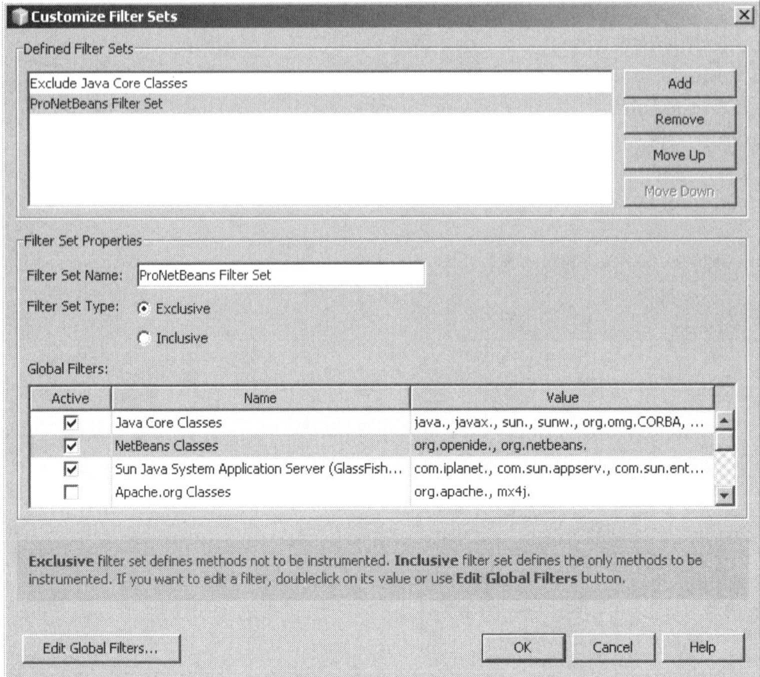

Figure 5-9. *The Customize Filter Sets window*

In Figure 5-9, I have selected a filter type of Exclusive and the global filters Java Core Classes, NetBeans Classes, and the Sun Java System Application Server Classes. Once you have selected the list of global filters the filter set should contain, click the OK button to return to the Profile Project window. When I run the Profiler using the defined global filters, any class that matches the patterns defined will be excluded from any performance data results.

Running the Profiler

Once you have configured what you're going to analyze and which filters to apply, you can execute the Profiler. In the Profile Project window in Figure 5-6, click the Run button. This will launch the Profiler tab in the Output window, which will list multiple lines of data. It should state that it is compiling the classes, starting the Profiler Agent, and initializing the Profiler Agent.

■ **Tip** After the first Profiler run, you should be prompted to choose whether you always want a snapshot of data taken and saved after the profiling session has finished. I typically set this to Yes. I accumulate many snapshots but can delete them later. Better to delete useless snapshots than to miss some important data when profiling.

If the profiled class runs through quickly, you may not get a chance to click the Live Results icon in the Profiler window. If the Live Results window is not open during the profiling session, you can open it at any time, even after the session is complete. The last accumulated results should still appear in the Live Results window. The data that appears is specific to the type of profiling you conducted.

You can easily run the same profiling session again. In the Controls section of the Profiler window you can click the Rerun Last Profiling Session icon (the green double arrows). This will immediately relaunch the Profiler with the same settings you last used. This can save you several clicks by not having to go through the Profile Project all over again.

Viewing the Results

Once you have initialized and executed a profiling session, you will need to view and interpret the results. The accumulated CPU Analyze Performance data should be listed in the Live Results window, as shown in Figure 5-10. The Live Results window contains a small toolbar along the top of the window and a data grid of columns at the bottom.

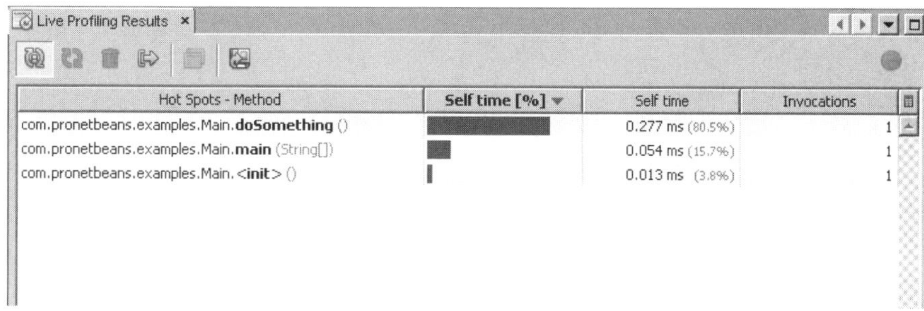

Figure 5-10. *The Live Results window after profiling*

For CPU profiling, the data grid contains four columns:

Hot Spots - Method: The name of a method or constructor with a measurable amount of execution time.

Self time [%]: The overall percentage of time that the hot spot spent executing as compared to the entire profiling session.

Self time: The specific amount of time, in milliseconds, that the hot spot spent executing. The percentage of overall execution time compared to the entire profiling session is listed next to it as well.

Invocations: The number of times the hot spot method or constructor was executed. This column is very important since it can help clarify performance data. Just because a method took a long accumulated time to execute doesn't mean it is necessarily a bottleneck if the number of invocations is very high.

The toolbar along the top of the Live Results window contains six icons:

Update Results Automatically: If you select this icon, the Live Results window will poll the NetBeans Profiler continually for updates to the data and will display them in the data grid. If you don't select it, you must update the results manually.

Updates Results Now: This icon allows you manually to trigger an update to the accumulated results displayed in the Live Results window.

Run Garbage Collection: Instructs the JVM to run garbage collection and update the results displayed in the Live Results window.

Reset Collected Results Buffer: This icon will trigger deletion of the data accumulated in the buffer. All results displayed in the Live Results window will disappear and no data will be displayed until the next automatic or manual results update.

Take Snapshot of Collected Results: If you click this icon during an active profiling session, the Profiler will open a new tab in the Source Editor area that contains a snapshot of the data from the Live Results window. This data is thus "frozen," in that it won't be updated or change. It allows you to capture moments in time during the profiling session and to examine them later.

Saves Current View to Image: If you click this icon, a file chooser window will appear prompting you to select a directory. This will take a screenshot of the results displayed in the Live Results window and save them as a PNG image.

Tip Save Current View to Image is a great feature for professional developers who must document code performance data. If your company or organization requires you to document test results, units test results, and performance test results, you can save multiple screenshots of the results in PNG format to include in your documentation.

An additional feature of the Live Results window is the ability to right-click any method and select Go To Source from the context menu. This will open the related Java source file in the Source Editor. This lets you investigate code in your projects or associated libraries to see why it might be performing the way the data reports.

Analyzing CPU Performance Example

As discussed in the previous section, the ability to profile CPU performance can prove crucial when developing software applications. I have run into performance bottlenecks numerous times when testing and deploying applications. One of the most common areas is that of generating content for web applications.

I've lost track of the number of times I have had to examine a JSP page and attempt to figure out why it took a long time to load. Sometimes the cause was a slow database or inefficient SQL calls or too much recursion, sometimes even just poorly written code. One problem I continue to run into is generating HTML code inside a loop in a Java class. I have created a mockup of this issue, as shown in Listing 5-1.

Listing 5-1. *The ProfileStringAppending Class*

```
public class ProfileStringAppending {

    public static void main(String[] args) {

        ProfileStringAppending psa = new ProfileStringAppending();

        String dataResults = psa.getCustomersByCountry(1234);

        String dataResults2 = psa.getCustomersByCountry2(1234);

        System.out.println("ProfileStringAppending done");
    }

    public String getCustomersByCountry(int countryId) {

        String results = "";

        // assume this is simply a list of customer names
        ArrayList<String> customers = getCustomers(countryId);

        for (int i = 0; i < customers.size(); i++) {
            results += "<tr><td width=300>";
            results += customers.get(i);
            results += "</td></tr>";
        }

        return results;
    }

    public String getCustomersByCountry2(int countryId) {

        StringBuffer results = new StringBuffer();

        // assume this is simply a list of customer names
        ArrayList<String> customers = getCustomers(countryId);

        for (int i = 0; i < customers.size(); i++) {
            results.append("<tr><td width=300>");
            results.append(customers.get(i));
            results.append("</td></tr>");
        }

        return results.toString();
    }

    private ArrayList<String> getCustomers(int countryId) {
```

```
        //connect to database, generate customer list
        ArrayList<String> mylist = new ArrayList<String>();
        // let's fake a list
        for(int i=0; i<2000; i++) {
            mylist.add("John Smith " + i);
        }

        return mylist;
    }
}
```

In this class, the main method instantiates an instance of the ProfileStringAppending class and calls two similar methods using the same input value. The results are returned and captured in two String variables but are otherwise ignored.

The two methods, getCustomersByCountry and getCustomersByCountry2, demonstrate the point of this example. What I have seen occur too often in generating content for JSPs is inefficient String appending.

Seasoned programmers may know the performance difference between appending Strings and using a StringBuffer. It has been discussed and well documented in Java articles and web sites for some time. However, I still see this problem crop up all too often. Even when you know it can be a problem, you may not adhere to the best practice until you see the performance data for yourself.

You can use the NetBeans Profiler to analyze the methods in the ProfileStringAppending class to determine the specific performance data. For starters, take a look at the getCustomersByCountry method:

```
public String getCustomersByCountry(int countryId) {

    String results = "";

    // assume this is simply a list of customer names
    ArrayList<String> customers = getCustomers(countryId);

    for (int i = 0; i < customers.size(); i++) {
        results += "<tr><td width=300>";
        results += customers.get(i);
        results += "</td></tr>";
    }

    return results;
}
```

It takes an input parameter called countryId, which is in turn passed to the getCustomers method. The getCustomers method returns an ArrayList of customer names. In real life, this would probably be an ArrayList of customer objects, where each customer object contained numerous fields to identify the customer.

The getCustomersByCountry method then loops through the ArrayList, extracts each customer name, and appends it to a String of HTML that is being dynamically built using String concatenation. The generated HTML would then typically get returned to a calling JSP page and embedded inside <table> and </table> tags for display on a page. In this example it simply returns the results back to the calling main method.

The number of times the loop iterates is controlled by the size of the ArrayList of customers that is returned by the getCustomers method:

```
private ArrayList<String> getCustomers(int countryId) {

    //connect to database, generate customer list
    ArrayList<String> mylist = new ArrayList<String>();
    // let's fake a list
    for(int i=0; i<2000; i++) {
        mylist.add("John Smith " + i);
    }

    return mylist;
}
```

The getCustomers method takes in the countryId variable and does nothing with it. In a real lookup method, a java.sql.Statement or java.sql.PreparedStatement might use the countryId variable to retrieve the matching customers from a database. In this sample method I create a new ArrayList list and specify that it will contain Strings. I then loop 2000 times and add the name John Smith + i to the list. This is done simply to generate a unique list of names to return to the calling code.

The getCustomersByCountry2 method does the same thing as the getCustomersByCountry method, except for one important difference. Instead of using String concatenation, it uses a StringBuffer to append the Strings together. As you might guess, this is more efficient than the String concatenation:

```
public String getCustomersByCountry2(int countryId) {

    StringBuffer results = new StringBuffer();

    // assume this is simply a list of customer names
    ArrayList<String> customers = getCustomers(countryId);

    for (int i = 0; i < customers.size(); i++) {
        results.append("<tr><td width=300>");
        results.append(customers.get(i));
        results.append("</td></tr>");
    }

    return results.toString();
}
```

Just seeing the two versions of a nearly identical method won't convince anyone. We actually need to profile the code to see any performance difference that may exist. Perform the following steps to profile the ProfileStringAppending class:

1. With the `ProfileStringAppending` class open in the Source Editor, select Profile ➤ Profile Other ➤ Profile "ProfileStringAppending .java" from the main menu.
2. In the Profile Project window click the CPU section at the left of the window.
3. Select the "Entire Application" radio button at the right of the window.
4. Select "Profile Only Project Classes" from the "Filter" drop-down field.
5. Click the Run button.

When the Profiler finishes running, the Live Results window should open, as shown in Figure 5-11. The first column will list the method names, which you can use to find the `getCustomersByCountry` and `getCustomersByCountry2` methods.

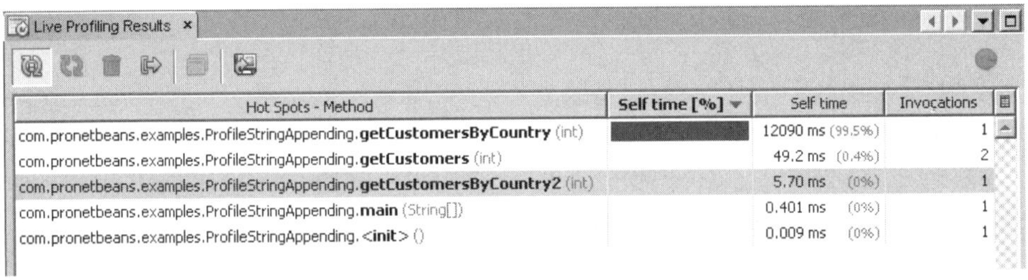

Live Profiling Results

Hot Spots - Method	Self time [%]	Self time	Invocations
com.pronetbeans.examples.ProfileStringAppending.**getCustomersByCountry** (int)		12090 ms (99.5%)	1
com.pronetbeans.examples.ProfileStringAppending.**getCustomers** (int)		49.2 ms (0.4%)	2
com.pronetbeans.examples.ProfileStringAppending.**getCustomersByCountry2** (int)		5.70 ms (0%)	1
com.pronetbeans.examples.ProfileStringAppending.**main** (String[])		0.401 ms (0%)	1
com.pronetbeans.examples.ProfileStringAppending.**<init>** ()		0.009 ms (0%)	1

Figure 5-11. *The results of the profiled class*

The next column to look at is the third column. The Self time column lists the number of milliseconds each method took to execute. Notice that the `getCustomersByCountry` method took 12,090 milliseconds (or about 12 seconds) to execute. Also notice that the `getCustomersByCountry2` method took only 5.70 milliseconds (or about 1/20 of a second). This should demonstrate the difference between `String` concatenation and `StringBuffer` appending as well as how to use the NetBeans Profiler to analyze CPU performance.

Analyzing CPU Performance with Profiling Points

Profiling points are markers in the code, similar to debug breakpoints, that trigger some sort of profiling-related action to occur. You can use profiling points to do many things, such as capture a snapshot of the accumulated profiler data, start a timer, reset the buffer of accumulated results, and run a load generator.

Profiling points are saved with the project data for each project. Similar to breakpoints, they persist when you close NetBeans and exit the JVM. When you open a project in NetBeans, the profiling points related to that project are available to run, view, edit, or remove, as discussed in the following sections.

Adding a Profiling Point

The easiest way to create a profiling point is directly in the code. Open a Java source file in the Source Editor, such as the `ProfileStringAppending` class from one of the previous sections, as shown in Listing 5-1. In the source file, right-click on the line where you want to locate the profiling point and select Profiling ➤ Insert Profiling Point from the context menu.

The New Profiling Point window will open, as shown in Figure 5-12. The Choose Type & Project screen is initially displayed. In the "Profiling Point Type" field, select one of the available options, such as Stopwatch. A stopwatch profiling point is a timer that lets you measure the start and end times of an event.

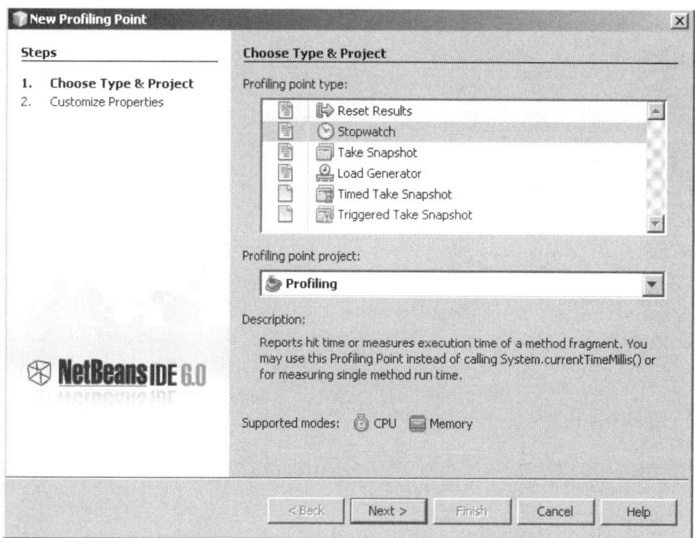

Figure 5-12. *The New Profiling Point window*

Once you have selected the stopwatch profiling point type, click the Next button. The Customize Properties screen will display, allowing you to customize the stopwatch profiling point.

The "Name" field will typically display the type of profiling point followed by the class name and line number in the code where the profiling point will appear. This name is a default and can be set to whatever you want it to be. I usually leave the name as is, unless I plan on having multiple profiling points initiated at the same line of code.

The Settings section lists the type of measure the stopwatch profiling point will use. You can set it to Timestamp or Timestamp and Duration. If you set it to Timestamp, then the profiling point merely takes a snapshot of the system time. It also means that the Stopwatch profiling point has only a starting location, specified by the Location (begin) section. If you set it to Timestamp and Duration, then the profiling point measures the duration of time between a starting point and an ending point. The ending point is specified by the Location (end) section on the screen. Set the "Measure" field to Timestamp and Duration.

You can then set the "Location (begin)" and the "Location (end)" fields. Set the two "File" fields to the name of the Java source file you initially used to create the profiling point. Set the "Line" field to the line number in the `ProfileStringAppending` class where you right-clicked in the Source Editor. Also select the Begin radio button, to designate the line as the starting point.

The "Line" field for the Location (end) section can be set to the same line or any other line you want to use to stop the stopwatch. Also select the End radio button. For the code snippet I am profiling from the `ProfileStringAppending` class, I have set the end point at line 40, or immediately after the end of the `for` loop in the `getCustomersByCountry` method. The Customize Properties screen should now look like Figure 5-13. Click the Finish button to add the profiling point.

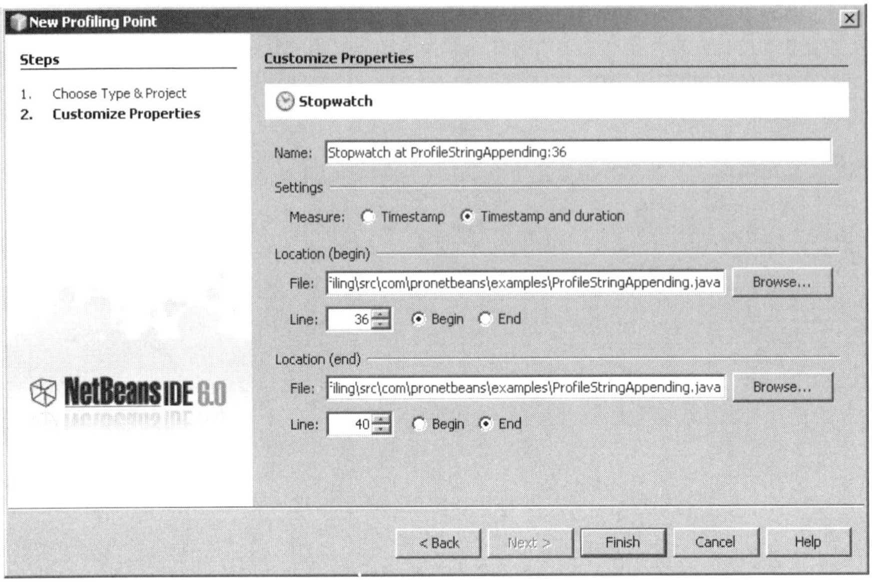

Figure 5-13. *The Customize Properties screen for a stopwatch profiling point*

The code snippet the stopwatch profiling point was used for is listed as follows:

```
for (int i = 0; i < customers.size(); i++) {
        results += "<tr><td width=300>";
        results += customers.get(i);
        results += "</td></tr>";
}
```

The first line of the `for` loop is number 36. The last line, where the closing curly brace appears, is number 40. These are the beginning and ending locations for the Stopwatch profiling point. Once the profiling point has been added, you should be able to see a set of visual glyphs in the Source Editor for the beginning and ending profiling points, as shown in Figure 5-14.

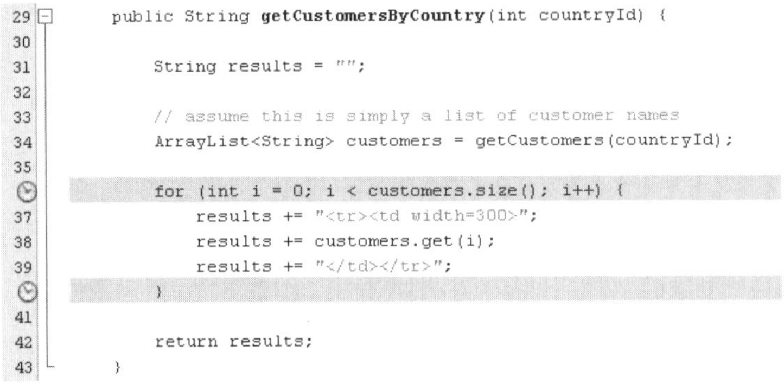

```
29     public String getCustomersByCountry(int countryId) {
30
31         String results = "";
32
33         // assume this is simply a list of customer names
34         ArrayList<String> customers = getCustomers(countryId);
35
           for (int i = 0; i < customers.size(); i++) {
37             results += "<tr><td width=300>";
38             results += customers.get(i);
39             results += "</td></tr>";
           }
41
42         return results;
43     }
```

Figure 5-14. *Profiling point glyphs in the Source Editor margin*

Modifying Profiling Points

Once a profiling point has been created, you can edit, delete, or disable it at any time. Right-click the profiling point glyph in the margin and look at the options on the Profiling Point submenu that appears in the context menu.

If the profiling point is enabled and active, the Enabled menu item will have a check mark next to it. If you want to disable a profiling point, simply select the Enabled menu item; the check mark will disappear, and the Profiling Point icon is grayed out. To re-enable it, right-click the profiling point glyph in the margin and select Profiling Point ➤ Enabled.

The Profiling Point submenu also contains a Delete option. If you select it, the profiling point will be completely deleted. Note that there is no way to undo the delete action. You will have to add the profiling point again.

You also can edit a profiling point if you need to change line numbers or other options. Right-click the profiling point glyph in the margin and select Profiling Point ➤ Customize from the context menu. The Customize Profiling Point window will appear, as shown in Figure 5-15. The Customize Profiling Point window lets you edit all the properties of the profiling point. You can rename the profiling point, change the beginning and ending lines, or even the type of measure.

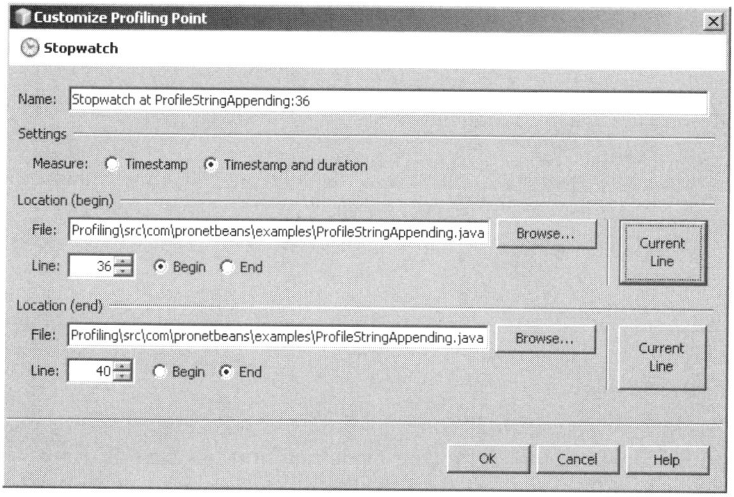

Figure 5-15. *The Customize Profiling Point window*

Two of the most important items to note in the Customize Profiling Point window are the Current Line buttons. These conveniently let you quickly change the line numbers for the beginning and ending of the stopwatch profiling point. Move the Customize Profiling Point window off to the side. Click a line in the `ProfileStringAppending` class that is open in the Source Editor. Once you have selected a line in the class, go back to the Customize Profiling Point window and click one of the Current Line buttons. Notice how the line number field has changed. These buttons allow you quickly and easily to update the line numbers by looking right in the source code. Once the line number and other properties are correct, click the OK button to save your changes to the profiling point.

The final option on the Profiling Point submenu is labeled Go To End Point. This menu item is specific to the profiling point you right-clicked in the margin. If you selected a stopwatch's start point, the context menu will have the Go To End Point option. If you selected a stopwatch's end point, the context menu will have the Go To Start Point option. These menu items let you jump to a stopwatch's matching point, whether it is the start point or the end point. This menu option will differ between the profiling points, depending on the type of profiling point.

Locating Profiling Points

For each type of profiling point you add to a Java source file, a different glyph will appear in the margin denoting its placement and existence. This lets you quickly identify where the profiling points are in your code. The difficulty arises when you want to locate profiling points across multiple classes or projects. If you want to track all the profiling points in your source code, you can use the Profiling Points window.

To open the Profiling Points window, go the main menu and select Window ➤ Profiling ➤ Profiling Points. The Profiling Points window will list every profiling point that has been defined in all currently opened projects, as shown in Figure 5-16. The Profiling Points window also allows you to control each profiling point, view its results, and open the Profiling Point report. The toolbar that appears along the top of the Profiling Points window contains several icons and filter fields, as shown in Figure 5-16.

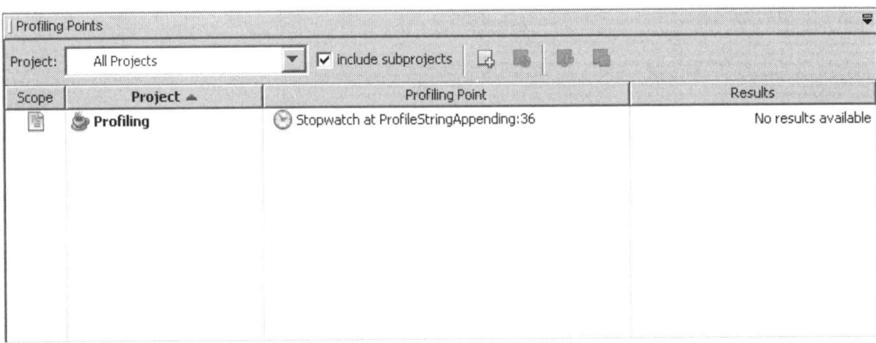

Figure 5-16. *The Profiling Points window*

The first field is a drop-down that is set to All Projects by default. You can use this drop-down to filter the list of displayed profiling points based on all projects or on a specific project. You can also enable or disable the check box next to the "include subprojects" field. If you have filtered the list by a specific project, the "include subprojects" field will also display the profiling points for the selected project's referenced subprojects.

There are also four icons next to the "include subprojects" field. These icons, in order, allow you to add a profiling point, remove a profiling point, edit a profiling point, or enable or disable a profiling point. Clicking the first icon will open the same Add Profiling Point window you see when you add a profiling point by right-clicking in a source file. Clicking the third icon, Edit Profiling Point, opens the Customize Profiling Point window discussed earlier in this chapter.

For the items displayed in the Profiling Points window, you can access additional options by right-clicking each line. The context menu for each profiling point will contain an option to edit, remove, and disable the profiling point. It should also contain an option to view the report for that profiling point (discussed further in the next section).

The context menu may also contain menu items specific to each type of profiling point. For instance, right-clicking a stopwatch profiling point will display a context menu with options such as Show Start in Source and Show End in Source. Right-clicking a "Reset Results Profiling Point" will display an option to Show in Source.

Similar to the Breakpoints window, the Profiling Points window allows you to gain a quick view of all the profiling points with which you need to work. It also allows you a single point of access to edit, remove, or disable them. If you are profiling an application that has multiple profiling points, this window will prove to be very useful.

Viewing a Profiling Point Report

After a profiling session has finished executing against one or more profiling points, a report is generated for each profiling point, as shown in Figure 5-17. The report can list data about the profiling point, such as its:

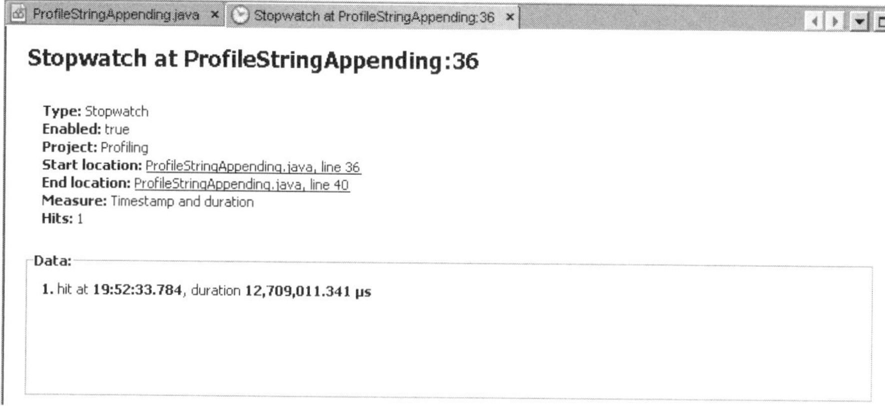

Figure 5-17. *The Profiling Points Report*

- Name
- Type
- Project in which it is located
- Status (enabled/disabled)
- Start location
- End location (if applicable)
- Measure
- Number of hits
- Result data

The number of hits tells you how many times the profiling point was hit by the running program. The Data section, as shown in Figure 5-17, will list each unique hit registered for the profiling point as well as the specific measurement that was taken at the time it was hit. If multiple hits occurred for this profiling point, then the Data section would contain one line per hit.

Memory Profiling

Memory analysis is the second type of code profiling you can perform using the NetBeans Profiler. It allows you to record the creation and garbage collection of objects, track object allocations, view the stack traces of object allocations, and compare results. This type of profiling can be useful when trying to track down `OutOfMemoryErrors`, code that consumes a lot of memory in the JVM, or basic inefficient code.

Running a Memory Analysis

For this section, I use two Java classes as examples: `ProfileMemory` and `ProfilePerson`. The `ProfilePerson` class is shown in Listing 5-2. The `ProfileMemory` class is shown in Listing 5-3.

Listing 5-2. *The ProfilePerson Class*

```
public class ProfilePerson {

    private String lastName;
    private String firstName;
    private String email;

    public String getEmail() {
        return email;
    }

    public void setEmail(String email) {
        this.email = email;
    }

    public String getFirstName() {
        return firstName;
    }

    public void setFirstName(String firstName) {
        this.firstName = firstName;
    }

    public String getLastName() {
        return lastName;
    }

    public void setLastName(String lastName) {
        this.lastName = lastName;
    }
}
```

The ProfilePerson class serves as a simple data bean. The class has three class variables: firstName, lastName, and email. There are also standard getter and setter methods for each class variable. This class will have a number of instances of itself created and stored to track object creation and allocation.

Listing 5-3. *The ProfileMemory Class*

```
import java.util.ArrayList;
import java.util.List;

public class ProfileMemory {

    public static void main(String[] args) {

        List<ProfilePerson> allPeople = new ArrayList<ProfilePerson>();

        for(int i=0;i<100000;i++) {
            ProfilePerson person = new ProfilePerson();
            person.setFirstName("Adam");
            person.setLastName("Myatt");
            person.setEmail("adam AT pronetbeans DOT com");

            allPeople.add(person);
        }

        System.out.println("Number of people = " + allPeople.size());
    }
}
```

The ProfileMemory class contains a main method that does the work. It defines an instance of ArrayList that will hold ProfilePerson objects. It then loops through 100,000 times, creates a new ProfilePerson object, sets the various properties to identical values, and stores each ProfilePerson object inside the ArrayList.

To profile the memory of the two classes, you can perform the following steps:

1. Locate the ProfileMemory class in the Projects window and open it in the Source Editor.
2. On the main menu select Profile ➤ Profile Other ➤ Profile "ProfileMemory.java."
3. In the Project Profiling window select the Memory block on the left side of the window.
4. Select the radio button labeled "Record Object Creation Only."
5. Set the number of object allocations to track to 10.
6. Select the "Record stack trace for allocations" check box.
7. Click the Run button.

Viewing the Memory Analysis Results

Once the Profiler has finished executing, you may be able to view the results in the Live Results window. I have found that the Live Results window tends to display the last set of accumulated results when running a CPU analysis but not for the memory analysis.

I have set up the Profiler so that it records a snapshot after every run. In my list of snapshots in the Profiler Control Panel window I can select the most recent snapshot generated and open it in the Source Editor area. The snapshot that was generated shows the allocated objects for the code that executed from Listings 5-2 and 5-3, as shown in Figure 5-18.

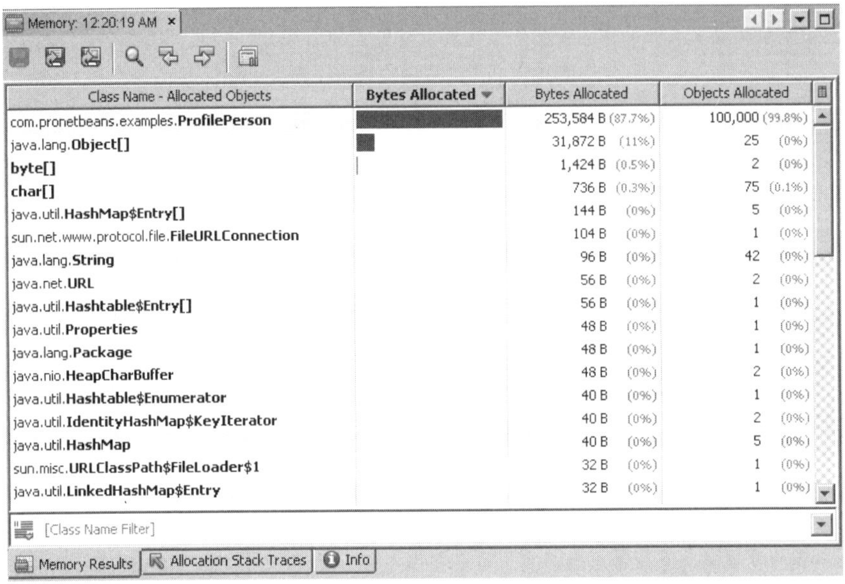

Memory: 12:20:19 AM

Class Name - Allocated Objects	Bytes Allocated	Bytes Allocated	Objects Allocated
com.pronetbeans.examples.**ProfilePerson**		253,584 B (87.7%)	100,000 (99.8%)
java.lang.**Object[]**		31,872 B (11%)	25 (0%)
byte[]		1,424 B (0.5%)	2 (0%)
char[]		736 B (0.3%)	75 (0.1%)
java.util.**HashMap$Entry[]**		144 B (0%)	5 (0%)
sun.net.www.protocol.file.**FileURLConnection**		104 B (0%)	1 (0%)
java.lang.**String**		96 B (0%)	42 (0%)
java.net.**URL**		56 B (0%)	2 (0%)
java.util.**Hashtable$Entry[]**		56 B (0%)	1 (0%)
java.util.**Properties**		48 B (0%)	1 (0%)
java.lang.**Package**		48 B (0%)	1 (0%)
java.nio.**HeapCharBuffer**		48 B (0%)	2 (0%)
java.util.**Hashtable$Enumerator**		40 B (0%)	1 (0%)
java.util.**IdentityHashMap$KeyIterator**		40 B (0%)	2 (0%)
java.util.**HashMap**		40 B (0%)	5 (0%)
sun.misc.**URLClassPath$FileLoader$1**		32 B (0%)	1 (0%)
java.util.**LinkedHashMap$Entry**		32 B (0%)	1 (0%)

[Class Name Filter]

Memory Results | Allocation Stack Traces | Info

Figure 5-18. *The memory analysis snapshot for Listings 5-2 and 5-3*

The snapshot in Figure 5-18 shows several columns. The first column displays the fully qualified class name of each object allocated. The second column displays a visual percentage bar of the total number of bytes allocated for each object compared to the total for all objects during the profiling session. The third column displays the actual number of bytes allocated for each object, with the percentage in parentheses next to it. Finally, the fourth column displays the number of objects allocated.

Based on the `ProfileMemory` code in Listing 5-3, you might expect the number of `com.pronetbeans.examples.ProfilePerson` objects allocated to be 100,000. The first line in the memory snapshot in Figure 5-18 does indeed list the `ProfilePerson` class as having had 100,000 objects allocated, with approximately 253,000 bytes allocated. This isn't bad and is pretty much expected.

The second line is a little more interesting. It shows that there were almost 32,000 bytes and 25 objects allocated for the `Object` arrays. This may or may not be expected, depending on the JVM code that was running in the target JDK. The memory analysis in the NetBeans Profiler picks up all objects allocated in the JVM and not just the objects allocated from your projects' files. The point here is that the 32,000 bytes allocated for the `Object` arrays may or may not be necessary. You can attempt to determine this by tracking where the objects were allocated.

Right-click the `java.lang.Object[]` item in the Memory snapshot. Select Show Allocation Stack Traces from the context menu. The Allocation Stack Traces tab of the snapshot will open and display the stack traces. You cannot actually click the Allocation Stack Traces tab directly and expect to see any results. It must be initiated by right-clicking an item in the snapshot data grid.

The Allocation Stack Traces tab will list each top-level location where the `Object` arrays were created. Clicking the plus icon next to each item will expand the entire stack trace and allow you to see where the objects were allocated from, as shown in Figure 5-19.

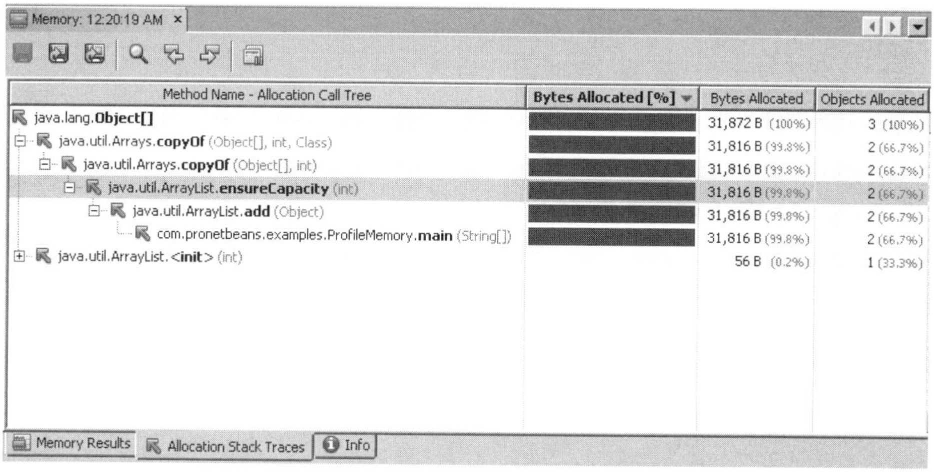

Memory: 12:20:19 AM

Method Name - Allocation Call Tree	Bytes Allocated [%]	Bytes Allocated	Objects Allocated
java.lang.**Object[]**		31,872 B (100%)	3 (100%)
java.util.Arrays.**copyOf** (Object[], int, Class)		31,816 B (99.8%)	2 (66.7%)
java.util.Arrays.**copyOf** (Object[], int)		31,816 B (99.8%)	2 (66.7%)
java.util.ArrayList.**ensureCapacity** (int)		31,816 B (99.8%)	2 (66.7%)
java.util.ArrayList.**add** (Object)		31,816 B (99.8%)	2 (66.7%)
com.pronetbeans.examples.ProfileMemory.**main** (String[])		31,816 B (99.8%)	2 (66.7%)
java.util.ArrayList.**<init>** (int)		56 B (0.2%)	1 (33.3%)

Memory Results | Allocation Stack Traces | Info

Figure 5-19. *The Allocation Stack Traces tab for the Object[]*

The first stack trace shows that the `ProfileMemory.main` method called `ArrayList.add`. Inside the `ArrayList.add` method, the `ArrayList,ensureCapacity` method was called. If you have ever looked inside the internals of `List`, `ArrayList`, and similar classes you may be starting to understand where I am going with this. The `ArrayList` is a data structure that maintains an internal array of `Objects` to hold each `Object` that is added into it.

When the internal `Object` array is nearly filled or filled, the `ArrayList` creates a new internal array and copies the contents of the old one into the new one. This allows code that calls the `ArrayList.add` method not to have to worry about resizing the data structure. However, when this call is made, you lose CPU cycles and memory, since the internal data structure is modified and copied.

You can attempt to address this issue by specifying a default size the `ArrayList` should use to set the size of the internal `Object` array. The `ArrayList` class has a single-argument constructor that takes an `int`. This lets you specify the size of the internal array. If the internal array is larger than the number of items you add into it, then it does not need to resize dynamically when you add multiple items. This can save CPU cycles and memory.

To correct the code, change the `ArrayList` instantiation in the `ProfileMemory` class to

```
List<ProfilePerson> allPeople = new ArrayList<ProfilePerson>(100000);
```

In the modified code, the `ArrayList`'s constructor had the value of 100,000 passed in. This will set the internal array size. Now rerun the profiling session to generate fresh results. When the Profiler is done, open the snapshot that was generated and compare the results.

Comparing Memory Analysis Results

Once you have more than one memory analysis snapshot, you can compare them directly in the IDE. The Profiler's snapshot comparison tool is basically a Diff tool. Instead of seeing only generic differences between the two snapshot files, you can actually see an intelligent, well-formatted view of the difference between the memory analyses.

To perform a memory analysis comparison, open a memory snapshot from the Profiler Control Panel window. In the snapshot toolbar, click the last icon on the right. If you mouse over the icon before clicking, the pop-up tooltip displays the message "computes the difference between two comparable memory snapshots." Once you click the icon, the Select Snapshot to Compare window will appear, as shown in Figure 5-20.

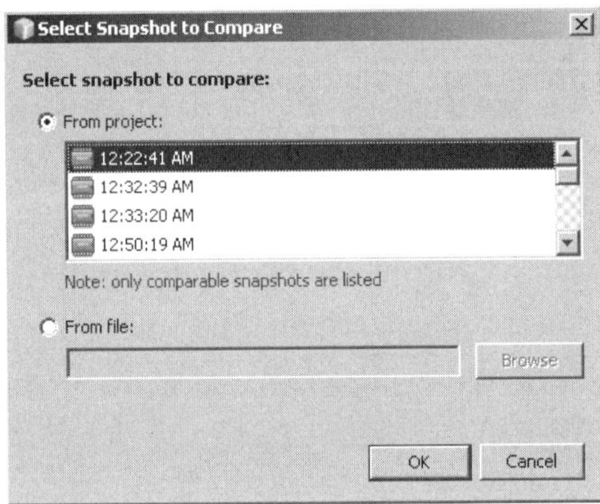

Figure 5-20. *The Select Snapshot to Compare window*

The Select Snapshot to Compare window lets you choose, in two ways, the second memory snapshot to use in the comparison. First you can choose from the list of memory snapshots that are stored with the project and available in the list of saved snapshots in the Profiler Control Panel window. Otherwise, you can click the "From file" radio button, which activates a Browse button. You can then use the Browse button to locate a snapshot file on the disk drive to use in the comparison. Once you have determined the file you want to use, click the OK button.

The Allocations Comparison window will appear as a tab in the Source Editor window area. It will display in a format similar to a memory analysis snapshot, but with a few differences. The columns Bytes Allocated and Objects Allocated do not display totals: they display the differences, as shown in Figure 5-21. In the figure, you can see the top line that lists `java.lang.Object`. This shows that the second memory analysis that ran against the modified `ProfileMemory` class allocated 31,816 fewer bytes and 23 fewer `Objects`.

Initially, this might seem like too small a gain to care about. However, if you examine this with scalability in mind, you can start to understand why examining a memory analysis like this might be useful. Imagine if you ran a very popular web site that received millions of hits per day. If the original `ProfileMemory` class were executed on a web server by 5000 users simultaneously, the 31,816 allocated bytes used in the original `ProfileMemory` class would balloon into approximately 159,000,000 bytes (or about 155 megabytes) of allocated memory. On a web server with only have a few gigabytes of memory allocated to the JVM, those 155 megabytes could be crucial to performance.

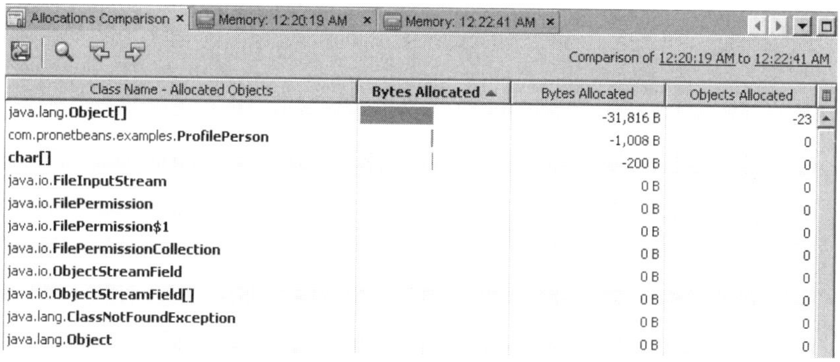

Figure 5-21. *The Allocations Comparison window*

Working with the HeapWalker

The HeapWalker is a new tool in the NetBeans 6 Profiler that allows you to evaluate the Java heap and search for memory leaks. You can examine the heap at any time by taking snapshots, as previously described in this chapter. Once you have taken a snapshot, you can examine the classes and instances that exist in the heap.

In Figure 5-1 the Profiler tab of the Basic Options window displays a field named "On OutOfMemoryError." As described in that section of this chapter, you can set the field to Save heap dump to profiled project. If an OutOfMemoryError occurs, then a heap dump snapshot is saved into the list of snapshots for the project. This setting will be necessary for testing the HeapWalker, because we review it in this section.

Review the `CauseOutOfMemoryError` class in Listing 5-4.

Listing 5-4. *The CauseOutOfMemoryError Class*

```
public class CauseOutOfMemoryError {

    private int count;

    public void setCount(int count) {
        this.count = count;
    }

    public static void main(String[] args) {

        List myList = new ArrayList();
        int total = 20000000;

        for(int i=0;i<total;i++) {
            CauseOutOfMemoryError calc = new CauseOutOfMemoryError();
            calc.setCount(i);
            myList.add(calc);
        }
    }
}
```

The CauseOutOfMemoryError class initializes an ArrayList, loops 20 million times, and fills the ArrayList with instances of itself. It also sets a counter variable in each instance so that they can be distinguished. Add the CauseOutOfMemoryError class to a Java application project and profile it by doing the following:

1. Right-click the class under the Source Packages node in the Projects window and select Profile File.
2. Select the Memory panel on the left of the Profile Project window.
3. Select the radio button next to the "Record object creation only" field.
4. Change the number in the "Track every X object allocations" field from 10 to 1000.
5. Click the Run button.

The Profiler will initialize, instrument the class file, and perform the profiling while the class runs. The Output window should log a message similar to "java.lang.OutOfMemoryError: Java heap space." You will also see a message that the heap dump is saved into the location nbproject\private\profiler\java_pid3012.hprof inside your project. The specific filename will differ, but the directory structure will be the same.

An Application Finished pop-up window will appear, asking if you want to take a snapshot of the collected results. If you click Yes, a standard memory snapshot will be taken of the profiled results collected up to when the OutOfMemoryError occurred.

You will then see a Question pop-up window appear that states that the application crashed and generated a heap dump. It will prompt you to open it in the HeapWalker. If you click the Yes button, NetBeans will load the heap dump in a tab in the Source Editor, as shown in Figure 5-22. It contains several tabs that allow you to view the information in the heap dump, such as Summary, Classes, and Instances.

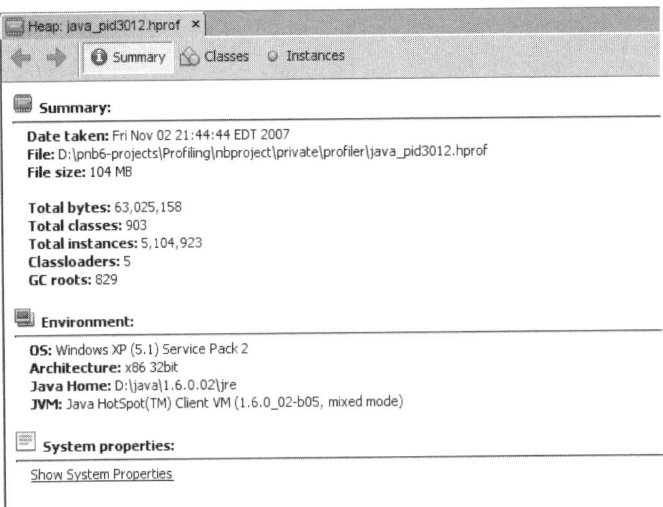

Figure 5-22. *The heap dump displayed in the Source Editor*

The Summary tab of the heap dump displays several sections of summary information. It lists the date the heap dump was taken, the file size of the heap dump, and the total instances of classes on the heap at the time when the OutOfMemoryError occurred. It also displays the basic environment information of the machine running the JVM.

The Classes tab of the heap dump, as shown in Figure 5-23, is similar to the standard memory analysis results in Figure 5-18. It lists the class name, the number of instances, and the size in bytes of all the instances. You can sort the data displayed by clicking the column headers.

Heap: java_pid600.hprof | Summary | Classes | Instances

Classes

Class Name	Instances [%]	Instances	Size
com.pronetbeans.examples.**CauseOutOfMemoryError**		3221693 (100%)	38660316 (71%)
java.lang.**String**		3867 (0%)	92808 (0%)
char[]		3695 (0%)	226308 (0%)
short[]		1181 (0%)	76206 (0%)
byte[]		960 (0%)	1348373 (2%)
int[]		917 (0%)	59988 (0%)
java.lang.**Object[]**		534 (0%)	13587844 (25%)
java.lang.reflect.**Method**		290 (0%)	22330 (0%)
java.util.**HashMap$Entry**		261 (0%)	6264 (0%)
java.lang.**String[]**		259 (0%)	5808 (0%)
java.lang.**Class[]**		165 (0%)	1524 (0%)

Figure 5-23. *The Classes tab of a heap dump in the HeapWalker*

The Instances tab of the heap dump displays instances of a specific class. It must be activated from the Classes tab by right-clicking a class in the list and selecting "Show in Instances View." The HeapWalker will display the instances of the selected class in the Instances tab, as shown in Figure 5-24.

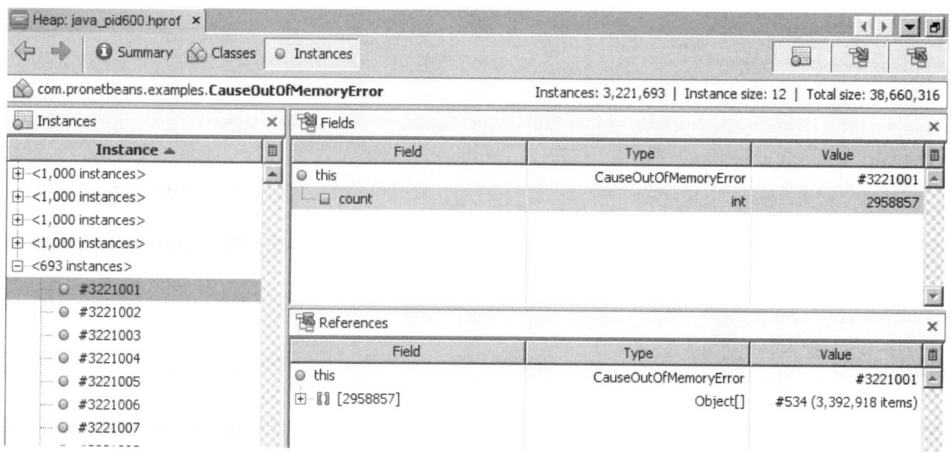

Figure 5-24. *The Instances tab of a heap dump in the HeapWalker Monitor Application (Thread Profiling)*

The Instances tab displays the individual instances in the left pane. It groups the instances together by the number you specified in the "Track every X object allocations" field in the Profile Project window. You can click the plus sign next to the group of instances to display each individual instance number.

When you select a unique instance, the top-right panel of the Instances tab will display the related fields. Each item listed in the Fields section of the Instances tab is displayed as well as the type and value of the instance field. This allows you to identify specific instances that existed in the JVM at the time the OutOfMemoryError occurred. This can be a powerful tool when trying to diagnose what caused the OutOfMemoryError.

The third and final type of profiling you can do with the NetBeans Profiler is monitoring threads. With the Profiler tools, you can track the runtime and state of all threads inside the JVM. This can obviously come in handy if you are developing multithreaded code, such as a server-based listener, a client-server program, or some type of computational engine.

You can enable thread monitoring when a profiling session starts or after it is already under way. For instance, I have created a new Web Application project in NetBeans and assigned it to run on Tomcat 6. If I want to monitor the threads for the application and the application server, I can start a profiling session.

To enable thread monitoring when a profiling session starts, go to the main menu and select Profile ➤ Profile Main Project. When the Profile Project window appears, make sure to select the Monitor section on the left side of the window. Once you have done this, the right side of the window will contain a single field: "Enable Threads Monitoring." This check box allows you to specify that thread monitoring should be enabled immediately when the profiling session starts. If it is not selected, then you can choose to enable it after the profiling session has started. I usually select the check box to activate thread monitoring right away.

Once the profiling session has initialized and started, the Threads window will appear. If you enabled thread monitoring to start right away, the Threads window should start displaying results, as shown in Figure 5-25.

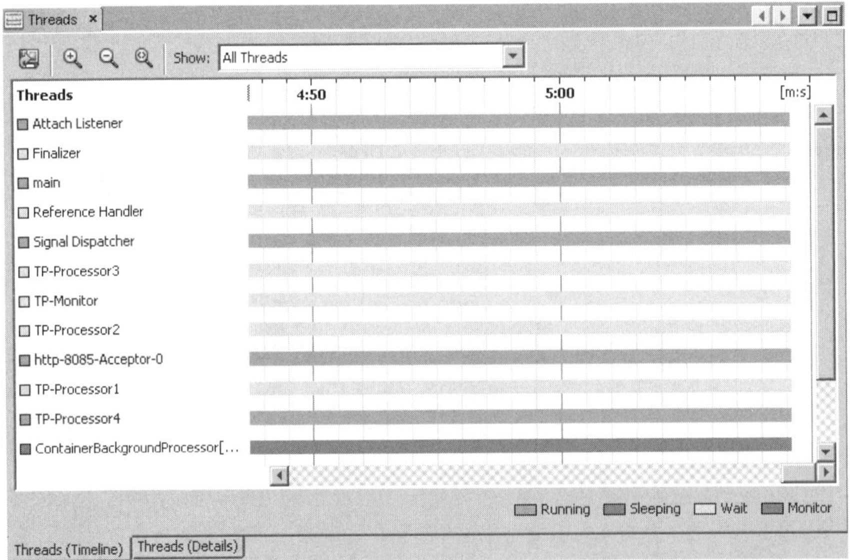

Figure 5-25. *The Threads (Timeline) tab during a profile-monitoring session*

The Threads window lists each thread name along with a running color-coded timeline for each thread. As the profiling session proceeds, the timeline continues to expand, tracking the state of the threads. Each thread state has a different color assigned for quick visual identification. Running threads are green, Sleeping threads are purple, Waiting threads are yellow, and threads waiting on a Java Monitor are red.

The Threads window also contains several fields in the toolbar along the top. If you mouse over each icon from left to right, you will be able to see the tooltip that appears to identify the icon.

The first icon is labeled "Saves Current View to Image." It allows you to create a screenshot of the results currently displayed in the Threads window and to save it to disk as a PNG file.

The next two icons are the Zoom In and Zoom Out actions. You can use these icons to zoom into the thread timeline to a very precise point. The smallest unit of measure I believe I found I could zoom in to was 10 milliseconds. However, the timeline was scrolling by so quickly it was difficult to tell precisely. You can also zoom out to be able to view a longer period of time on the timeline.

The fourth and final icon is labeled "Scale To Fit." If you select it, the timeline will display from start to finish on one screen. You can click the icon again to toggle back to the Fixed Scale mode, which allows you to zoom in and out.

The last field on the toolbar of the Threads window is the "Show" drop-down box. This serves as a filter for the threads that are displayed. By default it is set to All Threads. You can also select to view Live Threads Only or Finished Threads Only. This filter can help with displaying large numbers of threads you are trying to monitor during a profiling session.

The Threads window lets you filter by one or more specific threads. You can select a thread (or multiple threads using your OS-specific multiselect key) and right-click to view the context menu. One option that appears is Show Only Selected Threads. If you select this, then the Threads window will display only the thread or threads you selected. The "Show" drop-down box in the toolbar is set to Selected Threads, allowing you to turn off the filter by selecting any of the other values.

The context menu displayed when you right-click a thread also has a menu item named "Thread Details." If you select it, then the Threads (Details) tab will be displayed, with the specific information about the selected thread. You can also double-click a thread listed in the Threads window to load the thread details.

The Threads (Details) tab will display the individual timeline for the thread along with a chart of the thread states, as shown in Figure 5-26. In the figure, the percentage of time the thread spent in each state is listed, in minutes and seconds, as well as the overall percentage. You can also click the Details tab to see a text-based listing of the timestamp for each thread state.

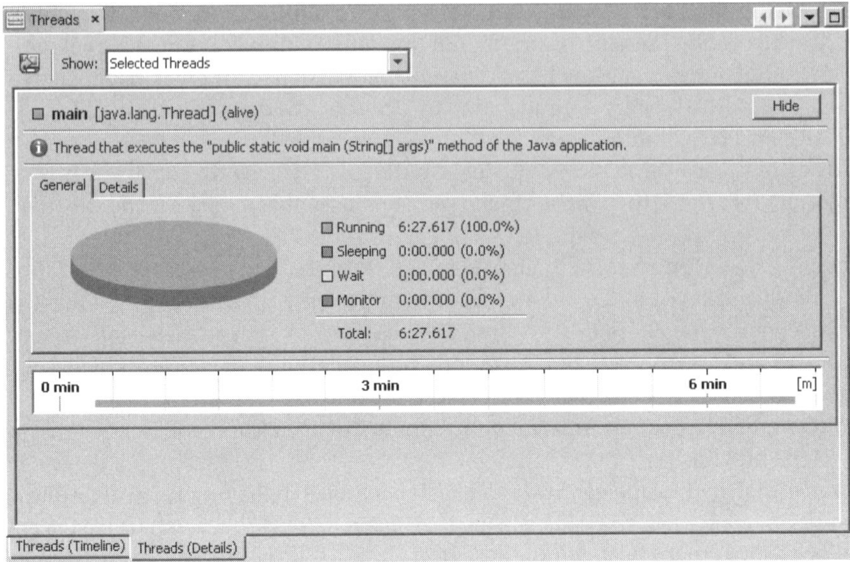

Figure 5-26. *The Threads (Details) tab for a selected thread*

The chart and timeline on the General tab can be saved to a PNG file for display in a Word document or PowerPoint using the toolbar icon labeled "Saves Current View to Image."

Understanding the Profiler Telemetry

When a NetBeans Profiler session is under way, you can monitor various telemetry graphs. These graphs let you watch a near-real-time display of several important pieces of information, such as the memory allocated to the JVM heap, the amount of memory used by the JVM heap, the number of threads, and the number of classes loaded in the JVM.

Viewing the Telemetry Overview

You can activate the Profiler Telemetry from the Profiler Control Panel window, as shown in Figures 5-4 and 5-5. The last icon along the top of the Profiler Control Panel window is the Telemetry Overview icon. If you click it, the Telemetry Overview window will appear, as shown in Figure 5-27. The three graphs that are displayed give you a quick glance at the internals of the JVM during the profiling session.

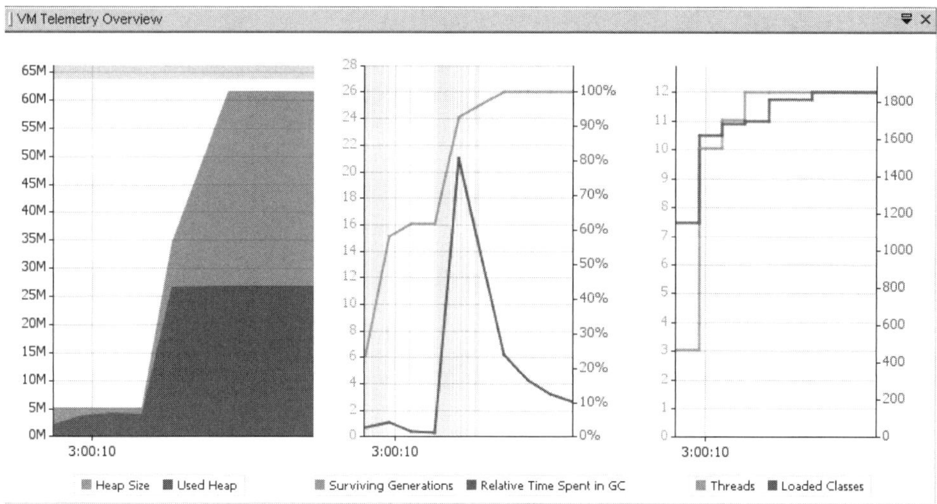

Figure 5-27. *The VM Telemtry Overview window with graphs*

The first graph in the Telemetry Overview window displays the heap size and the used heap. This lets you see the amount of memory that has been allocated to the JVM heap as well as the actual amount of memory *used* by the JVM heap.

The second graph displays the number of surviving generations and the relative time spent in garbage collection. If you are not exactly clear what a "surviving generation" is or what it can tell you, review the following explanation from the online NetBeans.org Profiler documentation:

> *A Generation is a set of instances created within the same GC interval (between two garbage collections). A Surviving Generation is a Generation that survives at least one garbage collection. The number of survived garbage collections—the generation's age—is its unique identifier. Surviving Generations (metrics) value is the number of different Surviving Generations that are currently alive on the heap (number of Generations with different generation ages).*

This lets you identify how many objects are living in the heap past garbage collection. If you have a higher-than-expected number of objects staying "alive" on the heap, then you may have a memory leak.

The third graph displays the number of threads being profiled vs. the number of classes loaded in the JVM.

Viewing the Main VM Telemetry Window

The Telemetry Overview window is convenient because all three types of graphs are displayed at once. However, it does not allow you much control over the display or let you perform any actions with the graphs. The VM Telemetry Window does.

You can use the VM Telemetry window in several ways. The Profiler Control Panel window contains an icon in the View section labeled "VM Telemetry." You can also access it from the main menu by selecting Window ➤ Profiling ➤ VM Telemetry. If you open the VM Telemetry window during a profiling session, the Memory (Heap) tab will be shown by default and actively display results, as shown in Figure 5-28.

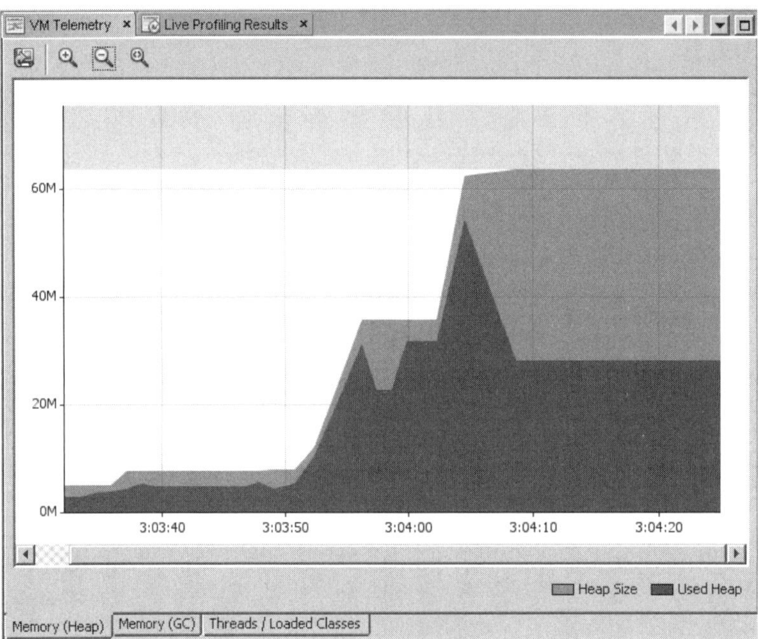

Figure 5-28. *The main VM Telemtry window*

The VM Telemetry in Figure 5-28 has three tabs: Memory (Heap), Memory (GC), and Threads / Loaded Classes. These tabs are for the same graphs that were displayed in the Telemetry Overview window. The main difference is that you have some additional capabilities available to you in the VM Telemetry window.

The toolbar along the top contains several icons. You can use the icons to save the currently displayed graph to a PNG file, to zoom into a more precise length of time in the graph, to zoom out to a more general length of time on the graph, or to scale the graph timeline to fit on the screen.

Profiling External and Remote Applications

One of the truly interesting features of the NetBeans Profiler is that it lets you profile code running external to NetBeans or on a remote machine. This allows you to monitor the threads, CPU performance, and memory usage of any type of Java application running on your machine or in a remote server.

Profiling a Remote Java Application Server Running in NetBeans

The Profiler lets you profile a wide variety of Java web application servers. The server can be running locally on your machine or remotely. Select Profile ➤ Attach Profiler from the main menu to configure the Profiler to be able to connect to the remote application server.

The Attach Profiler window appears. The "Attach To" drop-down is set to External Application. The text along the very bottom of the window states that the Attach Mode has no attach settings defined. It also provides a link to define the attach settings. The first time you run the Attach Profiler window, you can also click the Attach button to define the attach settings. On subsequent runs, the Attach Profiler window will list the last-used configuration under the Attach Mode area of the window. You must click the Define link to edit the attach settings if you want to change them.

Once you click the Attach button in the Attach Profiler window, the Attach Wizard window will appear. The "Target Type" field is initially set to <Select Target Type>. Select the value J2EE Web/App Server. For this example, I am profiling a Tomcat 6 Java application server that is running remotely inside an instance of NetBeans 6. I have done so because I can run the Tomcat server in Profile mode, thereby bypassing the need for configuring the remote profiling pack.

In the Attach Wizard, select the application server version from the "J2EE Web/App Server Type" field. Choose Tomcat 5.5 from the drop-down.

Note At the time of this writing, the latest Tomcat version listed was Tomcat 5.5, even though NetBeans 6 is bundled with Tomcat 6. I have selected Tomcat 5.5 for profiling and found little difference in the direct attach capabilities, even though the remote server is Tomcat 6.

Once you select the application server, choose the Remote radio button in the Attach Method section. The Direct radio button will be selected automatically in the Attach Invocation section. The Dynamic (JDK 1.6) radio button will be disabled. The Attach Wizard screen's fields should be set as depicted in Figure 5-29.

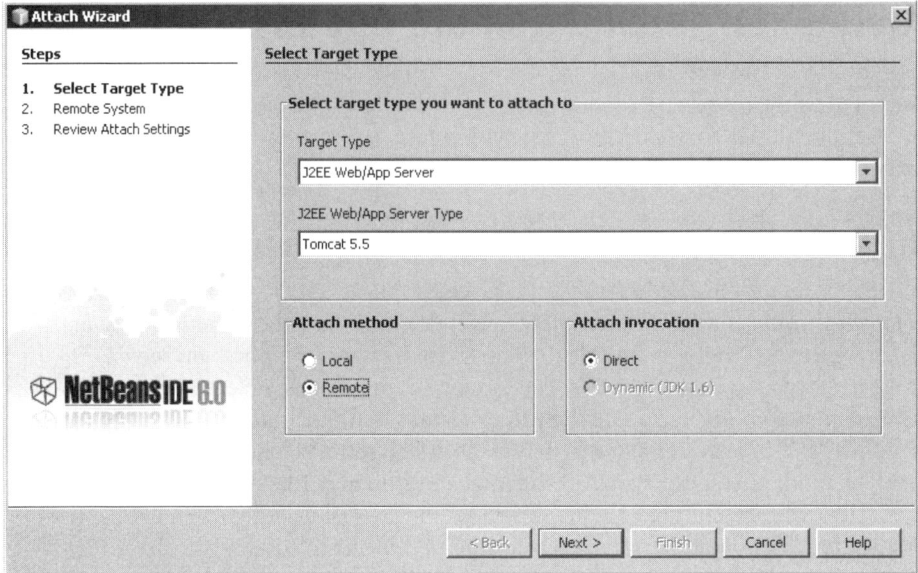

Figure 5-29. *Remote application server setting in the Attach Wizard window*

Click the Next button to proceed to the Remote System screen. In the Remote System screen, set the Hostname or IP Address of the remote application server you wish to profile. Also set the Host OS to the operating system of the target server. Then click the Next button.

The Review Attach Settings screen displays each Attach Profiler property you selected for verification and review. Make sure you have entered the correct data, and then click the Next button.

The Manual Integration screen will appear to describe how to install and run the Profiler remote pack for the target server. Since I will be connecting to a Tomcat server running in Profile Mode directly in NetBeans, I do not need to configure the remote pack. NetBeans and the NetBeans Profiler will handle this for me.

Finally, from the drop-down at the top of the screen select the target platform that will run your application server. Follow the instructions displayed to integrate the Profiler pack with your application server, if applicable, and click the Finish button to initiate the profiling session.

After the Profiler has connected to the remote server, you should be able to view results in the Live Results window, open the VM Telemetry window, take snapshots of results, and even take a heap dump from the remote server's JVM.

Profiling a Remote Java Application Server Using the Profiler Remote Pack

In the previous section, I took the easy way out when attempting to connect to a remote Java application server. Since the Tomcat server was invoked from NetBeans in Profiling mode, I did not need to configure it to be profiled remotely. However, if you want to profile a remote Java application server, you can use the Profiler Remote Pack. This allows you to connect and profile a remote server directly from NetBeans.

Almost any standard Java application server can use the Profiler Remote Pack. You can download an operating system–specific version from the http://profiler.netbeans.org project site. Versions are available in both 32 and 64 bits.

Once you have downloaded the remote pack, unzip, untar, or unpack the files into a directory where you want the pack to be located. Since I typically install NetBeans and the JDKs into a d:\java directory, I installed the remote pack to the location d:\java\netbeans-6-rp.

Next, locate the root directory for the application server. In this case I will be installing the remote pack for Tomcat 5.5 configured to run on JDK 1.6.0_02 in Windows. In the server's bin directory, locate the catalina.bat file (or catalina.sh file for Unix/Linux users). Near the beginning of the file, and after the comments, add a JAVA_HOME variable that points to an installation of the JDK 1.6. If you already have a JAVA_HOME environment variable, ignore this step.

On the next line of the catalina.bat file, add the following command all on one line, with no line breaks:

```
SET CATALINA_OPTS=-agentpath:D:\java\netbeans-6-➥
rp\lib\deployed\jdk16\windows\profilerinterface.dll=D:\java\netbeans-6-rp\lib,5140
```

When the Tomcat server loads, this will pass it the location of the remote pack's DLL and communication port to use when waiting for a connection from the Profiler. For Linux/Unix users, the profilerinterface.dll reference in the CATALINA_OPTS line in the preceding code can usually be changed to libprofilerinterface.so. You can find the precise path and filenames on the last screen of the Attach Wizard as described in the previous section.

Once the changes have been made, save them, exit the file, and run the catalina.bat file. Tomcat will initiate, but wait for a connection from the Profiler, as shown in Figure 5-30. Once the Tomcat server is initiated, you can follow the instructions in the previous section to have the NetBeans Profiler configured to connect remotely to the server.

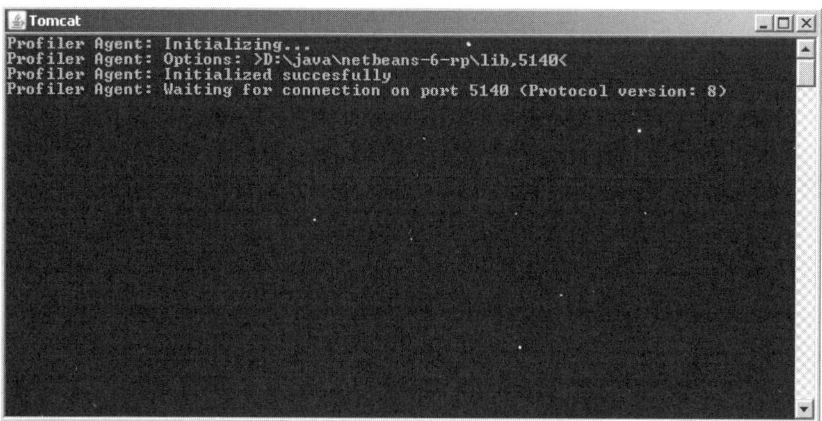

Figure 5-30. *Tomcat waiting for a remote Profiler connection*

Profiling an External Java Application

You can also attach the NetBeans Profiler to a Java application that is external to NetBeans (other than a web server). If the application is running in JDK 1.6, you can use the dynamic attach capability.

For this example, I run a Java application that some people may know: the Eclipse Java IDE. I have configured Eclipse to use the same JDK 1.6 instances as NetBeans. Once Eclipse is open, you can configure the NetBeans Profiler to attach to it. On the main menu, select Profile ➤ Attach Profiler. In the Attach Profiler window that opens, click the Change link in the Attach Mode section at the bottom. The Attach Wizard window will open and the Select Target Type screen will be displayed.

In the Select Target Type screen, choose the Target Type "Application." Set the "Attach method" field to Local and the "Attach invocation" field to Dynamic, as shown in Figure 5-31. Then click the Next button to display the Review Attach Settings screen.

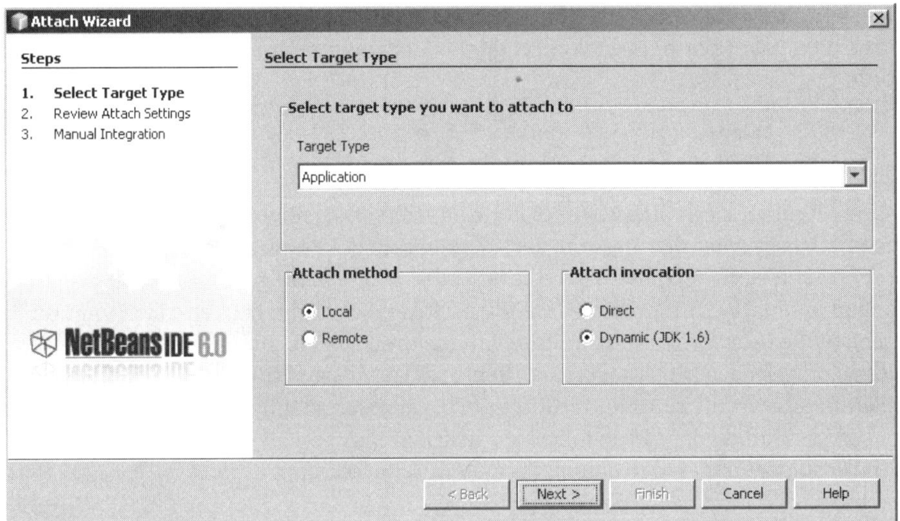

Figure 5-31. *The Select Target Type screen for attaching to an external application*

The Review Attach Settings screen displays a short summary of the settings you have configured. Click the Next button to proceed to the Manual Integration screen. This screen will allow you to select the target Java platform that will run your application. Once you select a target platform, a set of specific instructions will be displayed. For Java 6 applications, no additional manual integration is needed. Click the Finish button to exit the Attach Wizard.

In the Attach Profiler window, configure the type of profiling you wish to conduct (monitoring, CPU, memory) and click the Attach button. The Profiler will display the Select Process window. This contains a drop-down list of Java-based process IDs that are running in your operating system.

Select the PID of the application to which you wish to connect and the summary information about the PID will be displayed on the screen, as shown in Figure 5-32. Click the OK button in the Select Process window. It will close and the NetBeans Profiler will initialize. There may be a short or long delay while the Profiler instruments the Java application and before it is able to begin retrieving results. However, once it connects, you can open the Live Results and VM Telemetry windows to watch the application's performance.

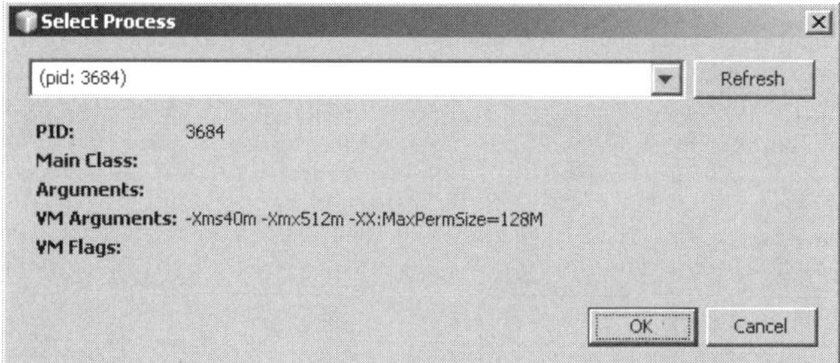

Figure 5-32. *The Select Process window*

Summary

This chapter discussed how to configure, execute, and work with the NetBeans Profiler. It showed how to configure the Profiler's settings in the Basic Options window and discussed how these settings affect the Profiler's operation. The chapter then went on to explain how to navigate the Profile Control Panel, use the controls, and initiate a profiling session.

The chapter reviewed in depth the three main types of profiling, starting with CPU analysis. You learned how to initiate a profiling session, execute a CPU analysis on a Java application, and review the accumulated results. Sample code was also presented that demonstrated the benefits of using profiling points to conduct CPU analysis in identifying bottlenecks in your code.

The chapter then discussed memory analysis as the second main type of profiling and examined and profiled several sample methods. You learned how to review the results, track the allocated stack traces for objects, and determine areas for reducing the memory usage of the Java application.

The third type of profiling the chapter reviewed was thread monitoring. The different windows and timelines were explained as well as the benefits of being able to watch the various thread states that exist in the JVM.

Finally, the chapter reviewed different ways the Profiler can connect to external applications and remote Java servers.

CHAPTER 6

Managing Version Control

An important aspect of software development is controlling your source code. In single-developer and multideveloper projects, it is essential to ensure the longevity of your code by storing the files somewhere other than on the developers' computers. It is also important to be able to track versions of individual source files and to be able to control changes.

Two popular version control systems are the Concurrent Versioning System (CVS) and Subversion. Out of the box, NetBeans provides full support for CVS and Subversion. However, to use Subversion with NetBeans you must download and install the Subversion executable. This chapter covers working with CVS, Subversion, and the new Local History feature.

Using CVS

CVS allows you to back up your project into a system that is external to your development machine. You can store files in CVS, have it manage individual unique versions of code, and retrieve those versions as you need them. A good CVS tool also allows you to perform comparisons between different versions of a file to see the changes. The NetBeans CVS module provides all of these capabilities.

Note Obviously, you could be running a CVS server on your local machine. But it is a best practice, even for small programming shops, to have a separate computer running a source code repository. This increases the likelihood that your project code will survive a hardware crash or other problem. Like any database, web, or file server, your source code repository server should be backed up regularly.

When NetBeans is initially installed, support for CVS is activated by default. You should see the Versioning menu on the NetBeans menu bar, as shown in Figure 6-1.

If there are other version control system modules installed, such as Subversion, they will also be listed on the Versioning menu. Many of the standard CVS commands are available by navigating to Versioning ➤ CVS.

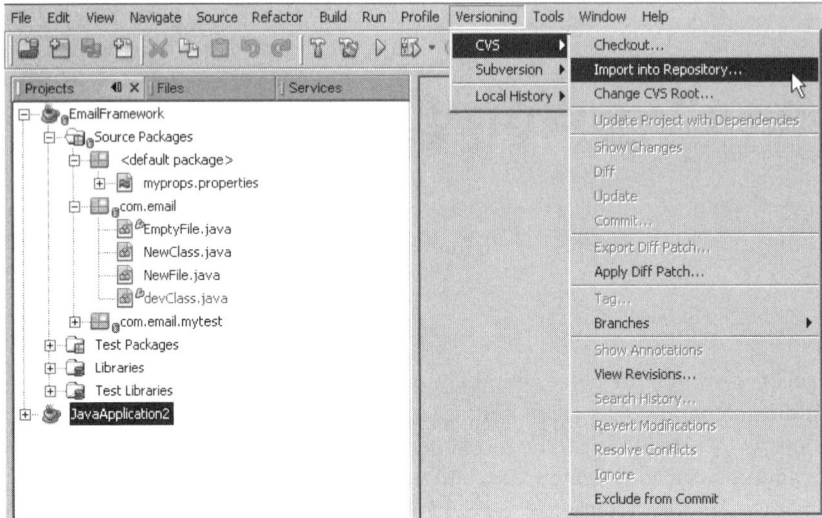

Figure 6-1. *The CVS main menu*

If a project has already been configured to use CVS, the Versioning menu will change dynamically. Open a project that was checked out of CVS and select the Versioning menu. You will see that the menu differs from Figure 6-1, in that it lists the CVS commands directly and not in a submenu, as shown in Figure 6-2.

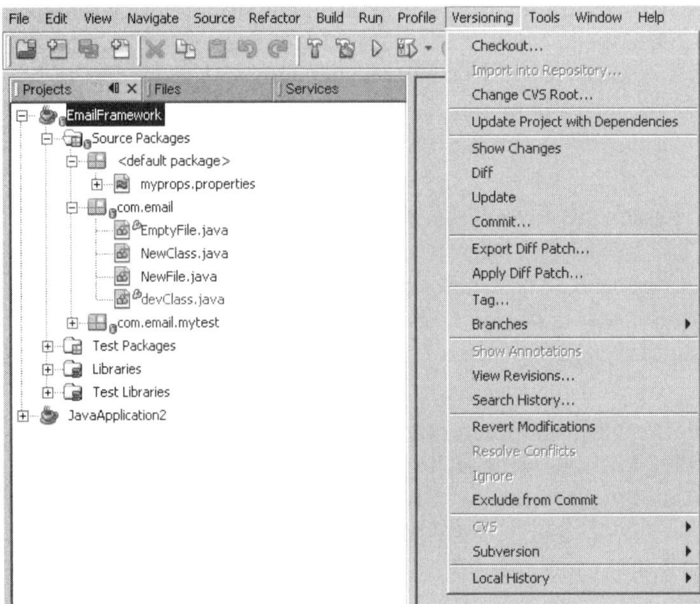

Figure 6-2. *The CVS-specific commands listed in the Versioning menu*

Configuring a Project to Use CVS

You can start using CVS in a NetBeans project in two main ways:

- Create a new project and import the project's code into your CVS repository. This assumes there is no prior code stored for your module or project in the repository.
- Download the most recent copy of the source code from the repository (also referred to as "grabbing the latest version" or "checking out the latest version").

Importing a Project into the Repository

If you have a new or existing NetBeans project, you can easily import it into the repository. To begin, right-click the project in the Projects window and select Versioning ➤ Import into CVS Repository. You will see the first step of the Import Project Options window, CVS Root, as shown in Figure 6-3.

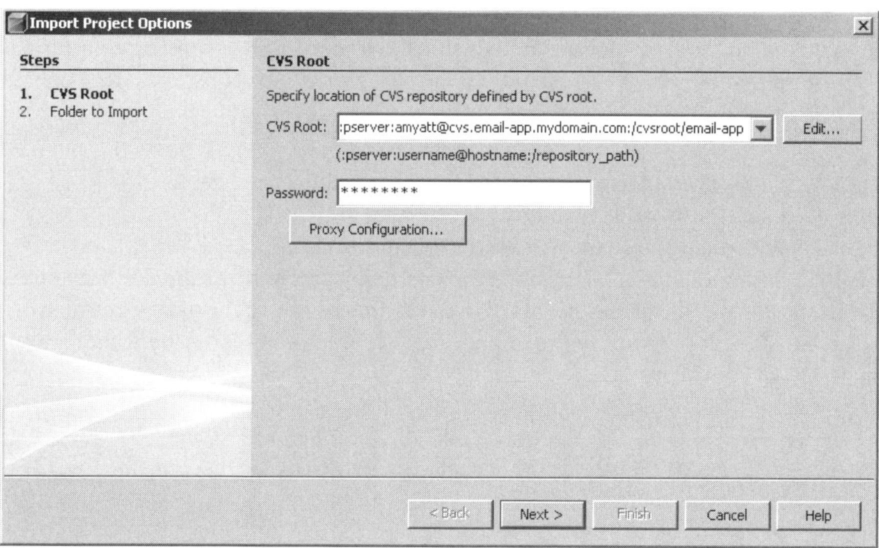

Figure 6-3. *The CVS Root window*

The first field requests the CVS root string. If you are unfamiliar with setting the CVS root, you can click the Edit button next to the field to use the Edit CVS Root dialog box to enter the string, as shown in Figure 6-4. If you are relatively new to CVS, using the Edit CVS Root dialog box can help you avoid making syntax errors in the CVS root string.

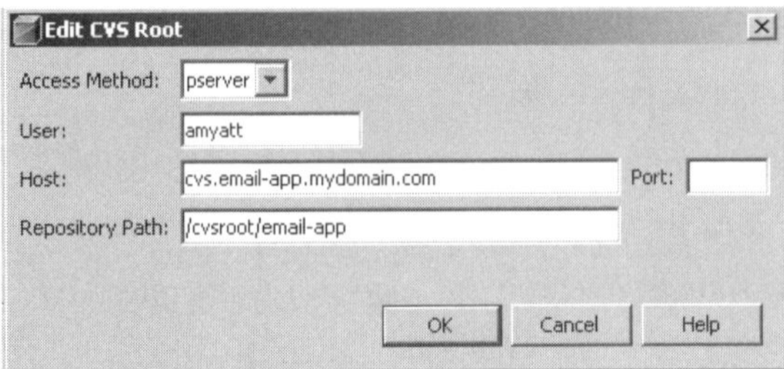

Figure 6-4. *The Edit CVS Root dialog box*

In the Edit CVS Root dialog box, select a method from the "Access Method" drop-down list. You have four choices:

- `pserver` allows you to connect to a remote server with a username and password.
- `ext` is similar to `pserver`, except it uses Secure Shell (SSH).
- `local`, as the name implies, allows you to connect to a source code repository running locally on your machine.
- `fork` is just an alternate version of `local`.

In most environments, you would use `pserver`, unless you are concerned about the source code's traveling across the network as plaintext.

In the Edit CVS Root dialog box, you also need to fill in the "User," "Host," "Port," and "Repository Path" fields. In the "User" field, enter the username you were assigned in your code repository. The Repository Path value is normally in the format of `/cvsroot/myproject`. After entering the values, click OK to return to the Import Project Options window, where your string will appear in the "CVS Root" field.

■ **Tip** If your CVS repository is configured to use the standard port of 2401, you can leave the "Port" field blank.

Once you have configured the correct CVS root string, click Next in the CVS Root window. NetBeans will attempt to validate the connection and then display the next step, Folder to Import, as shown in Figure 6-5. In this window, specify the project folder on your local machine to import. It should already be set to the project root folder of your NetBeans project. You can also specify the repository folder. This is the name under which the module will be placed in the CVS repository. When you are finished, click the Finish button.

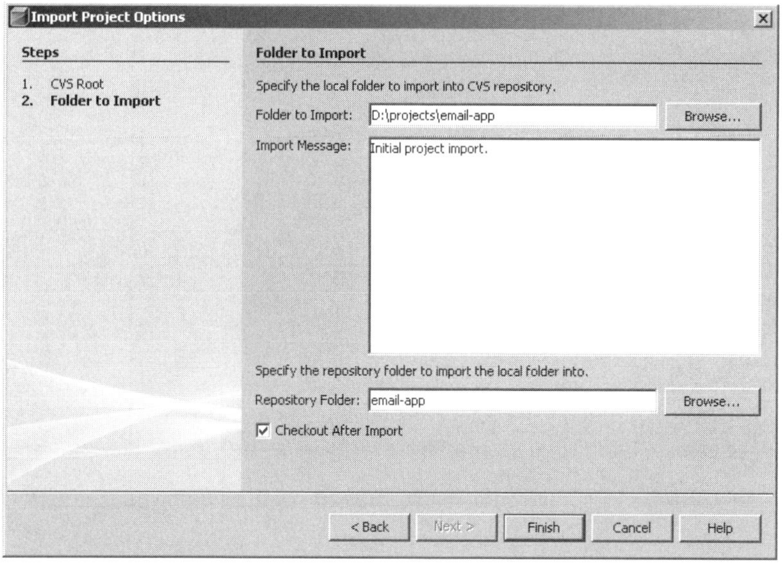

Figure 6-5. *The Folder to Import window*

Checking Out Code from the Repository

For an existing project, you may need to check out the code from the repository. This assumes that the code you have in your repository is structured in a NetBeans project hierarchy.

To check out an existing project, select Versioning ➤ CVS ➤ Checkout. In the first window that appears, specify the CVS root string, as discussed in the previous section, and then click the Next button.

In the Module to Checkout window, you need to specify several properties. The module is the actual code from the repository you want to download. If you know the name of the module, you can type it directly in the "Module" field. Alternatively, click the Browse button next to the "Module" field to browse the repository and select the module from a list, as shown in Figure 6-6. In the Browse CVS Module dialog box, you can drill down through the nodes to find the module under the root (`/cvsroot/email-framework` in the example shown in Figure 6-6). You can have multiple modules defined under the root. Select the one you want and click the OK button.

You can also choose to check out code using a CVS branch or tag, if such is used in your repository. In the Module to Checkout window, click the Browse button next to the "Branch" field to open the Browse Tags dialog box, as shown in Figure 6-7. If there is no specific branch or tag to use, click the HEAD node, and then click the OK button.

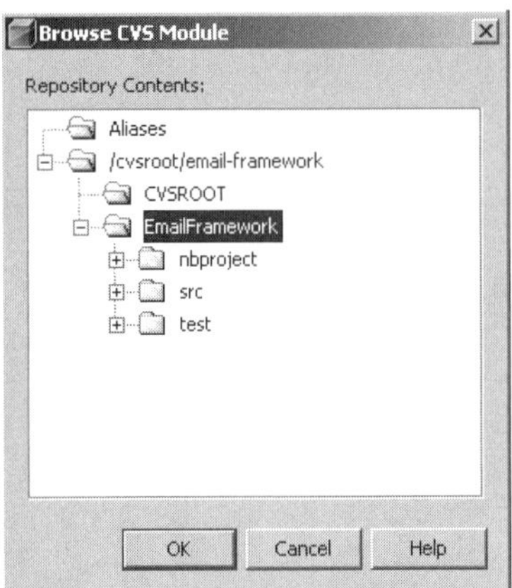

Figure 6-6. *The Browse CVS Module dialog box*

Figure 6-7. *The Browse Tags dialog box*

In the Module to Checkout window, you also need to specify the local folder to which the code will be copied. I usually use a standard location, such as a folder named `projects`, to store all my code. Your team or organization may have a standard directory structure, so be sure to pick the correct location. Click the Finish button after you have set the properties. The checkout operation will proceed.

When the checkout operation is finished, you will see a dialog box stating that the checkout is complete and asking if you want to open the project or close the window. If you click the Open Project button, the dialog box will close, and the project will now be listed in the Projects window.

Performing Common CVS Operations

You can perform many types of operations when working with a source code repository—adding code, updating, checking differences between two versions, tagging, branching, and searching. Sometimes the terms can be a little confusing. Learning the version control system features can take a little patience and experimentation.

Showing Changes

When working with CVS, you need to know when files have changed, when files have been added to the project, and when they have been deleted.

When a source file is checked out of CVS and edited, the filename appears in blue in the interface. This flags the file as having been changed. You will also see a blue cylinder icon next to the name of the source package and project name in the Projects window, as shown earlier in Figure 6-1. This visually flags a package as having one or more files that were altered.

The NetBeans CVS tool also provides a Versioning window that allows you to see what has changed, as shown in Figure 6-8. To open this window, right-click the name of the project and select CVS ➤ Show Changes.

■ Note The dynamic naming of the versioning menus can be confusing at first, but quickly makes sense after using it. As previously mentioned, if a project is configured to use CVS and you right-click the project name, the CVS submenu will appear on the context menu. If the project was not configured to use CVS, then the Versioning submenu would appear on the context menu. Similarly a Subversion submenu would appear on the context menu if you had checked out a project from a Subversion repository.

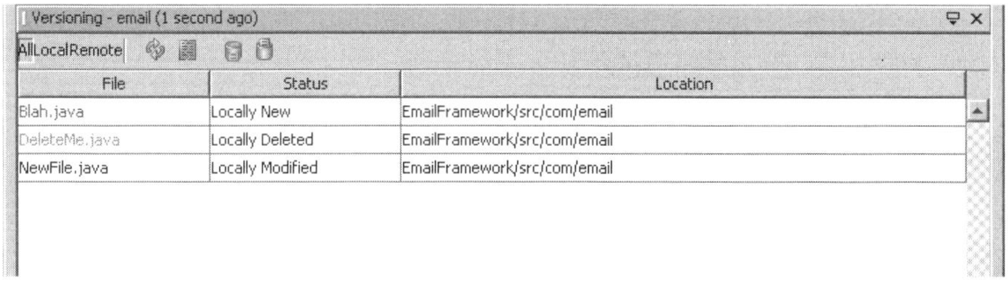

File	Status	Location
Blah.java	Locally New	EmailFramework/src/com/email
DeleteMe.java	Locally Deleted	EmailFramework/src/com/email
NewFile.java	Locally Modified	EmailFramework/src/com/email

Figure 6-8. *The Versioning window displayed by the Show Changes option*

The Versioning window displays any files that were added, modified, or deleted. For each file listed, you can individually choose to commit the file, ignore the file and exclude it from the commit, or revert the file modifications back to the repository version. The Status column will contain one of the following:

Locally New: Files that were added have a status of Locally New. They exist in the NetBeans project but have not yet been added to the code repository. If you right-click the file in the Versioning window, you can choose to open the file in the Source Editor or to commit the file, which adds it to the CVS repository.

Locally Deleted: Files that were deleted from the project have a status of Locally Deleted. You can right-click the deleted file and choose to commit it. This confirms the deletion with the CVS repository. You can also select to update the file, which downloads the latest version of the file from the repository, effectively undoing the deletion.

Locally Modified: Files that were modified have a status of Locally Modified. You can commit and update these files. If you commit a modified file, the changes you made are saved into the CVS repository. If you update the file, the local changes you made are undone. You may also want to know what you changed in a file and compare the differences. (These CVS options are covered in the following sections.)

Another way to view changes is to select Versioning ➤ Show All Changes from the main menu. This shows all the changes to all the open projects that are CVS-enabled. You should be careful, since different projects may have files with the same name. It is safer to view CVS changes project by project rather than by using the Show All Changes option.

Committing Changes

When you want to commit the changes made in your project, you have several options. You can commit a single file, multiple files, an entire package, or an entire project.

To commit a file that is locally new, right-click the file and select CVS ➤ Commit from the context menu. In the Commit dialog box, shown in Figure 6-9, you see the name of the file to commit, the status, the commit action, and the repository path. The commit action is the only option you can modify.

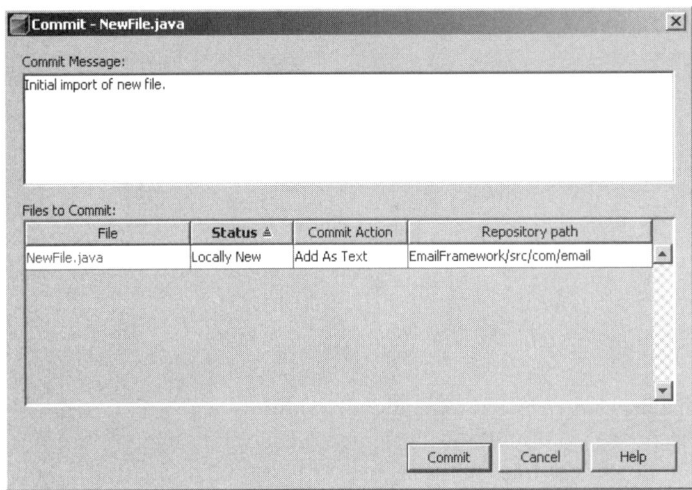

Figure 6-9. *Committing a new file*

By default, a Java source file's commit action is set to Add As Text. By clicking the field, you can change it to Add As Binary or Exclude from Commit. The Add As Binary option should be used for images, compiled class files, or other binary files. The Exclude from Commit option is useful when you are working with multiple files and want to exclude one or more of them from being committed, such as if you want to commit an entire project but exclude one file that you are still developing.

In the text box at the top of the Commit dialog box, you can add a commit message, which is intended to provide a clue to the changes being committed. It should be brief but still convey the reason for the change to the code. The "Searching History" section later in this chapter explains how to view the history of a file and see the comments made for each version of a file.

To commit multiple files, hold down the Ctrl key (in Windows) and click each file one at a time. You can also commit an entire package or the entire project by selecting it, right-clicking, and choosing CVS ➤ Commit. The Commit All Changes option is available from the CVS main menu, but make sure you are certain you know the ramifications of performing this action. All added, modified, and deleted files in *all* open projects will be committed if you use the Commit All Changes option. This will look very similar to Figure 6-6 except that multiple files would be listed.

Note When you commit multiple files, the commit message that is entered is applied to all the files. If you want your files to have different commit messages, you should commit them in separate batches.

Updating Files

Performing a CVS update on a file can sometimes be a little confusing. A CVS update operation grabs the latest copy of the file from the CVS repository and tries to merge it with the local copy. If changes have not been made to the local copy, then the file is said to be *patched*. Updates on a code base should always be performed prior to making any local changes so that you are sure you are working with the latest code.

When code is updated and a merge performed, CVS tries to figure out the changes that differ between the two files (the local copy and the repository copy). A simple scenario can demonstrate the functionality. Assume you have the following class named NewFile:

```
public class NewFile {

    public NewFile() {
        System.out.println("In the constructor");
    }
}
```

You have just retrieved a fresh copy of version 1.4 of the file onto your local machine. Another developer, John, does the same and immediately modifies the code. He adds a new method and commits the code, thereby creating version 1.5. He should really run the code through unit tests *before* committing it, but we'll let him off the hook this time. Here is the modified code:

```
public class NewFile {

    public NewFile() {
        System.out.println("In the constructor");
    }

    public void doNothing() {
        System.out.println("In the doNothing method");
    }
}
```

You still have the original code. If you modify the constructor and want to commit your changes, there is a problem. Your copy of the file does not have the new doNothing method. If you were able to commit the code, you would essentially overwrite John's changes and they would be lost. You could review the file's versions, but not if you didn't know John had made the changes.

Assume you went ahead and tried to commit the file. The commit will fail, and you will receive an error message similar to "Up-to-date check failed for file." This is warning you that the copy of the file in the CVS repository does not match what you have. This situation is where the CVS update function comes in handy.

When you choose CVS ➤ Update for the file, the CVS tool compares the files, line by line, to see what changed. Suppose you made the following change to the string in the `println` method in the `NewFile` class:

```
public class NewFile {

    public NewFile() {
        System.out.println("******** In the constructor ********");
    }
}
```

When you update the file, the tool sees that only one line differs in your local file and the three lines for the `doNothing` method differ in the remote file in the repository. It then combines these lines into one file:

```
public class NewFile {

    public NewFile() {
        System.out.println("******** In the constructor ********");
    }

    public void doNothing() {
        System.out.println("In the doNothing method");
    }
}
```

From a developer's perspective, this feature is fantastic. You no longer need to compare files manually to see changes or copy and paste the new or updated code. However, you should use it with caution, since conflicts may occur. If you and the other developer modify the same line or lines, CVS cannot make automatic assumptions. It merges the files and warns of a conflict during the update operation, as shown in Figure 6-10.

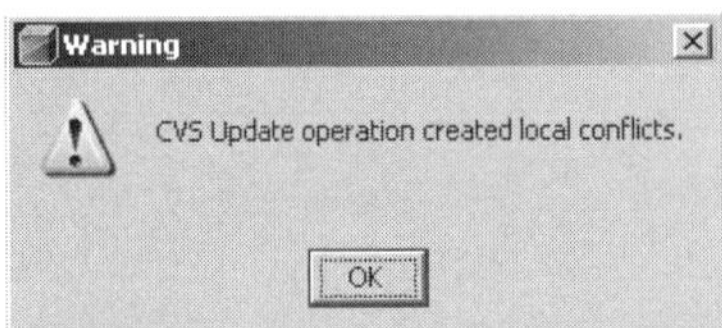

Figure 6-10. *Merge conflicts warning during a CVS update operation*

The filename will be shown in red in the Projects and Files windows. You can open the file and see what conflicts occurred. The file now contains invalid Java syntax, since CVS inserted text into the file during the update operation to identify the conflicting lines, as shown in Figure 6-11.

```
NewFile.java
 *
 * @author Adam Myatt
 */
public class NewFile {

    /** Creates a new instance of NewFile */
    public NewFile() {
        System.out.println("Hi made changes locally 3");
    }

   public void nextNewMethod() {
<<<<<<< NewFile.java
       System.out.println("next new method goes here 1234567890 ");
=======
       System.out.println("next new method goes here 4");
>>>>>>> 1.9
   }
```

Figure 6-11. *The line conflicts in the merged file*

In this example, both developers modified the text in the `System.out.println` statement in the `nextNewMethod` method. The text that was added identifies the following changes:

- `<<<<<<< NewFile.java` denotes the start of the section where text in the local file differs from that of the file in the repository.
- `System.out.println("next new method goes here 1234567890 ");` is the text that differs and is present in the locally modified file.
- `=======` denotes the end of the section of text that differs in the locally modified file.
- `>>>>>>> 1.9` denotes the end of the section of text that differs in the remote repository file.

If there were multiple consecutive lines of code, they would appear between the section delimiters. If lines of code differ in multiple sections of the file, these delimiters appear in each location of conflict. This allows you to review the conflicting code and attempt to choose which line you want to include in the file prior to committing it. The NetBeans CVS module also provides a Resolve Conflicts tool that attempts to help you in this process, as discussed in the next section.

Resolving Conflicts

When a filename shows up in red in the Projects window, as described in the previous section, right-click the filename and select CVS ➤ Resolve Conflicts. The Resolve Conflicts tool opens, as shown in Figure 6-12. This tool makes it very convenient to edit files that have conflicts. It takes out some of the guesswork in reading the CVS merge text that was inserted into the file. It also allows you to see a side-by-side comparison of the changes.

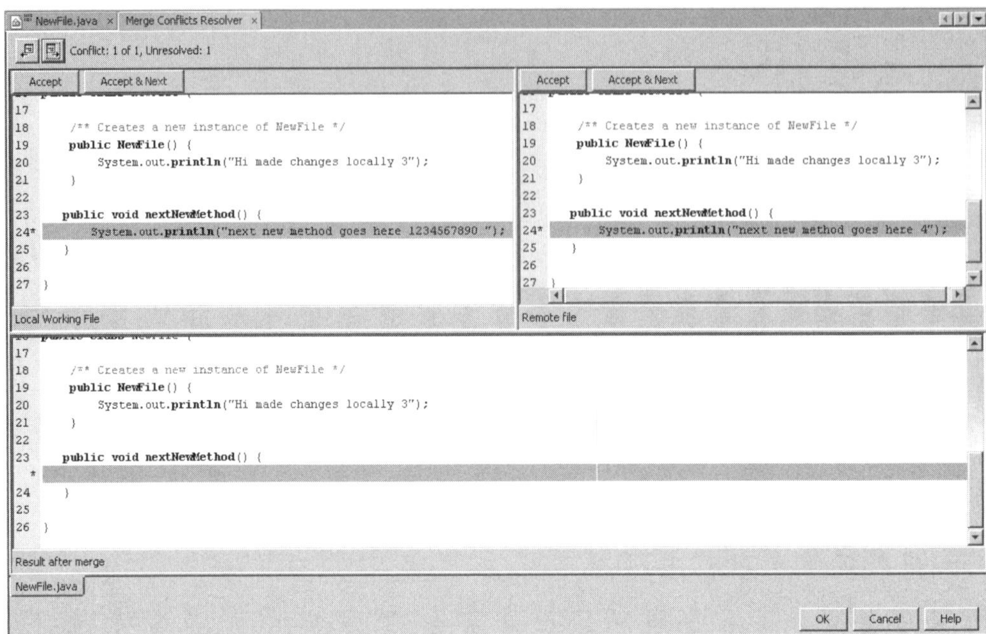

Figure 6-12. *The Resolve Conflicts tool*

It may not be easy to see all the text in Figure 6-12, since it is a wide screenshot, but I wanted to show the general screen layout. The top-left section shows the locally modified file, with each conflict highlighted. The top-right section shows the CVS repository version (remote file). Each conflict is highlighted. The lower half of the window shows the results that occur after the merge operation. In either the top-left or top-right pane, you can review and accept each conflicting line, one at a time. If you decide to accept the locally modified file's changes, click the Accept or Accept & Next button in the top-left pane. If you want to accept the changes from the remote file, use the buttons in the top-right pane.

When you are finished accepting changes, click the OK button at the bottom of the window. The CVS merge text will be removed from the file. If you accepted any changes from the locally modified file, you still need to commit the file before the changes are saved into the repository.

You may also encounter conflicts when you attempt to commit changes to a file that was modified by another user. If you run a commit operation before an update operation, you may receive a warning such as this:

```
cvs commit: Up-to-date check failed for `NewFile.java'
cvs [commit aborted]: correct above errors first!
```

This message means you need to run an update operation. After you do so, the NetBeans CVS tool should warn you that conflicts were created between the local and repository versions. After you resolve the conflicts, you will be able to commit the changes to the file.

Reverting Modifications

When programming, you probably frequently write some code and then immediately want to undo what you changed. Whether it is incorrect code or you were just experimenting with some new algorithms, you need to be able to roll back one or more code changes. The NetBeans CVS tool allows you to do so.

If you have locally modified a file and need to undo the changes, right-click and select CVS ➤ Revert Modifications. You will receive a Yes/No prompt asking if you want to overwrite your locally selected files with the current versions from the repository. If you click Yes, the changes to your code are undone, and the file should match the latest version of code stored in the CVS repository. You can also use the Revert Modifications option at the package or project level. Right-click a specific package or project and select CVS ➤ Revert Modifications.

Comparing Differences

One of the most important features of any CVS tool is the ability to compare the differences between two files. When you make changes to a local file, you may need to compare it against the remote version stored in the repository. This is useful if you modify a file and forget to commit it for a period of time. If you later come back to the file and need to know what changed, you can easily check it against the repository version. For this, you can use the Diff tool, which is one of my favorite NetBeans features.

To compare differences in locally modified files, right-click the file or files and select CVS ➤ Diff. The Diff window opens, as shown in Figure 6-13.

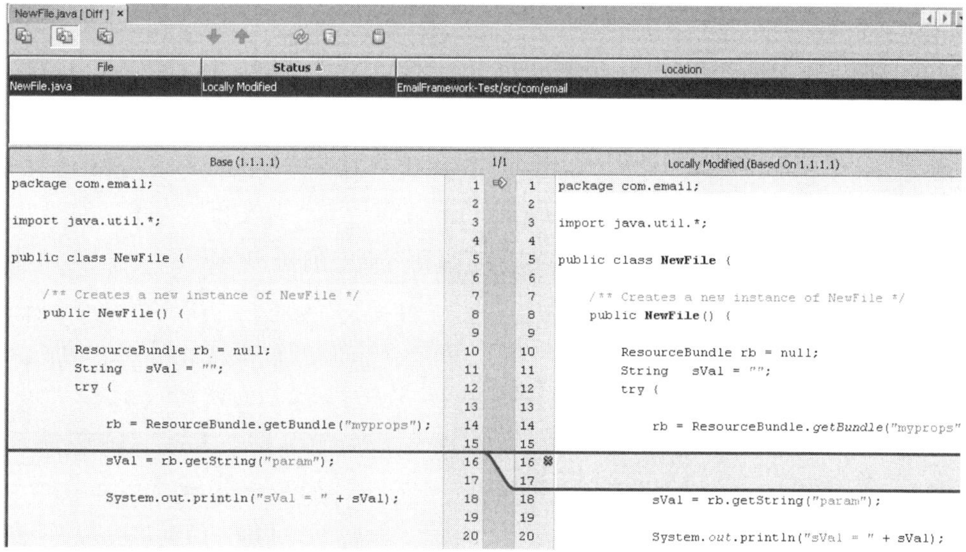

Figure 6-13. *The Diff window*

The Diff tool was significantly reworked in NetBeans 6 and is explained in more detail in the "Working with the Local History" section later in this chapter. This feature serves for version control system (VCS) file comparisons as well as local history file comparisons. When you use it for a VCS file comparison, you'll see the VCS toolbar displayed along the top.

Note that changes to the files are highlighted line by line. Different lines are highlighted in different colors. Typically, green lines were added, blue lines were modified, and red lines were removed. However, it has been my experience that the CVS color-coding in Diff tools is not an exact science and sometimes appears incorrectly.

In the Diff tool, you can use the up and down arrow icons along the top to navigate the differences between the files. You can also use the toolbar icons either to update the local file or to commit it.

To compare differences in multiple files or the entire project, select CVS ➤ Diff. In this case the top pane of the Diff window will include the selected files and display their status and location. Choosing a file from the list will open the file's difference comparison in the bottom pane of the window.

Searching History

One of the nice features of the NetBeans CVS tool is the ability to search the history of files in the repository. Using the Search History tool, you can query versions of files for several parameters and perform a variety of important operations.

To search the history of an individual file, package, or project, right-click the element and select CVS ➤ Search History. If you are searching an individual file, the Search History tool automatically queries the repository and displays all the versions of that file. If you are searching multiple files at the package or project level, the Search History tool will open but not display results. You will need to enter search terms manually or just click the Search button to execute the search without any filtering parameters. Figure 6-14 shows the results of searching on the `com.email` package without any filtering parameters.

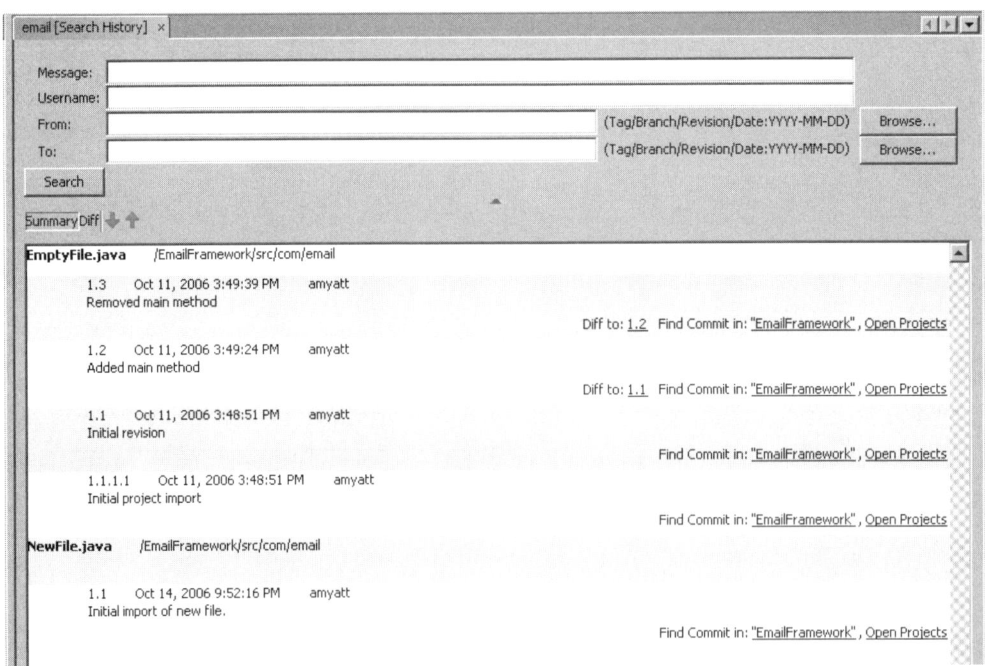

Figure 6-14. *The CVS history for the com.email package*

You can use the fields at the top of the Search History window to filter the search results.

- The "Message" field allows you to query the commit messages that were saved for each file in the range you are searching (package, project, and so on).
- The "Username" field allows you to query for all the versions that were added by a specific user in the CVS repository.
- The "From" and "To" fields allow you to query by revision date, branch, and tag.

These search filters are very useful if you are looking for a specific version of a file that might have dozens or hundreds of versions.

Each file and version that matches the filter parameters is displayed in the search results pane in the lower half of the Search History window. Versions are grouped under a file heading, and the version number and date, username, and commit message are listed.

For each version, several convenient links are listed on the right side of each row. The first link, Diff to *#.#*, allows you to perform a diff operation on the current version of the file against the previous version. This feature can help you understand what historic changes to a file took place over time. This is frequently used if something breaks in your application and you need to go back and see where it broke and who broke it. The other two links are for the Find Commit In feature. Clicking the first link allows you to query the current project for any files that were committed at the same time as the file you selected. Clicking the second link for Open Projects allows you to query all open projects in their respective CVS repositories for any files that were committed at the same time. This makes it easier to identify the 5, 10, or 200 files that were all committed simultaneously as a batch.

Right-clicking a version row in the Search History window opens a context menu with more options. For example, if you right-clicked the row for version 1.3 in the example shown in Figure 6-14, you would see the following options:

Diff to 1.2: Runs a diff operation between versions 1.3 and 1.2.

Rollback Changes: Runs an update operation based on the previous version's code.

Rollback to 1.3: Overwrites the local file with the specified version.

View 1.3: Downloads and opens the specified version in the Source Editor.

Find Commit in "Email-Framework": Finds matching committed files in the project.

Find Commit in Open Projects: Finds matching committed files in all open projects.

The one feature that may not be obvious is the ability to perform diff operations on nonsequential versions. Select a file in the Search History window and click the small Diff button next to the Search button. The selected file appears in the Search History window as a single node that you can expand to see individual versions. The difference is that you can use the multiple-item select key (the Ctrl key in Windows) to select two rows. The differences between the files appear in the two panes below the list. Figure 6-15 shows an example of comparing the local copy with version 1.1 of the `NewFile` class. You can use this tool to select and compare any two versions of a file.

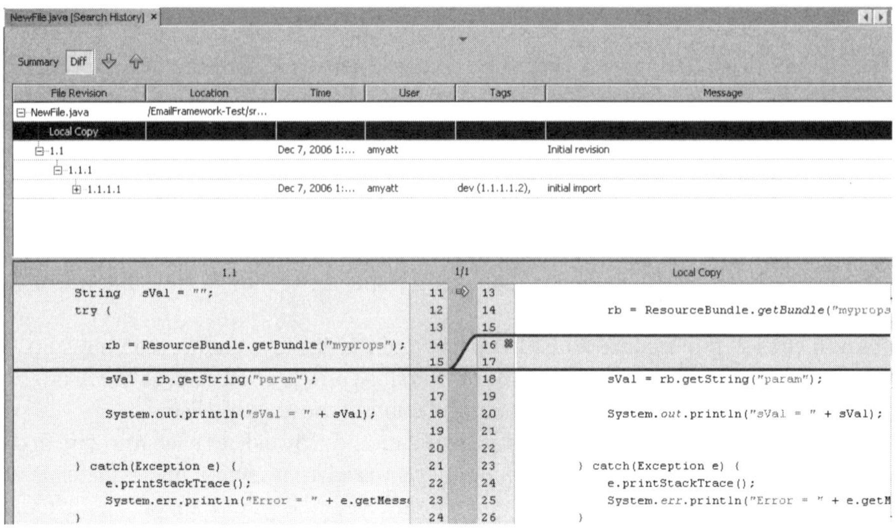

Figure 6-15. *Seeing differences in two nonsequential versions*

Adding Annotations

The Annotation tool is simple but powerful. It displays two important pieces of information on a line-by-line basis directly in the Source Editor window: the version number when the line was last modified and the username of who made that modification.

To view annotations, select a file in the Source Editor or the Projects window and select CVS ➤ Show "*File.java*" Annotations. In the example shown in Figure 6-16, the source file contains numerous modifications, ranging from version 1.1 to 1.18. Being able to view these annotations can quickly help you understand when changes were made and who made them. This is much faster than reviewing each version of a file manually or performing numerous diff operations between the different versions.

```
NewFile.java

1.17 amyatt   package com.email;
1.1 amyatt
1.1 amyatt
1.1 amyatt    public class NewFile {
1.1 amyatt
1.1 amyatt        /** Creates a new instance of NewFile */
1.1 amyatt        public NewFile() {
1.12 amyatt           System.out.println("Hi made changes locally 3");
1.18 amyatt
1.18 amyatt
1.1 amyatt        }
1.1 amyatt
1.5 amyatt       public void nextNewMethod() {
1.16 amyatt          System.out.println("next new method goes here 4");
1.5 amyatt       }
1.3 amyatt
1.1 amyatt    }
```

Figure 6-16. *The CVS annotations for a source file*

To turn off the display of annotations, select CVS ➤ Hide Annotations.

Using Subversion

Subversion is rapidly becoming a popular version control system. CVS is probably still the leader as far as number of users, but Subversion is rapidly gaining ground. It was built in an attempt to replace CVS and improve on its functionality. For a tutorial on Subversion features and how it differs from CVS, refer to the Subversion web site at `http://subversion.tigris.org`.

Installing Subversion

In NetBeans 6, the Subversion module became a standard part of the IDE. There is no longer a need to download and install it. Unlike with the CVS module, this is only half the battle.

You also need to install the actual Subversion client on your machine. You can download the Subversion software by visiting the Subversion web site at `http://subversion.tigris.org`. On the Subversion site is a section on the main menu titled Documents and Files. This contains several How-To documents that describe the installation steps, Subversion best practices, and also a CVS-to-Subversion Crossover Guide.

■ **Note** For those of you on a Windows platform, the installation of the Subversion software is quite easy. Just click the Next button about seven or eight times. The Subversion installer takes care of the rest.

Once you have installed the Subversion client and the NetBeans Subversion module, you are ready to begin working with Subversion repositories.

Performing Common Subversion Operations

Many of the version control features for CVS and Subversion are nearly identical in NetBeans. The Update, Commit, Diff, and Search History tools function the same, have the same look and feel, and contain the same information. Here we'll cover some of the areas where the two version control tools differ.

Checking Out Code

When you choose Versioning ➤ Subversion ➤ Checkout, the Subversion Checkout wizard starts. The first step to check out code is to specify the protocol. The Subversion module allows you to check out code using several protocols: File, HTTP, HTTPS, SVN, and SVN+SSH.

To check out the Subversion project code, use the URL `http://svn.collab.net/repos/svn/trunk`, as shown in Figure 6-17. After you enter the URL, you can optionally either enter a username or password if you have one assigned or leave the fields blank for anonymous access. Click the Next button to move to the Folders to Checkout window.

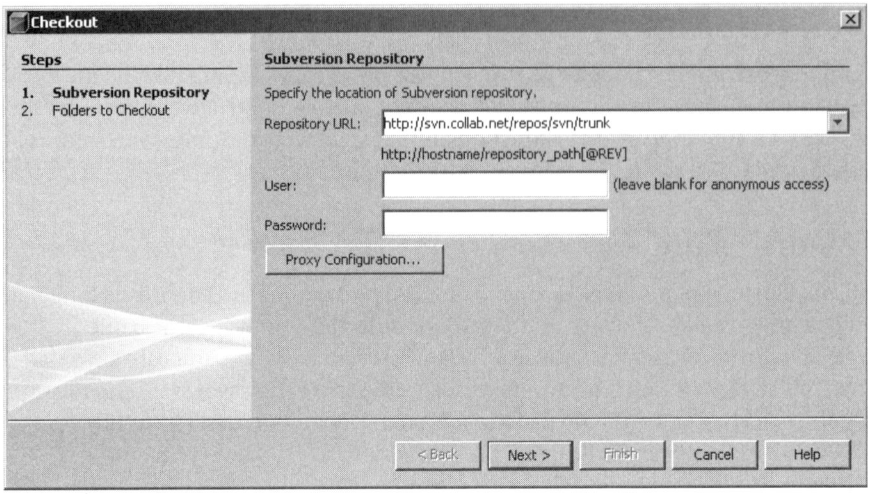

Figure 6-17. *Checking out a Subversion project*

In the Folders to Checkout window, specify the repository folder. You can enter the folder name manually in the "Repository Folder" field or click the Browse button to connect to the repository and browse the available options. You can also select the revision and the local folder for which to check out the code. Once you complete the fields, click the Finish button.

The Subversion module connects to the repository and attempts to download the code. In the Output window, you will see Subversion logging such as the following:

```
co -r HEAD http://svn.collab.net/repos/svn/trunk@HEAD
D:\projects\trunk --non-interactive --config-dir
C:\Documents and Settings\adam\.netbeans\5.5rc2\config\svn\config

U    D:\projects\trunk\www\project_license.html
...
U    D:\projects\trunk\subversion\libsvn_client\compat_providers.c

Checked out revision 22009.

==[IDE]== May 29, 2007 7:11:35 PM Checking out... finished.
```

The first few lines of the output show the Subversion statements that have run, then the downloading of individual files is indicated, and finally some summary information appears.

Once the code has finished downloading, if it contains NetBeans project metadata, the tool attempts to open the project. Otherwise, you will see a dialog box that asks if you want to create a new project. If you click the Create Project button, the New Project wizard appears and prompts you through its steps.

Working with Branches

One of the features that differs between Subversion and CVS is working with branches. In the Subversion module, you can create a branch, or copy, of a file, folder, or entire project and place it in your repository. The previous commit messages and history for the copied file are linked to the original. You can then later merge changes between these branches if necessary.

In the NetBeans Subversion module, you can copy a file by right-clicking the name and selecting Subversion ➤ Create Copy. The Copy dialog box appears, as shown in Figure 6-18. There you can select the destination folder in the repository for the copy of the file or files, or you can click the Browse button to view the existing tags and branches and choose where to copy the file. If you are branching an entire project, you can create a new folder under the branches node. You can also enter a description in the "Copy Description" text box. This description will be attached to the copy of the file. When you have the fields set correctly, click the Copy button.

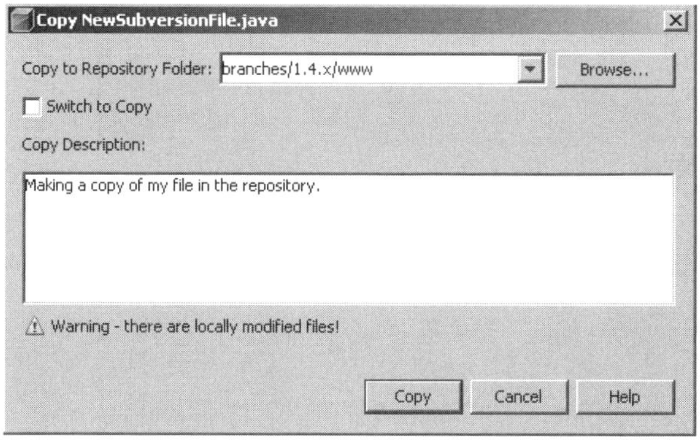

Figure 6-18. *The Subversion Copy dialog box*

You can also choose to switch the local working copy of a file or project to a specific branch or tag. Right-click the item to which you wish to switch and select Subversion ➤ Switch to Copy. The Switch dialog box opens, as shown in Figure 6-19. There you select to which branch or revision you want to switch. Once the switch is complete, you can edit and make changes to the file locally. The changes to the file occur to the branch to which you switched, not to the original file.

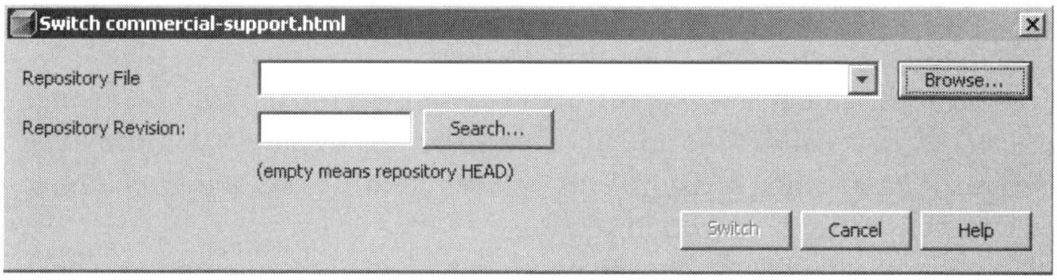

Figure 6-19. *The Subversion Switch dialog box*

Merging Changes

One of the other differences between the CVS and Subversion modules is the Merge Changes tool. This Subversion tool allows you to merge changes made in one or two different repository revisions and pull them into your local working code.

To merge changes, right-click a file and choose Subversion ➤ Merge Changes from Branch. If you select One Repository Folder from the "Merge From" drop-down list, you will see the fields in Figure 6-20. You must fill in the "Repository File" field or use the Browse button to query the repository and choose an item. You must also set the "Starting Revision" and "Ending Revision" fields. The Search button next to each field lets you query the repository and pick a revision from a list.

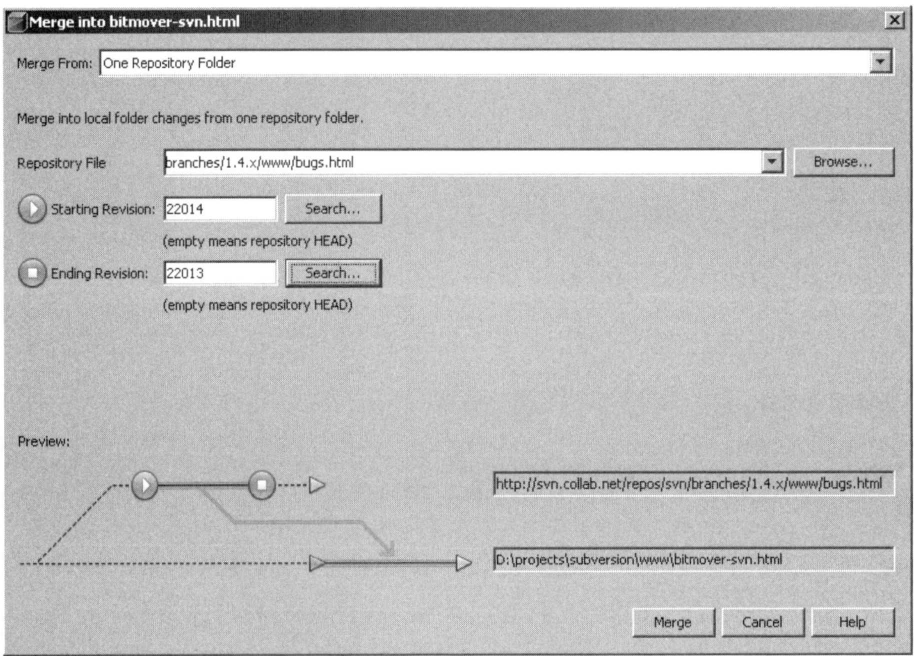

Figure 6-20. *The Subversion Merge into dialog box*

When you are ready, click the Merge button. The Subversion tool grabs the changes from the specified revision or revisions and merges them into your local working code. If merge conflicts occur, you must follow the standard version control process of resolving conflicts, as discussed earlier in this chapter.

If you specify a Merge From value of Two Repository Folders, then the fields to set change slightly. First you must specify a repository file and matching starting revision. Then you must pick a separate repository file and ending revision. This process allows you to merge changes from two separate revisions into your local working code.

If you specify a Merge From value of One Repository Folder Since Its Origin, only two fields need to be set: "Repository File" and "Ending Revision." This allows you to merge changes in a local working file since it was first created until the ending revision that you specify.

Using Local History

The Local History tool is new in NetBeans 6. Several other Java IDEs contain this type of feature. Previous versions of NetBeans lacked a local history, which has long been a sticking point mentioned during the Java IDE wars that take place online. I'm personally very glad that it was added in NetBeans 6, since it is a very useful feature.

A Local History tool is quite similar to a VCS, such as CVS or Subversion. It serves as a local repository of file versions as each change is made and saved to a file. It allows a programmer to recover content that was removed, discover content that was added, or identify content that changed, using an easy-to-understand Diff comparison. This type of tool is extremely useful to have since it helps you recover code that may have been deleted but not committed to your VCS. The NetBeans Undo feature can usually catch code deletions, but only up to a certain point (and not at all if you closed NetBeans).

Configuring Local History Properties

NetBeans allows you to configure several properties related to the Local History tool. To access the properties, navigate to Tools ➤ Options. In the Basic Options window, select the Miscellaneous icon to display a list of tabs. Select the Versioning tab, and you will see a list of versioning systems displayed on the left side of the tab.

If you select Local History from the list of versioning systems, the Local History settings will be displayed in the center of the tab, as shown in Figure 6-21.The "Keep Local History Files for" field allows you to specify the number of days that local versions of files are saved. The default value for the field is 7, but you may want to set this much higher.

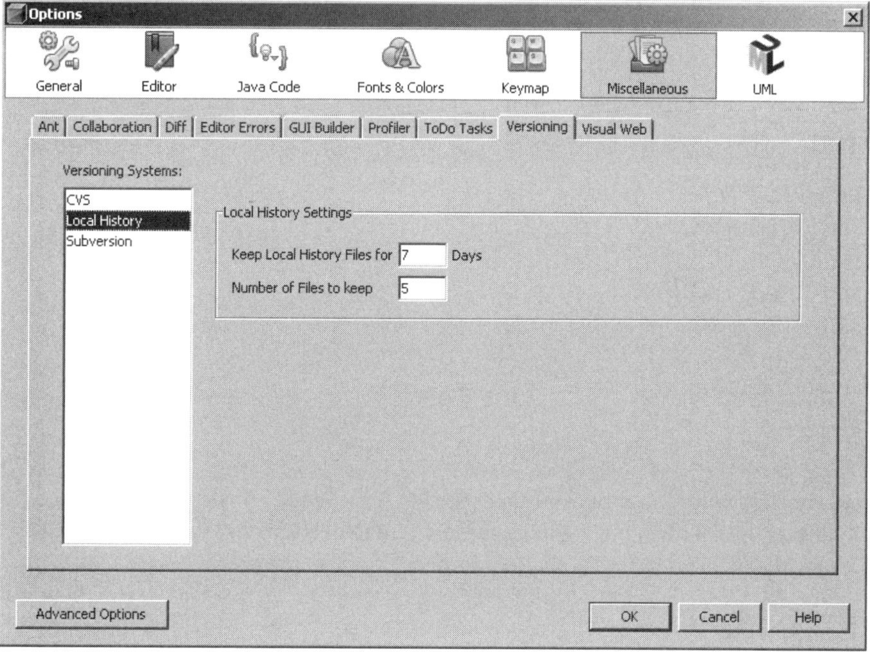

Figure 6-21. *The Local History properties*

I often write code, only to change it quickly for something I believe to be better. If I commit this modified file, then I have that code stored in my VCS, but the original version is lost. It may very well have been code I should not have committed to a VCS, but there may have been an interesting algorithm or idea expressed in it. If the "Keep Local History Files for" field is set too low, I could lose that code. You might ask why I don't just commit the original version of code. In many professional software shops, you can't commit code to a VCS unless it compiles and doesn't break the build.

The second field, named "Number of Files to Keep," specifies the number of files the Local History tool persists.

Working with the Local History

To demonstrate the capabilities of the Local History tool, create a new Java class in any project. Navigate to File ➤ New File and generate a new Java class. For this example I'll start with the following source file:

```
package com.pronetbeans.examples;

/**
 * @author Adam Myatt
 */
public class Calculate {

    public Calculate() {
    }

    public int checkNum(int origVal) {

        int returnVal = 0;

        if (origVal > 10) {
            returnVal = origVal - 1;
        } else {
            returnVal = origVal + 1;
        }

        return returnVal;
    }
}
```

The `Calculate` class contains a method `checkNum`. If I remove the constructor and add a `main` method, such as the following, I will have some original, deleted, and new content to display in the file's local history:

```
public static void main(String[] args) {
    System.out.println("Hello Calculator");
}
```

You can view the local history for a file by right-clicking its name in the Projects or Files window and selecting Local History ➤ Show Local History. A new tabbed window will open in the Source Editor, with the name `File.java [Local History]`, where `File.java` is the name of the file you selected. For the `Calculate` class, the tab would read `Calculate.java [Local`

History]. The Show History window displays information in two main sections: the version history on the top and file comparisons (Diff) on the bottom, as shown in Figure 6-22.

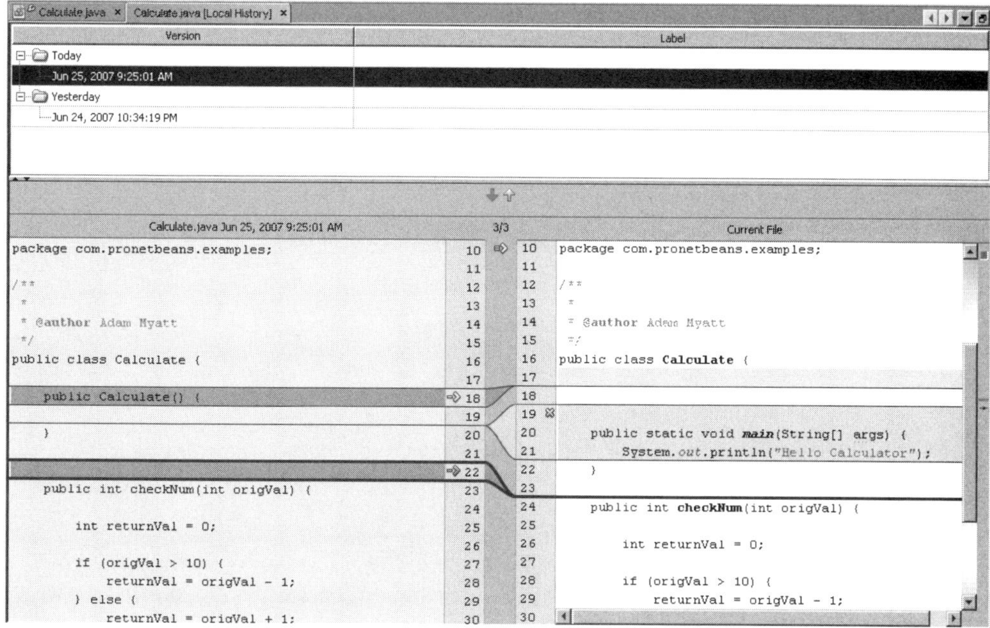

Figure 6-22. *The local history for the Calculate.java source file*

In Figure 6-22 the local history for `Calculate.java` shows two versions. The first version, listed at the bottom of the list, was the default class when I initially created the file. It contained only a class and a constructor. The second version, which appears at the top of the list, contained a default constructor and the `checkNum` method. The important thing to note is that the topmost version is not the current version of the file; it is only the most recent version prior to the current file. Figure 6-22 shows the Current File pane on the right side of the window. It contains the most current content of the file.

If the `Calculate.java` file were modified in any way, a new version would appear in the versioning pane at the top of the window. Using this tool, you can now perform an intelligent Diff between the current file content and any previous version.

Closely examine the code highlighting and lines that connect the version in the left pane and the current file in the right pane. In the left pane in Figure 6-22, line 18 is highlighted pink, indicating it has been removed. The coloring scheme here is nearly identical to that of a CVS or Subversion Diff. You should also be able to see the small arrow icon next to line 18 in the left pane. If you mouse over this arrow, the pop-up tooltip will display "Insert." If you click the arrow, the highlighted text in the left pane will be added back into the current file automatically. The line in the left pane will no longer be highlighted, since the Local History Diff tool no longer sees a difference between the two files for this line.

One of the nicest features about this Diff window is the ability to edit code right in the Current File window. The source code displayed is no different than a normal source file tab in the Source Editor. You can perform code editing, debugging, refactoring, etc. As you change each line of code, you can watch the Diff highlighting change.

Labeling Versions

As previously mentioned, the top pane of the Local History tool contains the list of versions for a file. Notice that the list of versions has two columns: the Version column and the Label column. The label column allows you to make short notes about specific local versions of a Java source file, as shown in Figure 6-23.

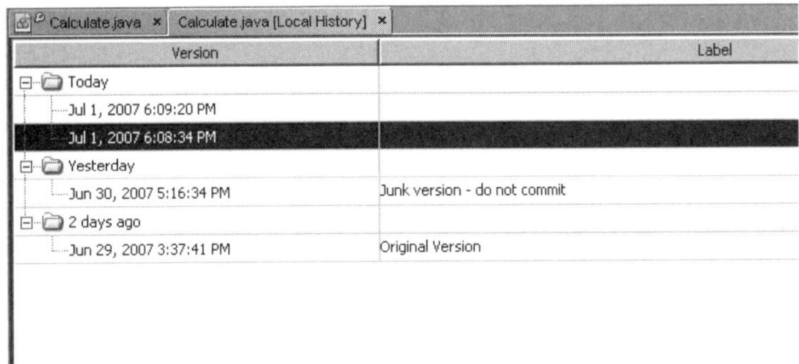

Figure 6-23. *The local history versions and labels pane*

To add a label to a version, simply click anywhere in the label column on the same line as a listed version and type some text. After you enter the text, click out of the box to save it. Labeling versions of files can prove useful if you are trying to remember the content of a specific version. This is nice if you want to make several recoverable versions of a file without committing them to a remote VCS. The labels can help you identify the different versions.

Deleting Versions

Individual versions from the list of versions in the top pane of the Local History tool can be deleted. To delete a specific version, right-click a version from the list and select Delete from History on the context menu. The version is immediately removed from the list and cannot be recovered.

This feature is particularly useful if you have rapidly created a number of versions and want to remove the unnecessary ones from the list.

Reverting to Versions

The Local History tool also allows you to revert the current file back to a previous version. This may be necessary if you want to roll back a number of changes.

The earlier discussion of the Diff tool explains how to insert content or changes from a previous version into the current file. If you want to revert the current file completely back to a previous version, you should not have to use the Diff tool and manually update the content. The "Revert to" feature allows you to switch version content instantly.

To revert back to a previous version, right-click a Java source file in the Projects window and select Local History ➤ Revert to. This will open the "Revert to" window, as shown in Figure 6-24. Once there, select a version and click the Revert button. This will revert the current file's content back to the selected version. You can also revert back to a previous version using the list of versions in the top pane of the Local History window. You can right-click any version in the version list and select Revert from History.

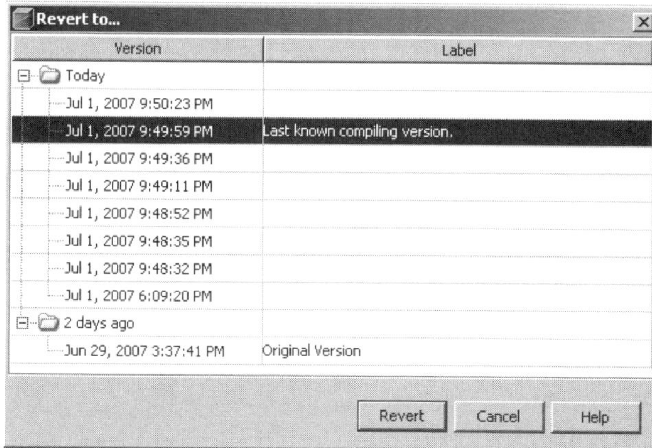

Figure 6-24. *The Local History "Revert to" window*

Summary

This chapter covered one of the core practices of software development: storing code in a source repository. It gave a brief crash course in version control and how to perform specific operations using a version control module in NetBeans. There are many additional operations that we did not cover. I encourage you to experiment with the version control module of your choice to understand all of its features fully.

Regardless of which version control software you use (CVS, Subversion, or another system), NetBeans tries to provide a standard user interface. As discussed in this chapter, many operations, such as update, commit, diff, search history, and show annotations, behave similarly. The important thing to remember is how to perform the core operations that allow you to store and retrieve your code.

One of the new features of NetBeans 6 is the Local History tool. This allows you to see changes to your Java source files without having to store them in a VCS. You can use the Local History tool to view, compare, delete, and revert to previous versions of files. You can also use the new Diff tool to compare versions of files and add, update, or remove content from the current version of the file.

CHAPTER 7

Generating and Accessing Javadoc

One of the most important aspects of writing code is documentation. Project documentation should not only cover system design, architecture, and logic, but also include details on how each class and method functions. The Java platform provides a very useful documentation tool called *Javadoc*.

The Javadoc tool scans source code and extracts special types of comments to create a bundle of HTML files. These files are linked together in a cross-referenced documentation web site commonly referred to by programmers as *Javadoc* or the *project Javadoc*. Developers traditionally generate this Javadoc bundle and store it with the rest of their project documentation.

Future project developers can then use the Javadoc as a quick reference for the functionality of the code. It is also useful to project architects and project managers who want a handle on what code does without having to read through the actual source.

This chapter describes the NetBeans features for creating and working with Javadoc.

Elements of Javadoc

Adding Javadoc comments to source code is extremely simple. You can use a variety of special documentation elements, or tags, that the Javadoc tool will recognize as having special meaning. During the generation of the HTML files, these special elements are formatted and marked for each Java member for which they are provided.

The following sections provide a quick overview of the main elements used in writing Javadoc. This is not a complete list, of course, but covers the elements you will probably use most often.

Class Description

The first Javadoc element that should be written for a class is the overall class description. The first sentence of this description should be as brief and direct as possible. The Javadoc tool will insert the first sentence from the class description into the index page for each package that lists the classes it contains.

The entire class description can be as brief or detailed as you feel is necessary. There are no rules or best practices regarding the length of class descriptions. You should attempt to describe the overall purpose and function of the class. Some programmers provide sample usage code in the class description that can serve as a type of user manual. Here is an example of a class description in Javadoc:

```
package com.pronetbeans.chapters;

/**
* Utility class for representing static constant color values.
* The color constants used in this class are string representations
* of HTML color codes.
*/
public class ColorConstants {
    // code for class here
}
```

Notice that the first line starts with the characters `/**`. This is how you flag a comment as a Javadoc comment and not just as a regular comment. The last line ends with the characters `*/`. The asterisks in between are optional as of Java 1.4, but they are usually added to provide a consistent visual flow.

Class Tags

The following are some class tags commonly used in Javadoc:

`@author`: Specifies who wrote the class. Multiple `@author` tags are allowed. The text for the author of a class can be just a name or can include an email address, web site URL, or other contact information. You can format the information that is displayed using the HTML `<br>` tag.

`@version`: Specifies the version of the class. Certain source code repositories allow you to use wildcard variables in this field, so when the code is checked out, the actual version and date can be inserted in place of the wildcard variables.

`@since`: Specifies the version of the code in which this class was added. This can be useful if you are writing an actual API that other programmers will use. As your API evolves over time, it is important to note in which version a specific class was added.

`@see`: Allows you to include a reference to an element in the class or another Java class or package. You can link directly to a specific method or to a section in the Javadoc.

■ **Note** By default, NetBeans does not include the `@author` and `@version` tags during the generation of a project's Javadoc. To include the tags, you need to edit the properties of a project, as described later, in the section "Configuring Project Javadoc Settings."

The following shows the class tags added to the sample Javadoc in the previous section:

```
package com.pronetbeans.chapters;

/**
* Utility class for representing static constant color values.
* The color constants used in this class are string representations
* of HTML color codes.
*
* @author John Doe<br>john.doe@somesite.com<br>John Doe Consulting
* @author Jane Doe
* @version 1.45
* @since 2.1.0
* @see com.pronetbeans.chapters
*/
public class ColorConstants {
    // code for class here
}
```

Class Member Variables

Each member variable defined in a class should have a matching Javadoc statement. Public member variables usually represent some type of constant and thus should have a full description explaining how to use them. The following shows the `ColorConstants` class in an abbreviated form. Notice that each member variable has a description.

```
public class ColorConstants {

    /** The HTML code for the color blue. */
    public static final String BLUE = "#0000FF";

    /** The HTML code for the color red. */
    public static final String RED = "#FF0000";

}
```

Constructors

Javadoc descriptions can also be added for constructors. For constructors that have parameters, the description should include what effect the parameters might have on the state of the object as it is instantiated.

If a constructor has a parameter, you can use the `@param` Javadoc tag to describe it. The `@param` tag should be followed by a space, the name of the parameter, another space, and the description of the parameter, as in this example:

```
public class ColorConstants {

    /** Default constructor */
    public ColorContstants() {

    }

    /** This constructor allows the debug mode to be enabled or disabled.
    *
    * @param debug true if logging should be enabled, false otherwise.
    */
    public ColorConstants(boolean debug) {
        // do something with the debug variable
    }
}
```

Methods

Javadoc for class methods is probably the most common type of documentation you will write as a programmer. A method has a description, just like a class, a member variable, and a constructor. The first sentence of the description is listed in the method summary section.

Method Javadoc can also include tags for the method parameters, method return type, and any exceptions that the method may throw, as follows:

`@param`: Describes a method's parameter. The `@param` tag should be followed by a space, the name of the parameter, another space, and the description of the parameter. If there are multiple parameters in a method definition, use multiple `@param` tags.

`@return`: Documents the return type of a method. The `@return` tag specifies the description of the parameter being returned to the calling code. A method can have only one return parameter, so only one `@return` tag is valid. Methods with a return type of `void` do not need a `@return` tag.

`@throws`: Describes an exception thrown by a method. You must use one `@throws` tag per exception. This lets programmers know what type of exceptions to expect to have to handle in their code.

Here is an example of Javadoc for a method:

```
public class ColorConstants {

    /**
    * Retrieve a list of all color code constants.
    *
    * @param filter A filter value to retrieve color codes that match.
    * @return An ArrayList of the color code values.
```

```
    * @throws NullPointerException If the filter parameter is null.
    */
    public ArrayList listColorCodes(String filter)
        throws NullPointerException, NumberFormatException {

        // do something

    }
}
```

Creating Javadoc in NetBeans

In NetBeans, you can write Javadoc directly in a source file in the Source Editor window. One of the nice features that the editor provides is the ability for Javadoc comments to utilize code folding. Sections of Javadoc can be collapsed and expanded for ease of viewing.

■ **Tip** Javadoc for certain classes can be quite long. Sometimes when you are developing, it can visually get in your way. You can fix this with the menu option View ➤ Code Folds ➤ Collapse All Javadoc. You can also set Javadoc to be collapsed by default by choosing Tools ➤ Options ➤ Editor and selecting the Javadoc Comments field.

Configuring Javadoc Hint Settings

Beginning with NetBeans 6, the Source Editor contains a set of hints for creating and correcting Javadoc. You can configure some basic properties of this functionality in the NetBeans Options window.

To configure the Javadoc Hint Settings, navigate to Tools ➤ Options. In the Basic Options window, click the Java Code icon in the top of the window and select the Hints tab that appears. The Hints tab contains areas for enabling or disabling specific types of hints in Java code.

The Hints tab allows you to activate a hint for creating Javadoc and for errors in Javadoc, as shown in Figure 7-1. If you click the node labeled "Create Javadoc," the Options panel in the upper right of the tab will activate and allow you to choose a value from the "Show As" drop-down list. The possible values you can select are Error, Warning, and Warning on Current Line.

These values affect how inline code hints are displayed in the Source Editor for a Java file. If Javadoc does not exist for one or more elements of a Java file, then NetBeans will prompt you to do so using the status notifications mentioned earlier.

Set the Create Javadoc hint to show as an error. This denotes a hint that checks for a complete lack of Javadoc for one or more elements in a Java source file. If a Java source file is open in the Source Editor, then each class name, member variable, constructor, and method that has no Javadoc will be highlighted red as an error, as shown in Figure 7-2.

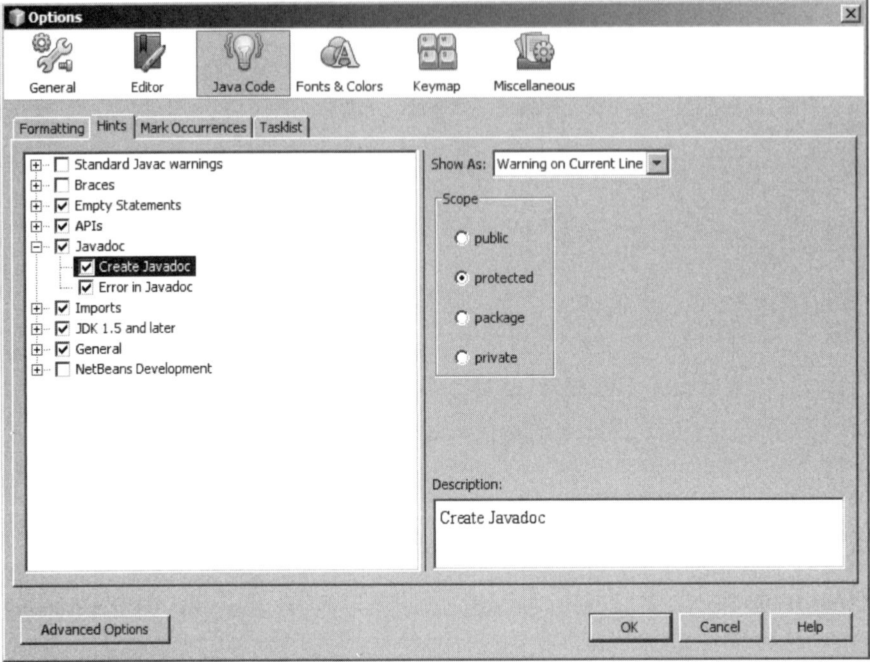

Figure 7-1. *The Javadoc Hints properties in the Basic Options window*

```
package com.pronetbeans.examples;

public class Main {


    public static void main(String[] args) {

        int x = 0;

        for (int i = 0; i < args.length; i++)
        {
            if(i>0) {
                System.out.println("TEST");
            }
        }
    }
}
```

Figure 7-2. *Missing Javadoc highlighted as an error*

Once the hints appear in the gutter, you can click each one to generate the appropriate Javadoc comments. When you click the hint lightbulb in the gutter, a single pop-up option will ask you to “Create missing Javadoc for <element-name>.” Clicking it will generate the skeleton Javadoc for the element.

You can also set the Create Javadoc hint to show as a warning instead of as an error. This denotes a hint that checks for a complete lack of Javadoc for one or more elements in a Java source file. If a Java source file is open in the Source Editor, then each class name, member variable, constructor, and method that has no Javadoc will be highlighted in the gutter as a warning-style lightbulb. You can then click each lightbulb to see the generate Javadoc prompt, as shown in Figure 7-3.

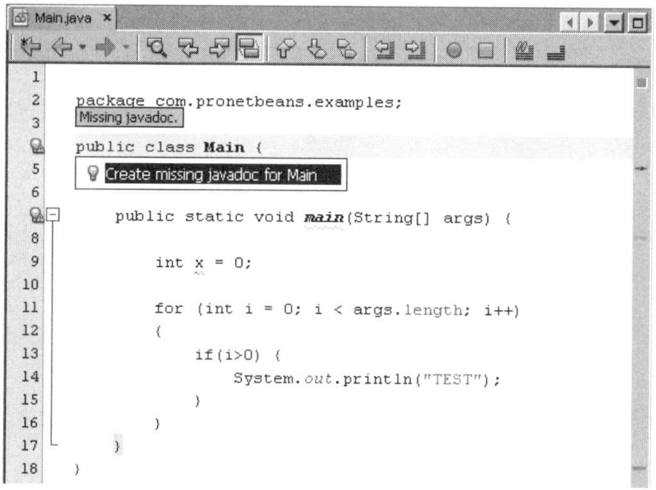
Main.java
package com.pronetbeans.examples;
Missing javadoc.
public class Main {
Create missing javadoc for Main
public static void main(String[] args) {
int x = 0;
for (int i = 0; i < args.length; i++)
{
if(i>0) {
System.out.println("TEST");
}
}
}
}

Figure 7-3. *Missing Javadoc highlighted as a warning*

Finally, you can also set the Create Javadoc hint to show as a warning on the current line. This is nearly the same as the previous two options, except the lightbulb warning icons will not display unless you click in the line for a specific element that is missing Javadoc. This is visually less invasive but not as thorough a warning system if you care about being notified of missing Javadoc in your code.

Configuring Project Javadoc Settings

Each Java-based project has a settings window you can use to configure Javadoc properties. With a Java project open in NetBeans, right-click the project and select Properties from the context menu. When the Project Properties window opens, click the Documenting node under the Build node. This will display the Javadoc properties for the project, as shown in Figure 7-4.

The first check box in the Javadoc Project Properties window is the "Include Private and Package Private Members" field. Selecting this field tells the Javadoc tool to include the Javadoc for all private and package private elements in the generated report. Typically these elements are not included, especially if you are writing a public API or code that others will use. By their very nature, private and package private elements shouldn't be used by others, so it is doubtful you would need to include them.

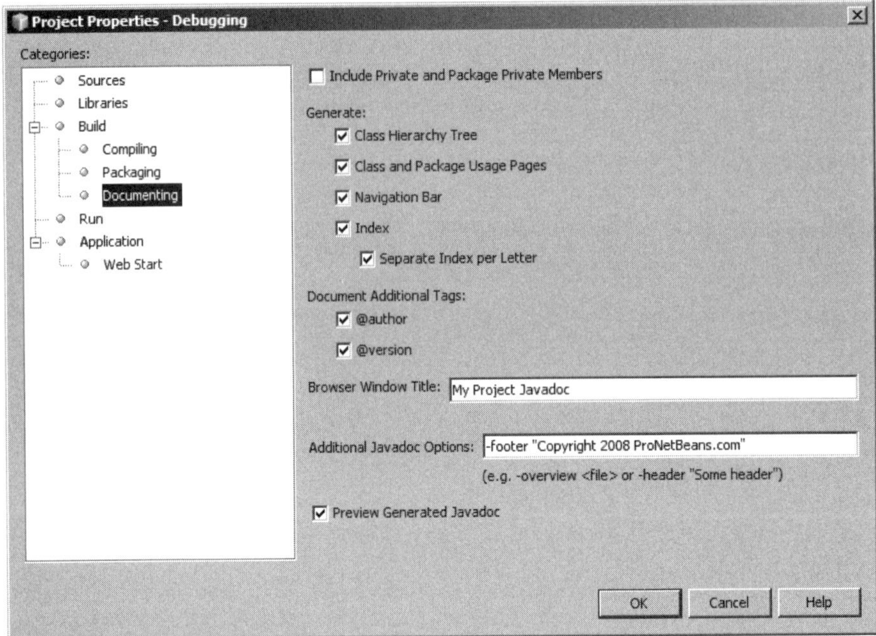

Figure 7-4. *Javadoc Project Properties window*

The next five check boxes under the Generate section are options that affect specific elements that appear in the generated report. They instruct the Javadoc tool as to what to include or exclude, such as a navigation bar, a complete index of Java elements, an alphabetized and separate index by letter, and various other pages.

Under the Document Additional Tags section are two check boxes: @author and @version. By default these are not selected, but they can easily be enabled for the project by selecting the check boxes.

The field "Browser Window Title" allows you to specify how the name of the generated Javadoc appears in the title bar of the web browser you use to view it. I typically enter the project name in this field, just to be thorough.

The field "Additional Javadoc Options" allows you to specify command-line arguments to the Javadoc tool. There are numerous additional settings you can use for which the NetBeans Project Properties window could not possibly contain fields. The "Additional Javadoc Options" field allows you to specify them, such as a header HTML file that includes a company logo or a footer with a copyright notice, as shown in Figure 7-4.

The final field is the "Preview Generated Javadoc" check box. It is selected by default and prompts NetBeans to open the default web browser and load the initial page for the generated Javadoc report. Once the report opens, you can see the affect of any additional command-line options you specified, such as a copyright notice, as shown in Figure 7-5.

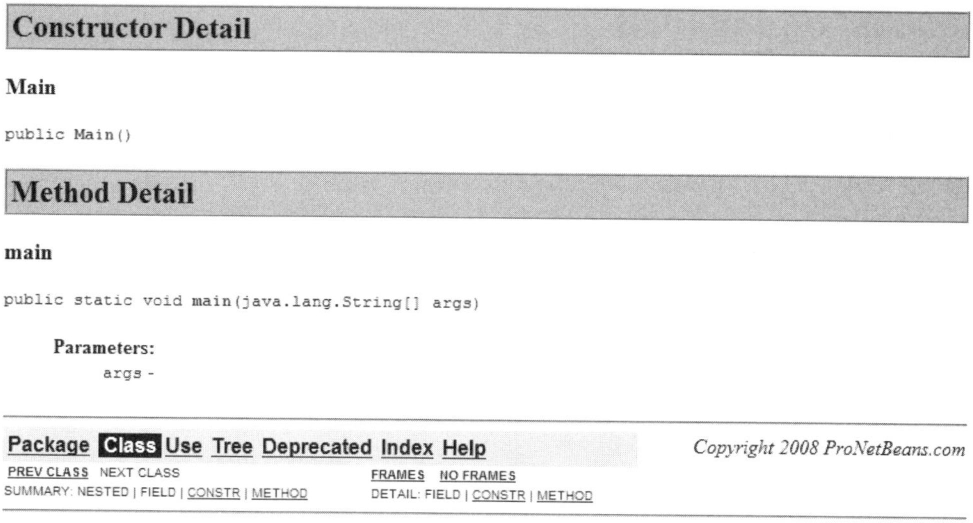

Constructor Detail

Main

```
public Main()
```

Method Detail

main

```
public static void main(java.lang.String[] args)
```

Parameters:
args -

Package Class Use Tree Deprecated Index Help
PREV CLASS NEXT CLASS
SUMMARY: NESTED | FIELD | CONSTR | METHOD
FRAMES NO FRAMES
DETAIL: FIELD | CONSTR | METHOD
Copyright 2008 ProNetBeans.com

Figure 7-5. *Javadoc report with copyright notice in footer*

Generating Project Javadoc

Once you have finished writing Javadoc comments in your source, you need to generate the HTML files. NetBeans makes this extremely easy to do. Simply select a project and choose Build ➤ Generate Javadoc for "*ProjectName*". You can also right-click a project in the Projects window and select Generate Javadoc for Project.

Once you have directed NetBeans to generate the files, the Output window appears, and you can watch the logging statements fly by as your project Javadoc is generated. After the process is complete, the project Javadoc homepage (typically `index.html`) should open in your Internet browser. If it does not open, then in the Files window, locate the `javadoc` directory in the `dist` directory and open the `index.html` file.

■ **Tip** The directory where the Javadoc is generated is typically `dist/javadoc`. While currently there is no setting to change this systemwide, you can set this individually for each project. Look in `nbproject/project.properties` for the `dist.javadoc.dir` property. You can set this to whatever you want, but I recommend leaving it as is unless you have a specific requirement to change it.

Accessing Javadoc

Along with tools for creating Javadoc for your projects, NetBeans provides several features to help you access existing Javadoc quickly and easily.

Attaching to Libraries and Platforms

If your project makes use of third-party libraries, you may want to consider attaching the associated Javadoc. Doing so allows you quick access to the documentation for that code and speeds up your development process.

Adding Libraries

NetBeans allows you to specify one or more JAR files as a library. Libraries are a good way to organize the third-party JAR files you want to use. You can define the binary class files that are executed, the matching source code, and the path to the Javadoc documentation.

To work with libraries, select Tools ➤ Libraries. In the Library Manager, you can add new libraries, remove libraries, or modify existing libraries. The window has three tabs for managing a library: Classpath, Sources, and Javadoc. Each tab allows you to add a reference to one or more JAR or zip files for the class files, source code, or Javadoc. If the Javadoc resides in a directory, you can add a reference to that directory using the Javadoc tab, as shown in Figure 7-6.

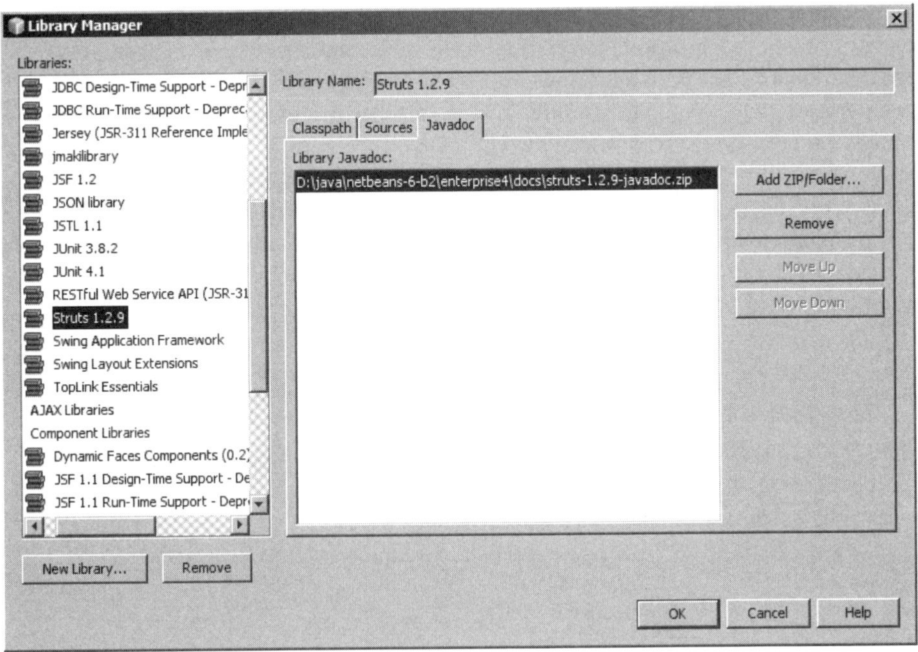

Figure 7-6. *The Javadoc tab in the Library Manager*

Adding Javadoc for Platforms

You can also add Javadoc for each Java platform that is defined in NetBeans. When you download and install a JDK, you should also make sure to download the source and the Javadoc. These can prove to be valuable resources, especially to novice programmers. Even pros can't remember every class and method usage in the entire Java platform. Having local access to the Javadoc for your JDK, as opposed to having to go online to look it up, can save valuable time.

In NetBeans, you can add the Javadoc to each platform by selecting Tools ➤ Java Platforms. In this window, you can view the default platform with which NetBeans is configured as well as any additional platforms you may have installed.

For each platform, the window has three tabs: Classes, Sources, and Javadoc. The JAR files should have been included automatically when you originally added the new platform. You need to reference the sources and Javadoc on each tab manually, as shown in Figure 7-7. Once you have added Javadoc to your libraries and Java platforms, you can view the context-sensitive Javadoc during coding.

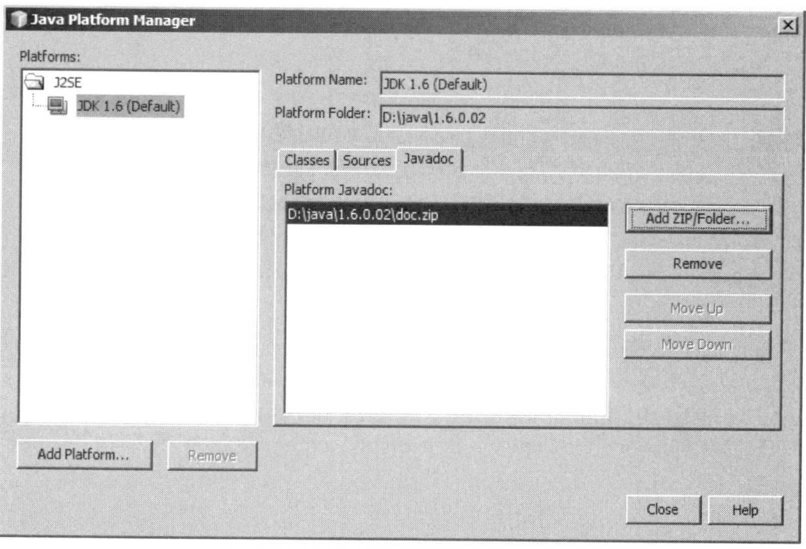

Figure 7-7. *Adding Javadoc in the Java Platform Manager*

Viewing Context-Sensitive Javadoc

During the code-editing process, you can view context-sensitive Javadoc. This allows you quick access to documentation and usage information directly in the Source Editor window.

As you code, you may have already seen the first method of viewing Javadoc, if you have the code completion feature activated (see Chapter 3). When you type a period after a package or class name, the code completion box appears. For the Java element highlighted in the code completion box, an additional pop-up window also appears, displaying the Javadoc for the currently selected element. If you use the keyboard arrow keys to scroll up and down the list, the Javadoc window should update accordingly, as shown in Figure 7-8.

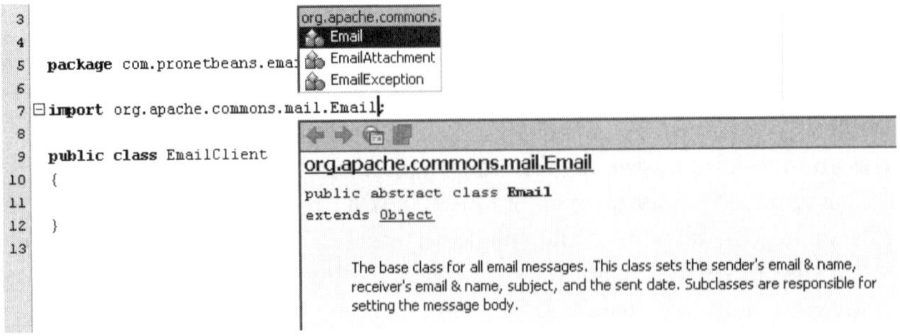

package com.pronetbeans.ema
import org.apache.commons.mail.Email;
public class EmailClient
{
}
org.apache.commons.
Email
EmailAttachment
EmailException
org.apache.commons.mail.Email
public abstract class Email
extends Object
The base class for all email messages. This class sets the sender's email & name, receiver's email & name, subject, and the sent date. Subclasses are responsible for setting the message body.

Figure 7-8. *Context-sensitive Javadoc during code completion*

You can also force the Javadoc window to appear. Highlight the class or package for which you wish to view the Javadoc and press Ctrl+Shift+Spacebar. The pop-up window will display the Javadoc for the selected item. This can sometimes prove faster than opening the Javadoc in a web browser.

■ **Tip** You can also highlight or select an element and right-click. On the context menu that appears is an item called Show Javadoc. The Show Javadoc option will attempt to open the Javadoc page specific to the element you selected. If you have not attached the Javadoc to the library or platform to which the element belongs, you will see the status message "Javadoc Not Found" at the bottom of the Source Editor window.

One additional way you can view context-sensitive Javadoc is by using the Javadoc View window. You can access this window by navigating to Window ➤ Other ➤ Javadoc View. This opens a small window along the bottom of the Source Editor that is similar to the Output window, as shown in Figure 7-9. The Javadoc View window displays the WYSIWYG view of Javadoc embedded in Java code.

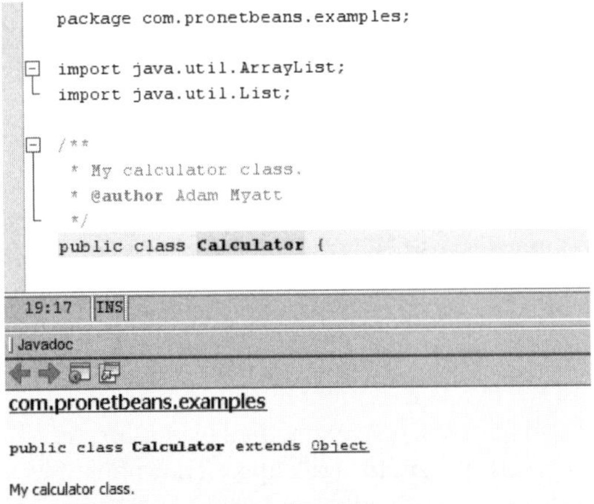

package com.pronetbeans.examples;
import java.util.ArrayList;
import java.util.List;
/**
* My calculator class.
* @author Adam Myatt
*/
public class Calculator {
19:17
INS
Javadoc
com.pronetbeans.examples
public class Calculator extends Object
My calculator class.

Figure 7-9. *The Javadoc View window*

If a Java source file is open in the Source Editor, you can select a specific element and see the Javadoc displayed in the Javadoc View window. Open a Java source file in the Source Editor and select the class name. The Javadoc for the class is displayed in the Javadoc View window, as shown in Figure 7-9.

As you select different elements, such as method names, class member variables, or constructors, the Javadoc View window will change accordingly. This assumes you have added some Javadoc for the selected element. Otherwise the Javadoc View window will not display anything.

Searching Javadoc

The Javadoc Search tool, shown in Figure 7-10, provides quick and convenient access to search Javadoc registered with NetBeans. Any Javadoc that has been referenced for a library or platform can be searched and displayed using the tool. It can also display any Javadoc that was generated for any open project.

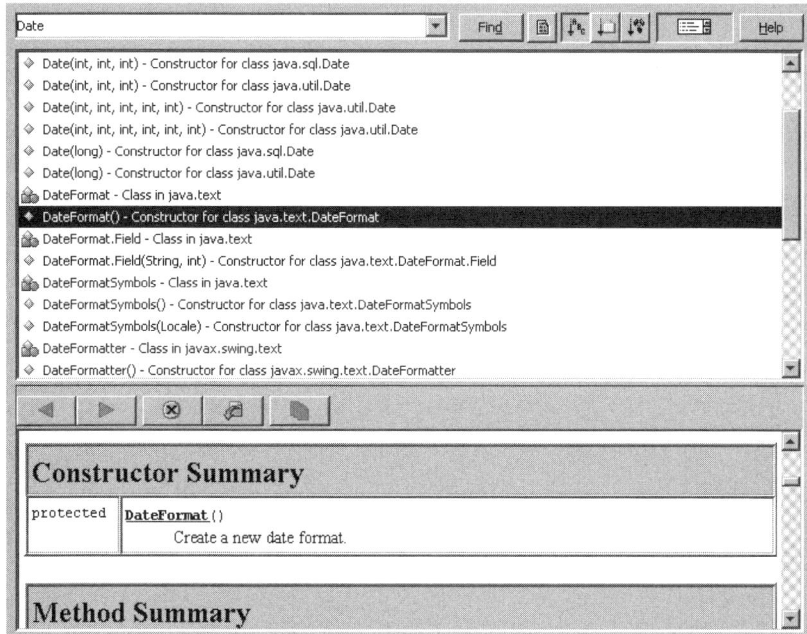

Figure 7-10. *The Javadoc Search tool*

If you are in the Source Editor writing code, highlight the term you wish to display in the Search tool and press Shift+F1. The Javadoc Search tool will immediately open and display the search results for the selected text. I have found this to be one of the fastest and easiest methods for viewing Javadoc.

The Javadoc Search window is divided into two sections: searching and viewing. The top pane allows you to search for Javadoc elements based on partial name matching. In the example in Figure 7-10, I started off by typing `Date` in the search field. When you have finished entering the phrase you want to search for, press the Enter key or click the Find button next to the search field.

The tool scans all the known Javadoc and displays the results. If you select any result in the list, the matching Javadoc page is displayed in the lower pane. You can jump directly to the source code for an element by clicking the View Source button. You can also sort the search results by name, package, and type by clicking the corresponding buttons. There is also a button to toggle the display of the HTML viewer window (lower pane). Move your mouse over each button to see a tooltip describing its function.

In the HTML viewer pane at the bottom of the window, you can scroll up and down a page of Javadoc for the selected element, exactly as if you were viewing it in an external browser. You can also click the hyperlinks in the Javadoc, just like in an external browser.

The buttons along the top of the HTML viewer pane allow you to navigate back and forth through the Javadoc you have viewed. Similar to a browser, the pane has Back, Forward, Stop, Reload, and History buttons.

The Javadoc Search tool can be docked as a window inside the Source Editor section of NetBeans, just like a page of source code. It is often faster and easier to leave the Search tool open for viewing Javadoc rather than use an external browser window. It can provide quick access to Javadoc for your associated libraries and source code.

Summary

This chapter provided a quick overview of the Javadoc-related features available in NetBeans. Writing Javadoc to go along with your code is a best practice for any new or seasoned developer to follow. NetBeans tries to make working with Javadoc simple by providing some helpful tools. This includes the Javadoc Search tool for querying all the Javadoc associated with your code and libraries.

As you saw in this chapter, there are many different tags you can use in your Javadoc. The entire list can be quite complex, but many developers who first start out using Javadoc need only the basics. To learn more about Javadoc, visit `http://java.sun.com/j2se/javadoc`.

CHAPTER 8

Managing Builds with Ant and Maven

Many problems can occur while building and developing software. One of the biggest challenges is attempting to build and compile a software application on a platform other than the one for which it was developed. Imagine three programmers working on the same application on three different platforms: Linux, Windows, and Mac.

Many existing build tools work fine but do not offer as much flexibility as some developers would like and are usually specific to a particular operating system. It can also prove difficult to extend their functionality and integrate them with Java IDE tools.

Ant was created to address many problems in the arena of cross-platform source code compilation. Because Ant is written in Java, tasks that are performed by Ant are executed by Java objects. Ant can also be extended using standard Java classes. This makes it an ideal tool for structuring cross-platform software builds (at least for the platforms that support a JDK).

Because Ant runs entirely in Java, no operating system–specific build configurations need to be written. You can create and structure a single build configuration and execute it across multiple platforms. This helps ensure that a build process is reliable and repeatable, which is a key foundation to developing quality software.

Maven, another project management and build tool, is similar to Ant. You typically run it via the command line to manage project builds. You can use it to compile Java source files, update library dependencies, generate Javadoc, generate WAR files, build project documentation, and so on. It also helps enforce consistency and standardization.

Ant and Maven can be tightly integrated with NetBeans 6. NetBeans makes full use of Ant and its capabilities for each type of project. If you install the Maven module, you can use it, instead of Ant, as the build tool for several types of projects. In this chapter, we explore how Ant and Maven work with NetBeans.

Ant Tasks and Targets

Ant uses XML files to store build configurations. Typically named `build.xml`, the build configuration file contains the definitions of specific tasks and targets. A *task* is a specific operation to be executed by an Ant Java class. A *target* is a group of one or more tasks that can then be executed by Ant.

One of the key things to remember regarding Ant targets is that they can be dependent on each other. For example, a target can contain an attribute named depends that directs Ant to process other targets first. This can lead to a cycle such as the following pseudo-build configuration:

```
target = "build-full", depends on ➥
"compile source, create javadoc, package classes to jar"
target = "package classes to jar", depends on "compile source, create javadoc"
target = "create javadoc", depends on "compile source"
target = "compile source"
```

These targets contain dependencies on other targets. Ant resolves any conflicts in duplicate dependencies and does not execute the same target more than once. In the example, when build-full is executed, the three targets on which it depends are executed in order from left to right. The first target could also be defined as follows:

```
target = "build-full", depends on "package classes to jar"
```

This line is valid because the build-full target depends on the package classes to jar target. In turn, that target depends on the create javadoc and compile source targets.

Needless to say, there are numerous ways you could structure targets and their dependencies, but this is just a very quick overview. For more discussion and information on Ant targets and semantics of dependencies, you can read *Pro Apache Ant* by Matthew Moodie (Apress, 2005).

As mentioned previously, targets are just groups of tasks. A task is basically a Java class that performs the actual processing and work. In the build configuration file, tasks can contain attributes and tags that further define how they function. See Table 8-1 for a partial list of Ant tasks with brief descriptions.

Table 8-1. *Some Common Ant Tasks*

Task	Description
java	Executes a Java file in the current JVM
javac	Compiles one or more source files
jspc	Compiles one or more JSP files into Java source files
javadoc	Runs the Javadoc tool for the specified Java source files
copy	Copies one or more files to a specific location
delete	Deletes one or more files
mkdir	Makes a new directory on the file system
move	Moves one or more files to a specific location
rename	Renames a file or directory
mail	Sends an SMTP email message
input	Interacts with the user to retrieve command-line input
jar	Packages a set of source or class files into a JAR file
unjar	Extracts the source or class files from a JAR file
war	Packages a set of files (an entire application) into a WAR file

Task	Description
unwar	Extracts a set of files from a WAR file
zip	Packages a set of source or class files into a zip file
unzip	Extracts the source or class files from a zip file
ftp	Performs an FTP operation
scp	Transfers files to a remote machine via SSH
cvs	Performs various CVS operations
junit	Executes a set of JUnit test classes
junitreport	Creates a JUnit report based on JUnit test data

Many additional tasks are available for use in Ant. You can even extend Ant and implement your own custom tasks. Once you understand a few of the Ant tasks, you can write your own build scripts, such as the one shown in Listing 8-1.

Listing 8-1. *Sample Ant Build Script*

```
<?xml version="1.0" ?>

<project name="pronetbeans" default="dist" basedir=".">

    <property name="dir.src" value="src" />
    <property name="dir.build" value="build" />
    <property name="dir.build.classes" value="${dir.build}/classes" />
    <property name="dir.dist" value="dist" />

    <target name="init">
        <mkdir dir="${dir.build}" />
        <mkdir dir="${dir.build.classes}" />
        <mkdir dir="${dir.dist}" />
    </target>

    <target name="compile" depends="init">
        <javac srcdir="${dir.src}" destdir="${dir.build.classes}" />
    </target>

    <target name="dist" depends="compile">
        <jar jarfile="${dir.dist}/pronetbeans.jar"
             basedir="${dir.build.classes}" />
    </target>

</project>
```

The build file in Listing 8-1 contains several important sections. The first section defines the project name:

```
<project name="pronetbeans" default="dist" basedir=".">
```

The `project` tag has an attribute named `default`, which defines the target that is executed by Ant if no target is specified on the command line when Ant is run. It also defines a `basedir` attribute, which specifies where the root directory for the project's files is located. Using the `basedir` attribute makes specifying directory paths easy, since you do not need to have a full path defined throughout the build file.

The `property` tags define a variable that can be specified once and referred to numerous times in the build file:

```
<property name="dir.src" value="src" />
<property name="dir.build" value="build" />
<property name="dir.build.classes" value="${dir.build}/classes" />
<property name="dir.dist" value="dist" />
```

This is a convenient and easy way to define directory paths, directory names, filenames, and so on. To refer to the value of a defined property, you can use the syntax `${variable}`.

The first target that is defined is named `init`. This target contains three `mkdir` tasks:

```
<target name="init">
    <mkdir dir="${dir.build}" />
    <mkdir dir="${dir.build.classes}" />
    <mkdir dir="${dir.dist}" />
</target>
```

Each `mkdir` task will create the directory specified by the `dir` attribute. Many Ant build files contain a target that initializes the overall build by creating directories and setting up any needed configurations.

The `compile` target will perform the actual compilation of the source code. It lists a dependency on the `init` target that will execute before the `compile` target:

```
<target name="compile" depends="init">
    <javac srcdir="${dir.src}" destdir="${dir.build.classes}" />
</target>
```

The dependency ensures the `build` and `build/classes` directories are created. The `javac` task performs the compilation of the source and is essentially the same as calling the `javac` executable on the command line. The `srcdir` attribute specifies the location of the source code that will be compiled. The `destdir` attribute specifies the location where the compiled classes are placed.

The `dist` target serves as a wrapper for the `jar` task. It depends on the `compile` task, since the source code should be compiled before being packaged into a JAR file:

```
<target name="dist" depends="compile">
    <jar jarfile="${dir.dist}/pronetbeans.jar"
            basedir="${dir.build.classes}" />
</target>
```

The `jarfile` attribute specifies the location and name of the JAR file to create. The `basedir` attribute specifies the location of the class files that should be compiled and packaged.

■ **Note** Listing 8-1 is a very simple and basic example of a build file. A single target can wrap many tasks. Tasks can contain numerous subelements and other tasks. For further examples, see the Apache Ant documentation or any NetBeans project `build.xml` file.

When NetBeans creates a project, it also creates a `build.xml` file and supporting files for the project. It defines the targets and tasks it needs to manage the compilation and build of the project. The structure and location of the `build.xml` file and supporting files is discussed later in this chapter in the section "NetBeans Project Build Files."

Configuring Ant Properties in NetBeans

You can configure several Ant properties directly in NetBeans. These allow basic control over several pieces of Ant functionality.

To access the Ant properties, select Tools ➤ Options. In the Basic Options window, click the Miscellaneous icon and make sure the Ant tab is selected. You will see the Ant properties, as shown in Figure 8-1.

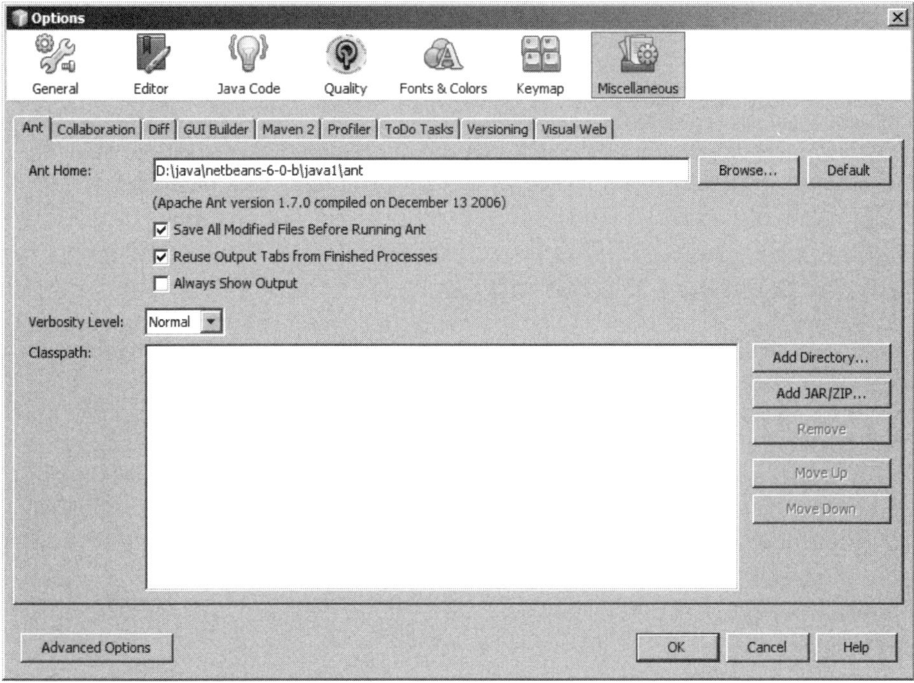

Figure 8-1. *The Ant properties in the Basic Options window*

The following properties are available:

Ant Home: This defines the directory location where the Ant program executable and supporting files are installed. When NetBeans is initially installed, a distribution of Ant is installed along with it. You can also download and install a separate version of Ant and change the Ant Home property to reference that location. Each major version of NetBeans supports a slightly newer version of Ant. Go to the NetBeans web site to determine the supported Ant versions.

Save All Modified Files Before Running Ant: If you are modifying several files at a time and need to execute a target, NetBeans will save each modified file before executing the Ant target specified. This can save you a lot of time and is also convenient.

Reuse Output Tabs from Finished Processes: This is a space saver. If you uncheck this option, every time you execute an Ant task, a new tab will open in the Output window. This doesn't sound too bad until you have spent several hours executing build targets and end up with dozens of tabs. If the property is checked, each time you execute an Ant target, NetBeans will reuse an existing tab for any target process that previously was complete.

Always Show Output: This directs NetBeans to bring the Output window to focus if it is not already and there is an error.

Verbosity Level: This specifies the amount of output that should be logged in the Output window. Several tasks, such as `copy`, `delete`, and `move`, have a `verbose` attribute that can be set. Your choices for this property are Quiet, Normal, Verbose, and Debug. This property is set to Normal by default.

Classpath: This section allows you to add JARs and directories that can be used by all Ant scripts in NetBeans. Click the Manage Classpath button to open the Classpath Editor.

NetBeans Project Build Files

NetBeans uses several related files to structure the build environment for a Java project. It uses targets and tasks, as in a normal Ant build file, but specific menu items and shortcuts are linked directly to targets, making for a tight integration between Ant and NetBeans.

Ant build files are not visible in the Projects window. NetBeans tries to abstract away the details of how projects are maintained and built during the normal day-to-day development tasks. You can view the Ant build files by switching to the Files window for a project. In this view, you can see the `build.xml` file for the project. Additional files are located in the `nbproject` directory. The following sections describe each of the project build files.

The build.xml File

The `build.xml` file is what Ant initially executes whenever a target needs to be executed. If you open the file, you will notice immediately that it contains very little information except for some comments. This is done to provide a flexible environment for you to work with NetBeans and Ant.

The targets that wrap Ant tasks are placed in the `build-impl.xml` file, which is explicitly referenced in the `build.xml` file via an `import` tag:

```
<import file="nbproject/build-impl.xml"/>
```

The import tag essentially makes the content of the build-impl.xml file function as if it were located in the build.xml file. Any targets defined in the imported file can also be overridden in the build.xml file.

The system-generated build-impl.xml file should *never* be modified (not that it can't be changed, but it's a best practice to leave it as is). If you need to modify or augment the behavior of a target, you can override it be redefining it in the build.xml file with a different set of tasks that it will perform.

You may want to override Ant targets for various reasons, such as to modify how an existing target works, add custom behaviors to the NetBeans build process, or integrate third-party tools into your Ant build scripts.

For example, for code I have written, I have needed to use the java.util.ResourceBundle class to read name/value pairs from a .properties file. In a project of type Java Application or Java Class Library, I will add the .properties file to the default package in the Source Packages node. When the code is compiled, the .properties file is compiled into the corresponding default package in the build/classes directory and is subsequently packaged into the JAR file. The problem arises when I do not want the .properties file to be included in the JAR but still want it copied into the build/classes and dist directories for easy access. I can arrange this in NetBeans by doing two things: excluding the .properties file from the JAR file and overriding a target defined in the build-impl.xml file.

First, to exclude the .properties file from the list of files that are included in the JAR file during the packaging process, I open the Project Properties window (right-click the project name and select Properties) and select the Packaging node on the left. The "Exclude from JAR File" field typically contains the value **/*.java,**/*.form. As shown in Figure 8-2, I add **/*.properties to the end of the value. Now when the JAR file is created, the .properties file will not be included.

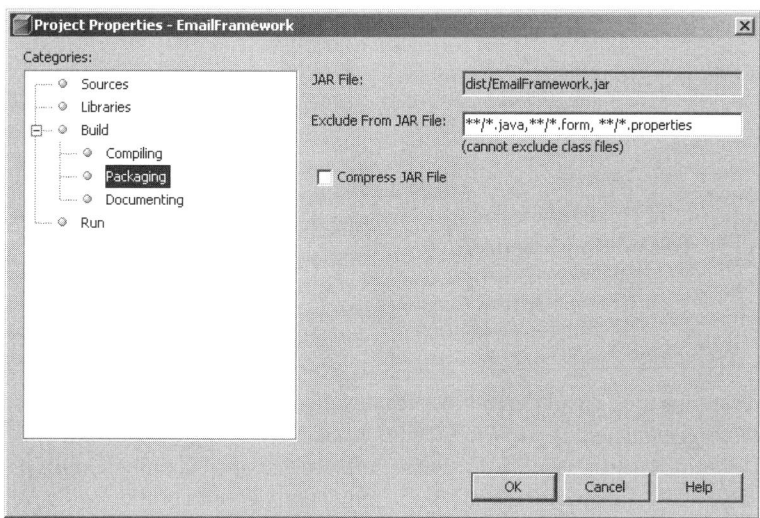

Figure 8-2. *Setting the "Exclude from JAR File" field for a project*

At this stage, the .properties file will also not be copied to the build/classes or dist directory. I remedy this by overriding the -post-jar target. If you open the build-impl.xml file and locate the target named jar, you will see its dependencies listed in the following order:

- init
- compile
- -pre-jar
- -do-jar-with-manifest
- -do-jar-without-manifest
- -do-jar-with-mainclass
- -do-jar-with-libraries
- -post-jar

The last target in the dependency chain is -post-jar. If you look at the definition of this target, you will see the following XML code:

```
<target name="-post-jar">
    <!-- Empty placeholder for easier customization. -->
    <!-- You can override this target in the ../build.xml file. -->
</target>
```

Notice that no tasks are in the -post-jar target. This is an empty placeholder target, provided so that you can define custom behaviors by overriding this task in the build.xml file. Here is the new -post-jar target I define at the bottom of the build.xml file:

```
<target name="-post-jar">
    <copy todir="${build.classes.dir}" >
        <fileset dir="${src.dir}" includes="**/*.properties" />
    </copy>
    <copy todir="${dist.dir}" >
        <fileset dir="${src.dir}" includes="**/*.properties" />
    </copy>
</target>
```

The new -post-jar target contains two copy tasks. Each task copies any .properties files from the source packages to the corresponding location in the build/classes directory and also into the dist directory.

The build-impl.xml File

The build-impl.xml file contains the core of the Ant tasks that NetBeans uses to execute and manage the project build. Project-related actions include Build, Clean and Build, Run Main Project, Run File, Test, and Generate Javadoc. Whether these actions are activated via menu items or via keyboard shortcuts, they tie directly to Ant targets in the project build configuration.

As discussed in the previous section, the content of the build-impl.xml file is imported into the build.xml file. Any target can be overridden, but for the most part you should not need to override the core targets. The build-impl.xml file for a Java Application or Java Class Library project is divided into several sections, as detailed in Table 8-2.

Table 8-2. *Sections of the build-impl.xml File*

Section	Description
Initialization	Initialize properties defined in the build file and in separate `.properties` files. Perform several conditional checks on project parameters and settings.
Compilation	Create build directories, compile the project code, or compile single files.
Dist	Create the distribution directory and package the compiled class files into a JAR file.
Execution	Execute the project class files or a single class file.
Debugging	Provide tasks for debugging projects and code in NetBeans.
Javadoc	Run the Javadoc tool against the project code and open a browser to view the generated report.
JUnit compilation	Compile all the project test files or a single test file.
JUnit execution	Execute one or all tests in a project.
JUnit debugging	Provide debugging tasks for project tests.
Applet	Provide Ant tasks for executing a Java applet.
Cleanup	Delete the `build` and `dist` directories and all the files inside them.

The build files for a Web Application project (and other project types in NetBeans) differ from those for a Java Application or Java Class Library project. The same types of files are created, but they may contain different sets of targets and tasks. For example, the `build-impl.xml` file for a Web Application project contains targets for compiling JSP files, packaging the application into a WAR file instead of a JAR file, and deploying the code to the target application server. However, the core targets and tasks are similar across each of the project types.

The build-before-profiler.xml File

The `build-before-profiler.xml` file is only a backup of the `build.xml` file. When you first initiate the NetBeans Profiler for a project, the `build.xml` file is copied and named `build-before-profiler.xml`. The original `build.xml` file is modified with the addition of an `import` statement:

```
<import file="nbproject/ profiler-build-impl.xml "/>
```

Note Chapter 5 describes how to install, configure, and use the NetBeans Profiler, the code profiling tool that allows you to profile for memory, CPU, and performance problems, as well as monitor threads. For more information about using the NetBeans Profiler, read Chapter 5 or visit `http://profiler.netbeans.org/`.

This `import` in the `build.xml` file allows the targets and tasks defined in the `profiler-build-impl.xml` file to be run during the normal project `build.xml` execution.

The profiler-build-impl.xml File

The profiler-build-impl.xml file defines the targets for profiling the project, a single file, applets, or tests, depending on how you activate the NetBeans Profiler. It is imported into the build.xml file so that the targets are part of the overall build configuration for a project. Similar to build.xml, the targets can be executed by using the menu items from the Profile menu. If you selected Profile ➤ Profile Main Project, then the profile target would execute:

```
<target name="profile" if="netbeans.home"
            depends="profile-init,compile"
            description="Profile a project in the IDE.">
    <nbprofiledirect>
        <classpath>
            <path path="${run.classpath}"/>
        </classpath>
    </nbprofiledirect>
    <profile/>
</target>
```

The profile target depends on the profile-init and compile targets to work correctly. You can't really profile code unless it compiles. It also wraps the nbprofiledirect task that defines the classpath for the classes to profile.

You can also profile a single source code file if a Main method is defined in the class. With the file open in the Source Editor, select Profile ➤ Profile Other ➤ Profile "*MyFile.java*". You can also right-click the file in the Projects window and select Profile from the context menu. The profile-single target will then execute:

```
<target name="profile-single" if="netbeans.home"
            depends="profile-init,compile-single"
            description="Profile a selected class in the IDE.">
        <fail unless="profile.class">Must select a file in the IDE</fail>
        <nbprofiledirect>
        <classpath>
            <path path="${run.classpath}"/>
        </classpath>
    </nbprofiledirect>
    <profile classname="${profile.class}"/>
</target>
```

The profile-single target contains a fail clause that requires a class be selected for profiling. The profile task explicitly defines which class should be profiled via the classname attribute.

Several other targets are included in this file, but the only other two to note are -profile-pre-init and -profile-post-init. These two targets are initially blank. The profile target depends on the profile-init target, which, in turn, depends on the -profile-pre-init and -profile-post-init targets. You can override them in the build.xml file if there are additional tasks you need to execute before and after a profiling session executes.

The project.properties File

The `project.properties` file contains the name/value pairs of properties used throughout the various Ant build files. It contains project settings, project configuration details, and directory definitions. The build file will recognize the properties after execution of the following target from the `build-impl.xml` file:

```
<target name="-init-project" depends="-pre-init,-init-private,-init-user">
    <property file="nbproject/project.properties"/>
</target>
```

This target uses a `property` task to reference and load the information in the `project.properties` file. The properties can then be referenced in the usual format of `${propertyName}`.

The following are some of the key values in the `project.properties` file:

```
build.dir=build
build.classes.dir=${build.dir}/classes
build.test.classes.dir=${build.dir}/test/classes
dist.dir=dist
dist.javadoc.dir=${dist.dir}/javadoc
javac.source=1.5
main.class=com.email.NewFile
src.dir=src
test.src.dir=test
```

Some of these properties define directory paths; others define project settings. Such properties as `java.source` and `main.class` can be set in the Project Properties window.

Working with Targets

You can activate the targets in the build configuration in several ways. The first and obvious is through the main menu items that correlate to specific targets. The second is by running the targets directly from the build files.

Locate the `build.xml` file in the Files window and right-click it to see the build file context menu. The context menu contains two relevant items: Run Target and Debug Target.

Running Targets

From the build file context menu, expand the Run Target submenu. You will see several target names displayed, as shown in Figure 8-3. If you click one of them, it will run that target. This is handy, especially if there is a target you want to run that performs a small chunk of work you need done without running the target that is at the beginning of a dependency chain.

Clicking the Other Targets option displays a submenu that allows you to execute the remaining targets that are not in the first submenu.

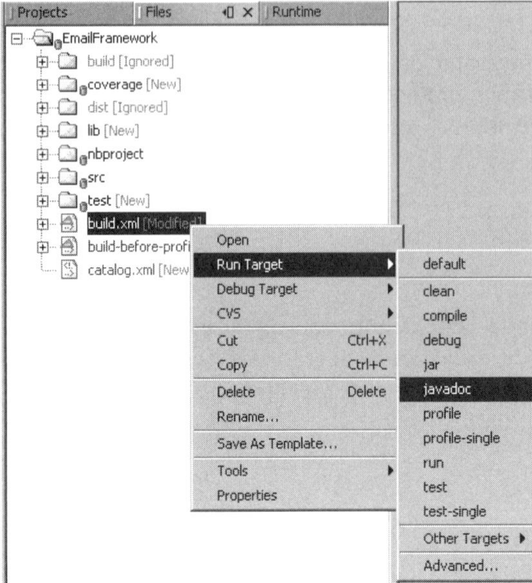

Figure 8-3. *Context menu for build files*

Debugging Targets

One of the many interesting features NetBeans provides is the ability to debug Ant files. In much the same way as you can debug Java source files, you can step through a build file line by line.

You can set a breakpoint in a build file, just as in a regular source code file: by clicking the line number in the glyph margin, as shown in Figure 8-4. You can then activate the debugging session for the target by right-clicking the `build.xml` file, selecting Debug Target, and choosing `run` from the submenu. This will trigger a debugging session for the `run` target and allow you to step through the build file.

```
<!--
=================
EXECUTION SECTION
=================
-->
<target name="run" depends="init,compile" description="Run a main class.">
    <j2seproject1:java>
        <customize>
            <arg line="${application.args}"/>
        </customize>
    </j2seproject1:java>
</target>
```

Figure 8-4. *Setting a breakpoint in an Ant build file*

Since Ant is so tightly integrated with NetBeans, you can access full debugging information using the IDE tools. For example, you can open the Local Variables window by selecting Window ➤ Debugging ➤ Local Variables or via the shortcut Alt+Shift+1.

As shown in Figure 8-5, a variety of variables are available during the debugging session. As you step through the build file, you can watch the values of those variables. This can be very useful if you need help debugging sporadic errors that occur while building your project code.

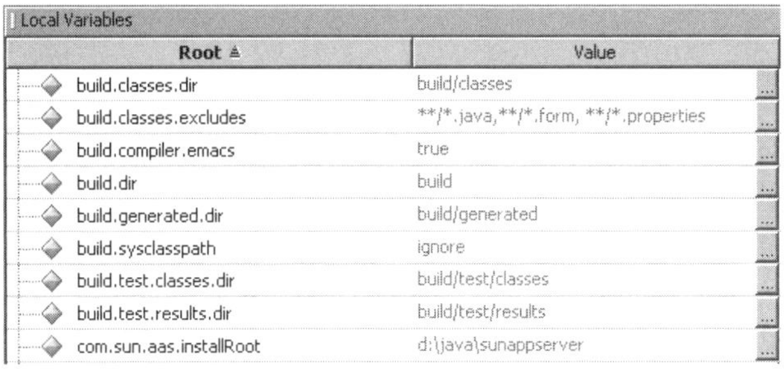

Local Variables

Root	Value
build.classes.dir	build/classes
build.classes.excludes	**/*.java,**/*.form, **/*.properties
build.compiler.emacs	true
build.dir	build
build.generated.dir	build/generated
build.sysclasspath	ignore
build.test.classes.dir	build/test/classes
build.test.results.dir	build/test/results
com.sun.aas.installRoot	d:\java\sunappserver

Figure 8-5. *Local variables during an Ant debug session*

Stopping and Rerunning Targets

One of the new features of NetBeans 6 is the ability to stop Ant targets that are executing. This can prove useful if you find an Ant target running for a long period of time or if you trigger a particular target and quickly decide you need to run another. You can also trigger an Ant target to run again. Rerunning a target is convenient if you are debugging a target and need to access it quickly.

The buttons to stop and rerun Ant targets were added to the margin of the Output window. If you execute a build of a Java Application project the Output window should appear, as shown in Figure 8-6. The build output displays as text with the message "BUILD SUCCESSFUL." Notice the margin to the left of the Output window. The Rerun Ant Target button displays two arrows pointing to the right. If you click it, the project build will execute again and the output will be displayed in the window.

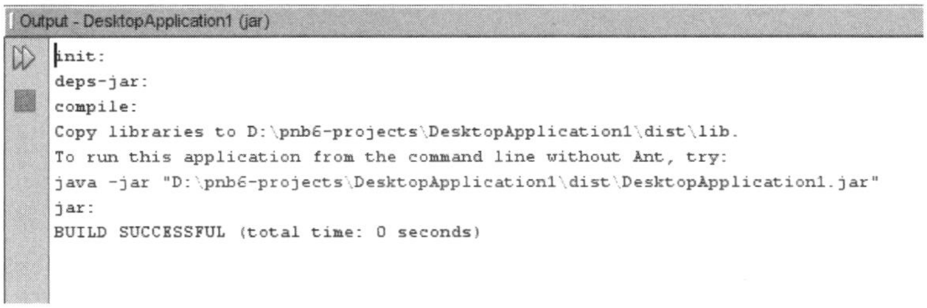

Output - DesktopApplication1 (jar)

```
init:
deps-jar:
compile:
Copy libraries to D:\pnb6-projects\DesktopApplication1\dist\lib.
To run this application from the command line without Ant, try:
java -jar "D:\pnb6-projects\DesktopApplication1\dist\DesktopApplication1.jar"
jar:
BUILD SUCCESSFUL (total time: 0 seconds)
```

Figure 8-6. *The Ant Stop and Rerun buttons in the Output window*

When the Rerun Ant Target button is pressed, notice that the square Stop button under it lights up. Even though it is enabled for only a moment, you can click this button to stop the Ant target at any time (assuming your target takes a few seconds to execute or if you're really quick with the mouse).

Creating Shortcuts to Ant Targets

For the past several versions, NetBeans has provided the ability to create shortcuts to Ant targets. If there is a specific target you access frequently when working on a project, you can create a shortcut, add it to a menu, or add it to a toolbar. This saves you the time of navigating the target tree of the `build.xml` file in the Files window.

You can create keyboard, menu, and toolbar shortcuts to Ant targets. Follow these steps to create all three types of shortcuts to the `Javadoc` Ant target:

1. In the Files window, find the `build.xml` file and click the plus sign next to the node to display the tree list of Ant targets. Right-click the `Javadoc` target and select Create Shortcut from the context menu.

2. In the "Create Shortcut to Ant Target" window, click the Add a Menu Item, Add a Toolbar Button check box, and Add a Keyboard Shortcut check box and click Next. As shown in Figure 8-7, you need to select the menu on which you want the shortcut to appear and name the shortcut. Once you have set the name and selected the menu, click the Next button.

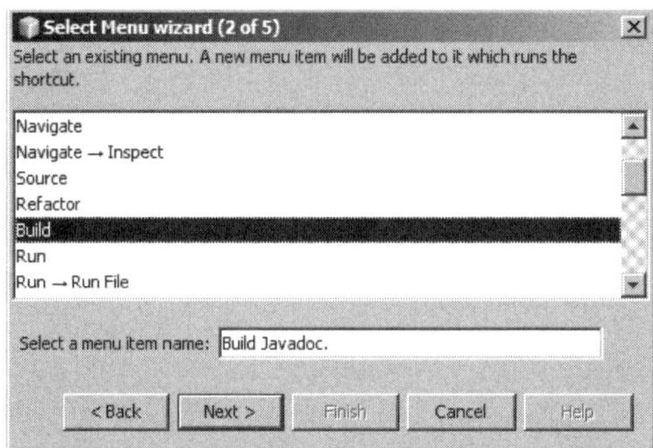

Figure 8-7. *Selecting a menu for the shortcut and naming the menu item*

3. On the next screen select the toolbar on which the Ant target shortcut will appear, such as the Build toolbar, as shown in Figure 8-8. Then enter a value for the "Select toolbar button text" field and click the Next button.

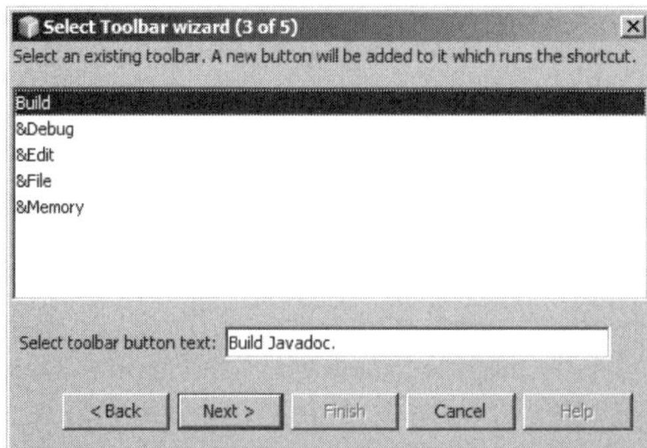

Figure 8-8. *Selecting a toolbar for the shortcut and naming the toolbar text*

4. Finally, press any combination of keys to select a keyboard shortcut for the Javadoc Ant target. You can avoid keyboard shortcut conflicts by navigating to Tools ➤ Options and viewing the existing shortcuts listed in the Keymap section of the Basic Options window.

With the new menu, toolbar, and keyboard shortcut, you have quick access to the "generate project JavadocAnt" target. An important thing to note is that these shortcuts are specific to your project, not the IDE. If you close the project and open another, the shortcuts will not apply to the newly opened projects.

■ **Tip** The procedure described in this section can be used to create a shortcut for any Ant target. You can create a set of toolbars and shortcuts to provide quick access to the Ant targets you plan to use most often.

Introduction to Maven

Maven is a project management and build tool similar to Ant. It allows you to manage your project builds in a consistent manner while enforcing strict dependencies between projects.

You can work with Maven 2.X directly in NetBeans 6. Throughout the rest of this chapter I refer simply to Maven, but I am referencing Maven 2, which is the version that the NetBeans 6 module supports.

Maven allows you to perform a build using a project object model (POM). It also uses a common set of features and plugins that are made available in the Maven build system. Thus, all projects you build using the Maven repository can share the same set of plugins, enabling a uniform build process and a simpler experience for the developer. The NetBeans Maven plugin attempts to make it even simpler by connecting pieces of Maven functionality to the menus and tools with which NetBeans users are familiar.

Working with Maven Projects

NetBeans provides an excellent plugin for Maven 2. It allows you to generate Maven projects directly in the IDE and perform many common actions with them. The Maven module is not part of the NetBeans install by default. You need to download it using the Plugin Manager.

To download the Maven plugin, perform the following steps:

1. Select Tools ➤ Plugins from the main menu.

2. Select the Available Plugins tab and click the Reload Catalog button. The list of modules displayed should refresh from the Update Centers you have previously configured.

3. Select the check box next to the Maven module and click the Install button.

4. On the confirmation pop-up that appears, click the Next button and accept the license agreement. The Maven module will download and be installed.

5. If prompted, select to Restart the IDE. When NetBeans restarts, the Maven module will be installed.

Configuring Maven Properties

The Maven plugin for NetBeans 6 allows you to configure a number of properties that affect how it works. You can access the properties by selecting Tools ➤ Options from the main menu to open the Basic Options window. Once it opens, click the Miscellaneous icon in the top navigation menu and select the Maven 2 tab from the list that appears. The Maven properties will be displayed, as shown in Figure 8-9.

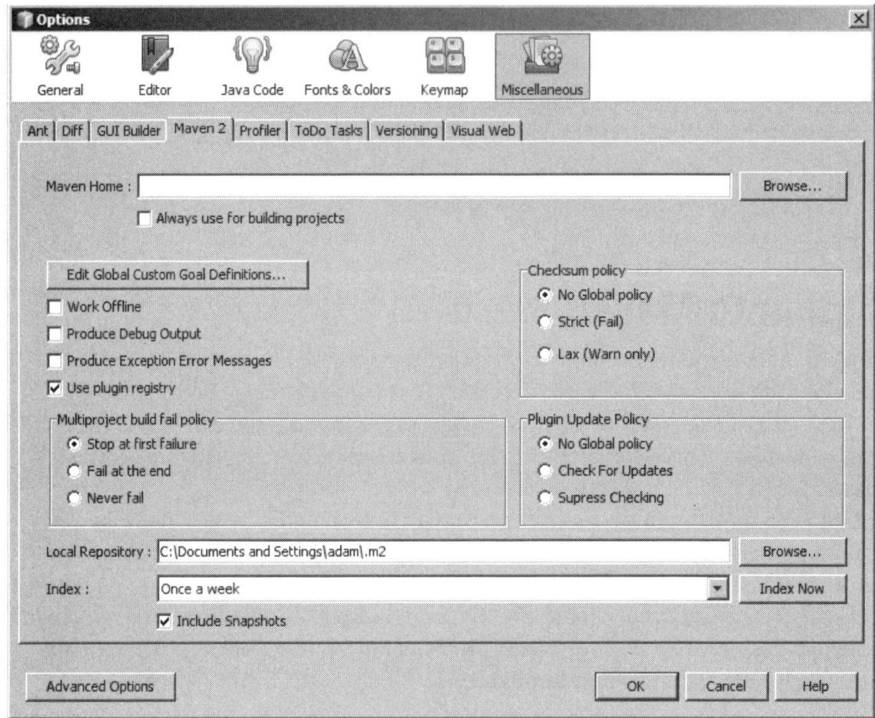

Figure 8-9. *The Maven properties in the Basic Options window*

The Maven 2 tab allows you to set a variety of properties. By default, NetBeans uses the Maven software that is bundled with the plugin. You can direct NetBeans to use an external version of Maven by setting the "Maven Home" field. Click the Browse button next to the field to select the local Maven repository on your machine.

There are also several sections in the Maven 2 tab that allow you to set the policy for checksum validation, plugin updates, and multiproject build failures. These sections allow you to customize how you want each event handled by selecting the appropriate radio button in each section.

The "Index" field allows you to specify how the Maven repository of plugins and projects is scanned for changes. You can set this field to various time periods or click the Index Now button to trigger an immediate indexing of the repository.

Creating Maven Projects

To create a new Maven project, do the following:

1. Select File ➤ New Project from the main menu.
2. Select Maven from the list of Categories in the left pane.
3. Select Maven Project from the list of Projects in the right pane.
4. Click the Next button.
5. On the Maven Archetype screen, select Maven Webapp Archetype to use as a template for your project, as shown in Figure 8-10. This will create a typical Maven project for a web application.

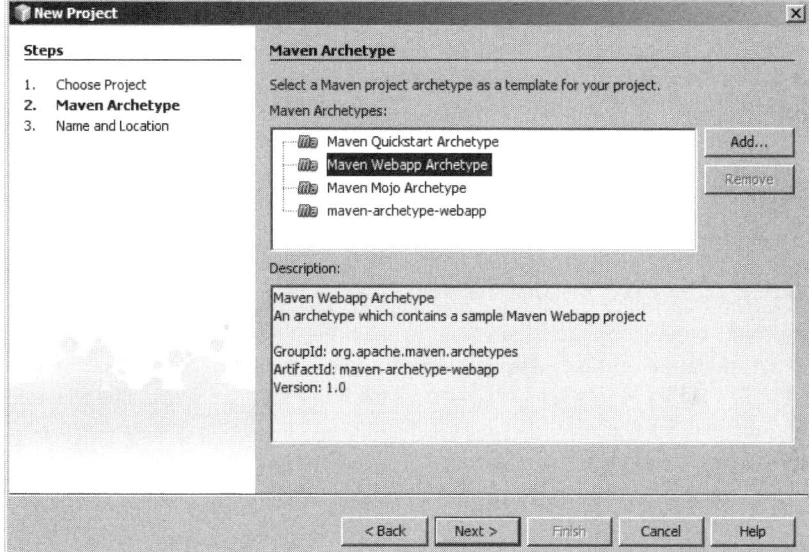

Figure 8-10. *The Maven Archetype screen in the New Project wizard*

6. Click the Next button to continue to the Name and Location screen.
7. On the Name and Location screen, enter a value for the "Project Name" field.
8. Select a value for the "Project Location" field by clicking the Browse button and choosing a base directory for the project.
9. At the bottom of the Name and Location screen, enter the Maven-specific information for the "Group Id," "Version," and "Package" fields, as shown in Figure 8-11. The "Package" field is optional because you do not need to specify a package hierarchy, but it is strongly recommended that you do so.
10. Click the Finish button to end the wizard and generate the project.

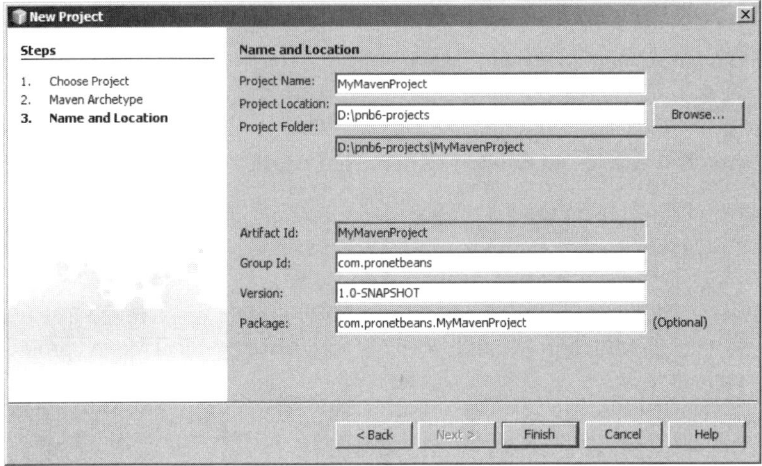

Figure 8-11. *The Name and Location screen in the New Project wizard*

The Maven project will be generated. If you look at the lines displayed in the Output window, you will see Maven attempt to download a number of libraries. The project will also attempt an initial build.

Configuring Maven Project Properties

Each Maven project can be configured and customized beyond the general Maven properties. Similar to Java Application and Web Application projects, you can right-click a project name listed in the Projects window and select Properties from the context menu. The Maven Project Properties window will appear.

The Maven Project Properties window provides several nodes in the Categories pane that allow you to customize how the Maven project functions. The Categories listed allow you to do the following:

General: Lets you set the Maven project data. You can change the "GroupId," "ArtifactId," "Version," "Packaging," "Name," and "Description" fields for the Maven project.

Sources: Displays the absolute directory path of the project folder. Also allows you to specify the Java Source/Binary Format for the project as well as the Encoding Format.

Run: Specifies properties for running the application. If the project is not a web application, then when you click it, the Run category will display fields that allow you to set the Main Class, Arguments, Working Directory, and VM options. These properties are similar to the runtime properties for a Java Application project. If the Maven project is a Web Application, the Run category node will display web server–related properties. You can specify the Java application server (Tomcat, WebLogic, and so on), set the Context Path for the web application, and set the Relative URL.

Actions: Lets you map the NetBeans project actions to the matching Maven goals. If you select an action from the pane on the right, you will see the matching goal displayed in the "Execute Goals" field, as shown in Figure 8-12. This lets you customize how Maven runs the goals and passes them properties.

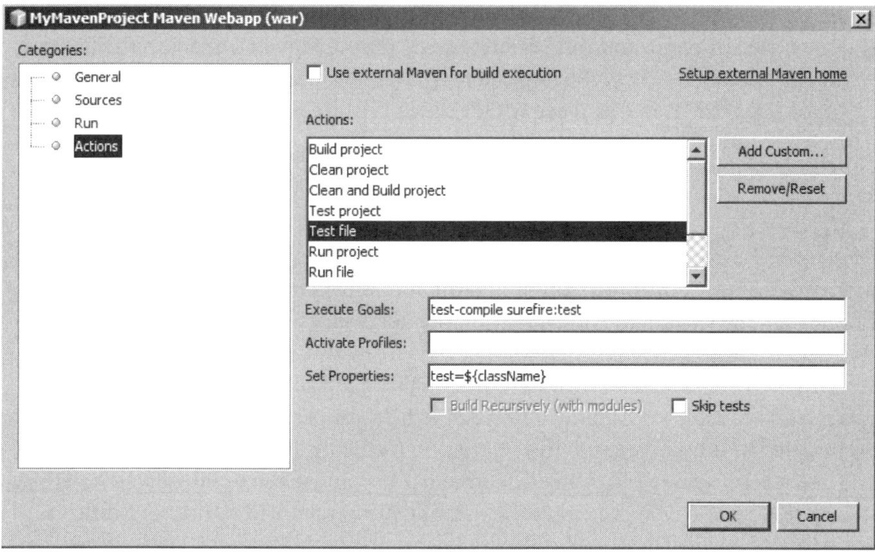

Figure 8-12. *The Actions node in the Maven Project Properties screen*

Adding Library Dependencies

As previously mentioned, one of the benefits of using Maven as a build system is its excellent ability to manage project dependencies. The NetBeans Maven plugin lets you take advantage of this via the Libraries node of the Maven project in the Projects window.

To add a project dependency to a Maven project, right-click the Libraries node and select Add Library from the context menu. The Add Library window will appear, prompting you to enter the fields to identify the dependency. You can enter the "GroupId," "ArtifactId," and "Version" fields to identify the dependency, as shown in Figure 8-13. The "Scope" field allows you to specify what type of library dependency you are adding, such as compile time, runtime, and so on.

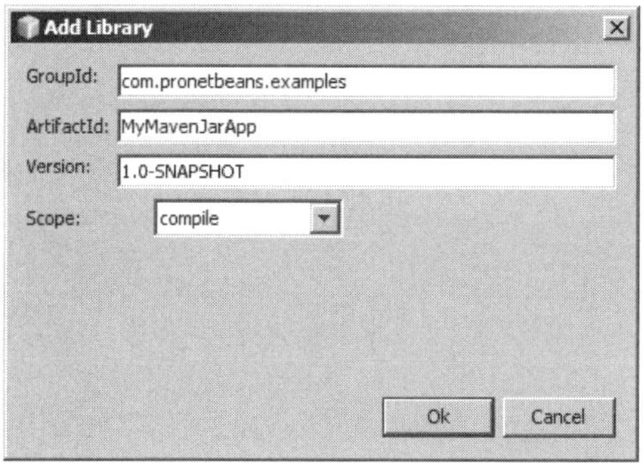

Figure 8-13. *The Add Library window for Maven project dependencies*

Once you fill out the required fields in the Add Library window, click the Ok button. The library dependency will appear under the Libraries node for the Maven project in the Projects window. You can view the contents of the dependent project by expanding the plus icon listed next to the node. You can drill down and see what classes exist inside the project as well as view the `pom.xml` for the dependent project.

Summary

This chapter provided a quick introduction to the Ant and Maven build tools. It covered the concepts of targets and tasks and how they provide the necessary functionality to the build process of your application.

Ant offers a full array of tasks that provide functionality such as compiling source code, packaging class files, sending SMTP email, and sending files via FTP. Much of this functionality is created and inserted into build files when you create a NetBeans Java project. The generated build files are linked directly to menu items in NetBeans. As you use the build-related tools available in the NetBeans IDE, you are actually executing Ant targets. Even though NetBeans abstracts away many of the details, you should still be familiar with Ant and its functionality, in case you want to customize or extend the build process.

Maven provides a project build tool similar to Ant but with better control over project dependencies. It lets you take advantage of a local repository of libraries and plugins. The NetBeans Maven plugin lets you create projects, configure dependencies, and take advantage of all the standard goals that Maven provides.

NetBeans makes it easy to work with Ant and Maven, including compiling, testing, running, and debugging projects. These build systems provide standard file structures, help enforce best practices on your projects, and provide a repeatable suite of functions for working with projects.

CHAPTER 9

JUnit Testing

Untested code has the potential to contain errors and bugs. Whether caused by an invalid assumption, an explicit coding mistake, or an otherwise-unknown issue, bugs that appear in code cause problems. Developers lose time trying to find such mistakes, organizations lose productivity, and companies lose money. For more critical systems, human lives can be lost if a software glitch occurs. This is why developers test code.

Testing should come as naturally as breathing. Every time code is being written, it should have a matching test. I won't go into the hotly debated topic of exactly when a test should be written. Some say after the code is finished, and some say before a single line of code is written. This chapter makes the general assumption that you write a class and then write a test. For those of you who write tests first, I also review how to create empty JUnit test classes.

An industry-standard mechanism for testing code is via a framework called *JUnit*. This framework defines a simple API to extend to implement tests. JUnit tests can be executed via the command line, Ant tasks, or numerous Java tools.

Full support for JUnit is bundled directly into NetBeans. NetBeans provides various wizards and code-generation tools for the supported JUnit version (JUnit 3 and 4 at the time of this writing).

Creating a JUnit Test Case

There are two scenarios for creating JUnit tests in NetBeans. The first is writing a test for a class that does not yet exist. The second is generating a JUnit class to test an existing Java source file.

Creating a New Test Class

NetBeans provides an option in the New File wizard for different types of JUnit classes. Here are the steps for creating a new empty test:

1. For any open Java project, right-click the project name in the Projects window and select New ➤ Other.

2. In the wizard, select the JUnit category. In the File Types section on the right, select the JUnit Test item. Then click the Next button.

3. In the New JUnit Test window, shown in Figure 9-1, enter a class name. It is predefined as `NewEmptyJUnitTest`, but can be changed to whatever you need. Typically, JUnit tests follow a standard naming convention. If the class that will be tested is called `MyFile`, then the matching JUnit test is usually named `MyFileTest`. Though not required, this is a best practice.

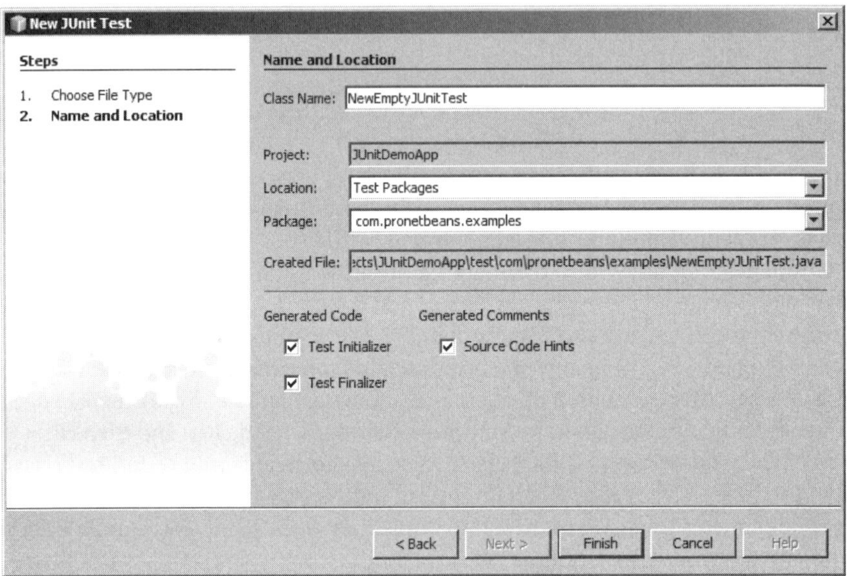

Figure 9-1. *Generating an empty JUnit test class*

4. If desired, you can change the values in the "Location" and "Package" fields. The "Location" field should be set to Test Packages, and the "Package" field is initially blank. If you right-click the name of a package that already exists in the Test Packages node and create a new empty test, this field is prepopulated with the package name.

5. You can select the check boxes to have the NetBeans New File wizard automatically generate method stubs for the "Test Initializer" and "Test Finalizer" fields. In simplest terms, these are generic utility methods used in a test class, but they are optional.

6. Optionally, select the Source Code Hints check box. If this is checked, NetBeans will insert some suggestions into the generated JUnit test file.

7. When you click the Finish button you will be prompted to choose a JUnit version for the JUnit test to use to generate the test skeleton.

8. Choose the radio button next to the appropriate version and click the Select button.

For ease of viewing, the comments have been stripped from the file, but the resulting code looks like the following for JUnit 3.x:

```
package com.pronetbeans.examples;
import junit.framework.*;

public class NewEmptyJUnitTest extends TestCase {

    public NewEmptyJUnitTest(String testName) {
        super(testName);
    }
    @Override
    protected void setUp() throws Exception {
        super.setUp();
    }

    @Override
    protected void tearDown() throws Exception {
        super.tearDown();
    }
    // TODO add test methods here. The name must begin with 'test'. For example:
    // public void testHello() {}
}
```

The `NewEmptyJUnitTest` class imports the standard `junit.framework` package. It also extends `TestCase`, which is the superclass for all JUnit tests. The empty method stubs for the `setUp` and `tearDown` methods have been generated and can be modified if desired.

Currently, there are no test methods in the `NewEmptyJUnitTest` class. If you selected the Source Code Hints check box in the wizard, you will see a `TODO` directive in the code (as in the preceding example), which will show up in the NetBeans Task List window.

Tip You can open the NetBeans Task List window by selecting Window ➤ Task List or using the keyboard shortcut Ctrl+6. The Task List window allows you to track all the `TODO` comments in your code. You can jump directly to them in the source by double-clicking any `TODO` listed in the window.

For the same JUnit test, the code that gets generated for JUnit 4.x looks like the following:

```
public class NewEmptyJUnitTest {

    public NewEmptyJUnitTest() {
    }

    @BeforeClass
    public static void setUpClass() throws Exception {
    }
```

```
    @AfterClass
    public static void tearDownClass() throws Exception {
    }

    @Before
    public void setUp() throws Exception {
    }

    @After
    public void tearDown() throws Exception {
    }

}
```

The JUnit 4.x version uses annotations to mark up the methods in the test class. The method names are unimportant in the JUnit 4.x version and can really be named almost anything you want, as long as they have the appropriate annotations applied.

Creating a Test for an Existing Class

You can also create a new JUnit test class by modeling the test on an existing Java source file. The NetBeans JUnit module will examine the source file and generate method stubs and sample test code in each method. For example, suppose you have the following `Calc` class:

```
public class Calc {

    public int checkNum(int origVal) {

        int returnVal = 0;

        if(origVal > 10) {
            returnVal = origVal - 1;
        }
        else {
            returnVal = origVal + 1;
        }

        return returnVal;
    }
}
```

This code contains a `checkNum` method, which takes a single parameter as an `int` primitive, performs a simple check comparison on it, and returns a modified value. To make sure this code functions as expected, you want to exercise the method using a variety of tests. You also want the tests to be repeatable, so you decide to create a JUnit test.

Using the Create Tests Dialog Box

To create the JUnit test based on the `Calc` class, right-click the `Calc` class name in the Projects window and select Tools ➤ Create JUnit Tests. With a class selected, you can also use the keyboard shortcut Ctrl+Shift+U. The Create Tests dialog box will appear, as shown in Figure 9-2.

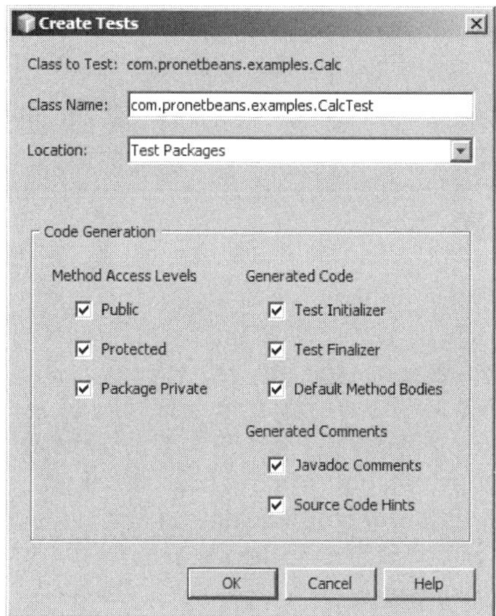

Figure 9-2. *The Create Tests dialog box for generating JUnit tests*

The Create Tests dialog box has several fields already filled out. The "Class Name" field contains a package and class name for the JUnit test. You can change this to whatever you want, but typically the package name should mirror the same package as the original source file.

■ **Note** Remember the NetBeans project structure. The `src` directory contains the source packages, and the `test` directory contains the test sources. You can have a test with the same package name as its matching source class without having them in the same directory.

In the Create Tests dialog box, you can also specify the method access levels that will be included for the new JUnit class. These determine which methods in the original source file will have matching JUnit test methods generated.

The Optional Code section allows you to specify what is autogenerated in the test. You can have the wizard generate the Test Initializer and Test Finalizer methods as well as the default method bodies for all the methods that will be tested.

The Optional Comments section has check boxes for comments and hints. The Javadoc Comments option directs the wizard to generate standard Javadoc for the test methods that are created. The Source Code Hints option inserts `TODO` directives or other comments into the code as hints to the programmer of actions to take.

Once you have specified the options you want, click the OK button. The JUnit test will be generated.

■ **Tip** During the process of creating a JUnit test, you are prompted to choose either JUnit 3.x or JUnit 4.x. Once you have made that choice, the IDE remembers it. The next time you create a JUnit test, it skips prompting you for the version. NetBeans adds the correct JUnit version's library to the list of compile-time test libraries. If you want to change the version of JUnit your project uses, simply remove the library from the Test Libraries node in the Projects window.

Using the New File Wizard

An alternate method of creating a test for an existing class is to use the New File wizard. Select New ➤ Other. In the JUnit category, select the Test for Existing Class option and click the Next button. You'll see the New Test for Existing Class window, as shown in Figure 9-3. This window looks very similar to the Create Tests dialog box (see Figure 9-2), but with two main differences. First, you need to specify the class you want to test. Click the Browse button and navigate the project package structure to find the class you want to test. Once you have selected which class to test, you will notice the other difference. In the "Created Test Class" field, you'll see that the wizard automatically named the JUnit test class for you based on the class you selected to test.

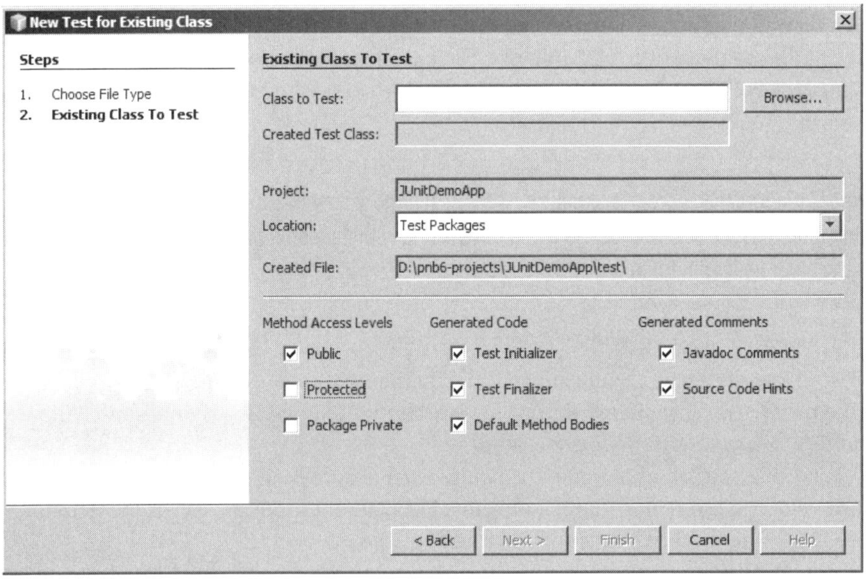

Figure 9-3. *Creating a JUnit test for an existing class*

Viewing the Test

Whether you use the New File wizard or the Create JUnit Tests wizard, once the test class is generated it will open in the Source Editor window. You will also see that the package and class are listed under the Test Packages node in the Projects window.

Here is an excerpt from the sample `CalcTest` class for JUnit 3.x:

```
/**
 * Test of checkNum method, of class com.pronetbeans.examples.Calc.
 */
public void testCheckNum() {
    System.out.println("checkNum");

    int origVal = 0;
    Calc instance = new Calc();

    int expResult = 0;
    int result = instance.checkNum(origVal);
    assertEquals(expResult, result);

    // TODO review the generated test code and remove the default call to fail.
    fail("The test case is a prototype.");
}
```

The wizard analyzed the `Calc` class, determined that the public method `checkNum` should be included, and generated a test method for it named `testCheckNum`.

The `testCheckNum` method includes sample test code. This is the result of selecting the Default Method Bodies check box in the wizard. This test code does the following:

- Declares an `int` named `origVal` and sets it to zero
- Creates an instance of the `Calc` class named `instance`
- Declares an `int` named `expResult` and sets it to zero
- Passes the `origVal` variable to the `checkNum` method of the `Calc` class instance
- Sets the `int` that is returned to an `int` variable named `result`
- Calls a JUnit method `assertEquals` to test if the expected result (`expResult`) matches the actual result (`result`)
- Automatically fails the test by calling the JUnit method `fail`

The intention of this test is to pass a sample value to `Calc.checkNum` and compare the expected return result with the actual return result. The call to the `fail` method is automatically inserted into the test method to make sure that you at least review the method prior to running it. The `fail` and `assertEquals` methods are inherited from the `TestCase` superclass.

The foregoing testCheckNum JUnit test method would appear as follows if you used JUnit 4.x to generate the test:

```
/**
 * Test of checkNum method, of class com.pronetbeans.examples.Calc.
 */
@Test
public void checkNum() {
    System.out.println("checkNum");

    int origVal = 0;
    Calc instance = new Calc();

    int expResult = 0;
    int result = instance.checkNum(origVal);
    assertEquals(expResult, result);

    // TODO review the generated test code and remove the default call to fail.
    fail("The test case is a prototype.");
}
```

The JUnit 4.x version of the test does not vary much from the JUnit 3.x version. The main difference is the @Test annotation that flags the method as a JUnit test. It also does not contain the word *test* in the name of the method.

■ **Tip** In the test file in the Source Editor, you can press Ctrl+Spacebar to open the code completion box. Here, you can review the numerous overloaded assertEquals methods and the other inherited JUnit methods available in the test class.

Modifying the Test

In this example, you will want to make a few changes to the code to make sure the test will pass. First, change the value of the origVal variable to 20. The Calc.checkNum method takes the value 20 and performs an if-else check on it. It should then subtract 1 from the value and return the value 19. Knowing what the method should return, you can set the expResult variable in the testCheckNum method to a value of 19. If you make these changes and remove the explicit call to fail, the resulting test method looks like this (JUnit 3.x):

```
public void testCheckNum() {
    System.out.println("checkNum");
```

```
        int origVal = 20;
        Calc instance = new Calc();

        int expResult = 19;
        int result = instance.checkNum(origVal);
        assertEquals(expResult, result);
    }
```

and this (JUnit 4.x):

```
@Test
public void checkNum() {
    System.out.println("checkNum");

    int origVal = 20;
    Calc instance = new Calc();

    int expResult = 19;
    int result = instance.checkNum(origVal);
    assertEquals(expResult, result);
}
```

When the JUnit test classes execute, the `testCheckNum` and `checkNum` methods should now pass.

You do not have to use one of the `assertEquals` methods to pass or fail a test method. You can perform any manual comparison you like and explicitly fail the test case. Suppose you want the expected result to be 18. Based on an original value of 20, the actual result should be 19. You could write a test to check if the expected and actual results were equal and fail the test, since they should *not* be equal, like this:

```
public void testCheckNumFail() {

    int origVal = 20;
    Calc instance = new Calc();

    int expResult = 18;
    int result = instance.checkNum(origVal);
    if(expResult == result) {
        fail("The expected result should NOT match the actual result.");
    }
}
```

Running JUnit Tests

Once you have written JUnit tests, you need to execute them. You can choose to run all the tests in a project or to run a test individually.

You can run the tests for an entire project in any of the following ways:

- Right-click the project name and select Test Project from the context menu.
- From the main menu, select Run ➤ Test "*Project-Name.*"
- Use the keyboard shortcut Alt+F6.

You can run a single test in any of the following ways (using the `Calc` class test from the previous section as an example):

- Right-click the test class under the Test Packages node in the Projects window and select Run File. NetBeans knows it should be run as a JUnit test.
- If the test class is open in the Source Editor, right-click anywhere in the code and select Run File from the context menu.
- If the test class is selected in the Source Editor, Projects, or Files window, then from the main menu select Run ➤ Run File ➤ Run "Calc.java."
- If the test class is selected, use the keyboard shortcut Shift+F6.
- If the test's matching source class is open, select Run ➤ Run File ➤ Test "Calc.java." This will execute the matching JUnit test in the Test Packages node.

Viewing Test Results

After one or more JUnit tests have executed, you can view the results in the JUnit Test Results window. To open this window, select Window ➤ Output ➤ JUnit Test Results. Figure 9-4 shows an example of test results.

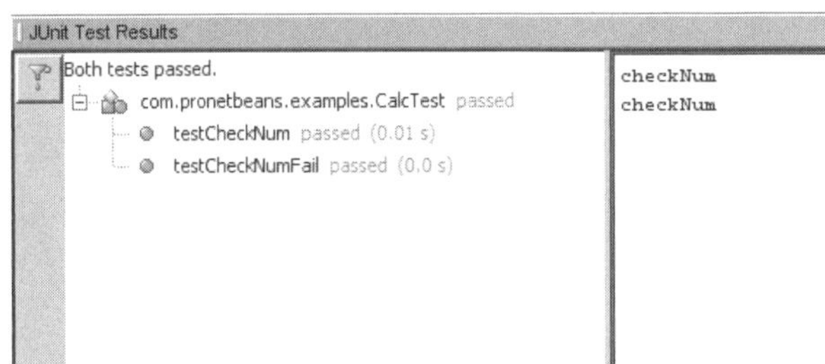

Figure 9-4. *The JUnit Test Results window after test case execution*

At the top of the JUnit Test Results window are two buttons that represent different views of the JUnit results and a button for filtering results. By default, the Statistics view appears. Clicking the Output button displays the standard output and error results from the JUnit test execution. If you used `System.out.*` or `System.err.*` in any of the tests or tested classes, the data will be listed.

The button to the right of the Output button allows you to filter the view to show only failed tests. If you click this filter button and execute the project tests, you will see lines displayed only for test classes that had at least one failure. This is a nice feature, especially if you are running hundreds of tests and receiving only a handful of failures. You can quickly see what is failing and avoid having to scroll down a long list of test classes that passed.

In the Statistics view for this example, you see the message “Both tests passed,” since only two test methods were created. For each JUnit test class in the test package, you should see an individual line, with the fully qualified class name and a pass/fail label next to it.

You can click the plus icon next to the class name to expand the class and display the individual method test cases. If a test method passed, it will be listed with a green “passed” label, along with the approximate time it took to execute.

To see what happens when a test fails, you can modify the `CalcTest` code from the previous section. In the `testCheckNumFail` method, change the code `int expResult = 18;` to read `int expResult = 19;`. The expected and actual results will then be equivalent, the `if` statement will pass, and the explicit call to the `fail` method will run, thereby failing the test case. After changing the code and running the JUnit tests, the JUnit Test Results window should display the results shown in Figure 9-5.

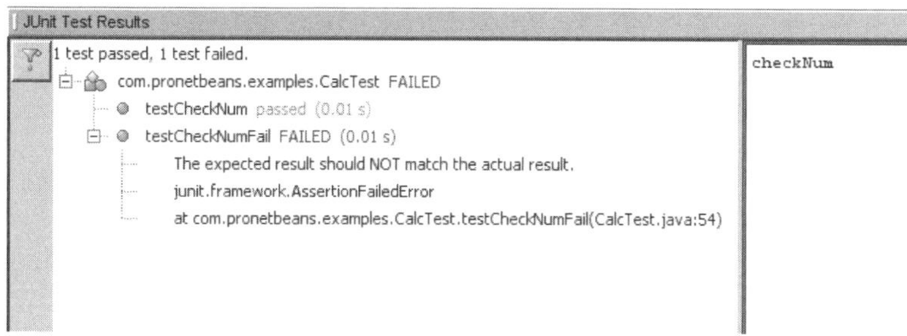

Figure 9-5. *The JUnit Test Results window after a test fails*

In this example, the Statistics view now shows the message “1 test passed, 1 test failed.” Alongside the fully qualified class name is a red “FAILED” message. If numerous classes were listed, you could quickly pick out which class had at least one failure in it. Clicking the plus icon next to the class displays the individual test methods.

One of the nice features of the JUnit Test Results window is that, for any test method that failed, you can see error-related output by clicking the plus icon next to it. The message “The expected result should NOT match the actual result” was the text that was logged with the explicit call to the `fail` method in the `CalcTest.testCheckNumFail` method. You can double-click the line that lists that the `testCheckNumFail` method failed, and the `CalcTest` class will open in the Source Editor.

Generating Test Case Reports

An additional option for viewing JUnit results data is available. Since NetBeans projects are layered on top of Ant, you can use the JUnit Ant tasks to generate test case reports. (See Chapter 8 for more information about Ant tasks.)

Listing 9-1 shows a sample Ant task that allows you to execute the project test classes and generate a special output of JUnit test results.

Listing 9-1. *Ant Task for Executing Test Classes and Generating Test Result Output*

```
<target name="JUnit-Tests-With-Reports" depends="compile,compile-test">
    <junit fork="yes" dir="${basedir}" failureProperty="test.failed">
        <classpath location="${build.classes.dir}" />
        <classpath location="${build.test.classes.dir}" />
        <formatter type="xml" />
        <test name="${testcase}" todir="${reports.junit.dir}" if="testcase" />
        <batchtest todir="${reports.junit.dir}" unless="testcase">
            <fileset dir="${test.src.dir}">
                <include name="**/*Test.java" />
            </fileset>
        </batchtest>
    </junit>

    <junitreport todir="${reports.junit.dir}">
        <fileset dir="${reports.junit.dir}">
            <include name="TEST-*.xml" />
        </fileset>
        <report format="frames" todir="${reports.junit.dir}" />
    </junitreport>

</target>
```

The target is named `JUnit-Tests-With-Reports`, so it stands out as a custom Ant task in your build file. It depends on the NetBeans project targets of `compile` and `compile-test`, so each time this target is executed, the code in the Source and Test Packages nodes is always compiled afresh.

It then uses the `junit` and `junitreport` Ant tasks. The script defines several classpath and directory properties to tell the Ant tasks where the source is located, which files to include, where to dump the output of the JUnit test execution, and where the final JUnit test results report is deposited. The property `${reports.junit.dir}` is defined higher up in the build file as follows:

```
<property name="reports.junit.dir" value="reports/junit/" />
```

I use a `reports` base directory so that my other plug-ins can deposit results into subdirectories within it.

Once you have created the new target, you can trigger it to run the project tests and generate the JUnit report files any time you wish. The JUnit test result format is similar to a Javadoc-style web site. It lists the tests by package and class and displays the pass/fail results for each individual method. Figure 9-6 shows a sample test results report. As you can see, this report provides information that is nearly the same as that in the NetBeans JUnit Test Results window. However, with this approach, you can zip or tar the report files and catalog the results or send them to a colleague.

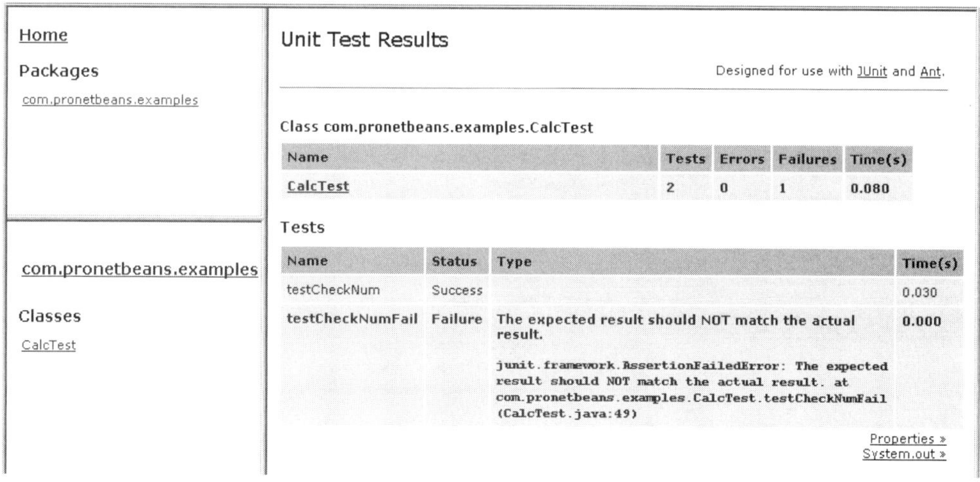

Figure 9-6. *A sample JUnit test results report*

Configuring JUnit Properties in NetBeans

You may have noticed that as you use the various JUnit wizards and tools, several properties are enabled or disabled by default (see Figures 9-1, 9-2, and 9-3).

As you create more and more test cases, you will not want to have to repeatedly check the same properties that you use most often. You can set which JUnit properties are enabled by default to save time when generating JUnit test classes.

To set the properties, select Tools ➤ Options. Click the Advanced Options button. In the left pane under the Testing folder, select the JUnit Tests option. The pane on the right will display the JUnit default properties, as shown in Figure 9-7. Using the check boxes, you can disable and enable properties as desired.

■ **Tip** The Test Skeleton Generator property contains the values JUnit 3.x, JUnit 4.x, and Ask. Using this property you can set JUnit either to generate test skeletons for a specific version of JUnit every time or to ask you which version. Since I do a lot of Java 5 work, I tend to set this to JUnit 4.x so that I can include annotations in my test classes.

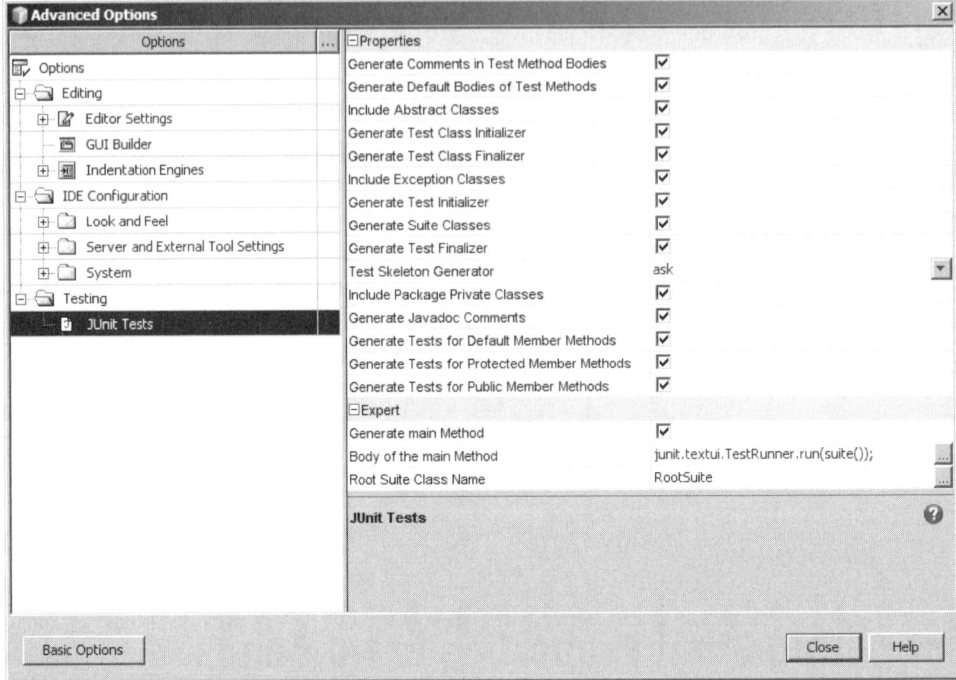

Figure 9-7. *The JUnit default properties in the Advanced Options window*

The properties in the Expert section offer additional settings:

Generate main Method: Specifies that a `main` method should be generated during the creation of the JUnit test.

Body of the main Method: Contains the default method body for the `main` method that is created. Adding a `main` method to your JUnit tests is necessary if you want to execute your tests from the command line.

Summary

This chapter covered how to run JUnit tests on your code, whether JUnit 3.x or 4.x. Writing tests that are thorough and repeatable provides a comfort level as source code evolves. Programmers can make enhancements to application code, run the set of project tests, and know what passes and fails.

The industry standard for testing is the JUnit framework. NetBeans provides support for JUnit via Ant build files and several integrated tools. You can use NetBeans to generate tests based on existing classes, execute all tests in a project, and view test results directly within the IDE.

CHAPTER 10

Refactoring

Refactoring capabilities are very important when working in the software industry. Anyone who has ever had to overhaul an existing code base has run into issues with changing code. One of the most common examples is moving classes between packages and having to edit the package statements manually at the top of each file. Another example is wanting to delete an element in code (such as a class member or an old utility method) and not knowing if code in your application still makes use of that element.

Performing these types of operations manually can be time consuming and prone to error. In the days before advanced development environments, programmers used simpler tools, like basic text editors, vi, or Emacs. While some of these tools allow you to search, match, and replace text, they are not Java-aware and thus may produce incorrect results.

With the advanced capabilities available in IDE tools like NetBeans, developers have tool sets for refactoring code. With access to parsed source files and near-real-time syntax validation, NetBeans can intelligently allow a developer to alter source code.

In this chapter, we review the NetBeans refactoring options.

NetBeans Refactoring Options

NetBeans provides many refactoring options on its Refactor menu:

- Move
- Rename
- Copy
- Safe Delete
- Use Supertype Where Possible
- Move Inner to Outer Level
- Encapsulate Fields
- Pull Up
- Push Down
- Convert Anonymous to Inner

- Introduce Variable, Constant, Field, or Method
- Extract Interface
- Extract Superclass
- Change Method Parameters

These refactorings are discussed in more detail in the following sections. Executing each refactoring presents a dialog box with options for the corresponding refactoring. All of them include a Preview button that allows you to simulate the refactoring.

When it comes to refactoring, no tool is perfect, so I recommend previewing changes before applying them. As shown in Figure 10-1, the preview window allows you to review each and every change that will be made to your code before it is applied. For most of the refactorings, the preview window will also display a Diff window. This will show the existing class compared to what the updated class would look like after the refactoring. This is a powerful new feature in NetBeans 6, since you can see each change actually highlighted in the source code.

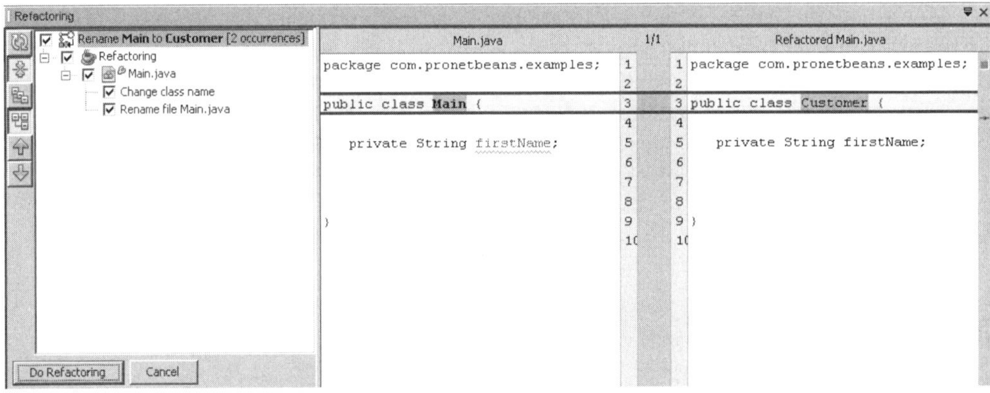

Figure 10-1. *Previewing changes for Rename refactoring*

The icons along the left side of the preview window let you work with the preview as follows:

- The top icon refreshes the refactoring changes listed in the window in case anything changes, such as code edits in the Source Editor.
- The second icon collapses or expands the tree hierarchy of the changes. This can be very useful when the list of changes is long.
- The third icon displays the logical view of the refactoring actions that will be performed. Each potential change is listed by each class underneath each package.
- The fourth icon displays the physical view of the refactoring actions that will be performed. Each potential change is listed by each class.
- The last two icons let you navigate up and down to each change.

As you use the icons to navigate up and down the changes in the preview window, the Diff comparison window will automatically jump to and display the matching change. This lets you examine each change if you are concerned about the validity of the refactoring. You can either click the Do Refactoring button to apply the changes or click Cancel if you don't want the changes to be made.

Move Class Refactoring

Moving a Java class from one package to another seems like a simple task at first glance. A developer can manually copy and paste a source file into the new directory and then edit the package statement at the top of the file. However, if other classes import or reference that class, then the developer must also search through and modify those files.

In NetBeans, Move Class refactoring does exactly what the name implies. It allows you to move a Java class to a different project or a different package hierarchy or between source and test packages. It also corrects the references to the moved class that exist in other classes.

To apply Move Class refactoring, select a class, and then choose Refactor ➤ Move. You will see the Move Class dialog box, as shown in Figure 10-2. In the Move Class dialog box, you can choose to move the class to a different project, source package location, or package.

■ **Tip** If you move one or more classes to the wrong package and apply the changes, don't panic. Most refactorings can be undone in NetBeans. From the main Refactoring menu, just select the Undo option.

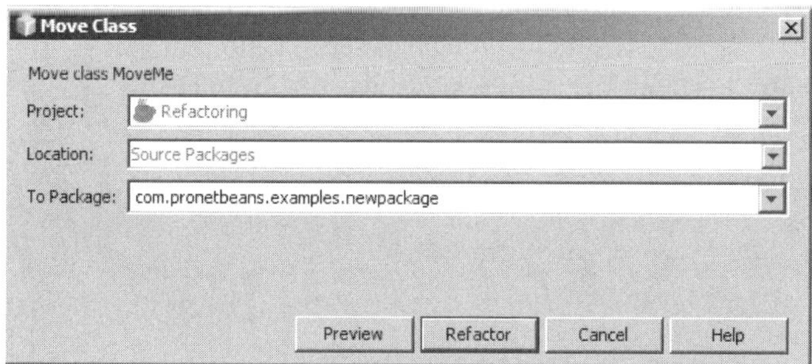

Figure 10-2. *The Move Class dialog box*

You can also activate Move Class refactoring by dragging and dropping a class in the Projects window into a different location. The only difference in using the refactoring in this manner is that an additional option appears in the Move Class dialog box: Move Without Refactoring. If this option is checked, NetBeans moves the class without scanning additional classes to correct references to the moved class. You might want to use this option if you need to move a class out of a package temporarily and move it back later. For example, while testing a package or running some analysis tool against a package, you may want to quickly exclude a class under development.

Rename Refactoring

Rename refactoring can serve two main purposes:

Renaming Java classes: Rename refactoring allows you to change not only the name of the class but also any constructors, internal usages, and references to the renamed class by other classes. If you need to rename a Java class, this is definitely the way to do it.

Renaming entire package structures: This can be useful if a programmer named a package incorrectly or misspelled a word that appears in the package structure. Rather than having to make the corrections manually, you can apply the Rename option to correct the errors all at once across the entire project.

To rename a class or package, select it and choose Refactor ➤ Rename. Enter the new name in the Rename Refactoring window and click the Refactor button. The changes will be made to the package name. If you want to preview the changes before executing the refactoring, click the Preview button instead. The Preview Refactoring window will appear listing each change to be made.

Safe Delete Refactoring

During the software development process, programmers frequently revisit previously written code. They review what was written and decide what can and cannot be cleaned up and removed. One common mistake is removing a class member variable that you think is not used, only to find out it does indeed appear in your code, and now your class does not compile.

With Safe Delete refactoring, you can identify each usage of a class, method, or field in code before deleting it. This functionality can be invaluable, especially if you are removing a class method that may be used by multiple classes.

For example, consider the following code fragment, which is a sample method that declares several method local variables and performs some nonsense operations:

```
public void calc() {

    int y = 2;
    int x = 0;
    int z = 0;

    z = x + y;

    if(z>3) {
        System.out.println("Z was greater than 3");
    }
    else if(y==2){
        System.out.println("x = "  + x);
    }
}
```

During a review of this class, you decide to delete the variable x. You could visually scan the class to see if the x variable is being used anywhere. In this example, it is pretty easy to find x as output in the `System.out.println` statement. However, if this method were a 100 lines long and contained multiple nested statements, spotting x would be much more difficult.

To execute the Safe Delete refactoring, highlight the variable you want to delete (x in the example) and select Refactor ➤ Safe Delete from the main menu. In the Safe Delete dialog box, checking the Search in Comments check box makes sure that the element is also deleted in any Javadoc comments in which it may appear. The only other option is the standard Preview button, allowing you to review each change before it is made.

If an element is used nowhere in your code, it is safe to delete. However, if the element you are attempting to delete is used somewhere in your code, some additional steps may be necessary. After clicking the Refactor button in the initial Safe Delete dialog box, a list of errors and warnings will appear, as shown in Figure 10-3. As long as only warnings are displayed, you can proceed with the refactoring.

If you see errors in the list, you'll need to do a bit of work. The Show Usages button is key to resolving any sections in your code that reference the variable being deleted. Click the Show Usages button to open the Usages window, as shown in Figure 10-4.

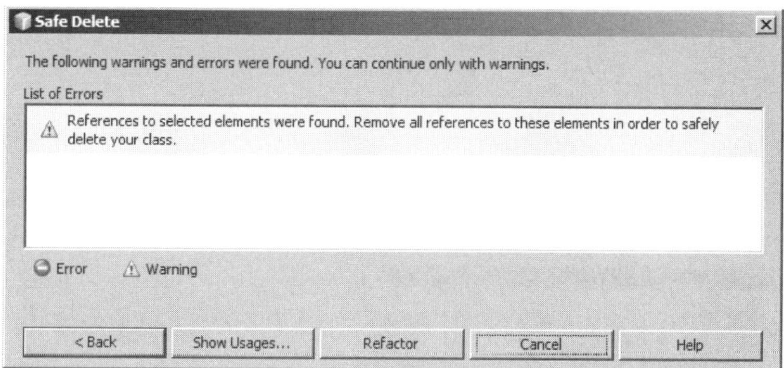

Figure 10-3. *List of errors and warnings for Safe Delete refactoring*

The Usages window displays each usage of the element you are trying to delete. Click a usage in the window, and the exact line in the source code will open in the Source Editor window. After navigating to each usage and manually correcting the code not to use the variable being deleted, you can click the Rerun Safe Delete button.

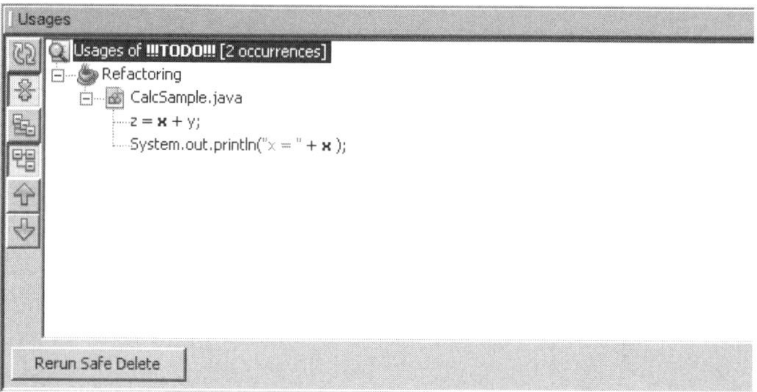

Figure 10-4. *Viewing usages of the element to delete*

Safe Delete refactoring may seem like a waste of time in certain circumstances. For instance, you may not need it if you are deleting a local variable in a method that is five or ten lines long. It is most useful if you have a class member variable or method that runs across numerous classes. The Safe Delete option allows you to review each usage and make sure you do not delete the element until there are no more references to it.

Use Supertype Where Possible Refactoring

Use Supertype Where Possible refactoring converts usage of a subclass to a superclass. Suppose you have the following code in a source file:

```
ArrayList myarray = new ArrayList();
```

If you want to convert it to use a specific superclass, double-click or highlight the object type `ArrayList` and select Refactor ➤ Use Supertype Where Possible. You'll see the Use Supertype dialog box, which allows you to select a superclass or interface, as shown in Figure 10-5.

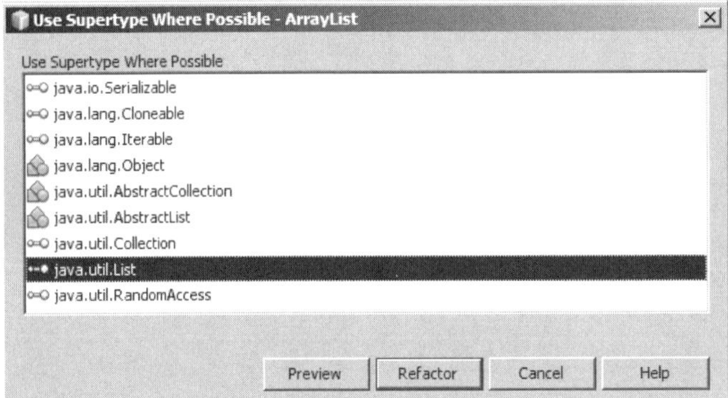

Figure 10-5. *Use Supertype Where Possible dialog box for java.util.ArrayList*

Obviously, this is a ridiculously simple example, but it demonstrates the core functionality. This method can also be used in conjunction with Extract Superclass refactoring, described later in this chapter.

Move Inner to Outer Level Refactoring

Move Inner to Outer Level refactoring converts an inner class to a separate external class declared in its own file. Suppose you have the following code, in which the `InnerClass` class is declared inside the `OuterClass` class.

```
public class OuterClass {
    public class InnerClass {
        public void execute() {
            System.out.println("execute...");
        }
    }
}
```

To move the InnerClass class to its own source file, highlight the class name and select Refactor ➤ Move Inner to Outer Level. In the Move Inner to Outer Level dialog box, you can specify a new name for the class that is being moved, as shown in Figure 10-6. This can be convenient, especially since inner classes are often named to make sense within the context of the containing outer class. Optionally, you can select to declare a field for the current outer class and enter a name for that field.

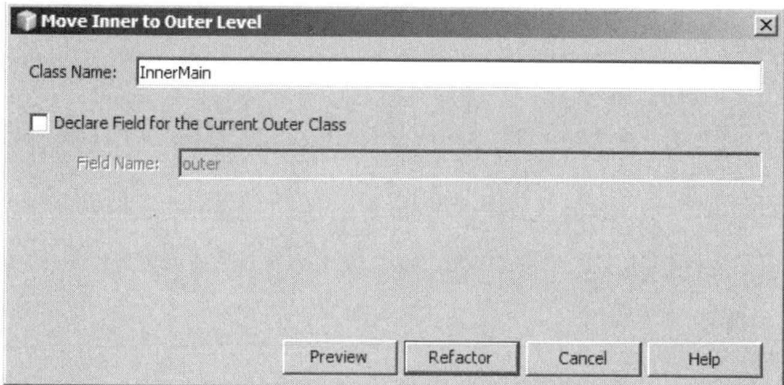

Figure 10-6. *The Move Inner to Outer Level dialog box*

If you apply the refactoring without selecting the Declare Field check box, then when you click the Refactor button, the following code results:

```
public class InnerMain {
    public void execute() {
        System.out.println("execute...");
    }
}
```

The InnerClass code is moved to its own individual source file with its new name, InnerMain, in the same package as OuterClass.

If you select the Declare Field for the Current Outer Class option and name a variable, the refactored code looks like this:

```
public class InnerMain {

    com.pronetbeans.examples.OuterClass outer;

    public void execute() {
        System.out.println("execute...");
    }
}
```

This option can be useful when separating the classes, especially if the InnerClass class made use of the members or methods of the OuterClass class.

Encapsulate Fields Refactoring

When writing applications, it is often useful to represent objects in the real world as classes with attributes. For example, you may choose to represent the fields for an employee as an Employee class with first name and last name public members:

```
public class Employee {
    public String FirstName;
    public String LastName;
}
```

Of course, you might also include address, phone number, organizational, and personal fields in the class.

Such an Employee class is quick and easy to work with, such as in the following code:

```
public class NewHire {
    public static void main(String[] args) {
        Employee newemp = new Employee();
        newemp.FirstName = args[0];
        newemp.LastName = args[1];
        saveEmployee(newemp);
    }
}
```

In the NewHire class, an instance of Employee is instantiated and the FirstName and LastName fields are set from the arguments passed on the command line. (Obviously, there are a lot of problems with the code in the NewHire class, such as no parameter or error checking, but here we are just focusing on the topic of encapsulation.)

As a programmer, you should be starting to realize this approach has some negative design features. For example, suppose your client has requested that the employee name be stored in the database with initial capital letters, such as John Smith. However, in the application the values need to be processed in uppercase. You could rewrite the entire application to add the usage of String.toUpperCase() anywhere the Employee.FirstName and Employee.LastName fields are output or processed throughout the entire code base. You could also encapsulate the fields.

Encapsulation involves controlling access to a class member variable using getter and setter methods. The class member variable is set to private so that no code outside the class can interact with it. The getter and setter methods are usually given a public accessor so that any code can retrieve or set the value of the member variable.

In the following code, the Employee class has been modified to use getters and setters for the FirstName and LastName member variables:

```
public class Employee {
   private String FirstName;
   private String LastName;

   public void setFirstName(String FirstName) {
       this.FirstName = FirstName;
   }
```

```
    public String getFirstName() {
        return this.FirstName;
    }

    public void setLastName(String LastName) {
        this.LastName = LastName;
    }

    public String getLastName() {
        return this.LastName;
    }
}
```

You can also modify the code in the `NewHire` class to interact with the updated `Employee` class. The `NewHire` class must now use the getter and setter methods:

```
public class NewHire {
    public static void main(String[] args) {

        Employee newemp = new Employee();
        newemp.setFirstName(args[0]);
        newemp.setLastName(args[1]);

        saveEmployee(newemp);
    }
}
```

With this type of design, you are in a better position to modify the code to handle special conditions. In the example, the code in the `Employee` class can be modified to convert the member variables to uppercase when they are set using `Employee.setFirstName` and `Employee.setLastName`:

```
public class Employee {
    private String FirstName;
    private String LastName;

    public void setFirstName(String FirstName) {
        if(FirstName!=null) {
            this.FirstName = FirstName.toUpperCase();
        } else {
            this.FirstName = null;
        }
    }

    public String getFirstName() {
        return this.FirstName;
    }
```

```
    public void setLastName(String LastName) {
        if(LastName!=null) {
            this.LastName = LastName.toUpperCase();
        } else {
            this.LastName = null;
        }
    }

    public String getLastName() {
        return this.LastName;
    }
}
```

Note It is usually preferable to perform any data conversion, checking, or modification in the setter method for a member variable rather than in the getter method. If the data conversion is implemented in the getter, each time the data is retrieved, the data conversion will take place, thus reducing performance slightly.

Generally, it is a common best practice never to have a public member of a class for which you write other code to set or get the value. Arguably, the only exception to the rule is with static constants.

Now that you have read a quick review of a key object-oriented concept, we can discuss how NetBeans can assist in encapsulation. (I apologize to those of you groaning about now, but this is one of the most frequent mistakes I see programmers make, so it deserves some review.)

Encapsulate Fields refactoring in NetBeans allows you easily to implement the design paradigm of encapsulation. It helps you to generate getter and setter methods for the members of a class to enforce good design.

Suppose you have the simple `Employee` class shown at the beginning of this section:

```
public class Employee {
    public String FirstName;
    public String LastName;
}
```

If you highlight the name of the class and select Refactor ➤ Encapsulate Fields, the Encapsulate Fields dialog box will list all the class fields, unselected by default. If you highlight a specific class field and select the Encapsulate Fields option, the dialog box will still display the entire list of fields in the class, but only the field you highlighted will be selected. For example, if you highlighted the `FirstName` field, the dialog box will list both the fields, as shown in Figure 10-7.

You can disable or enable creation of the getter and setter methods using the check box next to each one. In this dialog box, you can also manually alter the names of the getter and setters methods. The "Fields' Visibility" and "Accessors' Visibility" drop-down lists allow you to set the access level to the original fields (should be private) and to the getters and setters (should be public), respectively.

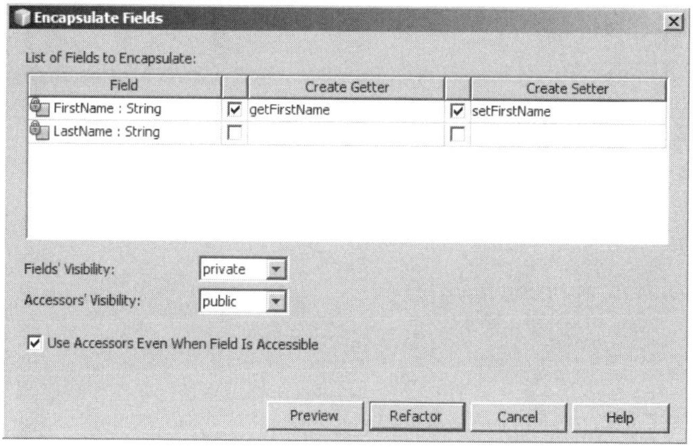

Figure 10-7. *Encapsulate Fields dialog box*

In my opinion, the Use Accessors Even When Field Is Accessible option should always remain checked. Then the refactoring procedure attempts to correct code in other classes that use the class member variables and convert it to use the accessors (getters and setters). The only time you might want to disable this option is when you set the Fields' Visibility option to anything other than private. The refactoring will then perform the Encapsulate Fields operation but will not convert code to use the accessors.

Once the overall refactoring is complete, the `Employee` class should look like this:

```
public class Employee {
    private String FirstName;
    private String LastName;

    public String getFirstName()
    {
        return FirstName;
    }

    public void setFirstName(String FirstName)
    {
        this.FirstName = FirstName;
    }

    public String getLastName()
    {
        return LastName;
    }

    public void setLastName(String LastName)
    {
        this.LastName = LastName;
    }
}
```

Pull Up Refactoring

Pull Up refactoring is useful when dealing with classes and superclasses. It allows you to move class members and methods from a subclass up into the superclass.

For example, suppose you have a Vehicle class and a Truck class that extends Vehicle:

```
public class Vehicle
{
    public void start()
    {
        // start the vehicle
    }
}

public class Truck extends Vehicle
{
    public void stop()
    {
        // stop the vehicle
    }
}
```

If you want to move the stop() method from the Truck subclass to the Vehicle superclass, select the stop() method and select Refactor ➤ Pull Up. In the Pull Up dialog box, select the destination supertype, the exact list of members to pull up, and whether or not to make them abstract, as shown in Figure 10-8.

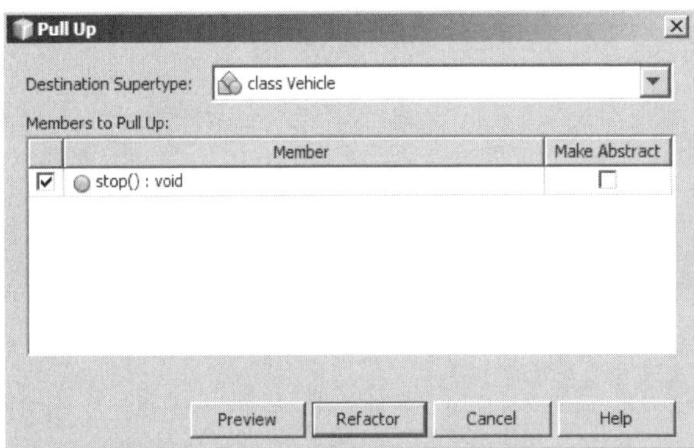

Figure 10-8. *The Pull Up dialog box*

Once the refactoring changes have been applied, the Truck and Vehicle classes look like this:

```
public class Vehicle
{
    public void start()
    {
        // start the vehicle
    }
```

```
    public void stop()
    {
        // stop the vehicle
    }
}

public class Truck extends Vehicle
{
}
```

Push Down Refactoring

Push Down refactoring is exactly the opposite of Pull Up refactoring. It pushes an inner class, field, or method in a superclass down into a subclass. For example, suppose that you added a `lowerTailgate()` method to the `Vehicle` class shown in the previous example:

```
public class Vehicle
{
    public void start()
    {
        // start the vehicle
    }

    public void stop()
    {
        // stop the vehicle
    }

    public void lowerTailgate()
    {
        // lower tailgate of vehicle
    }
}

public class Truck extends Vehicle
{
}
```

However, since many vehicles (such as cars, planes, and boats) do not have tailgates, you want to push the `lowerTailgate()` method down to the `Truck` subclass.

Select the `lowerTailgate()` method and choose Refactor ➤ Push Down. In the Push Down dialog box, select which class members you want to push down into the subclass, as shown in Figure 10-9. You can also choose whether you would like to keep them abstract if they already are abstract.

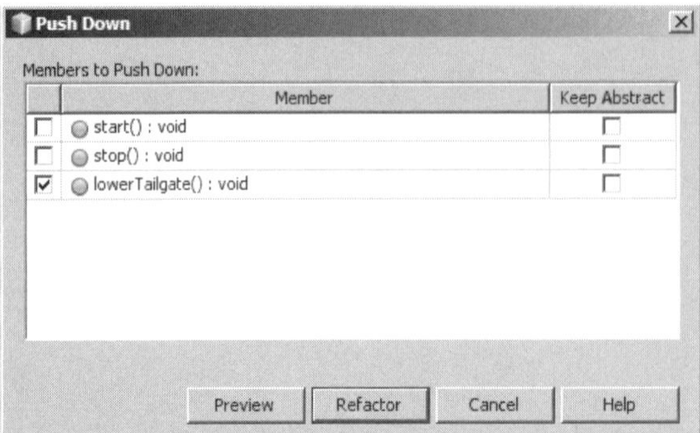

Figure 10-9. *The Push Down dialog box*

After you have applied the code changes, you can view the result. As expected, the `lowerTailgate()` method will now be in the `Truck` subclass:

```
public class Truck extends Vehicle
{
    public void lowerTailgate()
    {
        // do something
    }
}
```

If the superclass has multiple subclasses (which is usually the case), you could still perform a Push Down refactoring of a method from a particular class. For example, if you had a `Car` subclass that extended `Vehicle`, you could still push down a method from the `Vehicle` class. Suppose the `Truck`, `Car`, and `Vehicle` classes were defined as follows:

```
public class Vehicle
{
    public void changeTire()
    {
        // general method for changing tire
    }
}

public class Car extends Vehicle
{
   // car class
}

public class Truck extends Vehicle
{
  // truck class
}
```

The Truck class represents a large tractor-trailer. Changing a tire for this type of vehicle will most likely involve a different procedure than for a car. Thus, you might want to have the changeTire() method in the Car and Truck classes override the one in the Vehicle superclass. The changeTire() method in the Vehicle class should also be left as abstract (even though some vehicles, such as boats, do not have tires that need changing).

In the Push Down dialog box, you need to select the check box to keep the changeTire() method abstract in the Vehicle class. Preview the changes to make sure the code is modified as you expect. In Figure 10-10, notice that the third suggested operation is altering Vehicle.changeTire() to make it abstract. If the Keep Abstract option is not selected during the refactoring operation, then the line in the preview window would say, "Remove changeTire() element." You could prevent it from being removed from the Vehicle class by unselecting the check box next to this option.

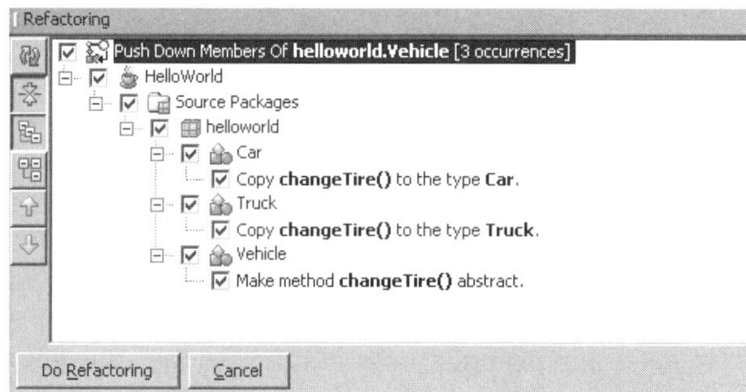

Figure 10-10. *Push Down refactoring with one superclass and two subclasses*

Convert Anonymous to Inner Refactoring

Convert Anonymous to Inner refactoring is used to separate an anonymous inner class into an actual inner class. There are several varieties of anonymous inner classes:

- Inner class for defining and instantiating an instance of an unnamed subclass
- Inner class for defining and instantiating an anonymous implementation of an interface
- Anonymous inner class defined as an argument to a method

For this section, we focus on the first type: unnamed subclasses.

Suppose you have the following code:

```
public class Item {
    public void assemble() {
        System.out.println("Item.assemble");
    }
}
```

```
public class Factory {
    public void makeStandardItem(int type) {
        if(type==0) {
            // make extremely unusual item .01% of the time
            Item myitem = new Item() {
                public void assemble() {
                    System.out.println("anonymous Item.assemble");
                }
            };
            myitem.assemble();
        } else {
            // make standard item 99.9% of the time
            Item myitem = new Item();
            myitem.assemble();
        }
    }
}
```

The code declares a class `Item` with a method named `assemble()`. The `Factory` class defines a variable `myitem` of type `Item` and instantiates an anonymous subclass of `Item` that overrides the `assemble()` method.

Why would you bother using an anonymous inner class instead of a normal inner or outer class? In this example, if the one-off case where the anonymous inner class is used were the only area where it is needed, you might not want to create a separate class. However, if you find that you need the code in the anonymous subclass in multiple areas, you might want to convert it to an inner class.

To convert the code to an inner class, click anywhere inside the anonymous class or highlight the name of the `Item` class constructor in the following section of the code:

```
Item myitem = new Item() {
    public void assemble() {
        System.out.println("anonymous Item.assemble");
    }
};
```

Then select Refactor ➤ Convert Anonymous Class to Inner. In the Convert Anonymous Class to Inner dialog box, you'll see the default class name of `NewClass`, as shown in Figure 10-11. You can set the name of the new inner class that will be created, the access level, and whether it should be declared static. If the constructor for the anonymous class has any parameters, the dialog box will also list them.

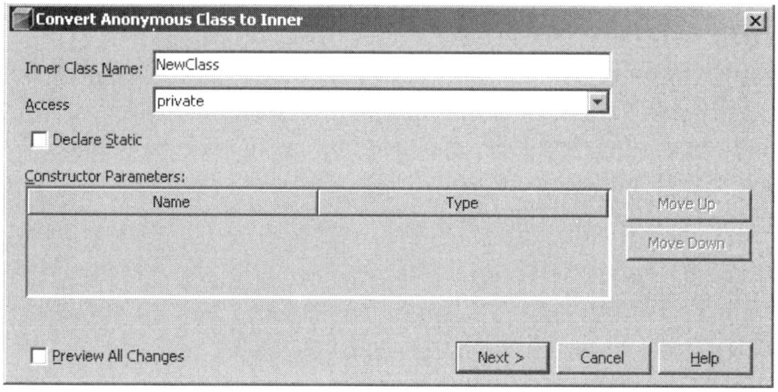

Figure 10-11. *The Convert Anonymous Class to Inner dialog box*

Suppose you named the new inner class `StrangeItem`. The refactored code would look like this:

```
private class StrangeItem extends Item {

    public void assemble() {
        System.out.println("anonymous Item.assemble");
    }
}
```

This class would be declared inside the `Factory` class, since that is where the original anonymous inner class resides.

In the following code, notice that the creation of the anonymous inner class has been altered to create an instance of the new inner class:

```
public void makeStandardItem(int type) {
    if(type==0) {
        // make extremely unusual item .01% of the time
        Item myitem = new StrangeItem();
        myitem.assemble();
    } else {
        // make standard item 99.9% of the time
        Item myitem = new Item();
        myitem.assemble();
    }
}
```

The purpose of this refactoring is to make your code more reusable and modular. Extracting the anonymous inner class into its own inner class helps improve many aspects of your code. It makes no sense to redefine the same anonymous inner class in multiple places in the `Factory` class, and Convert Anonymous to Inner refactoring can help correct the situation.

Introduce Method Refactoring

As you review code in a project, you may notice that certain sections of code, even small ones, contain similar-looking blocks of code. These blocks of code can be extracted into a separate method that can then be called. Separating out blocks of code makes your code more readable, more reusable, and easier to maintain.

As a simple example, suppose you have the following code:

```
public void processArray(String[] names)
{
    for(int i=0;i < names.length; i++)
    {
        names[i] = names[i].toUpperCase();
    }
    // rest of method here
}
```

This block of code contains a loop that iterates through a String array and converts each String to uppercase. You might want to put this code into a separate method. Introduce Method refactoring can do this for you.

To activate the refactoring, highlight the code you want to convert to a method and select Refactor ➤ Introduce Method. In this example, highlight the entire for loop in the processArray(String[]) method.

In the Introduce Method dialog box, you can set the name of the new method and the access level, as shown in Figure 10-12. The refactoring is even smart enough to assume that a String array should be passed into the method and lists it as a parameter for the new method.

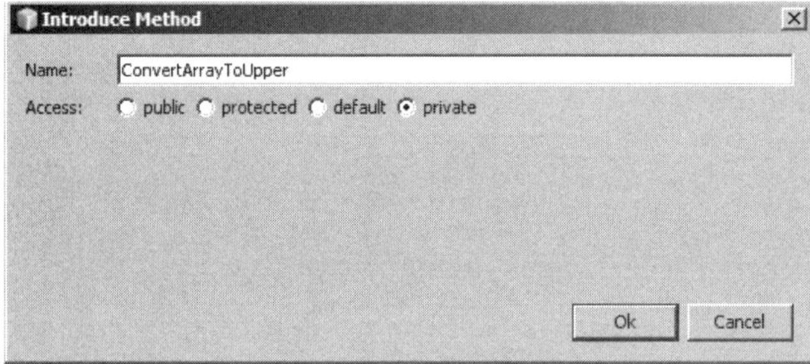

Figure 10-12. *The Introduce Method dialog box*

After applying the refactoring, the resulting code has the loop split out:

```
public void processArray(String[] names)
{
    ConvertArrayToUpper(names);
    // other method code here
}
```

```
private void ConvertArrayToUpper(final String[] names)
{
    for(int i=0;i < names.length; i++)
    {
        names[i] = names[i].toUpperCase();
    }
}
```

You can see that not only has the selected code been extracted into a separate method, but it was also replaced with the correct call to the new method with the correct parameter.

Extract Interface Refactoring

Extract Interface refactoring allows you to select public non-static methods and move them into an interface. This can be useful as you attempt to make your code more reusable and easier to maintain.

For example, suppose you want to extract two public non-static methods in the following `Item` class into an interface:

```
public class Item {
    public void assemble() {
        System.out.println("Item.assemble");
    }

    public void sell() {
        System.out.println("sell me");
    }
}
```

You can activate the refactoring by highlighting the class in the Projects window (or simply by having the class open in the Source Editor) and selecting Refactor ➤ Extract Interface. As shown in Figure 10-13, the options for the Extract Interface refactoring are quite straightforward. You can specify the name of the new interface that will be created. You can also select exactly which methods you want to include in the interface.

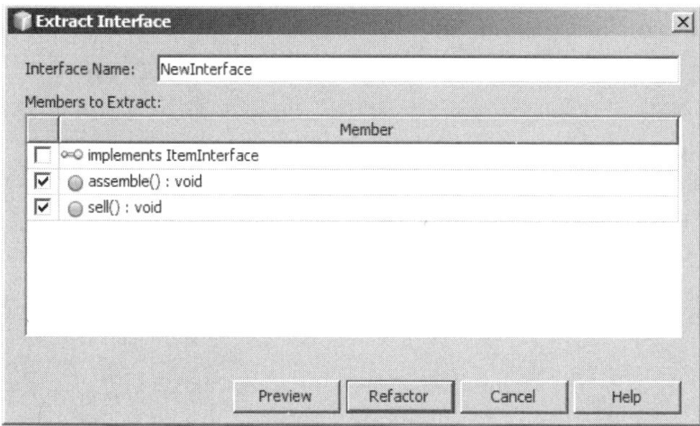

Figure 10-13. *The Extract Interface dialog box*

After applying the refactoring, the code for the interface looks like this:

```
public interface ItemInterface {
    void assemble();
    void sell();
}

public class Item implements ItemInterface {
    public void assemble() {
        System.out.println("Item.assemble");
    }

    public void sell() {
        System.out.println("sell me");
    }
}
```

The original `Item` class has been modified to implement the `ItemInterface`.

Extract Superclass Refactoring

Extract Superclass refactoring is nearly identical to Extract Interface refactoring. The only difference is that Extract Superclass pulls methods into a newly created superclass and extends the refactored class.

In the refactored code example from the previous section, you might want to modify the `Item` class to have a superclass:

```
public class Item implements ItemInterface {
    public void assemble() {
        System.out.println("Item.assemble");
    }

    public void sell() {
        System.out.println("sell me");
    }
}
```

Starting with the `Item` class selected, select Refactor ➤ Extract Superclass. As shown in Figure 10-14, the Extract Superclass dialog box allows you to set the name of the new superclass that will be created. You can select which members you wish to extract and place in the superclass. Since the `Item` class implements the `ItemInterface`, you can decide if you want to extract the `implements` clause into the superclass. You can also select whether or not the methods that are extracted are made abstract in the superclass. Selecting this option inserts abstract methods into the superclass and leaves the concrete implementations in the `Item` subclass.

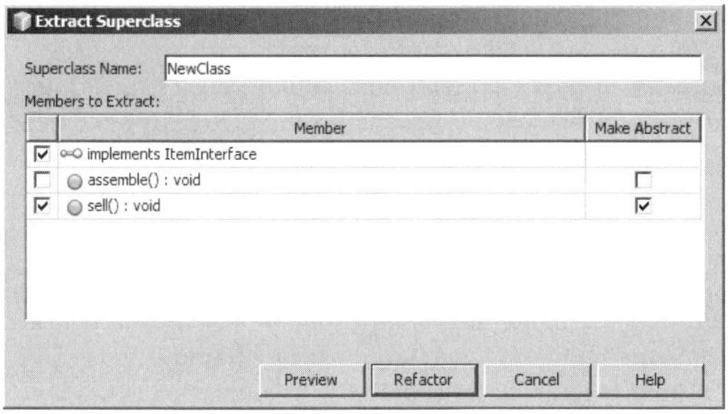

Figure 10-14. *The Extract Superclass dialog box*

For this example, select all the members for extraction. Then select the "Make Abstract" field only for the `Item.sell()` method. Preview the changes and apply the refactoring. The following code will be generated:

```
public interface ItemInterface {
    void assemble();
    void sell();
}

public abstract class ItemSuperclass implements ItemInterface {

    public void assemble() {
        System.out.println("Item.assemble");
    }

    public abstract void sell();
}

public class Item extends ItemSuperclass {

    public void sell() {
        System.out.println("sell me");
    }
}
```

Now you have an `Item` class with a concrete implementation of the `sell()` method. It extends the `ItemSuperclass`. `ItemSuperclass` implements `ItemInterface` and contains an abstract `sell()` method and a concrete implementation of the `assemble()` method. `ItemInterface` contains the definitions of the `assemble()` and `sell()` methods.

With refactoring options like Introduce Method, Extract Interface, and Extract Superclass, you can attempt to structure your code to take full advantage of good design principles. Ideally, for new code projects you would design classes correctly and wouldn't need refactoring. However, many programmers take over projects that have been implemented poorly and need refactoring.

Change Method Parameters Refactoring

Change Method Parameters refactoring is one of the most useful options in NetBeans. I have made extensive use of it on projects I inherited from other developers. In the old days of development, changing a method signature was time consuming. You would need to modify the method and then search through all your code to make sure all the references to it were updated. No sooner would you finish that task than you would decide to change the data types on the arguments or rearrange their ordering in the method. Change Method Parameters refactoring can reduce time spent on such operations.

Suppose you had the following code:

```
public class Item extends ItemSuperclass {

    public void sell() {
        System.out.println("sell me");

        System.out.println("Price(12345) : " + findPrice(12345));
    }

    public double findPrice(long itemNumber) {

        double price = 0.00;
        // look up itemNumber in database and set price variable
        return price;
    }
}
```

The `Item` class contains a `findPrice(long)` method. The method accepts an item number, looks it up in a database, and returns a price to the calling `sell()` method. If your client decided he also wants to be able to return the price and the currency in which the price is specified, you would need to alter the `findPrice(long)` method.

Assume you need to add a `String` argument to the `findPrice(long)` method that allows you to specify the type of currency. Highlight the name of the method and select Refactor ➤ Change Method Parameters. In the Change Method Parameters dialog box, you can add and remove parameters to the method. You can also change the order of the parameters and specify the method's new access level.

Tip You don't actually have to alter the parameters of a method to reorder them. You can use Change Method Parameters refactoring just to reorder parameters—a task I find myself doing often when I am developing code.

To add the new parameter, click the Add button. A new line appears in the parameters grid. Change the name, type, and default value fields, as shown in Figure 10-15. Then click the Next button, preview the changes, and apply the refactoring.

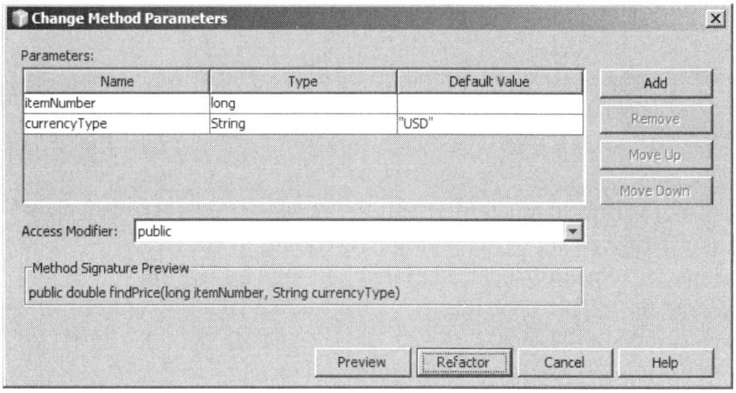

Figure 10-15. *The Change Method Parameters dialog box*

Your refactored code will look like this:

```
public class Item extends ItemSuperclass {

    public void sell() {
        System.out.println("sell me");

        System.out.println("Price(12345) : " + findPrice(12345, "USD"));
    }

    public double findPrice(long itemNumber, String currencyType) {

        double price = 0.00;
        // look up itemNumber in database and set price variable
        return price;
    }
}
```

Notice that the `findPrice(long)` method has been altered to include the new parameter. The `sell()` method has also been altered to call the modified method and pass it the default value of `"USD"`, which was specified during the refactoring operation.

Refactoring Keyboard Shortcuts

At the time of this writing, NetBeans 6 did not provide many shortcuts for the refactoring features. The only shortcut defined is for Rename refactoring, which you can activate by pressing Ctrl+R.

■Tip You can add your own shortcut for each refactoring option by selecting Tools ➤ Options ➤ Keymap ➤ Refactor. Make sure to explore the existing key mappings to get an idea of what is already used. NetBeans will prevent duplicates from being added.

Summary

In this chapter, you saw the wide variety of refactoring options available in the NetBeans IDE. You can use them to rework existing code or to make your new coding smoother.

Some of these refactorings will obviously be used more often than others, but you should become familiar with when and how to use each one. Applying these refactoring options when working with large code bases can be a lifesaver.

CHAPTER 11

Code-Quality Tools

Since the early days of computers, programmers have been striving to write "good" code. The exact definition of *good* varies greatly, depending on which programming language you are examining. It also depends on whom you ask to define what is and is not "good" code. For the purpose of the tools discussed in this chapter, I assume a practical definition of *good* Java code to include loosely the following:

- Consistent and easy-to-understand formatting (i.e., indentation and spacing)
- Consistent naming conventions
- No compile-time errors
- No runtime errors (or at least the ability to handle runtime errors)
- Adherence to best practices and good design
- Easy-to-understand and thorough in-code documentation

Some of the foregoing characteristics of "good" code are easy to enforce, while others are not. Many companies and organizations have documented standards that attempt to enforce (or at least suggest) that developers adhere to them. This in itself has proved difficult for many organizations. To adhere to coding standards, developers need to have read them thoroughly and to be reviewing their code constantly to make sure it conforms.

This can be a time-consuming and difficult process to do manually. This is where automated code-quality tools can be helpful, especially when used directly in a developer's coding environment, such as NetBeans. This chapter reviews the NetBeans plugins available for managing code quality in your Java projects.

Working with Checkstyle

Checkstyle is a development tool that Java programmers can use to scan code automatically for coding style violations. Released under the LGPL license, it is freely available from SourceForge at `http://checkstyle.sourceforge.net`.

Checkstyle can be used as a stand-alone tool, as part of an Ant build script, or as a NetBeans IDE plugin. It can also be integrated with other tools, such as Eclipse, Emacs JDE, Maven, and QALab.

Overview of Checkstyle Checks

The Checkstyle tool contains a number of "checks." Each check is a specific area of coding standards and styles that Checkstyle can identify. You can configure Checkstyle using one or more checks and apply those checks against your code. Checkstyle will then generate a report or list of violations. You can then use the list of violations to review and improve your code.

Checkstyle can scan your code and identify a number of areas that violate the generally accepted coding standards and styles. Some areas that can be identified include

- Duplicate imports
- Missing Javadoc comments
- Improper naming conventions
- Missing file headers
- Missing whitespace characters around identifiers
- Duplicate blocks of code
- Numerous coding best practices

Many of these areas have specific checks you can configure in Checkstyle, as discussed in the following sections.

The StrictDuplicateCode Check

Checkstyle can scan your code and help identify duplicate lines, including places where a developer may have copied and pasted blocks of similar code. Repeating large blocks of similar code can lead to more maintenance points, duplication of similar bugs, and harder-to-understand code.

You can configure Checkstyle to use the StrictDuplicateCode check to identify blocks of duplicate code. The StrictDuplicateCode check can be configured using the following listing in the Checkstyle configuration file:

```
<module name="StrictDuplicateCode">
   <property name="min" value="10"/>
</module>
```

This check contains a "min" property that allows you to specify the number of lines Checkstyle uses to consider a block of code to be duplicative. In this example it is set to 10. If Checkstyle finds any block of 10 lines of code in more than one place, this block will be considered a duplicate. It will locate duplicate matches even if the code is indented differently. However, code that is identical functionally but may use different variable names will not be identified as a duplicate.

Once Checkstyle has identified duplicate sections of code, you can examine them. If the functionality is generic enough, it may warrant the work to move the duplicative code into a reusable method that can then be called over and over. This will lessen the number of lines of code, make it easier to understand, and make it more reusable.

The UnusedImports Check

The UnusedImports check is one of the simplest sounding yet most useful that Checkstyle can provide. It can scan an entire code base and identify any Java import statements that are not actually used, are not needed (i.e., importing classes from the `java.lang` package), or are duplicates of other imports.

This can be useful for several reasons. Cleaning up unused imports can save you headaches. If you import classes from a third-party library, you need to maintain the project reference to that library, even if the imported classes are not actually used in your code. This can occur over time as multiple developers update code and comment out or remove pieces of functionality.

NetBeans can easily solve this on a class-by-class basis using the Fix Imports feature. This feature is typically available on the context menu when you right-click inside a Java source file open in the Source Editor. However, there is no easy way to enforce this across a project's large code base all at one time. This is where Checkstyle can help identify where you have unused imports. You can then open the Java source files where the issues are located and use the NetBeans Fix Imports feature to correct the situation.

If you are building your project code in a continuous-integration server, such as Hudson, Continuum, or Cruise Control, an unused import can actually cause your build to fail (thus costing you time and money to fix). During long-term maintenance of a Java application, you may upgrade different libraries, such as database drivers, logging packages, XML parsers, and database connection pooling drivers. An unused import from one of these libraries may reference a specific class or package that is not used in your code for one reason or another. If the JAR file that contains the imported classes is not correctly located in or referenced by the project, the build can fail. In this example, an unused import statement may cause you to waste time trying to figure out why the build failed, why your project is missing a required library, or where that library JAR file can be located so that it can be added back to the project.

Checkstyle contains an easy-to-use check that allows you to identify areas where imports are not used, are unnecessary, or are duplicated. The UnusedImports check can be configured using the following listing in the Checkstyle configuration file:

```
<module name="UnusedImports"/>
```

The MagicNumber Check

The concept of magic numbers is more of a coding best practice than a coding style. A magic number is considered to be any numeric literal other than `-1`, `0`, `1`, or `2` that may appear in your Java code.

Many experienced developers could tell you that magic numbers are typically a bad thing, though not always, depending on the situation. If you hard-code numeric literals in your code, it makes it more difficult to maintain the program and to understand the logic. Review the code in Listing 11-1.

Listing 11-1. *The MagicNumberExample Class*

```
public class MagicNumberExample {

    public List<String> calculate(List<String> data) throws Exception{
```

```
        List<String> returnData = new ArrayList();
        Iterator<String> mydata = data.iterator();

        while(mydata.hasNext()) {
            String nextVal = mydata.next();

            if(nextVal.length()<5) {
                returnData.add(nextVal);
            }

            // do something else

            if(nextVal.length()<5) {
               // log the data String
            }
        }

        return returnData;
    }
}
```

In Listing 11-1, the `MagicNumberExample` class has a method that iterates through a set of `String` data. It checks the length of each `String` and does something with it in several places if the length is less than 5. The value of 5 may have a special meaning throughout this class and other classes because it pertains to checking the length of a `String`. If you needed to change the value, you would have to ensure that you update the value 5 in multiple places. This leaves open the possibility of bugs if you do not update the value 5 in each and every place it occurs. You would typically create a class or method-scoped constant to replace each instance of the magic number.

Checkstyle can scan your code and identify areas where these magic numbers occur. This allows you to focus on determining whether or not they really are magic numbers and how you should handle them.

There are times when numeric literals appear in your code that should not necessarily be considered magic numbers. One example is when setting parameters for a `java.sql.PreparedStatement`, as shown in Listing 11-2.

Listing 11-2. *Code for Setting Parameters of a PreparedStatement*

```
public void updateCustomer(int custid,
                           String first,
                           String last,
                           String email,
                           String phone,
                           String company) {

        Connection conn;
        PreparedStatement pstmt;
```

```
        String sql = "UPDATE customer SET FIRST=?, LAST=?, EMAIL=?, " +
                     "  PHONE=?, COMPANY=? WHERE ID=?";
        try {
            // assume DataSourceFactory does a JDNI lookup
            // and returns a javax.sql.DataSource
            conn = DataSourceFactory.getDataSource().getConnection;

            pstmt = conn.prepareStatement(sql);

            pstmt.setString(1, first);
            pstmt.setString(2, last);
            pstmt.setString(3, email);
            pstmt.setString(4, phone);
            pstmt.setString(5, company);
            pstmt.setInt(6, custid);

        } catch (Exception e) {
            // error handling
        } finally {
            // database connection clean up
        }
}
```

Listing 11-2 uses numeric literals to specify the parameters of the `PreparedStatement`. Using Checkstyle to apply the MagicNumber check to the code would result in the identification of several violations. Since `-1`, `0`, `1`, and `2` are typically exempt, the lines that would get reported as violations would be

```
pstmt.setString(3, email);
pstmt.setString(4, phone);
pstmt.setString(5, company);
pstmt.setInt(6, custid);
```

I've seen programmers assume that since Checkstyle reports these as magic numbers, they must be evil. One way they try to "fix" the violation is by using a countervariable, such as this:

```
int i = 0;
pstmt.setString(++i, first);
pstmt.setString(++i, last);
pstmt.setString(++i, email);
pstmt.setString(++i, phone);
pstmt.setString(++i, company);
pstmt.setInt(++i, custid);
```

Whether or not this is good code is a matter of opinion. On one hand, you could argue that by not specifying parameter numbers explicitly, you can easily move the lines up or down to reorder the parameters if the SQL statement changes. On the other hand, you could argue that seeing the parameter numbers stated explicitly makes it easier to understand precisely which variable is being set to which field in the SQL that the `PreparedStatement` is executing. Regardless of your opinion, you need to be flexible when working with magic numbers.

Checkstyle has several configuration options available. The MagicNumber check can be configured using the following listing in the Checkstyle configuration file:

```
<module name="MagicNumber"/>
```

This simple listing will run Checkstyle, with the defaults applied to the MagicNumber check (that is, exclude `-1`, `0`, `1`, and `2`).

You can also set a parameter to ignore specific numbers, as in the following listing:

```
<module name="MagicNumber">
    <property name="ignoreNumbers" value="0, 1, 2, 3, 4, 6"/>
</module>
```

The "ignoreNumbers" property instructs the MagicNumber check to scan for magic numbers but to ignore `0`, `1`, `2`, `3`, `4`, and `6`. For the code in Listing 11-2, the only violation that would be identified would be the number `5` in the line of code

```
pstmt.setString(5, company);
```

You can also specify types of numeric literals to match using the MagicNumber check. Try the following check configuration:

```
<module name="MagicNumber">
    <property name="tokens" value="NUM_FLOAT, NUM_INT"/>
    <property name="ignoreNumbers" value="0, 1, 2, 3, 4, 6"/>
</module>
```

This check specifies the same list of numbers to ignore but also specifies a "tokens" parameter. This tells the MagicNumber check to look for all `floats` and `ints` in the code and to flag them as violations. In addition, the "ignoreNumbers" parameter instructs the code to ignore all values of `0`, `1`, `2`, `3`, `4`, and `6`.

The MultipleVariableDeclarations Check

Another useful Checkstyle check to run against your code is the MultipleVariableDeclarations check. This can identify places in your code where multiple variables are declared and initialized on the same line. Review the following code:

```
public void doSomething() {
    int a, b, c, d, e, f, g, h = 0;
    String firstName, lastName, email = "";
}
```

Code like this can be difficult to understand and document. For example, try writing some in-code documentation that correctly informs the reader how each variable differs and what it is used for. Furthermore, if future changes to the code cause the different variables to be initialized to different values, you will have to break them out onto separate lines anyway.

Having each variable declared on a separate line makes for cleaner code that is easier to document and easier to modify (i.e., you will be able to change initialization values quickly without having to worry about how the change affects other variables). The code would typically be written as follows:

```
public void doSomething2() {
        int a = 0;
        int b = 0;
        int c = 0;
        int d = 0;
        int e = 0;
        int f = 0;
        int g = 0;
        int h = 0;
        String firstName = "";
        String lastName = "";
        String email = "";
}
```

The MultipleVariableDeclarations check can be configured using the following listing in the Checkstyle configuration file:

```
<module name="MultipleVariableDeclarations" />
```

Sample Checkstyle Configuration File

Once you have identified the list of Checkstyle checks you want to use, you can put them into a single configuration file (Listing 11-3).

Listing 11-3. *A Checkstyle Configuration File*

```
<?xml version="1.0"?>

<!DOCTYPE module PUBLIC
    "-//Puppy Crawl//DTD Check Configuration 1.2//EN"
    "http://www.puppycrawl.com/dtds/configuration_1_2.dtd">

<module name="Checker">

    <module name="StrictDuplicateCode" />

    <module name="TreeWalker">

        <module name="UnusedImports" />

        <module name="MagicNumber">
            <property name="tokens" value="NUM_FLOAT, NUM_INT" />
            <property name="ignoreNumbers" value="0, 1, 2, 3, 4, 6" />
        </module>

        <module name="MultipleVariableDeclarations" />

    </module>
</module>
```

The configuration file lists several module definitions that were discussed in the previous section of the chapter. The other module definitions need a little explanation. The Checker module is the top-level module and references a Checkstyle class named `com.puppycrawl.tools.checkstyle.Checker`. This is the top-level check, encapsulating the other checks. Any module or check that runs under this parent node is one that typically applies checks across the entire code base, regardless of class or package.

The StrictDuplicateCode check appears as a child of the Checker module since Checkstyle compares code across all classes when trying to locate duplicates. The TreeWalker module references the `com.puppycrawl.tools.checkstyle.TreeWalker` class in the Checkstyle JAR file. The TreeWalker module is the parent module for all checks that run against an individual class. This module also creates a Java syntax tree of all the tokens that appear in the source file. The TreeWalker then iterates through each token and applies any child modules that are configured inside the TreeWalker module tag in the configuration file. In the sample file in Listing 11-3, the TreeWalker would execute the UnusedImports, MagicNumber, and MultipleVariableDeclarations checks on each token in a source file.

Regardless of the checks you include in the configuration file, they can be used to run Checkstyle in an Ant task, via the command line, or in an IDE as a plugin. The next section discusses using Checkstyle configuration files to enable the Checkstyle plugins for NetBeans.

Working with Checkstyle in NetBeans

At the time of this writing, several Checkstyle plugins were available for NetBeans. This section reviews two of those plugins, how to install them, and how to run them against a Java project.

Installing the Checkstyle-Task List Plugin

The Checkstyle-Task List plugin was written by Stanislav Aubrecht, a member of the NetBeans team at Sun Microsystems. One of his job duties involves working on the NetBeans Task List feature. The NetBeans Task List is the window that shows various TODO, FIXME, or VCS merge conflict statements that appear throughout your code. As a logical extension to it, he contributed a NetBeans Checkstyle plugin that displays results in the Task List.

You can download the plugin from the NetBeans Plugin Portal at `http://plugins.netbeans.org`. Once at the site, you can search for the term *Checkstyle*. Several results should be returned. Select the plugin labeled "Checkstyle-Task List Integration." You can then download a ZIP file that contains the `.nbm` modules needed to install it. To install the plugin, follow these steps:

1. Unzip the plugin into a directory.
2. In NetBeans, navigate to Tools ➤ Plugins.
3. Select the Downloaded tab and click the Add Plugins button.
4. Select the `.nbm` file and click the Open button. The module will then be listed in the Downloaded tab, as shown in Figure 11-1.
5. Click the Install button and accept the license when prompted. After the plugin has been installed, close the Plugins window.

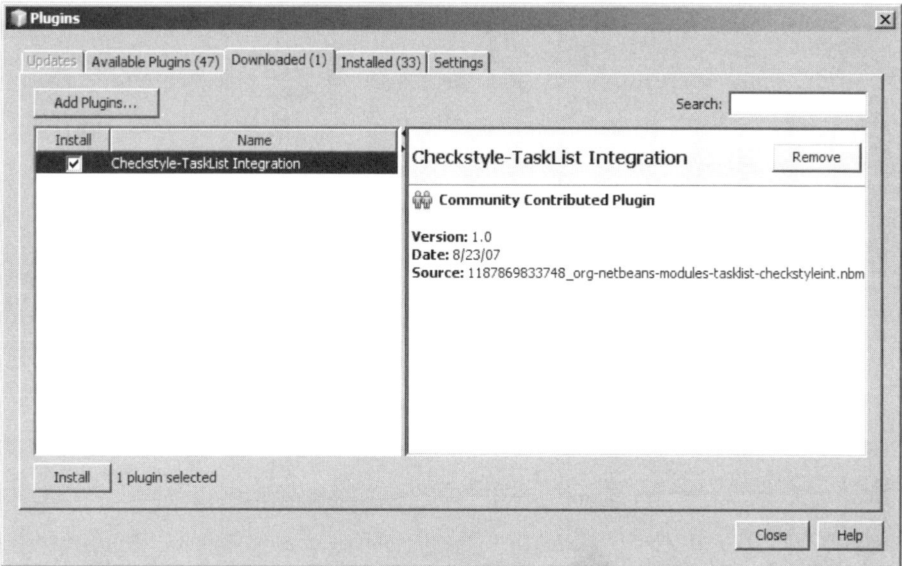

Figure 11-1. *The Plugins window listing the module ready to be installed*

Configuring the Checkstyle-Task List Plugin

Once the plugin has been installed you can configure which Checkstyle configuration file it uses. By default it points at a configuration file that includes the standard Sun Microsystems–recommended checks.

To change the configuration file, perform the following steps:

1. On the main menu, select Tools ➤ Options.
2. In the Options window, select the Miscellaneous icon in the top menu bar.
3. Click the Checkstyle tab to display the Checkstyle configuration settings.
4. Click the Browse button next to the "Configuration file location" field. Navigate your local file system and select a Checkstyle configuration file. The Checkstyle tab of the Options window should now display the updated Checkstyle file location, as shown in Figure 11-2.
5. Click the OK button to close the Options window.

The Checkstyle-Task List plugin will now be configured to use the new configuration file that was set in the Options window.

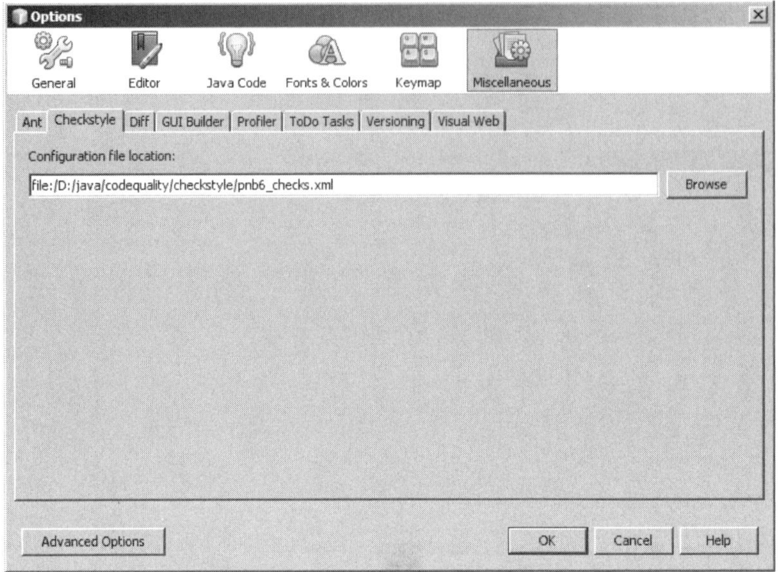

Figure 11-2. *The Checkstyle configuration file path in the Options window*

Running the Checkstyle-Task List Plugin

The Checkstyle-Task List plugin displays its results in the Task List. You do not actually have to run the plugin to see results. All you have to do is open the Task List window.

Once the Task List window is open, the resultant violations will appear in the list of tasks, as shown in Figure 11-3. It will display the different types of code violations identified by the Checkstyle checks contained in the configuration file you set up in the previous section. The second column displays the name of the file where the violation was found. The third column shows the line number where the violation was found. The fourth column displays the absolute path to the file where the specific violation was found.

Task List

Description	File	Line	Location
'5' is a magic number.	MagicNumberExample.java	26	D:/pnb6-projects/CodeQuality/src/com/pronetbeans/examples
'5' is a magic number.	MagicNumberExample.java	32	D:/pnb6-projects/CodeQuality/src/com/pronetbeans/examples
'100' is a magic number.	Main.java	28	D:/pnb6-projects/CodeQuality/src/com/pronetbeans/examples
'10' is a magic number.	Main.java	32	D:/pnb6-projects/CodeQuality/src/com/pronetbeans/examples
Each variable declaration must be in its own statement.	MultipleVariableDecs.java	23	D:/pnb6-projects/CodeQuality/src/com/pronetbeans/examples
Each variable declaration must be in its own statement.	MultipleVariableDecs.java	24	D:/pnb6-projects/CodeQuality/src/com/pronetbeans/examples
Found duplicate of 17 lines in D:\pnb6-projects\CodeQu...	NotAMagicNumber.java	18	D:/pnb6-projects/CodeQuality/src/com/pronetbeans/examples
'1.2f' is a magic number.	NotAMagicNumber.java	35	D:/pnb6-projects/CodeQuality/src/com/pronetbeans/examples
'5' is a magic number.	NotAMagicNumber.java	41	D:/pnb6-projects/CodeQuality/src/com/pronetbeans/examples

Checkstyle: 9

Figure 11-3. *The Checkstyle results displayed in the Task List window*

The Checkstyle violations displayed in the Task List can be double-clicked to jump directly to the matching line of source code for the file in the Source Editor. Once you correct the violation in your code, the matching violation will disappear from the Task List. This can be an effective way of locating coding-standard violations and fixing them.

Installing the Checkstyle Beans Plugin

The Checkstyle Beans plugin was written by Petr Hejl. It can be downloaded from `http://www.sickboy.cz/checkstyle/`. Once at the site, you should see a Download link in the main navigation menu. Download the ZIP file and extract the `.nbm` files to a directory on your local machine. You can then install the plugin by doing the following:

1. In NetBeans, navigate to Tools ➤ Plugins.
2. Select the Downloaded tab and click the Add Plugins button.
3. Select the `.nbm` files and click the Open button. The modules will then be listed in the Downloaded tab, as shown in Figure 11-4.

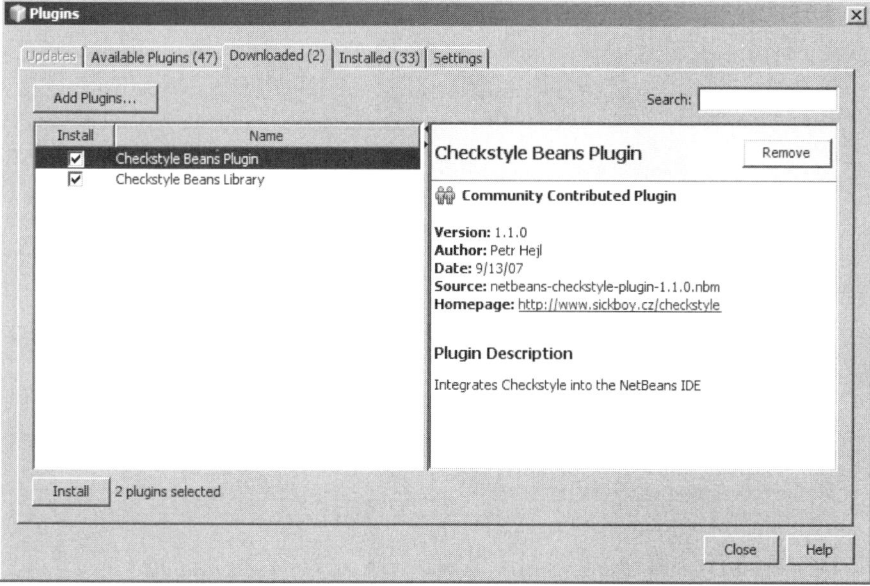

Figure 11-4. *The Checkstyle Beans plugin displayed in the Plugins window*

4. Click the Install button.
5. Click the Next button and accept the license.
6. After the plugin has been installed, click the Finish button to close the install wizard.
7. Click the Close button to close the Plugins window.

Configuring the Checkstyle Beans Plugin

Once the plugin has been installed, you can configure which Checkstyle configuration file it uses. By default it uses an internal configuration file that includes the standard Sun Microsystems–recommended checks.

To configure the plugin, perform the following steps:

1. On the main menu, select Tools ➤ Options.
2. In the Options window, select the Miscellaneous icon in the top menu bar.
3. Click the Checkstyle tab to display the Checkstyle configuration settings.
4. Click the check box next to the "Use custom configuration file" field. The text field and Browse button next to it will become enabled.
5. Click the Browse button to navigate to your local file system. Select a Checkstyle configuration file. The Options window should now display the updated Checkstyle file location, as shown in Figure 11-5.

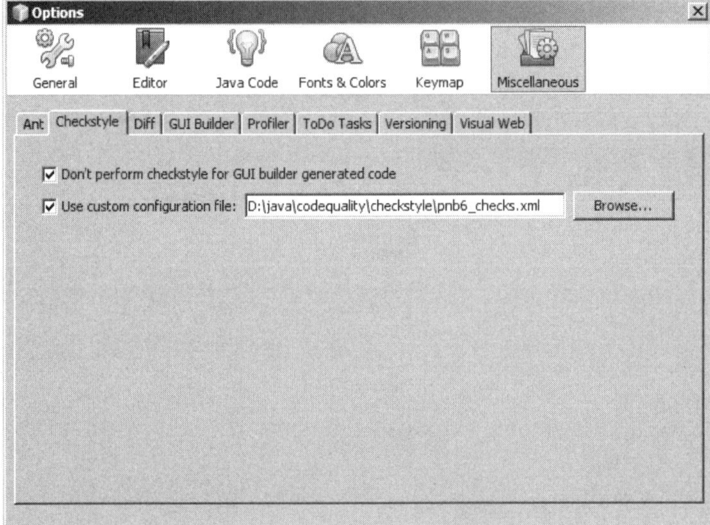

Figure 11-5. *The Checkstyle Beans properties in the Options window*

6. The "Don't perform checkstyle for GUI builder generated code" field is selected by default. If you uncheck it, then the Checkstyle plugin will scan areas of code generated by the Matisse GUI builder when working with Swing applications.
7. Click the OK button to close the Options window.

The Checkstyle Beans plugin will now be configured to use the new configuration file that was set in the Options window.

Running the Checkstyle Beans Plugin

The Checkstyle Beans plugin displays its results in two ways. The first is similar to the Checkstyle-Task List plugin. It will list the violations identified by Checkstyle in the NetBeans Task List. The second way it displays its results is via source code annotations.

You do not actually have to run the plugin to see results. All you have to do is open a Java source file in the Source Editor. Annotations should appear in the glyph margin if any Checkstyle violations are present in the file, as shown in Figure 11-6.

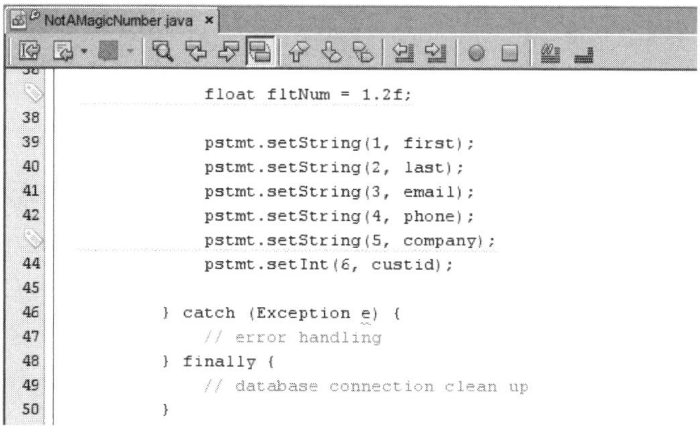

NotAMagicNumber.java ×

```
            float fltNum = 1.2f;

            pstmt.setString(1, first);
            pstmt.setString(2, last);
            pstmt.setString(3, email);
            pstmt.setString(4, phone);
            pstmt.setString(5, company);
            pstmt.setInt(6, custid);

        } catch (Exception e) {
            // error handling
        } finally {
            // database connection clean up
        }
```

Figure 11-6. *The annotations in the glyph margin for the Checkstyle violations*

The annotation glyphs may be difficult to see in Figure 11-6. It displays the source code discussed in the earlier section "The MagicNumber Check," but with a few changes. The following line is flagged as a violation:

```
float fltNum = 1.2f;
```

This line of source code is an addition to the code in Listing 11-2. It was added as an example to demonstrate the configuration settings for the MagicNumber check. The other line that is flagged is

```
pstmt.setString(5, company);
```

This line is flagged because the numeric literal `5` in the code is identified as a magic number. Checkstyle uses the configuration file from the earlier section "Sample Checkstyle Configuration File" to identify these violations.

You can also view the list of all the Checkstyle violations for the entire project by opening the Task List window. You can open the Task List window using the main menu and selecting Window ➤ Task List. You can also use the keyboard shortcut Ctrl+6.

Once the Task List window is open, the resultant violations will appear in the list of tasks, as shown in Figure 11-7. It will display the different types of code violations identified by the Checkstyle checks contained in the configuration file you set up in the previous section. The second column displays the name of the file where the violation was found. The third column shows the line number where the violation was found. The fourth column displays the absolute path to the file where the specific violation was found.

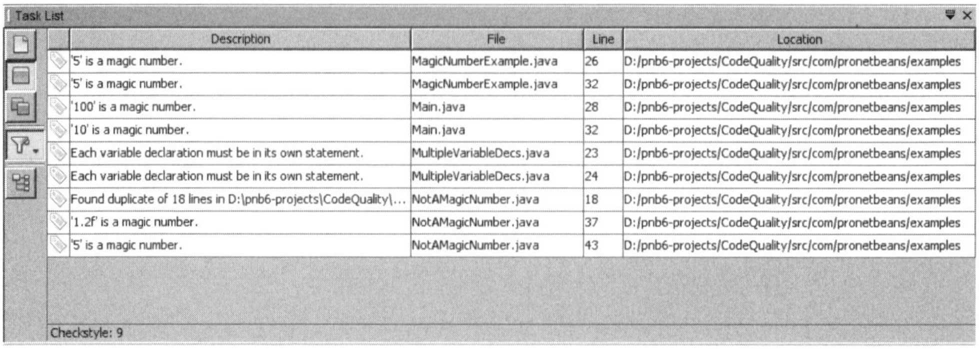

Task List

Description	File	Line	Location
'5' is a magic number.	MagicNumberExample.java	26	D:/pnb6-projects/CodeQuality/src/com/pronetbeans/examples
'5' is a magic number.	MagicNumberExample.java	32	D:/pnb6-projects/CodeQuality/src/com/pronetbeans/examples
'100' is a magic number.	Main.java	28	D:/pnb6-projects/CodeQuality/src/com/pronetbeans/examples
'10' is a magic number.	Main.java	32	D:/pnb6-projects/CodeQuality/src/com/pronetbeans/examples
Each variable declaration must be in its own statement.	MultipleVariableDecs.java	23	D:/pnb6-projects/CodeQuality/src/com/pronetbeans/examples
Each variable declaration must be in its own statement.	MultipleVariableDecs.java	24	D:/pnb6-projects/CodeQuality/src/com/pronetbeans/examples
Found duplicate of 18 lines in D:\pnb6-projects\CodeQuality\...	NotAMagicNumber.java	18	D:/pnb6-projects/CodeQuality/src/com/pronetbeans/examples
'1.2f' is a magic number.	NotAMagicNumber.java	37	D:/pnb6-projects/CodeQuality/src/com/pronetbeans/examples
'5' is a magic number.	NotAMagicNumber.java	43	D:/pnb6-projects/CodeQuality/src/com/pronetbeans/examples

Checkstyle: 9

Figure 11-7. *The Checkstyle results displayed in the Task List window*

The Checkstyle violations displayed in the Task List can be double-clicked to jump directly to the matching line of source code for the file in the Source Editor. Once you correct the violation in your code, the matching violation will disappear from the Task List. This can be an effective way of locating coding-standard violations and fixing them.

Working with PMD

PMD is another static analysis tool for identifying coding violations and code bugs. While Checkstyle focuses more on coding standards and styles, PMD focuses on code bugs, suboptimal code, and a variety of other coding problems.

You can download the PMD tool from its SourceForge site at `http://pmd.sourceforge.net/`. The PMD libraries allow you to use PMD from the command line, as part of an Ant build script, or as part of an IDE plugin.

Overview of PMD Checks

Just like Checkstyle, PMD has a large number of checks. Each check represents a specific area of coding issues, bugs, and problems that PMD can identify. You can configure PMD using one or more checks and apply those checks against your code. PMD will then generate a report or list of violations. You can then use the list of violations to review and improve your Java code.

PMD can scan your code and identify a number of areas that violate the generally accepted coding best practices. It can also identify potentials or issues with your code. Some areas that can be identified include

- Unused variables, methods, and parameters
- Unoptimized or inefficient code
- Poorly designed code
- Improper naming conventions
- Duplicate blocks of code
- Numerous coding best practices

Many of these areas have specific checks that you can configure in PMD, as discussed in the following sections.

MissingBreakInSwitch Check

PMD can scan your code and identify `switch` statements that have no `break` statements. A properly written `switch` statement contains a `break` in each and every case, including the `default` case, as shown here:

```
public void demoSwitch(int x) {

    switch(x) {

        case 0:
            System.out.println("x is 0");
            break;
        case 1:
            System.out.println("x is 2");
            break;
        default:
            System.out.println("x is default");
            break;
    }
}
```

If all the `break` statements were missing from the `case` statements, there could be a potential bug. For example, remove the `break` statements, pass in the value of `1` to the method, and execute the code that looks like this:

```
public void demoSwitch(int x) {

    switch(x) {

        case 0:
            System.out.println("x is 0");
        case 1:
            System.out.println("x is 2");
        default:
            System.out.println("x is default");
    }
}
```

With this code, if the value of the method parameter were `1`, the second `case` statement would execute. The standard output stream will output "x is 2". Program execution will then fall through to execute the `default` statement and "x is default" would print to the standard output stream. If the code's purpose were to modify records in a database or update financial transactions, then this type of code execution would definitely be identified as a bug.

You can configure PMD to use the MissingBreakInSwitch to identify `switch` statements with no `break` statement. The MissingBreakInSwitch check can be configured using the following listing in the PMD configuration file:

```
<rule ref="rulesets/design.xml/MissingBreakInSwitch"/>
```

The check may also be executed if the entire group of design checks is executed by specifying the following:

```
<rule ref="rulesets/design.xml"/>
```

This would execute all the design-related checks in PMD that belong to the design group. For an entire listing of these checks, see `http://pmd.sourceforge.net/rules/design.html`.

UseStringBufferForStringAppends Check

The UseStringBufferForStringAppends check can scan your code and identify incorrect `String` appending. Programmers typically write code that appends multiple `Strings`, especially in loops, which is inefficient. This check can scan for places where += is used to append `Strings` instead of a `StringBuffer` or `StringBuilder`.

Assume you have the following code that generates a meaningless HTML table structure:

```
public String getHtml(int numRows) {

    String returnValue = "<table>";

    for(int i=0; i < numRows; i++ ) {
        returnValue += "<tr><td>" + i + "</td><td>" + (i*i) + "</td></tr>";
    }

    return returnValue;
}
```

The `getHtml` method appends multiple `Strings` of HTML code into one long `String` that represents an HTML table. Inside the `for` loop, the table rows and columns are continuously appended to `returnValue` using the += construct. This is inefficient because it generates multiple redundant `String` and `StringBuffer` objects, leading to a slight degradation in memory and performance. If the `numRows` value was quite large, such as `10,000,000`, then the performance degradation would be much more noticeable.

The UseStringBufferForStringAppends check can locate the incorrect `String` appending, allowing you to identify and correct it. The check not only catches the += construct in the preceding code, such as this:

```
returnValue += "<tr><td>" + i + "</td><td>" + (i*i) + "</td></tr>";
```

it can also check the alternate syntax of this:

```
returnValue = returnValue  + "<tr><td>" + i + "</td><td>" + (i*i) + "</td></tr>";
```

You can configure PMD to use the UseStringBufferForStringAppends check to identify invalid `String` appending using the following listing in the PMD configuration file:

```
<rule ref="rulesets/optimizations.xml/UseStringBufferForStringAppends"/>
```

The check may also be executed if the entire group of optimization checks is executed by specifying the following:

```
<rule ref="rulesets/optimizations.xml "/>
```

This would execute all the optimization-related checks in PMD that belong to the optimization group. For an entire listing of these checks, see `http://pmd.sourceforge.net/rules/optimizations.html`.

Sample PMD Configuration File

Once you have identified the list of PMD checks you want to use, you can put them into a single configuration file (Listing 11-4).

Listing 11-4. *A PMD Configuration File*

```
<?xml version="1.0"?>

<ruleset name="My Ruleset"
    xmlns="http://pmd.sf.net/ruleset/1.0.0"
    xmlns:xsi="http://www.w3.org/2001/XMLSchema-instance"
    xsi:schemaLocation="http://pmd.sf.net/ruleset/1.0.0
                                     http://pmd.sf.net/ruleset_xml_schema.xsd"
    xsi:noNamespaceSchemaLocation="http://pmd.sf.net/ruleset_xml_schema.xsd">

    <rule ref="rulesets/coupling.xml"/>

    <rule ref="rulesets/unusedcode.xml">
        <exclude name="UnusedLocalVariable"/>
    </rule>

    <rule ref="rulesets/optimizations.xml/AvoidArrayLoops"/>
    <rule ref="rulesets/optimizations.xml/UseStringBufferForStringAppends"/>

    <rule ref="rulesets/design.xml/AvoidReassigningParameters"/>
    <rule ref="rulesets/design.xml/CloseResource"/>
    <rule ref="rulesets/design.xml/MissingBreakInSwitch"/>
    <rule ref="rulesets/design.xml/PreserveStackTrace"/>
    <rule ref="rulesets/design.xml/SingularField"/>

    <rule ref="rulesets/imports.xml/DontImportJavaLang"/>
    <rule ref="rulesets/imports.xml/ImportFromSamePackage"/>

    <rule ref="rulesets/logging-java.xml/SystemPrintln"/>

</ruleset>
```

The configuration file lists several methods for specifying PMD checks. The first listing, `<rule ref="rulesets/coupling.xml"/>`, contains the entire group of coupling checks. This will execute all the checks contained in the group. As previously mentioned, the entire list of checks is available at the PMD project site, `http://pmd.sourceforge.net`.

The second listing specifies the entire unused-code group of checks. However, it also specifies an explicit exclude of the UnusedLocalVariable check. Thus, all checks in the group will execute except for the UnusedLocalVariable.

The remaining entries in the file specify individual checks. The format is typically

```
<rule ref="rulesets/CATEGORY.xml/INDIVIDUAL-CHECK"/>
```

Once you have created the list of checks you wish to use, you can then apply those to your Java code projects. Having a standard list of checks you use to enforce good coding practices can be essential to writing and maintaining Java code. PMD can help dramatically in this area.

Working with PMD in NetBeans

At the time of this writing, the NetBeans PMD plugin had been updated by Radmin Kubacki. It contains support for the newest PMD library release, version 4.1. This section focuses on using the updated plugin. If you have an earlier version of the plugin, I strongly suggest updating it to support the PMD 4.1 release. This section reviews the plugin, how to install it, and how to run it against Java code in NetBeans.

Installing the NetBeans PMD Plugin

To download and install the NetBeans PMD plugin, go to the PMD project site, at `http://pmd.sourceforge.net`. The main navigation menu should contain a link to IDE plugins. Navigate the list and locate the NetBeans PMD plugin. The links will guide you to download a ZIP file for the plugin "pmd-netbeans 2.1."

To install the plugin, do the following:

1. Unpack the ZIP file onto your local machine.
2. In NetBeans, navigate to Tools ➤ Plugins.
3. Select the Downloaded tab and click the Add Plugins button.
4. Select the `pmd.nbm` file you extracted from the ZIP file.

5. Once the plugin is listed in the Downloaded tab, as shown in Figure 11-8, click the Install button.

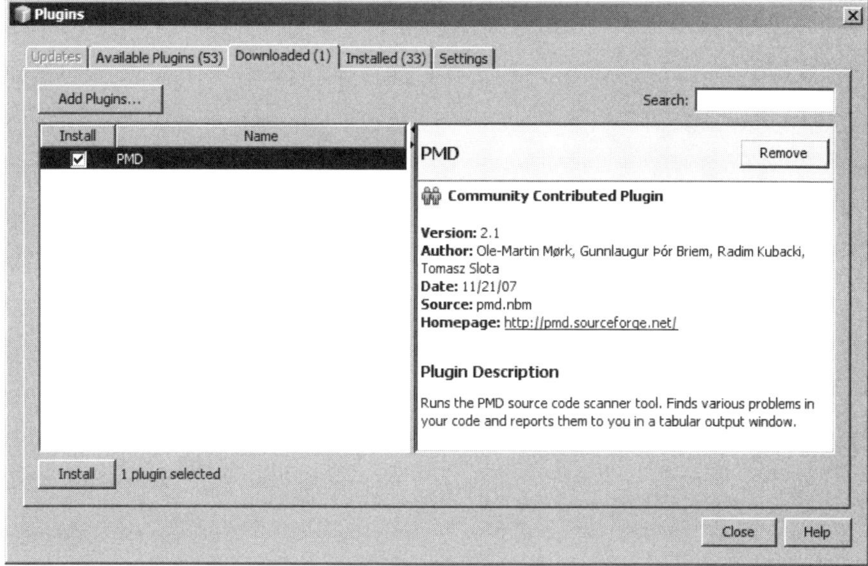

Figure 11-8. *The PMD plugin listed in the Downloaded tab of the Plugins window*

6. Click the Next button on the pop-up window and accept the license.

7. Once the plugin installs, click the Finish button. You will be prompted to restart the IDE.

Configuring the NetBeans PMD Plugin

Once the NetBeans PMD plugin is installed, you need to configure the checks it will use. Several configuration options are available for you to change that affect the plugin's behavior in NetBeans.

To change the plugin configuration options:

1. Select Tools ➤ Options from the main menu. The Basic Options window will appear.

2. Select the Miscellaneous icon in the main toolbar along the top.

3. Select the PMD tab. The PMD configuration screen will be displayed, as shown in Figure 11-9.

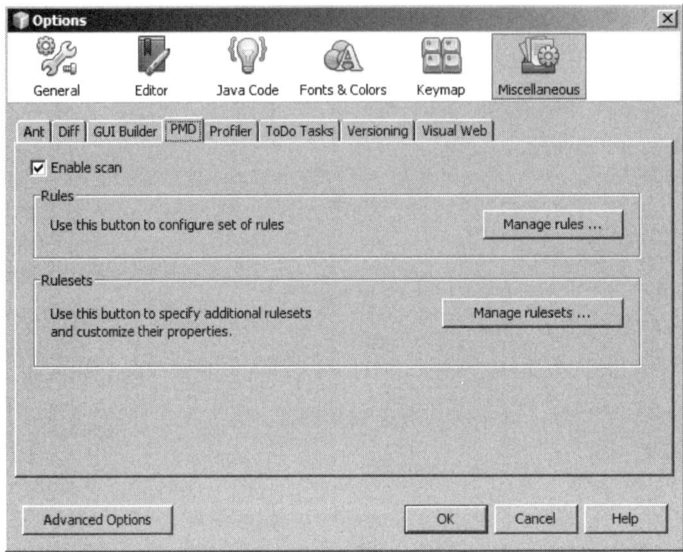

Figure 11-9. *The PMD configuration tab in the Options window*

The "Enable scan" property is unchecked by default. If you select it, PMD will automatically scan your code at certain intervals. If it identifies a piece of code that violates one of the rules specified in the configuration file, then it lists an annotation in the glyph margin. If you do not select the field, you would need to trigger PMD manually to run before the annotation would appear.

The rest of the PMD configuration tab includes the Manage rules button and the Manage rulesets button. If you click the Manage rules button, the PMD Rule editor window will appear, as shown in Figure 11-10. The Rule editor lets you easily manage the entire list of checks that the PMD plugin will use to apply to the code in your NetBeans project. The "Available rules" section lists all the checks you can use as defined in the PMD configuration file that is referenced. We'll discuss how to change which configuration file is referenced in a few moments.

You can select one or more rules from the "Available rules" section and click the right-facing arrows to move them into the "Chosen rules" section, as shown on the right of Figure 11-10. The rules come from the checks file included inside the module. Once a check appears in the list of chosen rules, you can click it to view its information and an example. The information about a check and an example of it are displayed in the middle of the PMD Rule editor window. The check's properties are also displayed at the bottom of the window. Click the OK button to save the list of checks you selected, and return to the PMD configuration tab in the Options window.

As previously mentioned, the PMD configuration tab also contains a Manage rulesets button. If you click it, the PMD Rulesets editor window will open. The top section of the window will display any referenced ruleset files. If none are displayed, you can click the Add RuleSet button, browse for a local ruleset file, and click Open. The selected ruleset file will appear in the top section of the PMD Rulesets editor, as shown in Figure 11-11.

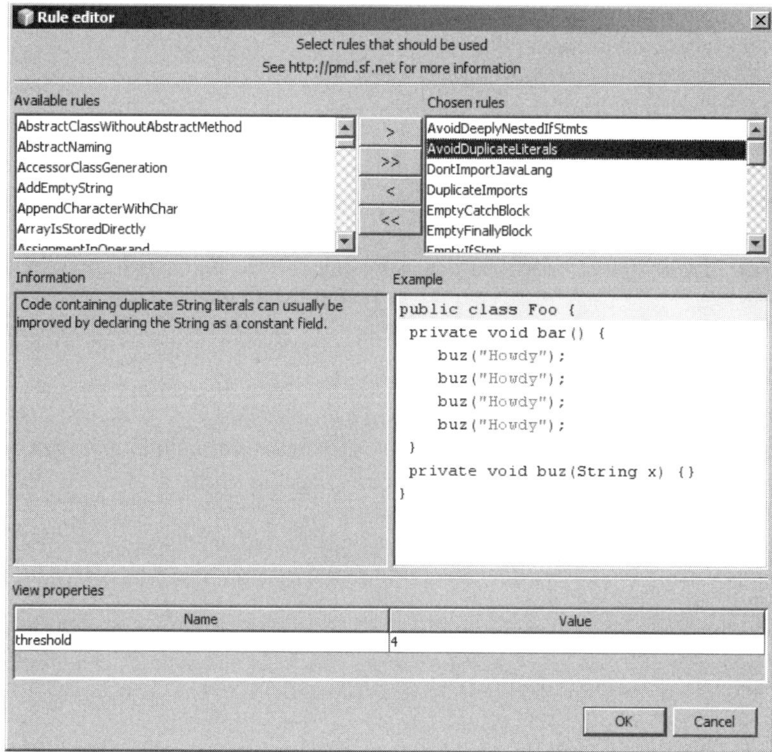

Figure 11-10. *The PMD Rule editor window*

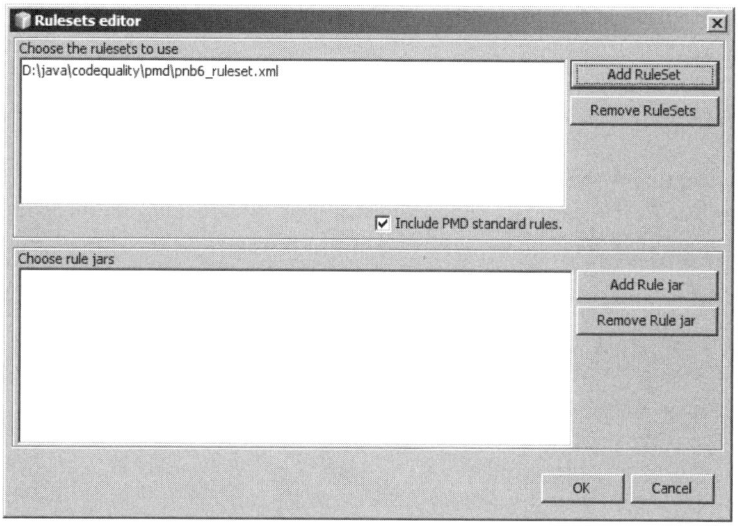

Figure 11-11. *The PMD Rulesets editor window*

Once you have selected a ruleset file, I recommend unchecking the "Include PMD Standard Rules" check box in the middle of the Rulesets editor window. If you select it, PMD will use the default PMD rulesets instead of your ruleset file.

The bottom section of the PMD Rulesets editor window allows you to specify ruleset JAR files, as opposed to individual ruleset files.

Once you have configured which rulesets you want the plugin to use, click the OK button to return to the Options window. You can then click the Manage rules button on the PMD configuration tab to view and manage the individual rules from the ruleset file. For information on how the rules are written and how to write your own rules, see the PMD site, at `http://pmd.sourceforge.net/howtowritearule.html`.

Running the NetBeans PMD Plugin

Once you have configured the PMD plugin, you will then want to run it against your Java code. If the "Enable scan" property from the previous section is enabled, then PMD annotations should appear in the glyph margin of the Source Editor when you open a class, as shown in Figure 11-12.

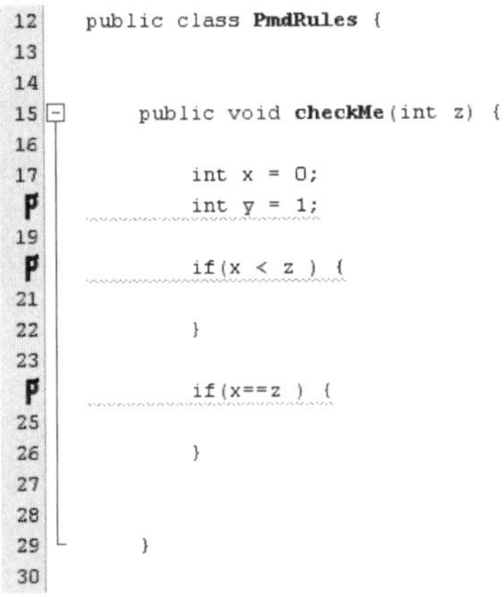

```
public class PmdRules {


    public void checkMe(int z) {

        int x = 0;
        int y = 1;

        if(x < z ) {

        }

        if(x==z ) {

        }


    }

```

Figure 11-12. *The PMD violation annotations in the Source Editor glyph margin*

Alternatively, you can right-click the Source Package node for a project in the Projects window and select Tools ➤ Run PMD. The PMD plugin will scan your source code and display a list of violations that matches the PMD checks in the PMD Output window, as shown in Figure 11-13.

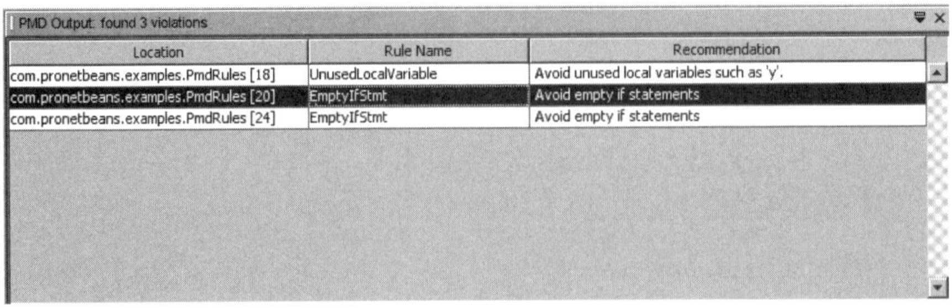

PMD Output: found 3 violations

Location	Rule Name	Recommendation
com.pronetbeans.examples.PmdRules [18]	UnusedLocalVariable	Avoid unused local variables such as 'y'.
com.pronetbeans.examples.PmdRules [20]	EmptyIfStmt	Avoid empty if statements
com.pronetbeans.examples.PmdRules [24]	EmptyIfStmt	Avoid empty if statements

Figure 11-13. *The PMD violations listed in the PMD Output window*

The PMD Output window displays a three-column list of violations. The columns include

Location: The fully qualified class name and line number where the issue is located

Rule Name: The PMD check name that flagged the code violation

Recommendation: The PMD description of the coding violation that was identified

You can also select a specific violation in the PMD Output window and double-click it. Doing so will open the matching source file in the Source Editor and place the cursor directly at the offending line of code. This can be a quick and easy way of navigating violations identified by PMD and correcting them.

Working with SQE

The Software Quality Environment (SQE) tool is a NetBeans plugin that aims to provide a one-stop shop for static analysis of Java code. It brings together in one platform multiple code-quality tools such as Checkstyle, PMD, FindBugs, and Dependency Finder.

With this plugin, you can execute each tool individually or as a group and view the results. It attempts to provide a consolidated section for configuring the tools as well as an area for graphing and trending the resultant violations that are identified. This section discusses how to download, install, and use the SQE plugin to support your code-quality processes.

Installing the SQE Plugin

To download and install SQE, perform the following steps:

1. Go to the project web site, at `https://sqe.dev.java.net/`.
2. The project site should contain a link to the SQE Update Center URL, such as `https://sqe.dev.java.net/updatecenters/sqe/updates.xml`.
3. In NetBeans, select Tools ➤ Plugins from the main menu. The Plugins window will open.
4. Select the Settings tab to display the list of Update Centers.
5. Click the Add button, enter `SQE` in the "Name" field, and paste the SQE Update Center URL into the URL field. Click the OK button, and the SQE Update Center will appear in the list of registered Update Centers in the Plugins window.
6. Click the Available Plugins tab. The SQE modules will be displayed, as shown in Figure 11-14.
7. Select the check boxes next to the modules and click the Install button.
8. Click the Next button, accept the license, and proceed with the installation.
9. After the modules have been installed, click the Close button to exit from the Plugins window.

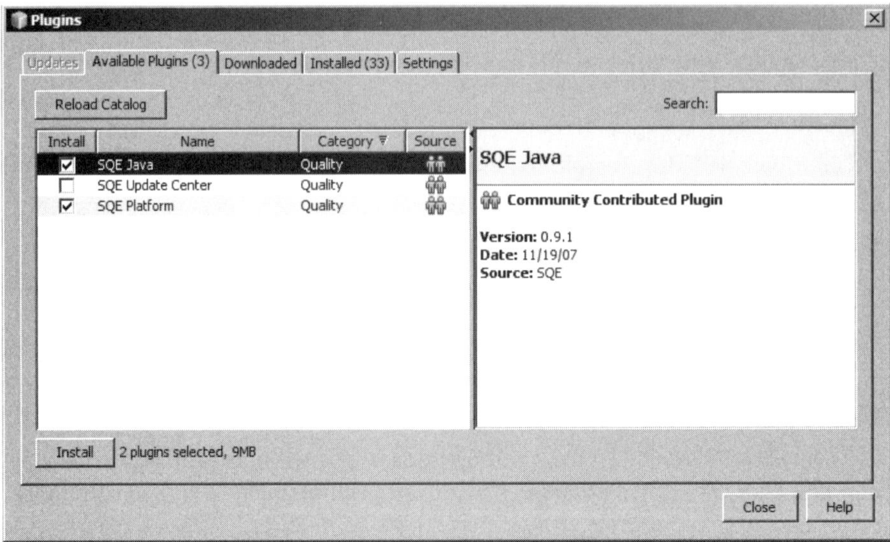

Figure 11-14. *The SQE modules available to download in the Plugins window*

Configuring the SQE Plugin

Once the SQE plugin has been installed, you can configure each of the individual static analysis tools that come with it. I discuss the configurations only briefly. The tool is still under heavy development, and parts of the tool configuration screen either are not complete or are subject to change.

To access the SQE configuration, select Tools ➤ Options from the main menu. The Options window will open. Select the Quality icon in the top navigation menu. The SQE configuration options will appear as individual tabs for the tools that came with the plugin, as shown in Figure 11-15.

You can select each icon to display the properties for the specific tool, such as Checkstyle, FindBugs, and PMD. At the time of this writing, the Checkstyle properties section was not complete and so it displays a blank tab. However, you can select the FindBugs and PMD icons to edit those tools' configuration options.

The PMD options in the Options window allow you to select or unselect from a single master list which checks are applied to the code. You can unselect the Enabled check box next to a rule to disable it from being applied to your code. As you select each check in the Rule column, a description and code sample of the check are displayed in the bottom part of the Options window.

The FindBugs options tab is very similar. It allows you to enable or disable individual checks via the check box in the Enabled column.

Future versions of the SQE plugin will have more configuration options available, but, as I mentioned before, it is still under development.

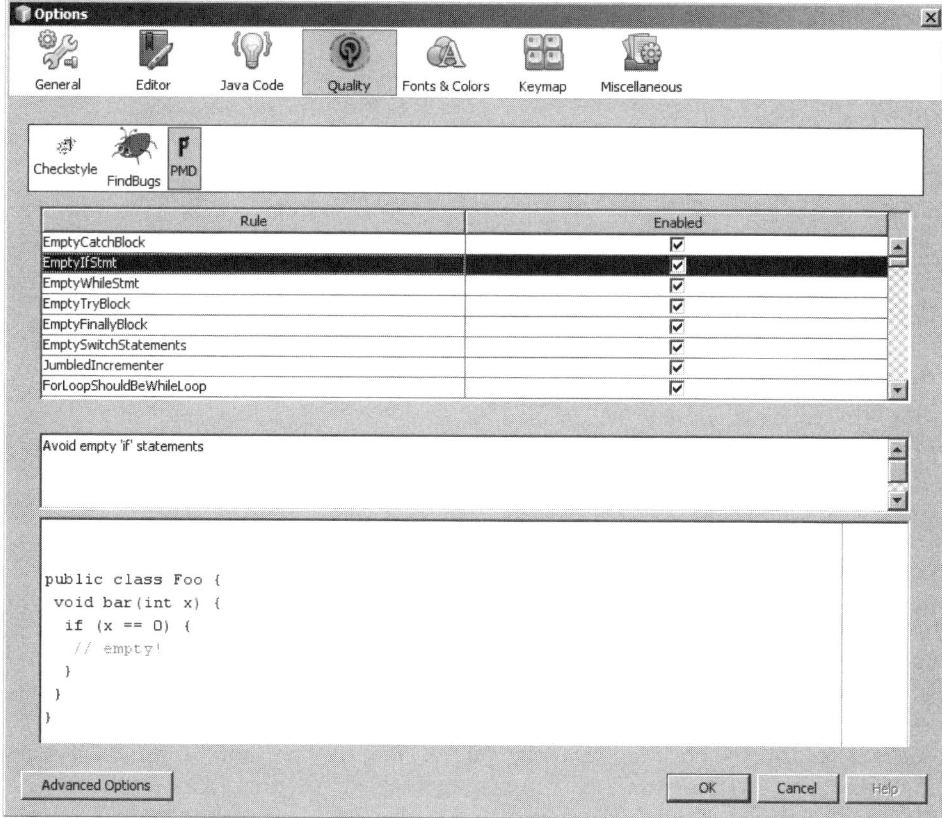

Figure 11-15. *The PMD options for the SQE plugin in the Options window*

Running the SQE Plugin

Once the SQE plugin is installed and configured, you have several options for running it. You can trigger all the code-quality tools to run at the same time or run each tool individually.

To run all the tools at once, select Quality ➤ Code Defects ➤ Check Quality from the main menu. This will immediately trigger a scan of your code and display the SQE Result window. If for some reason it does not display, you can open it manually by selecting Window ➤ Quality ➤ SQE Result from the main menu.

Once the scan completes, the SQE Result window will display the violations that were identified by each tool. However, the violations are displayed for only one tool at a time, as shown in Figure 11-16. At the top of the SQE Result window is a drop-down field labeled "Provider." If you expand the drop-down, you can see each of the code-quality tools that executed. Selecting PMD from the list will display the violations identified by PMD, as shown in Figure 11-16.

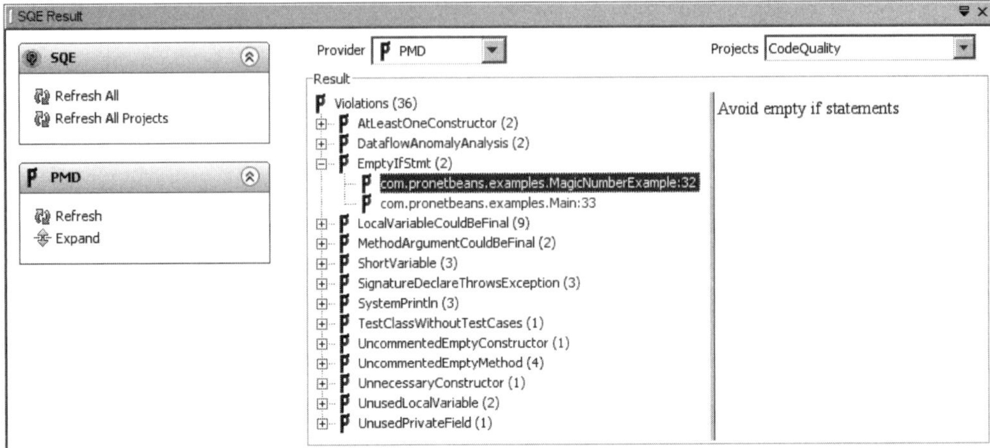

Figure 11-16. *The PMD results displayed in the SQE Result window*

The violations in the SQE Result window are listed by category, with a count of the total violations and a count of each group of violations. You can click the plus icon and expand the groups to view individual violations. Each violation will list the fully qualified class name and line number where the violation is located. Additionally, if you select a violation, the right pane of the SQE Result window will display a description of it. You can also double-click a violation to open the matching source file in the Source Editor.

After you have run the code-quality tools, you can open any Java source file in the Source Editor. If it contains a violation, you will see an annotation in the Source Editor glyph margin. This allows you to see at a glance in the source code how many code-quality violations exist. You can place the mouse over each annotation to see a tooltip explaining the violation, as shown in Figure 11-17.

MagicNumberExample.java

```
        while(mydata.hasNext()) {
            String nextVal = mydata.next();

            if(nextVal.length()<5) {
                returnData.add(nextVal);
            }

            // do something else

            if(nextVal.length()<5) {
                // log the data String
            }
        }
```

UCF: Useless control flow in com.pronetbeans.examples.MagicNumberExample.calculate(List)

Figure 11-17. *A code-quality annotation tooltip displayed in the Source Editor*

Instead of running all the code-quality tools as a group, you can run them individually. If you select Quality ➤ Code Defects from the main menu, the submenu displays the options Run FindBugs, Run PMD, and Run Checkstyle. Selecting any of these submenu items will run the matching code-quality tool individually. The results will display in the SQE Result window.

The SQE plugin has another feature that some developers will find useful. It can track the history of code-quality violations and display a trended graph, as shown in Figure 11-18. To activate this feature, select Window ➤ Quality ➤ SQE History.

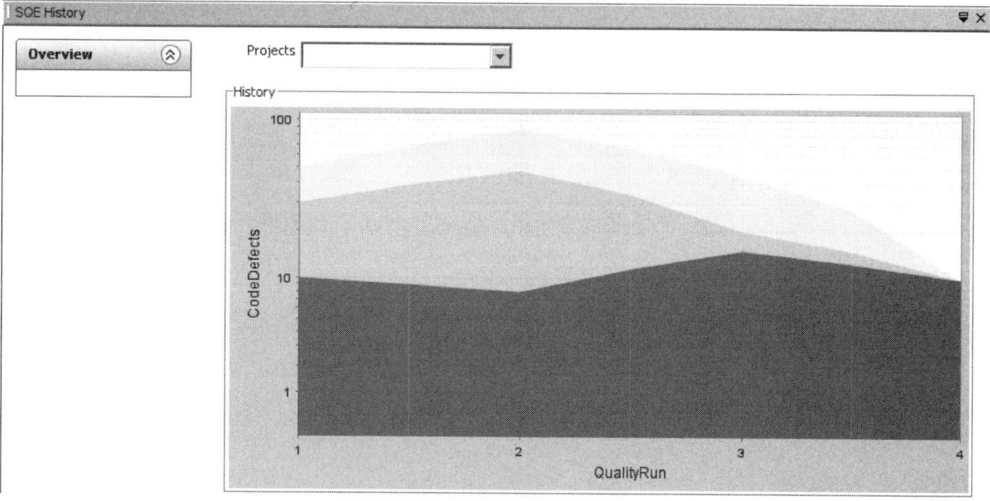

Figure 11-18. *The History graph of code-quality results*

At the time of this writing, the history feature was not quite complete. Eventually it is intended to provide a graph of the violations of each code-quality tool. You will be able to select a project from the drop-down and see its trended results. From your perspective as a developer, this can be useful in showing the history of the quality of your code. If, over time, the number of violations goes up, then either your tool configuration has changed or your code contains more bugs than it should.

Summary

This chapter reviewed the concepts of code quality, coding styles, and development best practices. It discussed the importance of being able to identify coding bugs, bad code formatting, and potential performance issues. Manually reviewing code can take developers too long and can prove to be error prone and difficult. Coding tools like Checkstyle and PMD can help automate and standardize the process.

This chapter reviewed the Checkstyle and PMD code-quality tools. It discussed an overview of each tool, some of the items they can check for, and a sample configuration file for each. It then went on to review how to use each as a NetBeans plugin, discussing how to download, install, configure, and run each of them.

Finally, the chapter discussed the SQE plugin. This plugin attempts to consolidate various code-quality tools, such as Checkstyle, PMD, and FindBugs, into one tool. It provides a number of interesting features, such as the ability to run all the tools at once, view the results in one window, and monitor the history of violations in each project for each code-quality tool. This can lead to a productivity savings for developers as well as identify sudden increases in coding bugs, issues, or bad formatting.

CHAPTER 12

Developing JRuby/Ruby on Rails Applications

For me, the most exciting new feature of NetBeans 6 is its support for Ruby and the Ruby on Rails framework. I struggled a bit with the organization of this chapter, since the two project types are relatively distinct. To me they're analogous to a General Java Application (Ruby) and a Web Application (Ruby on Rails). Add JRuby to the mix and an entire book could easily (and may someday) be dedicated to just the subject of Ruby, Ruby on Rails, and NetBeans.

I was initially going to discuss Ruby and Ruby on Rails as separate topics. However, that would have meant repeating too much information (editing, testing, and so on). So, following the DRY (don't repeat yourself) principle, I've decided to talk about the features of Ruby and Ruby on Rails together, especially since Ruby on Rails is really just a superset of Ruby—anything you can do in Ruby you can do in Ruby on Rails (but not vice versa).

Given the large amount of material to cover in this one chapter, I will assume that you already have a basic understanding of Ruby and the Ruby on Rails framework. I will go into more depth when discussing JRuby. Over the following pages I cover

- How to get the Ruby support in NetBeans
- Creating, editing, testing, debugging, and running Ruby and Ruby on Rails projects
- Managing RubyGems and Rails plugins
- IRB and the Rails Console
- JRuby

I also struggled with how much to talk about the Ruby and Ruby on Rails concepts. I'm really limited to covering the ways that NetBeans supports Ruby and Ruby on Rails development. For a more tutorial approach to learning Ruby, please see the NetBeans web site at `http://www.netbeans.org/kb/60/ruby/index.html`.

Installing Ruby Support

Keeping with the NetBeans IDE tradition of excellent "out of the box" productivity, Ruby language support, the Ruby on Rails framework, and the JRuby runtime all come bundled with the full distribution of NetBeans.

However, if you happen to have one of the smaller distributions of NetBeans without Ruby, you can easily install it via the Plugin Manager by doing the following (see Figure 12-1):

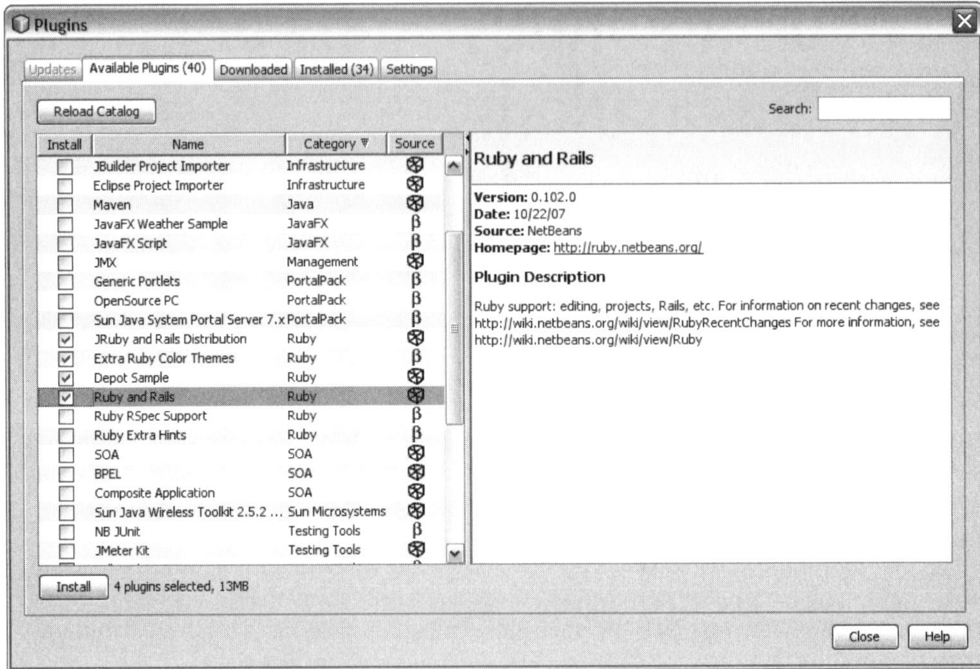

Figure 12-1. *Adding Ruby via the Plugin Manager*

1. Open the Plugin Manager by navigating to Tools ➤ Plugins.
2. Select the Available Plugins tab and click the "Category" column header to sort the list.
3. Select the check box next to the Ruby modules of interest. At a minimum, you will need "Ruby and Rails," which provides all of the NetBeans support for Ruby and Ruby on Rails (projects, editing, and so on). Unless you already have a Ruby or JRuby runtime installed, you will also want to select the "JRuby on Rails Distribution." All of the other plugins in the Ruby category are optional (Depot Sample, Color Themes, and so on), but there's really no reason not to install them as well.
4. Click the Install button to launch the Plugin Installer.
5. Accept the license and click Install to complete the Installation.

For more, see: `http://www.netbeans.org/kb/60/ruby/setting-up.html#downloading`.

Configuring Your Environment

NetBeans comes bundled with the JRuby interpreter, and its location is specified in the Ruby page of the Options dialog (see Figure 12-2).

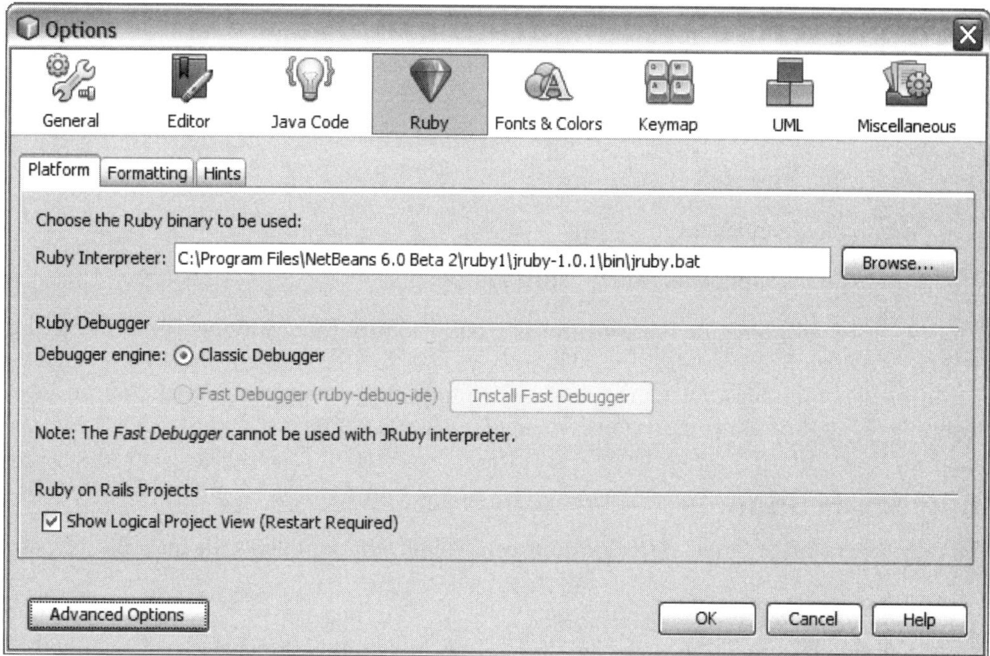

Figure 12-2. *Ruby Options dialog*

For those of you using NetBeans to learn Ruby and Ruby on Rails, the JRuby interpreter is all you need to begin your journey. However, if you already have a native Ruby interpreter installed, you can use this dialog to point NetBeans to the location of that interpreter by doing the following:

1. Select Tools ➤ Options (NetBeans ➤ Preferences on the Mac).
2. Select Ruby on the Toolbar.
3. Type the location of your Ruby executable in the list or click Browse to navigate to its location.

■ **Note** The next version of NetBeans, 6.1, will allow the Ruby interpreter to be set on a per-project basis, very similar to how the Java Platform Manager works today in NetBeans.

The Ruby Options page also includes settings for debugging and the Rails project view. Configuring the Ruby debugger is covered later, in the section “Debugging Your Project.” The Show Logical Project View setting is covered later, in the section “Creating a Ruby on Rails Project.”

Creating a Ruby Application Project

NetBeans provides four Ruby project types:

- Ruby application
- Ruby application with existing sources
- Ruby on Rails application
- Ruby on Rails application with existing sources

In this section I talk about the first two project types. I address the second two in the following section.

As the names implies, you can create a Ruby application either from scratch or from an existing Ruby application you previously created outside of NetBeans.

Ruby Application

The steps for creating a Ruby project are quite consistent with the other NetBeans project types.

1. Select File ➤ New Project.
2. Select Ruby under Categories and Ruby Application under Projects.
3. Give the project a name, if you so desire, and change the default project location (by default, NetBeans provides the last location at which you created a project).
4. Select whether you want your project to be the main project (the project acted on by menu selections such as Run) and whether you want to create a Main file (the file executed when the project is Run). A customizable default name of `main.rb` is suggested for you.
5. The dialog also indicates the Ruby interpreter in use, with an option to change it. As noted earlier, the Ruby interpreter is currently set for the entire IDE and not at a project level. However, clicking the Change button will open the IDE's Options dialog so that you can change it if you so desire (see "Configuring Your Environment," earlier, for more information).
6. Click Finish. Once the New Project wizard completes, you have a fully functional "Hello World" Ruby application—just press F6 to run it.

The only other files present in a new Ruby project are `Rakefile.rb`, which I address later, in the section "Running Rake Tasks," and `README`, which provides basic documentation on your project (see Figure 12-3).

By default the Source Files node maps to the underlying `lib` directory, where Ruby source files generally reside (see "Customizing the Ruby Project" for instructions on how to change the location of the `Source Files` directory). The Test Files node maps to the underlying test directory and is the intended location for your Ruby tests (see the later section "Testing Your Ruby Project" for more information).

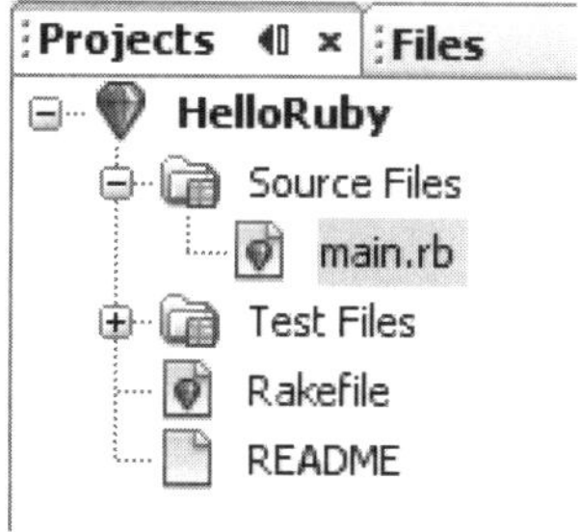

Figure 12-3. *Ruby Project layout*

Ruby Application with Existing Sources

If you already have Ruby sources laying around, you can easily and harmlessly work with them in NetBeans by choosing to create a new Ruby application with existing sources. The wizard asks for the location of your existing Ruby project folder as well as the names of your Source and Test folders. These values can later be changed or added to via the Project Properties dialog.

I say "harmlessly" because NetBeans simply adds an `nbproject` directory to your project, from which it maintains metadata used by NetBeans. Once you delete the folder, it's no longer a "NetBeans Project" (and this is exactly what NetBeans does when you delete a project from the IDE).

Creating a Ruby on Rails Project

As with Ruby projects, you have two options for creating your Rails application, either from scratch or from existing sources if you have them.

Ruby on Rails Application

In the New Ruby on Rails Application dialog (Figure 12-4), you specify a project name and location and whether you want the project to be the main project recognized by the IDE. You can also select the database that will be preconfigured for you in the `database.yml` file. Don't worry about the "If Using JRuby" options; I discuss these later when I talk about JRuby.

NETBEANS VS. THE COMMAND LINE

It's important to remember while working with NetBeans and Ruby on Rails that NetBeans is simply a veneer (albeit a very powerful one) on top of the existing Ruby on Rails framework. Most of the tasks that are run by NetBeans (creating a new project, running a generator, and so on) are calling out directly to the underlying Ruby interpreter. So the wizards you see in NetBeans are nice graphical interfaces to the parameters and options you'd alternatively have to specify on the command line. I often find myself thinking, "Gee, I wish NetBeans did such and such," only to realize it's really the Ruby on Rails script that I wish had that feature.

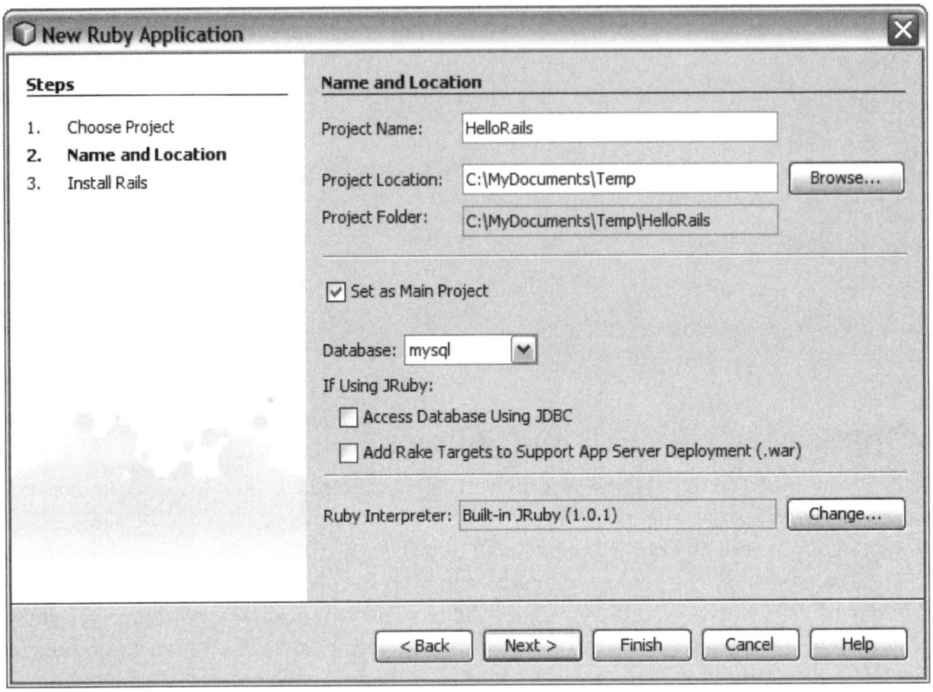

Figure 12-4. *New Ruby on Rails Application dialog*

■Note For the examples in this chapter, I assume that MySQL is the database, because that is what is most commonly used by Rails developers.

The second page of the New Project wizard will detect the installed version of Rails, with the option to update to the latest version if one is available.

When you click Finish, the wizard will run the `rails` command to create the project and show the results in the Output window. This would be equivalent to running `rails <project name>` from the command line. Note that the created files appear as a hyperlink that you can click to open that file in the editor (Figure 12-5).

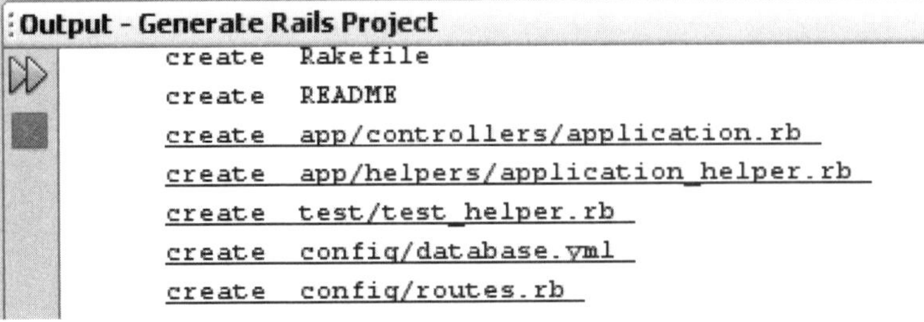

Figure 12-5. *New Ruby on Rails application output*

■ **Note** By default, the Project window shows a logical view of the project structure (Figure 12-6), which may be unfamiliar to existing Rails developers. To see your project by physical view, open Ruby Options (see the earlier section "Configuring Your Environment") and deselect "Show Logical Project View." To see the effects of this change, however, you will need to restart the IDE.

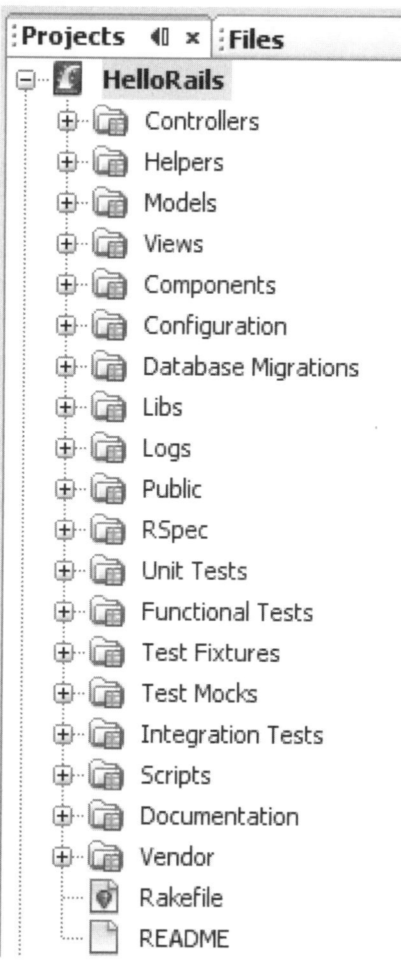

Figure 12-6. *Project view*

Unlike with creating a Ruby application, there is no Hello World version of the application that's ready to run. This is because NetBeans just runs the underlying `rails` command (see the sidebar "NetBeans vs. the Command Line").

Ruby on Rails with Existing Sources

The process for creating a Ruby on Rails application from existing sources is practically identical to creating a Ruby on Rails application from scratch. This is because there's no need to tell NetBeans the location of your project sources and test directories (since all Ruby on Rails applications share an identical project structure). Just point NetBeans to your project directory and go. Ah, the beauty of Rails conventions.

Adding Files to the Project

Whether you've created a Ruby application or a Ruby on Rails application, you need to add new files and make it actually do something more constructive than just saying hello to the world.

NetBeans provides several Ruby file templates (types) to help get you started, with Ruby File being the most generic, requiring simply a name and a location. A Ruby Module will let you specify an optional parent module, while a Ruby Class will let you specify an optional parent module and/or class. All three file types can be used interchangeably; the Ruby Module and Ruby Class templates just help you set up the file structure a bit.

For example, to create a new class, do the following (see Figures 12-7 and 12-8):

1. Select File ➤ New File.
2. Select Ruby from the Categories list and Ruby Class from the File Types list.
3. Give your class a name.

■ **Note** Ruby on Rails convention dictates that filenames always be lowercase and with underscores separating the words. So, for example, if you create a new class `CreditCheck`, the recommended filename will be `credit_check`. Also note, however, that the file can be called anything you want and doesn't have to match the class name.

---

4. In the "File Name" field, NetBeans has suggested a filename, but feel free to change it.
5. Using this dialog you can also specify whether your new class is in a module or extends a class.
6. The "Project" field is an informational, read-only field.
7. The "Location" drop-down will default to Source Files. You can alternatively use the "Folder" field to create the file in any location you like.
8. The "Created File" field is an informational, read-only field, showing the full name and location of the new file.

In a Ruby on Rails project you'd probably want to run a couple of generators before adding more files.

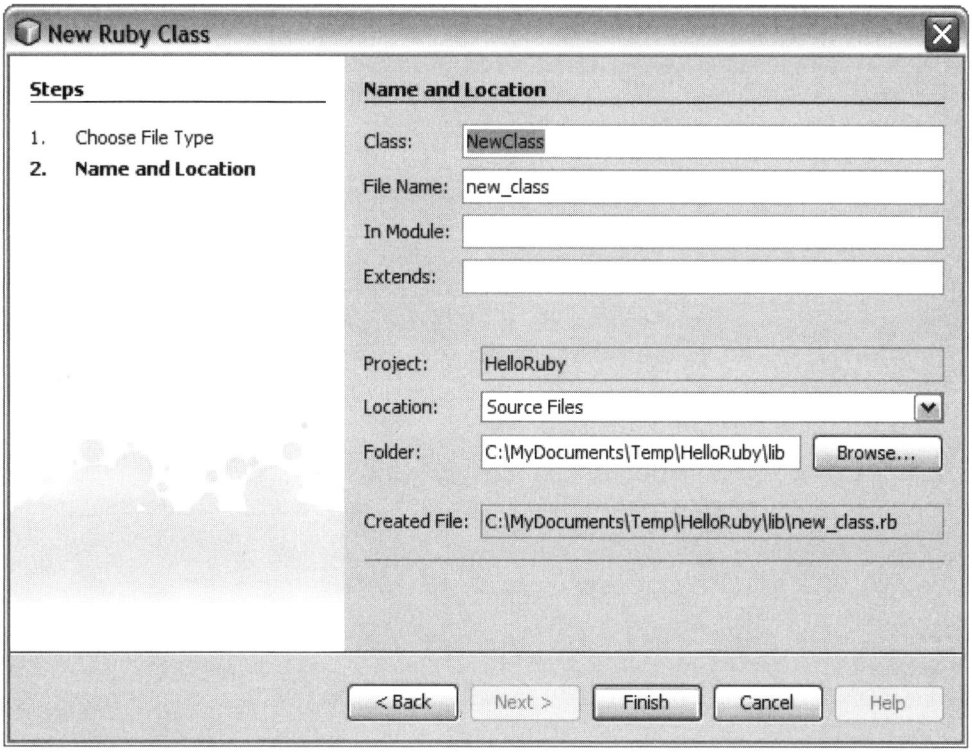

Figure 12-7. *New Ruby Class dialog*

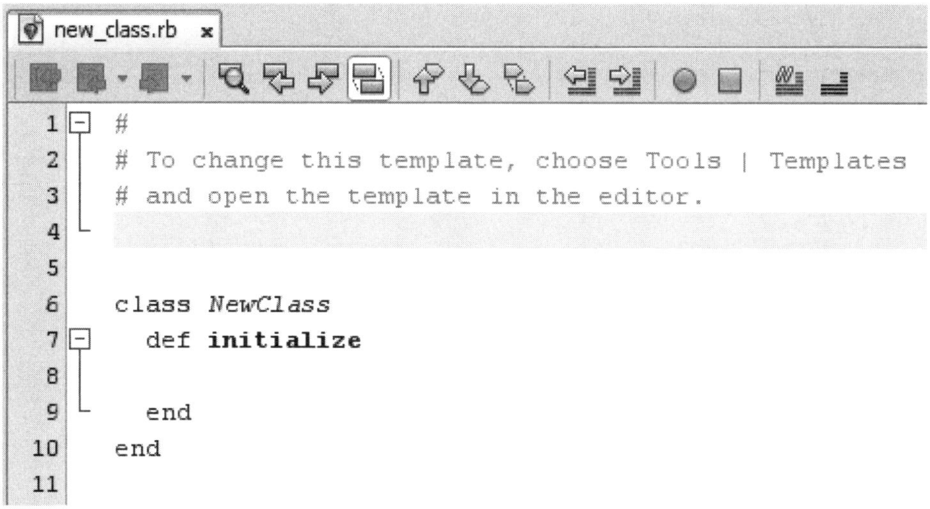

Figure 12-8. *New Ruby class*

Working with Generators

Working from the command line, you can run a command such as "ruby script/generate <generator> <options>". NetBeans gives you a nice graphical interface on top of this (Figure 12-9).

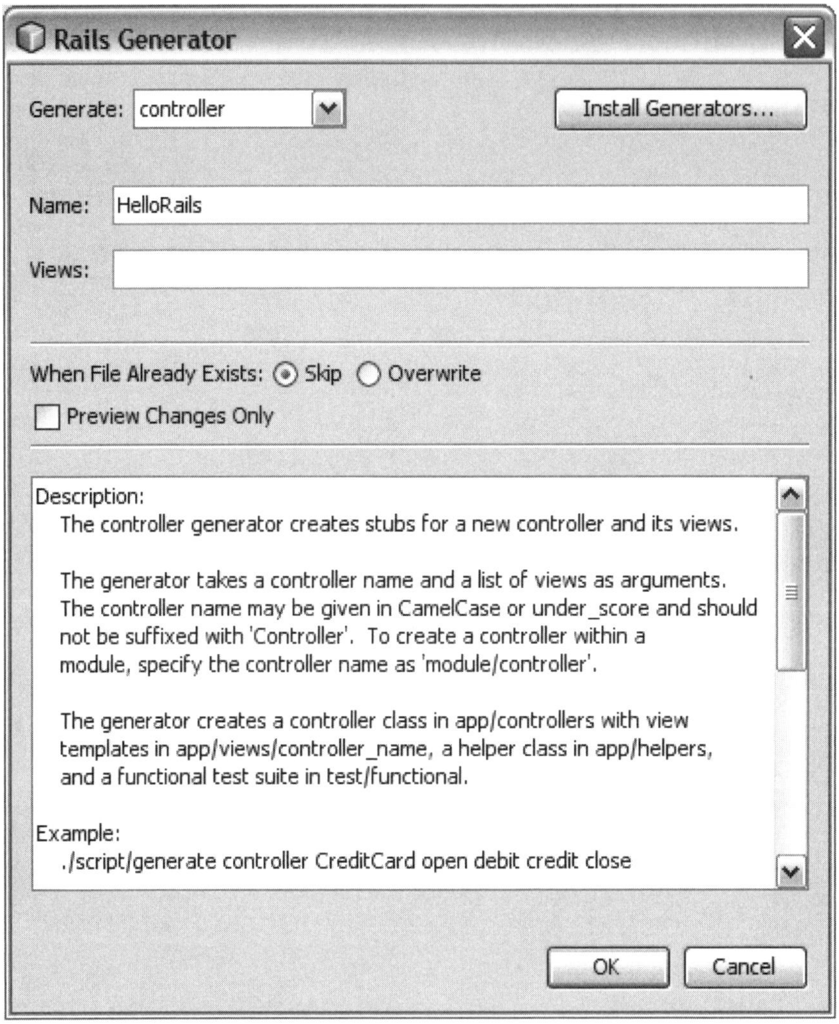

Figure 12-9. *Rails Generator dialog*

To access the generators, right-click the project and select Generate from the context menu. The command is context sensitive such that if you have the Controllers node selected, the dialog will assume you want to generate a new controller (Figure 12-10). This also works for Models and Database Migrations.

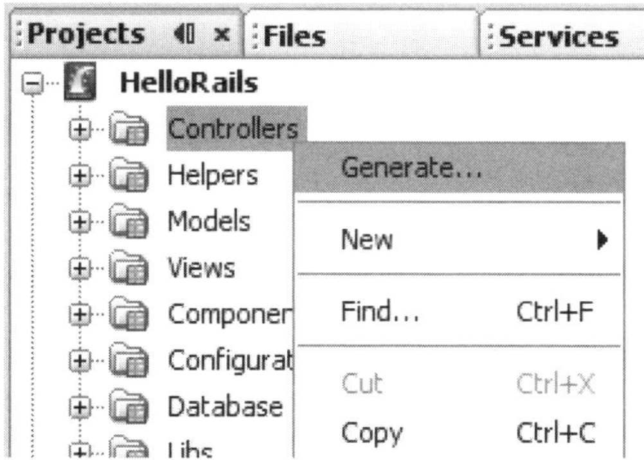

Figure 12-10. *Accessing the Rails generators for a project*

The input fields for the generator will change based on the generator you select. You can see from Figure 12-9 that *controller* takes "Name" and "Views" arguments. If you look at *model*, it just has a single arguments field. You also have the option to skip or overwrite existing files or merely to preview the changes made by the generator. All of these options are available via the command line, so NetBeans makes them available as well. The other nice thing about the Generator dialog is that it gives you the Rails help text for that generator. For the Controller generator, for example, this would be the same text you'd see if you typed on the command line the following from the project directory:

```
ruby script/generate controller -h
```

Finally, the Install Generators button will launch the Ruby Gem Manager, filtered by gems with *generator* in the title or description.

Note After installing a generator, restart the IDE to see it appear as an option in the Rails Generator dialog.

As the generator is running, its output appears in the Output window (Figure 12-11). Once complete, artifacts that were created are presented as hyperlinks, so you can quickly open them up in the editor.

```
Output - Rails Generator
      exists  app/controllers/
      exists  app/helpers/
      create  app/views/hello_rails
      exists  test/functional/
      create  app/controllers/hello_rails_controller.rb
      create  test/functional/hello_rails_controller_test.rb
      create  app/helpers/hello_rails_helper.rb
```

Figure 12-11. *Rails Generator output with hyperlinks*

The Ruby Editor

The Ruby Editor is a cornerstone of the IDE's first-class Ruby language support. Most of the features covered in Chapter 2, "The Source Editor," are also supported for the Ruby language, so I will not repeat them here. But I do think it's worth pointing out some of the features unique to Ruby.

Code Completion

Code completion for a dynamic language is much trickier than for a statically typed language such as Java because types generally have to be inferred based on usage patterns. Regardless, NetBeans steps up to the challenge and provides you with first-class code completion for Ruby.

As with Java, if you press Ctrl+Space as you are typing, completion is provided for variables, method names, class names, and constants. In addition, various Ruby built-ins, such as keywords and predefined constants, are provided. In all cases, Ruby documentation (rdoc) is also displayed, if it exists for the associated element.

In many contexts, NetBeans knows the exact type. For example, if you type `Dir.c` and invoke code completion, the editor shows you only the methods of class `Dir` that start with *c* as well as inherited methods and module mixins (Figure 12-12).

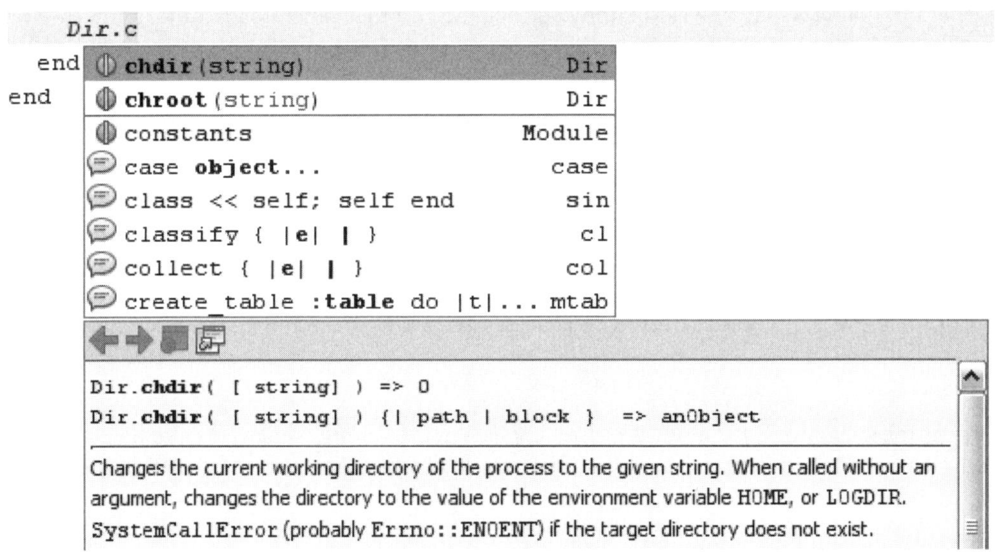

Figure 12-12. *Code completion*

Code completion also works for all kinds of literals in your code: strings, regular expressions, arrays, hashes, symbols, numbers, and so on, and you can even use it with the nil keyword. For example, with arrays, try code completion with `[1,2,3].ea` to see the each method and its documentation (Figure 12-13).

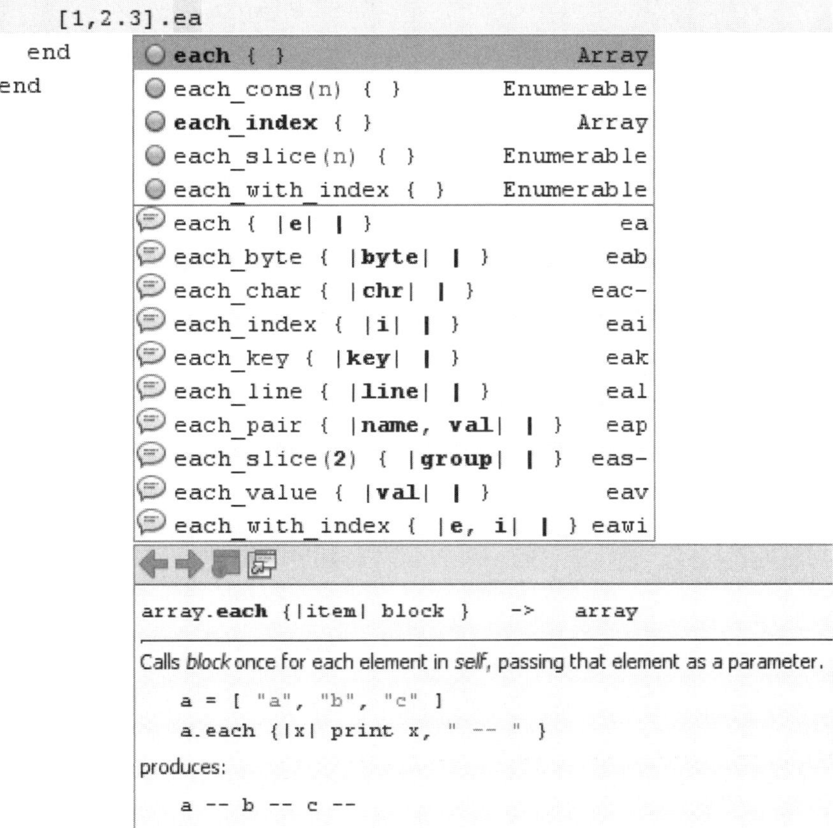

Figure 12-13. *Code completion on literals*

Code completion also provides help in specific contexts. For example, if you invoke code completion within the string of a `require` or `load` statement, you see a list of available imports, as shown in Figure 12-14.

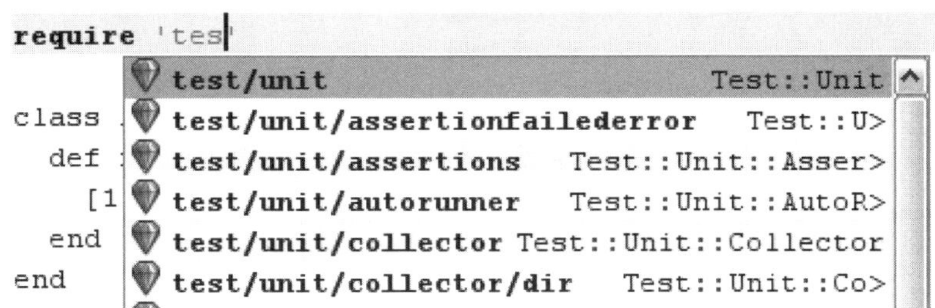

Figure 12-14. *Code completion: require statement*

If you invoke code completion while typing a regular expression, you get help with regular expression syntax, as shown in Figure 12-15.

```
    %r{this is a regex\}
  end           \A      Beginning of string
end             \B      Non-word boundary
                \D      Non-digit character
                \S      Non-space character
                \W      Neither letter or digit
                \Z      End of string (except \n)
```

Figure 12-15. *Code completion: regular expression*

If you're typing Ruby code and can't remember the names or meanings of global variables or what the escape codes are following a percent sign, use code completion, as shown in Figures 12-16 and 12-17.

```
$
$!      Latest error message
$$      Interpreter's process ID
$&      String last matched by regexp
$*      The command line arguments
$.      Line number last read by interpreter
$/      Input record separator
```

Figure 12-16. *Code completion: global variables*

```
%
%Q     String (double-quoting rules)
%W     String Array (double quoting rules)
%q     String (single-quoting rules)
%r     Regular Expression
%s     Symbol
%w     String Array (single quoting rules)
%x     Commands
```

Figure 12-17. *Code completion: escape codes*

There are more scenarios. For example, invoking code completion after a def keyword lists only the inherited methods from the superclasses.

In Ruby on Rails applications there's even code completion for `ActiveRecord` classes. This is a handy feature because, as you may already know, most methods in a model class are generated dynamically. However, NetBeans parses the migration files to determine the methods that the Ruby on Rails framework will make available to you, as shown in Figure 12-18.

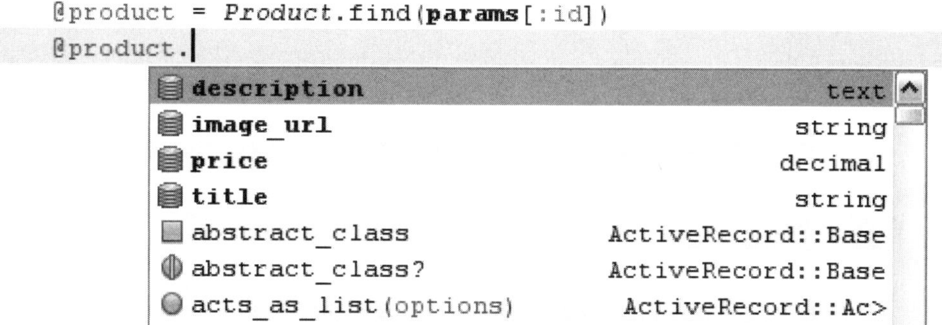

Figure 12-18. *ActiveRecord completion*

Code Templates

Code templates are covered in depth in Chapter 3. However, I think it's worthwhile to discuss some of the benefits that are particular to Ruby. If you're a TextMate developer, then you already know the benefit of code templates, and you'll be happy to learn that all of the TextMate templates have been incorporated into NetBeans. Templates exist for both Ruby and RHTML files, as shown in Figure 12-19.

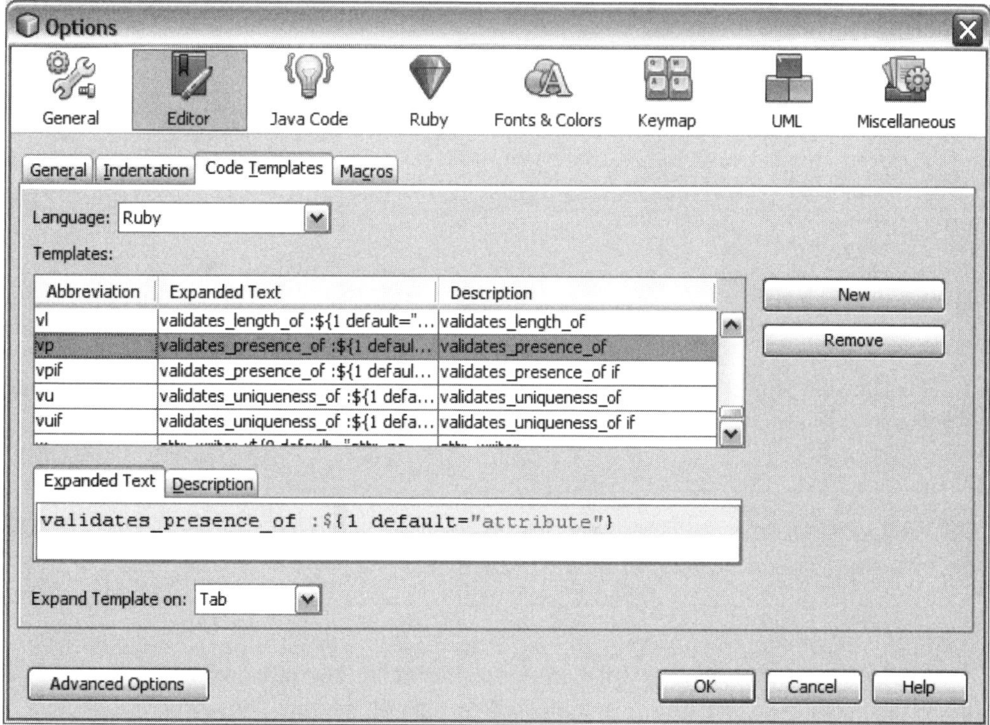

Figure 12-19. *Ruby template for vp (validates_presence_of)*

Running Rake Tasks

Both Ruby and Ruby on Rails applications support the running of Rake tasks via the project's context menu option Run Rake Task (Figure 12-20). Pausing on a particular task will cause a tooltip to appear with an explanation of that task, as shown in the figure.

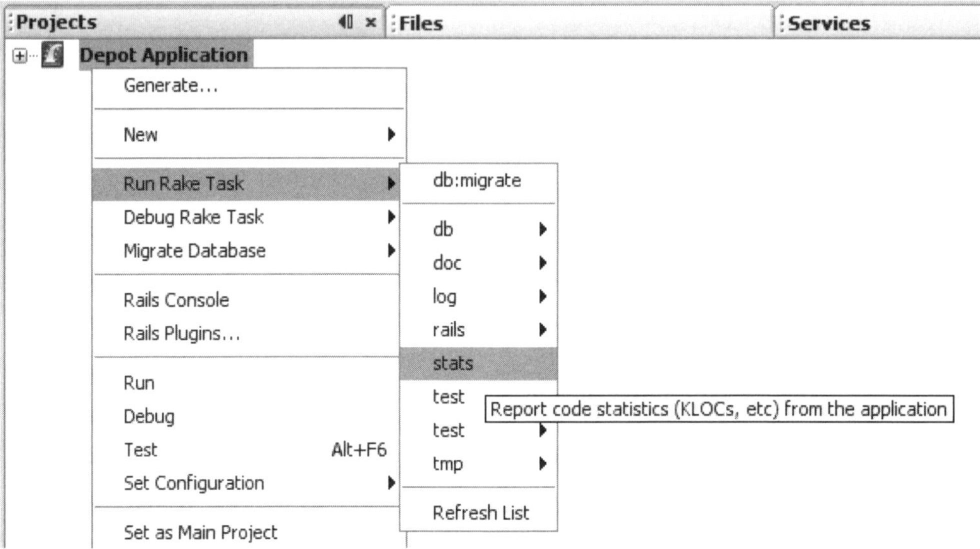

Figure 12-20. *Run Rake Task menu*

You'll notice that the last menu option is Refresh List. If you add a new Rake task to your project, just run the Refresh List task to get your tasks to appear in the Run Rake Task menu.

For example, if you add the following into `Rakefile.rb`:

```
desc "My Rake Task"
task :my_rake_task do
  puts "My Rake Task"
end
```

just right-click the project and choose Run Rake Task ➤ Refresh List to get the test task into the list. You may now run the task from the project's context menu.

Note A Rake task needs a description before the task name will appear in the Run Rake Tasks menu. The task description appears in the tooltip, as show in Figure 12-20.

As you can see in Figure 12-20, all of the predefined Rails Rake tasks are available from the context menu of the project. The most popular Rake task, db:migrate, has been given its own top-level menu, Migrate Database (Figure 12-21). Via this menu you can migrate to any version of your database schema. The "To Current Version" option is always the same as the highest version in the list, "To Version 7 – CreateUsers" in Figure 12-21. "To Version 0 – Clear" deletes all the tables in your database.

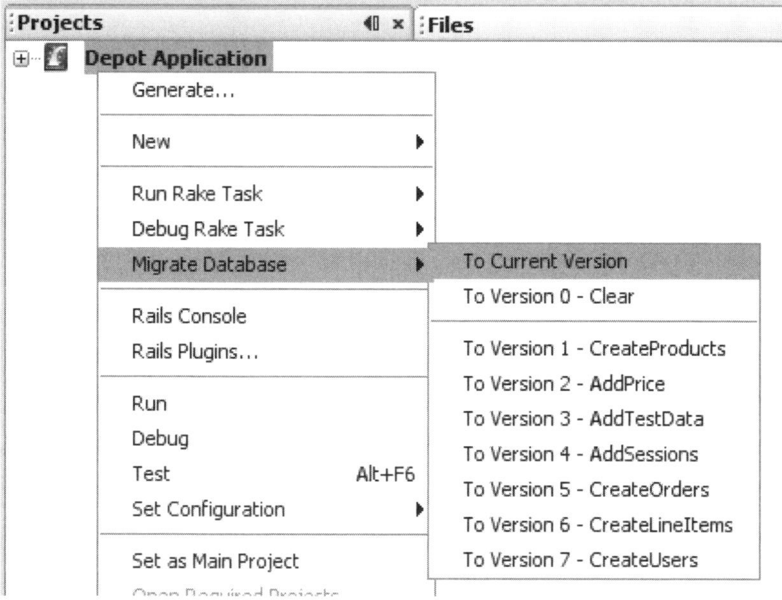

Figure 12-21. *Migrate Database context menu*

Customizing the Ruby Project

The project properties are one area where Ruby and Ruby on Rails projects are quite different, so I cover each project type separately.

Ruby Project Properties

To access the project's properties, right-click the project and select Properties at the bottom of the menu. There are three categories of project properties: Sources, Run, and Java. The Sources properties allow you to customize the name and location of the Source Files and Test Files folders in the Projects view. Again, this works similarly to other NetBeans project types.

In the Run category, you can change the Main Script that's run when the project is run. Additionally, you can set project arguments. For example, set "Argument" to "World" and change `main.rb` to the following:

```
puts "Hello " + ARG[0]
```

The working directory defaults to the `Source Files` directory (`lib` by default), and this can be changed with the Working Directory property. For example, if you have in the project's `lib` directory a file named `hello.txt` containing the text "Hello World," then adding the following to `main.rb` reads the file's contents and displays it in the Output window:

```
puts gets
```

If you prefer to have `hello.txt` in a different location, you can set your working directory to that location so that it can still be found. As their names imply, Ruby Options and Rake Arguments are used to pass values to the Ruby interpreter or Rake command. The Java category is covered later in this chapter.

Ruby on Rails Project Properties

Ruby on Rails doesn't have a Sources category, since the source and test file locations are fixed by the Ruby on Rails conventions. However, under the Rails category, you can configure the default port on which the server will start. You can also set the "Encoding" field and the arguments passed to Rake (see Figure 12-22).

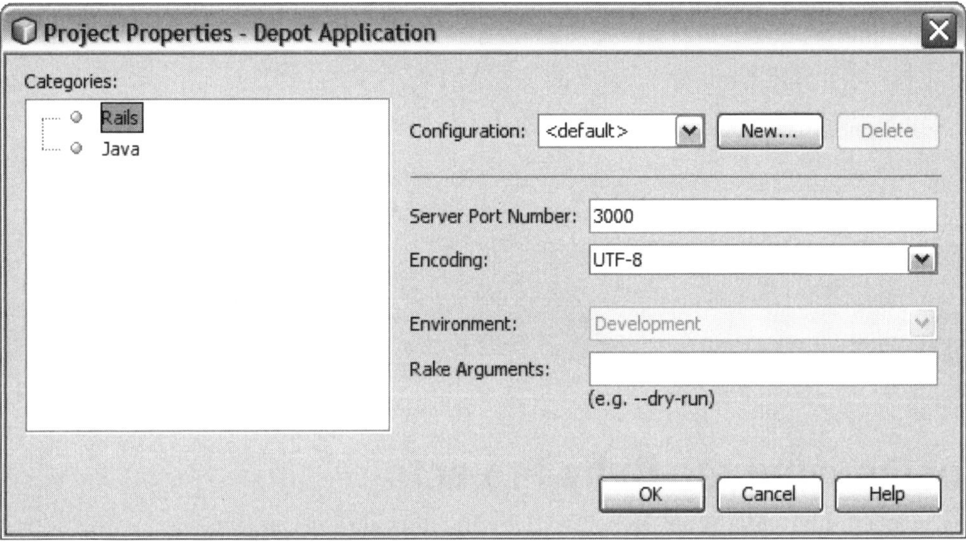

Figure 12-22. *Ruby on Rails Project Properties window*

The Ruby Gem Manager

The Ruby Gem Manager allows you to install new RubyGems as well as view and update existing gems. To access the Gem Manager, select RubyGems from the Tools menu.

On most systems other than Windows, the Ruby installation directory that the Gem Manager is trying to access is often privileged. Several solutions to this problem are documented at `http://wiki.netbeans.org/wiki/view/RubyGems`. For the purposes of this book, I'm going to change my gem repository permissions via the following steps:

- Open a terminal window and `cd` to #{NetBeans Installation Directory}/ruby1.
- Type `sudo chown -fR #{username} gems`, which for me would be `sudo chown -fR bleonard jruby1.0.1`.

The Ruby Gem Manager has four tabs (Figure 12-23):

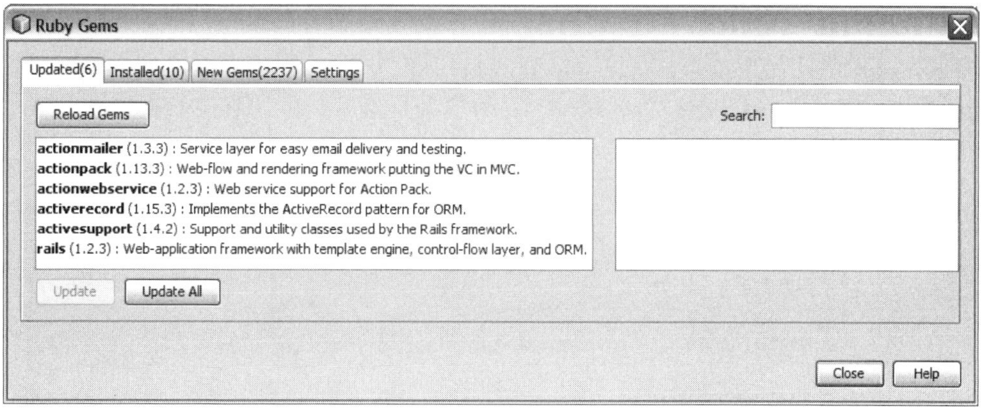

Figure 12-23. *Ruby Gem Manager*

Updated: This tab shows you installed gems for which new versions are available. The list includes the name of the gem, its currently installed version, and a short description. Selecting a gem will display the same information as well as the number of the new version available. From here you can choose to update the selected gem or all of the updated gems.

Installed: This tab shows you the gems you currently have installed, with a button to uninstall the selected gem.

New Gems: This tab allows you to add new gems to your Ruby installation. This is best done using the Search text box, which is also available for the Updated and Installed tabs but is most useful here, where more than 2,200 gems (and growing rapidly) appear in the list. After you perform a search, the total in the tab will update to indicate how many gems were found that match your search criteria, as shown in Figure 12-24.

Settings: This tab allows you to configure proxies.

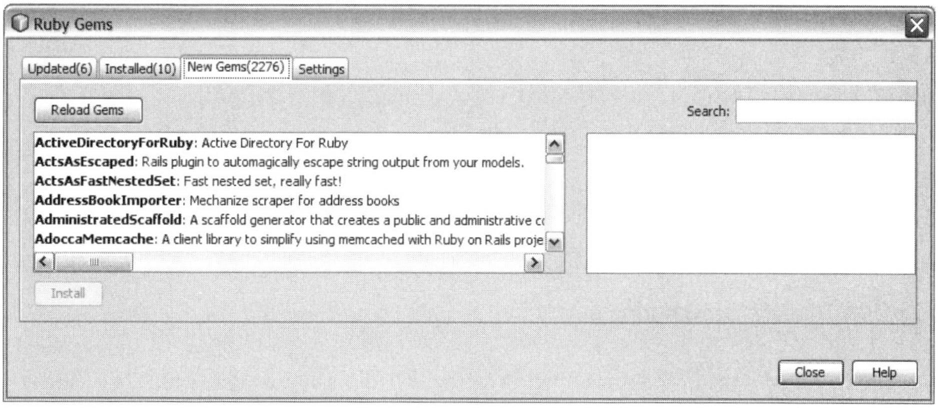

Figure 12-24. *Ruby Gems: new gems*

Managing Rails Plugins

Like gems for Ruby, plugins extend the functionality of Rails. Rails plugins are configured on a project-by-project basis and are accessible via the Rails Plugins context menu item off of the particular project (Figure 12-25).

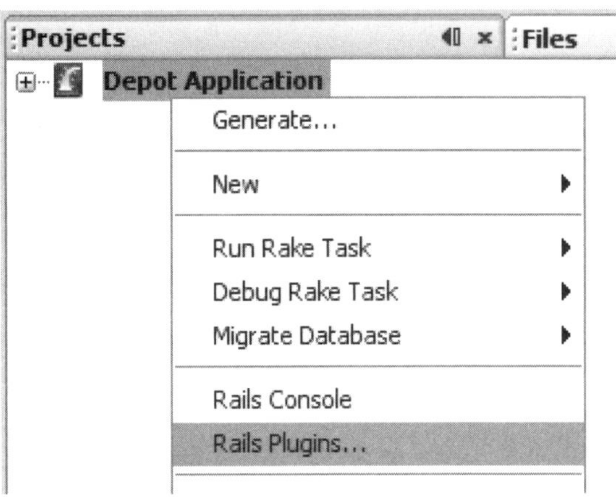

Figure 12-25. *Rails Plugins context menu item*

The Rails Plugins dialog has four pages: Installed, New Plugins, Repositories, and Settings (Figure 12-26).

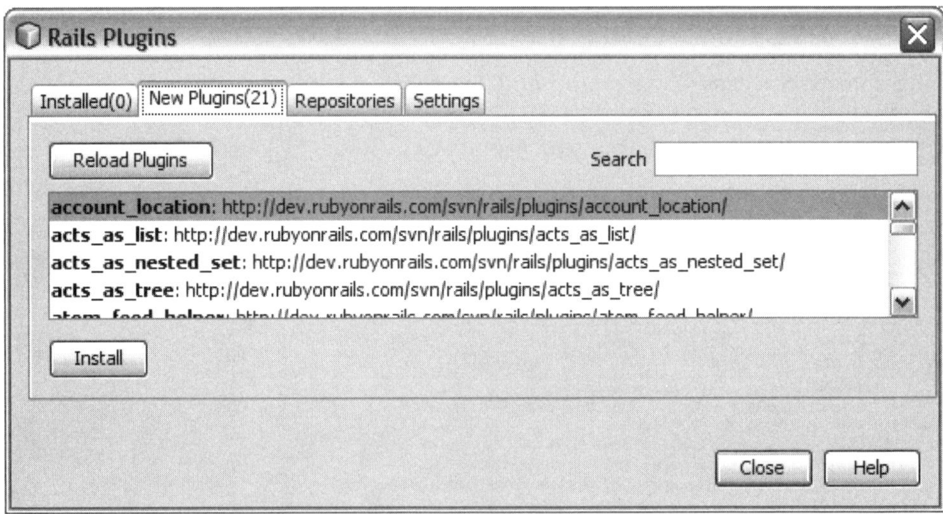

Figure 12-26. *Rails Plugins dialog*

The Installed page of the Rails Plugins dialog will show all installed plugins, whether installed via NetBeans or using the `script/plugin` install command from the command line. By default, no plugins are installed in a Rails project. From this page, Rails plugins can be uninstalled from the project or updated to their most current version.

The New Plugins page will list all Rails plugins available on the configured repositories, which, by default, is only `http://dev.rubyonrails.com/svn/rails/plugins/`. The Repositories page allows you to add new repositories or unregister existing repositories. You have the following options when adding a new Rails plugin repository:

1. Click the Find New button to display a list of known Rails plugin repositories.
2. Click the Add URL button to add your own repository manually.

Finally, the Settings tab allows you to configure a proxy if necessary. Clicking the Configure Proxies button takes you to the General page of the Options dialog, where proxy settings are configured for the entire IDE.

Testing Your Ruby Project

Ruby's Test::Unit framework is well integrated into the NetBeans IDE.

Creating Tests

The dialog for creating a new unit test is identical to that for creating a new class, as described earlier, in the section "Adding Files to the Project," the only difference being that the class will extend Test::Unit::TestCase.

Follow these steps to create a new unit test:

1. Select File ➤ New File.
2. Select Ruby from the Categories list and Ruby Unit Test from the File Types list (Figure 12-27).

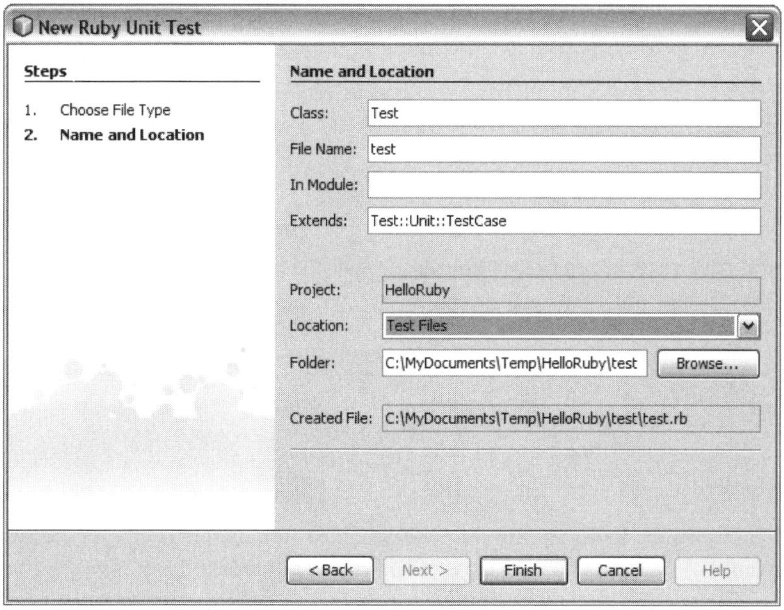

Figure 12-27. *New Ruby Unit Test dialog*

At a minimum, set the class name and ensure that "Location" is set to "Test Files."

Note For Ruby projects, the test class name generally matches the name of the class being tested, prefixed by "Test". Following this pattern, NetBeans will automatically add the `require` statement for the test following the "Test" prefix. For example, to test an existing class named "ShoppingCart", you would name your test class `TestShoppingCart` and NetBeans would produce the test template shown in Figure 12-28.

---

test_new_class.rb

```
#
# To change this template, choose Tools | Templates
# and open the template in the editor.


$:.unshift File.join(File.dirname(__FILE__),'..','lib')

require 'test/unit'
require 'new_class'

class TestNewClass < Test::Unit::TestCase
  def test_foo
    assert(false, 'Assertion was false.')
    flunk "TODO: Write test"
    # assert_equal("foo", bar)
  end
end

```

Figure 12-28. *Unit testing template*

Tip Once the test class is created, you can easily navigate from the test class to the tested class by choosing Navigate ➤ Go to Tested Class. From the tested class you can navigate back to the test class by choosing Navigate ➤ Go to Test.

Running Tests

Run your unit test by selecting Run ➤ Run File ➤ Test <class name>. This will execute your test whether you're currently viewing the test class or the class under test. Alternatively, you can select Run ➤ Run File ➤ Run <test class name>, but this works only when viewing the test class.

Test results will appear in the Output window, as shown in Figure 12-29. The output is hyperlinked, so you can easily navigate back to the failed tests for investigation.

```
Output - test_new_class.rb
Loaded suite C:\MyDocuments\Temp\HelloRuby\test\test_new_class
Started
F
Finished in 0.491 seconds.

  1) Failure:
test_foo(TestNewClass)
    [C:\MyDocuments\Temp\HelloRuby\test\test_new_class.rb:13:in `_wrap_assertion'
     C:\MyDocuments\Temp\HelloRuby\test\test_new_class.rb:13:in `test_foo']:
Assertion was false.
<false> is not true.

1 tests, 1 assertions, 1 failures, 0 errors
```

Figure 12-29. *Unit test results*

Debugging Your Project

If you're familiar with the Java debugging capabilities in NetBeans, you'll be very comfortable working with the Ruby debugger. Therefore, I don't go into too much detail here since the concepts covered in Chapter 4, "Debugging," also apply here.

However, it is worth noting that you currently can't debug Ruby on Rails projects using the bundled JRuby interpreter. This will be addressed when JRuby 1.1 is released. Even with the native Ruby interpreter, debugging Ruby applications leaves a lot to be desired, which is why NetBeans provides an option to install the Fast Debugger gem (ruby-debug-ide).

If you attempt to debug a Ruby project that is running on the native Ruby interpreter without the Fast Debugger installed, NetBeans will prompt you to install it, as shown in Figure 12-30.

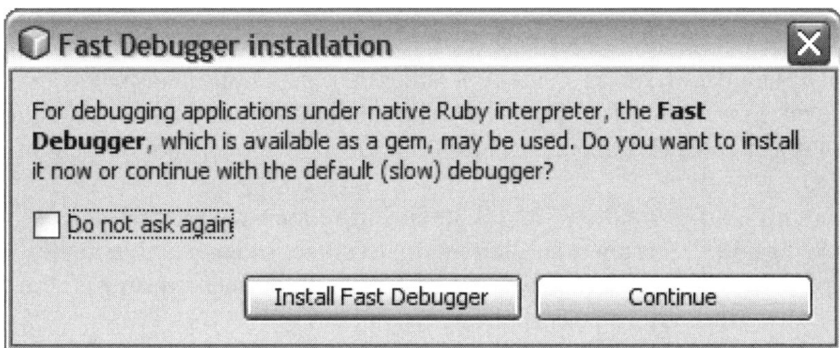

Figure 12-30. *Fast Debugger installation prompt*

Alternatively, you can install the Fast Debugger using the Ruby Gem Manager. See the earlier section "The Ruby Gem Manager" for more information.

Once you've installed the Fast Debugger, debugging a Ruby on Rails application will be as slick as with any Java application, giving you visual access to the call stack, threads, and local variables. All of these features are even supported for RHTML files in Ruby on Rails applications.

IRB and the Rails Console

Two interactive tools that you currently start from the command line are available from within NetBeans: IRB (for Ruby) and the Rails Console (for Rails).

You access IRB by choosing Window ➤ Other ➤ Ruby Shell (IRB). IRB opens at the root of your system, so you probably want to change to your project directory. You can do this using the `Dir.chdir` method.

A nice feature of the IRB console integrated in NetBeans is tab completion. For example, typing `[1, 2, 3].ea` and then pressing the Tab key produces what is shown in Figure 12-31.

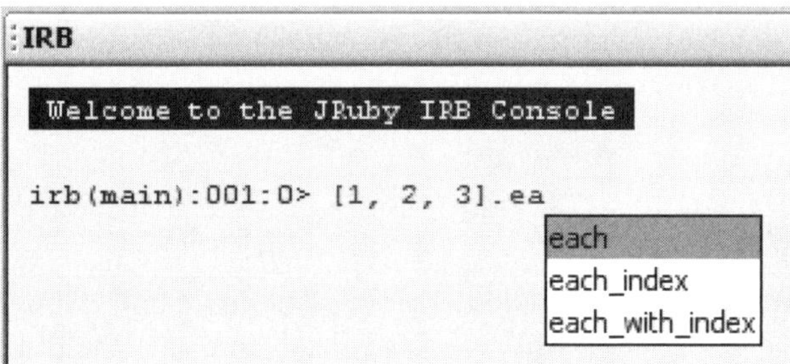

Figure 12-31. *Code completion in IRB*

From within NetBeans you can also open the Rails Console for any given Ruby on Rails project. You can access the Rails Console from the project's context menu by right-clicking the Ruby on Rails project and selecting Rails Console.

JRuby

JRuby is simply the Ruby language running on the JVM rather than the CRuby interpreter. Everything I've discussed up to this point is applicable to both Ruby and JRuby, and you should notice little difference in switching between the two runtimes. To learn more about JRuby, visit `http://www.jruby.org`.

Being able to run Ruby on the JVM does bring an interesting dimension to the mix. First of all, you can now leverage the vast array of Java libraries in existence today, whether in the public domain or in your own private domain. Second, and probably more interesting for the enterprise, is that you can write Ruby on Rails applications that will run on your existing deployment infrastructure, be that WebSphere, WebLogic, JBoss, GlassFish, or any other servlet container. In this section I give examples of both.

Calling Java from Ruby

JRuby allows you to define and interact with Java classes from within Ruby, and the best part is that you continue to use the Ruby syntax to which you're already accustomed.

The first step to working with your Java classes is making them available to the JRuby interpreter, and NetBeans can help with this step.

Note If you're working with any of the standard Java libraries (those that ship with the JVM), then this step is unnecessary because they are already bundled with the JRuby runtime.

If you open the project properties page, we can now address the Java category. From here you can configure JRuby with the Java libraries you want to use in your project (essentially just as you would need to do when working from a Java project).

The second step is to include Java:

```
include Java
```

The third step is to import the Java classes you're going to use. For example, if you wanted to work with a `java.util.ArrayList`, you would need to type the following:

```
include Java
import java.util.ArrayList
```

However, working with the `java.util.ArrayList` in Ruby becomes much more interesting, for types are not declared and we use the Ruby syntax to create new objects. For example:

```
dogs = ArrayList.new
dogs.add "Spaniel"
dogs.add "Hound"
dogs.add "Retriever"

dogs.each do |dog|
  puts dog
end
```

This is fun stuff because we're using a Java class as if it were a Ruby class, iterators and all. This demonstrates how you can easily make use of your existing Java APIs directly from a Ruby class.

Running Rails on Your Favorite Servlet Container

As discussed in the beginning of this section, one of the more exciting aspects of JRuby is the ability to deploy Ruby on Rails applications to a Java servlet container. This lets you take advantage of all the agility the Ruby on Rails framework has to offer while leveraging your existing deployment infrastructure.

From speaking with a lot of developers, I've learned that getting a new deployment runtime onto a production server can be a challenge. Several developers have even told me that they notified their server administrators that the application was written in Rails only after it was in production!

All of this is possible through a Rails plugin called GoldSpike, which packages your Ruby on Rails application as a WAR file for easy deployment to a servlet container. You can learn more at `http://wiki.jruby.org/wiki/Goldspike`.

If you think you'll want to deploy your application as a WAR file, then when creating the project select the option to "Add Rake Targets to Support App Server Deployment (.war)" (see Figure 12-32).

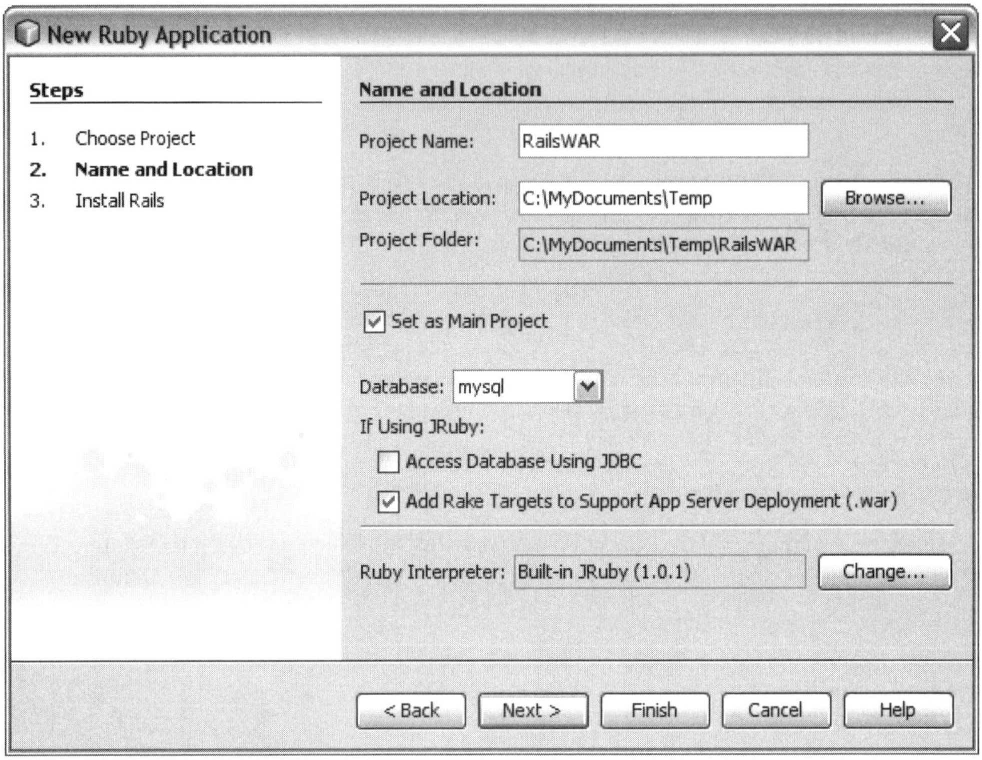

Figure 12-32. *Configuring a new Rails project with GoldSpike*

If you have an existing project you'd like to WAR, you can use the Rails Plugin dialog to add the GoldSpike plugin to your project.

In order to run the Rake targets added by the GoldSpike plugin, you also need to install the ActiveRecord-JDBC Ruby gem, which you can do via the Ruby Gem Manager. See the earlier section "The Ruby Gem Manager" for details.

■Note The war:standalone:create Rake target expects the Java `jar` command to be accessible on the path. Configure your environment to ensure that your Java `bin` directory is on your path (you should be able to run `jar -version` successfully from the command line).

Once these components are installed, you're ready to create a WAR of your Rails project. To accomplish this, run the Rake task war:standalone:create (Figure 12-33). The process takes several minutes to complete, and once you're done you'll have a deployable WAR file in your project's root directory.

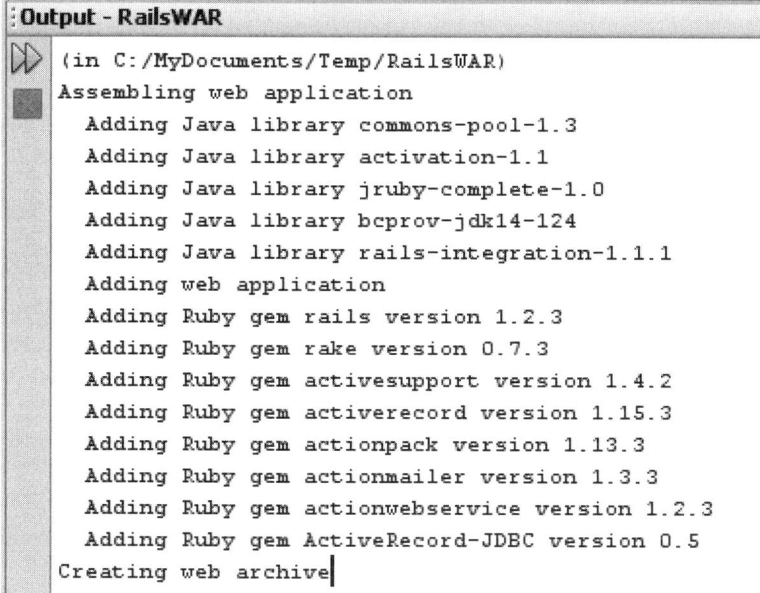

Output - RailsWAR
(in C:/MyDocuments/Temp/RailsWAR)
Assembling web application
Adding Java library commons-pool-1.3
Adding Java library activation-1.1
Adding Java library jruby-complete-1.0
Adding Java library bcprov-jdk14-124
Adding Java library rails-integration-1.1.1
Adding web application
Adding Ruby gem rails version 1.2.3
Adding Ruby gem rake version 0.7.3
Adding Ruby gem activesupport version 1.4.2
Adding Ruby gem activerecord version 1.15.3
Adding Ruby gem actionpack version 1.13.3
Adding Ruby gem actionmailer version 1.3.3
Adding Ruby gem actionwebservice version 1.2.3
Adding Ruby gem ActiveRecord-JDBC version 0.5
Creating web archive

Figure 12-33. *war:standalone:create output*

You can now deploy and run the WAR file on your favorite servlet container.

Putting It All Together

Here you'll use many of the features you learned about in the previous sections to build a simple Ruby on Rails application: an online visitor log, just like the kind you might find at a bed and breakfast, but digital.

Creating the Database

Before creating your project, you'll create your project's database. As noted earlier, the examples in this chapter assume MySQL as the database.

1. Select Window ➤ Services.
2. Expand the Database node.
3. If you already have a connection to a MySQL database in the list, skip to step 6.
4. Right-click the MySQL (Connector/J driver) and select Connect Using....
5. Set the Database URL to "`jdbc:mysql://localhost/mysql`" and the User Name to Root. Click OK to establish the connection. Using this connection you can create another MySQL database.
6. Right-click the MySQL connection and select Connect and then OK.

7. Right-click the MySQL connection again and select Execute Command.
8. Enter the command `create database visitor_log_development`.
9. Right-click the file and choose Run Statement.
10. Verify in the Output window that execution was successful.

Creating the Project

To create the project, do the following:

1. Select File ➤ New Project.
2. Select Ruby in the Categories list and Ruby on Rails Application in the Projects list. Click Next.
3. Name your project visitor_log and click Finish.

■ **Note** It's generally a Rails convention to name your project using lowercase, rather than CamelCase, lettering.

---

4. In the Projects window, right-click the Models node and select Generate.
5. The selected generator should already be Model. If not, please set it to such.
6. Set the "Arguments" field to "VisitorLog name:string comments:text data:datetime" and click OK to run the model generator.
7. Right-click the visitor_log project and select Migrate Database ➤ To Current Version.
8. Right-click the visitor_log project and select Generate.
9. Set the generator to scaffold. Set both the Model and Controller names to VisitorLog.

Running the Project

1. Choose Run ➤ Run Main Project to see the fruits of your labor. NetBeans will start the WEBrick server and launch the browser to `http://localhost:3000/`. Append `visitor_log` to the end of the URL to see your application.

■ **Tip** If you would like Rails to run a specific controller on launch, open `routes.rb`, uncomment the line `map.connect '', :controller => "welcome"`, and replace the controller value with the name of the controller you'd like to run. You also need to delete `index.html` from the Public folder. Alternatively, you can have NetBeans launch directly into the page you want to run by choosing Run ➤ Run File while viewing that page in the editor. For example, in the editor, open Views ➤ visitor_log ➤ list.rhtml and then select Run ➤ Run File > Run "list.rhtml". This feature also works from the controller. For example, while viewing `list.rhml` in the editor, select Navigate ➤ Go to Rails Action or View to open the list controller action associated with this view. From here you can also select Run ➤ Run File ➤ Run "visitor_log_controller.rb".

Notes:

1. The port number used by the server is configurable in the project's properties.
2. If another Rails project is already running at port 3000, NetBeans will automatically increment the port number, to prevent a "port in use" error when starting the server.
3. If you have installed Mongrel, then Mongrel will be started. NetBeans starts whatever is configured as the default server.

Summary

The Ruby features come bundled with the full download of the IDE, yet they're easy to get as plugins if you've already installed one of the smaller distributions. NetBeans comes bundled with the JRuby interpreter, but it is also easily configurable to work with an existing interpreter on your system, whether it be JRuby or native Ruby.

Out of the box, NetBeans has support for creating or working with your existing Ruby and/or Ruby on Rails applications. Once the projects are opened in NetBeans, you can easily add additional files or run Rails generators.

The Ruby language editor in NetBeans is first class, providing all the features you'd expect for a statically typed language (code completion, rdoc integrations, go to type, go to declaration), even though Ruby is a dynamic language.

Testing and debugging are also supported, with debugging at the same level as Java debuggers—a real treat for Rails developers who are used to running the debugger from the command line.

NetBeans also supports running Rake tasks as well as managing your Ruby gems and Rails plugins. Additionally, you do not have to leave NetBeans to launch either the IRB or the Rails Console.

The chapter concluded with JRuby, where I went into a bit more depth on the technology, for which the big benefits are the abilities to call Java libraries from your Ruby code as well as to deploy your Rails applications to a Java servlet container.

As stated at the beginning of this chapter, the topic of Ruby, Ruby on Rails, and JRuby is quite a bit to condense into a single chapter. I've been more broad then deep, showing you what's possible and providing you an opportunity to explore further on your own. To that extent, here are a couple of resources to continue your learning:

- Project homepage (maintained by NetBeans engineering): `http://ruby.netbeans.org`
- Product homepage (maintained by NetBeans Documentation Team): `http://www.netbeans.org/products/ruby`
- Mailing list: `users@ruby.netbens.org`

CHAPTER 13

Developing Web Applications

Several options are available in NetBeans for creating and working with web applications. The first is the Web Application project type. This includes standard HTML, JSP, and visual JSF support. There are also additional types of web application support available through plugins, such as Struts, JSF, and jMaki.

Prior to NetBeans 6, two types of Web Application projects were available in NetBeans: Web Applications and Visual Web Applications. These project types have been combined into one standard type of project named Web Application. With this type of project you can choose whether or not to add visual JSF support through the ability to add frameworks such as Struts and JSF.

This chapter focuses on providing an overview to each type of web application tool available while highlighting the updated and new features available in NetBeans 6.

Create a Web Application Project

To create a new web application, select File ➤ New Project. In the New Project window, choose the Web category. You will see the following project type choices:

- Web Application
- Web Application with Existing Sources
- Web Application with Existing Ant Script

The first item in the list is the one on which this chapter focuses. The second and third items are the same as the Web Application type. They differ only in how the project is created.

Follow these steps to create a Web Application project:

1. In the New Project window, select Web Application from the list, and then click the Next button to continue. As you can see in Figure 13-1, several options are available when creating a Web Application project.
2. The first few items to set in the wizard are the project name and location. Enter a value in the "Project Name" field. It will be appended to the value in the "Project Location" field to create what is displayed in the third field, "Project Folder." You will want to pick a generic location for the "Project Location" field. In Figure 13-1, you can see that I selected the folder `D:\projects`.

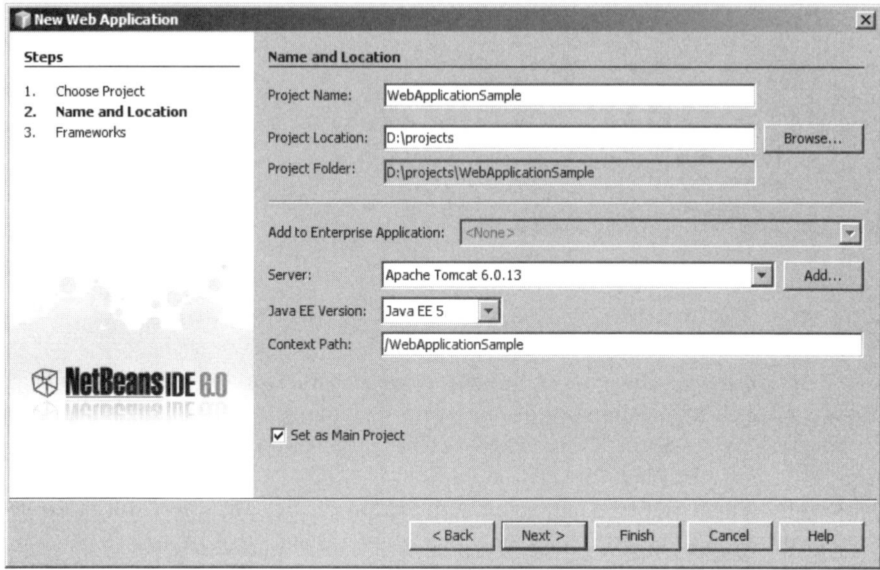

Figure 13-1. *Web Application properties in the New Web Application wizard*

Tip If you want your project to have a long, meaningful name but not an identical directory structure, you can do that. When creating your project, start by picking a short name, such as `surveytool`. When the project is created, you will see a path structure like `c:\projects\surveytool` (assuming your root location was `c:\projects`). Then in the Projects window, right-click the project name and select Rename Project. Enter the full name you want to assign the project, such as `MyCustomer Survey Tool`. The project structure will stay the same, but the project name displayed in the Projects window will have the long name you originally wanted.

---

3. Set the "Server" field to specify to which application server you will deploy the project. This can easily be changed later through the Project Properties window, so don't panic if you feel you've selected the wrong server. The options that appear in the "Server" field drop-down list may vary, depending on the NetBeans bundle you downloaded and installed. For the most part, NetBeans comes bundled with Tomcat. If you selected the correct option during installation, the Sun Java System Application Server (GlassFish) will also appear in the list. If the server you wish to use does not appear in the list, click the Add button to activate the Add Server Instance wizard. See the "Defining Java Application Servers" section later in this chapter for details on setting up an application server.

4. Fill in the "Context Path" field to define the URL where your application can be accessed once deployed to the application server.

5. Set the other fields to specify the Java Enterprise Edition (EE) version of the application and the source level and that the new project should be the main project.

6. Once you have set the configuration options for your application, click the Next button.

7. In the next window, the New Project wizard prompts you to add a framework to the web application. This list will vary, depending on which modules you have installed and activated. By default, you should see Visual Web JavaServer Faces, JavaServer Faces, and Struts in the list. Click the check box next to the Struts option, and you should see additional fields appear in the bottom half of the window, as shown in Figure 13-2.

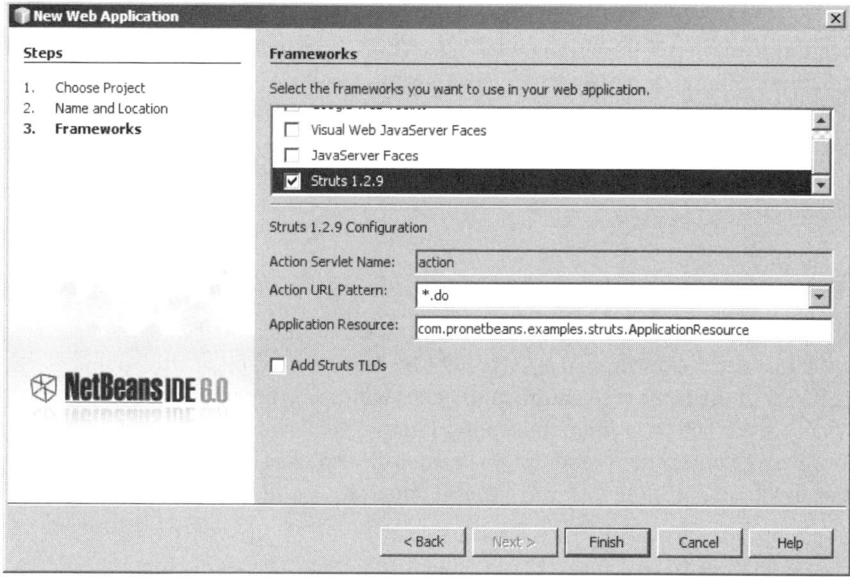

Figure 13-2. *Specifying the framework and properties for the Java web application*

8. The Struts Configuration section allows you to set the main high-level properties that the Struts framework will use for your web application. You can set the "Action URL Pattern" field, which is initialized by default to `*.do`. This is the pattern that your web application will use to map file URLs to Struts actions, as defined in the Struts configuration files. Before continuing, you should also modify the package structure in the "Application Resource" field to conform to the Java package structure your application will use.

9. Once you're satisfied with the settings, click the Finish button to generate the web application.

Once the new web application has been created, you can browse the nodes in the Projects window.

Navigating the Web Application Project

Like every other project type, Web Application projects are structured as a set of parent–child nodes with special designations. For the Web Application project type, the files are sorted into the following nodes:

- Web Pages
- Configuration Files
- Server Resources
- Source Packages
- Test Packages
- Libraries
- Test Libraries

This structure is how NetBeans arranges the files. The Source Packages, Test Packages, Libraries, and Test Libraries items should look familiar. They are the same as for a regular Java Application or Java Class Library project, as discussed in Chapter 2, on the Source Editor. They contain the Java source files, the source of the test files, any project libraries, and any test-specific libraries, respectively. The new nodes you have not seen before are Web Pages, Configuration Files, and Server Resources.

Web Pages

The Web Pages node in the Projects window defines where the actual web content should be located. This is where you can add HTML, JSP, CSS, images, and folders to your application.

If you look at the project structure in the Files window, you will see a top-level directory named `web`. This directory is where the content in the Web Pages node is located.

You will see that it contains a sample `index.jsp` file as well as the standard `WEB-INF` directory. If you look in the `WEB-INF` directory, you will also find a `web.xml` file and the `struts-config.xml` file.

Configuration Files

Configuration Files is a special node that does not represent an actual folder in the project structure. The items that appear under this node are categorized as items to which you would normally need access when making configuration changes to the application. It also contains the deployment descriptor for the web application.

The Configuration Files node contains the `web.xml`, `struts-config.xml`, and other project configuration files. These are the same files that appear under the `WEB-INF` directory in the Web Pages node.

■ **Note** The files under the Configuration Files node are not copies of the files under other nodes. They simply represent an alternative method for viewing and accessing them. If you find it confusing, you don't even need to use the Configuration Files node.

If you have captured any database schemas, you will be able to view the schema file under this node as well.

Server Resources

The Server Resources node is used primarily with Enterprise projects; however, there are a few uses for it in Web Application projects. Several files and objects are placed under this node after they have been created.

If you define a JDBC Resource, JDBC Connection Pool, JMS Resource, Persistence Resource, or JavaMail Resource, it will be listed under the Server Resources node. This is handy, since it gives you quick access to related resources. The items under the Server Resources node appear under the `Setup` directory in the Files window.

JavaScript and CSS File Support

NetBeans 6 has improved built-in support for CSS and JavaScript. The Source Editor allows you to open these file types and work with them in an intelligent manner.

Working with CSS Files

Out of the box, NetBeans 6 provides good support for CSS files. You can use the New File wizard to add a CSS file to your project and have a visual editor for modifying the style properties. You'll also be able to benefit from syntax coloring, rule creation, and CSS validation. If you are developing a web application, then as a best practice you make frequent use of CSS files. Any tools that can assist you in working with them are very valuable.

To add a new CSS file to your current Web Application project, select File ➤ New File from the main menu. In the New File window, select the Web category, choose the Cascading Style Sheet file type, and then click Next. Enter the filename. Do *not* add the `.css` extension. Select the folder in which the file will be located, and then click Finish.

The CSS file will be added to your project and will open in the Source Editor window. The file contains a comment block that lists the name of the file, the date it was originally created, the author, and a sample explanation of the purpose of the file. It also contains a `TODO` directive suggesting that the initial text in the file be modified. You can see this listed in the Task List window by selecting Window ➤ Task List or by pressing Ctrl+6.

Figure 13-3 shows the CSS file in the Source Editor. The toolbar along the top of the window includes a CSS-specific icon: Create Rule.

Tip In the NetBeans IDE, you can see the function for each icon by placing the mouse over it and reading the tooltip that is displayed.

```
/*
    Document   : app
    Created on : Oct 2, 2007, 12:37:33 AM
    Author     : Adam Myatt
    Description:
        Purpose of the stylesheet follows.
*/

/*
   TODO customize this sample style
   Syntax recommendation http://www.w3.org/TR/REC-CSS2/
*/

root {
    display: block;
}
```

Figure 13-3. *Default content in new CSS file*

The Create Rule button is on the far-left side of the toolbar. When you click the Create Rule icon, the Style Rule Editor dialog box appears. It allows you to define a new style class or element definition. You can use the Style Rule Editor to define a set of styles for an HTML element. The dialog box provides a drop-down list of HTML elements and allows you to choose multiple HTML elements. To add elements to the Style Rule Hierarchy list on the right, click the > button.

For example, in Figure 13-4, the `<h1>`, `<h2>`, and `<h3>` elements were chosen from the "HTML Element" drop-down list and added to the Style Rule Hierarchy list. Once you have created a Style Rule Hierarchy list to your liking, click the OK button. The new style rule is then added to the CSS file (but without any style definitions), like this:

```
h1 h2 h3 {

}
```

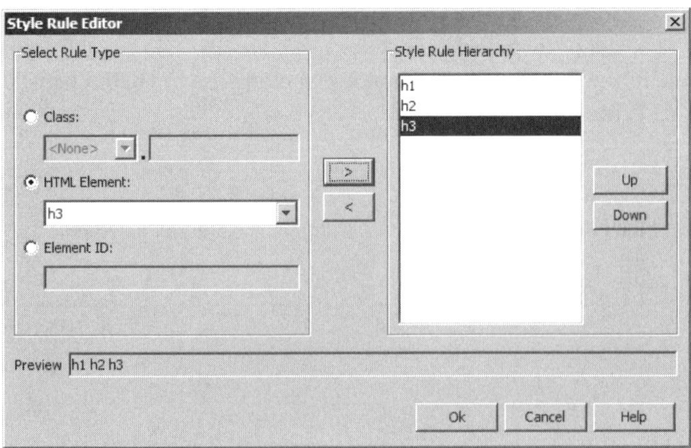

Figure 13-4. *The Style Rule Editor dialog box*

Once you have created the empty style rule, you need to define styles. You can do so manually in the text displayed in the Source Editor, or you can use the Style Builder. To open the Style Builder window, go to the main menu and select Window ➤ Other ➤ Css Style Builder. The Style Builder window should open and be visible along the bottom of the screen, as shown in Figure 13-5. (This may vary slightly, depending on how many windows you have open at the time.)

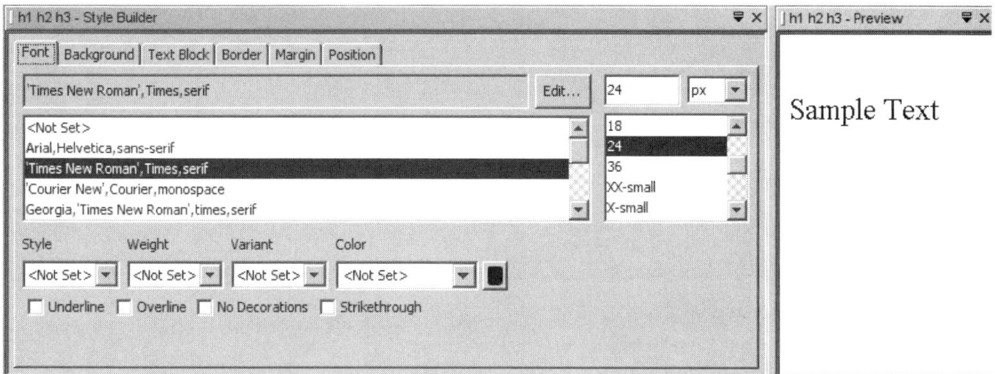

Figure 13-5. *Editing styles in the Style Builder*

The Style Builder provides a graphical interface for editing styles. You can use it to set font attributes, margins, borders, background attributes, and more. To use the Style Builder for a specific element in a CSS file, place the cursor anywhere inside the corresponding style. As you select different properties from the list, the Css Preview window on the right will show what the text will look like with the style applied. (If you are defining a style for a nontext HTML element, the preview pane will not display anything.)

As you set the various properties for the style, you will see the text in the Source Editor change to correspond to your selections. Once you are finished, you can close the CSS file from the Source Editor window. The Style Builder will also close.

Note The CSS Preview window is a separate window that can be opened, docked, or closed independent of the Css Style Builder window. You can close it to save screen space or to have more room to view the Css Style Builder window. To reopen the window, go to the main menu and select Window ➤ Other ➤ Css Preview.

Working with JavaScript Files

NetBeans 6 also provides improved JavaScript support. You can now take advantage of basic code completion, improved syntax highlighting and recognition, and code templates.

There are several ways you can work with JavaScript in a Web Application project. First, add a block of JavaScript directly to an HTML file. Open an HTML file in the Source Editor, such as the following:

```
<html>
    <head>
        <title>My Page</title>
        <meta http-equiv="Content-Type" content="text/html; charset=UTF-8">
    </head>
    <body>
    </body>
</html>
```

Then add a script tag and several simple JavaScript methods:

```
<script type="text/javascript">

    function showPopup(textVal) {
          alert(textVal);
    }

    function showWarning(warnText) {
          // do something with warning text
          showPopup(warntext);
    }

    function showError(errorText) {
          // do something with error text

    }
</script>
```

After adding this JavaScript to the HTML file, place your cursor on the blank line below the comment inside the showError method. Then press Ctrl+Spacebar to activate the code completion window. You will see a list of suggestions displayed in the code completion window, as shown in Figure 13-6.

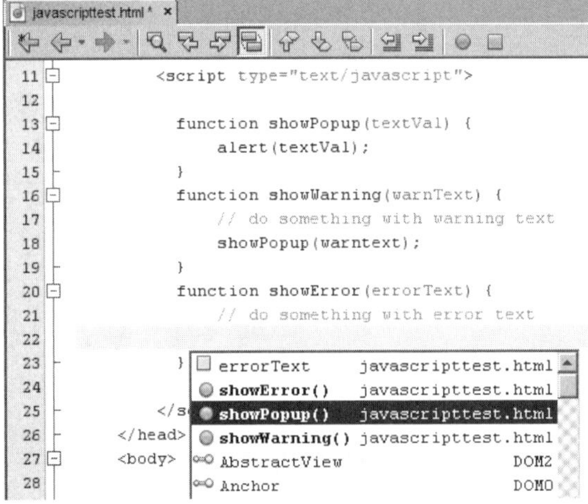

Figure 13-6. *Code completion menu for Javscript embedded in HTML files*

For JavaScript, the code completion will typically list any objects or functions defined in the HTML file in which you are currently working. The list also contains a listing of objects from the DOM, core JavaScript method (denoted as JS Core), and any JavaScript keywords. You can use the up and down keys to navigate the list and press the Enter key to select the item you want from the list.

Note At the time of this writing, JavaScript code completion did not allow you to type a partial method or object name to filter the list of results. Hopefully, this feature will make it into the final release of NetBeans 6.

As any web developer knows, you can also work with stand-alone JavaScript files ("`.js`" files). To create a stand-alone JavaScript file, do the following:

1. Right-click the Web Pages node for a project in the Projects window and select New ➤ Other.
2. In the New File wizard that appears, select Web from the Category section.
3. In the File Types section, select JavaScript File and click the Next button.
4. Specify the JavaScript file's name in the "File Name" field.
5. Using the "Folder" field, specify the folder where the JavaScript file will be located. If you activated the New File wizard by right-clicking the Web Pages node, then the "Folder" field will be set to web. Otherwise you must use the Browser button to select the folder where you want to place the file.
6. Click the Finish button to create the file and open it in the Source Editor.

With the new stand-alone JavaScript file open in the Source Editor, paste in the same functions you embedded in the HTML file. Change the function names to `showPopup2`, `showWarning2`, and `showError2`. You will be able to see the syntax coloring displayed. You can also click inside the code and place the cursor next to a parenthesis or curly brace. The matching curly brace or parenthesis will be highlighted for easy identification, as shown in Figure 13-7.

```
app.js

function showPopup2(textVal) {
    alert(textVal);
}

function showWarning2(warnText) {
    // do something with warning text
    showPopup2(warntext);
}

function showError2(errorText) {
    // do something with error text
    showPopup2(errorText);
}
```

Figure 13-7. *Identifying matching braces in JavaScript*

Once you have placed JavaScript code inside a stand-alone file, you can use it from within any JSP or HTML file. Insert the following code between the <head> and </head> tags in the document:

```
<script type="text/javascript" src="my-standalone-js-file.js"></script>
```

Once you have added the script tag that references your stand-alone JavaScript file, the methods and objects within it will appear in the code completion pop-up window if activated from within the HTML file.

Building a Web Application

In NetBeans, you can choose to compile and build an entire web application without necessarily having to deploy it to an application server. Building an application in NetBeans is quite simple. Select the Build ➤ Build Main Project menu option. This assumes the project you want to build is set as the main project. If it is not, you can set it to the main project by right-clicking the project name in the Projects window and choosing Set Main Project. You can also right-click a project name and choose Build Project from the context menu if you want to build a specific project.

Once you have started the project build process, the Output window will appear. You will see a number of lines scroll through the Output window. The output lines are caused by the actions that are taking place in the background, based on the project's build configuration (in other words, the project's Ant build file). Choosing the Build menu option actually activates an Ant target for the current project. For more details on how NetBeans projects are structured and integrated with Ant, see Chapter 8.

The basics of what happened during the build are abstracted away for the most part. You should see a "Build Successful" message as one of the last lines in the Output window. This tells you that the Java source files compiled correctly and that the web application was packaged as specified in the project properties. You can now run the application, work with the compiled application files externally from NetBeans, or continue with your development work.

Cleaning and Building a Project

You may also choose the Build ➤ Clean and Build Main Project menu option. This does the same set of tasks as the Build option, with one difference: all content inside the `build directory` in the NetBeans project structure is deleted. This ensures that no class files or other resource files are present.

After deleting the content of the `build` directory, the project is then recompiled into the `build` directory. This is sometimes necessary if you have built an application, made numerous code changes, and want to feel confident that the compiled code is using the most current version of the source files. This also comes in handy after updating your application from a source code repository such as CVS.

Caution In NetBeans, you may occasionally have a problem cleaning and building a running web application. If JAR files in the `WEB-INF/lib` directory are in use by the application server, they often cannot be deleted by the clean operation. You need to go to the Runtime window and stop the running application server (as described in the "Defining Java Application Servers" section later in this chapter) before initiating the clean and build operation.

Compiling JSP Files

For web applications, you may also want to make sure that all the JSP files are compiled during the project build operation. This is a configurable option that is disabled by default. It is highly recommended that you enable it, since it will let you know if your JSP files will compile correctly. To enable this property, do the following:

1. Right-click the project name in the Projects window and select Properties.
2. Under the Build category, choose Compiling.
3. Select the check box next to the Test Compile All JSP Files During Builds field.
4. Click the OK button.

The next time you build your project, you should notice some additional text in the Output window under the heading `compile-jsps`. With each project build, all the JSP files will be compiled.

Repeating and Stopping Builds

Two new features added as of NetBeans 6 are the options to repeat a build and to stop a currently running build. These menu options appear on the main Build menu.

If you initiated at least one build or run operation, you should be able to select Repeat Build/Run *AppName* (*operation*) from the main Build menu. The *AppName* will be the name of the application in which the last build or run operation occurred, and the *operation* will be either Build or Run. This helps clear up any confusion, especially if you are working in multiple open projects.

The Build ➤ Stop Build/Run option is useful when the build operation takes a long time and you need to stop it. This saves you from having to wait through the entire build process.

You will also see new icons in the Output window as of NetBeans 6, as shown in Figure 13-8. These represent the Repeat Build and Run and Stop Build/Run options. The two green triangles activate the repeat build/run operation, and the square under it will stop a currently running build or run operation.

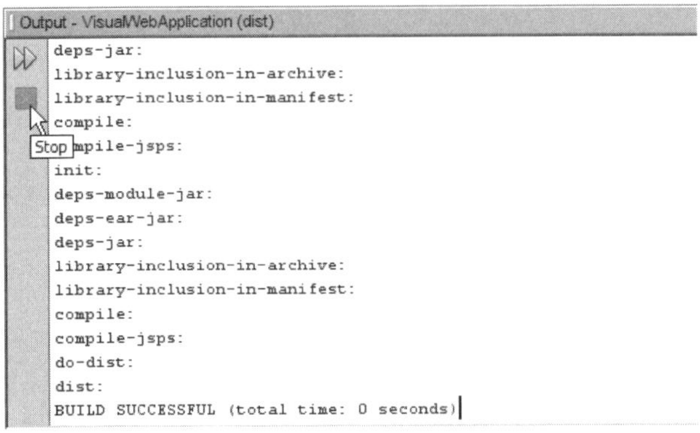

```
Output - VisualWebApplication (dist)
deps-jar:
library-inclusion-in-archive:
library-inclusion-in-manifest:
compile:
compile-jsps:
init:
deps-module-jar:
deps-ear-jar:
deps-jar:
library-inclusion-in-archive:
library-inclusion-in-manifest:
compile:
compile-jsps:
do-dist:
dist:
BUILD SUCCESSFUL (total time: 0 seconds)
```

Figure 13-8. *The Repeat Build/Run and Stop Build/Run icons in the Output window*

Running a Web Application

A large component of developing web applications is being able to test and run them in an application server. During the regular course of development, most programmers will run a JSP page dozens of times to make sure it functions as expected.

When a web application is run, it is first built, packaged, and deployed. If the associated Java application server is not started, NetBeans attempts to start and deploy the application to it. When you choose to run an application, NetBeans uses the project's Ant build file to compile, package, and run the application files.

To run the web application, select Run ➤ Run Main Project, or press F6. The Output window will appear. As the various steps in the build configuration process, you will notice a separate tab for the run operation in the Output window.

The various build steps will execute—compiling any Java source files, compiling JSP files, copying files to the project build directory, and so on. Before the application actually runs, you will notice that the application files are packaged into a distribution file. For a Java Application project, a JAR file is created. For Web Application projects, a WAR file is created. The WAR file is a glorified JAR file that allows the entire web application to be packaged and distributed together. You can then take this WAR file and deploy it to one or more servers.

If the application WAR file is not created, you can set the project to create one. To force a Web Application project to generate a WAR file, perform the following steps:

1. Right-click the project name in the Projects window and select Properties.

2. Select Packaging from the Categories list on the left.

3. Check the Create WAR File property check box.

Once the run and run/deploy steps in the build process execute, the target application server will be started. Additional tabs will open in the Output window for the application server. Figure 13-9 shows an example of the tabs and output for an application running and deployed to the Tomcat application server.

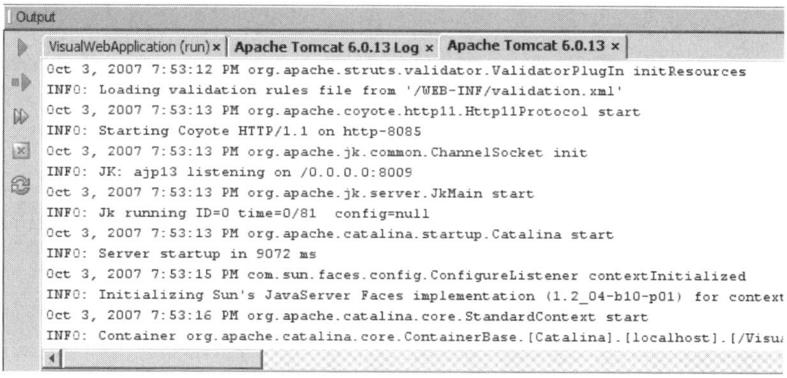

Output

VisualWebApplication (run) × | Apache Tomcat 6.0.13 Log × | Apache Tomcat 6.0.13 ×

```
Oct 3, 2007 7:53:12 PM org.apache.struts.validator.ValidatorPlugIn initResources
INFO: Loading validation rules file from '/WEB-INF/validation.xml'
Oct 3, 2007 7:53:13 PM org.apache.coyote.http11.Http11Protocol start
INFO: Starting Coyote HTTP/1.1 on http-8085
Oct 3, 2007 7:53:13 PM org.apache.jk.common.ChannelSocket init
INFO: JK: ajp13 listening on /0.0.0.0:8009
Oct 3, 2007 7:53:13 PM org.apache.jk.server.JkMain start
INFO: Jk running ID=0 time=0/81  config=null
Oct 3, 2007 7:53:13 PM org.apache.catalina.startup.Catalina start
INFO: Server startup in 9072 ms
Oct 3, 2007 7:53:15 PM com.sun.faces.config.ConfigureListener contextInitialized
INFO: Initializing Sun's JavaServer Faces implementation (1.2_04-b10-p01) for context
Oct 3, 2007 7:53:16 PM org.apache.catalina.core.StandardContext start
INFO: Container org.apache.catalina.core.ContainerBase.[Catalina].[localhost].[/Visu
```

Figure 13-9. *The output tabs when running a JSP page*

The five icons along the left margin of the tab shown in Figure 13-9 allow quick access to the application server and the ability to start, stop, and restart it. From top to bottom, the icons are Start the Server, Start the Server in Debug Mode, Restart the Server, Stop the Server, and Refresh the Server Status. The Refresh the Server Status option is useful when the application server takes a long time to stop or shut down. Sometimes application servers can hang or time out, and the ability to refresh the status can save you some headaches.

Defining Java Application Servers

Web applications can be deployed to a variety of Java application servers. Among that list are Tomcat, BEA WebLogic, GlassFish, the Sun Java System Application Server (SJSAS), JBoss, and others. Web applications can be associated only with application servers that have been identified in NetBeans through the Servers window.

The Servers window allows you to define an application server, reference the root directory where it is installed, and configure a variety of server properties. Once this process is complete, you can manage the server directly in NetBeans, control it (starting, stopping, restarting, and so on), and deploy web applications to it.

To access the tool, select Tools ➤ Servers. The initial list of servers registered with NetBeans will vary, depending on what you originally installed. If you downloaded any web-related bundle, you may have either Tomcat or GlassFish listed in the Servers window.

The Servers window will list the currently configured application servers in the left pane. If a specific server is selected, its properties appear in the right pane. Click the Add Server button on the lower-left side of the window to define a new application server for use with your NetBeans Web Application projects. When adding a new server, you will need to know the base directory location for the installed server as well as some additional parameters.

Once an application server is configured, you will see it listed under the Servers node in the Services window. From there, you can control the server, view information about it, and access the various web applications that may be deployed.

With an application server configured for use in NetBeans, you can configure web applications to use it through the project properties for the application.

The following sections discuss how to add specific types of servers and then how to set your web applications to deploy to your configured servers.

Using Tomcat

NetBeans currently ships with a bundled version of the Tomcat Java application server. Tomcat is a de facto standard widely used by the programming industry to deploy Java applications.

Setting Tomcat Properties

You can use the Tomcat properties available in the Servers window to configure the server. As shown in Figure 13-10, the Servers window displays multiple tabs for the bundled Tomcat server: Connection, Startup, Platform, Deployment, Classes, Sources, and Javadoc. Each tab contains a set of properties you can modify. For example, on the Connection tab, you can change the port on which the server listens and the username and password for the manager role.

■ **Note** If you plan on running multiple instances of Tomcat on your machine, you will need to change the value in the "Server Port" field. The default is 8080, but this can be set to any port that is not in use. If you accidentally set the server port to one in use, you will see an error message in the Server Output tab in the Output window when the server starts up.

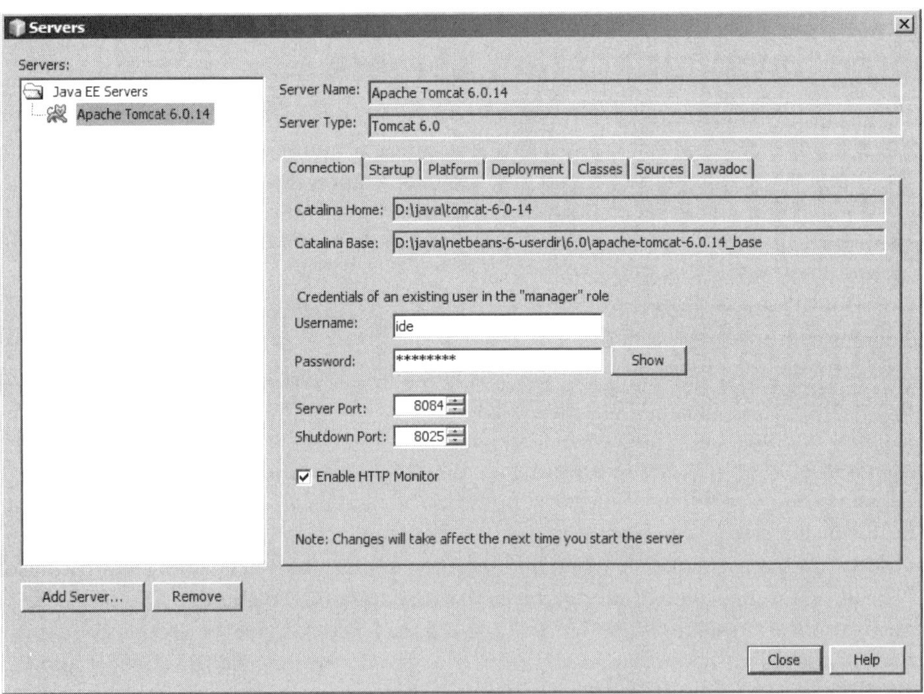

Figure 13-10. *The Tomcat server selected in the Servers window*

Click the Platform tab to view two very important fields:

Java Platform: Allows you to select in which version of Java the application will run. If you have a heterogeneous development environment, you may need to be able to test Tomcat in different versions of the JVM.

VM Options: Allows you to pass command-line parameters to the JVM during startup. One issue you may encounter is memory constraints. You may be testing or profiling your application code in Tomcat and receive an "out of memory" error. This happens when your application code uses up the maximum amount of memory the JVM is allowed to allocate. You can adjust the initial and upper limit for memory allocation by passing parameters to the JVM via the VM Options field. The value `-Xms200m -Xmx500m` sets the initial amount of memory allocated to the JVM to around 200MB and the maximum amount it can expand to consume to around 500MB.

The Deployment tab in the Servers window is new for Tomcat in NetBeans 6. It contains two important fields:

Deployment Timeout: The amount of time NetBeans waits while deploying an application before it considers the deployment to have failed.

JDBC Driver Deployment: Instructs NetBeans to deploy database drivers to the application if necessary.

Once you have modified the properties to your needs, click the OK button to close the Servers window. You will need to restart the Tomcat application server for the changes to take effect.

Working with Applications Deployed to Tomcat

The Tomcat server should appear in the Servers window and under the Servers node in the Services window. In the Services window, you'll see a Web Applications node under the Tomcat listing. (Other servers may have different nodes available.) Tomcat simply lists the applications that have been deployed in the server instance, as shown in Figure 13-11.

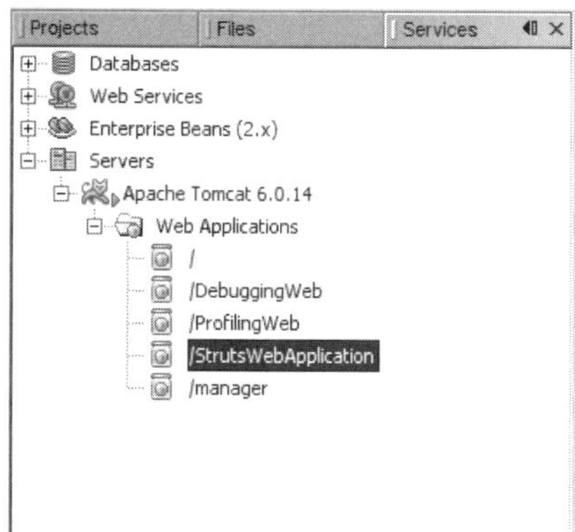

Figure 13-11. *Web applications deployed to the Tomcat server listed in the Services window*

For each deployed web application listed under the Web Applications node, you have several options. Right-click the application name to see a context menu with the following options:

Start: Allows you explicitly to start a web application instance that is deployed to Tomcat. The Tomcat server itself may be started, but that does not mean every web application instance has also been started. When you run a web application in NetBeans, then by default it is deployed to the application server and started. It should not be stopped unless you have done so explicitly.

Stop: Allows you to stop a running web application. This will make the application unavailable via a web browser, but it does *not* undeploy it from Tomcat. Tomcat will still recognize it, and you can restart the application whenever you wish.

Undeploy: Stops the web application and undeploys it from the server. The server will no longer list the application under the Web Applications node. You will need to redeploy it to Tomcat to be able to view it.

Open in Browser: Opens the NetBeans default web browser and navigates to the URL for the web application. The server URL and port are defined in the Tomcat properties. The context path for the URL that is opened is project specific and defined in the project properties. This is basically the same as using the Run Main Project option for a web application, in that it opens the application in the browser.

Controlling the Tomcat Server

NetBeans also provides the ability to control the Tomcat server in the Services window. Right-click the server name in the Services window to see a context menu with the following options:

Start, Start in Debug Mode, and Start in Profile Mode: Allow you to start the Tomcat application server for the specified purposes.

Stop: Allows you to shut down the application server so no web applications can be accessed. Note that this does not explicitly stop each individual web application as does the Stop option on the context menu for an application under the Web Applications node. The next time you start Tomcat, the web applications will all be available, unless you explicitly used the Stop option for a specific application.

Restart: Stops and restarts the Tomcat server. This is useful if you want to clear any sessions in progress or clean up any potential memory leaks caused by your application code.

Refresh: Polls the application server to see what state it is in and refreshes the menu items that may be available.

Edit server.xml: Opens Tomcat's main configuration file, `server.xml`, in the Source Editor. If you need to make changes to the overall server configuration, you can conveniently access it directly in NetBeans.

View Admin Console: Opens a new web browser window and navigates to the Tomcat admin console. You can log in to this web application and perform administrative functions for Tomcat.

View Server Log and View Server Output: Open the Output window in NetBeans and give focus to the Server Log tab and Server Output tab, respectively.

Properties: Opens the Servers window, with the Tomcat server selected. This allows you quick access to the Tomcat configuration properties that you are allowed to change directly in NetBeans, as described earlier.

Using GlassFish

The GlassFish Java application server is an open source product that branched from the Sun Java System Application server. It is a Java EE5-compliant server that comes with the Full or Web & Java EE installation bundles of NetBeans 6.

Setting GlassFish Properties

Like Tomcat, you can use the Servers window to view and edit GlassFish properties. Select Tools ➤ Servers from the main menu and the Servers window will open. Select GlassFish from the list of Java EE Servers and the tabbed properties will display in the right-hand pane.

Many of the properties are similar to Tomcat, in that you can specify the admin user's username and password and instruct NetBeans to use the HTTP Monitor with the server. The Classes, Sources, and Javadoc tabs are also quite straightforward. The final tab, Options, allows you to specify the startup timeout and the deployment timeout, as shown in Figure 13-12.

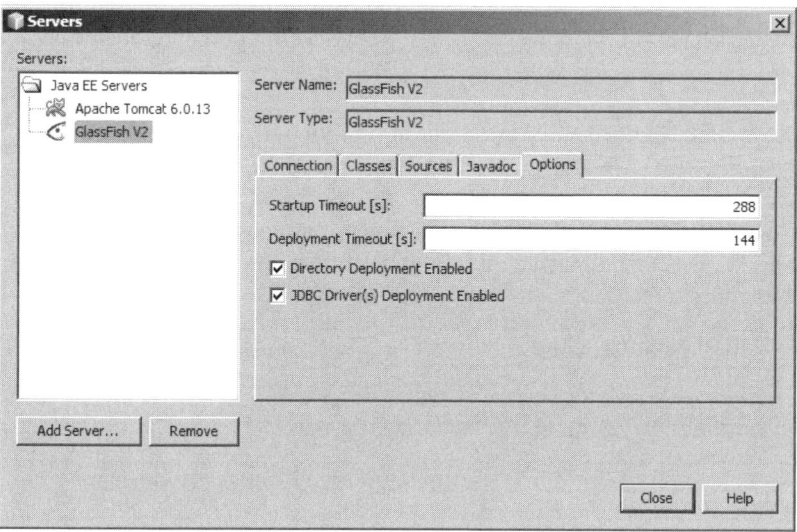

Figure 13-12. *The Options tab for GlassFish in the Servers window*

The Options tab shown in Figure 13-12 also lets you specify two additional values. The Directory Deployment Enabled check box instructs GlassFish to deploy and run the application directly from the project's `build` directory. If it is not selected, then the application is deployed to the default GlassFish domain. The location of the domain folder can be found by clicking the Connection tab for GlassFish in the Servers window.

If you look inside that directory, you'll see an applications directory. This is the directory where GlassFish deploys the web application if you unselect the Directory Deployment Enabled check box in the Options tab. This can impact the speed of the deployment process negatively.

Working with Applications Deployed to GlassFish

The GlassFish server will also appear in the Services window under the Servers node. From there, you can control the server and the applications that are deployed to it.

If you expand the plus icon next to the GlassFish node, you will see nodes labeled Applications and Resources. The Applications node is where the web, enterprise, and EAR applications have been deployed. You can expand the Applications node to view the individual applications.

If you right-click an application under the Applications node, a context menu appears. This lets you undeploy an application from the server, disable it from running while leaving it deployed, and view the properties of the application.

Controlling GlassFish

If you right-click the GlassFish node in the Services window, you will see options for controlling it. This is similar to Tomcat in that you can start, stop, and restart the GlassFish server. You can also start the server in debug or profile mode, remove the server from the list of servers, view the server log, or open a browser to the admin console.

When you start GlassFish, you may notice that it takes quite a bit of memory (especially on the Windows platform). You can use the GlassFish admin console to adjust the startup memory parameters. Right-click the GlassFish node in the Services window and select View Admin Console. Assuming the GlassFish server is already started, a web browser will open and load the admin console login page.

When you are presented with the login page, enter the admin username and password that you configured when GlassFish was installed. The default username and password are typically *admin*.

Once you have logged into the admin console, there are numerous options from which to choose. You have to drill down through several menus to locate the JVM startup parameters. To locate them, follows these steps:

1. In the left navigation pane, click Application Server. The right pane will display a set of tabs.

2. Click the JVM Settings tab. A submenu of tabs will appear.

3. Click the JVM Options tab. A list of JVM startup options will appear, as shown in Figure 13-13.

4. Locate the –Xmx512m property in the list and change it to a lower value. I have found 300 to work nicely without sacrificing too much performance.

5. Click the Save button. The window will refresh and you should see the message "New values successfully saved."

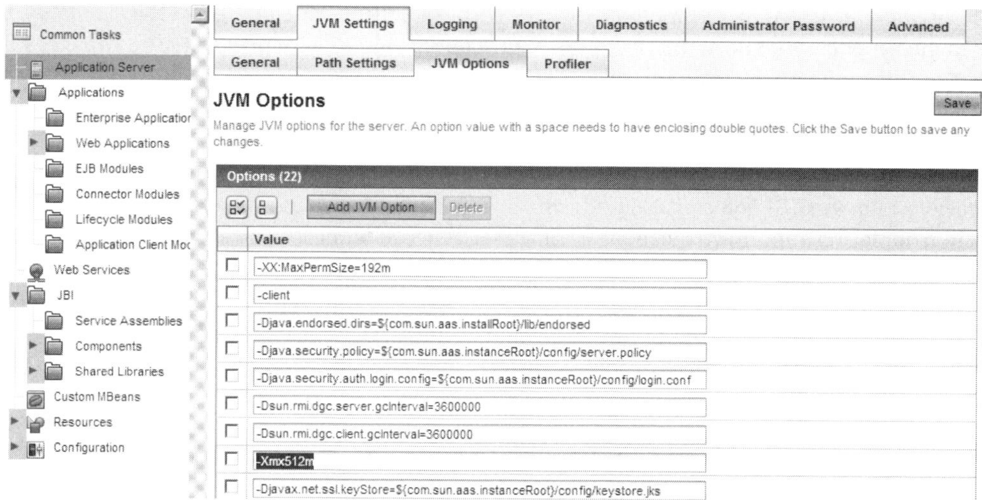

Figure 13-13. *Setting the max memory for GlassFish startup in the admin console*

The maximum amount of memory GlassFish should use will be lowered. If you restart GlassFish, it should consume less memory on your system.

Setting the Application Server for a Project

After you have added an application server in the Servers window, it is available for use. You can modify which application server a project will use by doing the following:

1. Right-click the name of a project in the Projects window and select Properties.
2. Select the Run category in the left pane.
3. Select the desired application server from the "Server" field drop-down list.
4. Click the OK button.

Once you have switched the application server in the project properties, no further actions are necessary.

NetBeans makes it extremely easy to toggle the application server a project will use. This is invaluable if you need to test your application across different types of servers to ensure compatibility. It can also come in handy if you must develop an application that will be deployed onto one server for development and testing purposes but deployed to a different server for production.

HTTP Monitoring

One of the most annoying things about developing web applications is not knowing what is going on behind the scenes when you are testing a particular page. Often, you read and write from the Request, Response, and Session objects and need to know what the values for session attributes were for a specific page request.

At one time or another, many web developers have written code that grabs the values from the Session or Request objects, iterates through the names, and prints out the current values. This is often done in an attempt to know the precise values passed to a JSP page or servlet. The HTTP Monitor can help make that type of debugging a thing of the past. In my opinion, the HTTP Monitor is one of the best features available in NetBeans.

The HTTP Monitor allows you to view all the state information for a particular page request directly within the IDE. You can also perform powerful actions such as modifying the state information, replaying a specific page request from a sequence of requests, and saving a page request for later viewing.

The HTTP Monitor must be supported by and enabled for the application server to which you are deploying. At the time of this writing, only Tomcat, GlassFish, and the SJSAS supported the HTTP Monitor.

Enabling the HTTP Monitor

You can enable the HTTP Monitor for a server in the Servers window as follows:

1. Select Tools ➤ Servers.
2. In the Servers window, select a server from the left pane.
3. In the server properties displayed in the right pane, you will see an Enable HTTP Monitor check box if the server supports the HTTP Monitor (see Figure 13-10 earlier in this chapter). Check this box, and then click Close.

Using the HTTP Monitor

Once you configure an application server to work with the HTTP Monitor, you can start using the tool. When you run a single JSP page or an entire web application, the HTTP Monitor will automatically activate. After the browser has finished processing the initial request, the HTTP Monitor window will open and display any results, as shown in Figure 13-14.

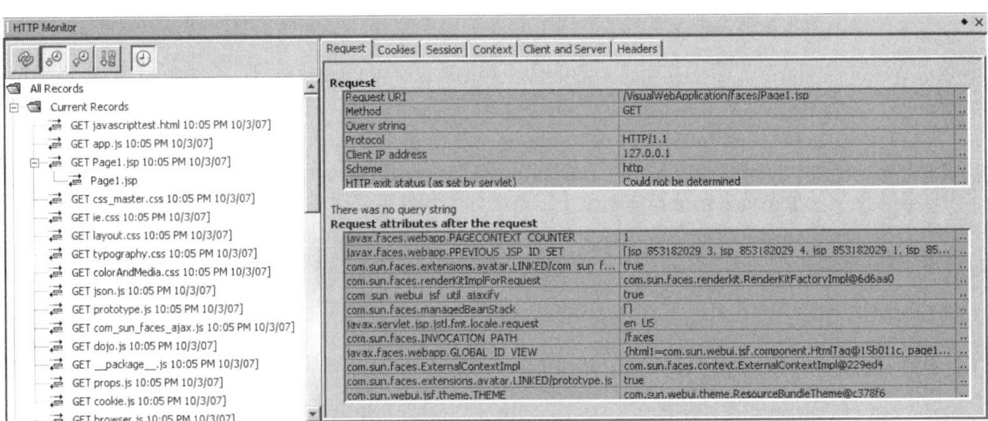

Figure 13-14. *Sample output in the HTTP Monitor*

Viewing Record Information

In the example in Figure 13-14, the HTTP Monitor displays several records under the Current Records node on the left side of the window. The current records are HTTP requests that have been made in the application you have deployed to the server. You can click any record to view the data for it.

Once you select a record, the fields and values for that specific record will display in several tabs on the right side of the HTTP Monitor window:

Request: Displays request information, such as the URI, method, protocol, and client IP address. Also shows an individual listing of parameters and values from the query string. Additionally, it displays request attributes that exist after the request.

Cookies: Displays the incoming and outgoing cookies.

Session: Displays general information about the session, such as the session ID, the time it was created, and the time it was last accessed. This tab also displays the session attributes that existed before the request and the attributes that exist after the request.

Context: Displays general servlet context data as well as context attributes and initialization parameters.

Client and Server: Displays client information, such as the protocol, client IP address, character encoding, locale, software used, and accepted file formats. Also displays server information, such as the hostname, port, application server platform, and Java version.

Headers: Displays the typical HTTP headers, such as `user-agent`, `host`, `connection`, and `cookie`.

You can use the data displayed in the HTTP Monitor to perform a forensic analysis of all the request-related variables. If you examine the records displayed in Figure 13-14, you will see they are formatted as HTTP protocol, page name, and date/time. The records listed in the figure were all done via a `GET` request.

Manipulating Records

When you right-click a single request under the Current Records node, you will see several options on the context menu:

Delete: Permanently deletes the request record. There is no undo for this type of operation, so make sure you really want to delete the record.

Save: Moves the record under the Saved Records node. It will then be saved for further examination. Once you close the NetBeans IDE software, the items under the Current Records node will be lost. Only the records that have been saved will be accessible.

Replay: Directs NetBeans to perform the exact HTTP request again automatically. All request attributes, session variables, context parameters, and cookies are put in place to simulate the original request exactly. A web browser window will open, and the requested page will load. After the request is completed, a new record will appear at the end of the Current Records list. The fields and values that result from the request may or may not be identical to the original request. You may have changed application code before replaying the request, which may affect the values.

Edit and Replay: Allows you to select a request record, alter some of the fields and values, and replay the request in the web application. This is invaluable for testing things like query string parameters, cookies, and header variables. This is one of the particularly interesting features I use most often, as described next.

Editing and Replaying Records

When you select the Edit and Replay item from the record's context menu, the Edit and Replay window appears. Via the Add Parameter button, you can specify a name/value pair for a new query string parameter. You can also edit or delete any of the existing query string parameters. Figure 13-15 shows an example of three query string parameters displayed in the Edit and Replay window.

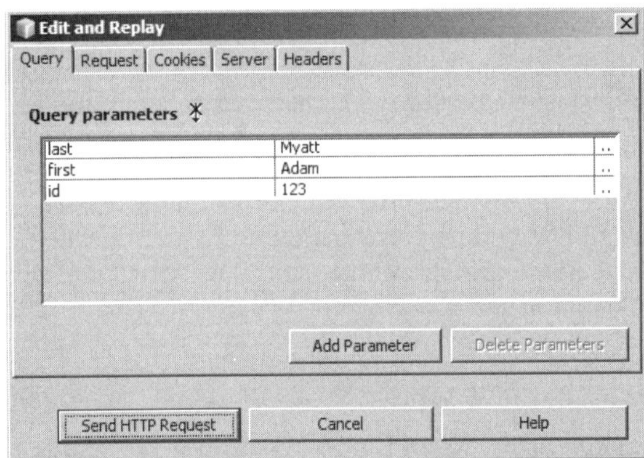

Figure 13-15. *Editing the query string in the HTTP Monitor*

Once you have added, modified, or deleted the request parameters, you can trigger the replay operation by clicking the Send HTTP Request button. If you change your mind and decide to not replay the request, click the Cancel button.

Here are several scenarios where the Edit and Replay feature may come in handy:

- You need to test a JSP page that displays different data based on the value of a query string parameter.
- You want to add a cookie value to test a "remember my username" feature on a login form.

- You want to change the server hostname to which the request will be sent during a test of a clustered server.
- You need to change the HTTP header `accept-language` to an alternate value to test the internationalization capabilities of your web application.
- You want to change the HTTP header `user-agent` to test the cross-platform, cross-browser capabilities of some JavaScript in a web application.

There are many reasons for using the HTTP Monitor. It is a simple yet powerful tool, which every web application programmer should get to know. I encourage you to try it out and experiment.

Working with Web Application Frameworks

Web application frameworks provide some great functionality. They can extend your web applications and provide many nonstandard features, widgets, and tools that can drastically improve both the backend architecture and the front GUI.

Many frameworks provide plugins that integrate the frameworks into NetBeans. You can generate content, use new file wizards, and view and manage framework widgets.

Leveraging Struts

Craig McClanahan originally kicked off the Apache Struts framework around mid-2000. The first major version was released in 2001, providing a Java Model-View-Controller (MVC) framework. Since then, Java developers have been using it to build web applications that cleanly separate business logic, control flow, and presentation.

This section assumes you have a working knowledge of Struts. If you are new to Struts, I strongly suggest learning about its capabilities. You can find information at the official web site (`http://struts.apache.org`) or refer to a book on the topic, such as *Beginning Apache Struts: From Novice to Professional* by Arnold Doray (Apress, 2006).

Adding Struts Support

In the opening section of the chapter "Create a Web Application Project," you saw how to add Struts support to a new application. In the New Project window, the Frameworks screen lets you select the Struts framework. You can also specify the Action URL Pattern, the Application Resource file, and whether you want to add the Struts TLDs, as shown in Figure 13-2.

You can also add Struts support to an existing web application. To add the Struts framework to an existing web application, follow these steps:

1. Right-click the project name in the Projects window and select Properties.
2. Click Frameworks in the Categories section, and then click the Add button on the right side of the window.
3. Select Struts in the list of options and click the OK button.
4. Customize the text in the "Action URL Pattern" field if necessary.

5. Customize the package hierarchy text in the "Application Resource" field.

6. Optionally, select the Add Struts TLDs check box.

7. Click the OK button.

Once Struts support has been added to the project, you will notice additional files under the various nodes in the Projects window. A welcomeStruts.jsp file is listed under the Web Pages node. The default index.jsp page will also be modified to include a link to the new welcomeStruts.jsp page using the Struts action URL pattern Welcome.do, which maps to welcomeStruts.jsp.

You will also see a file named struts-config.xml listed under the Configuration Files node. This file contains the basic Struts configuration information, the action mappings, plugin definitions, and so on. The web.xml file has also been modified to include references to the necessary Struts servlets. Some additional XML configuration files may appear in the WEB-INF directory that do not appear under the Configuration Files node.

The Struts resource file ApplicationResource.properties will appear in a package hierarchy under the Source Packages node. This file contains name/value pairs used throughout the application code and the Struts superclasses.

The Struts JAR file and supporting JAR files will be listed in the Libraries node.

If you chose to add Struts TLD files when you added the Struts framework support to the project, a few changes are made to the project. The files struts-logic.tld, struts-bean.tld, struts-html.tld, struts-nested.tld, and struts-tiles.tld are added to the WEB-INF directory under the Web Pages node. These files contain basic configuration information for the various Struts constructs. The web.xml file is also modified to include the correct references to the local TLD files. You should see the following added to the web.xml file:

```
<jsp-config>
    <taglib>
        <taglib-uri>/WEB-INF/struts-bean.tld</taglib-uri>
        <taglib-location>/WEB-INF/struts-bean.tld</taglib-location>
    </taglib>
    <taglib>
        <taglib-uri>/WEB-INF/struts-html.tld</taglib-uri>
        <taglib-location>/WEB-INF/struts-html.tld</taglib-location>
    </taglib>
    <taglib>
        <taglib-uri>/WEB-INF/struts-logic.tld</taglib-uri>
        <taglib-location>/WEB-INF/struts-logic.tld</taglib-location>
    </taglib>
    <taglib>
        <taglib-uri>/WEB-INF/struts-nested.tld</taglib-uri>
        <taglib-location>/WEB-INF/struts-nested.tld</taglib-location>
    </taglib>
    <taglib>
        <taglib-uri>/WEB-INF/struts-tiles.tld</taglib-uri>
        <taglib-location>/WEB-INF/struts-tiles.tld</taglib-location>
    </taglib>
</jsp-config>
```

Note One of the disadvantages of the NetBeans Struts support is that you cannot change the overall settings after initial setup. When you add Struts support to a project, you can set the various parameters. Once you have clicked OK, you are locked into the settings you have chosen. If you go back to the Frameworks node in the Project properties, you will see the fields grayed out. If you need to make any changes to those parameters, you must make them directly in the configuration files. Perhaps this feature will be improved in a future version.

Adding Forms

As you build a Struts-based web application, you may need to create your own `ActionForm` classes. In Struts, when you need to validate and store the input data from users, you create a subclass of `org.apache.struts.action.ActionForm`. These classes are used to transfer data between JSP pages and other Struts classes, such as `Actions`.

To create a new Struts `ActionForm` class, follow these steps:

1. Right-click the project name in the Projects window, select New, and choose File/Folder.
2. Select the Struts category from the list on the left and choose the Struts ActionForm Bean from the File Types list on the right. Click the Next button to move to the next step of the wizard, as shown in Figure 13-16.

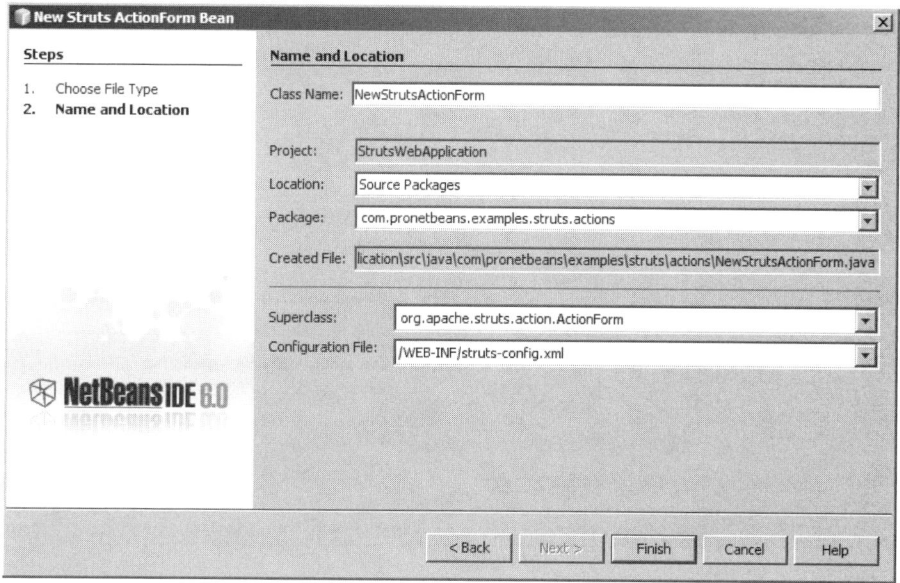

Figure 13-16. *Customizing ActionForm Bean fields*

3. Most of the `ActionForm` Bean fields are already filled out for you. The "Project," "Location," "Superclass," and "Configuration File" fields are preset to the suggested values. All you need to specify is the "Class Name" and the "Location" values. Then click the Finish button.

Tip When naming Struts classes, I usually end the names of `ActionForm` Beans with the word `Form` and end Struts actions with the word `Action`. It also helps to separate them into distinct packages, such as `com.mydomain.projectname.forms` and `com.mydomain.projectname.actions`.

Once the file has been created, it should open in the Source Editor window. You will notice that the `ActionForm` class has several default properties and basic content in the standard `validate` method.

Adding Actions

Actions are Struts' way of handling the Request and Response objects in the web application server container. You can use Struts actions to read information to the request, respond back to the calling client, and dispatch work to other classes.

To create a new Struts `Action` class, follow these steps:

1. Right-click the project name in the Projects window, select New, and choose File/Folder.
2. Select the Struts category from the list on the left and Struts Action from the File Types list on the right. Click the Next button to move to the next step of the wizard, as shown in Figure 13-17.

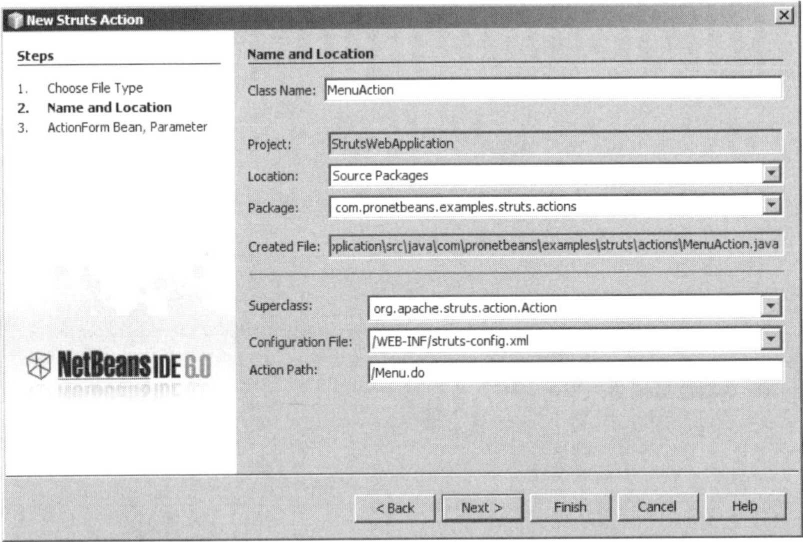

Figure 13-17. *Adding a new Struts action*

3. In the example in Figure 13-17, the "Class Name" has been set to `MenuAction`. The "Superclass" field is set to `org.apache.struts.action.Action`. The "Configuration File" field references the `struts-config.xml` file that was generated when you added Struts support to the project. When the `Action` class is created, its definition and action mapping will be listed in the `struts-config.xml` file. Once the properties are set, click the Next button.

4. You can choose to associate an `ActionForm` Bean with the Struts action you are about to create. If you select the Use ActionForm Bean check box, the remaining properties will be enabled, as shown in Figure 13-18.

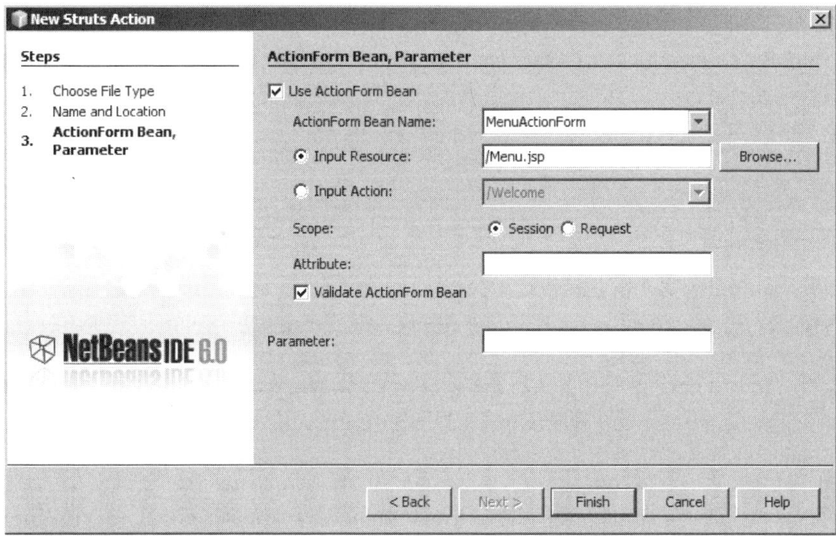

Figure 13-18. *Associating an ActionForm Bean with a Struts action*

5. Select an `ActionForm` Bean to associate with the Struts action. The "ActionForm Bean Name" field is a drop-down list of existing `ActionForm` Beans in the project. You must select an existing `ActionForm` Bean; otherwise, you cannot proceed.

6. The last field you need to set is the "Input Resource" text box. This is the view associated with the `ActionForm` Bean. You can use the Browse button next to the field to navigate the list of files under the Web Pages node in the Projects window and select the one you wish to use. Once you are finished, click the Finish button.

The new action will be generated and opened in the Source Editor window. The action mapping will also be added to the `struts-config.xml` file:

```
<action-mappings>
    <action input="/menu.jsp" name="MenuActionForm"
             path="/menu.do" scope="session"
             type="com.pronetbeans.struts.forms.MenuAction"/>
    <action path="/Welcome" forward="/welcomeStruts.jsp"/>
</action-mappings>
```

You will see that the path for the `welcomeStruts.jsp` file is `/Welcome` instead of `/Welcome.do`. This is due to the `forward` attribute, which specifies that requests for the path `/Welcome` should be forwarded immediately to the `welcomeStruts.jsp` file instead of to a Struts action.

Tip One problem with using Struts `Action` classes is with testing. In Chapter 9, you will learn about using JUnit in NetBeans to create tests for your code. The problem with trying to use JUnit to test Struts actions is that you need to be able to simulate the internal state of the Struts application. This is extremely difficult to do. Instead, you can use an open source project available from `SourceForge.net` called StrutsTestCase. This tool effectively extends JUnit and allows you to test Struts `Action` classes. For more detailed information on the project, visit the web site at `http://strutstestcase.sourceforge.net/`.

Configuring Struts

As previously mentioned, the `struts-config.xml` file is where many of the overall configuration settings for Struts are defined. It is also where navigation rules such as forwards and action mappings are defined.

The file allows a variety of tags, but the sections you will use most often are `form-beans`, `global-exceptions`, `global-forwards`, and `action-mappings`. If you read the previous sections on `Action` and `ActionForm` classes, the `form-beans` and `action-mappings` sections should look familiar. The `global-exceptions` section allows you to map an error response to a specific action. The `global-forwards` section allows you to map a URL pattern to an action. This is handy if you want to map a URL like `www.mydomain.com/tv` to a longer or more complicated action-mapping name.

NetBeans does not provide the same sort of interface for the `struts-config.xml` file as it does for the `web.xml` file (at least not yet). However, it does provide a few wizards, which are available from the context menu. With the `struts-config.xml` file open in the Source Editor, right-click anywhere in the file. You should see a Struts option on the context menu.

The Struts menu will contain options such as Add Action, Add Forward, and Add Exception. These wizards allow you to define new actions, forwards, and so on for existing Struts components without creating new classes. For example, the Add Action menu item gives access to a wizard that allows you to specify a new action mapping, as shown in Figure 13-19. In this dialog box, set the "Action Class" and "Action Path" values. You can then customize the other fields in the same manner as discussed previously. Then click the Add button. You should see the new action defined in the `struts-config.xml` file.

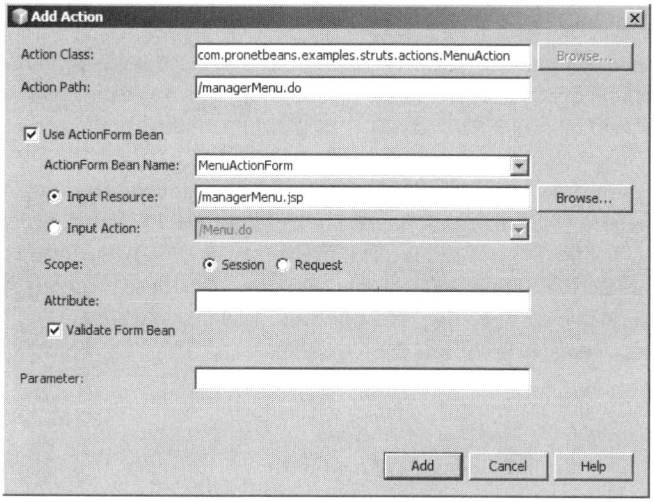

Figure 13-19. *The Add Action dialog box*

Leveraging Struts 2

The Struts framework currently supports two major versions: Struts 1.X and Struts 2.X. Struts 2 has been completely reworked, providing new features, easier configuration, and better support for more modern technologies.

Struts 2 provides a number of new and improved features, such as

Ajax support via special Struts-type tags

Usage of POJOs instead of ActionForms to capture form input

Better Spring integration

Enhanced form tags

Easier plugin installation

Struts 2 has been out for a while. However, at the time of this writing the Struts 2 plugin for NetBeans was still under development. You can go to the project web site at `https://nbstruts2support.dev.java.net/`. There were no binary releases when I last visited. I had to use the CVS client in NetBeans to download and build the source code from the project site. It should build fine and prompt you to open as a NetBeans project.

Currently, when I use the plugin there is basic support in the New Project window for adding the Struts 2 framework to the project. The plugin provides only a few other Struts-related integrations with NetBeans, but it is still early in the project.

If you use Struts 2, I strongly suggest you keep an eye on this project as it develops.

Leveraging Visual JavaServer Faces

The Visual JavaServer Faces support was previously known as the Visual Web Pack. It was ported over from Sun's Studio Creator Java IDE. Starting with NetBeans 6, there is no more Visual Web Pack. The Visual JSF capability has been integrated into the IDE (depending on the bundle you choose to download).

NetBeans Visual JSF gives you powerful features for working with JSF, Ajax, and data binding. It includes support for an impressive array of technology standards, including JSF 1.2, Struts, EJB 3.0, Java Servlets 2.5, JSP Standard Tag Libraries, Java API for XML Web Services (JAX-WS) 2.0, and a variety of XML- and web service–related APIs. Bundled with the NetBeans IDE, these technologies greatly enhance your ability to develop cutting-edge Java applications effectively. We next discuss how to configure and take advantage of the Visual JSF capabilities.

Getting Started

One of the biggest gaps in functionality of earlier versions of NetBeans was its lack of a good WYSIWYG web design tool. Java Studio Creator contained a pretty reasonable tool for performing visual JSF development, and many developers, including myself, secretly wished for it to become part of NetBeans.

At the JavaOne 2006 conference, I visited many of the Sun booths in the pavilion area. One of the NetBeans development team members was present and mentioned that the different Sun IDE products were being modularized for inclusion in other tools. He also made the comment that a visual web design tool was coming soon for the next major release of NetBeans, version 5.5. Suffice it to say, I was delighted at this news.

The Visual Web Pack was delivered with NetBeans 5.5 at the end of October 2006 as a technology preview. It was later released as a production-ready version in December 2006. Based on the JSF Visual Designer from Studio Creator, the VWP has been updated and made available as an add-on pack for NetBeans 5.5. For NetBeans 6, the concept of the Visual Web Pack has been done away with. The Visual JSF support is better integrated with the IDE and web applications.

The Visual JSF module provides a variety of time-saving and productivity-improving features that make working with JSF easy and fun. For example, you can drag-and-drop JSF components from a palette onto a JSP page. It also offers the usual types of components—buttons, form elements, text fields, and so on—but it also provides some nonstandard components, such as Trees, Tab sets, Remove lists, Breadcrumbs, and more. All of these components can be configured visually in the Visual Designer window or textually in the Properties window. They can also be bound to data without having to write a single line of code.

In the past, tools like Macromedia UltraDeveloper provided similar capabilities. However, as you used the automated capabilities, they generated multiple lines of obtuse code that was difficult to understand, hard to maintain, and not always the optimal method for obtaining the desired functionality. The automatic code generated by the Visual JSF module is quite different. It actually looks like Java code a programmer would write. This makes software written in NetBeans easier to work with and more maintainable.

The Visual JSF module also comes with the Visual Database Query Editor. This tool is very similar to Microsoft SQL Server's Enterprise Manager tool for working with SQL.

All these tools are brought together in NetBeans. When combined with the overall ease of use that NetBeans provides, you have an extremely powerful software development platform.

Configuring Visual JSF Options

The NetBeans Visual JSF module allows you to configure several options that affect its operation. You can view and modify these properties by selecting Tools ➤ Options from the main menu.

In the Basic Options window that appears, select the Miscellaneous icon to display a row of tabs. Select the Visual Web tab to display the Visual JSF properties, as shown in Figure 13-20.

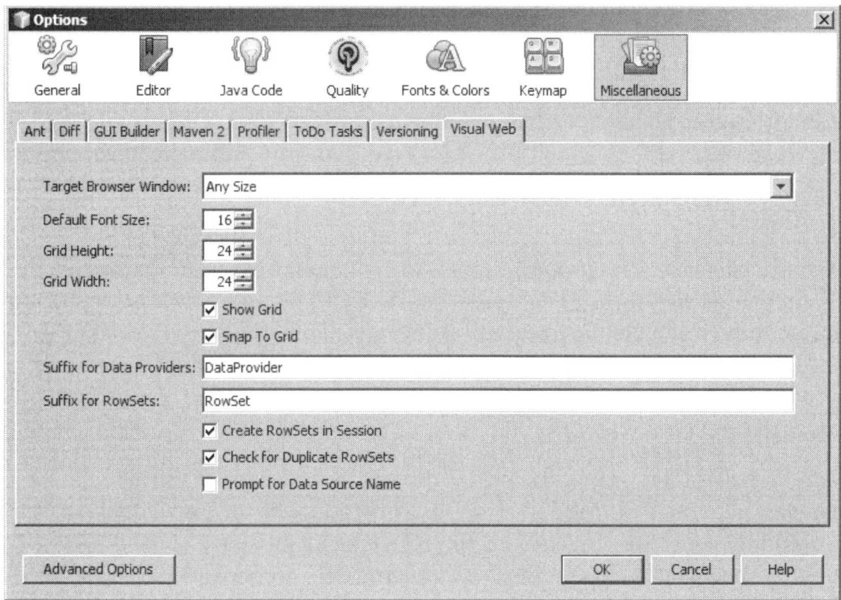

Figure 13-20. *The Visual Web properties in the Basic Options window*

You can set the following properties for it:

Target Browser Window: This property determines the specific screen resolution size for the web pages you develop. If you set it to the smallest size, 640×480 (600×300 page), and open a JSP page in the Visual Designer, the page visually denotes the shape and size. This allows you to add and arrange components according to the window size of your user community.

Default Font Size: This is the size of fonts for text components that are dropped onto the Visual Designer window for a JSP page. The font size displayed in the Visual Designer may differ from what is rendered in a web browser, due to default browser settings. You can set the default font size value for the Visual Designer to any standard font size.

Grid Height and Grid Width: These properties control the number of pixels between grid lines in the Visual Designer window. They define the height and width of each square that appears in the grid. This is a very important element to review, especially if the Snap to Grid property is enabled.

Snap to Grid: This property instructs the Visual Designer to snap components to the nearest grid line automatically. This affects almost all the work you do in the Visual Designer.

Show Grid: This property, enabled by default, determines if the grid lines are displayed in the Visual Designer window.

The remaining fields on the Visual Web tab deal with data sources and data binding. When you bind a database table to a component, several Java objects are created. (Data binding is covered later in this chapter in the "Data Binding" section.) These properties affect the creation of those Java objects as follows:

Create RowSets in Session: This property affects where a `CachedRowSet` object is created, regardless of where you drag-and-drop it. The property is enabled by default. If you unselect it, binding a database table to a component will result in the rowset's being created where you bind the data.

Check for Duplicate RowSets: This property affects the creation of rowsets as you drop them onto components. If you bind a database table to a component, NetBeans first attempts to determine if a matching rowset already exists. If the property is selected, which it is by default, NetBeans will prompt you either to reuse the existing rowset or to create a new one. If the property is unselected, NetBeans will automatically generate a new rowset.

Suffix for Data Providers: This property specifies the text that is added to the name of the data provider class generated during a data-binding operation. If you drop a database table onto a component, a data provider class is created using the name of the database table combined with the value of the Suffix for Data Providers property. For example, if you created a data binding for a table named `customers`, the data provider would be named `customersDataProvider`.

Suffix for RowSets: This property specifies the suffix for the rowset class that is created. For example, the rowset created for the `customers` table would be named `customersRowSet`.

Prompt for Data Source Name: If selected, you will be prompted to enter the name of the data source when you drag-and-drop the data source into a Visual Web page.

After you have set the Visual Web properties, click the OK button in the Basic Options window. You have now configured the Visual Web module and are ready to create your first project.

Creating a Visual Web Application

After you've configured the Visual Web module to suit your preferences, you can add the Visual JSF framework to a Web Application project type in NetBeans. Follow these steps to start a new project:

1. Select File ➤ New Project from the main menu.
2. In the New Project window, select Web from the Categories section on the left, select Web Application from the list of projects on the right, and then click the Next button.
3. Fill out the "Project Name" and "Project Location" fields.

4. Specify a Java package in the "Default Java Package" field.
5. Make sure you select either Tomcat 6 or GlassFish in the "Server" drop-down list.
6. Make sure that the "Java EE Version" field is set to Java EE 5.
7. Click the Next button to proceed to the Frameworks screen.
8. Select Visual Web JavaServer Faces from the list of frameworks. A list of JSF-specific properties will be displayed, as shown in Figure 13-21.

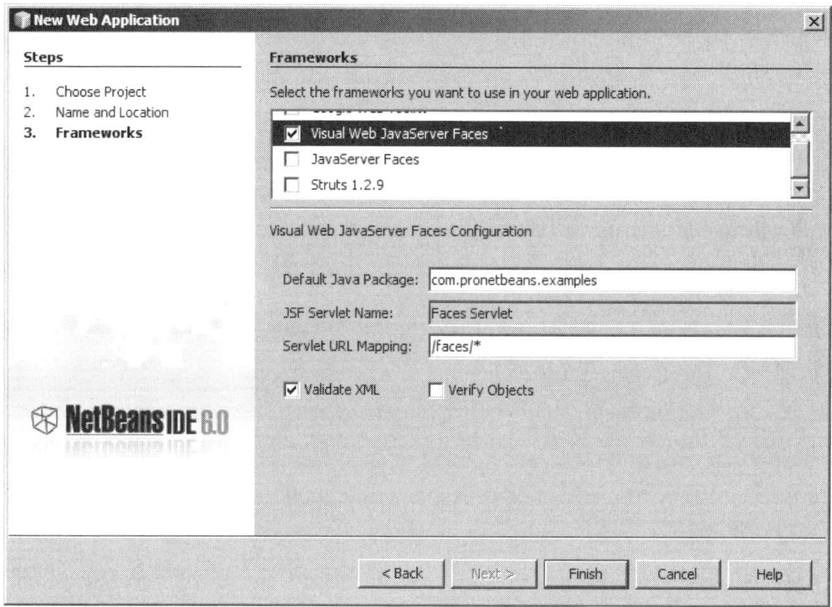

Figure 13-21. *The properties for the Visual Web JavaServer Faces framework*

9. Fill out the "Default Java Package" field with your application's correct package hierarchy.
10. Enter the desired "Servlet URL Mapping." The default is `/faces/*`. Then click the Finish button.

As you can see, adding Visual Web capabilities to a Web Application project is very simple. Your new project will be listed in the Projects window. Let's review the project structure in the Projects window.

Navigating the Visual Web Application Project Structure

A Web Application project has a standard structure. But when you add Visual Web JSF support, it modifies the list of nodes displayed in the Projects window. The Web Application project is still structured as a set of parent–child nodes, but there are some additions to the standard list. It better organizes the different components that make up a Visual Web Application project into easy-to-understand sections.

Let's take a look at what each of these nodes contains.

Web Pages

The Web Pages node is where the web-related content is stored. You can add JSP, HTML, CSS, images, and so on to this node.

One difference is that for a Visual Web–enabled project you can right-click any JSP file under the Web Pages node and select Set As Start Page. This option specifies that the file you clicked will be the default page displayed when the web application runs. The start page in the Web Pages node is denoted by a small green triangle next to the filename.

You can add new file types to this section by right-clicking the Web Pages node and selecting New ➤ Other. In the New File wizard, select JavaServer Faces from the Categories section in the left pane. The list of available file types will then appear in the right pane of the window. For a Visual Web Application project, the following file types are available:

Visual Web JSF Page: A JSP page with Visual JSF enabled. You can drag-and-drop components from the Palette and edit in WYSIWYG mode.

Visual Web JSF Page Fragment: A fragment of a JSP page with Visual JSF enabled. You can drag-and-drop components from the Palette and edit in WYSIWYG mode. This type of file is frequently used for common content that is dynamically included in other JSP pages.

JSF Managed Bean: Represents a managed bean class.

Visual Web JSF Request Bean: Represents a managed bean class that is stored in the request scope.

Visual Web JSF Session Bean: Represents a managed bean class that is stored in the session scope.

Visual Web JSF Application Bean: Represents a managed bean class that is stored in the application scope.

After you click the Finish button to complete the wizard, the new file will be added under the Web Pages node and will open in the Source Editor.

You should be aware of the differences between a Visual Web JSF Page and a standard JSP file. The Visual Web JSF Page is actually a standard JSP file with "special" features enabled. It is marked with a special icon and file type so that NetBeans knows to open it in the Visual Designer. The JSP file type is intended for use with standard HTML and JSP content. Even if you copied the JSP source content from a Visual Web JSF Page file into a JSP file, the Visual Web module will still treat the JSP file as a standard JSP file.

The Visual Web JSF Page Fragment file type is the same as the Visual Web JSF Page file type. However, you can include the Visual Web JSF Page Fragment file type inside a Visual Web JSF Page file type. In JSP code, you can use a special `include` directive to include the content of one JSP file inside another JSP. Many programmers use this approach when designing sites. If a site has a common page header, footer, or navigation menu, then each section can be contained in a JSP page and included into any page that needs to display that content. This way, the code for those sections is located in one place, making maintenance significantly easier. Visual Web JSF Page and Visual Web JSF Page Fragment file types are no different. They allow you to encapsulate commonly used sections into reusable pieces.

Load Generator Scripts

This node will appear for your project only if the JMeter Load Testing module has been installed in NetBeans. If it has not been installed, the node will not appear. It appears by default for most projects. You can use it to add JMeter scripts to test your project.

Configuration Files

The Configuration Files node does not represent an actual folder in the project structure. The items that appear under this node are categorized as items to which you would normally need access when making configuration changes to the application. It also contains the deployment descriptor for the web application.

The Configuration Files node contains the `web.xml`, `faces-config.xml`, and other project configuration files. These are the same files that appear under the `WEB-INF` directory in the Web Pages node.

■ **Note** The files under the Configuration Files node are not copies of the files under other nodes. They simply represent an alternative method for viewing and accessing them. If you find it confusing, you don't even need to use the Configuration Files node.

Server Resources

The Server Resources node is where various types of resources are located. If you define a Java Database Connectivity (JDBC) resource, JDBC connection pool, Java Message Service (JMS) resource, persistence resource, JavaMail resource, and so on, they will be listed under this node. This is handy, since it gives you quick access to related resources.

Any items under the Server Resources node will appear under the `Setup` directory in the Files window.

Source Packages and Test Packages

The Source Packages node is where you define the Java source code to be used in your application. Here, you can add and maintain the package statements you would normally use, such as `com.mycompany.projectname`. Adding packages is extremely easy. Right-click the Source Packages node and select New ➤ Java Package. In the New Java Package window, you can specify the name of the new package, such as `com.yourcompany.product`. After you click the Finish button, the new package name is added under Source Packages in the Projects window.

The Test Packages node is nearly identical to the Source Packages node. However, the Test Packages node specifies the package structure for your application's test classes and JUnit tests. If you were to execute the project tests by selecting Run ➤ Test *MyProjectName*, the classes in the Test Packages node would be executed.

Libraries and Test Libraries

The Libraries node is for defining class libraries that your application will use. If you need to use nonstandard libraries or classes from an external project, you can define them here. To add a JAR file to the libraries for your project, right-click the Libraries node and select Add JAR/Folder.

Similar to the Libraries node, the Test Libraries node contains class files or JAR files that your project test classes need to reference. You can add files to your test libraries by right-clicking the Test Libraries node and selecting Add JAR/Folder. The JAR file for JUnit exists by default in the Test Libraries section.

Themes

The Themes node contains the themes you can use with your project. Themes are a collection of look-and-feel configurations that can be applied to a Visual Web–enabled application. They are made up of properties files, JavaScript files, CSS files, and images. Any component that appears in the Palette window under the Basic, Composite, and Layout sections uses themes.

In JSF 1.2 and Java EE 5 Visual Web Application projects, there is only one default theme: Web UI Default Theme. A small arrow next to the filename indicates that it has been applied to the project.

The Visual Web module allows you to add your own themes and to apply them to your project.

Component Libraries

The Component Libraries node is used to add new component libraries to the project. A component library, such as BluePrints AJAX Components, can be imported into NetBeans via the Component Library Manager.

You can access the manager by selecting Tools ➤ Component Libraries. Once you have imported component libraries using the manager, they will be available to be added to a specific project.

To add a new component library to the project, right-click the Component Libraries node and select Add Component Library. The list of eligible libraries will appear, and you can add them to the project.

Data Source References

The Data Source References node contains a list of data sources configured for the Visual Web–enabled application. If you bind a database table to a component, then you instruct NetBeans to reference the associated data source.

This node is handy because it displays all the database-related connections that are used by your Visual Web Application projects. You do not have to go searching through your project code and configuration to discern which data sources you are using.

If you open a project that has incorrect or missing data sources, you can use the Data Source References node to resolve or correct the missing data source. To do so, right-click the Data Source References node and select Resolve Data Source(s) from the context menu.

Working with Visual Web Application Projects

In the NetBeans IDE, you'll use a variety of windows while working on your Visual Web–enabled project. Each window has a specific purpose, some specifically for the Visual Web module in NetBeans. Several of the most commonly used windows are described in the following sections.

Visual Designer Window

The Visual Designer window is where you'll perform the majority of the work for your Visual Web Application projects. The Visual Designer is the WYSIWYG interface for working with JSF in NetBeans, as shown in Figure 13-22. The Visual Designer window contains a white design surface with a dotted grid. You can drag-and-drop components onto this surface and arrange them any way you desire.

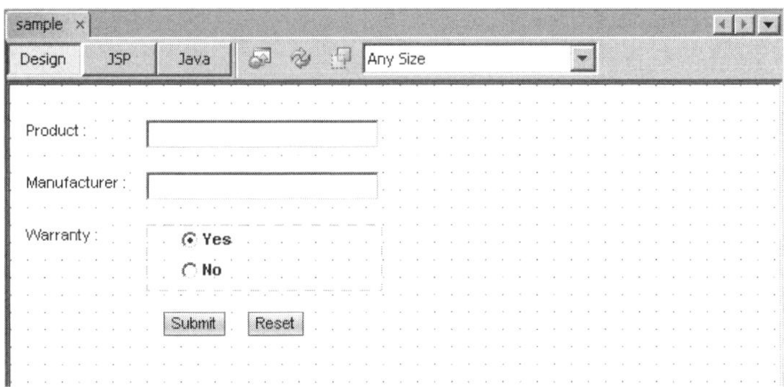

Figure 13-22. *The Visual Designer window*

At the top left of the Visual Designer window are three view buttons: Design, JSP, and Java. The Design view, which appears by default, shows the visual design surface. The JSP view shows the source code of the JSP page, and the Java view shows the Java source code for the backing bean that matches the JSP page.

Note Throughout the rest of this chapter, I refer to the Visual Web JSF Page file type as a *JSP page* or *JSP file*. The Visual Web JSF Page file type represents a JSF-aware JSP page that is specially recognized in the Visual Designer. Technically, you can add a non-JSF JSP page, but for the purposes of this chapter I use the term *JSP* to refer to a JSF-aware JSP file.

To the right of the view buttons are several icons that provide access to common functions, as described in Table 13-1.

Table 13-1. *Toolbar Icons in the Visual Designer*

Icon	Function	Description
	Preview in Browser	Allows you to generate an HTML view of the JSP page currently open in the Visual Designer window. It will then open in the default browser.
	Refresh	Refreshes the page and components in case they are not displaying correctly.
	Show Virtual Forms	Displays any virtual forms that have been configured in the JSP file and outlines the components that are associated with each virtual form.

The drop-down list on the right of the Visual Designer toolbar is the "Target Browser" property. It specifies a screen resolution size for the web page you are developing. If you set it to the smallest size, 640×480 (600×300 page), and open a JSP page in the Visual Designer, you will notice the page visually denotes the shape and size.

Navigator Window

The Navigator window displays a listing of the objects in a specific page. If you are viewing a Visual Web JSF Page in the Visual Designer window, the page name will appear as the top-level node in the Navigator window, as shown in Figure 13-23.

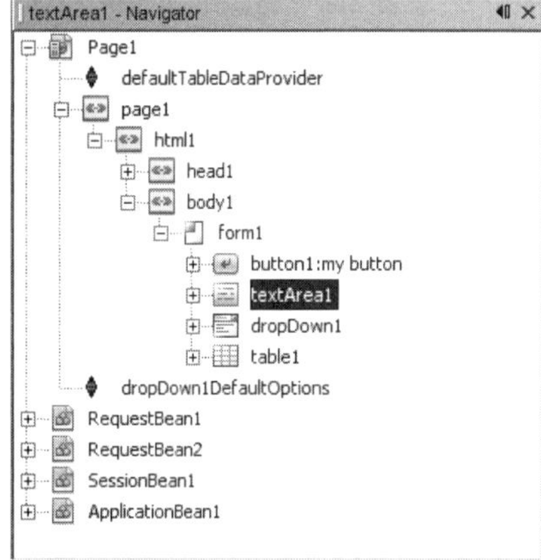

Figure 13-23. *The page node in the Navigator window*

You can expand the page node and view the components that are part of the page. In Figure 13-23, you can see that the body node contains several child nodes, including a form component with button, table, dropDown, and textArea components. This list of components represents the Visual Web JSF elements that appear for a Visual Web JSF Page in the Visual Designer. You can right-click any of the components listed in the Navigator window and manage them via the various context menu options.

The Navigator window also displays nodes for the request bean, session bean, and application bean. These nodes are identical to the RequestBean, SessionBean, and ApplicationBean nodes that appear in the Projects window for a Visual Web–enabled application. You can double-click each of the nodes in the Navigator window to open the corresponding source code in the Source Editor window.

If the Navigator window is not displayed in the NetBeans IDE, you can open it by selecting Window ➤ Navigating ➤ Navigator or by using the shortcut Ctrl+7.

Palette Window

The Palette window displays components specific to the file opened in the IDE. If you open a JSP file, the Palette window will display the JSF components you will use in the Visual Designer. You can click a component in the Palette window and drag-and-drop it into the JSP file open in the Visual Designer. The components available differ slightly, based on the Java EE version you configured for the project. Several of the components are discussed further in the "Working with JSF Components" section later in this chapter.

If the Palette window is not displayed, you can open it by selecting Window ➤ Palette.

Properties Window

The Properties window shows context-sensitive properties and values. As you select various elements in the NetBeans IDE, the associated properties are displayed in the Properties window. If you select an element or node in the Projects window, Navigator window, or Visual Designer window, its properties are listed in the Properties window.

If the Properties window is not visible in the IDE, you can open it by selecting Window ➤ Properties or by using the keyboard shortcut Ctrl+Shift+7.

Using the Page Navigation Tool

The Page Navigation tool is one of those technologies that really surprise you with how well they work. When I first started working with Visual Web JSF technology and read about the Page Navigation tool, I was excited but skeptical. It seemed too good to be true. After minutes of playing around and testing it, I realized it not only worked, but worked well.

Defining Navigation Rules

In NetBeans 5.5, the navigation rules defined in the `faces-config.xml` file were displayed in the Page Navigation window. It allowed a visual method for editing the navigation links between web pages. In NetBeans 6, the window has been reworked to be a GUI that is displayed only when you open the `faces-config.xml` file.

Here is an example of a `faces-config.xml` file:

```
<?xml version="1.0" encoding="UTF-8"?>
<faces-config version="1.2" xmlns="http://java.sun.com/xml/ns/javaee" ➥
              xmlns:xsi="http://www.w3.org/2001/XMLSchema-instance" ➥
              xsi:schemaLocation="http://java.sun.com/xml/ns/javaee ➥
              http://java.sun.com/xml/ns/javaee/web-facesconfig_1_2.xsd">

    <navigation-rule>
        <from-view-id>/addUsers.jsp</from-view-id>
        <navigation-case>
            <from-outcome>success</from-outcome>
            <to-view-id>/results.jsp</to-view-id>
        </navigation-case>
    </navigation-rule>
</faces-config>
```

The `faces-config.xml` file contains navigation rules that define the starting view, specified by the `from-view-id` tag. Each navigation result can also contain one or more cases that determine the destination view based on an outcome. In the preceding example, if the `addUsers.jsp` view returns an outcome of `success`, then the JSF controller routes page flow to the `results.jsp` view.

If you are confused by the format of the tags in the faces-config.xml file or simply don't like to work with it, you can use a GUI for editing the file.

Starting with NetBeans 6, when you open the faces-config.xml file it opens in GUI editing mode by default. The PageFlow tab is selected, which displays each Visual Web JSF Page and the associated links between them.

Using the faces-config.xml Editor

To open the faces-config.xml editor, double-click the faces-config.xml file in the Projects window under the Configuration Files node. The faces-config.xml editor window has a blank white background and dotted grid lines. If you have any JSP pages in your project, they are displayed in the Page Navigation window as rectangles that show an icon and the page name. You can use this window to create actual Visual Web JSF Pages and link them together.

Let's add several pages, configure some components, and create links to demonstrate use of the editor.

1. Within your Visual Web Application projects in the Projects window, double-click the faces-config.xml file under the Configuration Files node.

2. Right-click in a blank spot in the editor window and select New File. The standard New File wizard will appear.

3. Click through the New File wizard to generate a Visual Web JSF Page named Menu. You do not need to enter a file extension of .jsp, because it is assumed. When you complete the New File wizard, a new file icon labeled Menu.jsp is added to the faces-config.xml editor, as shown in Figure 13-24. The Menu.jsp file is also added in the Projects window under the Web Pages node. It is the same as if you had right-clicked the Web Pages node, selected New ➤ Other, and added the Menu.jsp file.

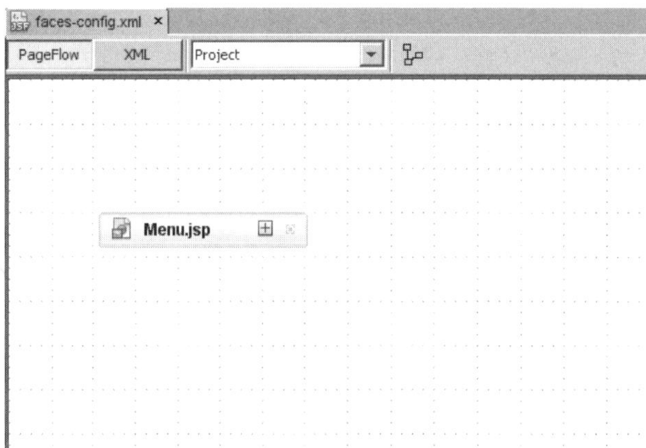

Figure 13-24. *The Menu.jsp file icon in the faces-config.xml editor*

4. Double-click the `Menu.jsp` icon in the `faces-config.xml` editor. The corresponding file will open in the Visual Designer window.

5. From the Palette window, drag-and-drop three Button components and one Hyperlink component onto the `Menu.jsp` file in the Visual Designer window.

6. Set the component properties as follows:

   - Select the first Button component. Set its `id` property to `btnProducts` and the `text` property to `Products`.
   - Select the second Button component. Set its `id` property to `btnServices` and the `text` property to `Services`.
   - Select the third Button component. Set its `id` property to `btnAboutUs` and the `text` property to `About Us`.
   - Select the Hyperlink component. Set its `id` property to `lnkSiteMap` and the `text` property to `Site Map`.

7. Save the changes by pressing Ctrl+S.

8. In the `faces-config.xml` editor, right-click in an empty space window and select New File.

9. Use the New File wizard to add four new Visual Web JSF Pages named `Products`, `Services`, `Aboutus`, and `Sitemap`.

10. Arrange the four pages you just created in a vertical column on the right side of the editor window. Put the `Menu` page on the left side of the window.

11. Click the plus sign next to the `Menu` page icon. It will expand and display a list of the Button and Hyperlink components contained within it. Next to each component name is a small icon denoting the type of link.

12. Click and hold the icon next to the `btnProducts` item. Then drag the cursor onto the `Products` page and release the mouse button. An orange line now connects the two pages.

13. You have just created a JSF navigation rule in the `faces-config.xml` file. Click the XML tab along the top of the window to toggle to the `faces-config.xml` file. You will see the new navigation rule:

```
<navigation-rule>
    <from-view-id>/Menu.jsp</from-view-id>
    <navigation-case>
        <from-outcome>case1</from-outcome>
        <to-view-id>/Products.jsp</to-view-id>
    </navigation-case>
</navigation-rule>
```

14. The rule basically states that once the `btnProducts` button is clicked, if the button's action method in the backing bean returns the value `case1`, then the page flow will be directed to the `Products.jsp` page. To verify this, click the `Menu.jsp` icon and double-click the `btnProducts` link. The backing bean for the `Menu.jsp` file will open in the Source Editor. Notice that the Java tab of the Visual Designer window is selected. The cursor will also be placed inside the `btnProducts_action` method so that you can alter the code if necessary. Notice that the return outcome is already set to `case1`, as shown in this code snippet:

```
public String btnProducts_action() {
    // TODO: Process the action. Return value is a navigation
    // case name where null will return to the same page.

    return "case1";
}
```

15. Use the faces-config.xml editor to link the other components in the `Menu.jsp` file to the other pages you've created:

    - Connect the `btnServices` Button component to the `Services.jsp` page.
    - Connect the `btnAboutUs` Button component to the `Aboutus.jsp` page.
    - Connect the `lnkSiteMap` Hyperlink component to the `Sitemap.jsp` page.

The resulting layout of the files displayed in the faces-config.xml editor should look something like Figure 13-25.

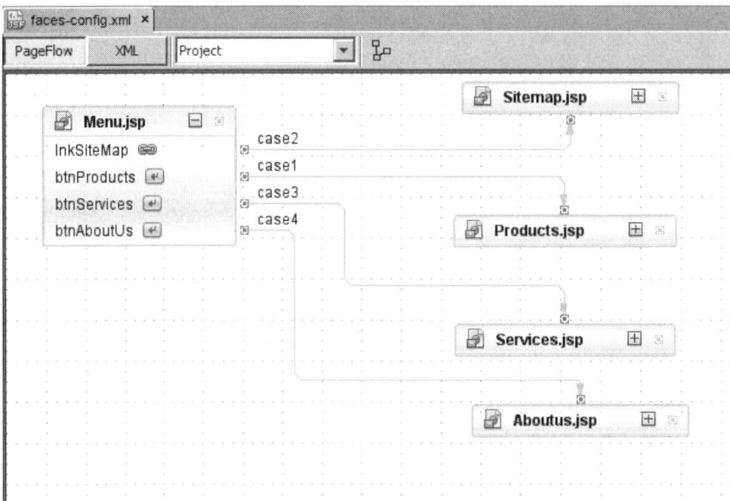

Figure 13-25. *The linked files in the faces-config.xml editor*

If your page links do not look like the ones in Figure 13-25, you can adjust them. You can click and drag the page icons up and down in the window so that they are ordered in any fashion you desire.

You can also move the connector lines that connect the pages. If you mouse over a connector line, you will see a small square anywhere the line changes directions. The little squares can be clicked and dragged around to change the layout of the link lines.

Working with JSF Components

The JSF components in NetBeans provide an amazing array of features and flexibility. They abstract away many of the mundane technical details of JSF so that you can focus on making your application work.

In simple terms, the JSF components are a combination of HTML tags and JSTL tags that have properties, trigger events, and the ability to bind to data. In many cases, you can add a component to a JSP page, configure its properties, and bind it to a database table, field, or Java object without having to write a single line of code.

Like other NetBeans components, the JSF components are available in the Palette window, primarily from three sections:

- The Basic section contains components for text, form elements, hyperlinks, images, and calendars. The components all share a similar look and feel due to the theme that has been applied to the project.
- The Layout section contains components such as forms, page separators, tabs, grid panels, and layout panels. These elements are typically used for page layout and grouping of items.
- The Composite section contains only a few components. These are combination components that provide nicely wrapped functionality representing commonly used widgets in a web application. Much of the programming for these widgets has already been done.

Setting Component Properties

After you've added a component to your page, you can click it and view its properties in the Properties window, where you can set the attributes for a component exactly as if you were writing code, only it's easier.

For example, Figure 13-26 shows a page with some components from the Basic section of the Palette window. If you click one of the Text Field components in the upper left of this page, you can edit its properties. Suppose that you set the `id` property to `txtName`, the `columns` property to `16`, the `text` property to `John`, and the `maxLength` field to `100`. You also enabled the `required` check box. You could then view the corresponding JSP code for the component by clicking the JSP tab in the Visual Designer window. It would look as follows:

```
<webuijsf:textField binding="#{formComponents.txtName}"
                    columns="16"
                    id="txtName"
                    maxLength="100"
                    required="true"
                    style="left: 72px; top: 24px; position: absolute"
                    text="John" />
```

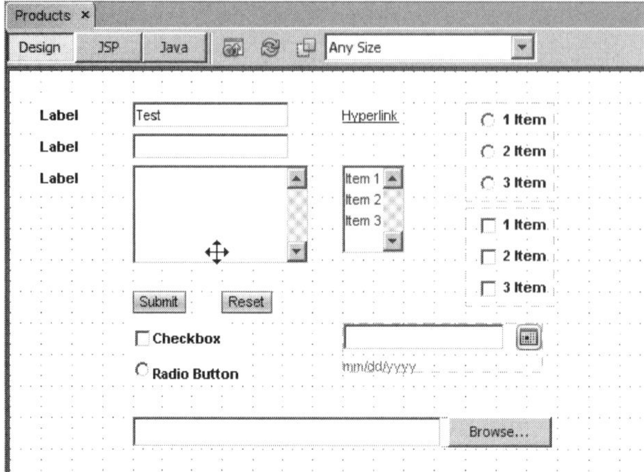

Figure 13-26. *Sample JSF components from the Basic section of the Palette window*

As you can see, the property settings in the Properties window are reflected in the code. Using the Properties window can often be faster than switching to the code view and trying to locate a specific line of code.

Setting Component Event Handlers

Most components have event handlers. There are client-side JavaScript behaviors that can be configured via the component properties in the Properties window. There are also server-side Java event handlers that are evoked when certain actions occur.

To set an event handler for a component, right-click it and select Edit Event Handler. This displays a submenu with a list of event handlers available for that specific type of component.

Let's return to the sample page in Figure 13-26. Suppose you want to set an event handler for when the value changes in the `txtName` Text Field component. Right-click that component and select Edit Event Handler ➤ processValueChange. The Java view of the Visual Designer window will open, displaying the source code for the JSP page's backing bean. The page should automatically scroll down to the `txtName_processValueChange` method. The method will be empty by default. You can use the `ValueChangeEvent` object passed in as a parameter to query the old and new values of the Text Field component whose value has changed. For example, you can retrieve the old and new values and output them to the standard output stream as in this code snippet:

```
public void txtName_processValueChange(ValueChangeEvent event) {

    Object objOld = event.getOldValue();
    Object objNew = event.getNewValue();

    if(objOld!=null) {
        System.out.println("Old=" + objOld.toString());
    }
    if(objNew!=null) {
        System.out.println("New=" + objNew.toString());
    }
}
```

If other components in the JSP page use event handlers, they will also be listed in the JSP page's backing bean source code. There is no guarantee that they will be placed sequentially in a file, so you might consider using the Navigator window (select Window ➤ Navigator or press Ctrl+7 to open this window) to view the list of methods in the file. Any event handlers will show up in the Navigator window, because they are implemented as Java methods.

Data Binding

Data binding is an important feature provided by the Visual Web module in NetBeans 6. It allows you to associate data with components automatically without having to write any code. You can bind a component to values in another component, a Java object, or a database table.

The really interesting aspect of data binding is that it can be performed via drag-and-drop in the NetBeans IDE. You can also change the data bindings at any time and use a powerful SQL editor to modify database-related bindings.

Binding to an Object

The NetBeans Visual Web module allows you to bind components to a Java object. You can create properties in the `RequestBean`, `SessionBean`, or `ApplicationBean` class and bind them to a component.

For example, suppose you wanted to display some application-scoped variables to the users of a web application. You can bind, or link, those application-scoped variables to specific components in a JSP file.

To see how this works, create a `HomeOffice` class with three encapsulated class members: `location`, `manager`, and `numEmployees`. Add the appropriate public getters and setters for each member variable. The code should look similar to the following:

```
public class HomeOffice {

    private String location;

    public String getLocation() {
        return this.location;
    }

    public void setLocation(String location) {
        this.location = location;
    }

    private String manager;

    public String getManager() {
        return this.manager;
    }

    public void setManager(String manager) {
        this.manager = manager;
    }
```

```
    private int numEmployees;

    public int getNumEmployees() {
        return this.numEmployees;
    }

    public void setNumEmployees(int numEmployees) {
        this.numEmployees = numEmployees;
    }

}
```

Next, create a member variable and associated getter and setter for the HomeOffice class in the ApplicationBean class for your Visual Web Application projects. The code added to the ApplicationBean class should look like this:

```
private HomeOffice homeOffice;

public HomeOffice getHomeOffice() {
    return this.homeOffice;
}

public void setHomeOffice(HomeOffice homeOffice) {
    this.homeOffice = homeOffice;
}
```

Finally, you can add several lines to the ApplicationBean.init method that will create an instance of the HomeOffice class, as follows:

```
private void _init() throws Exception {

    HomeOffice homeOff = new HomeOffice();
    homeOff.setLocation("Buffalo");
    homeOff.setManager("John Doe");
    homeOff.setNumEmployees(210);
    setHomeOffice(homeOff);
}
```

Then you will need to create a new JSP file in your Visual Web Application projects and add several components to it. Perform the following steps to create the JSP file for this example and bind some data:

1. Right-click the Web Pages node in the Projects window and select New ➤ Other.
2. Select the JavaServer Faces category and the Visual Web JSF Page file type, and then click the Next button.

3. Name the file and choose a folder location in the project. Then click the Finish button.

4. With the new file open in the Visual Designer window, add six Static Text components (by dragging them from the Palette window into the page's design area), as follows:

   - Set the first Static Text component's `id` property to `lblLocation` and the `text` property to `Office Location :`.
   - Place the second Static Text component beneath the first one. Set its `id` property to `lblManager` and the `text` property to `Manager :`.
   - Place the third Static Text component beneath the second one. Set its `id` property to `lblNumEmployees` and the `text` property to `# Employees :`.
   - Place the fourth Static Text component next to the `lblLocation` component. Set its `id` property to `txtLocation`.
   - Place the fifth Static Text component next to the `lblManager` component. Set its `id` property to `txtManager`.
   - Place the sixth Static Text component next to the `lblNumEmployees` component. Set its `id` property to `txtNumEmployees`.
   - Next, you need to bind the Static Text components `txtLocation`, `txtManager`, and `txtNumEmployees` to the corresponding data elements in the `HomeOffice` class in the `ApplicationBean`.

5. Right-click the `txtLocation` component in the Visual Designer window (or in the Outline window) and select Bind to Data.

6. The Bind to Data window will appear. If it is not already selected, click the Bind to an Object tab.

7. In the Bind to Data window, the `ApplicationBean1` node contains the `HomeOffice` class listing. Expand the `homeOffice` node to see the member variables that are part of the `HomeOffice` class.

8. To bind the `txtLocation` component to the corresponding application-level property, click the line `property: location String`, as shown in Figure 13-27. The Current Text property setting field at the top of the window should display `#{ApplicationBean1.homeOffice.location}`.

9. Click the OK button to apply the binding. You will see that the `txtLocation` component displays the value `abc`. This indicates that it has been bound to string data.

10. Repeat steps 5 through 9 to bind the `txtManager` and `txtNumEmployees` components to their corresponding `HomeOffice` properties.

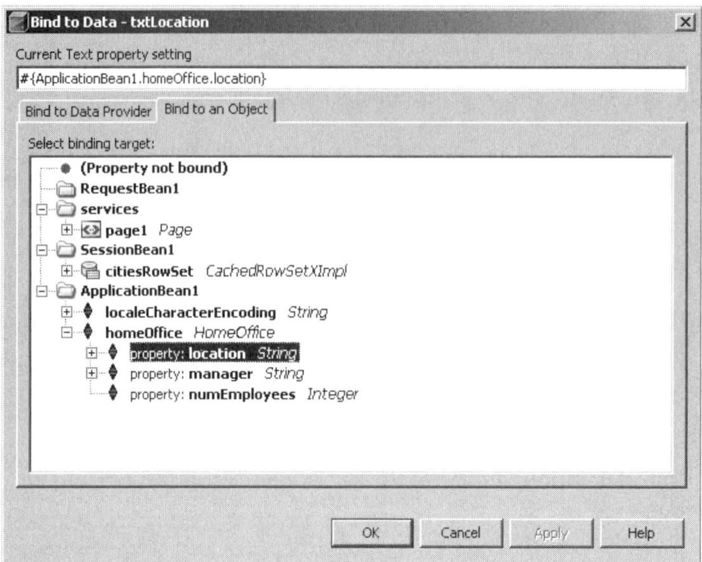

Figure 13-27. *The Bind to Data window*

You now have a JSP page that displays six Static Text components: three bound and three unbound, as shown in Figure 13-28.

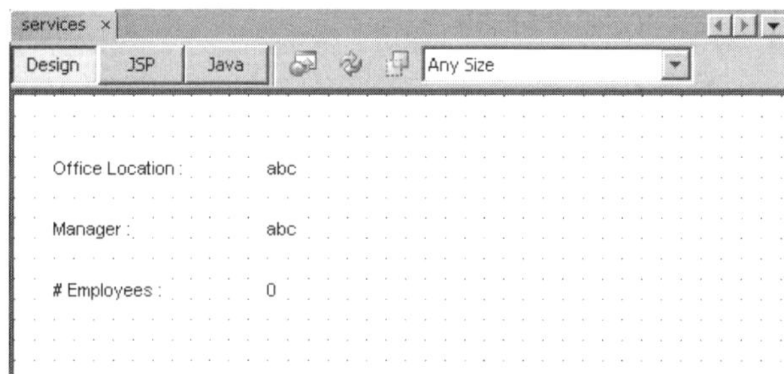

Figure 13-28. *The components after the data-binding operation*

If you run the application and navigate to the JSP page, you should see the following:

```
Office Location : Buffalo
Manager : John Doe
# Employees : 210
```

Binding to a Database Table

The NetBeans Visual Web module provides the ability to bind a database table to a JSF Table component. When you drag-and-drop the database table onto the component, NetBeans generates code in the page's backing bean and the JSP file.

To bind the data to the table, follow these steps:

1. Drag-and-drop a JSF Table component from the Palette window into a JSP page in the Visual Designer window. A table with three columns and several rows of filler data will be displayed, as shown in Figure 13-29. If you click the JSP tab in the Visual Designer window, you will see that the JSF tag `<webuijsf:table>` was added to the file. The `<webuijsf:table>` also contains the nested tags `<webuijsf:tableRowGroup>`, `<webuijsf:tableColumn>`, and `<webuijsf:staticText>`.

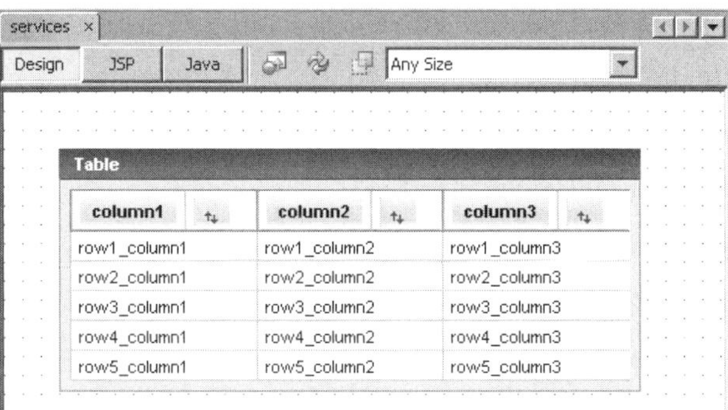

Figure 13-29. *A JSF Table component in the Visual Designer*

2. Now you need to connect to a database and bind data to the Table component. In the NetBeans Services window, expand the Database node to list the database connections you have defined. Expand the nodes in the Services window for the database connection you want to use until you locate a database table. For this example, I used an Oracle database table named `CUST`, which is defined as follows:

```
CREATE TABLE CUST
(
  LAST_NAME    VARCHAR2(50),
  FIRST_NAME   VARCHAR2(50),
  BUSINESS     VARCHAR2(200),
  JOBTITLE     VARCHAR2(100),
  ADDRESS1     VARCHAR2(100),
  ADDRESS2     VARCHAR2(100),
  CITY         VARCHAR2(100),
  STATE        VARCHAR2(20),
  ZIP          VARCHAR2(20),
  COUNTRY      VARCHAR2(100),
  CUST_ID      INTEGER
)
```

3. Click and drag the database table name in the Services window and drop it onto the JSF Table component. NetBeans will process for a moment, but it will eventually refresh the JSF Table component in the Visual Designer.

The table will be reformatted to display all the columns from the database table. The column names will appear as the column headers in the table. The column values are represented as the various data-binding placeholders, such as abc for character fields and 1 for numeric fields.

If you look in the Navigator window and expand the page node for the JSP file, you will see a node that defines an implementation of the CachedRowSetDataProvider class. The class name should start with the name of the database table you originally selected to bind and end with DataProvider.

The following code was also added to the JSP page's backing bean in the Managed Component Definition section near the top of the source file:

```
private CachedRowSetDataProvider custDataProvider = new ➥
CachedRowSetDataProvider();

public CachedRowSetDataProvider getCustDataProvider() {
    return custDataProvider;
}

public void setCustDataProvider(CachedRowSetDataProvider crsdp) {
    this.custDataProvider = crsdp;
}
```

The JSP page's backing bean must also specify the CachedRowSet that returns the data and add it to the CachedRowSetDataProvider class. The backing bean's init method contains the following line:

```
        custDataProvider.setCachedRowSet((javax.sql.rowset.CachedRowSet) ➥
getValue("#{SessionBean1.custRowSet}"));
```

As you can see in this code snippet, a CachedRowSet was retrieved from the SessionBean1 object and set in the custDataProvider class (the CachedRowSetDataProvider).

When you bind the database table to the JSF Table component, NetBeans generates an implementation of the CachedRowSet, which resides in SessionBean1. If you look in the Navigator window under the SessionBean1 node, you will see the listing for the CachedRowSet. Its name starts with the name of the database table you selected for binding and ends with RowSet. You should also be able to see a short description of the SQL query that the CachedRowSet represents. This is discussed in the "Working with the Visual Database Query Editor" section later in this chapter.

The SessionBean1 class defines the CachedRowSet as a member variable and creates the associated getter and setter methods. It also adds code to the init method that sets the CachedRowSet's data source name, table name, and SQL command. See the following code snippet:

```
private void _init() throws Exception {
    custRowSet.setDataSourceName("java:comp/env/jdbc/dataSource");
    custRowSet.setCommand("SELECT * FROM ITMSDB.CUST");
    custRowSet.setTableName("CUST");
}
```

```
private CachedRowSetXImpl custRowSet = new CachedRowSetXImpl();

public CachedRowSetXImpl getCustRowSet() {
    return custRowSet;
}

public void setCustRowSet(CachedRowSetXImpl crsxi) {
    this.custRowSet = crsxi;
}
```

The JSF Table component can then bind to the CachedRowSetDataProvider, which in turn retrieves the implementation of the CachedRowSet class (CachedRowSetXImpl) that retrieves the data from the database.

After you have added the appropriate objects and settings to the application code, you can customize the JSF Table component using the Table Layout window (Figure 13-30). Here, we'll look at the binding-related options.

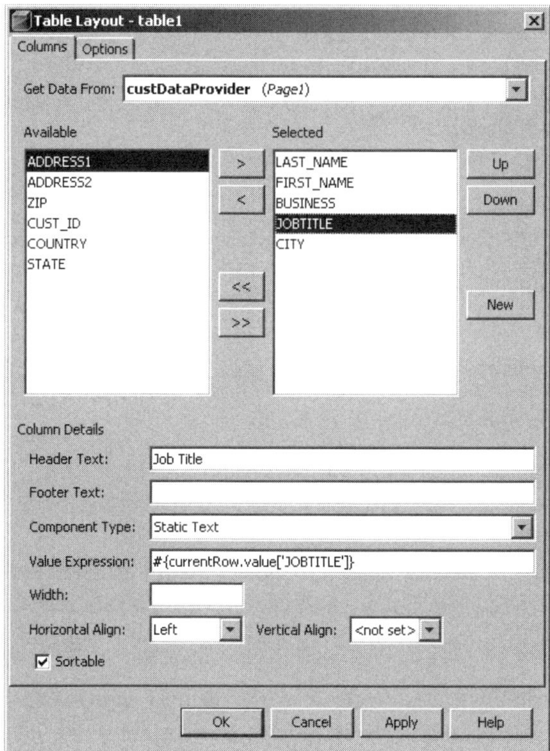

Figure 13-30. *Table Layout options for a Table component bound to a database table*

In the Columns tab of the Table Layout window, notice that the database table fields are listed in the Selected box, because all the fields were originally added during the automatic data-binding process. You can remove fields from the list (and the data binding) by selecting the field name in the Selected list and clicking the < button. The field you selected will be removed from the Selected list and appear in the Available list. When you click the OK button, the table will appear in the Visual Designer window without that column.

For example, to format the table that I bound to the `CUST` database table (shown in the previous section), I used the < button to remove all the fields from the Selected list, except for `LAST_NAME`, `FIRST_NAME`, `BUSINESS`, `JOBTITLE`, and `CITY`, as shown in Figure 13-30. Then I clicked each field in the Selected list and changed the "Header Text" field to an easier-to-read value: `Last Name`, `First Name`, `Job Title`, and so on.

Then I clicked the Options tab in the Table Layout window. In the "Title" field, I entered the text `List of Customers`. This title will display along the header of the table. I activated pagination by selecting the Enable Pagination check box, and then I set the "Page Size" field to `4`. (Normally, you would want between 20 and 50 records on a page, but that depends on the data, your application, and the software requirements.) Then I clicked the OK button, and the JSF Table component refreshed and appeared in its modified format.

If you want to view the JSP page in a browser and test it, you first need to set it as the start page so that it loads in the browser (assuming you haven't set up any page navigation). To do this, right-click the page in the Projects window and select Set As Start Page. A green arrow will appear next to the page name, denoting it as the start page.

Next, run the application by selecting Run ➤ Run Main Project (or pressing F6). After your application builds, the page will load in the browser. My sample table looks like Figure 13-31.

List of Customers				
Last Name	**First Name**	**Business**	**Job Title**	**City**
Doe	John	Microsoft	Programmer	Seattle
Smith	Bob	Sun Microsystems	Program Manager	San Francisco
Gonzalez	Pietro	Acme Widgets	Vice President	New York
Smith	Karen	New York Times	Senior Editor	New York
Philippe	Pierre	Acme Widgets	Software Architect	New York
Johnson	David	Acme Widgets	Technical Writer	New York
Lincoln	John	Microsoft	Financial Analyst	Seattle
Sully	Kathlene	Sun Microsystems	Vice President	San Francisco

Figure 13-31. *A data-bound JSF Table component displayed in a web browser*

Working with the Visual Database Query Editor

When you bind a JSF component to a database table, a `CachedRowSet` object maintains an SQL command that selects fields from a database table. You can use a SQL query-editing tool, called the Visual Database Query Editor, to manipulate the SQL query that was created automatically during the binding.

To open a query in the query editor, locate the `CachedRowSet` in the Navigator window. You can double-click the name or right-click and select Edit SQL Statement. The Visual Database Query Editor window opens and displays the SQL statement, as shown in Figure 13-32. If you have ever used the SQL tools in the Microsoft SQL Server Enterprise Manager, this tool should look familiar.

In the Visual Database Query Editor, you can select which columns you want to include in the query, set the sort order for each column, manually edit the SQL, and view the results of the query. This tool allows you to customize the SQL and the associated data completely in the `CachedRowSet` that is bound to a JSF component.

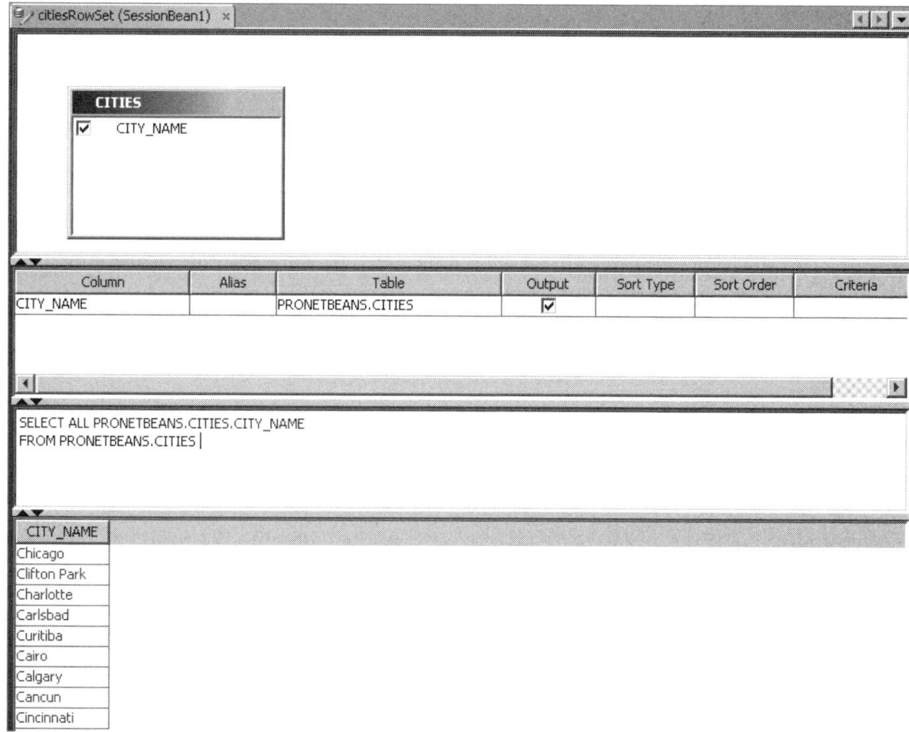

Figure 13-32. *The Visual Database Query Editor*

The editor window has four sections. The top section shows which tables are currently included in the query. You can right-click anywhere in the top section and select Add Table from the context menu. The Select Table(s) to Add dialog box lists the SQL tables available based on the defined database connection. You can select one or more tables and click the OK button. The tables will then appear in the top section of the query editor.

The second section allows you to perform several convenient actions:

- You can assign database table columns with aliases via the Alias column.
- You can also determine if columns should be included in the `SELECT` clause of the SQL statement by selecting or unselecting the check box in the Output column.
- In the Sort Type column, you can specify if the table field will be sorted in ascending or descending order.
- The Sort Order column allows you to specify in which order the table field will be sorted.
- The Criteria column allows you to specify a value (depending on the column's data type) to use in a SQL `WHERE` clause. For example, if you specified a value of `LIKE 'New%'` in the Criteria column for the `CITY` column, then the SQL would contain something similar to `WHERE CITY LIKE 'New%'`.

The third section contains the raw SQL text, which you can alter manually. If you modify any fields in the top two sections, you will see the changes to the SQL displayed here.

If you right-click in the window and select Run Query, any results that match the SQL query will be displayed in the bottom section.

Leveraging the jMaki Framework

jMaki is a JavaScript and Ajax framework that provides a variety of web-based widgets. It can be used directly in NetBeans via a wrapper plugin. The plugin can provide support to add jMaki to a web application, display the widgets in the Palette window, and allow you to drag-and-drop widgets into web pages.

Installing the jMaki Framework

The jMaki framework plugin is available from the jMaki project at `Java.net`. The project site makes available an update center module to download that allows you to download the actual plugin.

Go to the project site at `http://ajax.dev.java.net/`. In the Download section you can choose to download the NetBeans plugin or a smaller `.nbm` module that installs only the update center for the jMaki plugin.

If you download either plugin, save it to your local drive. In NetBeans, go to the Plugin Manager by selecting Tools ➤ Plugins. In the Plugin window click the Downloaded tab and locate the downloaded plugin by clicking the Add Plugins button. After locating the plugin, click the Install button and proceed through the remainder of the installation. If you selected to install the jMaki update center, you can then go to the Available Plugins tab and Reload Catalog to see the list of jMaki plugins. Select the jMaki plugins from the list and perform a normal installation. You may be prompted to restart NetBeans.

Adding jMaki Support to a Web Application

Once jMaki has been installed, you can add the framework to a project. During the New Project wizard, the Frameworks screen will display a list of frameworks you can add to your framework. The jMaki Ajax Framework can be selected from the list.

If you select the jMaki Ajax Framework, the bottom portion of the screen will display the jMaki Ajax Framework configuration. The CSS Layout section lets you choose a web page layout to apply to the initial JSP file in the project. If you scroll through the list, you will see a variety of layouts, such as left sidebar, right sidebar, and no layout. Select the Right Sidebar layout, as shown in Figure 13-33. Then click the Finish button to generate the project.

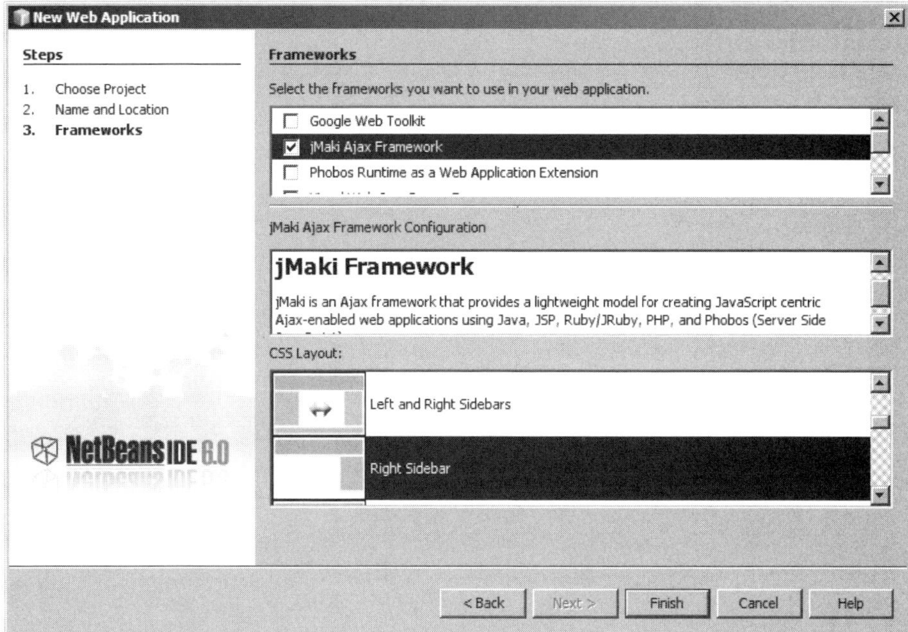

Figure 13-33. *Adding the jMaki framework to a project*

The project will be generated and displayed in the Projects window. The default web application page is named `index.jsp`. It contains the layout that was specified in the Frameworks screen of the New Project wizard. An additional file was also generated. The `jmaki-right-sidebar.css` file was created during project generation. It is based on the type of CSS layout that was specified in the New Project wizard. The `index.jsp` file contains a `<link>` tag that imports the styles from the `jmaki-right-sidebar.css` file. This allows the `index.jsp` to have the specified formatting that you chose.

If you run the project, you can view the initial page layout. Select Run ➤ Run Main Project from the main menu. The application server will start, the project will build, and a web browser will open displaying the `index.jsp`. You will see that it contains a top section, left content area, and right sidebar, as shown in Figure 13-34. It should match the CSS layout you chose in the New Project wizard.

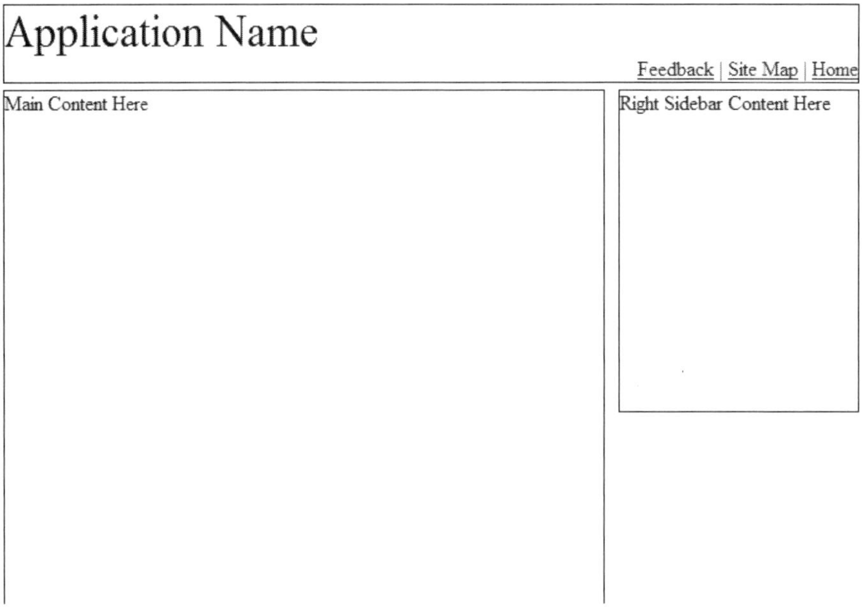

Figure 13-34. *The index.jsp page display for the right sidebar layout*

The page layout shown in Figure 13-34 is just one example that jMaki can provide. As you saw in the New Project wizard, you can create pages with different layouts. To add a new JSP page to the project with a different layout, do the following:

1. Right-click the Web Pages node in the Projects window and select New ➤ Other.
2. In the New File wizard, select the Web category from the left pane and Stylized JSP (jMaki) from the right pane. Then click the Next button.
3. Provide a value for the "JSP File Name" field. Use the Browse button next to the "Folder" field to choose a folder under the Web Pages node where the new page will be located.
4. Scroll through the list of CSS Layouts and select a value.
5. Click the Finish button to complete the New File wizard. The new JSP file will open in the Source Editor.

Working with jMaki Widgets

jMaki provides widgets in the form of JSP tag libraries that generate Ajax-enabled JavaScript and HTML components. jMaki itself is composed of several of these modules, but it also provides components from other popular JavaScript frameworks, such as Google, Dojo, Flickr, Scriptaculous, Spry, and Yahoo.

The available components are displayed in the Palette window, as shown in Figure 13-35. You can click and drag a component from the Palette into one of the Stylized JSP (jMaki) pages you created in the project.

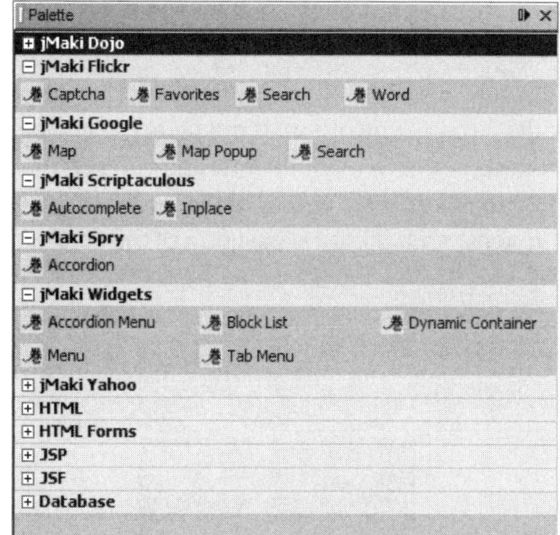

Figure 13-35. *The jMaki widgets in the Palette window*

You can use any of the widgets in the different jMaki categories in the Palette. One of my favorites is the Spry Accordion. If you click and drag it into a JSP page, the following code will be added:

```
<a:widget name="spry.accordion"
   value="{ items :
    [{ label :'Books', content : 'Book content'},
     { id : 'bar', label :'Magazines', include : 'test.jsp', lazyLoad : true},
     { label :'Newspaper', content : 'Newspaper content', selected: true}
     ]}"/>
```

This Spry Accordion code will generate a set of sliding layers. Each layer will have a visible area with text that identifies which layer it is. As each layer is clicked, it slides completely open, showing the entire layer's content. All other layers visible slide shut.

The foregoing Spry Accordion code uses an array to store the different layers. Each array element can have several attributes used to customize the layer. The first array element looks like this:

```
[{ label :'Books', content : 'Book content'},
```

The layer's label is identified with the `label` attribute. The `content` attribute can be a block of text that will appear in the layer.

Each layer can include an external page in case you want dynamic content or a lot of content to be displayed. The second array element shows you how to do so with the following code:

```
{ id : 'bar', label :'Magazines', include : 'test.jsp', lazyLoad : true},
```

The `id` attribute denotes the unique identifier used for the specific layer. The `include` attribute lets you specify a web page to include as the content of the layer. The `lazyLoad` attribute specifies the way to load the page.

The third and final element of the layer array has this code:

```
{ label :'Newspaper', content : 'Newspaper content', selected: true}
```

The only difference with this element is its usage of the `selected` attribute. If the `selected` attribute is set to `true`, then that layer is selected and displayed in the rendered content. If you run the page to which you added the widget, the generated content will look similar to Figure 13-36. In this example, I added the Spry Accordion code to the right sidebar content section of the Stylized JSP page from the previous section.

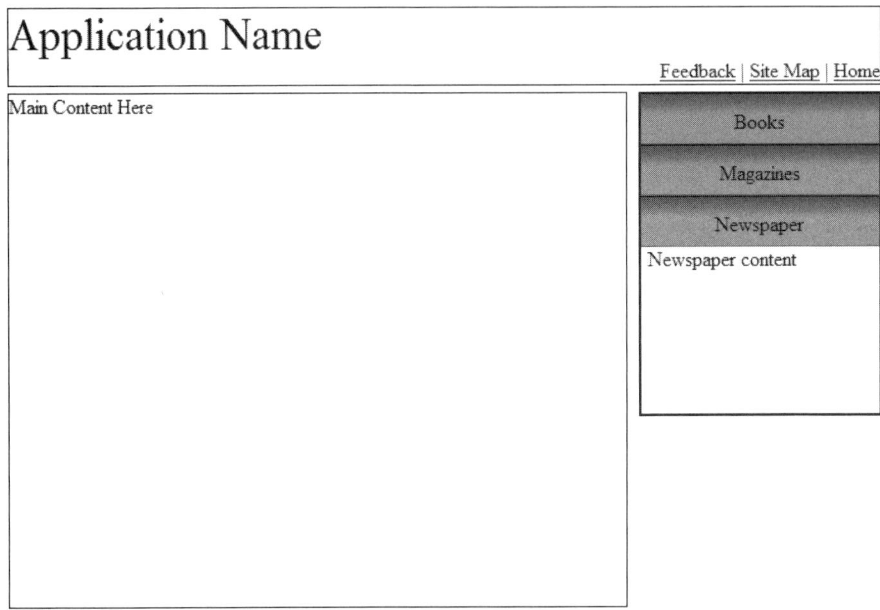

Figure 13-36. *The Accordion widgets displayed in the web browser*

Customizing Widgets

You can customize jMaki widgets directly by editing the code displayed in the Source Editor. You can also use the jMaki Customizer window. This window allows you to edit the widget's text and any attributes it may have.

To use the Widget Customizer window, click inside the code for a widget that is displayed in the Source Editor. Then click the jMaki button in the Source Editor toolbar. The Widget Customizer window will appear, with the Spry Accordion widget's attributes and code displayed, as shown in Figure 13-37.

The top section contains any arguments the widget may have. Initially the Spry Accordion widget did not have an `args` attribute displayed in the code. The widget was thus using the default value. If you look at the Args section, you will see an argument named `gradient`. The value for the argument is set to `Blue`. If you click inside the "Value" attributes field, you can select a new color from the drop-down list that appears. This allows you to change the default arguments for the widget.

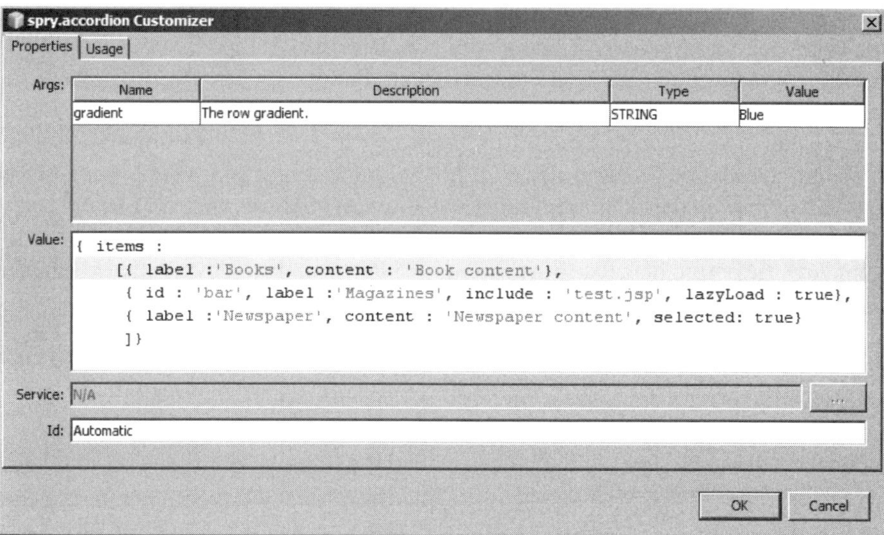

Figure 13-37. *The Widget Customizer window*

You can also edit the main body of the widget. The bottom half of the Widget Customizer window shows the value of the widget. It lists the layer array text that you can edit and change as you see fit.

The Widget Customizer window also has a Usage tab. If you select it, the tab will display the name of the widget, its description, and an image that shows you what the widget typically looks like. If you click the OK button the Widget Customizer window will close and any changes you made to the widget code will be displayed in the Source Editor.

Summary

This chapter focused on creating web applications in NetBeans. In it we covered how to create a web application and manage its properties and settings and the overall structure and layout of its files. We discussed building, running, and deploying an application along with the various properties and tools for controlling those operations. We reviewed working with web application files, such as HTML and CSS.

The chapter also provided an overview of the NetBeans tools for working with Struts in a web application. It covered how to use the IDE wizards to add actions and forms as well as how to make modifications to the overall Struts configuration.

As you learned in this chapter, before you can deploy an application to a Java application server, that server must be registered in NetBeans. We covered how to set up and work with the Tomcat and GlassFish application servers.

Next, you learned about one of my favorite NetBeans tools, the HTTP Monitor. The HTTP Monitor is a valuable tool for examining HTTP request data, modifying values such as query string parameters and HTTP headers, and replaying specific HTTP requests.

The chapter also covered the NetBeans Visual Web JavaServer Faces framework, beginning with how to install it and configure its options. Then it ran through the process of creating a Visual Web–enabled application, reviewing the project structure, and setting project properties.

Visual Web–enabled projects make use of several standard NetBeans windows and tools, including the Palette, Properties, and Navigator windows. They also use special windows called the Visual Designer window and the Visual Database Query Editor.

You also saw how to create Visual Web–enabled pages, add JSF components to them, and configure the navigation links between them. The `faces-config.xml` editor is a powerful tool to drag-and-drop links between JSP pages and create JSF navigation rules in the `faces-config.xml` file. We also explored the NetBeans data-binding capabilities. With these, you can automatically connect JSF components to database tables by simply dragging-and-dropping items. You can easily configure the bound data using the various properties and windows that NetBeans provides.

Finally, we covered the jMaki framework. You can add this powerful JavaScript and Ajax framework to your web application. It gives you quick access to some amazing Ajax-enabled widgets on the Palette. You can drag-and-drop these widgets into your source code and edit their code to quickly configure and customize them.

The frameworks discussed in this chapter can extend the functionality of the standard Web Application projects. Each framework offers a different set of features that can make you more productive and deliver better functionality to end users. Understanding how to use the widgets in NetBeans can help you when working with them.

CHAPTER 14

Developing Web Services: JAX-WS, SOA, BPEL, and RESTful

The concept of software as a service is not new. People in the IT community have been discussing it for years. A related idea in software architecture, *modularization*, involves making portions of software separate and loosely coupled. Web services provide this loose coupling by separating software components.

Many of the tools that implement the alphabet soup of web service technologies are difficult to work with and have a steep learning curve. The NetBeans IDE attempts to supply simple solutions to working with these technologies. It provides support for the latest web service specifications, such as Java EE 5 and the Java API for XML Web Services (JAX-WS). These tools allow you to use Java EE 5 and annotations for defining web service servers and clients quickly and easily.

NetBeans 6 also provides support for service-oriented architecture (SOA) tools like the Business Process Execution Language (BPEL) and its supporting features. You can use visual tools to design a business process, invoke web services, and test the entire process. These tools let you construct what is known as a composite application, made up of various logical processes and web services. This helps enforce the modularization that web services aim to provide and allows you to interact with them quickly and easily.

Installing the Web Services Modules

To use the XML, SOA, and BPEL tools available in NetBeans, you can download and install the full NetBeans 6 bundle. You can also download one of the smaller bundles and later install the needed modules. For working with the web services in this chapter you will need to download the following NetBeans 6 modules: SOA, BPEL, Composite Application.

To locate and install the module, do the following:

1. Go to the main menu and select Tools ➤ Plugins. The Plugin Manager window will open.

2. Select the Available Plugins tab and click the Reload Catalog button. The remote update centers will be checked for new plugins.

3. Scroll down the list of available plugins and locate the ones named SOA, BPEL, and Composite Application.
4. Select the check box next to the module name and click the Install button. A plugin installer prompt will pop open. Click the Next button.
5. Select the radio button next to the "I accept the terms" field and click the Install button.
6. You should see a message denoting the success or failure of the plugin installation process. Click the Finish button to close the window and return to the Plugin Manager.
7. Click the Close button to exit the Plugin Manager.

The modules are now ready to be used. You can verify their installation by searching for them in the Installed tab of the Plugin Manager.

Creating Web Services

One of my first experiences with web services was several years ago. As a beginner, I started using the several Apache libraries for working with XML and web services. These were a little unwieldy and took quite some time to learn, considering the numerous acronyms, specifications, and implementations to sift through. Eventually, I began to comprehend the technology, and I found I could do some interesting web service calls via the Simple Object Access Protocol (SOAP).

SOAP provided some nifty capabilities, particularly RPC-type calls via HTTP that communicated on the standard port 80. This allowed web services to bypass many corporate firewalls and also added some flexibility in the web services paradigm, laying the groundwork for web applications to evolve into SOA applications.

Up to this point, working with the various web service technologies was a little difficult. When Sun introduced the Java EE 5 platform, it included JAX-WS, a new API combined with annotations that greatly simplified the process of working with web services. This XML-based document approach is similar to SOAP and replaces the XML-RPC type of web services that existed in the past.

NetBeans 6 provides several convenient tools for creating web services using JAX-WS. These tools can help you quickly create web service servers and clients as well as get rid of much of the boilerplate code you typically write.

In NetBeans, you can specify several different web service file types via the New File wizard:

Web Service: Creates an empty web service that is part of an EJB or web container that is called by a client application.

Web Service Client: Specifies the client application that calls a web service.

Web Service from WSDL: Generates a web service based on a Web Services Description Language (WSDL) file. A WSDL file is an XML-based file that describes a web service as defined by the W3C specification. It acts like an interface to the web service by describing its network bindings, protocol, and messages.

WSDL Document: Creates an empty WSDL file that describes a web service using XML.

Logical Handler: Creates a Java class that allows you to perform preprocessing and post-processing of web service messages.

Message Handler: Creates a Java class that allows you to perform preprocessing and post-processing of web service messages. This handler differs from the Logical Handler in that it affects the body and header of the message. This file type is typically used for security and/or logging purposes.

Secure Token Service (STS): Creates an empty, secure web service that is part of an EJB or web container that is called by a client application.

These file types can be employed in several different types of NetBeans projects. The following examples use a Web Application project type for the web service and a Java Application project type for the client.

Creating a Web Service

Let's say you wanted to create a web service in a Web Application project that allowed client applications to retrieve customer information. Define a simple `Customer` class such as the following:

```
package com.pronetbeans.examples.services;

public class Customer {

    public Customer() {}

    private long Id;
    private String FirstName;
    private String LastName;

    public long getId() {
        return Id;
    }

    public void setId(long Id) {
        this.Id = Id;
    }

    public String getFirstName() {
        return FirstName;
    }
```

```
    public void setFirstName(String FirstName) {
        this.FirstName = FirstName;
    }

    public String getLastName() {
        return LastName;
    }

    public void setLastName(String LastName) {
        this.LastName = LastName;
    }
}
```

The Customer class contains three member variables. The Id variable represents the number used to identify a customer uniquely in a database system. The FirstName and LastName variables define the customer's name. I've used a simple example for demonstration purposes. Obviously, a Java class that represents a real customer would have numerous fields for items such as billing address, shipping address, phone numbers, payment details, and so on.

■ **Tip** You don't actually have to type all the getter and setter methods in the example. You can highlight the three member variables, right-click in the Source Editor window, and select Refactor ➤ Encapsulate Fields, which will generate the getter and setter methods for you. See Chapter 10 for details on refactoring.

In this example, the Customer class will be populated with data and sent to the client applications that execute the web service. To create the web service, follow these steps:

1. Right-click the project name in the Projects window and select New ➤ Other.
2. In the New File wizard, select Web Services from the list of categories in the left pane and Web Service from the list of file types in the right pane. Then click the Next button to continue.
3. In the Name and Location screen, shown in Figure 14-1, specify a value for the "Web Service Name" field, such as CustomerInfo. This is the name that client applications will use to call the web service, so try to make it a meaningful one. You can also specify the "Location" and "Package" fields in this window.
4. Choose how your web service is generated by selecting either the Create an Empty Web Service option or the Delegate to Existing Session Enterprise Bean option. Specify an EJB if necessary. Then click Finish.

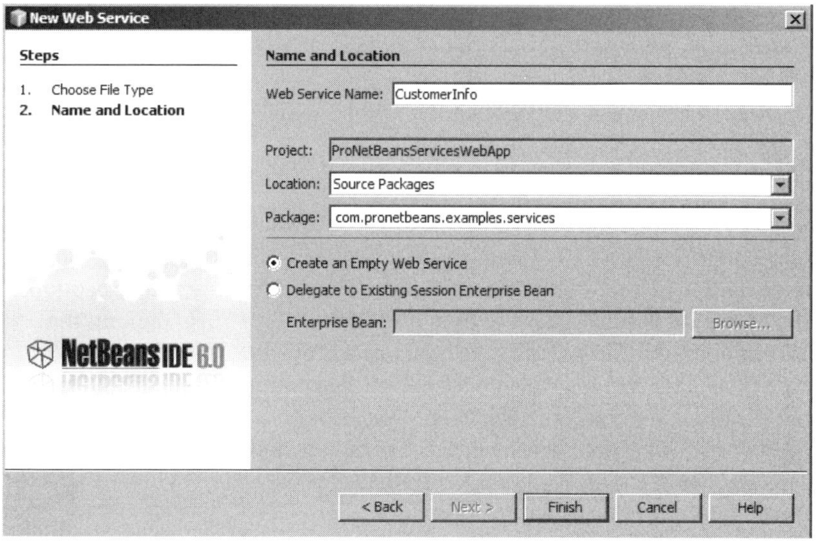

Figure 14-1. *Adding a web service in the Name and Location screen*

The Create an Empty Web Service option will simply generate a skeleton web service class with no code or operations. More often than not, you will choose this default option. If you leave it selected and click the Finish button, the following web service class will be generated (the package and import statements are not included):

```
@WebService()
public class CustomerInfo {

}
```

The Delegate to Existing Session Enterprise Bean option allows you to expose an EJB as a web service. When you click the Browse button to select an EJB, a dialog box will display a list of any enterprise modules or projects currently open in the Projects window. Once you have selected an EJB from this dialog box, you can click Finish to complete the new file creation process. The new web service class is created with the following code:

```
@WebService
public class CustomerInfoImpl {

    @EJB
    private com.pronetbeans.examples.NewSessionLocal newSessionBean;

}
```

In this example, the `NewSessionLocal` class is the EJB selected to expose as a web service. It is marked with the `@EJB` annotation.

Regardless of how you choose to generate a web service, you should end up with a class that is marked with the `javax.jws.WebService` annotation. This annotation allows JAX-WS to handle the Java class like a web service.

Once you have created a web service, you need to give it functionality by adding operations.

Adding an Operation to a Web Service

You can add an operation to a web service by right-clicking inside a class displayed in the Source Editor and selecting Web Service ➤ Add Operation. The Add Operation dialog box will appear, allowing you to specify a Java method name, parameters, return type, and exceptions.

The name of the operation is what the client calls. The "Return Type" field denotes the type of value that is returned to the client. The field contains a drop-down list of suggested values, such as `long`, `String`, and `int`. You can choose one of these values or type directly in the field. If the return type is not listed, you can click the Browse button to open the Browse Class dialog box. This dialog box allows you to type a partial or complete name of a Java class and view the matching results. For example, if you search on the value `Cust`, the `Customer` class created in the previous example will appear in the results.

You can then choose to add an input parameter to the operation. The bottom half of the Add Operation dialog box allows you to add, edit, and remove parameters. Each parameter has a type and a name associated with it. You can also order the parameters in the operation using the Up and Down buttons in the dialog box.

For this example, I have specified a name of `getCustomerById`, a return type of `com.pronetbeans.examples.services.Customer`, and a single parameter of `long lngCustomerId`. Once the fields are properly set, the Add Operation dialog box should look like Figure 14-2.

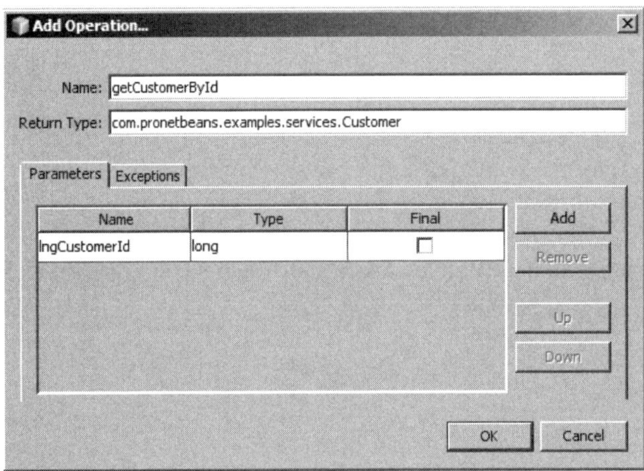

Figure 14-2. *The Add Operation dialog box for a web service*

Finally, click the OK button to create the operation. The code that is generated will look similar to the following:

```
@WebMethod(operationName = "getCustomerById")
public Customer getCustomerById(@WebParam(name = "lngCustomerId")
    long lngCustomerId) {
        //TODO write your implementation code here:
        return null;
}
```

In the preceding code, you can see that the method is marked with the `@WebMethod` annotation. The matching `import` statement for the `@WebMethod` annotation is also added to the class as `import javax.jws.WebMethod;`. This annotation identifies the method as a web operation that should be exposed through the web service. The input parameter is also marked with an annotation named `@WebParam`, which contains a `name` attribute that defines the name of the parameter explicitly. You can learn more about this class (and all of the annotation classes) by reviewing the Java EE 5 Javadoc available at `http://java.sun.com`.

The body of the method is empty, but you can quickly add content to make the web service functional. In the following code, I have defined and instantiated an instance of the `Customer` class. I then perform an `if-else` check on the input parameter to see whether it matches a certain value. If it matches either of two values, I populate the `Customer` object with fake data to be returned to the calling client application. This is to simulate a query to a data source. If the `lngCustomerId` parameter does not match either of the two hard-coded values, the `Customer` object is populated with meaningless values and returned.

```
@WebMethod(operationName = "getCustomerById")
public Customer getCustomerById(@WebParam(name = "lngCustomerId")
    long lngCustomerId) {

    Customer cust = new Customer();

    if(lngCustomerId ==1234567890) {
            cust.setId(1234567890);
            cust.setFirstName("Adam");
            cust.setLastName("Myatt");
    } else if(lngCustomerId ==123) {
            cust.setId(123);
            cust.setFirstName("John");
            cust.setLastName("Doe");
    } else {
            cust.setId(-1);
            cust.setFirstName("");
            cust.setLastName("");
    }
    return cust;
}
```

The web service operation I defined here will accept a customer identification number as a parameter, retrieve the customer data from a data source, and return a `Customer` class filled with customer data.

Yes, Virginia, there is a Santa Claus! With a few quick clicks, you have a real working web service in NetBeans using Java EE 5 and JAX-WS.

Testing the Web Service

The GlassFish server comes with a web service testing application, which you can use to test your web service without having to write a client application. To test the web service, follow these steps:

1. Press F6 or select Run ➤ Run Main Project. Once the project runs and deploys, the application server will start automatically.
2. Expand the Web Services node in the Projects window, right-click the web service, and select Test Web Service. A web browser will open.
3. Once the web browser has opened, you will see the web service testing page for the specific service you are testing. In this example, the `CustomerInfo` web service is exposed and available to be tested using a simple HTML form, as shown in Figure 14-3. The text field represents the input parameter for the web service method. For this example, enter the value `1234567890` in the input field. Then click the `getCustomerById` button to submit the value.

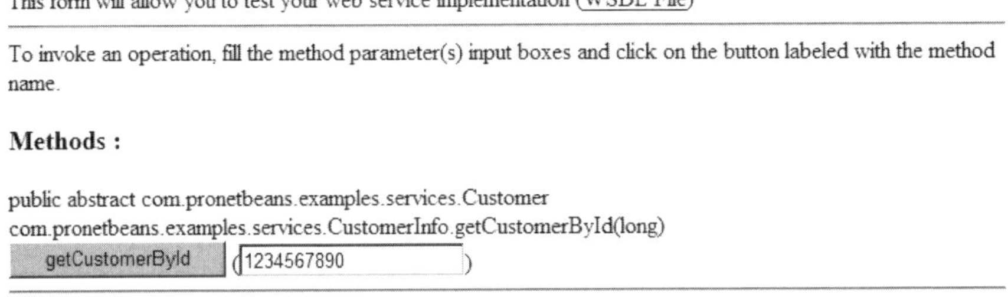
CustomerInfoService Web Service Tester
This form will allow you to test your web service implementation (WSDL File)
To invoke an operation, fill the method parameter(s) input boxes and click on the button labeled with the method name.
Methods :
public abstract com.pronetbeans.examples.services.Customer
com.pronetbeans.examples.services.CustomerInfo.getCustomerById(long)
getCustomerById
(1234567890)

Figure 14-3. *The GlassFish web service testing application*

The testing application returns a `Customer` object filled with data as specified in the definition of the `getCustomerById` method. The results page will display the SOAP request XML:

```
<?xml version="1.0" encoding="UTF-8"?>
<S:Envelope xmlns:S="http://schemas.xmlsoap.org/soap/envelope/">
    <S:Header/>
    <S:Body>
        <ns2:getCustomerById xmlns:ns2="http://services.examples.pronetbeans.com/">
            <lngCustomerId>1234567890</lngCustomerId>
        </ns2:getCustomerById>
    </S:Body>
</S:Envelope>
```

This SOAP envelope defines the body of the request, the function name `getCustomerById`, and the input parameter `lngCustomerId`. The value that was specified in the web service testing application is listed between the opening and closing tags that define the `lngCustomerId` parameter.

The application also displays the SOAP response XML:

```
<?xml version="1.0" encoding="UTF-8"?>
<S:Envelope xmlns:S="http://schemas.xmlsoap.org/soap/envelope/">
    <S:Body>
        <ns2:getCustomerByIdResponse
                  xmlns:ns2="http://services.examples.pronetbeans.com/">
            <return>
                <firstName>Adam</firstName>
                <id>1234567890</id>
                <lastName>Myatt</lastName>
            </return>
        </ns2:getCustomerByIdResponse>
    </S:Body>
</S:Envelope>
```

The data returned in the SOAP response shows that the web service actually functioned correctly and returned the correct values for the `id`, `firstName`, and `lastName` fields.

Creating a Web Service Client

A web service client represents the application code that executes a web service. It can be created as part of a Web Application project or a standard Java Application project. This allows you to call a web service from almost any type of Java application.

For the purposes of this chapter, I show you how to create a new web service client in a Java Application project. To create the project and the web service client, follow these steps:

1. Select File ➤ New Project from the main menu.

2. In the New Project window, select Java from the list of categories on the left and Java Application from the list of available project types on the right, and then click the Next button.

3. In the Name and Location window, name the project, select a project location, and specify the name and package of the `Main` class for the application. Click the Finish button to generate the project.

4. In the Projects window, right-click the project name and select New ➤ Other.

5. In the New File wizard, select Web Services from the list of Categories in the left pane and Web Service Client from the list of file types in the right pane. Then click the Next button.

6. In the WSDL and Client Location window, shown in Figure 14-4, first specify the WSDL file. Your choices are Project, Local File, and WSDL URL. If you select "Local File," you can browse to and select a WSDL file on the local file system. If you select the "WSDL URL" field, you must enter a complete URL to the WSDL file, such as `http://www.myhost.com/webapp/mywebService?wsdl`. For this example, select the "Project" radio button, and then click the Browse button. In the Browse Web Services dialog box, expand the project name node, select the web service, and click the OK button.

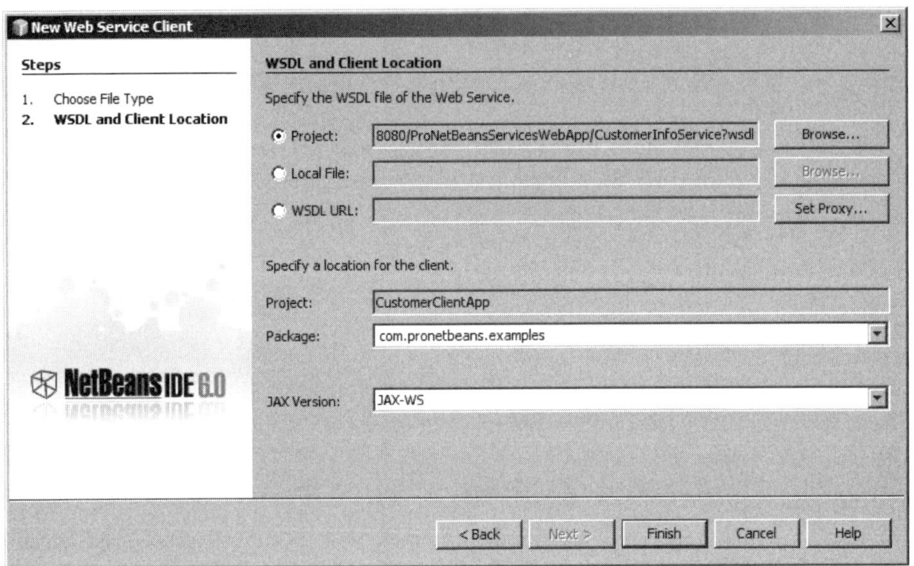

Figure 14-4. *The WSDL and Client Location window for creating a web service client*

7. Specify the Java package hierarchy for the web service client.

8. Click the Finish button to complete the process.

As NetBeans generates the web service client, you will see a progress bar and a status message indicating that it is importing the WSDL file. After the web service client is generated, a new node named Web Service References appears under the project name in the Projects window. The WSDL file is located under the Web Service References node. Double-click the WSDL file node (CustomerInfoService in this example), to open the WSDL file in the Source Editor window. The following is a snippet of XML from the WSDL file:

```
<message name="getCustomerById">
    <part name="parameters" element="tns:getCustomerById"></part>
</message>
<message name="getCustomerByIdResponse">
    <part name="parameters" element="tns:getCustomerByIdResponse"></part>
</message>
```

```
<portType name="CustomerInfo">
    <operation name="getCustomerById">
        <input message="tns:getCustomerById"></input>
        <output message="tns:getCustomerByIdResponse"></output>
    </operation>
</portType>
<binding name="CustomerInfoPortBinding" type="tns:CustomerInfo">
    <soap:binding transport="ashttp://schemas.xmlsoap.org/soap/http"
                          style="document"></soap:binding>
    <operation name="getCustomerById">
        <soap:operation soapAction=""></soap:operation>
        <input>
            <soap:body use="literal"></soap:body>
        </input>
        <output>
            <soap:body use="literal"></soap:body>
        </output>
    </operation>
</binding>
```

Calling the Web Service

The WSDL file defines several configuration options for the service and allows web service clients to interact with the service via the defined port, binding, and message. The WSDL file allows you to use JAX-WS and the NetBeans web services tools to create Java code easily that calls the web service, as follows:

1. Open the `Main` class that was generated during the project creation process. You will see that the `main` method is empty.

2. Right-click anywhere inside the `main` method and select Web Service Client Resources ➤ Call Web Service Operation. The Select Operation to Invoke dialog box will appear, as shown in Figure 14-5.

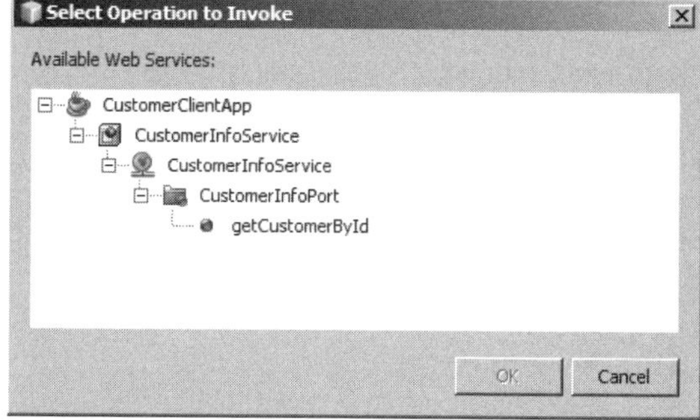

Figure 14-5. *The Select Operation to Invoke dialog box*

3. Expand each node in the Select Operation to Invoke window until you can see the `getCustomerById` web service.

4. Click the web service name, and then click the OK button. NetBeans will generate code to call the web service inside the `main` method.

For this chapter's example, the following template code is generated:

```
public static void main(String[] args) {

    try { // Call Web Service Operation
        com.pronetbeans.examples.CustomerInfoService service = new ➥
com.pronetbeans.examples.CustomerInfoService();
        com.pronetbeans.examples.CustomerInfo port = service.getCustomerInfoPort();

        // TODO initialize WS operation arguments here
        long lngCustomerId = 0;

        // TODO process result here
        com.pronetbeans.examples.Customer result = ➥
port.getCustomerById(lngCustomerId);
        System.out.println("Result = "+result);
    } catch (Exception ex) {
        // TODO handle custom exceptions here
    }
}
```

The first two lines in the `try` block define and instantiate instances of the `CustomerInfoService` and `CustomerInfo` classes. Creating these instances initializes the web service for execution. The code then calls the `getCustomerById` method, passing in the `lngCustomerId` parameter. You can specify any value for the `lngCustomerId` field other than the default value of 0 that is listed. The `getCustomerById` method returns a `Customer` instance, which can then be used to retrieve the desired values.

You can modify the `main` methods as follows:

```
public static void main(String[] args) {
    try {
        CustomerInfoService service = new CustomerInfoService();
        CustomerInfo port = service.getCustomerInfoPort();

        long lngCustomerId = 1234567890;

        Customer result = port.getCustomerById(lngCustomerId);

        System.out.println(" Cust Id = " + result.getId());
        System.out.println(" First   = " + result.getFirstName());
        System.out.println(" Last    = " + result.getLastName());
```

```
        } catch (Exception ex) {
            ex.printStackTrace();
        }
    }
```

You can remove the fully qualified package names for the classes and add the necessary imports by selecting Source ➤ Fix Imports (or use the shortcut Ctrl+Shift+I).

The modified `main` method also contains a value for the `lngCustomerId` field, which is passed to the `getCustomerById` method, which calls the web service on the remote server. Once the `Customer` object is returned, you can call the getter methods to retrieve the values that were passed along by the web service.

Running the Web Service Client

To run the web service client, you can simply press F6 to run the project, assuming you used the `Main` class that was specified during the project creation process. If you added the web service code to a different class, select Run ➤ Run File ➤ Run "<*YourFile*.java>" to execute that specific class.

Once the `Main` class runs, the web service client is invoked and passes the request to the remote web service via the SOAP request. It then receives the SOAP response via the XML and translates the returned values into the `Customer` object. (The SOAP request and response are described in the earlier section "Testing the Web Service.")

Testing the Web Service Client

To understand fully what is taking place between the web service client and the web service, you can use a network-monitoring program such as Ethereal to monitor the TCP/IP traffic that is exchanged between the client and server. You can also use the HTTP Monitor built in to the NetBeans IDE, as described in Chapter 13, but certain nonparameterized pieces of data do not display in the HTTP Monitor.

Using a network-monitoring program allows you to view the protocols, IP address, and entire set of data exchanged between the client and server. You can start by following these steps:

1. Activate your network monitor to track the incoming and outbound data.
2. Make sure that the web service has been deployed to a running Java application server.
3. Open the client application and run it. The `Main` class should execute, call the web service client, and retrieve data from the remote web service.
4. Disable your network-monitoring program and view the accumulated data.

In the results, you should be able to see that the application performed an HTTP `GET` on the WSDL file:

```
GET /ProNetBeansServicesWebApp/CustomerInfo?WSDL HTTP/1.1
```

The contents of the WSDL file are returned from the server to the client. The web service client then performs an HTTP POST operation and passes the request as follows:

```
POST /ProNetBeansServicesWebApp/CustomerInfo HTTP/1.1
Content-Length: 302
SOAPAction: ""
Content-Type: text/xml; charset=utf-8
Accept: text/xml, application/xop+xml, text/html, image/gif, ➥
 image/jpeg, *; q=.2, */*; q=.2
User-Agent: Java/1.5.0_10
Host: localhost:8080
Connection: keep-alive

<?xml version="1.0" encoding="UTF-8"?>
<S:Envelope xmlns:S="http://schemas.xmlsoap.org/soap/envelope/">
    <S:Header/>
    <S:Body>
        <ns2:getCustomerById xmlns:ns2="http://services.examples.pronetbeans.com/">
            <lngCustomerId>1234567890</lngCustomerId>
        </ns2:getCustomerById>
    </S:Body>
</S:Envelope>
```

The SOAP response that appears as part of the server response will look similar to this:

```
X-Powered-By: Servlet/2.5
Content-Type: text/xml;charset=utf-8
Content-Length: 364
Date: Wed, 13 Sep 2007 19:00:51 GMT
Server: Sun Java System Application Server Platform Edition 9.0_01

<?xml version="1.0" encoding="UTF-8"?>
<S:Envelope xmlns:S="http://schemas.xmlsoap.org/soap/envelope/">
    <S:Body>
        <ns2:getCustomerByIdResponse
                xmlns:ns2="http://services.examples.pronetbeans.com/">
            <return>
                <firstName>Adam</firstName>
                <id>1234567890</id>
                <lastName>Myatt</lastName>
            </return>
        </ns2:getCustomerByIdResponse>
    </S:Body>
</S:Envelope>
```

You can see that the SOAP XML passed back and forth between the client and server is nearly identical to the SOAP XML you saw when testing the web service using the GlassFish web testing application.

■Note In the preceding examples, I've formatted the XML on multiple lines and added spaces to make it easier to read. In the actual `GET` and `POST` HTTP operations, the XML is typically sent in one long string, without spaces, to minimize the number of characters that are transmitted.

Once your web service client's code has finished running, look at the Output window. As expected, the `Customer` logging text should appear as shown here:

```
Customer
   Id      = 123456
   First   = Adam
   Last    = Myatt
```

Creating a Web Service from a WSDL File

NetBeans also provides a wizard for generating a new web service based on an existing WSDL file. If you want to import an existing WSDL file or create a new one manually in an application and then model a web service from it, you can do so using the New File wizard.

To create a new web service from a WSDL file, follow these steps:

1. Right-click the project name in the Projects window and select New ➤ Other.
2. Select Web Services from the list of categories in the left pane and Web Service From WSDL from the list of file types in the right pane. Click the Next button to proceed.
3. In the Name and Location screen, specify the web service name as well as values for the "Location" and "Package" fields, as shown in Figure 14-6.
4. Click the upper Browse button to locate the local WSDL file. The dialog box allows you to browse your entire file system, not just WSDL files in open projects. Once you have located the WSDL file you want to use, click the Open button and review the settings in the Name and Location window.
5. If the WSDL file defines multiple services and ports, click the Browse button next to the "Web Service Port" field to specify the port you wish to use.
6. Click the Finish button to complete the process. NetBeans will generate the web service and list it in the Projects window under the Web Services node. The Java source file that represents the web service should also open in the Source Editor.

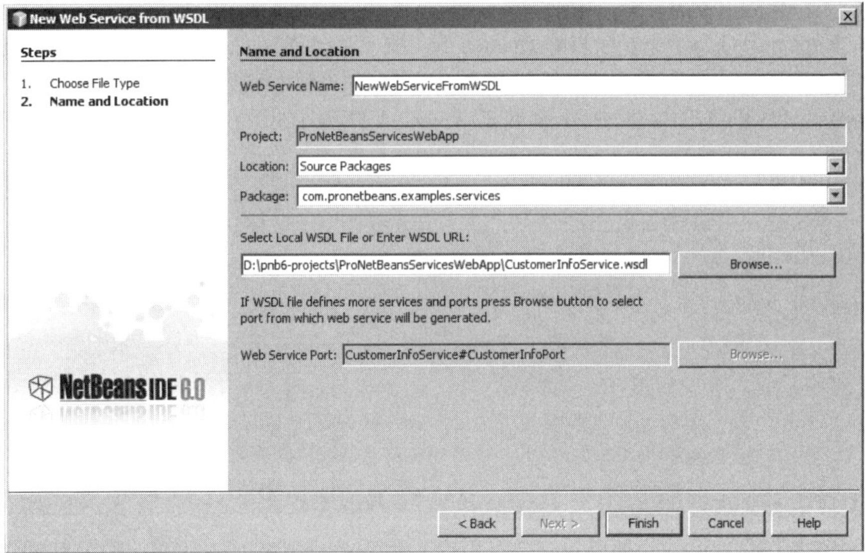

Figure 14-6. *Creating a web service from a WSDL file*

Creating a Message Handler

A message handler is a Java class that can typically access the header and body blocks of a SOAP message in a web service or client.

Generating a New Message Handler

To create a message handler, follow these steps:

1. Right-click the project name in the Projects window and select New ➤ Other.
2. In the New File window, select Web Services from the categories list in the left pane and Message Handler from the file types list in the right pane. Click the Next button to proceed.
3. In the Name and Location screen, you need to specify values for the "Message Handler Name," "Location," and "Package" fields. After entering values in these fields, click the Finish button to generate the new handler class.

The skeleton code for the message handler that is generated will look similar to the following:

```
public class PnbMessageHandler implements SOAPHandler<SOAPMessageContext>{

    public boolean handleMessage(SOAPMessageContext messageContext) {
        SOAPMessage msg = messageContext.getMessage();
        return true;
    }
```

```
    public Set<QName> getHeaders() {
        return Collections.EMPTY_SET;
    }

    public boolean handleFault(SOAPMessageContext messageContext) {
        return true;
    }

    public void close(MessageContext context) {
    }
}
```

In the preceding code, the `handleMessage` method is processed for all incoming and outgoing messages. You can use the `SOAPMessage` object to gain access to various bits and pieces of information for each message that passes into and out of the web service (for example, if you wanted to log a specific header for each request).

Adding the Message Handler to a Web Service

To configure the web service to use the new handler, you must add it to the service, as follows:

1. Under the web application's Web Services node, right-click the web service name and select Configure Handlers.

2. The Configure Message Handlers dialog box will appear. Click the Add button to open the Add Message Handler Class dialog box, as shown in Figure 14-7.

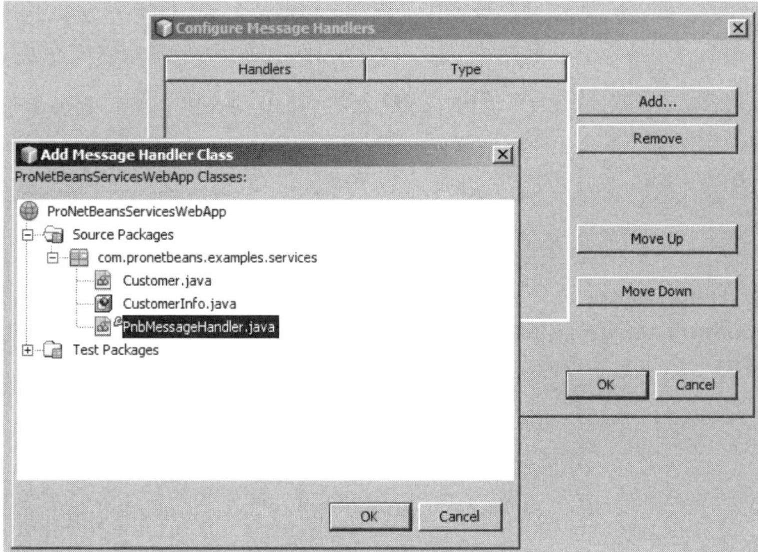

Figure 14-7. *The Add Message Handler Class dialog box*

3. Expand the Source Packages node and select the message handler class. Then click the OK button.

4. The class you selected will now appear in the Handler Classes list in the Configure Message Handlers dialog box. Click the OK button to complete the process.

A new file named `CustomerInfo_handler.xml` is created and added to the package where the Message Handler class exists. Its content defines the basic handler chain for the web service and lists the name and class for each handler that is configured for a web service.

```
<?xml version="1.0" encoding="UTF-8"?>
<handler-chains xmlns="http://java.sun.com/xml/ns/javaee">
  <handler-chain>
    <handler>
      <handler-name>
          com.pronetbeans.examples.PnbMessageHandler
      </handler-name>
      <handler-class>
          com.pronetbeans.examples.PnbMessageHandler
      </handler-class>
    </handler>
  </handler-chain>
</handler-chains>
```

The web service class itself is also modified to reference the handler chain:

```
@WebService()
@HandlerChain(file = "CustomerInfo_handler.xml")

public class CustomerInfo {
    // class content removed for brevity
}
```

Now when you build, deploy, and execute the web service, the message handler class is invoked.

Creating a Logical Handler

A logical handler is a Java class that can handle blocks of a SOAP message in a web service or client for the purpose of reading or modifying the message to augment its processing. Typical uses for a logical handler in a web service are logging and security.

To create a logical handler, follow these steps:

1. Right-click the project name in the Projects window and select New ➤ Other.

2. In the New File wizard, select Web Services from the categories list in the left pane and Logical Handler from the file types list in the right pane. Click the Next button to proceed.

3. In the Name and Location screen, you need to specify values only for the "Logical Handler Name," "Location," and "Package" fields. Once you have specified the values, click the Finish button to generate the new handler class.

The skeleton code for the logical handler that is generated will look similar to the following:

```
public class PnbLogicalHandler implements LogicalHandler<LogicalMessageContext> {

    public boolean handleMessage(LogicalMessageContext messageContext) {
        LogicalMessage msg = messageContext.getMessage();
        return true;
    }

    public boolean handleFault(LogicalMessageContext messageContext) {
        return true;
    }

    public void close(MessageContext context) {
    }
}
```

As with a message handler, the `handleMessage` method of a logical handler is executed for each incoming and outgoing message. You can use the `LogicalMessage` object to gain access to the internals of the SOAP message.

Working with SOA and BPEL

NetBeans 6 provides a variety of tools for working with SOA and BPEL applications. You can use tools to create and manage a WSDL file, create and modify a BPEL process, define a Composite Application project, and execute and test a business process.

Creating a BPEL Module Project

A BPEL Module project contains the design logic for a business process. You can visually define a flow of data, perform various conditional branches and checks, and invoke web services, depending on the desired functionality of your business process.

To create the BPEL Module project, follow these steps:

1. Select File ➤ New Project from the main menu.
2. In the New Project window, select SOA from the list of categories in the left pane and BPEL Module from the list of projects in the right pane. Then click the Next button.
3. In the Name and Location screen, enter the name for the BPEL Module project, and then click the Finish button.

The BPEL Module project will be generated and listed in the Projects window. It contains a single subnode called Process Files, which is where the BPEL processes and WSDL files are created. You can add the BPEL process files directly to this node.

Creating the BPEL Process File

The BPEL process file is what allows you to define an actual business process in a visual representation. To create a BPEL process, follow these steps:

1. Right-click the Process Files folder under the BPEL Module project name in the Projects window and select New ➤ Other.
2. In the New File window, select SOA from the categories listed in the left pane and BPEL Process from the file types listed in the right pane. Click the Next button to continue.
3. In the Name and Location screen, as shown in Figure 14-8, enter the filename for the new BPEL process and select a folder. The default folder that is suggested for use is the `src` directory in the project.
4. Enter a value for the "Target Namespace" field. This field specifies the XML namespace for the BPEL process that aligns with the `targetNamespace` attribute in the XML definition.
5. Click the Finish button to complete the process.

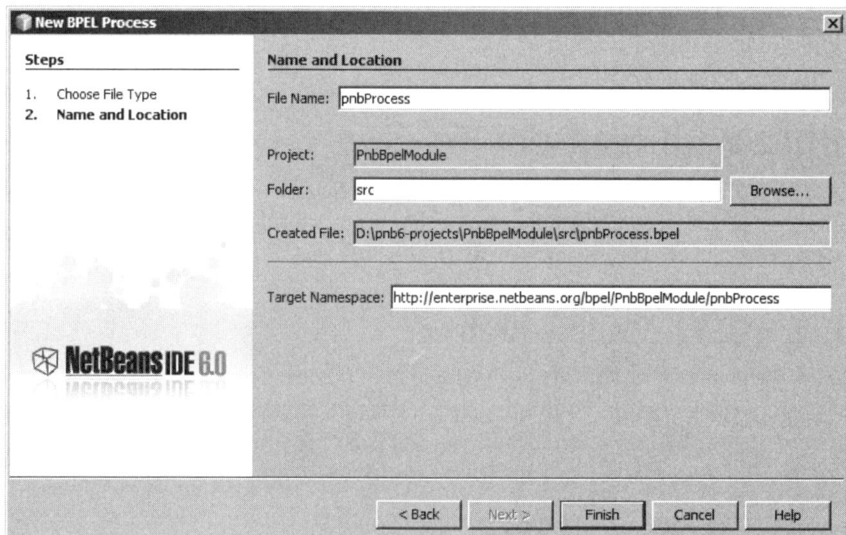

Figure 14-8. *The Name and Location screen for creating a BPEL process*

The BPEL process file will be generated and listed under the Process Files node in the Projects window.

The BPEL process file will also open in the BPEL Design window in the center of the IDE. An empty BPEL process will be displayed in the window. It contains a Process Start point, an empty Sequence component (represented by a rectangle), and a Process End point, as shown in Figure 14-9.

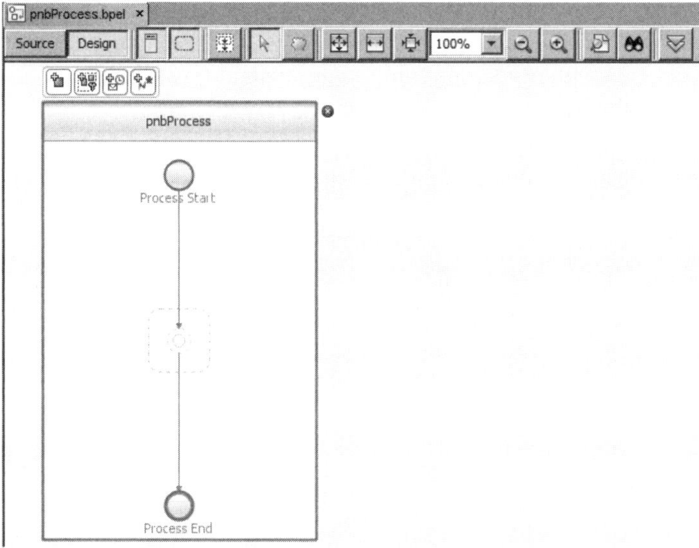

Figure 14-9. *A BPEL process displayed in the BPEL Design window*

Navigating the BPEL Design Window

The BPEL Design window, which currently shows the empty BPEL process, offers two views for working with the business process: Source and Design. The Design button is selected by default. Click the Source button to see the mostly empty XML code that defines the current process:

```
<?xml version="1.0" encoding="UTF-8"?>
<process
    name="pnbProcess"
    targetNamespace=" http://enterprise.netbeans.org/bpel/PnbBpelModule/pnbProcess"
    xmlns=" http://docs.oasis-open.org/wsbpel/2.0/process/executable/"
    xmlns:xsd="http://www.w3.org/2001/XMLSchema"
    xmlns:tns=" http://enterprise.netbeans.org/bpel/PnbBpelModule/pnbProcess ">

   <sequence>
   </sequence>

</process>
```

Once you have visually created the BPEL process, this XML definition will include the detailed XML code. As you make changes in the Design view, NetBeans updates the XML code.

Along with the Source and Design buttons, the BPEL Design window toolbar, shown in Figure 14-10, includes the following buttons:

Figure 14-10. *The BPEL Design window toolbar*

Show Partner Links: Toggles the display of BPEL components called *partner links*. This button is selected by default so that the components are displayed in the diagram. Once you have created a large diagram with numerous components, you may want to hide these components by clicking the button.

Show Sequences: Toggles the display of BPEL components called *sequences*. This button is selected by default, and you can click it to hide these components.

Expand All: Expands any minimized/collapsed nodes displayed in the BPEL process Design view.

Editing Mode: If selected, enables editing of the BPEL process in the Design view.

Navigation Mode: If selected, allows you to click and drag around a BPEL process displayed in the Design view. This is particularly useful when you are zoomed in or have a large process layout.

Fit Diagram: Automatically scales the content displayed in the window so that it fits in one window.

Fit Width: Automatically scales the content displayed to fit horizontally, which may or may not add a vertical scrollbar to the window.

Zoom: Displays the content in the window at a zoom level of 100%. Depending on the size of the content displayed in the window, there may or may not be horizontal and vertical scrollbars. You can manually enter a percentage for the zoom level in the small text field displayed to the right of the button. Next to that is a sliding bar you can click and drag to set the zoom level.

Zoom In / Out: Allows you to zoom in or out of the BPEL process displayed in the Design view.

Print Preview: Displays a paginated preview of the BPEL process, allowing you to print it out.

Advanced Search: If clicked, will open a small Advanced Search pop-up window that allows you to search the BPEL process for any type of BPEL component.

Validate XML: Allows you to validate XML.

The Validate XML feature is available for most XML files. For BPEL process files, it validates the content to ensure that it follows the defined XSD and rules. If you click the Validate XML button without adding any content to the newly created BPEL process, the Output window will open and display an error message:

```
XML validation started.
D:/projects/website/PnbBpelModule/src/pnbProcess.bpel:2,0
To be instantiated, an executable business process must contain at least
one <receive> or <pick> activity annotated with a createInstance="yes" attribute.

1 Error(s),  0 Warning(s).
XML validation finished
```

The BPEL process displayed in the BPEL Design window also denotes the error with a white *X* in a red circle in the upper-right corner of the Process component. If you click the red circle, you will see a small dialog box that lists any errors for the BPEL process, as shown in Figure 14-11.

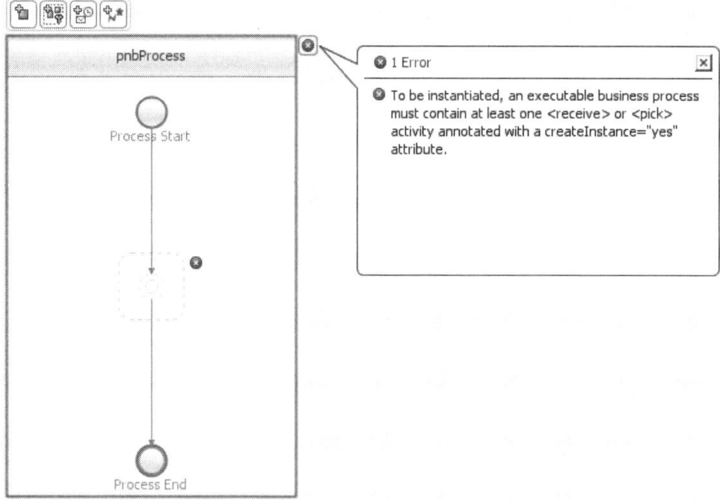

Figure 14-11. *The error dialog box in the BPEL Design window*

Creating the WSDL File

A BPEL process uses web services and WSDL files to define a link into and out of the business process. You can use NetBeans to create and manage a WSDL file that describes that interaction. Once the WSDL file has been created, you can add it to the business process and associate it with the various component operations in the process.

To create a WSDL file in the BPEL Module project, follow these steps:

1. Right-click the Process Files node in the Projects window for the BPEL Module project and select New ➤ WSDL Document.

2. The Name and Location screen will appear, because you already elected to create a WSDL document. Define the filename and the target namespace, and click the Finish button to proceed to the Abstract Configuration screen.

3. In the Abstract Configuration screen, shown in Figure 14-12, specify a value for the "Port Type Name" and "Operation Name" fields. The port type defines one or more operations for a web service. The operation name defines the initial web service function you want to create in the WSDL file.

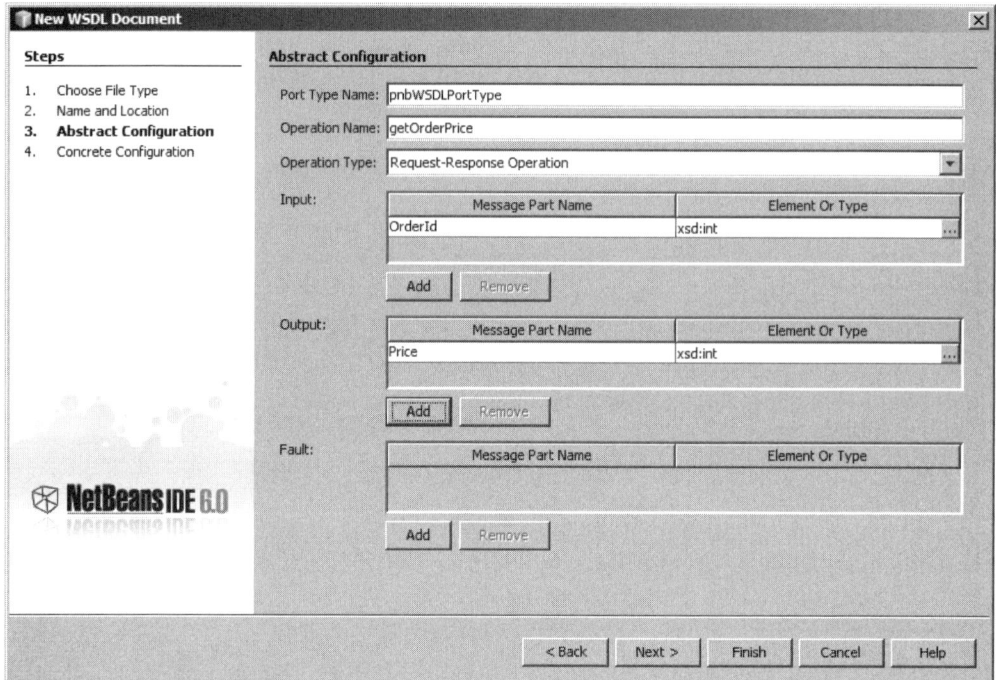

Figure 14-12. *Creating a WSDL file in the Abstract Configuration screen*

4. The "Operation Type" field defines the functioning of the web service in the WSDL file. The drop-down lists offers four choices:

   - *Request-Response Operation*: The web service will receive a value and send a response. This is most commonly used in services that receive an input parameter, perform a lookup or calculation, and return a result to the calling client. Possible uses for this type of service include an authentication or authorization service, a product order querying system, and a financial calculation service.

   - *One-Way Operation*: The web service operation will only receive an input message and will not send any output. This type of operation could be useful when creating a logging application that can be called by other services.

   - *Solicit-Response Operation*: The web service operation sends an output message to another service and waits to receive the reply. This type of service might be used with a process that monitors a local resource waiting for a condition to be true. If the condition occurs, it activates and notifies another service and waits for a response.

   - *Notification Response*: The web service operation sends an output message only and does not wait for a response.

5. The remainder of the Abstract Configuration screen prompts you to specify the input and output parameters for the operation. Depending on the value for the "Operation Type" field, these input and/or output sections may or may not be filled out. To add an input or output parameter, click the Add button that appears under each section. A new line will be added to the grid in the specific section and allow you to type directly in the column fields. You can also optionally add any faults (errors) that occur in the process. Once you have specified the input, output, and fault parameters, click the Next button.

6. In the Concrete Configuration screen, shown in Figure 14-13, specify the binding name. The binding name defines the binding type and subtype for the web service.

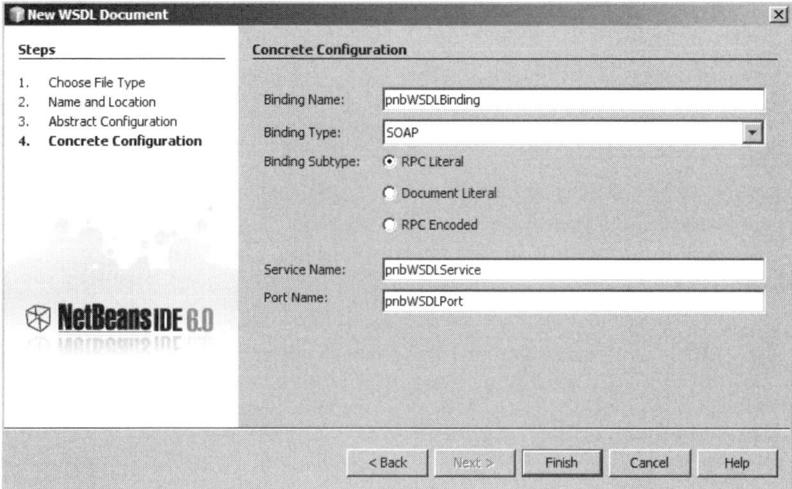

Figure 14-13. *The Concrete Configuration screen when creating a WSDL file*

7. The only available value for the "Binding Type" field is SOAP.

8. Choose a value for the "Binding Subtype" field. The binding subtype defines how the binding will be translated into a SOAP message. You have three choices:

   - *RPC Literal*: The SOAP binding will be defined as `<soap:binding style="rpc" transport="http://schemas.xmlsoap.org/soap/http"/>`.
   - *Document Literal*: The SOAP binding will be defined as `<soap:binding style="document" transport="http://schemas.xmlsoap.org/soap/http"/>`.
   - *RPC Encoded*: The SOAP binding will be defined as `<soap:binding style="rpc" transport="http://schemas.xmlsoap.org/soap/http"/>`.

9. Set the values for the "Service Name" and "Port Name" fields. These names affect how the web service is called, so specify something meaningful.

10. Once you have finished specifying the values for the WSDL file, click the Finish button to complete the process.

The WSDL file will be generated and listed under the Process Files node in the Projects window. The WSDL file is also opened in the WSDL Editor.

The WSDL XML will define the SOAP binding according to your selection for the binding subtype. If you chose RPC literal (the default), the SOAP binding will appear as follows:

```
<operation name="getOrderPrice">
  <soap:operation/>
  <input name="input1">
    <soap:body use="literal"
              namespace="http://j2ee.netbeans.org/wsdl/pnbWSDL"/>
  </input>
  <output name="output1">
    <soap:body use="literal"
              namespace="http://j2ee.netbeans.org/wsdl/pnbWSDL"/>
  </output>
</operation>
```

Notice that the `<soap:body>` tag has an attribute of `use` with a value of `literal`, based on the selection in the Concrete Configuration screen (Figure 14-13).

If you selected Document Literal for the binding subtype, the SOAP operation defined following the SOAP binding will appear as follows:

```
<operation name=" getOrderPrice">
  <soap:operation/>
  <input name="input1">
      <soap:body use="literal"/>
  </input>
  <output name="output1">
      <soap:body use="literal"/>
  </output>
</operation>
```

If you selected RPC Encoded for the binding subtype, the SOAP operation is defined as follows:

```
<operation name=" getOrderPrice">
  <soap:operation/>
  <output name="output1">
    <soap:body use="encoded"
          encodingStyle=http://schemas.xmlsoap.org/soap/encoding/
          namespace="http://j2ee.netbeans.org/wsdl/wsdl232232323"/>
  </output>
</operation>
```

Navigating the WSDL Editor

As the name implies, the WSDL Editor allows you to edit a WSDL file. It has three main views: Tree, Source, and Column. Since the WSDL file contains metadata that describes the web service and how to access it, you should be familiar with creating and modifying WSDL files.

The WSDL Editor displays the Tree view, a parent-child node view of the XML elements in a WSDL file, by default. (You can also toggle Tree view off and on by clicking the Tree icon in the toolbar, to the right of the WSDL button.) As you can see in Figure 14-14, it is intended to provide a simple view of the data in the file.

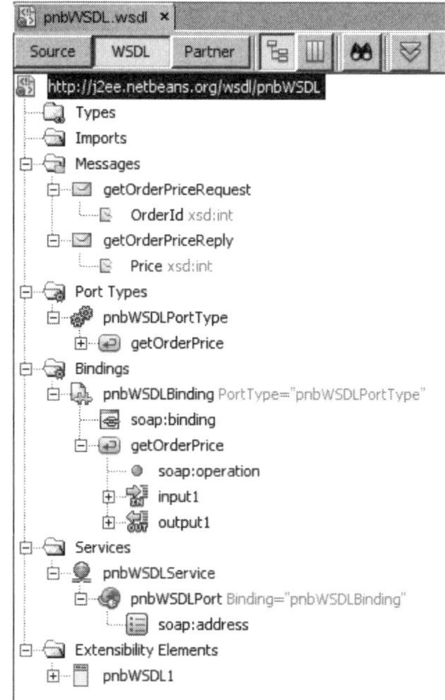

Figure 14-14. *The Tree view of a WSDL file in the WSDL Editor*

For each of the nodes that appear in the Tree view of the WSDL Editor, you can access specific sets of actions by right-clicking the node. You can right-click most nodes and select Go to Source, which toggles the WSDL Editor to the Source view and places the cursor in the section of XML that corresponds to the node you selected. This is useful if the WSDL file is quite long and you do not want to search through numerous lines of XML for a specific element.

You can also modify the WSDL file by adding new elements to it. In several sections, you can right-click a node and select Add ➤ *Element*, where *Element* is a context-sensitive element that can be added to the node. Using the context menus, you can add additional services, port names, bindings, operations, input/output parameters, and so on. All of this can be done without having to write any XML code.

The WSDL Editor also offers the Column view, which can be accessed by clicking the Column icon in the editor's toolbar. This is a great way to work with XML-based data, such as a WSDL file, because it gives you a left-to-right view of the parent-child relationships, as shown in Figure 14-15. If you select an element that contains a subnode (or child), a new column appears to the right of the current column and displays the child nodes. This provides a type of navigation that is similar to the standard Tree view but can be easier for some people to follow.

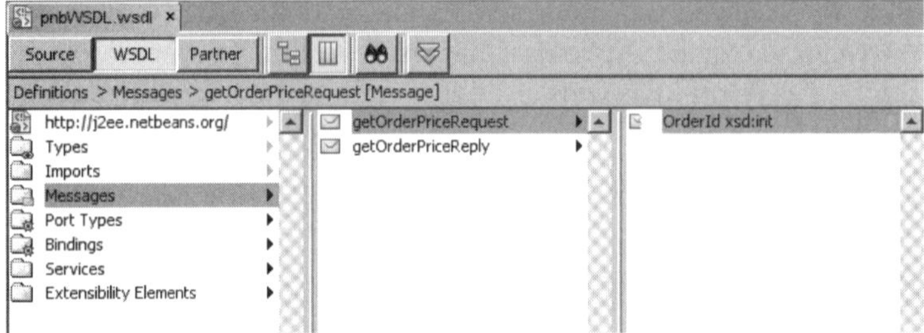

Figure 14-15. *Column view of a WSDL file in the WSDL Editor*

The Column view of the WSDL file provides the same sort of context menu features that are available in the Tree view. You can right-click any node to access the context-specific settings and options for it.

You can also view the WSDL file using the Partner view. The Partner view provides a nice GUI for viewing the web service information. You can view and modify the Partner Link Types as well as any Messages, as shown in Figure 14-16.

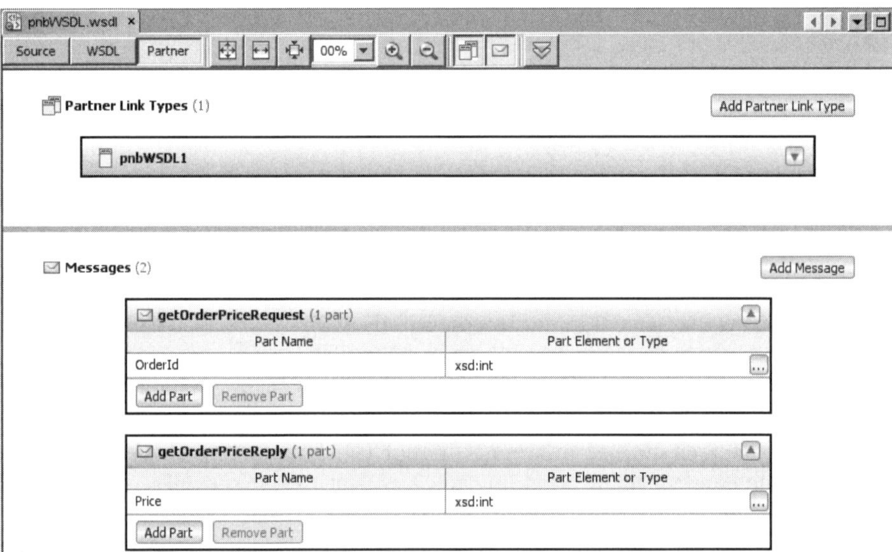

Figure 14-16. *Partner view of a WSDL file in the WSDL Editor*

The Partner view also lets you add and edit the messages displayed. If you double-click the `getOrderPriceRequest` message name, it will turn into a text field that allows you to change the value. You can also add part names and specify their types by clicking the Add Part button.

You can even add a new message to the WSDL file by clicking the Add Message button displayed on the right side of Figure 14-16. This adds a new box to the screen directly under the `getOrderPriceReply`. You can then use the GUI to modify the message name and the parts it contains.

Now that you've seen how to create a WSDL file and how to navigate the WSDL Editor, let's get back to the BPEL process we created earlier and add to it.

Working with the BPEL Designer and the BPEL Mapper

The `pnbProcess` BPEL process you created in the section "Creating the BPEL Process File" is relatively blank, as shown earlier in Figure 14-9. You need to add functionality to it.

You can add BPEL components to the BPEL process in the BPEL Design window by dragging-and-dropping them from the Palette window. The Palette window contains components specific to web services and BPEL, as described in Table 14-1. (You can open the Palette window by selecting Window ➤ Palette or pressing Ctrl+Shift+8.)

Table 14-1. *The BPEL and Web Service Components in the Palette Window*

Category	Component	Description
Web Service	Invoke	Sends a message to a partner web service defined by a partner link.
Web Service	Receive	Waits for an incoming message from a web service defined by a partner link that was originally initiated by the Invoke component.
Web Service	Reply	Sends a message to a web service defined by a partner link in reply to a message that came in through the Receive component.
Web Service	Partner Link	Defines a web service that will interact with the BPEL process.
Basic Activities	Assign	Copies data between different variables and allows you to assign new data type values to variables.
Basic Activities	Empty	Represents an empty activity that does nothing. You can use this component if your BPEL process needs to ignore certain outcomes or paths.
Basic Activities	Wait	Causes the BPEL process to pause for a specified amount of time according to various criteria.
Basic Activities	Throw	Generates an error or exception from within a BPEL process.
Basic Activities	Exit	Halts the flow of a BPEL process.
Structured Activities	If	Represents a conditional process that allows you to determine separate paths of execution for a BPEL process.
Structured Activities	While	Repeats a branch in the process as long as a condition continues to succeed.
Structured Activities	Repeat Until	Repeats a branch in the process as long as a condition continues to succeed after each loop iteration.
Structured Activities	For Each	Repeats a branch inside a Scope component as defined by specific criteria.
Structured Activities	Pick	Executes an activity after an event has occurred.
Structured Activities	Flow	Allows a BPEL process to perform multiple actions in parallel sequence.
Structured Activities	Sequence	Defines a group of activities that are executed in a sequential order.
Structured Activities	Scope	Defines an activity with an individual scope that contains its own internal local variables, links, and errors.

To have a BPEL process receive a message, perform a conditional check, and send a reply, you need to configure the conditional check in the If component. You do this through the BPEL Mapper window, which allows you visually to construct logical expressions, assign values to input and output parameters, and create logical checks of data.

When the If component is selected in the BPEL process, the BPEL Mapper window will display the list of variables in the left pane and a result node in the right pane, allowing you to map a `true` or `false` Boolean condition to it. The toolbar along the top of the BPEL Mapper window contains several drop-down menus that allow you to choose from specific categories of components, such as date and time elements, Boolean elements, and operators (addition, subtraction, multiplication).

Once you have reviewed the web services and BPEL components that are available, you can begin to add them to your BPEL process. The following sections walk you through creating a sample BPEL process.

Adding a Partner Link Component

To be able to interact with a web service, a BPEL process needs to have a Partner Link component:

1. Select the Partner Link component in the Palette window and drag it to a blank spot on the BPEL process canvas in the BPEL Design window. (You can also click a WSDL file in the Projects window and drag-and-drop it onto the BPEL process canvas.) Once the Partner Link component has been added, the Partner Link Property Editor window will open, as shown in Figure 14-17.

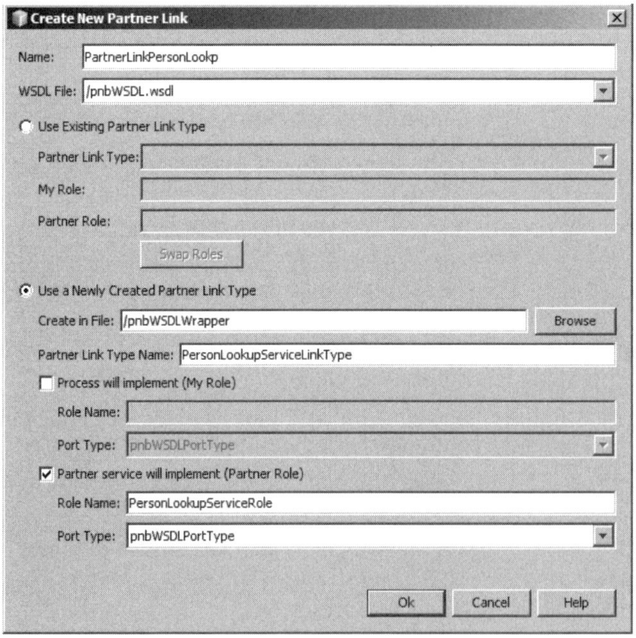

Figure 14-17. *The Partner Link Property Editor*

2. In the Partner Link Property Editor, specify a value for the "Name" field and select a WSDL file to which to apply the partner link.

3. Choose to use an existing partner link type or create a new partner link type. The partner link type is defined in the WSDL and specifies interaction rules.

4. Click the OK button. A square representing the partner link is added to the BPEL process.

Adding a Receive Component

The next task in this example is to add a Receive component to the BPEL process:

1. Click the Receive component in the Palette window and drag it over the Process Start circle.

2. While still holding down the mouse, move the component straight down until you see a small dotted circle light up, as shown in Figure 14-18 (it will appear orange on your screen).

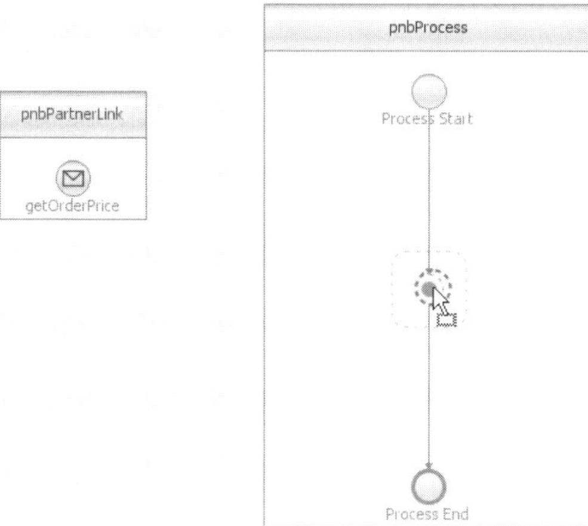

Figure 14-18. *Adding a Receive component to the BPEL process*

3. Once the circle is filled with orange, release the mouse, and the Receive component will be added to the BPEL process.

4. Next, you want to associate the Receive component with a partner link so that when a web service sends a message, the BPEL process will receive and act on it. Double-click the Receive component to open the Receive Property Editor window, as shown in Figure 14-19.

5. In the Receive Property Editor window, specify the name of the Receive component as it will appear in the BPEL process, define the partner link from which the component will receive a message, and specify the web service operation that will send the Receive component a message.

6. In the "Input Variable" field, create or use an existing local variable to store the message received from the web service via the partner link.

7. Click the OK button. The Receive component will be configured to receive a message from the partner link. You should also be able to see an orange dotted line connecting the Partner Link and Receive components.

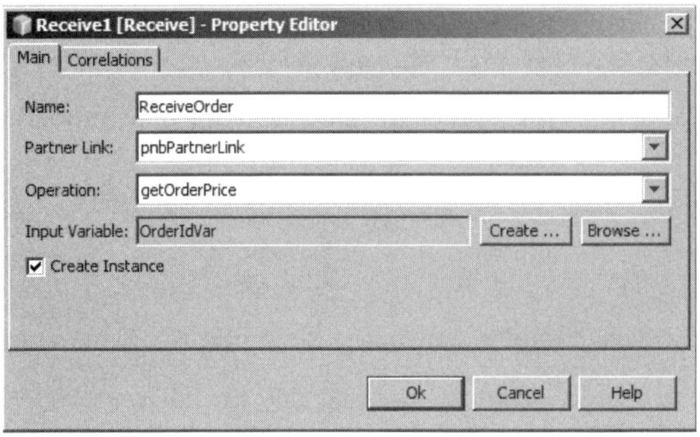

Figure 14-19. *The Receive Property Editor*

Adding a Reply Component

Next, you will add the Reply component, which responds to the partner link with a message allowing the calling web service to retrieve a value. To do so, follow these steps:

1. Select the Reply component in the Palette window and drag it over the Receive component in the BPEL process.
2. While holding down the mouse button, move the mouse straight down until the orange dotted circle target below the Receive component becomes filled in. This indicates that you are over a target location where you can drop the component.
3. Release the mouse button to add the Reply component to the BPEL process.
4. Double-click the Reply component to open the Reply Property Editor window, as shown in Figure 14-20.

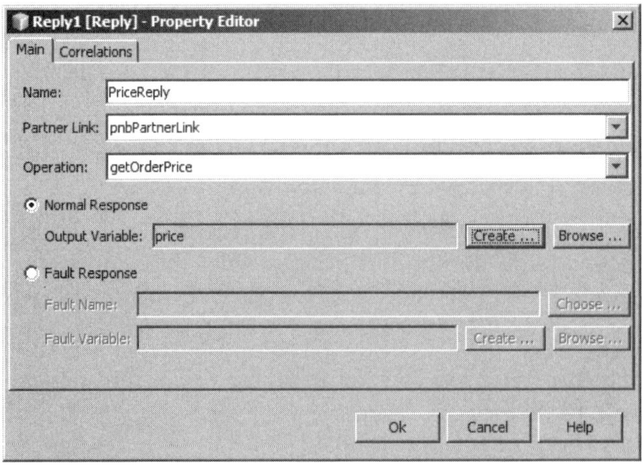

Figure 14-20. *The Reply Property Editor*

5. In the Reply Property Editor window, specify the name of the Reply component as it will appear in the BPEL process. Also specify to which partner link and operation the component will send a reply.

6. In the "Output Variable" field, create a new variable or specify an existing variable that will hold the reply message to be transmitted back to the partner link.

7. Click the OK button to proceed.

At this point, the BPEL process should contain a Partner Link component, a Receive component, and a Reply component, as shown in Figure 14-21. The remaining steps you will perform determine how the input variable is checked, what conditions apply, and how the output variable is set.

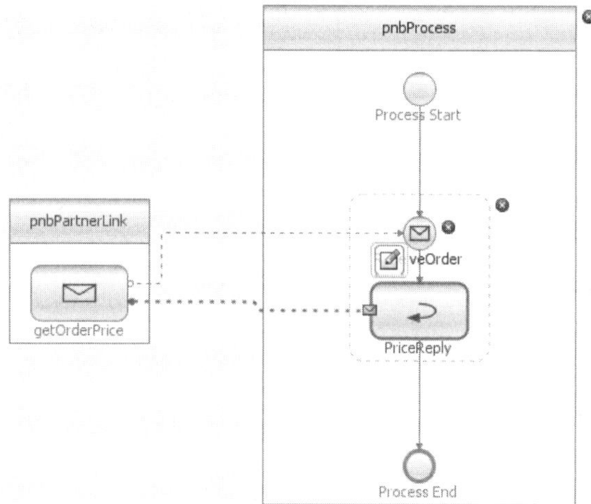

Figure 14-21. *The BPEL process containing Partner Link, Receive, and Reply components*

Adding an If Component

Next, to add a conditional check to the BPEL process, do the following:

1. Click the If component in the Palette window and drag it over the BPEL process.

2. Move the mouse directly below the Receive component and drop the If component into the circle target below the Receive component. Now you need to configure the If component using the BPEL Mapper.

3. Open the BPEL Mapper window by selecting Window ➤ Other ➤ BPEL Mapper or pressing Ctrl+Shift+9.

4. To configure the If component to check an input variable and return true if a certain condition is met, click Operator in the BPEL Mapper window menu bar and select EQUAL. The EQUAL element appears in the center section of the BPEL Mapper window. It contains two lines with variables `any1` and `any2` and a third line labeled `return Boolean`.

5. Select Number ➤ Number Literal. This adds a single-line element labeled Number Literal. Double-click the empty line and enter a value, such as `1000`.

6. In the left pane, expand the Variables node until you find the `OrderIdVar` variable.

7. Drag the `OrderIdVar` variable to the right and drop it onto the `any1` line of the EQUAL element. A line connecting the two elements will appear.

8. Click and drag a line between the Number Literal element connecting it to the `any2` line of the EQUAL element.

9. Click and drag a line between the return Boolean line of the EQUAL element and the Result node in the right pane of the BPEL Mapper window. The final result should look similar to Figure 14-22.

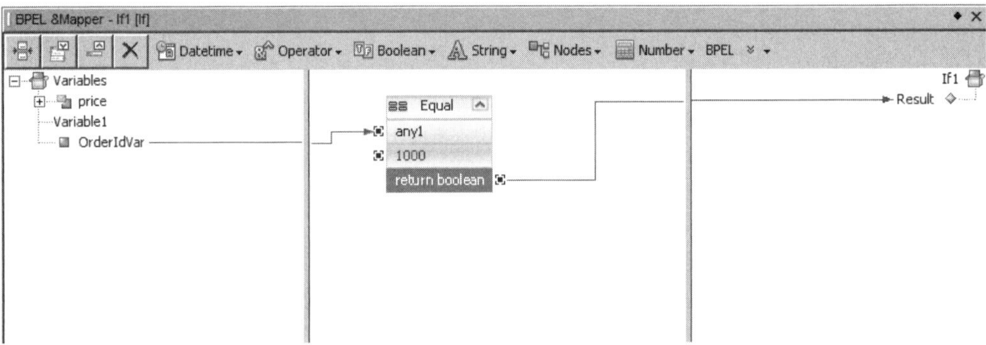

Figure 14-22. *The If component configured in the BPEL Mapper*

Adding an Assign Component

Continue with the following steps to add an Assign component and finish creating the sample BPEL process:

1. Drag an Assign component from the Palette window onto the BPEL process in between the two pieces of the If component.

2. Click the Assign component in the BPEL process and open the BPEL Mapper window (select Window ➤ Other ➤ BPEL Mapper or press Ctrl+Shift+9).

3. Add a Number Literal element by selecting Number ➤ Number Literal.

4. Once the Number Literal element is displayed in the center pane of the BPEL Mapper window, double-click it and enter a number, such as `123456789`.

5. Click and drag a line from the Number Literal element over to the `Price` variable in the right pane of the BPEL Mapper window, as shown in Figure 14-23.

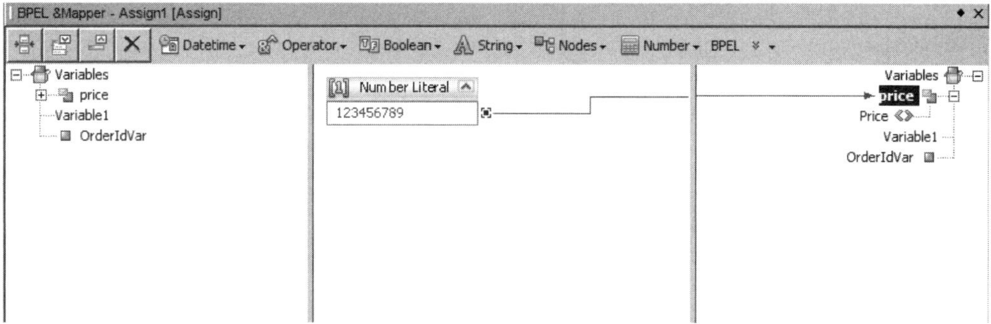

Figure 14-23. *Configuring the Assign component in the BPEL Mapper window*

Reviewing the Completed BPEL Process

The finished BPEL process should look similar to Figure 14-24 and perform the following steps:

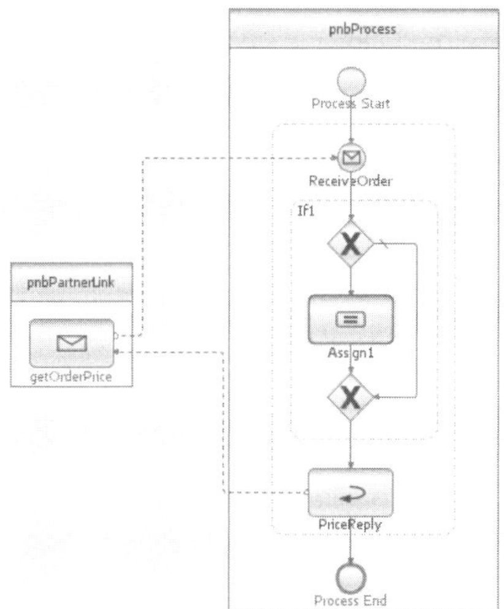

Figure 14-24. *The completed BPEL process*

- The BPEL process receives a message from a web service and assigns it to the `OrderIdVar` variable.
- The process compares the `OrderIdVar` variable to a numeric value of `1000`. If the variable is equal to `1000`, the If condition succeeds and activates the Assign component.
- The Assign component will assign the value of `123456789` to the `Price` variable.
- The If component finishes and hands off control to the Reply component.
- The Reply component passes the `Price` variable back as a response to the partner link web service.

■ **Tip** You can print a copy of the BPEL process design from the IDE. To see a print preview first, with the BPEL file open in the BPEL Design window, select File ➤ Print Preview.

Once the BPEL process is complete, you need to add it to a Composite Application project in order to use it, as described in the next section.

Creating a Composite Application

A Composite Application project is deployed to a Java Business Integration (JBI) server. The GlassFish server mentioned in previous chapters fully supports JBI server functionality. You can add a JBI module to it to execute your business application (also known as a BPEL Module).

Creating a Composite Application Project

To create a new Composite Application project, perform the following steps:

1. Select File ➤ New Project from the main menu.
2. In the New Project window, select SOA from the categories section on the left and Composite Application from the list of projects on the right. Click the Next button.
3. In the Name and Location screen, enter a project name and location.
4. Click the Finish button to generate the Composite Application project.

Setting Composite Application Project Properties

You can review and configure several project properties that affect the Composite Application project. To access the properties, right-click the project name and select Properties from the context menu.

In the Project Properties window, you will see several nodes in the left pane. If you select a node, the related properties appear in the right pane of the window. The different nodes and their properties are as follows:

General: Displays properties such as Service Assembly Alias, Service Assembly Description, Service Unit Alias, and Service Unit Description.

Packaging Project: Displays properties that define the target components and service assembly artifacts for the Composite Application project, as shown in Figure 14-25. Also allows you to specify the JBI filename, which is typically a JAR file that is deployed to the target application server.

Running Project: Displays a drop-down list of available application servers that support JBI functionality.

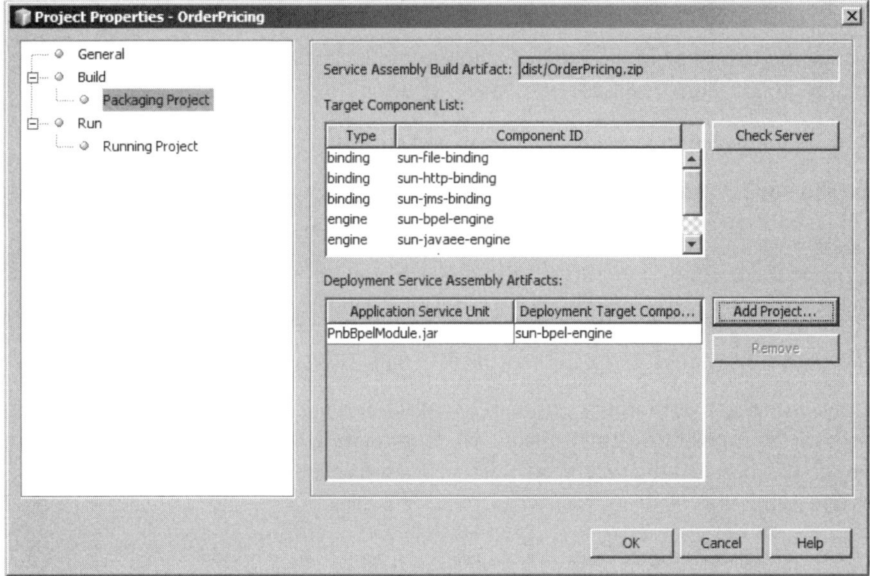

Figure 14-25. *The Composite Application project's Packaging Project properties*

Adding a JBI Module

To enable the Composite Application project to use the BPEL Module project created in the previous section, you need to add a JBI module by following these steps:

1. Right-click the JBI Modules node in the Projects window and select Add JBI Module.
2. In the Select Project dialog box, locate and select a BPEL Module project, and then click the Add Project JAR Files button. The JAR file for the BPEL Module project will appear under the JBI Modules node.
3. Once the JBI module has been added to the Composite Application project, deploy it to the JBI application server by right-clicking the project name and selecting Deploy Project.

■ **Note** You must first start the target application server before you can deploy the Composite Application project.

Testing the Composite Application and BPEL Process

NetBeans composite applications allow you to write test cases similar to JUnit tests. You can generate a test case that exercises a web service that, in turn, runs the BPEL process.

To create a new test case for your Composite Application project, do the following:

1. Right-click the Test node in the Projects window and select New Test Case from the context menu. The New Test Case wizard will appear.
2. In the first window, enter the test case name and click the Next button.
3. Expand the node for the BPEL Module and select the WSDL file that contains the operation to test. Click the Next button to proceed to the next window.
4. Select the actual operation defined by the WSDL file you previously selected.
5. Click the Finish button to generate the test. The new test will appear under the Test node in the Projects window for the Composite Application project.

The new test contains two subnodes: Input and Output. If you double-click the Input node, a file will open in the Source Editor named `Input.xml`. It contains XML content that represents a SOAP message, as shown in Figure 14-26, which will be passed to the web service and, in turn, passed to the BPEL process.

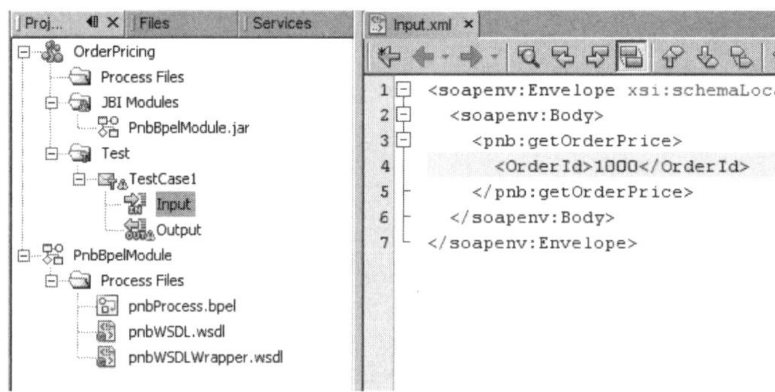

Figure 14-26. *The input SOAP message*

To customize the input passed to the web service, you can change the text inside the `<OrderId>` and `</OrderId>` tags. This is the value assigned to the `OrderId` variables received by the Receive component in the BPEL process. Once you have configured the Input node text, you can execute the test in one of two ways:

- Right-click the project name and select Test Project, or press Alt+F6 to execute all of the tests in a project. For this example, this executes the single test contained under the Test node in the Composite Application project.
- To execute a specific test, right-click the test and select Run from the context menu.

Once your test runs, it will load the results into the Output node and the matching `Output.xml`. The `Output.xml` file shows the output SOAP message that results, which contains the value `123456789` in this example:

```
<soapenv:Envelope
xsi:schemaLocation="http://schemas.xmlsoap.org/soap/envelope/ ➥
http://schemas.xmlsoap.org/soap/envelope/" ➥
```

```
xmlns:xsi="http://www.w3.org/2001/XMLSchema-instance" ➥
xmlns:xsd="http://www.w3.org/2001/XMLSchema" ➥
xmlns:soapenv="http://schemas.xmlsoap.org/soap/envelope/" ➥
xmlns:pnb="http://j2ee.netbeans.org/wsdl/pnbWSDL">
  <soapenv:Body>
    <pnb:getOrderPriceResponse>
      <Price>123456789</Price>
    </pnb:getOrderPriceResponse>
  </soapenv:Body>
</soapenv:Envelope>
```

Creating RESTful Web Services

One of the myriad new technologies in the area of web services is the concept of Representational State Transfer (also known as REST). It's a type of architecture for defining and addresses web resources without the use of messaging layers like SOAP.

This section assumes you have a basic working knowledge of RESTful Web Services using Java. It will explain how best to use NetBeans to work with them. At the time of this writing, the Java API for RESTful Web Services, JSR-311, was still being finalized. Some of the APIs, and the NetBeans support of them, are thus subject to change.

Installing the RESTful Module

To begin taking advantage of RESTful technologies in NetBeans, you must first install the module. It is available from the NetBeans Beta update center and in the near future hopefully will be part of the standard NetBeans module offerings.

To locate and install the module do the following:

1. Go to the main menu and select Tools ➤ Plugins. The Plugin Manager window will open.
2. Select the Available Plugins tab and click the Reload Catalog button. The remote update centers will be checked for new plugins.
3. Scroll down the list of available plugins and locate the one named RESTful Web Services.
4. Select the check box next to the module name and click the Install button. A plugin installer prompt will pop open. Click the Next button.
5. Select the radio button next to the "I accept the terms" field and click the Install button.
6. You should see a message denoting the success or failure of the plugin installation process. Click the Finish button to close the window and return to the Plugin Manager.
7. Click the Close button to exit the Plugin Manager.

The module is now ready to be used. You can verify its installation by searching for it in the Installed tab of the Plugin Manager.

Creating RESTful Web Services from Patterns

NetBeans allows you to create RESTful Web Services in several ways. The New File wizard lets you generate web services from a pattern catalog. The patterns you can use include:

Singleton: Typically a single class with `GET` and `PUT` for wrapping a web service resource.

Container-Item: Creates an item resource class and a container resource class. Utilizes a `POST` method for adding to the container.

Client-Controlled Container-Item: Creates an item resource class and a container resource class. Utilizes a `PUT` method for adding to the container.

Creating the Service

Before you can create a RESTful Web Service, you need to create a web application to contain it. Use the New Project wizard to create a new Web Application. Once the Web Application has been generated, locate it in the Projects window. To create a RESTful Web Service from a pattern, do the following:

1. Right-click the project name and select New ➤ Other. The New File wizard will appear.
2. Select Web Services from the list of Categories.
3. Select RESTful Web Services from Patterns from the list of File Types.
4. Click the Next button. The Select Pattern screen will appear, as shown in Figure 14-27.

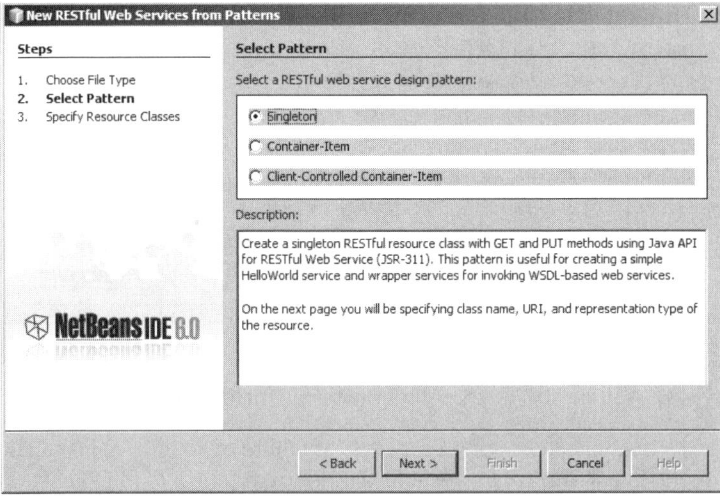

Figure 14-27. *The Select Pattern screen*

5. Select the radio button next to the Singleton item. Then click the Next button. The Specify Resource Classes screen will appear.
6. For the "Resource Package" field, enter the value `com.pronetbeans.examples`.

7. For the "Resource Name" field, enter the value `Customer`.

8. Select the value `text/html` from the MIME Type drop-down field.

9. Enter the value `java.lang.String` for the "Representation Class" field. The Specify Resource Classes screen should contain the values displayed in Figure 14-28.

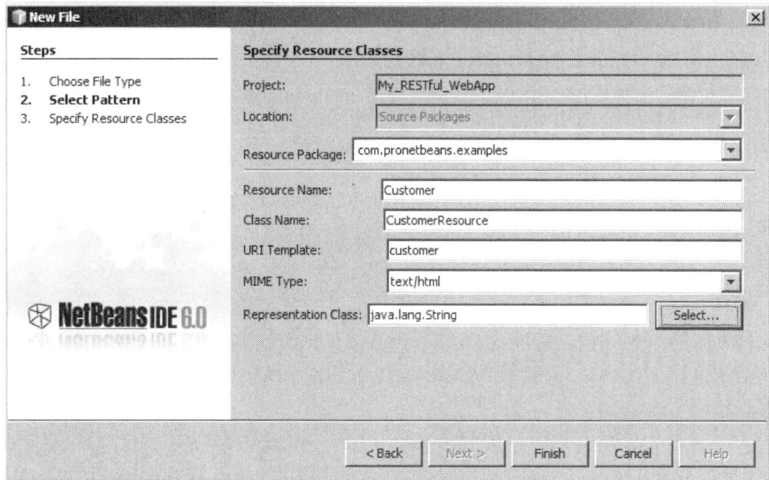

Figure 14-28. *The Specify Resource Classes screen*

10. To generate the web service, click the Finish button. The New File wizard will close.

The web service will be generated and will be available in the project. If you look at the Projects window, the project will now contain a node named RESTful Web Services. If you expand the node, the CustomerResource you created will appear under it. You can double-click it to open the matching CustomerResource.java source file.

The stub code that was generated by the New File wizard looks like the following (plus the Javadoc statements that were removed for brevity):

```
@UriTemplate("customer")
public class CustomerResource {

    @HttpContext
    private UriInfo context;

    public CustomerResource() {
    }

    @HttpMethod("GET")
    @ProduceMime("text/html")
    public String getHtml() {
        //TODO return proper representatin object
        throw new UnsupportedOperationException();
    }
```

```
    @HttpMethod("PUT")
    @ConsumeMime("text/html")
    public void putHtml(String content) {
    }
}
```

This gives you the basic code you need to get started with writing your web service.

You should modify the getHtml method so that it does not throw an UnsupportedOperationException. I changed it as follows:

```
public String getHtml() {
    return "Hello RESTful World";
}
```

The RESTful Web Services can now be tested.

Testing the Service

To test a RESTful Web Service in NetBeans, you can use a special testing page that can be generated. Right-click the project name in the Projects window and select Test RESTful Web Services from the context menu.

The application will trigger a build, the associated Java application server will start, and the default web browser should open, pointing to the test page. The test page lists each service on the left. If you select the hyperlinked service, you can see the resource and an area for Test Input, as shown in Figure 14-29.

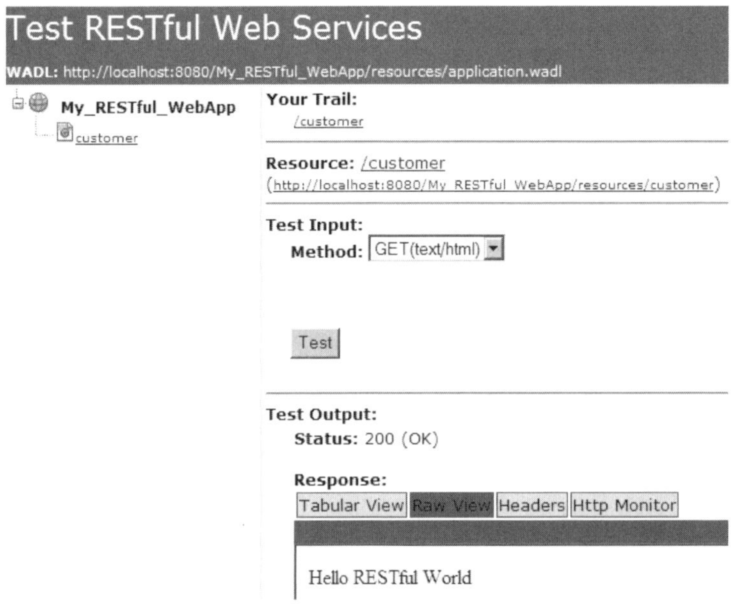

Figure 14-29. *The test page for a RESTful Web Service*

The Test Input section lets you select the method to test. The methods are the Java methods in the `CustomerResource` class that you annotated with `@GET`, `@POST`, and so on. If you select the GET option and click the Test button, the page will refresh. Select the Raw View tab in the Test Output section and you should see the output shown in Figure 14-29.

Creating a Client to Read the Service

NetBeans also contains a wizard for generating a RESTful client to read the web services you created. Using the Web Application project from the last section, you can create the client. Perform the following steps:

1. Right-click the project name and select New ➤ Other. The New File wizard will appear.
2. Select Web Services from the list of Categories.
3. Select RESTful Web Service Client Stubs from the list of File Types.
4. Click the Next button. The Select Projects Containing RESTful Web Services screen will appear, as shown in Figure 14-30.

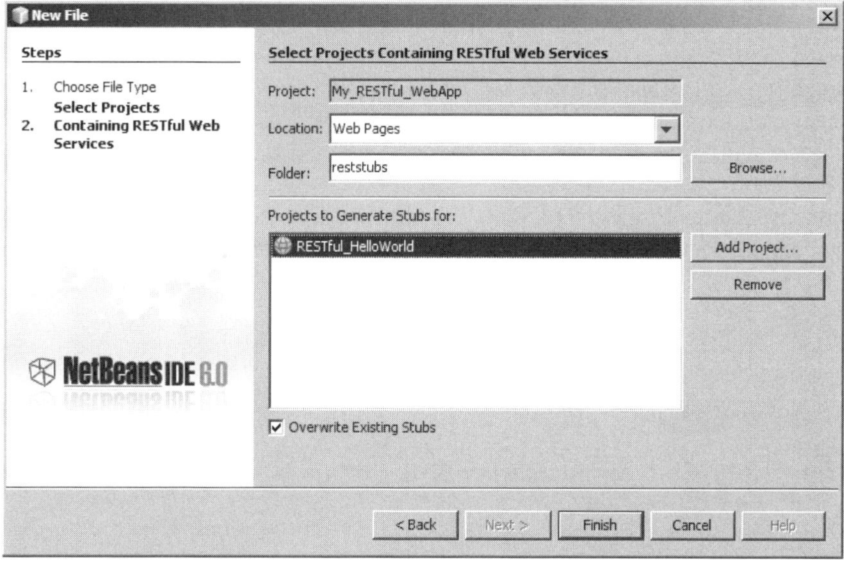

Figure 14-30. *The Select Projects Containing RESTful Web Services screen*

5. Specify a value for the "Folder" field. It is set to `reststubs` by default.
6. Click the Add Project button to select a project that contains the RESTful Web Services. Select the RESTful_HelloWorld project you created in the previous section.
7. Click the Finish button to end the New File wizard and generate the client stubs.

The wizard will generate a folder named `reststubs`. It will contain an HTML file, `reststub.html`, and several JavaScript files: `RESTful_HelloWorld.js`, `helloworld.js`, and `support.js`. These files make up the client stub you can use to call the RESTful Web Service you generated in the previous section.

Summary

In this chapter, we discussed working with web services using JAX-WS, SOA, BPEL, and REST. The NetBeans IDE provides a variety of tools for making it easier to work with these technologies. You first learned how to install SOA and BPEL support. Then you moved on to creating web services using JAX-WS and Java EE 5 annotations, adding an operation, and testing it. Creating a web service is extremely easy in NetBeans, and you can use the available wizards to generate operations. The GlassFish server provides a web testing application that you can use to test a web service.

As you learned, NetBeans also allows you to create a web service client that executes a remote web service, and you have the option to create empty skeleton web services and generate web services from a WSDL file. You can also create message and logical handlers that allow you to read and modify the header and body of a SOAP message.

You also learned how to model a business process using BPEL visual design tools. You can add a variety of BPEL components onto a canvas and use a visual mapping tool to create logical expressions. The BPEL process can interact with web services using components called partner links, which allow a web service to pass in and retrieve variables from a business process. You can then add the BPEL module to a composite application, which can be deployed and tested on a JBI application server.

Finally, the chapter discussed RESTful Web Services. It walked through the process for installing the module and using the NetBeans wizards to generate a new web service and client.

CHAPTER 15

Developing GUI Applications

NetBeans has some impressive capabilities for developing Java GUI applications. First, it provides the Matisse GUI Builder, which allows for what-you-see-is-what-you-get (WYSIWYG) design of applications. The GUI Builder includes intuitive, easy-to-use features, such as guides, anchors, and the GroupLayout approach to component layout. When combined with the other NetBeans features, this gives developers a professional coding environment for developing full-fledged desktop applications.

JSR-296 defines the Swing Application Framework, which intends to simplify the building of Java Desktop Applications. NetBeans 6 provides some basic support for this framework and allows you to utilize some of its features.

NetBeans 6 also provides support for JSR-295, Beans Binding, which allows you to synchronize values of GUI components with values in entity classes.

In this chapter we review how to create, develop, and build a simple GUI application. The main features of NetBeans GUI building tools are covered, such as the main GUI Builder window, the GUI components available in the Palette window, and the different database-related and Beans Binding features added in NetBeans 6.

Creating a Simple GUI Application

This section shows how to create a simple GUI application in NetBeans. You will learn how to generate the project, add the visual Java components into the project, and execute the application. In this section you will build a simple GUI application for enabling text-to-speech capabilities using the FreeTTS library.

Working with the Palette Window

One of the first tools to understand when working with GUI applications is the list of available components in the Palette window. When you have a Swing- or AWT-based Java class open in the IDE, the contextual nature of the Palette window allows it to display the various GUI-related components, as shown in Figure 15-1.

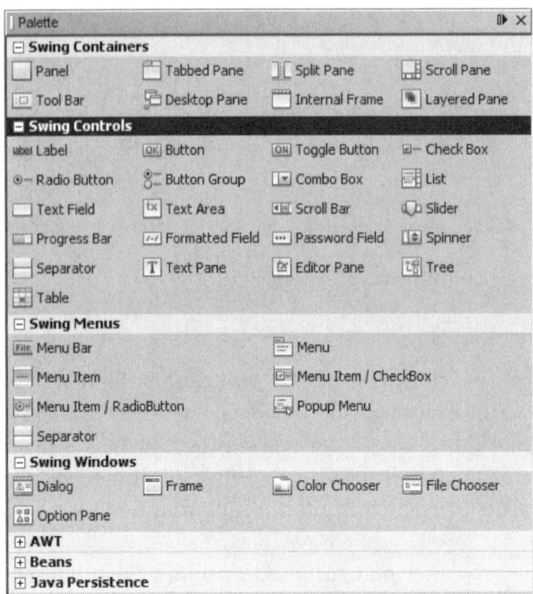

Figure 15-1. *The Palette window, displaying the available GUI components*

As you can see in Figure 15-1, the Palette window provides components for Swing Containers, Swing Controls, Swing Menus, and Swing Windows that are part of the `javax.swing` package, as shown in Tables 15-1, 15-2, 15-3, and 15-4.

Table 15-1. *Swing Container Components Available in the Palette Window*

Component Name	Representative Class
Panel	`javax.swing.JPanel`
Tabbed Pane	`javax.swing.JTabbedPane`
Split Pane	`javax.swing.JSplitPane`
Scroll Pane	`javax.swing.JScrollPane`
Tool Bar	`javax.swing.JToolBar`
Desktop Pane	`javax.swing.JDesktopPane`
Internal Frame	`javax.swing.JInternalFrame`
Layered Pane	`javax.swing.JLayeredPane`

Table 15-2. *Swing Control Components Available in the Palette Window*

Component Name	Representative Class
Label	`javax.swing.JLabel`
Button	`javax.swing.JButton`
Toggled Button	`javax.swing.JToggleButton`
Check Box	`javax.swing.JCheckBox`
Radio Button	`javax.swing.JRadioButton`
Button Group	`javax.swing.ButtonGroup`
Combo Box	`javax.swing.JComboBox`
List	`javax.swing.JList`
Text Field	`javax.swing.JTextField`
Text Area	`javax.swing.JTextArea`
Scroll Bar	`javax.swing.JScrollBar`
Slider	`javax.swing.JSlider`
Progress Bar	`javax.swing.JProgressBar`
Formatted Field	`javax.swing.JFormattedTextField`
Password Field	`javax.swing.JPasswordField`
Spinner	`javax.swing.JSpinner`
Separator	`javax.swing.JSeparator`
Text Pane	`javax.swing.JTextPane`
Editor Pane	`javax.swing.JEditorPane`
Tree	`javax.swing.JTree`
Table	`javax.swing.JTable`

Table 15-3. *Swing Menu Components Available in the Palette Window*

Component Name	Representative Class
Menu Bar	`javax.swing.JMenuBar`
Menu	`javax.swing.JMenu`
Menu Item	`javax.swing.JMenuItem`
Menu Item/CheckBox	`javax.swing.JCheckBoxMenuItem`
Menu Item/RadioButton	`javax.swing.JRadioButtonMenuItem`
Popup Menu	`javax.swing.JPopupMenu`
Separator	`javax.swing.JSeparator`

Table 15-4. *Swing Window Components Available in the Palette Window*

Component Name	Representative Class
Dialog	`javax.swing.JDialog`
Frame	`javax.swing.JFrame`
Color Chooser	`javax.swing.JColorChooser`
File Chooser	`javax.swing.JFileChooser`
Option Pane	`javax.swing.JOptionPane`

The Palette window also provides AWT components that are part of the `java.awt` package, as shown in Table 15-5. The Beans and Java Persistence sections in Figure 15-1 are interfaces from the `javax.persistence` package for working with persistence units.

Table 15-5. *AWT Components Available in the Palette Window*

Component Name	Representative Class
Label	`java.awt.Label`
Button	`java.awt.Button`
Text Field	`java.awt.TextField`
Text Area	`java.awt.TextArea`
Checkbox	`java.awt.Checkbox`
Choice	`java.awt.Choice`
List	`java.awt.List`
Scrollbar	`java.awt.Scrollbar`
Scroll Pane	`java.awt.ScrollPane`
Panel	`java.awt.Panel`
Canvas	`java.awt.Canvas`
Menu Bar	`java.awt.MenuBar`
Popup Menu	`java.awt.PopupMenu`

Creating the Project

You can create Java GUI applications inside a standard NetBeans Java Application project. You can create the project by performing the following steps:

1. Select File ➤ New Project from the main menu.
2. In the New Project window, select Java from the Categories list and Java Application from the Projects list. Click the Next button to continue.
3. In the Name and Location screen, enter a value for the "Project Name" field.

4. Next, select a value for the "Project Location" field by using the Browse button.
5. Finally, uncheck the "Create Main Class" field. There is no need to generate an empty `Main` class at this point. This will set up the correct properties for the project, as shown in Figure 15-2. Click the Finish button to finalize the creation of the project.

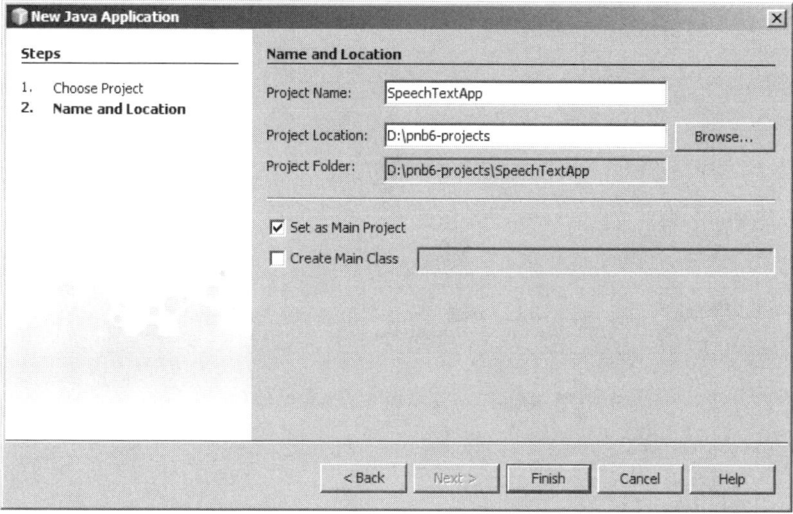

Figure 15-2. *The Name and Location screen in the New Project window*

Once the project has been generated, it will open in the Projects window. You can now add classes to it and continue creating the text-to-speech application.

Creating the Initial JFrame Class

To add a Java `JFrame` class, do the following:

1. In the Projects window, right-click the Source Packages node and select New ➤ Other from the context menu.
2. In the New File window, select Swing GUI Forms from the Categories list on the left and JFrame Form from the File Types list on the right. Click the Next button to continue.
3. In the Name and Location screen, enter a value for the "Class Name" field, such as `SayIt`.
4. Next, enter a Java package hierarchy in the "Package" field, such as `com.pronetbeans.examples`, as shown in Figure 15-3.
5. Finally, click the Finish button to generate the class. It will open in the Form Editor (a special GUI editing tool discussed in the next few sections).

The new `SayIt` class will be generated. The matching form will display in the Form Editor, as discussed in the next section.

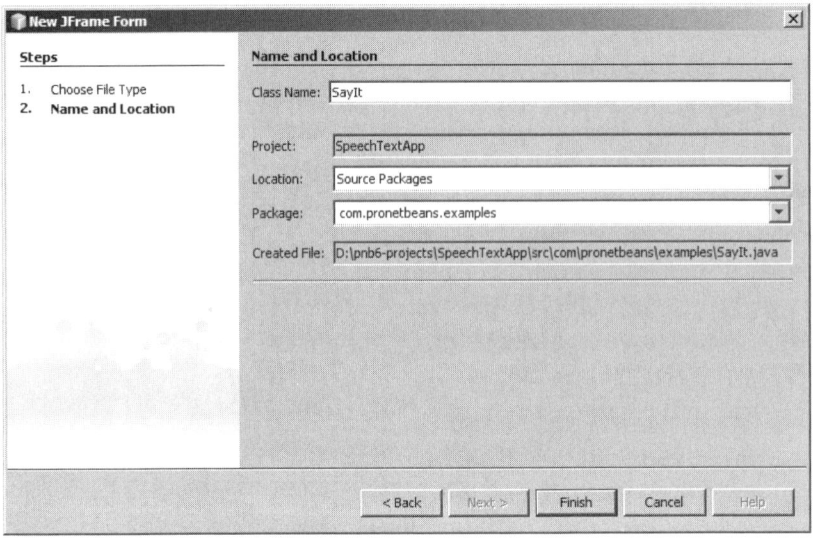

Figure 15-3. *The Name and Location screen for the new JFrame class*

Working with the Form Editor

Once you have created a Java class to represent the GUI, you can begin to work with it in the NetBeans Form Editor. The Form Editor is similar to the standard Source Editor. It provides a code-based view of the Java `SayIt` class and a WYSIWYG view of the GUI form of the `SayIt` class.

The first time you open the `SayIt` class in the Form Editor, it will show the Design view by default, with the Design icon selected. It will display a rectangular grey area, as shown in Figure 15-4, where you can add components from the palette to design visually the GUI form you will create.

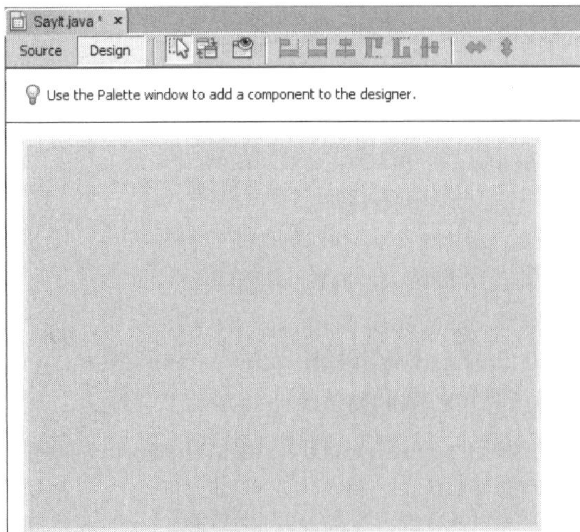

Figure 15-4. *A blank JFrame displayed in Design view in the Form Editor*

Understanding the Form Editor Toolbar

Along the top of the Form Editor is a toolbar displaying GUI-related items and actions. As shown in Figure 15-4, the Source and Design icons appear on the left side of the toolbar. If you select the Source icon, the Form Editor will display the Java source code for the `SayIt` class. The toolbar will also change to look nearly identical to the standard source code–based toolbar displayed by the Source Editor, except for one difference. The toolbar still includes the Source and Design icons. If you select the Design icon, you will toggle back to the WYSIWYG Design view of the `SayIt` class in the Form Editor.

The toolbar displayed in the Design view of the Form Editor, as shown in Figure 15-4, contains other useful icons. If you place the mouse over each icon, a pop-up tooltip is displayed. The icons and their intention are as follows:

Selection Mode: The default mode of the Form Editor. It allows you to select components, move them around on the form, and add new components to the form.

Connection Mode: An alternate mode for the Form Editor. It allows you to generate code that modifies one component (the target) via an action from another component (the source). This is discussed in more detail in the later section "Adding Events Using Connection Mode."

Preview Design: Opens the form in a new pop-up window, allowing you to see how it would look if you actually built and ran the project. Note that no event-handling code is actually triggered, even though you can click buttons, enter text, and so on.

Align left in column: Aligns the left edge of two or more components in the form.

Align right in column: Aligns the right edge of two or more components in the form.

Center horizontally: Horizontally aligns two or more components in the form using the exact center of each component.

Align top in row: Aligns the top edge of two or more components in the form.

Align bottom in row: Aligns the bottom edge of two or more components in the form.

Center vertically: Vertically aligns two or more components in the form using the exact center of each component.

Change horizontal resizability: Enabled or disabled for each component. If enabled, it allows the component to be automatically resized horizontally when the parent `JFrame` is resized horizontally. You can resize the `JFrame` by clicking and holding the lower-right corner of it and moving the mouse.

Change vertical resizability: Enabled or disabled for each component. If enabled, it allows the component to be automatically resized vertically when the parent `JFrame` is resized vertically. You can resize the `JFrame` by clicking and holding the lower-right corner of it and moving the mouse.

Adding Components to the Form

Once you have created a form, you can add components to it. There are several ways to do this, such as using the components displayed in the Palette window and using the Add Mode icon on the toolbar.

The Add Mode icon on the Form Editor toolbar is not displayed by default. To display it, right-click on an empty place on the toolbar and select Show Add Button from the context menu that appears. A new icon will appear on the Form Editor toolbar that looks like a plus sign, as shown in Figure 15-5. If you place the mouse over the icon the tooltip should state "Add Mode."

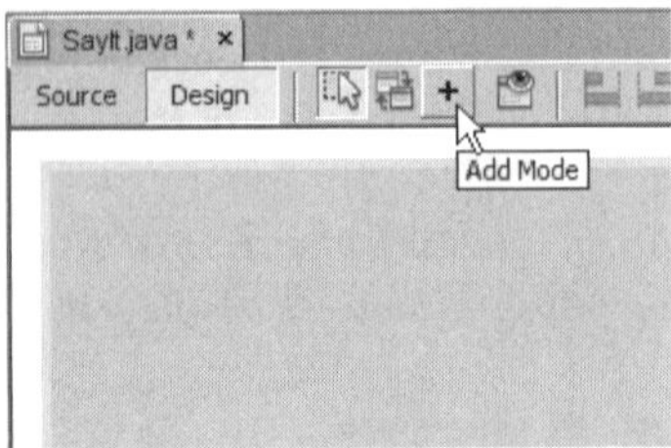

Figure 15-5. *The Add Mode icon on the Form Editor toolbar*

You can now click the Add Mode button to display a set of menus for adding Swing and AWT components to the form. Click the Add Mode icon and select Swing Controls ➤ Text Area. A text area component will appear on the Palette. You can move the mouse anywhere and the component will follow. When you are ready to finalize the component's position, click the form and the component will be positioned accordingly.

You can also add components to the form by dragging-and-dropping them from the Palette window. With the Palette window displayed, click a component, keep the mouse button pressed, and move the mouse over the form in the Form Editor. The Form Editor will display alignment guidelines for aligning the component with other components, as shown in Figure 15-6.

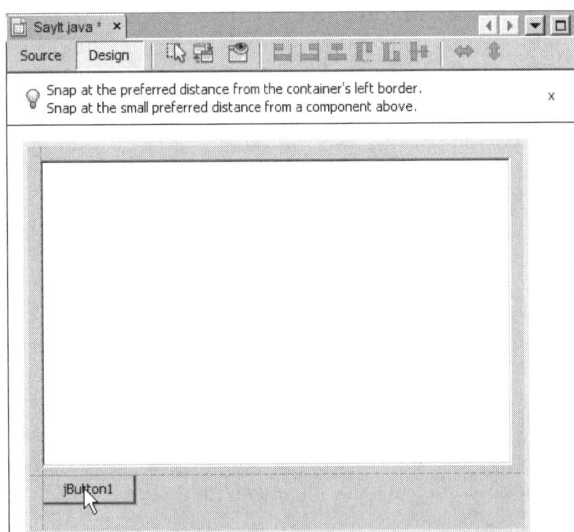

Figure 15-6. *The Form Editor, displaying the text area and button*

Figure 15-6 shows a text area component stretched across most of the form. It also shows an attempt to place a new button component below the text area component. As you move the button component around the form, a series of dashed lines appear in different locations, depending on the component's alignment. It may be difficult to see in Figure 15-6, but a dashed alignment guideline is displayed aligning the left edges of the text area and button components. With the button component selected, if you were to move it away from the left edge of the text area component, then the alignment guideline would disappear.

Next, we will place a second button component onto the form. Drag-and-drop a button component from the Palette and position it in the lower-right corner of the form. With the mouse button still pressed, move the component so that it looks horizontally centered with the first button component shown in Figure 15-6. When the second button component is actually horizontally centered with the first, an alignment guideline will appear confirming that the two components are indeed centered, as shown in Figure 15-7.

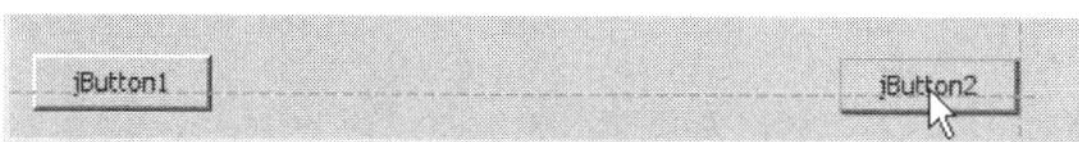

Figure 15-7. *A horizontal alignment guideline centering the buttons*

Modifying Component Properties

Once you have added a text area and two button components to the form, you can modify their properties. Each component, including the JFrame, has a large number of properties you can set directly in NetBeans using the Properties window.

To display the Properties window, select Window ➤ Properties from the main menu or use the keyboard shortcut Ctrl+Shift+7. The Properties window will appear, typically on the right side of the Form Editor. As with any other window, you can click and drag the window's title bar to dock it in a more convenient location.

If you do not have a specific element selected in the Form Editor, the Properties window will appear blank. Select the text area component in the Form Editor, and the Properties window will display properties specific to that component, as shown in Figure 15-8.

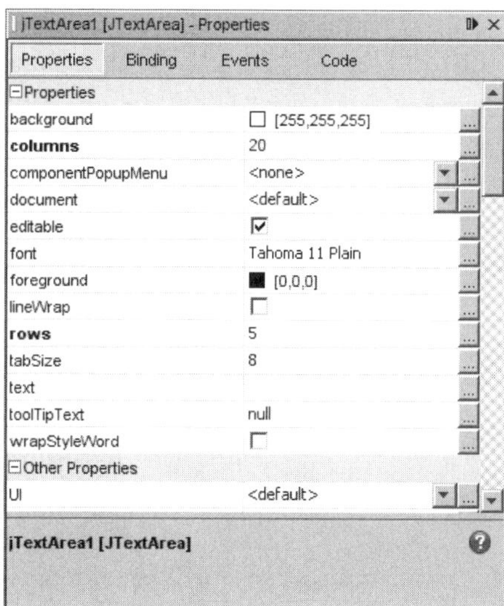

Figure 15-8. *The Properties window, displaying the properties for the text area*

Configure the text area component by doing the following:

1. Select the Properties tab in the Properties window, as shown in Figure 15-8.
2. Set the toolTipText property to "Enter text to be spoken here."
3. Select the Code tab in the Properties window.
4. Set the Variable Name property to "TextToBeSpoken."

Configure the first button component (labeled "jButton1") by doing the following:

1. Select the Properties tab in the Properties window, as shown in Figure 15-8.
2. Set the text property to "Speak Text."
3. Set the toolTipText property to "Click to hear the text in the text area spoken."
4. Select the Code tab in the Properties window.
5. Set the Variable Name property to "SpeakTextButton."

Configure the second button component (labeled "jButton2") by doing the following:

1. Select the Properties tab in the Properties window, as shown in Figure 15-8.
2. Set the text property to "Clear Text."
3. Set the toolTipText property to "Click to clear the text from the text area."
4. Select the Code tab in the Properties window.
5. Set the Variable Name property to "ClearTextButton."

Once you have finished modifying the various properties of the form components, the finished form should look like Figure 15-9.

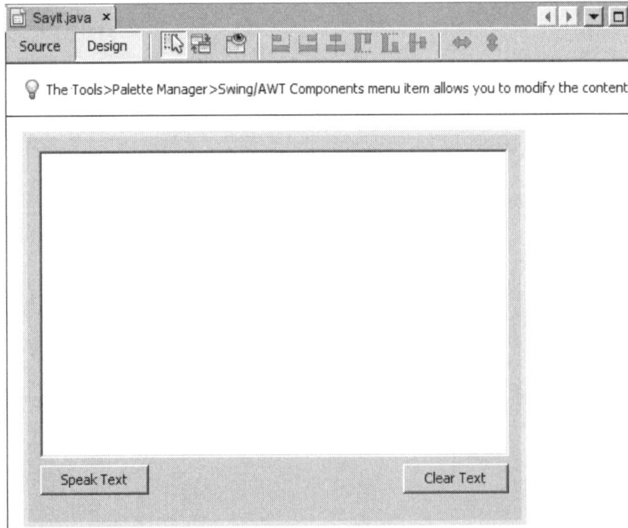

Figure 15-9. *The finished GUI form of the SayIt class*

The SayIt class contains the following autogenerated main method:

```
public static void main(String args[]) {
    java.awt.EventQueue.invokeLater(new Runnable() {
        public void run() {
            new SayIt().setVisible(true);
        }
    });
}
```

This initiates the constructor, which is defined as

```
public SayIt() {
    initComponents();
}
```

The constructor calls the initComponents method, which is private to the class and performs the actual initialization of the components that appear on the form:

```
// <editor-fold defaultstate="collapsed" desc="Generated Code">
private void initComponents() {

    jScrollPane1 = new javax.swing.JScrollPane();
    TextToBeSpoken = new javax.swing.JTextArea();
    SpeakTextButton = new javax.swing.JButton();
    ClearTextButton = new javax.swing.JButton();

    setDefaultCloseOperation(javax.swing.WindowConstants.EXIT_ON_CLOSE);

    TextToBeSpoken.setColumns(20);
    TextToBeSpoken.setRows(5);
    TextToBeSpoken.setToolTipText("Enter text to be spoken here.");

    jScrollPane1.setViewportView(TextToBeSpoken);

    SpeakTextButton.setText("Speak Text");
    SpeakTextButton.setToolTipText(➥
"Click to hear the text in the text area spoken.");

    ClearTextButton.setText("Clear Text");
    ClearTextButton.setToolTipText("Click to clear the text from the text area.");

     // additional GroupLayout initialization code removed
}
```

The private initComponents method initializes an instance of each component that was placed in the Java GUI form of the JFrame class. It then sets several properties of the jTextArea TextToBeSpoken, such as the number of columns, the number of rows, and the text displayed in the tooltip. It also sets the text and tooltip text for each of the buttons.

One of the benefits the Matisse GUI Builder in NetBeans provides is accurate code generation and the ability to keep the autogenerated code up to date, especially when components are changed. The text area and two button components were given default names and properties when they were first added to the form. Changing their properties in the Properties window causes Matisse to rename the instances of the components and to set their properties accordingly.

Adding Events Using Connection Mode

An important concept when working with GUI applications is that of event handling. Whether it is the pressing of a key on the keyboard, the click of a mouse, or some other occurrence, events need to be handled appropriately. Events are how users interact with an application. For the sample speech-to-text application we are developing in this section, we will discuss only a few types of events.

First, the application will allow users to type text into the text area. Then they can click the Speak Text button, causing the FreeTTS code to activate (discussed in the next section). Finally, users can click the Clear Text button to clear the text from the text area and start over. The two events we focus on here are the two button clicks. First we focus on the Clear Text button click event.

There are several ways to add event-handling code using the Matisse GUI Builder. The first is to use the Connection Mode button on the Form Editor toolbar to open the Connection Wizard. Connection Mode allows you to select two components displayed in the form for which event handling is related. For example, if the Clear Text button is clicked (event 1), then the text area component's text property should be set to blank (event 2). Thus, we can use the Connection Mode as follows to generate event-handling code:

1. Click the Connection Mode icon in the Form Editor toolbar.
2. Click the Clear Text button. It will be highlighted with a red border.
3. Click the text area. It will be highlighted with a red border, and the Connection Wizard window will appear.
4. In the Select Source Event screen of the Connection Wizard, expand the plus icon next to the mouse node. This will display the possible mouse-related events.
5. Select the mouseClicked event. The Method Name will suggest a name for the event-handler method that will be generated, as shown in Figure 15-10, but you can edit the text field to any value you wish. Unless you have a good reason, it is usually a best practice to name event handlers with the name of the component to which the event applies, followed by the name of the event. In Figure 15-10, the suggested name is ClearTextButtonMouseClicked. ClearTextButton is the instance name of the component and MouseClicked is the name of the event.
6. Click the Next button to proceed to the Specify Target Operation screen.

7. In the Specify Target Operation screen, the component `TextToBeSpoken` is listed as the target for the operation. This is because it was clicked second when in Connection Mode. Here you can specify that the target component have a property set, a specific method called, or other custom code executed in the class. Click the Set Property radio button.

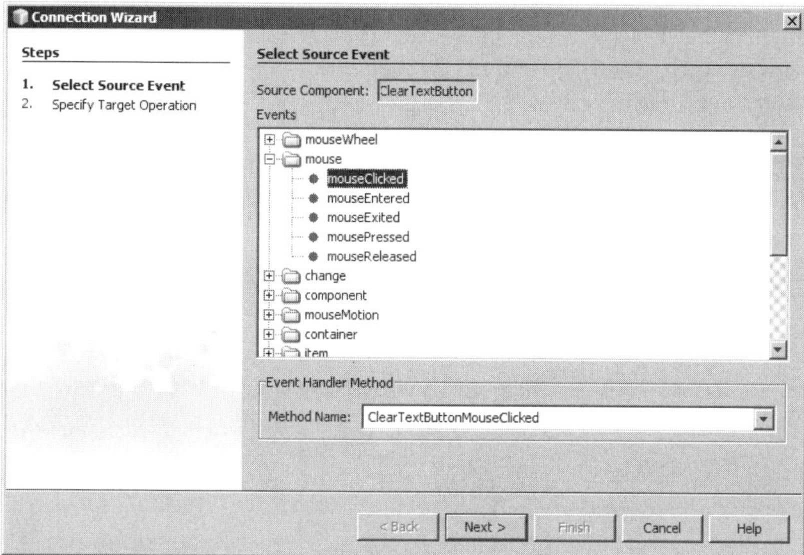

Figure 15-10. *The Select Source Event Screen in the Connection Wizard*

8. Select the text property displayed in the list of properties. The Specify Target Operation screen will look like Figure 15-11.

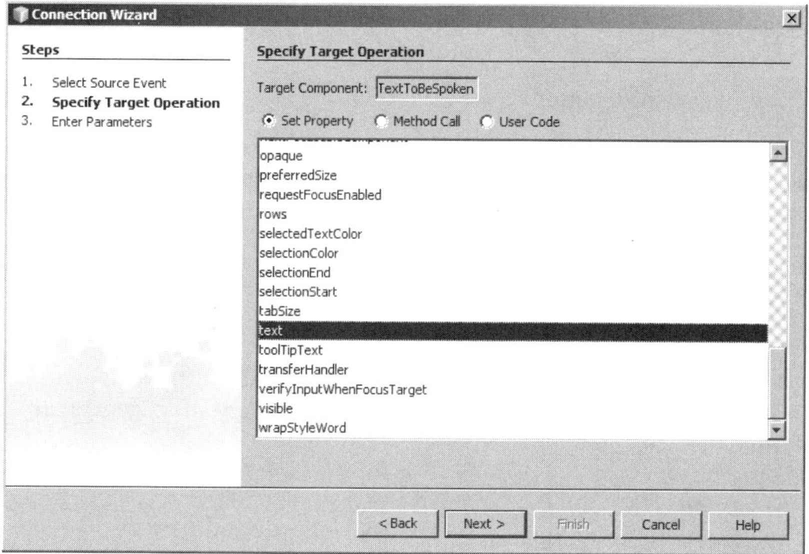

Figure 15-11. *The Specify Target Operation screen in the Connection Wizard*

9. Click the Next button to proceed to the Enter Parameters screen. In this screen you can specify a parameter to use to set the text property of the TextToBeSpoken text area component.

10. Select the Value radio button. The field will become enabled and allow you to enter text. It is empty by default, representing an empty String. Notice that the "Generated Parameters Preview" field at the bottom of the screen shows two quotation marks symbolizing as much, shown in Figure 15-12. This essentially sets the text property of the text area to be blank.

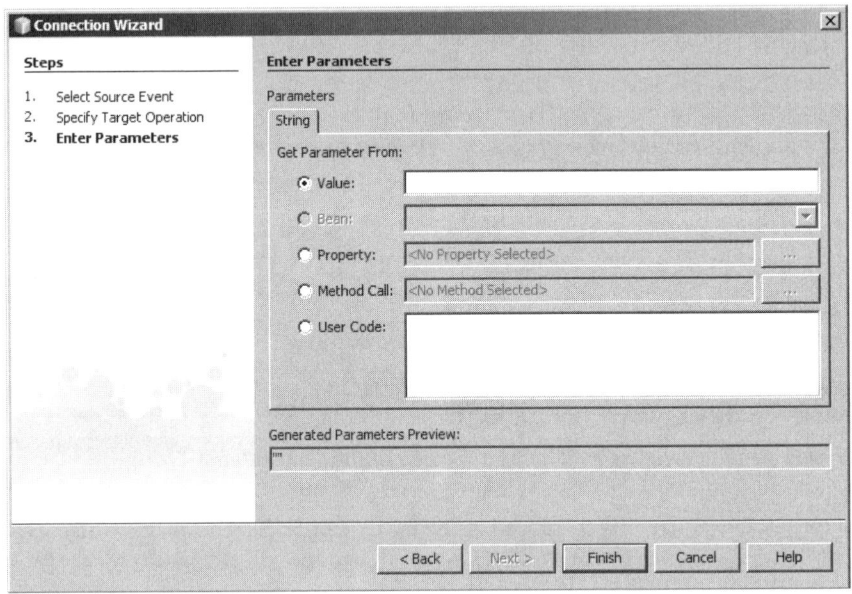

Figure 15-12. *The Enter Parameters screen of the Connection Wizard*

11. Finally, click the Finish button.

After you click the Finish button in the Enter Parameters screen, the Connection Wizard window will disappear. The Form Editor window will automatically switch to the Source view and display the newly added Java source code for the event handler as shown:

```
private void ClearTextButtonMouseClicked(java.awt.event.MouseEvent evt) {
    TextToBeSpoken.setText("");
}
```

The `ClearTextButtonMouseClicked` event-handler method is in turn called by a MouseListener that is added to the ClearTextButton button in the Matisse-generated code in the form:

```
ClearTextButton.addMouseListener(new java.awt.event.MouseAdapter() {
    public void mouseClicked(java.awt.event.MouseEvent evt) {
        ClearTextButtonMouseClicked(evt);
    }
});
```

Adding Events Manually

Obviously, you do not always have to use the Connection Mode to create event-handling code. If you did, then the Matisse GUI Builder tool would not be as useful or easy to use. You can also add event-handling code manually via the context menus for each component of the form.

Right-click the SpeakTextButton and select Events ➤ Mouse ➤ mouseClicked, as shown in Figure 15-13. The Form Editor will switch to the Source view and display the newly generated event-handler method, `SpeakTextButtonMouseClicked`.

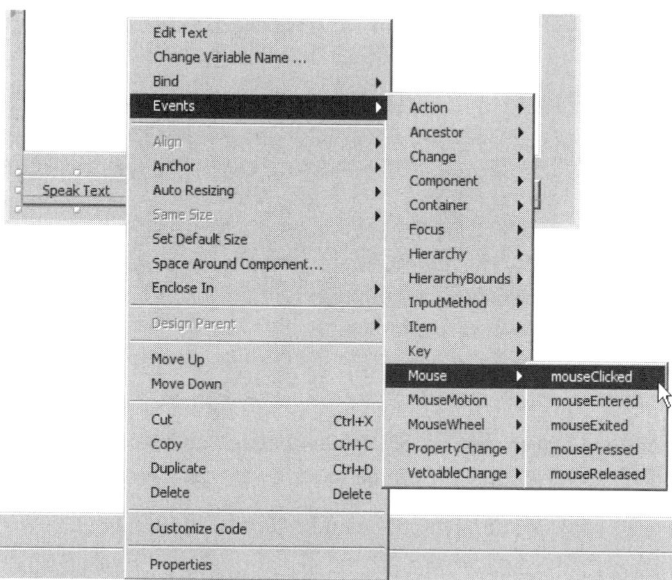

Figure 15-13. *The event-handling submenus on the context menu*

The empty event handler in code looks like the following:

```
private void SpeakTextButtonMouseClicked(java.awt.event.MouseEvent evt) {
    // TODO add your handling code here:
}
```

This also triggers the Form Editor to generate code automatically inside the initComponents method to register the event handler. A new MouseListener is added to the SpeakTextButton, which in turn calls the `SpeakTextButtonMouseClicked` method:

```
SpeakTextButton.addMouseListener(new java.awt.event.MouseAdapter() {
    public void mouseClicked(java.awt.event.MouseEvent evt) {
        SpeakTextButtonMouseClicked(evt);
    }
});
```

You will then need to add the code inside the SpeakTextButtonMouseClicked event handler that takes the text from the text area and enables it to be spoken. This is covered later, in the section "Adding FreeTTS Code to an Event Handler."

Using FreeTTS

The FreeTTS project is a 100 percent pure Java speech synthesis system. Originally based on Flite from Carnegie Mellon University, it was written by Sun Microsystems Laboratories. It provides a Java speech synthesis engine, support for a variety of voices, and partial support for the Java Speech API (JSAPI).

Downloading the Library

To download FreeTTS, go to the project site at `http://freetts.sourceforge.net`. FreeTTS provides several different types of packages for download. For our purposes you will need to download the `bin` package, which contains the compiled binaries of FreeTTS. Once you have downloaded FreeTTS, extract it to a directory on your local machine.

Adding FreeTTS as a Project Library

For the speech-to-text application to be able to use FreeTTS, you need to add it as a library for the project. To add FreeTTS to the project, do the following:

1. In the Projects window, right-click the Libraries node and select Add JAR/Folder.
2. Browse the file system and locate the `freetts.jar` file that was included in the FreeTTS `bin` package you downloaded.
3. Click the Open button in the Add JAR/Folder window. The `freetts.jar` file will then be listed under the Libraries node in the Projects window.

You can now import FreeTTS classes into the project and voice-enable the application that was developed earlier in this chapter.

Adding FreeTTS Code to an Event Handler

Earlier in this chapter, you added the SpeakTextButtonMouseClicked event handler to the SpeakTextButton in the form. The empty event handler in code looks like the following:

```
private void SpeakTextButtonMouseClicked(java.awt.event.MouseEvent evt) {
    // TODO add your handling code here:
}
```

To voice-enable the application, you can modify the method as follows:

```
private void SpeakTextButtonMouseClicked(java.awt.event.MouseEvent evt) {
    String sText = TextToBeSpoken.getText();
    if (sText != null && sText.trim().length() > 0) {
        VoiceManager voiceManager = null;
        Voice syntheticVoice = null;

        try {
            voiceManager = VoiceManager.getInstance();
            syntheticVoice = voiceManager.getVoice("kevin");
            syntheticVoice.allocate();
            syntheticVoice.speak(sText);

        } catch (Exception e) {
            e.printStackTrace();
        } finally {
            syntheticVoice.deallocate();
        }
}
```

First, the method retrieves the text from the SpeakTextButton using the following code:

```
String sText = TextToBeSpoken.getText();
```

It then checks to make sure that the text from the text area has a value. Next, it declares a `VoiceManager` and a `Voice` class. These classes allow you to access the speech engine. The method then retrieves an instance of `VoiceManager` using the `VoiceManager.getInstance` static method and in turn retrieves an instance of `Voice` using `voiceManager.getVoice`.

The code in the SpeakTextButtonMouseClicked event handler then calls the `Voice.allocate` method. This internally creates an audio output thread and audio output handler. You can then call the `Voice.speak` method, which takes a `String` as an argument. This string is the text to be spoken. In the foregoing method, we pass in the text from the text area. In the "finally" clause we call `Voice.deallocate`. This cleans up the audio output thread and shuts down the voice processing.

With the code that is now included in the SpeakTextButtonMouseClicked event-handler, you can now test out the GUI application. To test it out fully, do the following:

1. Turn on your computer's speakers and make sure the audio volume is not on mute.

2. Run the application, selecting Run ➤ Run main project from the main menu.

3. In the form window that appears, type a sentence into the text area.

4. Click the button labeled "Speak Text." You should hear the text you typed spoken by the FreeTTS library.

Using the Swing Application Framework

NetBeans 6 introduces support for the Swing Application Framework, JSR-296. This framework has a set of Java classes that provide an infrastructure common to many Java desktop-based applications. The framework can help offer assistance with commonly used features. Here are several examples:

- GUI state persistence between application executions
- Creating and managing both synchronous and asynchronous actions
- Resource management (strings, images, component labels, tooltips, and so on)

The Swing Application Framework support in NetBeans 6 includes several template project types, various new file wizards, an Action Customizer window for managing actions, tight integration with the Matisse GUI Builder and Form Editor window, and more.

This section discusses how to create a NetBeans project based on the Swing Application Framework as well as how to use the IDE to take full advantage of the framework. For more information on the Swing Application Framework, visit the project site at `https://appframework.dev.java.net`.

Creating a Java Desktop Application Project

The Java Desktop Application is a new project type that provides support for the Swing Application Framework. Creating a project of this type will generate a skeleton application with basic features such as menus, a status bar, and persistence of the GUI state. To create a Java Desktop Application project, perform the following steps:

1. Select File ➤ New Project from the main menu. The New Project window will appear.
2. Select Java from the list of Categories in the left pane of the Choose Project screen.
3. Select Java Desktop Application from the list of Projects in the right pane of the Choose Project screen.
4. Click the Next button to proceed to the Name and Location screen.
5. Enter a value for the "Project Name" field, such as `ProNetBeansDesktopApp`.
6. Choose a value for the "Project Location" field. You can enter one by typing directly in the field or by clicking the Browse button to select one from your local file system.
7. Modify the "Application Class" field to contain an appropriate Java package hierarchy and class name for the initial project form.
8. Select Basic Application from the Choose Application Shell section. The Name and Location screen of the New Desktop Application window should look like Figure 15-14.
9. Click the Finish button to close the New Desktop Application window.

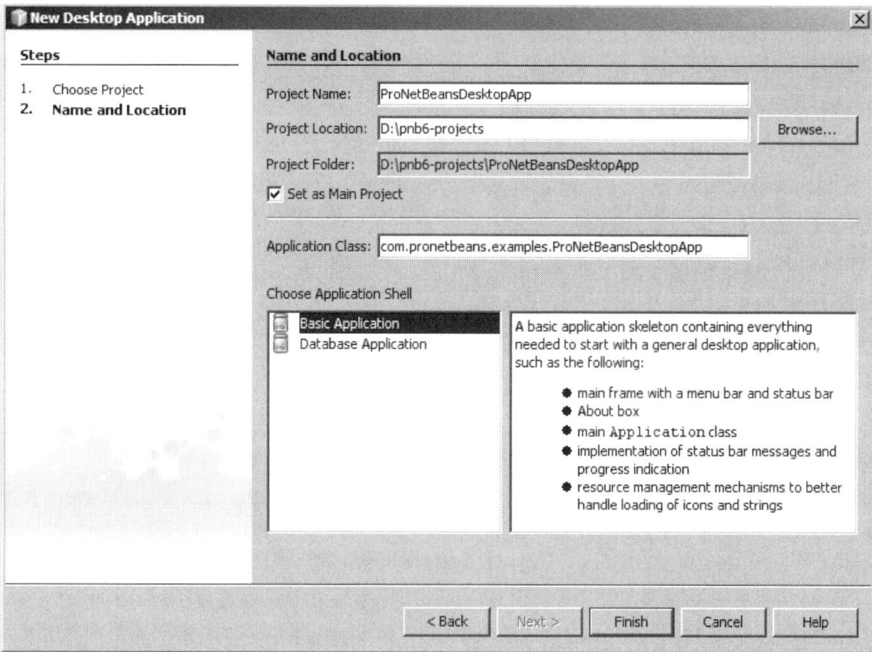

Figure 15-14. *The Name and Location screen for the new Java Desktop Application project*

After you generate the project, a form named `ProNetBeansDesktopView` class opens in the Form Editor, as shown in Figure 15-15. It contains several components, complete with initialization code. A `JMenuBar` is stretched across the top of the main `JFrame`. It contains two `JMenus` with their own `JMenuItems` contained within. The bottom of the `JFrame` also contains several `JLabels` and a `JProgressBar`, for creating a progress bar.

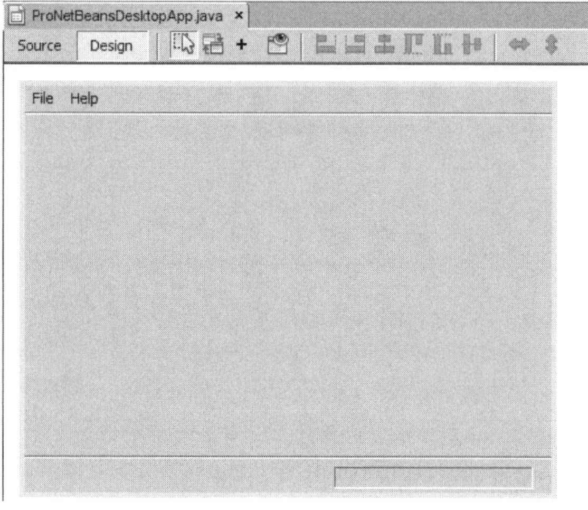

Figure 15-15. *The new skeleton form displayed in the Form Editor*

Next, switch to the Source view of the Form Editor for the ProNetBeansDesktopApp class. The first thing you should notice is that the ProNetBeansDesktopApp class extends the org.jdesktop.application.FrameView class. The FrameView class is the base class for forms in the Swing Application Framework.

The single argument constructor that exists in the class takes a SingleFrameApplication as the argument. It then passes it to the FrameView super class constructor and calls the initComponents methods to initialize the GUI components on the form.

The class defines and instantiates an instance of org.jdesktop.application.ResourceMap. The ResourceMap provides resource management for the entire Java Desktop Application project. It allows the application code to access the name/value properties stored in the ProNetBeansDesktopApp.properties file. The .properties file was generated automatically by the IDE when the project was originally generated.

The remainder of the code in the constructor deals with initializing and setting up the Timer and TaskMonitor classes for the progress bar. The progress bar is visible in the lower-right corner of the form, as shown in Figure 15-15.

The initComponents method was autogenerated by NetBeans when the class was created. It is guarded as autogenerated code and cannot be changed directly in the Form Editor. The code in the initComponents method can be changed by moving and resizing components in the Design view of the Form Editor, changing properties for each component in the Properties window.

It contains code for initializing the GUI components, such as mainPanel = new javax.swing.JPanel();. It also performs the component layout on the form, based on how the components are visually arranged:

```
javax.swing.GroupLayout mainPanelLayout = new javax.swing.GroupLayout(mainPanel);
mainPanel.setLayout(mainPanelLayout);
mainPanelLayout.setHorizontalGroup(
mainPanelLayout.createParallelGroup(javax.swing.GroupLayout.Alignment.LEADING)
    .addGap(0, 400, Short.MAX_VALUE)
    );

mainPanelLayout.setVerticalGroup(
    mainPanelLayout.createParallelGroup(javax.swing.GroupLayout.Alignment.LEADING)
    .addGap(0, 252, Short.MAX_VALUE)
    );
```

Using Actions

Once the main ProNetBeansDesktopApp class has been created, you can add a menu item and pop-up window using the GUI Builder actions. This section demonstrates how to create a new JDialog window, add components to it, and then use the GUI Builder's action capabilities to tie events together.

Creating the JDialog Window

To create the new JDialog window needed for this example, do the following:

1. Right-click the project name in the Projects window and select New ➤ Other.

2. Select Swing GUI Forms in the Categories list in the left pane of the Choose File Type screen.

3. Select JDialog Form in the File Types list in the right pane of the Choose File Type screen.
4. Click the Next button.
5. For the "Class Name" field, enter the value `HelloWorldBox`.
6. Enter `com.pronetbeans.examples` for the "Package" field.
7. Click the Finish button.

The `JDialog` form will open in the Form Editor window. It will appear as a square grey form, similar to a `JFrame`. Click anywhere on the grey part of the `JDialog`. Once it is selected, click and hold the lower-right corner of the component and resize it. Make the component look like a standard OK-Cancel dialog window, where it is a short but wide rectangle, as shown in Figure 15-16. Once you have made the `JDialog` component a similar size, you can perform the following steps:

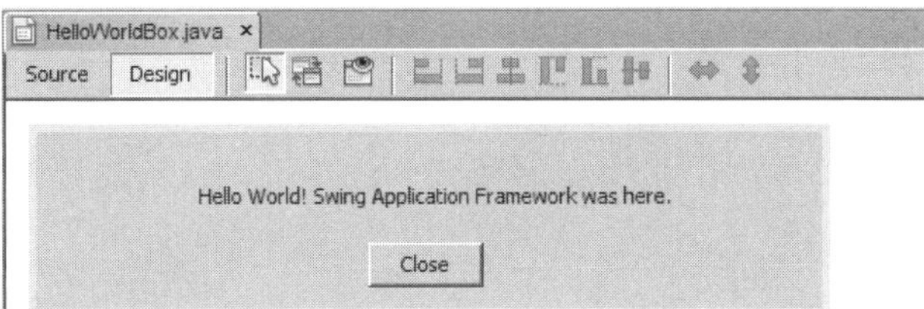

Figure 15-16. *The HelloWorldBox JDialog form*

1. Open the Palette window by selecting Window ➤ Palette (or by pressing Ctrl+Shift+8).
2. Drag a `JLabel` component from the Palette window and place it in the center of the form.
3. Drag a `JButton` component from the Palette window and place it in the center of the form, just below the `JLabel`.
4. Double-click the `JLabel` on the form. The text will become editable. Enter the value `Hello World! Swing Application Framework was here.`
5. Open the Properties window by selecting Window ➤ Properties (or by pressing Ctrl+Shift+7).
6. Click the `JButton` on the form.
7. With the `JButton` selected on the form, edit the text property in the Properties window and change the value to `Close`. The JDialog window should now look similar to Figure 15-16.

Creating New Actions

The Swing Application Framework has the ability to create actions based on the `org.jdesktop.application.Action` class. With these actions you can quickly and easily tie application functionality together.

In the example from the previous section, we created and customized a JDialog window. Now, we can enable its use via actions. To enable the first action, right-click on the Close button of the HelloWorldBox `JDialog` form from Figure 15-16 and select Set Action. The Set Action window will appear, as shown in Figure 15-17.

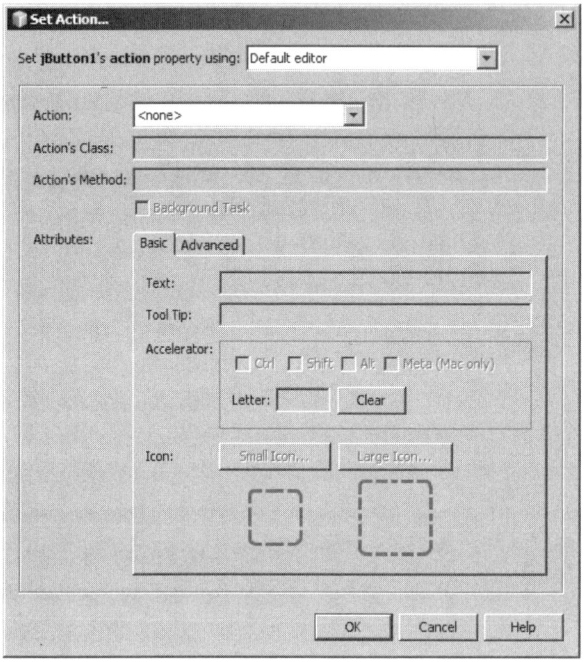

Figure 15-17. *The Set Action window*

The Set Action window allows you to specify an action to use when the button is clicked. You can specify an existing action by selecting one from the "Action" drop-down list, as in Figure 15-17. You can also create a new action, name it, and specify custom attributes.

To create a new action, perform the following steps:

1. Select Create New Action from the "Action" drop-down field.
2. Enter the value `closeWindow` in the "Action's Method" field.
3. Enter the value `Close` in the "Text" field.
4. Enter the value `Click this button to close this dialog window` in the "Tool Tip" field.
5. In the "Accelerator" section, select the Ctrl and Shift check boxes. In the "Letter" field, type the character `C`.
6. Click the OK button. The Set Action window will disappear.

When the Set Action window has closed, the `HelloWorldBox` class will contain this newly generated code:

```
@Action
    public void closeWindow() {

    }
```

The @Action annotation indicates that the method is an action of type org.jdesktop.application.Action from the Swing Application Framework API. If you look inside the Matisse-generated initComponents method, you will see that the new closeWindow action has been registered as the action for the jButton1 component (the Close button).

```
javax.swing.ActionMap actionMap = org.jdesktop.application.Application.getInstance(➥
com.pronetbeans.examples.ProNetBeansDesktopApp.class).getContext().getActionMap(➥
HelloWorldBox.class, this);

jButton1.setAction(actionMap.get("closeWindow"));
```

This code retrieves the ActionMap instance for the HelloWorldBox class. It then retrieves the ActionMap named "closeWindow," which matches the annotated closeWindow method that was generated. It is then up to the programmer to add code into the closeWindow method to make it do something.

For this example, we will add the code setVisible(false); so that when the button is clicked the HelloWorldBox JDialog disappears and gives the appearance of closing as intended. Thus, the final closeWindow method might look like this:

```
@Action
    public void closeWindow() {
        setVisible(false);
    }
```

Actions store resource strings in a .properties file that has the same name as the action's .java file. The file is formatted as a standard name/value pair, similar to using a ResourceBundle class to access it. The keys for each property are derived from the action name. The types of properties stored can include text, tooltips, accelerator shortcuts, blocking titles, blocking messages, and icon paths.

For the JDialog window displayed in Figure 15-16, there is a matching HelloWorldBox.properties file in the com.pronetbeans.examples.resources package in the Projects window. If you open the file, you will see content similar to the following:

```
jLabel1.text=Hello World! Swing Application Framework was here.
jButton1.text=Close
closeWindow.Action.text=Close
closeWindow.Action.accelerator=shift ctrl pressed C
closeWindow.Action.shortDescription=Click this button to close this dialog window
```

The property names, such as closeWindow.Action.text and jButton1.text, are used in the initComponents method of the class. As previously discussed, an instance of org.jdesktop.application.ResourceMap retrieves the value of each property, such as:

```
jLabel1.setText(resourceMap.getString("jLabel1.text"));
```

The property `jLabel1.text` is in the `HelloWorldBox.properties` file and matches the text "Hello World! Swing Application Framework was here."

The next step we take in demonstrating how to create and use actions involves adding a new menu item to the `ProNetBeansDesktopView` JFile menu. Open the `ProNetBeansDesktopView` class in the Form Editor and select the File menu along the top. It should display the default Exit menu item. In the Palette window, locate the Swing Menus section and drag a `Menu Item` component (representing a `JMenuItem` class) and place it just below the Exit menu item. As you move the mouse cursor near the Exit menu item, an orange dashed line should appear, either below or above it, depending on how close to the top or bottom of the Exit menu item you are. This denotes the location where the new `Menu Item` component will be placed when you drop it onto the menu. Once you drop the component, the File menu on the form will then contain a new menu item named "Item," with no shortcut display. The list of menu items will be displayed, as shown in Figure 15-18.

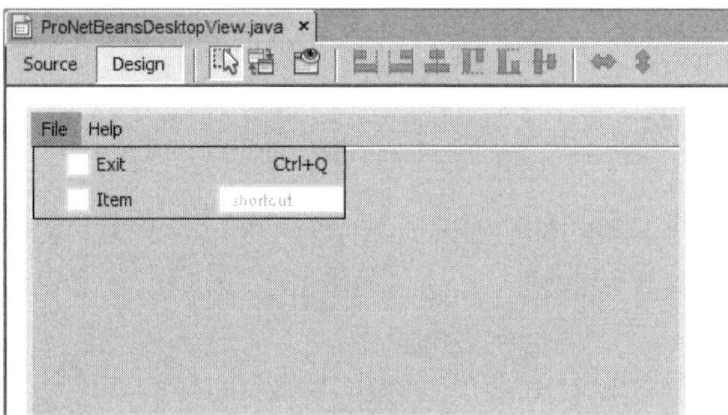

Figure 15-18. *The list of menu items on the File menu of the form*

Select the Item submenu. Once the Item submenu is highlighted with an orange border, right-click it and select Set Action from the context menu. The Set Action window will open. Do the following to configure the action:

1. Select Create New Action from the "Action" drop-down field.
2. Enter `showHelloWorld` in the "Action's Method" field.
3. Enter `Say Hello` in the "Text" field.
4. Enter `Click to open the Hello World JDialog` in the "Tool Tip" field.
5. Click inside the "Letter" field. Press and hold the Ctrl and Shift keys. Then press the R key. The Ctrl and Shift check boxes should be selected. The "Letter" field should display a capital R character.

Once you have entered the values into the fields, the Set Actions window will look like Figure 15-19.

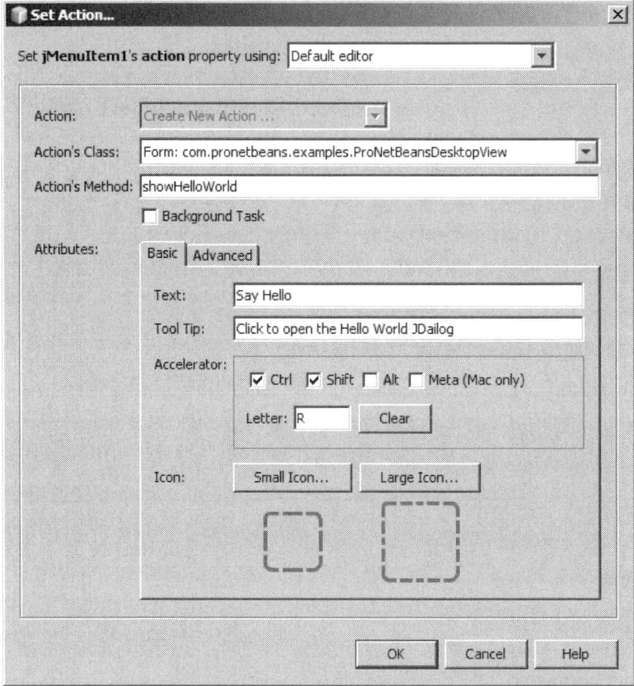

Figure 15-19. *The Set Action window for the showHelloWorld action*

The `showHelloWorld` method is then added to the `ProNetBeansDesktopView` class. It is defined as follows:

```
@Action
public void showHelloWorld() {

}
```

You can then add code to the `showHelloWorld` method to display the `HelloWorldBox` `JDialog` form:

```
@Action
public void showHelloWorld() {

    if (showHelloWorldBox == null) {
        JFrame mainFrame = ProNetBeansDesktopApp.getApplication().getMainFrame();
        showHelloWorldBox = new HelloWorldBox(mainFrame, true);
        showHelloWorldBox.setLocationRelativeTo(mainFrame);
    }

    ProNetBeansDesktopApp.getApplication().show(showHelloWorldBox);
}
```

This code retrieves the application's main `JFrame`, instantiates an instance of the `HelloWorldBox` form, and sets the location of it relative to the main `JFrame`. Finally, it calls the `show` method to display the `HelloWorldBox JDialog` form.

If you haven't already figured it out, the preceding list of steps is nearly identical to how the Java Desktop Application's project "About Box" works (see the Help menu item and the About submenu in the `ProNetBeansDesktopView` form). When the project is generated, the main GUI form for the project already contains menu items such as File ➤ Exit and Help ➤ About. If you look through the project code, you will see that the ability to show and hide the `ProNetBeansDesktopAboutBox` form is nearly identical to the steps described in this section.

Working with the Application Actions Window

The actions provided by the Swing Application Framework are useful, but they can be difficult to manage in a large code base, especially if you have to go searching to find them. NetBeans provides a convenient way to locate and manage all the actions in a project, via the Application Actions window.

You can open the window by selecting Window ➤ Other ➤ Application Actions from the main menu. The Application Actions window will appear and display a list of all methods annotated with `@Action`, which refers to the `org.jdesktop.application.Action` class. The Applications Actions window is shown in Figure 15-20.

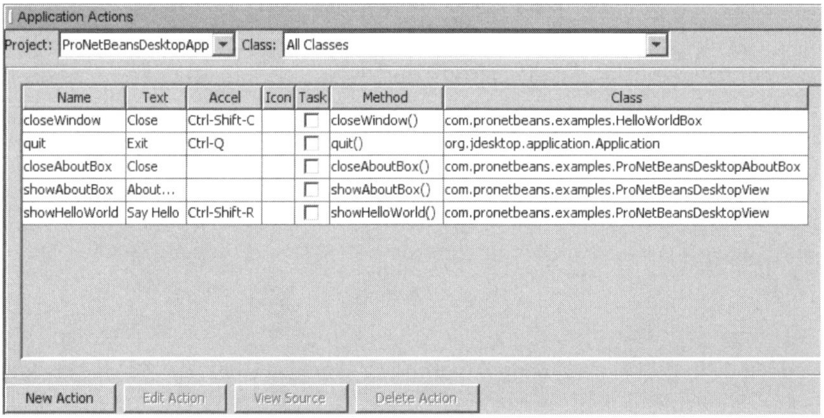

Application Actions

Project: ProNetBeansDesktopApp Class: All Classes

Name	Text	Accel	Icon	Task	Method	Class
closeWindow	Close	Ctrl-Shift-C		☐	closeWindow()	com.pronetbeans.examples.HelloWorldBox
quit	Exit	Ctrl-Q		☐	quit()	org.jdesktop.application.Application
closeAboutBox	Close			☐	closeAboutBox()	com.pronetbeans.examples.ProNetBeansDesktopAboutBox
showAboutBox	About...			☐	showAboutBox()	com.pronetbeans.examples.ProNetBeansDesktopView
showHelloWorld	Say Hello	Ctrl-Shift-R		☐	showHelloWorld()	com.pronetbeans.examples.ProNetBeansDesktopView

New Action | Edit Action | View Source | Delete Action

Figure 15-20. *The Application Actions window*

The Application Actions window will display a list of actions, which includes the Name, Text, Accelerator keyboard shortcut (if applicable), Icon, Task, Method, and Class. The list displayed belongs to the main project opened in the Projects window. However, if you have multiple projects open that use the Swing Application Framework, you can switch between them via the "Project" field at the top of the Application Actions window. When you select a project, only the actions for that project will be displayed in the window. You can also filter the list of actions to a specific class by selecting it from the "Class" drop-down field.

There are also several buttons along the bottom of Application Actions window that allow you to manage the list of actions. Clicking the New Action button opens the Create New Action window, which is similar in look and functionality to the Set Action window shown in Figure 15-17.

The Application Actions window also has an Edit Action button. You can select an action from the list, click the Edit Action button, and use the Edit Action Properties window that appears to customize the action, as shown in Figure 15-21.

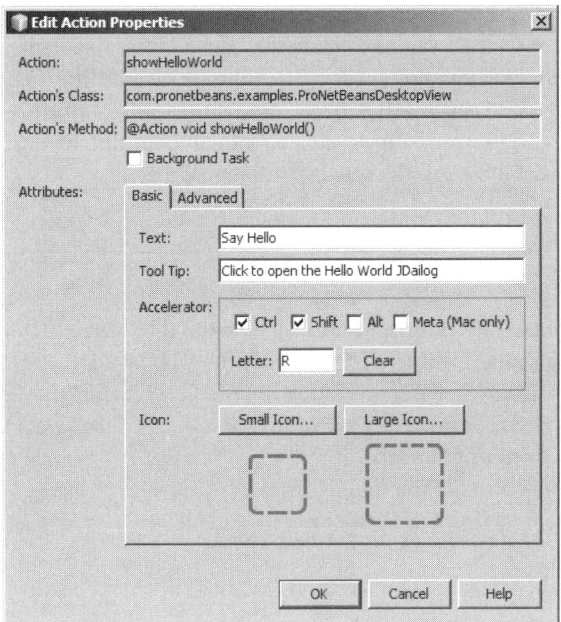

Figure 15-21. *The Edit Action Properties window*

The Edit Action Properties window does not allow you to change the "Action's Class" or "Action's Method" field. However, you can edit the "Text" and "Tool Tip" fields as well as change the Accelerator. You can also change the blocking-related properties on the Advanced tab if the Background Task check box is enabled. Once you have changed the properties to your liking, click the Close button to exit the Edit Action Properties window.

The Application Actions window in Figure 15-20 also contains a View Source button. Select an action from the list and click the View Source button. The Form Editor will open the file that contains the action and jump directly to the matching line of code in the Source view.

The Application Actions window also lets you delete an action from the list. Select an action from the list and click the Delete Action button. It will be deleted. The action will disappear from the list. However, the matching method in the class will not be deleted. All that will happen is that the `@Action` annotation will be removed. The `initComponents` method of the class will also have removed the association of the action with the component used to trigger it.

Using Beans Binding

Beans Binding, JSR-295, is new to NetBeans 6. It provides component and data-binding capabilities similar to those in the NetBeans 5.5 Visual Web Pack. In NetBeans 5.5 you could create Visual Web projects that tied the properties of components to beans, entity classes, database fields, or other component properties. Beans Binding is a similar concept, but applied to GUI development and Java Desktop Applications.

In this section I review the Beans Binding capabilities provided by NetBeans 6, how to create a database, how to create a Java Desktop Application project, and how to link a GUI form to the database table providing full create-read-update-delete (CRUD) capabilities. This specific set of steps has been extremely well documented in various online Beans Binding tutorials, so here I cover the steps as briefly as possible. I then break out when applicable and discuss various customizations, windows, and tools for effectively using Beans Binding in NetBeans. For more information on Beans Binding, see the official project page at `https://beansbinding.dev.java.net`.

Creating the Database

For this example of Beans Binding, we connect a GUI form to the data in a database table. This section assumes you have installed and configured the Java DB in NetBeans. The Java DB (formerly known as Derby) is included as part of Java SE 6 or can be downloaded and installed separately. You can point NetBeans at your Java DB install by selecting Tools ➤ Java DB Database ➤ Settings from the main menu and specifying the location.

To create the sample database for this section, do the following:

1. Select Tools ➤ Java DB Database ➤ Start Server from the main menu.
2. Once the database server has started, select Tools ➤ Java DB Database ➤ Create Database. The Create Java DB Database window will appear.
3. Enter a name for the database, such as ProNetBeansDoughnuts.
4. Enter values for the "User Name" and "Password" fields.
5. Click the OK button to generate the database.
6. In the Services window, expand the Databases node until you see the connection to your new database. Right-click it and select Connect from the context menu.
7. When the database has connected, expand the node. Right-click the Tables node that appears and select Create Table from the context menu. The Create Table window will appear.
8. Enter the value `doughnuts` for the "Table name" field.

9. Create four columns, as shown in Figure 15-22, named ID, NAME, DESCRIPTION, and PRICE.

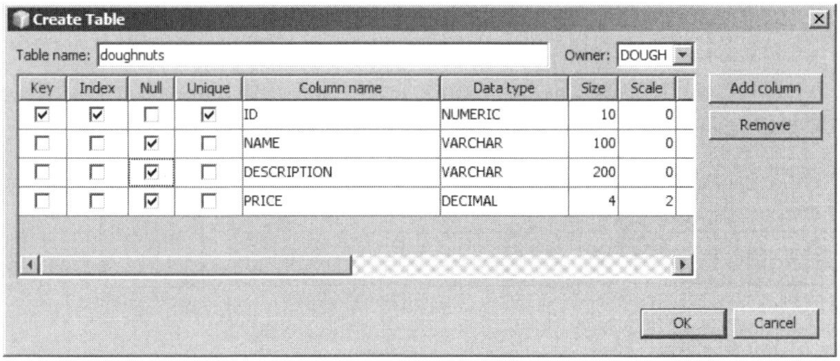

Create Table

Table name: doughnuts Owner: DOUGH

Key	Index	Null	Unique	Column name	Data type	Size	Scale
☑	☑	☐	☑	ID	NUMERIC	10	0
☐	☐	☑	☐	NAME	VARCHAR	100	0
☐	☐	☑	☐	DESCRIPTION	VARCHAR	200	0
☐	☐	☑	☐	PRICE	DECIMAL	4	2

Add column Remove

OK Cancel

Figure 15-22. *The DOUGHNUTS table schema*

10. Once the columns have been configured with the correct parameters, click the OK button to close the Create Table window.

The DOUGHNUTS table will be generated and listed under the Tables node in the Services window for the new database. You can now insert data into the table using a few simple SQL statements. Right-click the DOUGHNUTS table node in the Services window and select View Data from the context menu. An SQL Command window will open.

The SQL Command window allows you to enter SQL statements and execute them against the defined database connection. You can enter the following SQL statements one at a time into the SQL Command window. Execute them individually by right-clicking inside the window and selecting Run Statement.

```
insert into DOUGHNUTS values(1,'Glazed','Plain doughnut with glaze',1.25)
insert into DOUGHNUTS values(2,'Old Fashioned','Plain doughnut',1.25)
insert into DOUGHNUTS values(3,'Sugared','Plain doughnut with white sugar',1.25)
insert into DOUGHNUTS values(4,'Jelly','Jelly filled puff',1.25)
insert into DOUGHNUTS values(5,'Chocolate','Chocolate dough, no topping',1.25)
```

You can then enter a SQL query to view the entered data, such as

```
Select * from DOUGHNUTS
```

This will display the table data in a simple grid at the bottom of the SQL Command window. You can also use the newer Design Query window added in NetBeans 6. Previously, the Design Query tool was available to users of the Visual Web Pack in NetBeans 5.5. It allows visual manipulation of tables and columns to create and generate SQL queries. To use it, right-click the DOUGHNUTS table node in the Services window and select Design Query from the context menu. The Design Query window will appear, as shown in Figure 15-23.

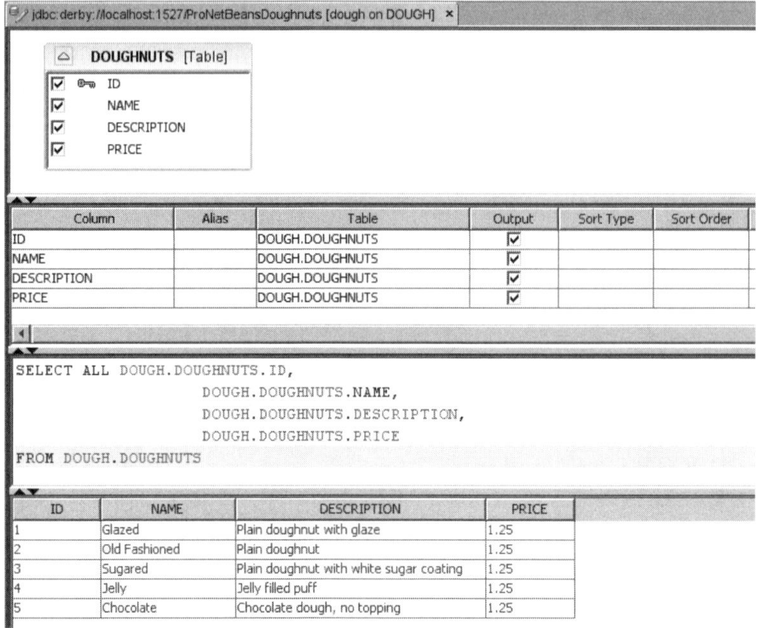

Figure 15-23. *The DOUGHNUTS table displayed in the Design Query window*

The Design Query window provides four sections. The first section, on top, allows you to visualize the database tables and their schema. To display additional tables and create SQL joins, right-click inside the blank space in this section and select Add Table from the context menu that appears.

The second section from the top displays the columns. It allows you to set if they appear in the SQL statement as well as if and how they are ordered. The third section from the top displays the SQL query. As items are modified in the top two sections, the SQL displayed in this third section is dynamically modified. You can also edit the SQL directly in this third section and have the changes updated in the other sections. The fourth and final section displays the results of the SQL statement in a simple grid.

I encourage you to explore this useful and handy database tool in more depth. There is more functionality available that has not been discussed here, since this is not an in-depth view of the tool.

Creating the Project

This section discusses how to create and configure a Java Desktop Application project. Earlier in this chapter we reviewed how to create a Java Desktop Application project that used the "Basic Application" Application Shell. This section deals with using the "Database Application" Application Shell.

To create the project, do the following:

1. Select File ➤ New Project from the main menu. The New Project window will open.

2. On the Choose Project screen, select Java from the list of Categories in the left pane and Java Desktop Application from the list of Projects in the right pane.

3. Click the Next button.

4. On the Name and Location screen, enter a value for the "Project Name" field, such as "BeansBindingSampleApp."

5. Enter a fully qualified package name and class name in the "Application Class" field.

6. Select Database Application from the list of available application shells. The Name and Location screen should look like Figure 15-24. Click the Next button to continue.

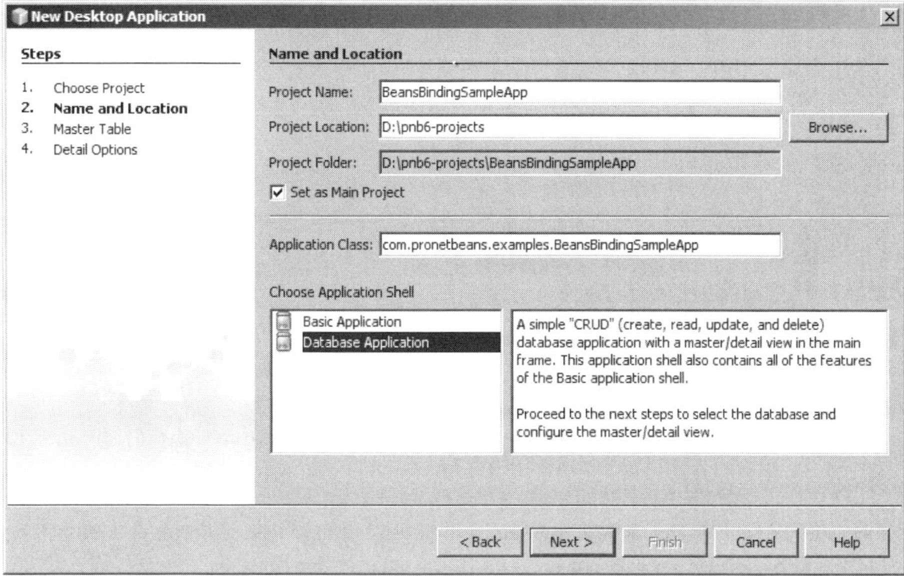

Figure 15-24. *The Name and Location screen*

7. On the Master Table screen, select the ProNetBeansDoughnuts database from the "Database Connection" drop-down list.

8. Select DOUGHNUTS from the "Database Table" drop-down list. The "Columns to Include" list should display the list of all the columns in the DOUGHNUTS table, as shown in Figure 15-25.

9. Then click the Next button to display the Detail Options screen.

10. On the Detail Options screen, select the ID column in the "Columns to Include" list on the right and click the < button. The ID column will disappear from the list and be displayed in the "Available Fields" list on the left. This will instruct NetBeans not to generate a text field for it in the detail section of the GUI form. Only the "Name," "Description," and "Price" fields will have text fields generated, since they appear in the "Columns to Include" list.

11. Click the Finish button to close the New Project wizard.

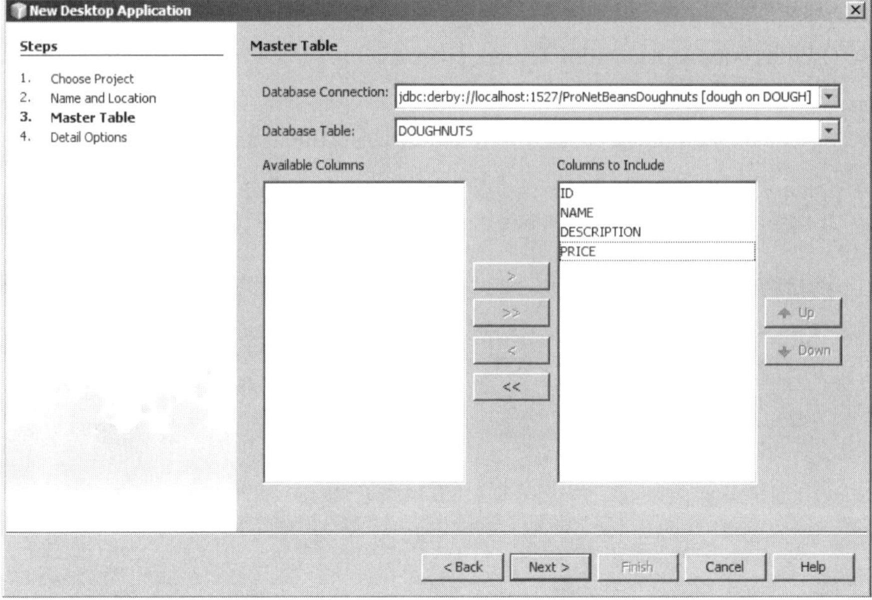

Figure 15-25. *The Master Table screen*

Once NetBeans has finished generating the project code, run the project by selecting Run ➤ Run Main Project from the main menu. The project code will compile, build, and run. A GUI form class named `BeansBindingSampleView` will display by default when the project runs, as shown in Figure 15-26. As you can see in the figure, a data grid is displayed listing the data from the DOUGHNUTS table. Underneath the data grid are three text fields that display the information for each record when a specific record is selected in the data grid.

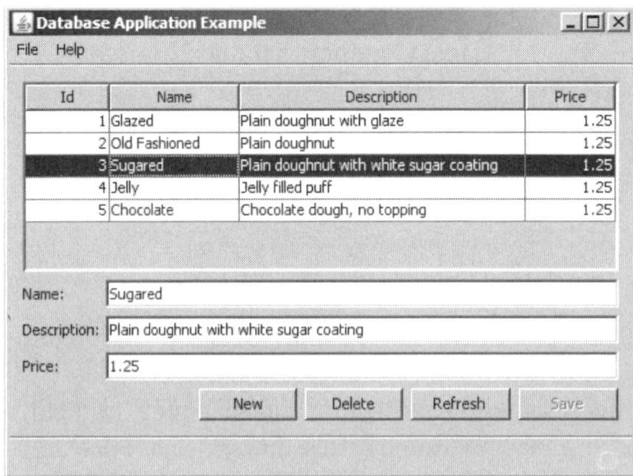

Figure 15-26. *The finished application window displaying the DOUGHNUTS table data*

If you experiment with the GUI form displayed in Figure 15-26, you will see that a number of capabilities are present. The GUI form uses a combination of the Swing Application

Framework, Beans Binding, and Java Persistence to provide a fully functional database table–editing tool. You can add, view, edit, and delete records from the table using the buttons at the bottom of the form. Once you make changes you want to persist, you can click the Save button, which becomes enabled when a change is made to the list of data.

You may also notice that as you select an item in the data grid, the corresponding details for that record are displayed in the text fields below the data grid. You can also resize the columns in the data grid and drag-and-drop the column headers around to rearrange the fields in the table.

To test whether the automatically generated code actually works, go ahead and edit the data. Select a row in the data grid. In the text fields below, change any of the values. As you do so, the Save button becomes enabled. Click the Save button, wait a second or two, and then close the entire application. In NetBeans, rerun the project by selecting Run ➤ Run Main Project (or pressing F6). The GUI form will open again and display the data, including the changes you made. As far as Java GUI applications go, this is an amazing set of features to have automatically generated for you.

Exploring the Generated Application

Now we explore the application in more detail. One of the features you may have noticed regards selecting items in the data grid. As you selected an item, the corresponding values for that record were displayed in the text fields at the bottom of the window. Also, as you changed the text in the text fields, the corresponding data in the data grid also changed. This "glue" between components is one part of Beans Binding.

Open the `BeansBindingSampleView` class in the Form Editor. The Design view should be displayed by default. Select the text field to the right of the Description label. The text field will then be highlighted with an orange border, and various anchors and guidelines will appear denoting its specific position on the form, as shown in Figure 15-27.

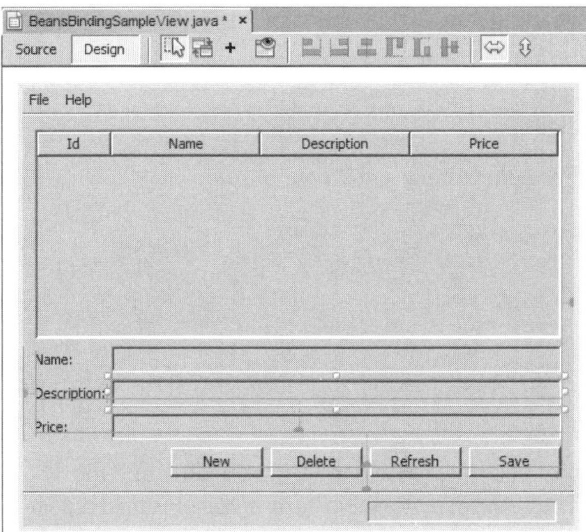

Figure 15-27. *The highlighted "Description" text field on the form*

Next, view the properties for the component. You can do so by opening the Properties window by selecting Window ➤ Properties from the main menu. You can also right-click the text field component and select Properties from the context menu that appears.

In the Properties window, look at the Binding tab and locate the text property. Click the ellipsis next to it to open the Bind window.

Working with the Bind Window

The Bind window contains two tabs: Binding and Advanced. The Binding tab contains two fields, named "Binding Source" and "Binding Expression," as shown in Figure 15-28.

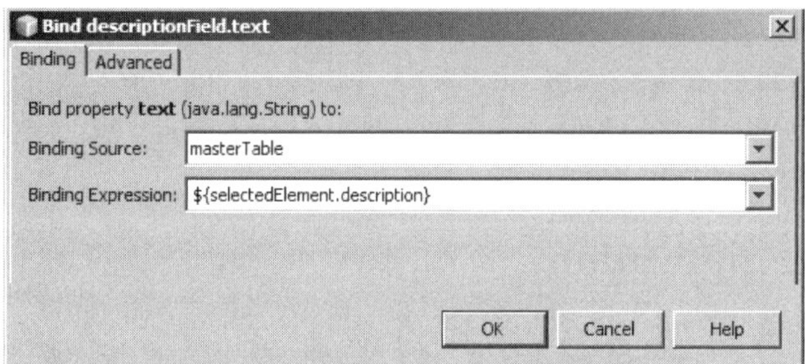

Figure 15-28. *The Binding tab of the Bind window*

The current settings in the Bind window denote that the "text" property of the Description text box is bound to the property `${selectedElement.description}` of the `masterTable` component, which is an instance of `javax.swing.JTable`.

This binding is defined and configured in the autogenerated `initComponents` method. A column binding is added to the `JTable`, as specified by the name `${description}`:

```
columnBinding = jTableBinding.addColumnBinding(➥
org.jdesktop.beansbinding.ELProperty.create("${description}"));
columnBinding.setColumnName("Description");
columnBinding.setColumnClass(String.class);
```

Then farther down the method, the text field component is configured:

```
binding = org.jdesktop.beansbinding.Bindings.createAutoBinding(
   org.jdesktop.beansbinding.AutoBinding.UpdateStrategy.READ_WRITE,
   masterTable,
   org.jdesktop.beansbinding.ELProperty.create("${selectedElement.description}"),
   descriptionField,
   org.jdesktop.beansbinding.BeanProperty.create(
         "text_ON_ACTION_OR_FOCUS_LOST"));
```

This code defines and creates a binding between the `JTable` named `masterTable` and the `descriptionField` text field component. The column in the table used in the binding is specified by the `ELProperty` expression `${selectedElement.description}`. This specifies that the description field of the element selected in the table should bind to the `descriptionField` component.

Other arguments of the `createAutoBinding` method are specified in the preceding code. The first argument specifies the binding update strategy. In this case it is set to `READ_WRITE` and will be discussed momentarily. The last argument of the `createAutoBinding` method defines how and when the data is synced between the two components. In this case it is set to sync when the field loses focus or the Enter key is pressed. The other options are discussed in a moment as well.

The Advanced tab of the Bind window displays a number of additional options you can configure, as shown in Figure 15-29.

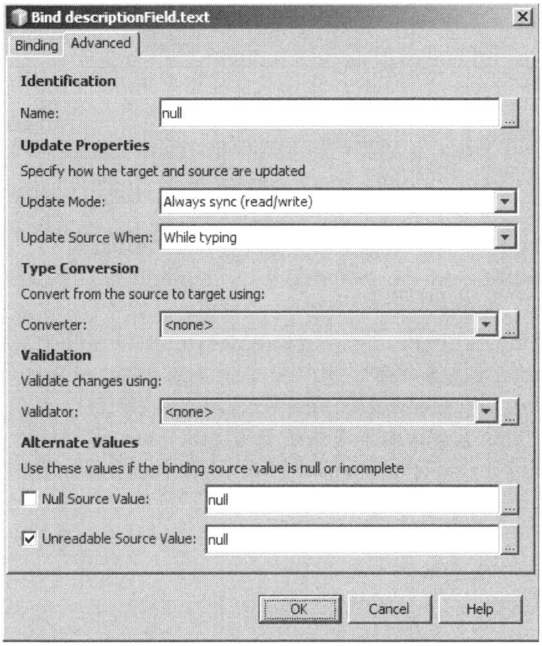

Figure 15-29. *The Advanced tab of the Bind window*

The "Name" field is set to `null` by default. You can enter any name you wish that helps identify the name of this specific binding. You can then later use that name to assist in retrieving the specific binding from the group of bindings if you need to customize the code or perform some binding-specific action.

The fields in the Update Properties section specify how the target and source components in the binding get updated. The "Update Mode" field can be set to

Always sync (read/write): If a change is made to the source component, then the target component gets updated (and vice versa). This is the default setting.

Only read from source (read only): The target component will receive updates from the source component only. The source component does not receive updates.

Read from source once (read once): The target component is updated only once, when the binding between the two components first takes effect.

The “Update Source When” field specifies when the sync between the target and source components is performed. It is normally only available to use to bind to the text property of either a text field or text area. It can be set to

Enter is pressed or focus is lost: As the name implies, the sync occurs either when the Enter key is pressed or the focus is lost, typically by pressing Tab or by clicking outside the component.

Focus leaves: The sync occurs when focus is lost on the component, typically by pressing Tab or by clicking outside the component.

While typing: The sync occurs when the user types a character inside the component.

If you are developing an application with a lot of text fields or text areas, the setting of the “Update Source When” property should be taken into consideration. This is discussed in the following section.

The Advanced tab of the Bind window also contains a “Converter” field. If you need to convert data types between the source and target components, you can do so by specifying a Converter that has been added to the form.

The “Validator” field lets you specify a class that extends `org.jdesktop.beansbinding.Validator` or custom code to validate the component input before the components are synced.

The remaining section on the Advanced tab of the Bind window allows you to handle either `null` or incomplete values from the source component. The “Null Source Value” field lets you specify a value or custom code to use when the source component value contains the value `null`. If you select the check box next to the “Null Source Value” field label, the text field immediately to the right will become enabled. Next, click the ellipsis button to the right of the field and the Null Value window will open, as shown in Figure 15-30.

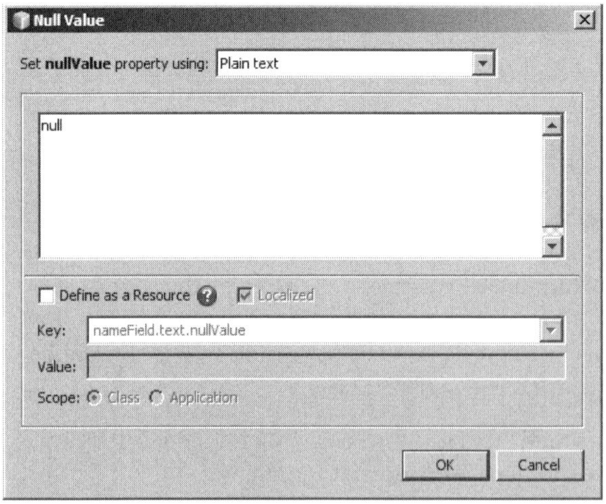

Figure 15-30. *The Null Value window*

The drop-down list at the top of the window is set to “Plain text” by default. This setting allows you to enter a value into the text area below it. You can then select the “Define as a

Resource" check box to enable the text you entered to be stored in a .properties file, using the ResourceMap functionality of the Swing Application Framework.

The drop-down list at the top of the Null Value window can also be set to "Resource Bundle." This displays several fields that allow you to browse the Source Packages of the project and choose a .properties file. You can then select a key that exists in the .properties file for which the value should be used.

The drop-down list at the top of the Null Value window can also be set to "Custom code." The window will then display a field for entering code specific to the data type that is expected for the field. For the text property of the text field component, a value for the data type java.lang.String is expected. You can enter a pair of empty quotation marks to signify that an empty String should be used if the value null occurs in the field.

Once you have selected the appropriate setting for the null value, click the OK button to close the Null Value window.

The "Unreadable Source Value" field on the Advanced tab of the Bind window can be configured nearly identically to the "Null Source Value" field.

Understanding the "Update Source When" Field

The "Update Source When" field is set to "While typing" by default. What this specifically means is that as each and every character is typed into the text field or text area component, the source and target components are synced. Whether this is a good idea or not depends on the needs of your application and the type of binding behavior you want to enforce.

I next demonstrate the effect of this setting on some sample code. Open the BeansBindingSampleView class in the Form Editor and select the Source view. At the bottom of the constructor, locate the following code:

```
bindingGroup.addBindingListener(new AbstractBindingListener() {
    @Override
    public void targetChanged(Binding binding, PropertyStateEvent event) {
        // save action observes saveNeeded property
        setSaveNeeded(true);
    }
});
```

This adds a binding listener (essentially an event listener) to the group of bindings. It is a new AbstractBindingListener that overrides the targetChanged method that fires when the target component is changed. This in turn sets the class member variable saveNeeded to true, which in turn enables the Save button that is displayed on the form.

Add a debugging statement to the code so that it looks like the following:

```
bindingGroup.addBindingListener(new AbstractBindingListener() {
    @Override
    public void targetChanged(Binding binding, PropertyStateEvent event) {
        // save action observes saveNeeded property
        setSaveNeeded(true);
        System.out.println("targetChanged:" + binding.getTargetValueForSource());
    }
});
```

Next, we need to change the "Update Source When" field for one of the components by performing the following steps:

1. In the Form Editor window, select the Design view for the `BeansBindingSampleView` class.
2. Right-click the text field next to the "Description" field label and select Properties from the context menu.
3. On the Binding tab of the Properties window, locate the text property and click the ellipsis button next to its value. The Bind window will open.
4. Click the Advanced tab in the Bind window.
5. For the "Update Source When" field, select the value "Enter is pressed or focus is lost."
6. Click the OK button to close the Bind window.
7. Click the Close button to close the Properties window for the "Description" text field.
8. Finally, run the project.

Once the project has run, make sure the Output window is open and select a record in the data grid. Click inside the "Description" text field and type several characters. If you look at the Output window, you will see nothing. Click outside the field. The Output window will display the following:

```
targetChanged : value: Plain doughnut with white sugar coatingTYPING
```

The characters "TYPING" represent the new characters that were added to the field. They were not output into the Output window until the text field lost focus due to the setting of the "Update Source When" field. When the focus of the component was lost, the `targetChanged` method that was overridden in the binding listener was executed, thereby triggering the `System.out.println`.

To see this more clearly, click inside the text field next to the "Name" label. Type the characters `12345` one at a time, pausing for a second after each character. If you watch the Output window, you will see one line of text at a time appear as the `targetChanged` method is executed, eventually displaying the following results:

```
targetChanged : value: Sugared1
targetChanged : value: Sugared12
targetChanged : value: Sugared123
targetChanged : value: Sugared1234
targetChanged : value: Sugared12345
```

This is due to the default setting for the "Update Source When" field of the "Name" text field, which is set to "While typing."

Writing a Custom Validator

As discussed earlier, you have the ability to specify a Validator for a source component in the Bind window. As input is entered into a source component, it can be validated and either accepted or rejected before syncing with the target component. In this section we create a custom validation component and tie it to the "Name" and "Description" text fields of the `BeansBindingSampleView` class.

First, create a new Java class using the New File wizard:

1. Right-click the project name in the Projects window and select New ➤ Other.
2. Select Java from the list of Categories in the left pane and select Java Class from the list of File Types in the right pane.
3. Click the Next button.
4. On the Name and Location screen, specify a value for the new class, such as `MyTextValidator`.
5. Specify a package, such as `com.pronetbeans.examples.validators`.
6. Click the Finish button.

Once NetBeans finishes generating the stub of the class, it will open in the Source Editor:

```
package com.pronetbeans.examples.validators;

/**
 *
 * @author Adam Myatt
 */
public class MyTextValidator {

}
```

To continue, change the code so the class extends the `org.jdesktop.beansbinding.Validator` class. If you do not use the fully qualified class name you can right-click in the Source Editor and select Fix Imports to add the missing `import` statement to your code.

An error glyph will appear in the margin, since the `MyTextValidator` class does not implement all the abstract methods from the `Validator` class. Click the glyph in the margin and select "Implement All Abstract Methods" from the suggestion that appears. A method stub will be generated as follows:

```
@Override
public Validator.Result validate(Object arg0) {
    throw new UnsupportedOperationException("Not supported yet.");
}
```

Change the method to actually validate the input, for example:

```
@Override
public Validator.Result validate(Object arg0) {

    Validator.Result result = null;
    if(arg0 instanceof String) {
        String sResult = (String) arg0;

        if(sResult.indexOf('$')!=-1) {
            result = new Validator.Result("123", "Invalid dollar sign");
            System.out.println("The text value contained a dollar sign.");
        }
    }

    return result;
}
```

The method now defines a `Validator.Result`. This is the expected object that will be returned. It is initialized to `null` since the method should return `null` if the input is valid. For the sake of sanity, I check the `Object` argument passed in to see whether it is a `String`. If it is, I then perform some sort of validation on the text. In this example I check for the existence of the dollar sign character. Perhaps in this application I do not want data entry staff entering pricing information into these fields

If the dollar sign character is found anywhere in the `String`, the code instantiates an instance of `Validator.Result`. The first argument to the constructor is a `String` representing a meaningless error code. This can be `null` or something meaningful in your application. The second argument in the constructor is the error message that is typically logged in the event that the `Validator` finds the input invalid.

To add the custom validator to the `BeansBindingSampleView` form, you have to copy and paste it. Look in the Projects window and locate the `MyTextValidator` class node in the `com.pronetbeans.examples.validators` package. Right-click the node and select Copy from the context menu.

Next, open the `BeansBindingSampleView` class in the Form Editor. If the Inspector window is not displayed, open it by selecting Window ➤ Navigating ➤ Inspector from the main menu. Right-click the top node, "Form BeansBindingSampleView," and select Paste from the context menu. If you look at the bottom of the list, an instance of the `MyTextValidator` class will be displayed.

To configure the "Name" and "Description" text fields, perform the following steps:

1. Select the "Name" text field. Right-click the component and select Properties from the context menu.

2. Select the Binding tab of the Properties window.

3. Locate the text property and click the ellipsis button next to it. The Bind window will open.

4. Click the Advanced tab in the Bind window.

5. Select the Validator drop-down field and choose the `MyTextValidator` instance.
6. Click the OK button to close the Bind window. Click the Close button to close the Properties window.
7. Repeat steps 1 through 6 with the "Description" text field component.

Once you have configured the text field component to use the `MyTextValidator`, run the project. When the `BeansBindingSampleView` form opens, select a record in the data grid. Then click inside the "Name" text field and type several characters, such as `ABC`. Remember that the "Update Source When" field in the Bind window for the "Name" text field is set to "While typing." As you type inside the text field, the corresponding value in the data grid is synced and displays each new character. Now, type a dollar sign character. Notice that the corresponding value in the data grid did not update. Type several other characters. The value in the data grid still does not update. If you delete the dollar sign from the "Name" text field, you will notice that the corresponding value in the data grid updates to the new value. This occurs because the dollar sign has been deleted and the `MyTextValidator.validate` returns `null`.

Summary

This chapter discussed a number of topics related to Java and Swing GUI development. First, it reviewed how to create a simple Java GUI application. It discussed the basics of creating a project, creating a basic JFrame class, and how to manipulate the class in the Form Editor.

The chapter then went on to review different tools that NetBeans provides along with the Matisse GUI Builder, such as the Palette window with Swing GUI components, the Form Editor, and handling component events.

A sample application was developed that demonstrated how to implement basic text-to-speech capabilities. The chapter reviewed how to create the form, add components to it, and download a third-party library and use it in the project.

Next, the chapter went on to discuss the Swing Application Framework, JSR-296. This provides a number of conveniences and tools for creating GUI applications. Step by step we created a sample Java Desktop Application project and demonstrated the usage of actions and how to develop a GUI form that uses them.

Finally, the chapter discussed Beans Binding, JSR-295. This API provides the ability to connect properties of two components together so that data between them is synced. You can use this to update a database field when a form component value is changed or change values of database fields or bean properties using visual components like sliders. NetBeans integrates well with Beans Binding by providing application shells, wizards, and tools to enable usage of the framework.

The chapter reviewed how to create a sample database, create a Java Desktop Application project, and configure a GUI form to use binding effectively. It concluded by using some of the binding-related tools and writing a custom validator for validating input.

CHAPTER 16

Developing Rich Client Applications

Rich client applications are applications written for the desktop. After several years in which the Web has been the dominant target for application developers, the desktop is increasingly undergoing a resurgence in popularity. This is especially true in the context of Java Web Start technology, which enables desktop applications to be distributed via the Web. Java and the Swing Toolkit on the desktop are both becoming a more viable option, particularly in light of the great performance strides made in Java and Swing in JDK 6.

However, a typical hindrance to the creation of medium- to large-size applications is the amount of boilerplate code that needs to be written at the start. Everything, from the application's life cycle to its windowing system, menu bars, and options settings, for example, need to be created from scratch, before the domain-level items, that is, the business logic, can begin to be added. Typically, developers spend more time on the infrastructure than on the domain, whereas the domain is the real added value they provide to their users. It is in this area that NetBeans offers a tailor-made solution.

The infrastructure, on top of which the IDE is created, called the *NetBeans Platform*, can be extracted and reused as a framework for your own applications. Similar to how the JavaServer Faces framework provides a predefined out-of-the-box starter kit for web development, so the NetBeans Platform provides an extensive infrastructure for application developers engaged in Swing-based desktop development.

The benefits of using the NetBeans Platform, the full range of features it provides, practical steps for getting started, and a demo of a complete application are covered in this chapter. The demo is necessarily small, but, despite that, several of the main principles of the NetBeans Platform will come to light when you work on that part of the chapter. However, for a full examination of the NetBeans Platform and all that it has to offer, you are advised to read *Rich Client Programming: Plugging into the NetBeans Platform* (Prentice-Hall, April 2007).

Features Provided by the NetBeans Platform

The NetBeans Platform provides the following main features:

- *User interface management*: The NetBeans Platform provides Windows, menus, toolbars, and other presentation components. You will write modules that the NetBeans Platform will automatically manage for you, saving you time and producing cleaner, more bug-free code.

- *Data and presentation management*: The NetBeans Platform, principally via the Window System API, Visual Library API, and Explorer & Property Sheet API, provides a rich set of user interface elements for presenting data to the user and for letting the user manipulate that data.

- *Setting management*: You can manage saving and restoring settings via the Options Settings API and the NbPreferences API. These are easy to implement and provide a mechanism for storage that is safe, simple, transparent, and often automatic.

- *Graphical editing*: By using NetBeans IDE as the SDK for the NetBeans Platform, you can use the "Matisse" GUI Builder to create drag-and-drop graphical views of data. In addition, the Visual Library API will let you put together complex modeling and graphing views.

- *Editor*: Applications built on the NetBeans Platform can reuse the NetBeans Editor, which is a powerful and extensible tool set that can be extended and customized. You can use it independent of the NetBeans Platform.

- *Wizard framework*: The NetBeans Platform provides NetBeans APIs for easily building extensible, user-friendly wizards to guide you through more complex tasks, generate common artifacts, and set up project source structures.

- *Storage management*: This is an abstraction of file-based data access. *Files* in the NetBeans Platform's paradigm may be local files, or they may exist remotely. For example, files could exist on an FTP server, in a CVS repository, in an XML file, or in a database. Where this data is stored is completely transparent to other modules that work with this data.

- *A huge selection of additional components*: The NetBeans IDE uses features such as its Favorites window and Component Palette that are provided by loosely coupled modules. Since they are loosely coupled, they lack strong dependencies on each other and can easily be reused by any other application created on top of the NetBeans Platform. As a result, you can simply adopt NetBeans IDE's versioning support, specialized editors, specialized UI components, remote data access via FTP, other transports, and most other features typical to NetBeans IDE. The NetBeans IDE modules, as well as many others, can provide convenient ways to work with a variety of Java and Internet technologies via plugins that any application can reuse.

- *Internet-based update delivery*: Applications based on the NetBeans Platform can use Java Web Start technology to deliver custom sets of modules as updates based on a user's role, for complex applications. A Web Start–enabled application is always up to date and combines the advantages of centralized management and deployment with the advantages of a rich client user experience. For non-Web Start applications, you can simply add a Plugin Manager, which lets the user download updates or new functionality via the Web.

Getting Started

Getting started with the NetBeans Platform is as simple as downloading the NetBeans IDE, which is a superset of the NetBeans Platform. NetBeans IDE is also the NetBeans Platform's software development kit (SDK). Obtaining the NetBeans Platform itself means removing the modules that are specific to theNetBeans IDE. Tools in the NetBeans IDE make this process very easy, as is shown later. Removing the NetBeans IDE's modules will leave you with the NetBeans Platform, the small subset of NetBeans IDE that forms its core.

Alternatively, however, you can use any other IDE, instead of the NetBeans IDE, for developing NetBeans Platform applications. In this case, you would download just the NetBeans Platform. A separate download providing only the NetBeans Platform is available via the Download section of `http://www.netbeans.org`. Once you have the NetBeans Platform, you can use it as a runtime container and deploy the modules you create to it. However, prior to the phase where you begin developing your modules in a different IDE, the wizards that NetBeans IDE provides for generating project source structures and NetBeans API stubs are unmissable, and, until alternative IDEs provide similar tools for setting up a source structure and creating API stubs, NetBeans IDE is a "must have" when it comes to getting started with the NetBeans Platform.

Though once you have the source structures and NetBeans API stubs available, you can simply use any other IDE to develop them and then return to the NetBeans IDE for deployment and debugging, this chapter assumes you are using the NetBeans IDE as the SDK for the entire development process on top of the NetBeans Platform.

Terminology

A small set of terms is germaine specifically to the NetBeans Platform. They are used repeatedly in this context, and, before continuing, we briefly outline them here.

- *NetBeans Platform*: The skeleton application that provides a common basis for Swing applications.
- *NetBeans Platform application*: An application created with the NetBeans Platform as its starting point.
- *NetBeans Runtime Container*: The minimal configuration needed for modular development. The container consists of the Utilities API, the Module System API, the FileSystems API, Bootstrap, and Startup, as shown in Figure 16-1. This last glues the other pieces together. This minimal subset of the NetBeans Platform provides a basis for headless deployment, class loading, and dynamic enablement/disablement of features in an application.
- *NetBeans System FileSystem*: The general registry of an application's configuration data. It is built from the `layer.xml` configuration files of all the modules in the application, together with a read/writable directory on disk. Among other things, NetBeans Platform applications store a wide variety of data relating to the user interface in the System FileSystem. For example, the System FileSystem contains a folder called "Menu," which contains subfolders with names such as "File" and "Edit." These subfolders contain files that represent Java classes that implement the actions that appear in the File and Edit menus in the application.

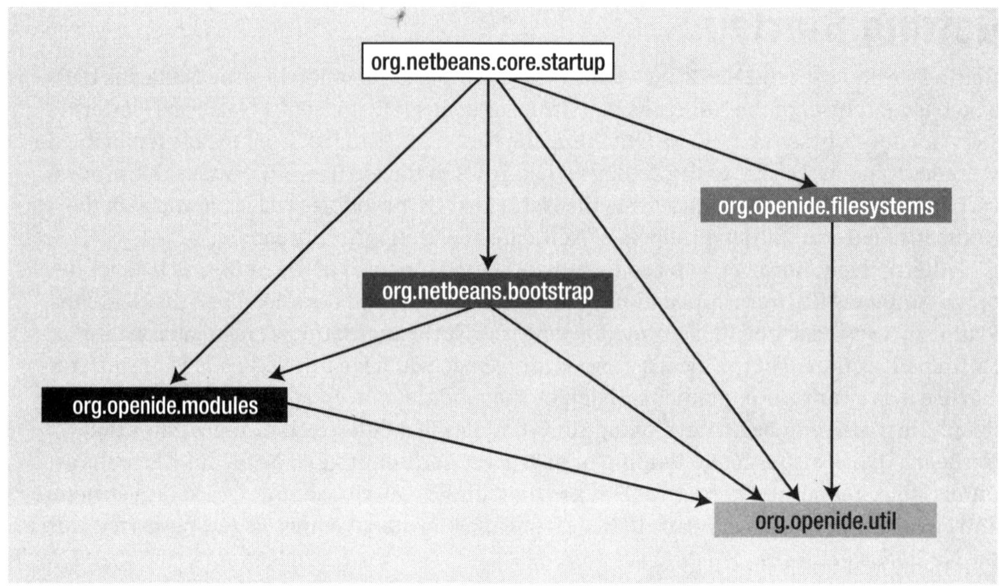

Figure 16-1. *Relationship of the APIs in the NetBeans Runtime Container*

- *NetBeans Module*: A single building block of a NetBeans Platform application. A module consists of a group of Java classes that provides an application with a specific feature. The Java classes use the Java Manifest file to declare the JAR as a module.
- *NetBeans layer file*: Each module provides an XML file known as a *layer file*. Normally, the file is named `layer.xml`. A module uses its layer file to register its functionality in the NetBeans System FileSystem. For example, if a module provides actions, it will register these actions in the layer file, where it will specify how the actions will be invoked. If the action will be invoked from the File menu, the module registers the action in the "Menus/File" folder.
- *NetBeans APIs*: The public interfaces and classes available to NetBeans Platform application developers. You'll find an overview at the end of this chapter.

For a full conceptual explanation of these terms and their relationships to one another, see *Rich Client Programming: Plugging into the NetBeans Platform* (Prentice-Hall, April 2007).

The next section explores the tools that NetBeans IDE makes available specifically for NetBeans Platform developers.

NetBeans Platform SDK

This section introduces you to all of the NetBeans Platform–related tools in the NetBeans Platform SDK, that is, the NetBeans IDE. You will find these tools very useful as you create NetBeans Platform applications. At the very least, it is good to be aware of them, for you might need them and at that point it will be good to know they're there.

Project Templates

The NetBeans IDE comes with a set of project templates that make setting up a module's source structure as simple as clicking through a wizard. Open the New Project wizard (Ctrl+Shift+N) and you will see three project templates, as shown in Figure 16-2, that set up three project structures that relate to NetBeans Platform development.

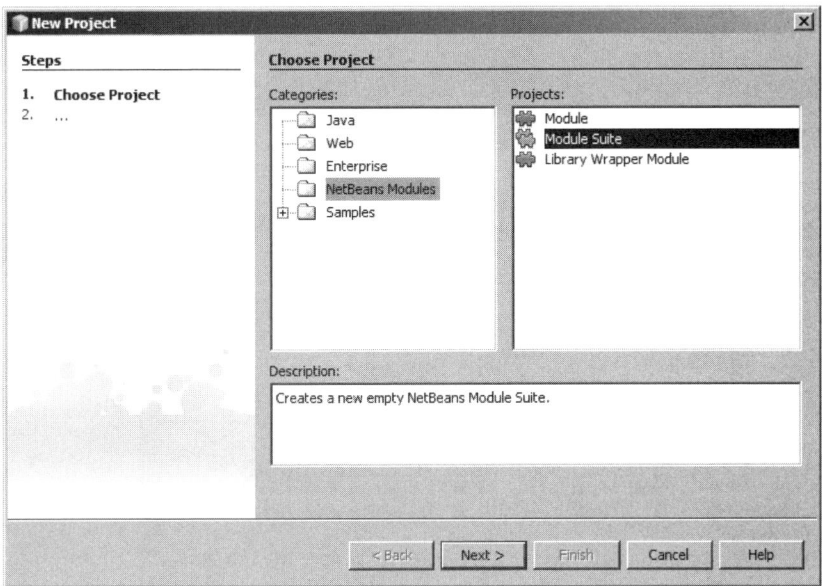

Figure 16-2. *New Project wizard category that provides the three NetBeans module project types*

The project templates shown in Figure 16-2 are as follows:

- *Module*: Creates the source structure of a single building block of your rich client application.
- *Module Suite*: Creates the source structure of a rich client application. By default, all the modules that make up the NetBeans IDE are included in the application this wizard creates. To exclude modules or clusters of related modules, you need to right-click the application project node, choose the Properties menu item, and use the Libraries tab to exclude the clusters and modules you do not need.
- *Library Wrapper Module*: Creates a module that holds one or more third-party libraries, such as Log4J and JDom. The libraries are those needed by one or more of the modules in the suite. It makes sense to create a separate module for each of your third-party libraries so that whenever one of them is updated by their owner, you can distribute updates easily and with as little impact on the existing modules as possible. For example, if you have a library wrapper module for library Log4J, when library Log4J's version number increments, you would create a new version of your module and distribute that module to your users while all the other modules remain unchanged.

File Templates

Once you have created a module, file templates are available to generate stubs for the most commonly used NetBeans APIs. To use these, right-click the module project that you have created; several of them will then be listed in a context pop-up menu. To see all of them, choose Other. Then, within the New File wizard, you will find a Module Development category, which contains all the file templates that relate specifically to NetBeans Platform development, as shown in Figure 16-3.

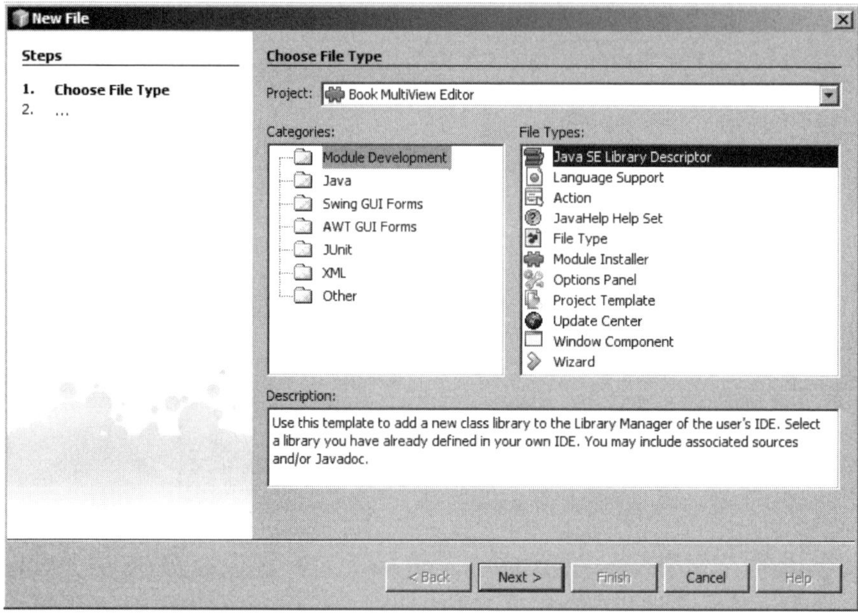

Figure 16-3. *New File wizard category that provides wizards for generating NetBeans API stubs*

The following file templates are listed in Figure 16-3:

- *Java SE Library Descriptor*: Wraps a library such that, when the application is deployed, the library is available in the Library Manager. The difference between this and the Library Wrapper Module, discussed earlier, is that the Java SE Library Descriptor provides a module to the *user*, while the Library Wrapper Module provides it to a *module*. In the latter case, the user does not see the library in the NetBeans IDE. In the former, it is selected from the Library Manager in order to be put on the classpath, such as the libraries used by applications making use of a web framework, such as Struts.

- *Language Support*: Provides a starting point for implementing a "Schliemann" declaration-based editor. The Schliemann Project was introduced in NetBeans Platform 6 as a wrapper around the more complex Lexer API, to provide a simplified underlying framework allowing for generic language support for languages such as JavaScript.

- *Action*: Creates a class that will perform an action from a menu item or toolbar button, depending on where it is registered in the `layer.xml` file. The wizard lets you register the action in the appropriate place.
- *JavaHelp Help Set*: Creates all the files required by a JavaHelp set. A dummy HTML file is also created.
- *File Type*: Lets the NetBeans Platform recognize a new file type. You can register a new file type either by its extension or by its XML root element, if you are working with XML files.
- *Module Installer*: Specifies code that should be executed at startup or shutdown of a module. The best module installer is an empty one, since module installers add to the startup time of an application.
- *Options Panel*: Lets you extend the Options window with new panels. In combination with the NbPreferences API, you can enable the user to set options that relate to your application.
- *Project Template*: Adds new samples to the New Project wizard in the NetBeans IDE.
- *Update Center*: Installs the URL to an XML file that defines an update center. The URL is installed in the Plugin Manager, so the user does not need to do so manually.
- *Window Component*: Creates a new window that integrates with the NetBeans Platform window system. Each window can be minimized/maximized, dragged/dropped, and undocked from the window frame. You can use the "Matisse" GUI Builder to design the content of the window.
- *Wizard*: Provides the stubs for a multistep set of dialogs, known as a "wizard." Once you have filled out the wizard stubs provided by the Wizard file template, the wizard can serve to let the user create files, specify settings, or something else that needs to be done over a guided series of steps.

As you can see from this list, some of the file templates are useful in adding something to NetBeans IDE specifically (such as the Project Template wizard), while others are useful in the context of any NetBeans Platform application (such as the Window Component wizard).

NetBeans Platform Manager

The NetBeans Platform Manager, shown in Figure 16-4, is a tool that lets you register multiple NetBeans Platforms in the NetBeans IDE. Once you have registered a NetBeans Platform, you can specify that modules or applications should compile against that specific NetBeans Platform. You may want to do that if, for example, you are creating an application for an earlier version of the NetBeans Platform. For example, you may want to use the tools provided by NetBeans IDE 6 while creating an application to run on the 5.0 version of the NetBeans Platform. In such a case, you would register NetBeans Platform 5.0 in the NetBeans Platform Manager and then specify, in your module's or your application's Project Properties dialog box, that the application should compile against NetBeans Platform 5.0.

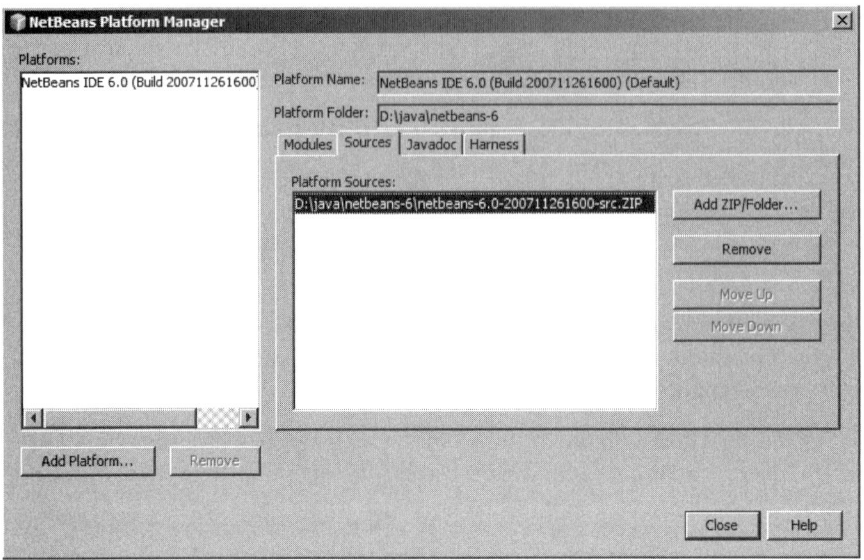

Figure 16-4. *The NetBeans Platform Manager*

Another use for the NetBeans Platform Manager is to allow quick and efficient browsing through NetBeans API Javadoc. To do this, register the ZIP file containing the NetBeans sources (which you can get from `www.netbeans.org`) by clicking the Add ZIP/Folder button in the NetBeans Platform Manager (shown in Figure 16-4) and then choosing the ZIP file from where you downloaded it on disk. Then you can hold down the Ctrl key and move the mouse over the identifier of a class or other item defined in the NetBeans API Javadoc. When you do so, the identifier becomes a blue hyperlink, as shown in Figure 16-5. When you click the link, the corresponding NetBeans API source file opens, as shown here, so that you can read the source code and related Javadoc, shown in Figure 16-6.

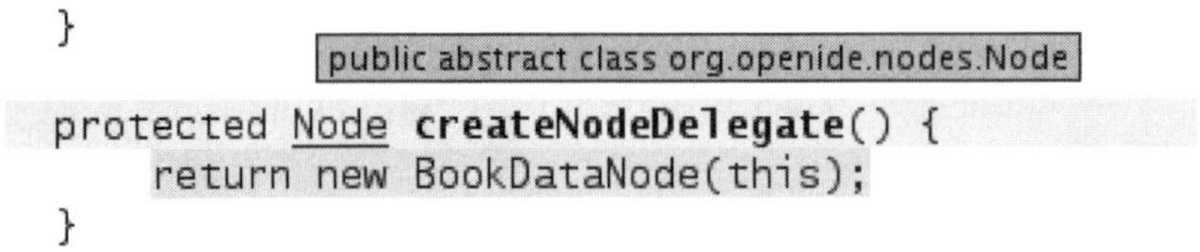

```
}              public abstract class org.openide.nodes.Node
protected Node createNodeDelegate() {
    return new BookDataNode(this);
}
```

Figure 16-5. *The editor, showing a hyperlink under the NetBeans API Node class*

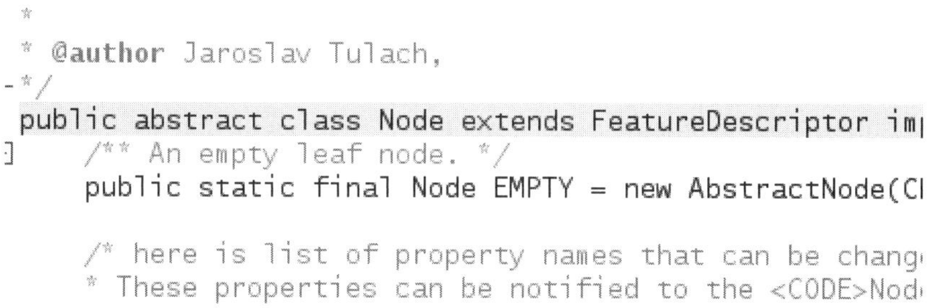

```
 *
 * @author Jaroslav Tulach,
-*/
public abstract class Node extends FeatureDescriptor im|
]    /** An empty leaf node. */
     public static final Node EMPTY = new AbstractNode(Cl

     /* here is list of property names that can be chang
      * These properties can be notified to the <CODE>Nod
```

Figure 16-6. *The editor, showing what happens when you click the hyperlink in Figure 16-5*

Navigating through NetBeans API Javadoc and sources in this way makes for easy reading of the code. It is recommended that you set up the NetBeans Platform sources in this way, to speed up your learning and simplify the development process.

Project Properties Dialogs

When you right-click on a module project's node in the Projects window or Files window, you can choose Properties. When you do so, you will see the Project Properties box shown in Figure 16-7.

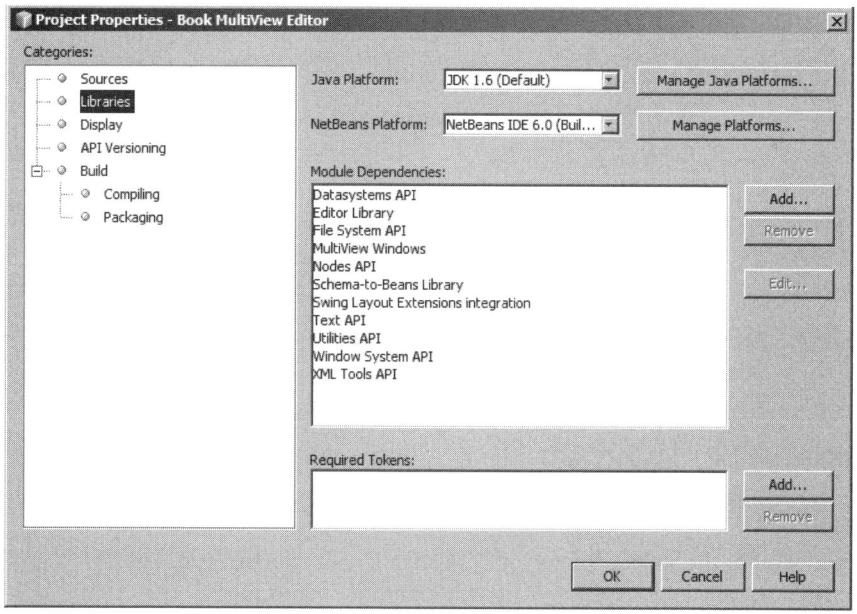

Figure 16-7. *The Project Properties dialog, showing the modules available to the current module*

A module project's Project Properties box lists the following categories:

- *Sources*: Shows the module's project folder on disk and sets the JDK of the sources.
- *Libraries*: Sets the modules containing the classes the current module can use.
- *Display*: Sets display name and other texts principally used by the Plugin Manager.
- *API Versioning*: Sets versioning information, including which packages are public.
- *Build*: Sets compiling and packaging information, such as the module's license.

An application also has a Project Properties box. You can specify application-level settings here, as indicated in Figure 16-8.

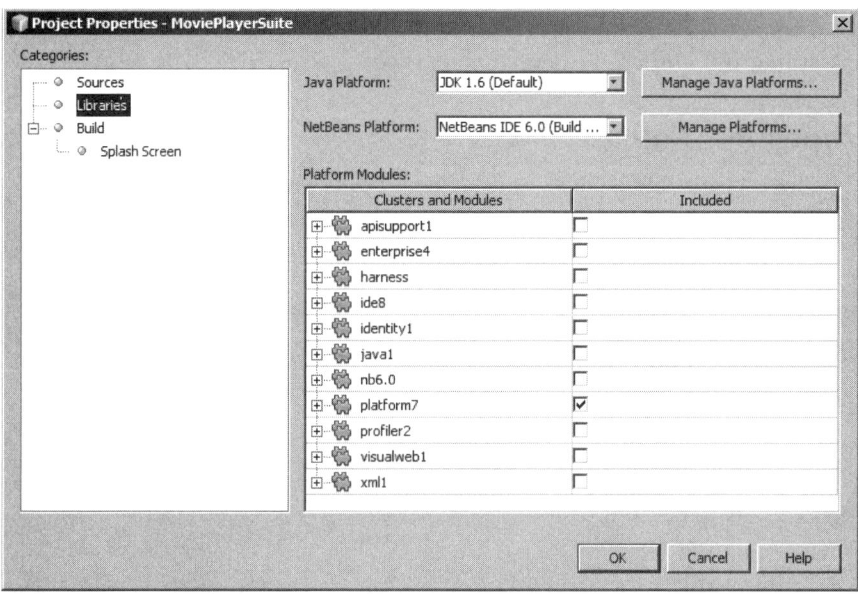

Figure 16-8. *Project Properties dialog, showing the modules available to the current application*

The Project Properties box for an application lists the following categories:

- *Sources*: Shows the application's project folder on disk and sets the modules in the suite.
- *Libraries*: Sets the modules and groups of modules available to the current application.
- *Build*: Sets whether the suite is for an application or a collection of modules as well as the display name, About box icon, and launcher name of the application.
- *Splash Screen*: Sets the application's splash screen as well as the splash screen's progress bar and progress bar text.

Context Menu Items

When you right-click a module, the module-related menu items shown in Figure 16-9 are available, that is, in addition to standard menu items such as "Close" and "Delete." The context menu lists the following items:

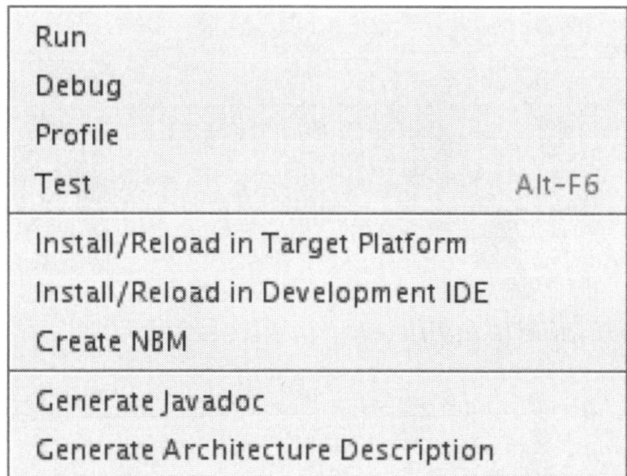

Figure 16-9. *A section of the context menu items available to module project nodes*

- *Run*: Runs the module, which installs it into a new instance of the IDE.
- *Debug*: Runs the module in debug mode.
- *Profile*: Attaches the Profiler to the module so that threads can be analyzed and bottlenecks identified.
- *Test*: Runs the module's JUnit tests.
- *Install/Reload in Target Platform*: Installs the module in a new instance of the IDE.
- *Install/Reload in Development IDE*: Installs the module in the current development IDE.
- *Create NBM*: Creates a binary file, similar to a ZIP file, that can be installed as a plugin.
- *Generate Javadoc*: Generate Javadoc for the module.
- *Generate Architecture Description*: Generates an architecture description document.

An application also has a set of menu items specifically tailored to applications, as shown in Figure 16-10. The context menu lists the following items:

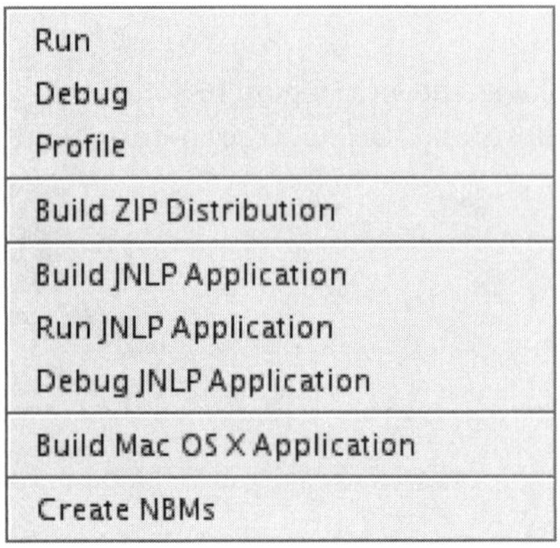

Run
Debug
Profile
Build ZIP Distribution
Build JNLP Application
Run JNLP Application
Debug JNLP Application
Build Mac OS X Application
Create NBMs

Figure 16-10. *A section of the context menu items available to application project nodes*

- *Run*: Runs the application.
- *Debug*: Runs the application in debug mode.
- *Profile*: Profiles the application, to analyze threads and identify bottlenecks.
- *Build ZIP Distribution*: Creates a binary of the application and archives it, with its distribution structure.
- *Build JNLP Application*: Creates a Web Start–capable application.
- *Run JNLP Application*: Creates and runs a Web Start–capable application.
- *Debug JNLP Application*: Creates and runs a Web Start–capable application in debug mode.
- *Build Mac OS Application*: Creates a distribution of the application for Mac OS X.
- *Create NBMs*: Creates a binary NBM file for each of the modules in the suite, together with an XML file, called the *autoupdate descriptor*, for defining an update center.

Now that I have introduced you to all the tools that NetBeans IDE, as the SDK of the NetBeans Platform, provides to ease the development process, it's time for you to create a NetBeans Platform application.

Meeting the APIs Outside of the Platform

Before creating your first NetBeans Platform application, create a simple Java application that makes use of some of the NetBeans APIs. Typically, an introduction to the NetBeans Platform would begin by getting you to work with the NetBeans Platform. Here, however, you will simply make use of some of its APIs and then, once you are comfortable with them, move the application to the NetBeans Platform. You will then look at the benefits of having done so. By the end of this section, you will have created the small application shown in Figure 16-11. When you run that application, you will have the file browser shown in Figure 16-12.

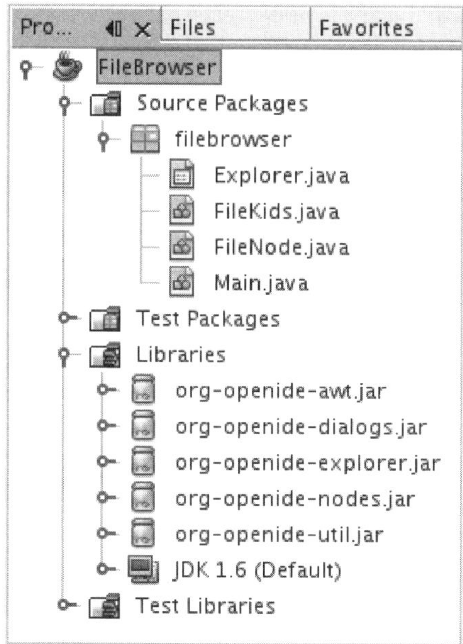

Figure 16-11. *The source structure of the simple Swing application you build in this section*

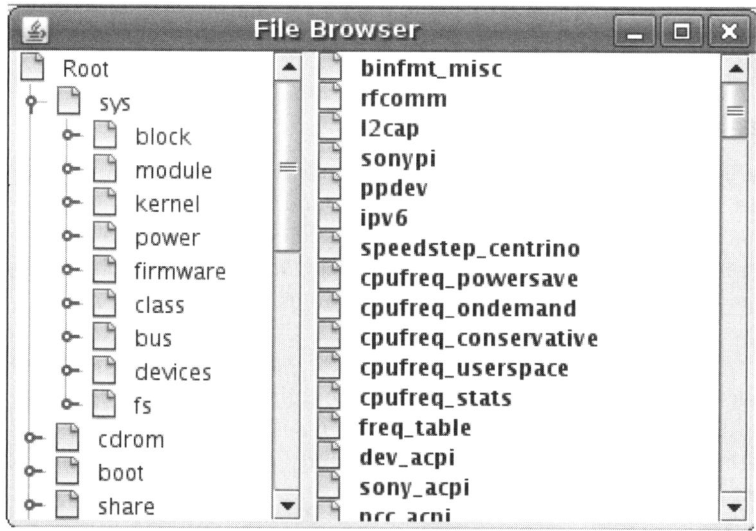

Figure 16-12. *The simple Swing application at runtime*

You begin by putting the necessary NetBeans APIs on the application's classpath. Then you use them in a JFrame, to create a simple file browser. You will use the following NetBeans APIs:

- User Interface (UI) Utilities API (`org.openide.awt.jar`)
- Dialogs API (`org.openide.dialogs.jar`)
- Explorer & Property Sheet API (`org.openide.explorer.jar`)
- Nodes API (`org.openide.nodes.jar`)
- Utilities API (`org.openide.util.jar`)

For a brief description of each of these APIs, see the section titled "Summary of the Main NetBeans APIs" at the end of this chapter.

Getting Started

You can begin creating your application by taking the following steps:

1. Create a Java application called "FileBrowser," by using the wizard obtained when you choose File ➤ New Project and then Java Application from the Java category.
2. Right-click the FileBrowser's Libraries node and add the JARs listed earlier to your application. You will find them in the `platform7` directory, within the root directory where you installed the NetBeans IDE. The first four are found in the `platform7/modules` subdirectory, while the last, that is, org.openide.util, is found in the `platform7/lib` subdirectory.

Using the Explorer & Property Sheet API

The Explorer & Property Sheet API provides a set of UI components that can render your application's data models. In the next section, you create a data model. A good thing about the NetBeans APIs is this separation of concerns: data models are handled by the Nodes API, while their views come from the Explorer & Property Sheet API. Changing the view on top of your data model is generally as simple as replacing one view with another. You will see this in action during this section.

Begin by exposing the UI components provided by the Explorer & Property Sheet API to the IDE's Component Palette. You do this so that you can drag-and-drop these views onto your Swing container, just like any other Swing component. Here, your Swing container will be a `JFrame`. You will see that the UI components the Explorer & Property Sheet API provides are very useful for interacting with the data model provided by the Nodes API in the next section.

1. To do so, choose Tools ➤ Palette ➤ Swing/AWT Components. In the Palette Manager, click "Add from JAR" and then browse to "org.openide.explorer.jar" in the NetBeans root directory's `platform7/modules` subdirectory.
2. Click Next. Select the beans shown in Figure 16-13.

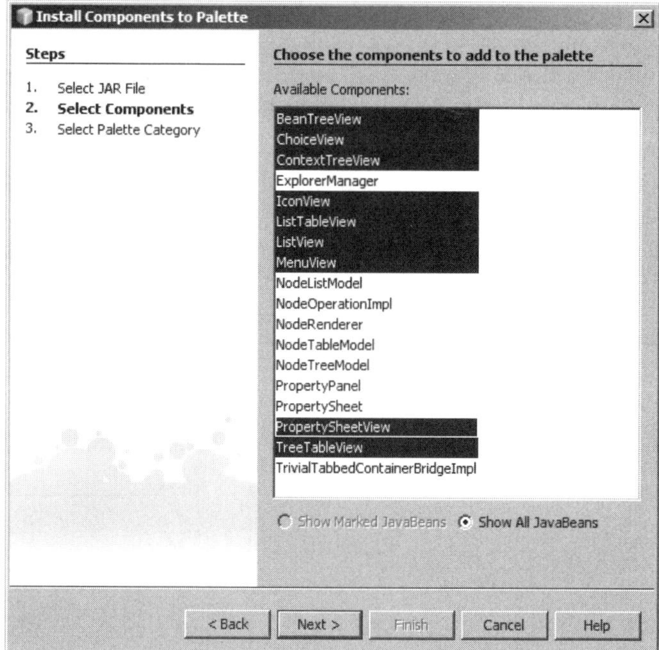

Figure 16-13. *The Palette Manager, showing the beans available in the Explorer & Property Sheet JAR*

3. Click Next. Choose Swing Containers and then click Finish. Once you have a Swing container, you will see that the Palette contains your new UI components, provided by your selected beans. You now have the following new UI components:

   - *BeanTreeView*: The class typically used for displaying nodes in a `JTree`-like hierarchical structure.
   - *ChoiceView*: Displays child nodes in a `JComboBox`.
   - *ContextTreeView*: Displays a tree of nodes but not its leaves.
   - *ListView*: Displays child nodes in a `JList`, optionally indented.
   - *MenuView*: Displays child nodes in a `JMenu`.
   - *PropertySheetView*: Displays node properties in a property sheet.
   - *TreeTableView*: Combines a tree with a table, showing nodes in the tree and their properties.

You will not use ListTableView and IconView very much, and you may find that they are being maintained less than the other views in the list. Explorer views are managed by the API's `ExplorerManager` class, which provides functionality to them, as needed. An explorer view finds its Explorer Manager by looking up the AWT hierarchy until it finds it. You will work with it in a later step.

1. In your FileBrowser application, create a `JFrame` called "Explorer." Do so by right-clicking the "FileBrowser" project node in the Projects window and then choosing New ➤ JFrame Form. Type `Explorer` in the "Class Name" field and `filebrowser` in the "Package Name" field. Click Finish.

2. Select the `JFrame` and open the Component Palette (Ctrl+Shift+8), if it isn't open already. From the Palette, drag-and-drop "ContextTreeView" and "ListView," which you added there earlier, onto your new "Explorer" `JFrame`. (These two views together will display the files on disk.) Then resize them to a more manageable size, to get the general layout shown in Figure 16-14.

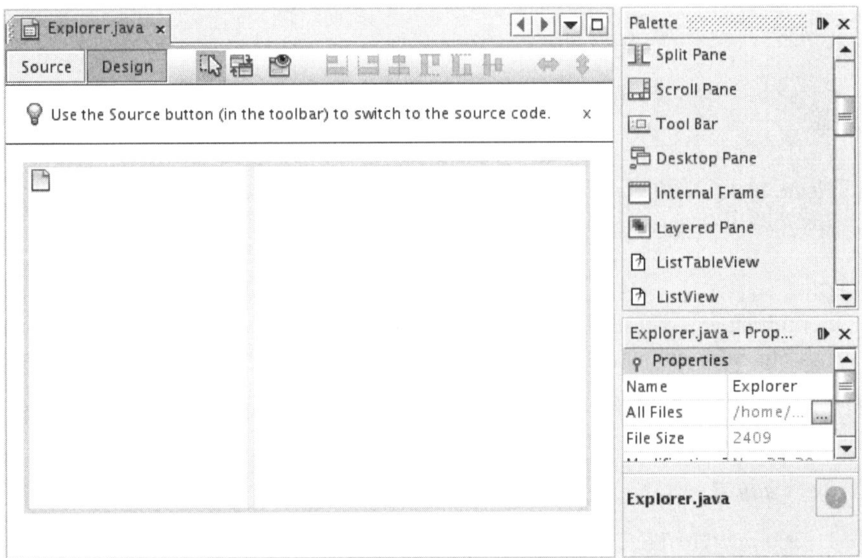

Figure 16-14. *The "Matisse" GUI Builder, showing the two dropped explorer views*

3. Click the Source button in the top left corner of the GUI Builder. In the source, change the class signature to implement `ExplorerManager.Provider`. The IDE's lightbulb hint prompts you to let it add an import statement for `org.openide.explorer.ExplorerManager`. Next, it will prompt you to let it create an abstract method for you, which it adds to the end of the class. You will fill this method out in the next step.

4. Declare an explorer manager to manage your explorer views:

```
private ExplorerManager em;
```

5. Next, instantiate it at the start of the constructor:

```
em = new ExplorerManager();
```

6. Return it in the `getExplorerManager` method, which was created in the previous step:

```
public ExplorerManager getExplorerManager() {
    return em;
}
```

7. Now set the root of the node hierarchy, in the constructor, right after the statement that creates the explorer manager:

```
em.setRootContext(FileNode.files());
```

Note The referenced class in the preceding statement does not exist yet; you will create it in the next subsection.

Using the Nodes API

In this subsection, you create the node hierarchy that will be shown by the explorer views you defined in the previous section. Create a new Java class and name it `FileNode`. This class will extend the NetBeans API `AbstractNode` class, a commonly used convenience base class. Set it as your root node, and then create the node's children beneath it:

```
public final class FileNode extends AbstractNode {

    public FileNode(File f) {
        super(new FileKids(f));
        setName(f.getName());
    }

    public static Node files() {
        AbstractNode n = new AbstractNode(new FileKids(null));
        n.setName("Root");
        return n;
    }

}
```

The Nodes API requires you to pass a `Children` object to an `AbstractNode`'s constructor. The `Children` object will create subnodes only when needed, such as when the user expands a node in one of the explorer views. At this point, the `addNotify` method is called and the child nodes are created. `Children.Keys` is typically used, here working with `java.io.File`, representing files on disk:

```
public final class FileKids extends Children.Keys<File> {

    File file;

    public FileKids(File file) {
        this.file = file;
    }

    @Override
    protected Node[] createNodes(File f) {
        FileNode n = new FileNode(f);
        return new Node[]{n};
    }

    @Override
    protected void addNotify() {
        if (file == null) {
            File[] arr = File.listRoots();
            if (arr.length == 1) {
                arr = arr[0].listFiles();
            }
            setKeys(arr);
        } else {
            File[] arr = file.listFiles();
            if (arr != null) {
                setKeys(arr);
            }
        }
    }
}
```

Your application is now complete. It consists of two explorer views, one that will list folders and files on disk, the other of which will not show leaves. That is how file browsers typically display files. You are using the Nodes API and the Explorer & Property Sheet API in combination, separating your data model from your views.

Running the Application

Finally, to run your application, use the `Main` class, which was generated for us when we created the Java application:

```
public class Main {
    public static void main(String[] args) {
        Explorer.main(args);
    }
}
```

Alternatively, or probably better, is to make the `Explorer` class be the main class instead and to discard the preceding class altogether.

Right-click the application and choose Run. This displays the file browser. You can browse through your file system, using an application built on top of the NetBeans APIs. Now remove one or both of the views and replace them with one or more of the other explorer views in the Component Palette. Then run the application again. For example, drag-and-drop IconView and then run the application again. You will see the same nodes, but displayed in a different view. The separation of concerns between data models and views provided by the NetBeans APIs makes this possible.

However, even though the NetBeans APIs have made life more convenient, if you move the application to the NetBeans Platform, you will gain a lot more besides. On the simplest level, you will have a highly flexible window system and be able to bundle the Plugin Manager, which will make it easy to add new plugins to extend your application. The next section goes into a lot of detail about how to port your application and, in the end, what to do with the result.

Assembling a NetBeans Platform Application

In this section, you create your first NetBeans Platform application, using the NetBeans IDE to do so. It will be a fully functioning application, with an independent life cycle, its own launcher, and a splash screen. You will refer back to the tools introduced in an earlier section, and you will get to know some more about the NetBeans APIs.

In creating your application, notice that you will be *assembling* it rather than creating it from scratch. You will begin by using a wizard to create the framework of your application. Next, you will add one single module, which will contain everything relevant from your original application. You will bundle all the NetBeans modules you want to reuse in your own application, such as the module that provides the Plugin Manager, so that your users will be able to extend their distribution of your application easily.

Toward the end, you will brand the application such that various user interface elements provided by the NetBeans Platform's own modules will be hidden, because your application will not need them. In taking these steps, you will be *assembling* the application, since most of its pieces exist already, and you will provide only one specific module, that is, the module containing the original application's features.

Getting Started

To begin creating your application on the NetBeans Platform, take the following initial steps to set up your framework.

1. Create a Module Suite project called "FileBrowser" by using the wizard obtained when you choose File ➤ New Project and then Module Suite from the NetBeans Modules category. Now you have the starting point of your application.

2. Create a Module project called "FileBrowserPlugin" by right-clicking the "FileBrowser" application's "Modules" node and choosing "Add New." You now have the basis of your application. It consists of a module suite called "File Browser," which is your application framework, containing one module called "FileBrowserPlugin," as shown in Figure 16-15.

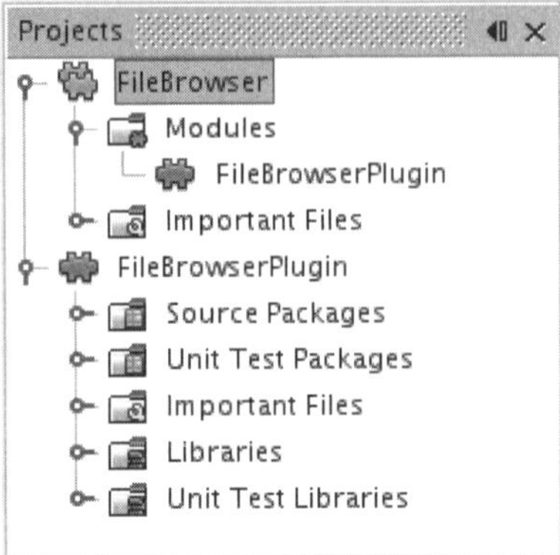

Figure 16-15. *The FileBrowser application, with one contributed module*

However, right now your new "FileBrowser" application contains a lot more than one module. In fact, it contains *all* the modules that are part of the NetBeans IDE. You do not need all these modules in the simple application you will be creating in this chapter. In the next step, you exclude all the unnecessary modules.

3. Right-click the "FileBrowser" application project node and choose Properties. The Project Properties dialog opens. In the Libraries node, *deselect* all the "clusters" except "platform7." A *cluster* is a group of related modules. When you click OK, the only set of modules your application provides will be those that make up the NetBeans Platform.

   In addition, though, the application will include the one module that you created in the previous step, that is, the module called "FileBrowserPlugin." In the remainder of this section, you move the relevant parts of the original "FileBrowser" application into that module's source structure.

Using the Window System API

Any GUI application needs to display an interface for user interaction. Typically, though, as applications expand in size, `JFrame`s simply are insufficient. Menus, toolbars, and a docking framework are common requirements for medium- to large-sized applications. The NetBeans Platform provides the framework for these features "out of the box." You can plug your own windows into its windowing system by means of the NetBeans Window System API's `TopComponent` class.

The Window System API provides several additional classes, for the placement and opening of windows. But for the purposes of this demo, you focus specifically on the `TopComponent` class. The `TopComponent` class is a `JPanel` with additional methods that let it integrate into the NetBeans Window System. In this section, you use a wizard to create a `TopComponent` class.

After you create your `TopComponent` class, you will use the "Matisse" GUI Builder to design its layout and content. The content will come from your original application. You will simply copy and paste the content of your original `JFrame` onto your `TopComponent`, in the "Matisse" GUI Builder's Design mode. You will also move the Java source files from your original simple Swing application into your module's source structure. For the purposes of this simple application, you will then have completed porting your application.

Typically, however, the porting process is much longer and more involved. For this reason, the NetBeans Platform Porting Tutorial (`http://platform.netbeans.org/tutorials/60/nbm-porting-basic.html`) provides a full step-by-step procedure you can follow to learn about the full process.

1. Right-click the "FileBrowserPlugin" project node and then choose New ➤ Window Component.

2. In the New Window wizard, choose "editor" in Window Position. By doing this, you specify that the window will appear in the "editor" area of your application, that is, the main area of your application where, in the NetBeans IDE, the editor is shown. Also, select "Open on Application Start," which adds code that will open the new window when the application first starts up. Click Next.

3. Type `FileBrowser` in the "Class Name Prefix" field. The wizard shows you the files that will be created, all prefaced by `FileBrowser`. Optionally, you could add an icon, which must have a dimension of 16×16 pixels. The icon, if you select it, will be shown in the window's tab. Click Finish. The IDE adds a new class that extends the NetBeans API `TopComponent` class to your module's source structure. In addition, some XML files are added, for persistence of the window's state. Typically, you never need to touch these XML files. A class that extends the NetBeans API `CallableSystemAction` class is also created. In the layer file, entries have been added that will let the user invoke the action from the Window menu. When the user invokes the action, the window will open, if it is closed.

4. Double-click the `FileBrowserTopComponent` class and notice that it opens in the "Matisse" GUI Builder. In the next step, you will copy the user interface from your original application onto this window class in the Design mode.

5. In your original application, expand the "Source Packages" folder and the `filebrowser` package, and then double-click the "Explorer" `JFrame`. It then opens in the Design mode of the "Matisse" GUI Builder.

6. Select both explorer views, right-click, and then choose Copy.

7. Open the `FileBrowserTopComponent` class in the GUI Builder's Design mode and then choose Paste.

8. Click the Source view of the `FileBrowserTopComponent` class. Notice that the class extends `TopComponent`, which is the NetBeans API class discussed earlier. Also notice the red error marks in the right sidebar. Click one of them and notice that the `org.openide.explorer` package is missing. To add this package, right-click the "FileBrowserPlugin" module and choose Properties. In the Libraries category, click Add Dependency. Put `org.openide.explorer` in the Filter field, and you will then see "Explorer & Property Sheet API" in the Module list. Select it and click OK. Click OK again to close the Project Properties box and to confirm that you want to declare this dependency. In the editor, notice that the red error marks have disappeared.

9. Now, as in the original "Explorer" JFrame, let the TopComponent class implement ExplorerManager.Provider. As before, click the lightbulb in the left sidebar and the appropriate import statement is added; click it again, and the required method is created at the end of the class. Return the ExplorerManager from this method, as you did in the "Explorer" JFrame.

10. Before going further, copy the FileNode class and the FileKids class from the original application into the module's main package, where the other files are already found. Open one of them and notice that the org.openide.nodes package is required but missing. Repeat step 8, and you will find that the Nodes API is needed. Make sure to set a dependency on it before continuing.

11. Back in the FileBrowserTopComponent class, instantiate the ExplorerManager and set its root context as before. The TopComponent constructor should now be as follows:

```
private FileBrowserTopComponent() {
    em = new ExplorerManager();
    em.setRootContext(FileNode.files());
    initComponents();
    setName(NbBundle.getMessage(FileBrowserTopComponent.class, ➥
"CTL_FileBrowserTopComponent"));
    setToolTipText(NbBundle.getMessage(FileBrowserTopComponent.class, ➥
"HINT_FileBrowserTopComponent"));
    //   setIcon(Utilities.loadImage(ICON_PATH, true));
}
```

12. Compile the FileBrowserPlugin class. Compilation should succeed without a problem. If it does not, make sure to fix the problem before continuing.

This simple porting exercise is now complete. The user interface you had originally is now defined in the TopComponent. The supporting Java source files are in the module's source structure. You have set the required dependencies on the Nodes API and the Explorer & Property Sheet API. The other required depdendencies were set for you by the New Window wizard.

Branding the Application

If you were to run your application right now, all the modules that make up the NetBeans Platform would be installed and the related user interface elements from all these modules would be displayed. However, even though you need all the modules provided by the NetBeans Platform, you do not need all their user interface elements. For example, you do not need all the menu items that the NetBeans Platform's modules provide. In this subsection, you create a new module.

You do so for one purpose only: to brand the application. You will do this by deleting items from this new module's layer file. When all the layer files are merged and the application starts, your branding module's layer file will cause the menu items you deleted not to be displayed.

Create a new module, as done in a previous section, and name it "FileBrowserBranding." In the Module wizard, make sure the new module will be added to your already existing FileBrowser application. When you complete the wizard, you should see Figure 16-16.

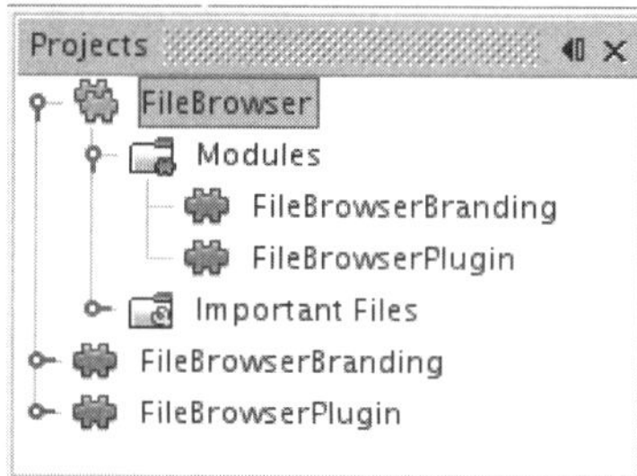

Figure 16-16. *The FileBrowser application, with functionality and branding module*

Now you will remove the unnecessary menu items from the new module's layer file. Expand the Important Files node. Then expand the XML Layer node. When you expand this specific node, two subnodes appear. The first shows all the contributions that the current module has made to the System FileSystem. The second shows everything provided by all the modules that make up the current application. Since you want to exclude menu items provided by other modules, expand the second node. Within that node, expand "Menu Bar," and then right-click all the nodes you want to exclude from your own application. Do the same within the "Toolbars" node.

You do not need any toolbars in your simple application, so you can right-click all the nodes within the "Toolbars" node, and then choose Delete. In the "Menu Bar" node, we only need "File|Exit," "Tools|Plugins," and "Tools|Options." You can delete all the other items within that folder. Figure 16-17 shows how the relevant part of the project structure will look while you are performing this task.

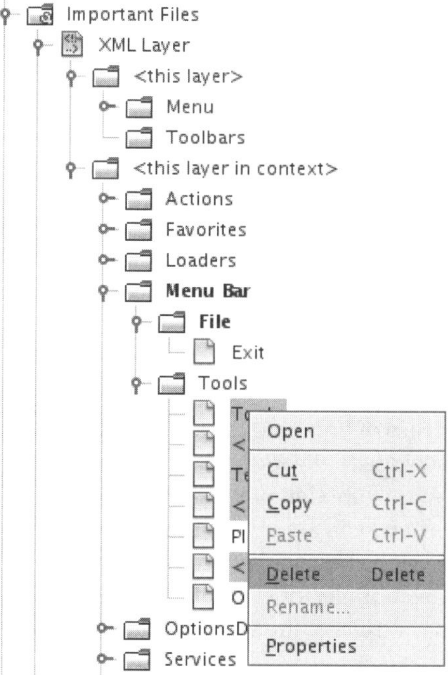

Figure 16-17. *Hiding menu items contributed by NetBeans Platform modules*

When you now open the layer file in the editor, you will see the effect of the deletions you performed in the previous step. Many folders and files are listed, with _hidden appended. You could have typed these into the layer file manually, but the user interface in the previous step simplified this process for you.

```
<filesystem>
    <folder name="Menu">
        <file name="Edit_hidden"/>
        <folder name="File">
            <file name="Separator2.instance_hidden"/>
            <file name="Separator3.instance_hidden"/>
            <file name="Separator4.instance_hidden"/>
            <file name="org-openide-actions-PageSetupAction.instance_hidden"/>
            <file name="org-openide-actions-PrintAction.instance_hidden"/>
            <file name="org-openide-actions-SaveAction.instance_hidden"/>
            <file name="org-openide-actions-SaveAllAction.instance_hidden"/>
            <file name="org-openide-actions-SaveAsAction.shadow_hidden"/>
        </folder>
        <file name="GoTo_hidden"/>
        <file name="Help_hidden"/>
        <folder name="Tools">
            <file name="Separator1.instance_hidden"/>
            <file name="Separator2.instance_hidden"/>
            <file name="Separator3.instance_hidden"/>
            <file name="org-netbeans-modules-favorites-templates- ➥
TemplatesAction.instance_hidden"/>
            <file name="org-openide-actions-ToolsAction.instance_hidden"/>
        </folder>
        <file name="View_hidden"/>
        <file name="Window_hidden"/>
    </folder>
    <folder name="Toolbars">
        <file name="Edit_hidden"/>
        <file name="File_hidden"/>
        <file name="Memory_hidden"/>
    </folder>
</filesystem>
```

You have now done some basic branding. Other types of branding could cover icons, localization, splash screen, and so on. You could brand your application within a separate module, as done here, or you could do so within one of the functionality modules. However, if you provide branding in a separate module, as done here, you are able to make multiple branding modules available, so your end user would have a choice. Possibly one branding module would hide different items to another branding module, for example. In this way, you could provide tailor-made solutions for different kinds of users of the same application. There are several ways of doing this, but this is one of them.

Running the Application

Right-click the FileBrowser application and choose Run. The application starts up, first showing the splash screen. Then the the file browser is deployed again, as before, but this time on the NetBeans Platform, as shown in Figure 16-18.

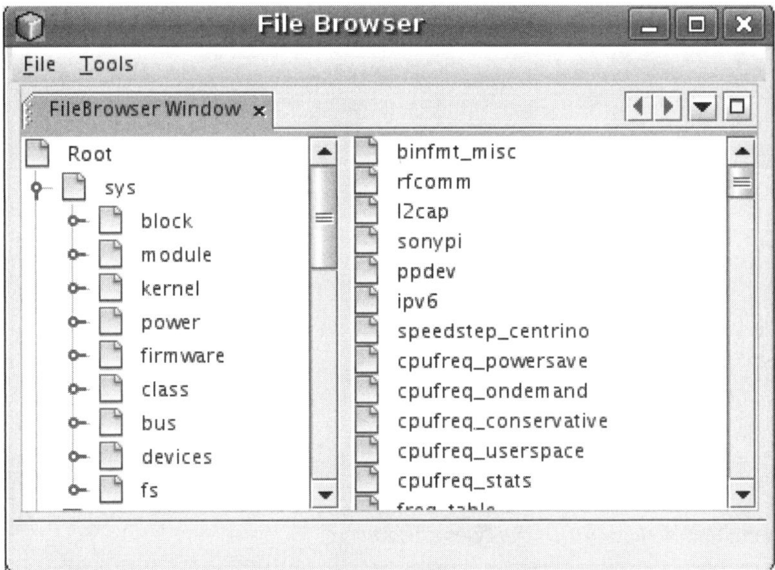

Figure 16-18. *The file browser deployed to the NetBeans Platform*

Since you have created a very simple application, it doesn't do much more than the original. However, it is now integrated into the NetBeans Platform, so you can easily extend it, as a later section in this chapter shows. You ported the user interface of our application to a TopComponent.

Distributing the Application

Now that our application is complete, we can distribute it. We can let the IDE create a ZIP distribution or a JNLP application. We begin by creating a ZIP distribution.

1. Right-click the application and choose Build ZIP Distribution. The IDE creates cross-platform launchers for your application and creates an archive in the application's "dist" folder.

2. Open the Files window (Ctrl+2) and then expand the "dist" folder to see the newly created archive file shown in Figure 16-19.

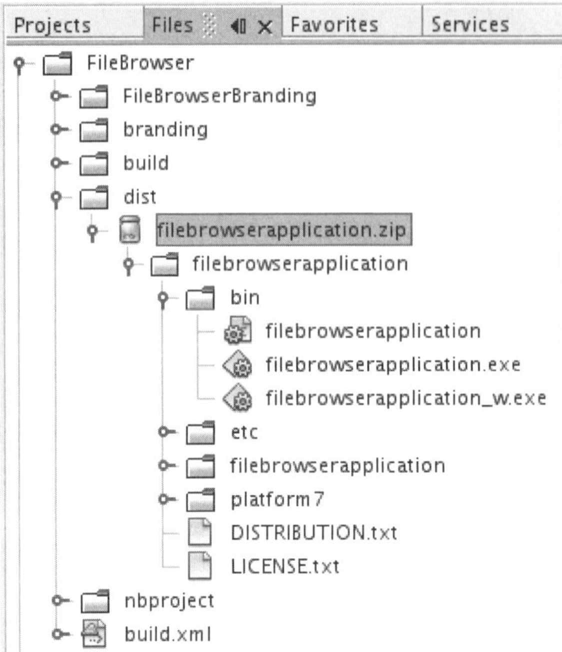

Figure 16-19. *The newly created archive file in the Files window*

In addition to creating a ZIP distribution, you can create and run a Java Network Launch Protocol (JNLP) application. Java Web Start, another name for JNLP, is a mechanism for program delivery through a standard web server. Typically initiated through the browser, these programs are deployed to the client and executed outside the scope of the browser. You can use this technology to deliver your NetBeans Platform application to your end users.

Right-click the application and choose "Build JNLP Application," "Run JNLP Application," or "Debug JNLP Application." The Files window (Ctrl+2) shows the JNLP files that are created as required by the Web Start technology. Refer to the JNLP product page (`http://java.sun.com/products/javawebstart/`) for details on how to use them, now that you have all the necessary files.

When you distribute your application via JNLP, you are making the complete application available to your users. You continue to be in full control of the application, and whatever is provided by the application is what all your users will have available to them. However, if you distribute your application as a ZIP file, the users will be able to run it locally, on their own system. In that case, you have less control. On the other hand, the users will be able to pick and choose the additional functionality they want to make use of. Additional functionality is provided by new modules, distributed as plugins to your end users. The next section discusses this aspect of application distribution.

Updating the Application

One of the menus you *did not* remove when you branded the application was the Tools menu. Within it, the users will see Options and Plugins. When they select Options, they will see the Options window. You can use the Options Dialog and SPI to extend the Options window with new panels to let your users define settings specific to your application. However, when your users select Plugins, they will see the Plugin Manager.

Via the Plugin Manager, they will be able to add new plugins. Distributing plugins can be done in several ways. You could put them on a server, for example. The users would then need to download them and use the Downloaded tab in the Plugin Manager to install them.

In addition, you can let the IDE generate an XML file called the "autoupdate descriptor." The descriptor defines the location of your modules as well as other information, such as their descriptions. When you put the descriptor on a server, your users will be able to register it in the Settings tab in the Plugin Manager. Then they will be able to use the Plugin Manager to access your plugins and install them into their application.

To create this descriptor, right-click the application and choose Create NBMs. Then look in the "build/updates" folder, in the Files window, where you will find the `updates.xml` file. That file is the application's autoupdate descriptor. Open it in the editor and notice that your modules are defined there, between `<module>` tags. Information between these tags is taken from various sources, such as a module's manifest.

Further Reading

The following resources will bring you further information:

- NetBeans IDE JavaHelp (Help ➤ Help Contents in NetBeans IDE 6.0)
- NetBeans Platform home (`http://platform.netbeans.org/`)
- NetBeans 6 API list (`http://bits.netbeans.org/6.0/javadoc/index.html`)
- NetBeans API changes from 5.5 to 6 (`http://bits.netbeans.org/6.0/javadoc/apichanges.html`)
- *Rich Client Programming: Plugging into the NetBeans Platform* by Tim Boudreau, Jaroslav Tulach, and Geertjan Wielenga (Prentice-Hall, April 2007)
- NetBeans developer FAQ (`http://wiki.netbeans.org/wiki/view/NetBeansDeveloperFAQ`)
- NetBeans Platform Porting Tutorial (`http://platform.netbeans.org/tutorials/60/nbm-porting-basic.html`)
- NetBeans Platform mailing list (`dev@openide.netbeans.org`)

Summary of the Main NetBeans APIs

Though there are many NetBeans APIs supporting the features described in the previous sections, the ones you will use on a daily basis, to a greater or lesser extent, are the following:

- *Actions API*: Provides system actions, such as Copy and Delete, which can optionally be implemented context sensitively. The actions can be invoked from a menu item, a toolbar button, a keyboard shortcut, or combinations of these.
- *Auto Update Services API*: Lets a module access the Plugin Manager to programmatically download, install, uninstall, enable, or disable modules made available there.

- *Command Line Parsing API*: Lets a module participate in parsing an application's command line.
- *Common Palette API*: Provides the infrastructure of a palette, which you can enable and then populate with items, enabling users to drag/drop items into an editor or window. One use is where you want to let the user add code snippets to the editor by dragging-and-dropping an item from the palette.
- *Datasystems API*: Sits on top of File Objects, provided by the File System API, to give File Objects logical behavior, such as a name and a set of operations.
- *Dialogs API*: Provides general classes for showing and working with dialogs, user messages, and wizards.
- *Editor Code Completion API*: Lets you add an autocomplete feature to your custom editor or to one of the existing editors.
- *Explorer & Property Sheet API*: Provides explorer views that render nodes. Swing components are provided for rendering nodes in structures such as trees, lists, combo boxes, tables, and menus.
- *File System API*: Provides access to the NetBeans concept of a file system, which is a virtual file system, with the flexible NetBeans File Objects instead of `java.io.File`.
- *I/O APIs*: Provides access to the Output window, together with the possibility of creating hyperlinks in the Output window, which link back to a line in an editor.
- *JavaHelp Integration API*: Provides integration with the JavaHelp API.
- *Lexer API*: Lets you create a sequence of tokens to enable, for example, syntax coloring, code completion, or hyperlinking in the editor.
- *Module System API*: Provides the pluggable modular architecture underpinning NetBeans Platform applications.
- *MultiView Windows API*: Lets you create an editor with multiple panels, which can be source editor panels or provided by Swing components.
- *Navigator API*: Provides a dedicated window for showing the structure or outline of a document.
- *Nodes API*: Lets you present hierarchical structures visually.
- *Options Dialog and SPI*: Lets you extend the Options window with your own panels for user settings.
- *Progress API*: Provides access to a progress bar integrated in the bottom right corner of your application.
- *Task List API*: Provides a dedicated window for showing problems, such as errors and warnings, associated with the current folders, documents, or both.

- *UI Utilities API*: Provides utility classes relating to the visual appearance of your application. For example, you use the `StatusDisplayer` class to write to the application's status bar.
- *Utilities API*: Provides general classes needed by your application, such as the classes for the registration and usage of the Lookup mechanism, enabling intermodular communication.
- *Visual Library API*: Provides reusable and extendable widgets and actions for visualization, graphs, and modeling.

Summary

Though the full length and breadth of the NetBeans Platform could not be covered within the space of a single chapter, you should now have a basic overview of several of its key aspects. The NetBeans IDE's tools for NetBeans Platform development have been covered in some detail. You have also built a basic application on top of the NetBeans Platform. Though simple, it shows several of the main advantages of NetBeans Platform applications. For example, the pluggability of your new application has been outlined, as well as its windowing system. In addition, you have seen how your application has been *assembled* from preexisting modules provided by the NetBeans Platform combined with your own modules. Your first module provided your application's new functionality; your second module branded the application.

The main feature that has not been touched on here is the NetBeans-specific approach to intermodular communication. In order to show you within one chapter how to create an application, this aspect could not be covered. Larger applications, containing multiple modules, need a coherent strategy for communicating in a decoupled way with each other. Details on this important aspect are described in *Rich Client Programming: Plugging into the NetBeans Platform* (Prentice-Hall, April 2007). It is my hope that this introduction to the NetBeans Platform has whetted your appetite for more. See the Further Reading section in this chapter for sources of more detailed information.

Index

Numbers and Symbols

A

D

J

O

P

XYZ